EntwiningofSouls

A Life-Changing Experience

Judy Roach

MBS Press (Mind Body Spirit)
A division of Pick-a-WooWoo Publishers

Copyright © 2014

The moral right of Judith Ann Roach to be identified as the author of the work has been asserted by her in accordance with the Copyright, Designs and Patents Act 1988. All rights reserved. No part of this book may be reproduced, stored in a retrieval system, or transmitted in any form, or by any means electronic, mechanical, recording, photocopying, or in any manner whatsoever, without permission in writing from the publisher, except for book reviews.

National Library of Australia Cataloguing-in-Publication entry

Author: Judy Roach
Title: Entwining of souls: a life-changing experience/ Judy Roach.
ISBN: 978-0-6459316-0-0(pbk.)
Roach, Judy.
Subjects: Past-life readings.
Women--Psychic ability.
Women psychics.
Dewey Number: 133.9

Publishing Details

Published in Australia – MBS Press (Mind Body Spirit)
(A division of Pick-A-WooWoo Publishers)

Printed & Channel Distribution in US/UK/AUS / Canada

Printed through Lightning Source (USA/UK/AUS)

Available via:

United States

Ingram Book Company; Amazon.com; Baker & Taylor

Canada

Chapters Indigo; Amazon Canada http://www.amazon.ca/

United Kingdom

Amazon.com; Bertrams; Book Depository Ltd; Gardners; Mallory International

Australia

DA Information Services; The Nile; Emporium Books Online; James Bennet (Australian Libraries); Dennis Jones and Associates; Brumby Books and Music

The author of this book is not dispensing medical advice or prescribing the use of any technique as a form of treatment for medical, physical or emotional problems without the advice of a physician, either directly or indirectly.

The authors intent is to offer information only, to help you in your quest for spiritual and emotional well-being. In the event you use any of the information in this book for yourself, which is your divine right, the author and the publisher assume no responsibility for your actions.

Some names have been changed to protect the privacy of individuals.

The author can be contacted through the publisher: info@mbspress.com

http://www.entwiningofsouls.com

Dedication

This book is for Tess, my beloved mother.

Mum, without your love, faith and support, this journey would not have been possible.

Acknowledgements

I wish to sincerely thank all the people who assisted with the manuscript and its journey …

You all know who you are.

A Special Note to the Reader

This book is written with the purest intent and is based on the diarised events and meticulous notes of the author. There is no wish to vindicate or to harm others. Its intent is to reveal how unresolved past lives and negative karmic attachments can and do have devastating effects and create trauma in one's present life. The author encourages the reader to read her account with an open mind and a generous heart, understanding that her sole purpose is to seek resolution and healing. Thanks to the events recounted here, a miraculous spiritual journey ensued, leading to the 'Ten Year Mary Project 1994' and the reuniting of an ancient soul group.

Soul Group

Conner believed seriously in reincarnation. He'd told me more than once of his belief that souls travel in flocks, like birds, following each other from life to life just as swallows go from tree to tree. Our roles change, he said, but the souls stay the same; someone who was your brother in a past life may be your best friend in this one, or your sister now may have been your wife in ancient Rome. He pooh-poohed my objection that this would be incest. 'What matters is that the souls are together,' he said. 'The bodies themselves are insignificant, and so is what we do with them.' Any numbers of soul combinations were possible. He even believed people changed gender from life to life, as easily as people change clothes.

Eddie's Bastard by William Kowalski (1).

Standing outside in the narrow street I felt apprehensive, yet with a sense of *I must buy this place*. The weather was wet and cold, the street busy, the people not seeing each other as they rushed past. I looked into my friend's face and she nodded as I knocked on the door. We would go inside.

The three-storey property was centuries old, set in a row of odd-looking buildings — odd because of their various styles. One building frontage had slates cut to represent the four card suits, an indication that it had once been a gambling house. People had told us the area had been a place of prostitution long ago.

Inside the shop an elderly lady greeted us, taking us past the cluttered antiques through to her kitchen, where she gave us Earl Grey tea in fine china cups. The property was for sale and we had plans to open a tearoom. Situated in the village of Ashburton on the edge of Dartmoor, the shop appeared ideal. Anne and I were in our thirties and totally without catering experience, but we were determined our plans would succeed.

We were shown up a narrow staircase to the first floor. The bathroom was a disaster, but a quaint sitting room overlooked the main street and at the rear was a largish bedroom with a floor that sloped towards the window. Outside were a shed and a long garden with a path leading to a lane. As we climbed the stairs to the second level I grew tense, but pushed the feeling aside as we made our way to a narrow landing and a huge room with a very large window.

'This will make a great double guest bedroom,' I said to Anne.

Tucked away at the other end of the landing was a small bedroom overlooking the rear. I was drawn to its tiny window, but as I looked out pain clutched my chest. It was as if someone was holding me close — too close — and my earlier feeling of apprehension returned. Anne hurried me towards the next room.

This was a large windowless empty space under an unlined roof, very dark, but with slivers of light coming through gaps in the slate tiling. I did not go in. *I could not go in.* Instead, I stood by the door trying to visualise how we could use this area. We continued on, reaching the third level via yet an even narrower, steeper staircase. At the top was a spacious attic with a modern skylight.

Anne whispered to me, at which the elderly lady gave us a questioning look. 'Anne has an eight-year-old son,' I explained. 'We think he'd love this space.'

We returned to the ground level and out through the kitchen door into the garden. I turned to look back and my eyes were drawn up to the tiny window of the small bedroom where I had felt so uncomfortable.

A movement.

How is that possible? I wondered. We were the only people in the house.

'This was a saddlery in the old days,' the lady said. 'The story is that the saddler had seven children and built the place next door to house his family. In the outbuilding by the kitchen he made and repaired the metal items that were worn by horses at that time.' As she continued her story I could imagine horses being brought down the now-enclosed passageway from the main street. 'Next door is a gift shop now, with a separate title,' she added, before leading us back to the kitchen.

As we followed her, my eyes were drawn again to the tiny window. Anne shivered, perhaps from the cold or maybe because of the major decision we had to make. We thanked the owner for her time and told her we would think it over.

I had reconnected with Anne three years before, in March 1980, when I returned to England after living in Australia for a few years. During our teens we had been good friends, playing hockey for our respective counties. In my early twenties I had travelled to America to work as a nanny, returning six months later to Devon to start a career in the local police force. After five years I resigned and eventually went to live in Australia. Anne and I always kept in touch. I was a guest at her wedding and she later invited me to be godmother to David, her younger son. Now, after many adventures, I was very reluctantly living in England once more due to serious health problems and the need to be with family, especially my mother.

On my return I joined a major retail company as their mobile head office detective, travelling extensively and working long hours. Too much time spent alone in hotels and poor eating habits did not improve my health, and in time I required two major operations. To avoid the knife again I sought alternative medicines and treatments, learning how stress can lead to illness and realising there must be folk like myself wondering where to turn for help. The concept of a *special place* began to form in my mind. I shared my thoughts with Anne and she in turn shared her fears that, without skills, she would not find employment. Three years earlier she had gone through an unpleasant divorce and was still a single parent. She needed to work, but also to be at home to care for her son David, determined he would not become a latchkey child. The tearoom would provide an income for us both and an ideal home environment for David.

Once the decision was reached, Anne and I approached my friend Geoff Coyte, a manager with Lloyds Bank, about a business loan. I explained that we were in a position to buy the property, but we couldn't go ahead without a loan to set the place up as a tearoom. With his positive response, we made an offer on the premises and it was accepted. The purchasing solicitor was not happy, however. Two women on a title: What if we fell out? He held that question in the air as we both sat there. I waited for Anne to speak, knowing her divorce had been the outcome of family business problems. I wanted her certainty regarding this legal step to becoming a business partner again. After a pause she said firmly that this was what she wanted. The solicitor handed us the contract to sign.

The restoration work was undertaken by a local firm that specialised in old buildings. I drew on my personal capital to pay for the early restoration. Anne and David moved in with my mother and me in her Torquay apartment while the work was done. As Anne was not yet receiving any maintenance, my finances and Mum's were stretched to the limit. To assist as much as we could with the work at the Old Saddlery, Anne and I made the thirty-to-forty-minute drive from Torquay daily.

At last it was our pre-opening buffet party. This was quite an event, with all my family there ahead of the official opening on 15 March 1983. A huge shield sign with the name 'Old Saddlery 14th Century Eating House' would soon swing outside above street level. Our planned tearoom had become an intimate restaurant. We would serve meals all day from a wholefood and vegetarian menu, using organic produce wherever possible. We had a BYO licence for those who wished to have wine with their meal, and offered bed-and-breakfast accommodation in the spacious double bedroom on the second floor: we needed every bit of income we could get because we now had a large business loan to repay. Neither of us would draw a real wage; everything had to be ploughed back into the business.

Old Saddlery, Ashburton, Devon

Our small restaurant looked wonderful inside, with its old-world atmosphere. The main feature was a fireplace with a long granite hearth. I had bought the single stone locally; it had come from the original London Bridge when it was dismantled. We chose Wayside china to focus on the wildflowers of the English hedgerow.

As well as the restaurant, we now had an excellent bathroom and the attic had been renovated for David. He loved it and played up there for hours. But the cost of the restoration was steadily mounting. While whitewashing the exterior walls, I looked up at the building and identified the extent of work needed. An idea came to me. We would seek a grant from the National Trust. Our property was a Grade Two Heritage Listed Building. A grant would not only ensure the property was restored, but also increase its value — a good investment for Anne and me and our individual futures.

The months of restoration were exhausting. Mum agreed to look after David at the Old Saddlery while Anne and I took a long-weekend break. When we returned, Mum was unusually tense and in a hurry to leave. I thought perhaps David had been a problem, but she was adamant he'd been fine. It was not until some time later, after I began to experience unusual events, that she shared her concerns.

I contacted the National Trust and, following an inspection, we began the process of applying for a grant. Meanwhile, Anne took a two-week *Cordon Verte* cookery course to increase her vegetarian cooking skills.

After the restaurant opened, we noticed that customers seemed to have problems entering. The main entrance was between two very large display windows and lined with potted plants to make its location more obvious, yet most customers tried to enter through the closed black door on the right that led into the passageway, the access point for horses in times gone by. Not having any knowledge, at that time, of energies and the effect they have, I watched in frustration as people tried in vain to open the locked black door. Some walked away, confused, even though our sign said, 'Open'. Others knocked until I came out to walk them through the main entrance. Weeks later, I relented and opened the passageway, closed the main entrance and arranged the potted plants across as a barrier. For several weeks the reverse happened — people tried unsuccessfully to use only the main entrance, some even stepping on the pot plants as they tried to enter. Then everything calmed down and people found their way in.

One of our early customers was a tall, smartly dressed woman in her fifties who announced she was from 'Cranks'. While she sat down in front of the fireplace to study the menu, I went out to the kitchen to Anne. 'The woman who runs Cranks at Dartington is here,' I told her quietly. Cranks was a famous restaurant specialising in vegetarian food.

She chose one of my maternal grandmother's recipes — potato cake with zest of lemon — a delicious and popular dish. As we had grown busier, parts of the menu had become my responsibility. The woman told me she had enjoyed her visit and we felt we had survived an important test.

Days later, a middle-aged woman wearing a flowing dress and with unkempt long grey hair came in. With a vivacious smile, she announced she was 'sussing us out'. She picked up the menu, read its contents and said, 'You'll be alright.' She introduced herself as Pat Densham. She lived outside the village and I later discovered she was an alternative practitioner.

We were approaching 21 September and my sister Barbara's forty-second birthday. Mum and I bought her air tickets to visit her friend Jan, in Guernsey. It was Barbara's first flight, and we went to the airport to see her off. She waved as she boarded the plane but we could see she was nervous. Mum stared after the plane as it took off — crying — so I took her arm as we walked away. I was slowly overwhelmed by a strange feeling. I was seeing the scene of Barbara's departure through the eyes of *another* — a male — I felt his smile on my mouth, and then his complete face covered mine. I recognised the smile — it was my father's. My father had passed over in April 1973. For several minutes as we walked I was not aware of any other part of my body, *only his smile*. When he left, I told Mum that Barbara would be okay and that Daddy was looking out for her. Mum absorbed this without comment but I could not help wondering why she had cried and why Daddy had felt compelled to communicate.

We had been running the Old Saddlery for seven months when we decided we were in need of a holiday. I was drawn to buy the *Here's Health* magazine and read a gardening article by a man called Jack Temple. The magazine also featured a ten-day trip to Austria, led by Jack himself, who would be giving daily lectures on alternative therapies and also leading walks into the mountains. *I had to go.*

We met Jack and other members of the group when we arrived in Austria. He was a strong, fit man in his early sixties who would later walk us off our feet, while our companions were mainly professional people. Each day we received a lecture on an alternative therapy: homeopathy, reflexology and other modalities. I noticed at meal times Jack would appear to confer mentally on his choice of both food and drink. Watching him, I wondered if he was a spiritual man. Having an open mind with regard to anything spiritual or connected with healing, I was determined to learn all I could from him.

As a child I had felt driven many times to wander outside during Sunday School and sit on the outside wall of a nearby building. Years later I discovered that building was a Spiritualist church. Later, in my teens, I visited Oberammergau in Germany, near the Austrian border, with a school party. On entering the place where the *Passion Play* is presented every ten years, we passed a huge cross defining a pale, injured figure of Jesus; vivid red blood flowed from the crown of thorns on his head. I stood there horrified. Before I could stop myself, I said loudly, 'This is not how it was, this is not how it is meant to be.' The voice came from deep within me. My friends became distressed and a teacher tried to calm me, but without success. She told me to sit on a seat outside. Alone and confused, I wondered from where such emotions and words had come.

Now I was in Austria, eager to learn more about Jack's personal gifts.

Before embarking on the Ashburton Old Saddlery project, I had undergone a total hysterectomy, due to endometriosis, followed months later by an emergency gall bladder operation. Instead of the usual small incision for gall bladder surgery, I was left with a long jagged scar that stretched from my chest across my stomach. As a result, I went from being a competitive swimmer to being barely able to float. Arm movements for swimming were difficult and I had to lean on my side in order to sit up.

On our second-last day, Jack was to demonstrate spiritual healing. He set up a massage table and then sat quietly as though waiting for instructions. At last he said, 'Judy, come and sit on the table.'

Anne was the only person present who was aware of the surgery I had undergone. Jack asked me to lie down and then turned away, still talking. I leant on my side in order to lie down. When Jack returned he held an object on a cord in his hand. He explained it was a pendulum and moved it slowly over my chest and stomach, about two inches above my clothing, announcing he was a muscle dowser. I watched fascinated as the pendulum moved in circles. Jack stopped to explain that I had undergone surgery and indicated the areas affected. He said my muscles had been incorrectly aligned and he began working on those areas, holding his hand above each area with the pendulum until it stopped circling and just moved slightly. I felt the muscles ping. He stopped and told me to sit up. I went to lean on my side.

'No, Judy, sit up,' he insisted.

Slowly and unaided for the first time since my operations, I sat up.

Before the course ended, Jack encouraged us to make pendulums and suggested we practise dowsing over our food and drinks to ask our higher self (the part of us that is all-knowing) which were most beneficial — the response being a *Yes* or *No* depending on each circular movement. It was a shambles; none of our pendulums would even move.

On the return flight, Jack sat beside me. He insisted that I obtain a pendulum and start using it. 'It's an important healing tool,' he said. 'You must learn to open your gift.' I agreed that I would, but wondered what he meant by my gift. I told him about the Old Saddlery and how we served mainly organic produce. He said he wanted to mention our restaurant in an article he was about to write and asked me to send him more information.

When Jack's article appeared in the *Here's Health* magazine it was read by the staff at a cancer clinic in Bristol. They recommended our restaurant, and we soon began to meet their patients. My dream of a special place, it seemed, was becoming a reality.

I bought a silver chain with a small silver ball from the gift shop next door and, as Jack had requested, I learnt how to dowse for our individual diets and supplements. We were able to discover that David had a sinus problem and was sensitive to dairy products. It was a small step in developing my abilities, but an important one.

Months went by. We had a steady flow of customers, including bed-and-breakfast guests. In quiet times I began to redecorate the double guest bedroom, coming down each day for breaks in the restaurant. A new customer by the name of Vincent began to visit. He was of Italian descent, middle-aged, with a Van Dyke beard. Anne commented that he gave her the creeps, but I liked him. We often talked, and one morning I took him on a tour of the building. He seemed to be drawn to the small bedroom with the tiny window.

Later that day while working in the guest bedroom I had an overwhelming feeling I must go downstairs. The restaurant was closed. As I started my descent, I heard a scream — a female scream — and thought Anne must have fallen. But instead of continuing down, I went into the back bedroom and looked out the window. Anne was hanging out the washing. I returned to the stairs to sit and to listen. The scream came again and I recognised it as a young girl's scream. I shook my head in disbelief; I knew the house was empty. In time I heard Anne come in from the garden. I felt no-one would believe it and decided it was best to say nothing to her.

The next day Vincent arrived as soon as we opened and took me to one side. 'A child followed me home yesterday,' he told me. 'I contacted her mother, but when she came, the child would not go with her.'

I stared at him, not comprehending. 'No child was here yesterday.'

Vincent sighed impatiently. 'It was a child in spirit.'

He obviously meant for me to take him seriously, so I kept a straight face.

'You must know what I'm talking about,' he persisted. 'What happened here yesterday? You must tell me.'

I told him of the screams I had heard.

'The child followed me home after you showed me around the house. When I brought her mother through from spirit, the child refused to go with her.'

By now I was at a loss for words. Vincent explained that he was a medium and he could communicate with the spiritual realm. After he left, I felt compelled to take our two dogs for a walk in the woods, where I spent the time trying to put what he had said into perspective. I drove to Mum's apartment and shared with her what had happened. It was then that she shared her experience when looking after David at the Old Saddlery, and her apprehension of being alone at the property.

Mum told me she and David had been reading in the sitting room when a loud knocking noise came from the surface of the coffee table next to her chair. David jumped out of his seat wanting to know what the noise was. Two more loud knocks followed. 'David went to the window overlooking the street to see who was at the door,' Mum explained, 'but no-one was there.'

She knew the sounds had come from the coffee table but said nothing. Instead, she reassured David and suggested he go up to bed, following him later to say goodnight. He'd calmed down and soon dropped off to sleep. Mum then checked both the restaurant and kitchen doors and on re-entering the sitting room sensed a *presence* so strongly that she felt compelled to firmly speak out, 'I am alive, I am alive.'

'I do not want to be there unless another adult is there as well,' Mum said. 'The building makes me feel uncomfortable.' Her words were a warning of what was to come.

'Who do I talk to about this? Acora! I'll visit him; he will know,' I said.

Acora was a friend, well known for his abilities as a clairvoyant. After my return from Australia in 1980, and prior to reconnecting in person with Anne, I had visited him on the Plymouth Barbican, built in Elizabethan times. He told me a friend with dark hair, a stocky build and the initial 'A' would re-enter my life. 'But,' he warned, 'keep in touch with all your friends, because one day you are going to need them.'

The Barbican is half an hour's drive from Ashburton. I rang Acora to arrange a meeting; I didn't have to explain why. As I sat beside him, he came out strongly with the observation 'There is a spiritual imbalance in your home and it concerns a child.'

The following morning a poorly dressed gypsy came into the restaurant. She was elderly and looked hungry. I offered her a hot drink and something to eat at no charge. She accepted a cup of tea and a slice of my potato and lemon cake and I sat with her while she ate. She reached out and took my hand. 'There is a black cloud over this house, lots of bad luck and misfortune,' she warned.

At that moment, Anne entered the restaurant from the kitchen. The gypsy looked long and hard at her. She remarked on Anne's watch, a Rolex, and asked Anne to give it to her. There was a deathly silence before Anne refused and walked away. The gypsy's next words stayed with me for the rest of the day. 'What little I have and with all that she has, she didn't give me the watch. I want you to know the character of this person.' I realised a point was being made. The gypsy had not intended to keep the watch.

She spotted my nephew Tim, who was my godson and one of my sister's teenage twin sons. He was helping in the kitchen when the gypsy asked me who he was. I introduced Tim to her. 'You and Tim have a bond and are close,' she said. 'He chose to be your nephew in this lifetime to be near you. One day he will follow.' Although I was not sure what she meant, I knew she was right to this extent: I had always felt that Tim and I had strong emotional links.

This was not the first time a gypsy had made an impression on me. When I was twelve years old I came across my mother talking to a gypsy at our front door. When she saw me she asked who I was. 'My younger daughter,' Mum said.

The gypsy walked towards me, stopped a distance away and drew an outline in the air around me, an unusual shape. 'The continent of

Australia is all around you,' she said. 'One day you will go there and never return.'

Later that day Vincent called in and asked if the house was calm. Anne didn't know what he was talking about, so I told her what had happened. She was sceptical, and it showed. I'll have to put an end to this before it gets out of hand, I thought.

Vincent went on to explain that when the child would not go with the mother, he asked the father to come, and the child had gone with him. Good, I thought. I don't understand this, but we seem to have a solution.

I asked him why the father and child had not passed over long ago. He explained that sometimes a person doesn't know how to or does not wish to. Grief felt by a partner can also hold them here. It may be necessary to use a medium to rescue them. Some time later Vincent came to ask whether he could write a story about his experience with the child, but I said I was not comfortable with the idea. We did not see him again.

I was surprised to receive a telephone call from Barbara. My sister and I rarely had personal contact — there seemed to be a gulf between us. I had been there for her and her four children both financially and emotionally when she went through her divorce and afterwards, but we had little in common. She had rung to tell me her current boyfriend, a man born in Ashburton, knew the history of the property. 'The story is that a young girl hanged herself there.'

Fine time to tell me, I thought, gathering the child had died in the empty room we called the roof room, from the large beam at the entrance. No wonder I was unable to enter the room when we had inspected the property. 'Why on earth didn't you tell me before we bought the place?' I asked.

Her reply was that I'd been so keen to buy that she hadn't wanted to tell me the house was haunted. Surely anyone hearing that a property a relative is buying is haunted would mention it to them? Again, I felt the lack of something between my sister and me, something I could not quite put my finger on. After her phone call I spent time pondering and comparing our relationship. My mother and her three sisters were so comfortable and full of love for one another, and yet Barbara and I lacked that rapport.

I decided to see Pat Densham. The memory of her visit and 'sussing us out' had stuck in my mind and I had learnt that she was good with stress issues. There had been a lot of tension at the Old Saddlery. David was reacting to the strain of his parents' divorce. His brother had chosen to stay with his father and the boy's visits to the Old Saddlery were stressful. Anne was distressed; her brother had been financially advantaged by their father, providing an educational advantage over her, a mere girl. Now David's brother was being financially advantaged by his father. History was repeating itself.

I told Pat about the feelings of dread that descended when I was inside the Old Saddlery. I would feel fine until this mood came, then I would curl up on the single bed in the small bedroom and cry. Eventually the mood would pass, only to be replaced by an undercurrent of anger. Pat generously invited me to visit her at her cottage when I was unable to cope. I tried to push the feelings aside but they became stronger and I had to use all my energy not to allow them to affect my working life.

More unusual happenings began. Small objects disappeared from my displays — miniatures, stones and shells. I asked David if he was playing with them and believed him when he said no. I became so edgy that I could not bear to be with David or Anne for long. I experienced strange physical sensations, but could not describe them when I spoke to Pat again.

One evening, the feeling of dread descended so forcibly that I ran from the property, through the garden and into the back lane, making my way towards the main street, crying and distressed, but feeling better now I was out of the house. As I walked along, a car stopped beside me and a woman shouted, 'Get in.'

Pat had been quietly reading at home when she felt compelled to drive through the village. Observing me in the street, she knew she had to take me home with her. While I sat recovering in her office, she took out a pendulum and ran a finger down a sheet of paper containing words, until the pendulum stopped moving. 'Spiritual imbalance,' she said. 'You have a spiritual problem in your home.' Acora had said the same thing and more. 'There is a spiritual imbalance and it concerns a child.' Pat recommended that I see a local clergyman who had dealt with negativity in other houses in the village. I asked her to explain to Anne that it was not my imagination and that something tangible was happening to me. She came, but Anne became impatient, not wanting to listen.

The clergyman, a gentle Catholic priest, came to the house one Sunday afternoon. He carried a Bible, lit a candle and sprinkled holy water through the house. He asked me to repeat prayers in each and every room. He was sincere, but within a few days the dread returned so strongly that I stayed at the local motel overnight. As I lay on the motel bed, the instruction, *Go back and speak to Acora,* entered my mind, so I drove to see him.

Acora took one look at me and remarked, 'The child's father has no intention of leaving. He wants you out because the child stays with you all the time. Don't bring the church in, it will make him worse.'

'Too late,' I said.

'Keep your mother away,' he warned. 'Sell and leave,' he insisted.

'Why is the child drawn to me?' I asked.

'With you she feels safe,' he replied.

I could sense truth in that statement.

My reason for joining the police force had been to learn how to protect and help women and children. I had specialised in that field. However, child or no child, I did not want to sell, and as I entered the Old Saddlery on my return, I was determined to keep the strange feelings of dread out of my mind.

Weekends were very busy for us. Folks would walk Dartmoor and call into the villages for refreshments. The Sunday following the visit by the priest I took an order for four cream teas. I was returning from the kitchen with a tray of cream, jam pots and scones; as I passed the fireplace, the tray was *forced* out of my hands. Stunned, I watched it crash to the floor. The feeling of dread was back with a vengeance. I looked around, but no-one in our small, crowded restaurant had stopped talking or was even looking in my direction. As I struggled to comprehend how this could be, David came from the kitchen and, seeing my distress, bent to clean up the mess. He asked whether it was happening again and I nodded. He helped me towards the kitchen door and Anne looked at us both as I put the tray down. I said nothing and went into the garden with David close behind me.

By this time tears were flowing. I walked to the top of the garden and stood under a tree. There was a plank of wood on the ground and I picked it up. I began hitting an old tree stump with all my might and with each blow the awful feeling rose through my body from deep inside me. It moved slowly through my chest to my throat, where it stayed for a few seconds. I could feel it boiling inside, until it came out as a scream … the scream of the young girl. I sat on the ground crying with relief.

David came over and hugged me, saying over and over, 'I love you Judy. I love you.'

The next morning I moved into a friend's flat. I needed a few days to think. Anne decided to take David on a weekend break, and when they were gone, I went back to the Old Saddlery. I was sitting by the street window in the sitting room, recalling how the wallpaper would peel off overnight when I tried redecorating, when the lights in the room and the rest of the house flickered and then went out. I looked outside but no-one else was in darkness and the street lights were on.

'Stay calm,' I told myself aloud, going to the fuse box only to discover the fuses were fine. This is the father, I decided, and went to find my hockey stick. What I was going to do with it was anyone's guess, but I stood in the sitting room and said loudly, 'I *am not* afraid of you. This is my home and I *am not* leaving. Now, leave me alone.'

As I stood there the phone rang, and as I answered it the lights came on again. It was another medium saying he wanted to see me. I wrote down his address and made an appointment for the next day. I'd never realised there were so many mediums.

When I went to bed I placed my hockey stick on the floor beside me. I was almost asleep when I heard a door open. It was the stable door from the passageway into the restaurant. The catch had a distinctive sound so that we could hear it in the kitchen. My heart began to race. I waited. The kitchen door opened and closed. The dogs slept in the kitchen overnight and I heard their agitation. Then the door from the kitchen to the stairs opened … then closed. Footsteps … a man's heavy footsteps … up they came.

When they stopped outside my bedroom, I was convinced whoever it was would enter, and I broke into a cold sweat. The apprehension was overwhelming. There was a moment of indecision outside the door before the footsteps carried on up to the attic.

I stayed where I was for a matter of seconds, then leapt out of bed and onto the stairs — brandishing my hockey stick. I had to know whether this was a human or a spirit. Nervously, I climbed the stairs to the attic. It was icy-cold and empty.

The next day I visited the medium. The first thing he said was, 'There is a man near you all the time. He wears a naval uniform and is protecting you. He stands by you at night.' Again, confirmation that my father was always near. I explained what had happened the night before in the Old Saddlery. 'That was a visitation.' Visitation! He was so calm about it, as if I had shared a cup of tea with a friend. 'A visitation is where *they* make their presence felt,' he explained. 'You are a very strong person. Because of this you will become a better person.'

'There must be other ways for me to become a better person, surely?'

He told me that when I returned home I was to light a candle and think blue. 'Fill the room with blue,' he said. 'Whoever is there will leave.' He finished by saying, 'You will soon live abroad and become very successful.'

'Fine,' I said, 'but I have to get through this first.' As I drove home I wondered how I was going to think blue. And why blue? I regretted I'd not probed further.

When Anne and David returned, he told me he often heard someone walk on the stairs outside his bedroom at night. To make light of our spirit-filled situation, we called the ghost Fred. Giving him a name seemed to take the apprehension out of it all.

I had not shared these events with my family, knowing Mum would be concerned. But someone I had confided in must have talked about what was happening. I was home alone one morning, with the feeling of dread strong again, when there was a knock at the main street passage door. I opened it and was confronted by a television camera and interviewer. Before I could stop them, they began filming. That night I was on the local news and seen by my mother. She was shocked and concerned.

During all this, the restaurant was visited by representatives from the Egon Roney Group, which publishes a guide to the top two hundred restaurants in Britain. They arrive inconspicuously, eat their way through your entire menu and decide if you are good enough to be included in their publication. I was thrilled, as I was the one who researched the various dishes served and made all the decisions regarding the daily menu. Much later we heard we were to be featured and life became busier than ever.

Regardless of time or circumstance, I had to leave the building when the distressing feelings returned. I spoke to Pat again and she recommended a psychiatrist who worked with spiritual disturbances. This gets worse! Now a psychiatrist! Anyway, I made an appointment to see Dr Bampty. She struck me as a wonderful woman, and I was comfortable with telling her my tale of woe. She explained that Ashburton was mentioned in the *Domesday Book*, Britain's oldest surviving public record, a detailed survey of lands held by William the Conqueror and his people in the 11th century. It was popularly considered to be as final as the judgments of doomsday, hence the name. She had other clients experiencing similar spiritual disturbances, all of whom were living in these old villages and townships surveyed in the *Domesday Book*. Her theory was that there was a link between these present disturbances and the distant past; and the people affected, such as myself, seemed to be drawn to live in these specific villages and townships in this present lifetime to resolve issues either for others in the spiritual realm or for themselves.

'Do you mean to resolve issues from a past life?' I asked in amazement.

'Yes,' she replied calmly.

The notion of one returning lifetime after lifetime was something I felt at ease with, but to be confronted with the reality of an unresolved past-life issue by Dr Bampty left me feeling a little apprehensive.

Anne started to withdraw for days, not wanting to speak to me or David, in fact ignoring our presence in the house. Our working atmosphere was fraught with tension. I felt it was important I record everything, so I began to write detailed notes every day. Then David began to withdraw, spending hours alone in his bedroom until I encouraged him to go for daily walks with me and our dogs.

During winter we took in a lodger to supplement our income. He complained that his room was icy-cold so I gave him an extra heater, but it seemed to make no difference. Then, one evening while out at a party, he felt dizzy. He later told us he had the sensation of 'being borrowed' and felt pressured to return to the Old Saddlery. I told him about Fred, our ghost, and the spirit child. He decided to leave and I wondered whether his feeling of being borrowed meant Fred was weakening. However, after he left, I was again disturbed by feelings ranging from bursts of anger to intense distress, and I was often forcibly drawn back to the small bedroom during the day.

When my mood swings became unbearable, I went to see Pat. After I told her of Dr Bampty's theory, she suggested a past-life reading. I was to understand these were not all of my past-life experiences, just those of importance at this time. I wrote down Pat's reading for my notes.

11th century: Born a Jewish male in what is now Israel.

12th century: Born in Ashburton, in the same street as the Old Saddlery. One of two sisters, I died in a fire at the age of sixteen. Following my death by fire, I chose to return as a male Aboriginal in Australia. I was killed with a spear during a tribal war. She said I had been born an Australian Aboriginal many times. I had not mentioned to her that I had lived in Australia in this present lifetime.

19th century: Born in England, again male. I lived in Cornwall, but while young was wrongly accused of theft and deported to Tasmania, where I chose death by suicide.

My life prior to this present lifetime: Again Jewish, as in the 11th century, born in Norway to a restrictive and wealthy family. Because I had a lover I was murdered by my jealous sister.

I pondered the two Jewish past-life experiences and recalled my six months in America in my early twenties as a nanny. I had chosen a Jewish family from a long list of employers and had lived on Long Island with them for six months. I had always been drawn to books about Jewish people. Being born in 1946, just after the Second World War, I was aware of the atrocities the Jews had suffered. Reconciliation was attempted by our teachers at school, who encouraged us to have German pen pals to help heal the rift between England and Germany, and hopefully pass some measure of healing on to the next generation. This was how Erika, who lived in Western Germany, came into my life. We became lifelong friends.

I visited Germany many times and loved it. But I recall one visit when I was driven to the beautiful Alsace region of France by Erika and her husband. In one village I was drawn to an alley where tourists were looking down into a pit that was covered by a metal grating. A plaque explained this was where Jews had been placed and people had walked over them. I was filled with an intense fear as I stared down into the darkness. I walked back to Erika, still carrying those feelings — I could not speak. I was aware only that she was German. At last, I saw her as my friend again and took her arm as we walked on down the street. Another strong feeling I'd experienced from time to time, though not a negative one as in this case, was a longing to visit the Wailing Wall in Jerusalem. Now I understood where that fear and that desire might well have come from — two specific past lives.

'Born in Ashburton during the 12th century, in the same street as the Old Saddlery.' This could explain the knowing that *I must buy this place*. I was beginning to accept that for some reason I was meant to live in North Street and in the Old Saddlery.

'Born an Australian Aboriginal many times.' I recalled the gypsy's prediction when I was twelve years old: 'The continent of Australia is all around you and one day you will go there and never return.' When I first sailed from Singapore to Western Australia in October 1974, my intention had been to spend a six-week holiday there. As I stood on the cruise ship *Fedor Shalyapin* watching the low white coastline of Australia appear, the feeling of returning home had been overwhelming. We docked at Fremantle and then I flew to Adelaide in South Australia. I looked for work and was offered a job as a security officer for Myer Department Stores. I applied for residency, and my holiday — much to my family's concern — became a two-year absence from England.

Within months of my arrival in Australia I had felt compelled to fly north to Alice Springs. I travelled to the Aboriginal sacred site of Uluru (Ayers Rock) in the Red Centre. I had been drawn to read about the Dreamtime, the foundation of Aboriginal culture. I spent time with Aboriginals in the outback during May 1979 and experienced the comfortable feeling of belonging. I loved it all — the children with smiling faces, full of fun and mischief, the women gathering and preparing food, the elderly men working at their various crafts with quiet dignity. I was affected by the horrific stories I'd heard of abuse towards Aboriginals. Now I understood why: Pat had confirmed my past lives as an Australian Aboriginal. The land, its original culture and peoples were part of me.

I also took a trip to the Australian island state of Tasmania, in March 1976, to visit the penal colony at Port Arthur, and stood on the ground that had been walked on by convicts from England. One vivid memory from that visit is of me standing on the cliffs looking out to the sea and being drawn to jump. Such a feeling of despair swept over me that I had to step back and walk away. Had I been wrongly charged with theft in the 19th century and removed from Cornwall in England by force, pleading my innocence? And if I had been innocent, was it any wonder I had chosen death by suicide rather than life imprisonment? I had now travelled once more to Australia from the south-west of England, but under very different circumstances and of my own free will.

Then there was Pat's statement that my life prior to this present lifetime came to its end by being murdered by a jealous sister because I had a lover. The word *lover* kept repeating in my mind until I recalled the day Anne and I moved into the Old Saddlery and I had found two miniature Willow Pattern chamber pots left behind by the previous owner: the Willow Pattern illustrates the Chinese legend of 'The Lovers'. At the time, the words *the lovers* had played on my mind all day, and I had not understood why. These pots were now in the kitchen window, and I sensed they had been left in the house for me. For some reason the word *lover* had importance for me, and I remembered Pat's words, 'These are by no means all your lifetimes, only those of importance at this time.'

Was the strained atmosphere between my sister and me from the 12th century? Had we been sisters in Ashburton, or Norway, or both? There was an animosity towards me over my closeness with our mother, but there was something else I could not identify. I felt a sense of unease, and so brought my mind back to the present.

I began to experience mood swings once again. Late one evening I went outside into the back garden for a while. I kept telling myself, 'I need help.' In bed that night I developed a headache and woke in pain. I opened my eyes and saw a long, dark tunnel with a bright white light at its far end. My head entered the tunnel, I was not aware of the rest of my body. The pain began to recede as I was washed by wave upon wave of the most beautiful blue colour. It soon disappeared and I fell asleep.

When I awoke the next morning I understood that I must dress, get into the car and drive. I headed towards Torquay and spotted a fair in a field by the main road. I wondered whether this was my destination, and a deeper level of my mind confirmed this. On a gypsy-style caravan I saw a sign 'Readings by Appointment' and knew I must take down the phone number. Later I made an appointment to see Dawn Davie. All that morning I had been acutely aware of the fact that when I formed a question in my mind another energy in the form of a thought would superimpose itself in reply. It was my first awareness of being *guided*, and I felt only total willingness to follow the directions.

At the last moment Anne decided to come with me when I kept my appointment. I was uncomfortable with this, but she insisted. She was invited to wait while I was led to a room by a plump woman in her fifties. I noticed a well-used pack of tarot cards on the table. As Dawn and I sat down opposite one another, she asked, 'Why is there so much aggression between you two?' I replied that it was a long story and offered no further information. I was weary of it all — my mood swings, Fred and the tensions that had arisen between the three of us. Dawn studied twenty-four cards that she'd asked me to select. 'You are walking parallel with the spirit world. Very near to going abroad again. There are three people from spirit standing behind me. The first is a motherly figure who sends her love.' I could see no-one, but I was drawn to my silver signet ring. It had been given to me by my sister, Barbara, and its central moonstone was from the jewellery box of our maternal grandmother, Lilian Storey-Smith. I wondered if she was the motherly figure. To my surprise, Dawn smiled at me in acknowledgement.

Then she said a smiling man had pushed forward. I knew that was my father. 'He has a mannerism you have inherited of putting your fingers to your mouth when concentrating,' Dawn told me. 'He has a message for you. You will be helped by spirit and he stands by you at night. You need a rescue to take place,' she continued. She went on to explain that she used to do the rescuer's work, but had not done so for some time. My heart sank and then she explained that it meant she would need a helper. 'I will come next Sunday the seventeenth, late in the afternoon,' she said.

There was no further reference to the third spiritual person, and she told me there would be a charge only for the reading, not for the rescue. I left wondering how I could be rescued from what was happening. I shared all this with Mum, telling her about my having asked for help and being sent to see Dawn, and that Daddy and her mother were waiting for me. I told her how he had conveyed the message and the assurance that I would be helped by spirit.

Sunday came and the restaurant was so busy I was kept occupied all day. When we closed at five o'clock I started to become agitated. Perhaps Dawn would not come. Then there was a knock on the passageway door and I opened it to her and her helper, Sue, a woman in her thirties, tall and slim with long brown hair. Anne was apprehensive, but I was curious. We sat in the restaurant while Dawn explained what might happen, and told me I was to do whatever I was asked by either herself or Sue — whoever was not influenced or taken over by a spirit entity or entities. This was important, she said, so I readily agreed.

Both Dawn and Sue fell silent, looking at one another and asking simultaneously whether the other could hear a ticking clock. There was no clock in the restaurant. Dawn stood and walked around, remarking that there was nothing here. We all walked out into the kitchen. The same comment: 'Nothing here.' We moved up to the first floor and into the sitting room. Dawn turned and asked if I had difficulty decorating or furnishing this room. I hadn't told her about the wallpaper that continually fell off the wall or of the knocking noise from the coffee table, though I was surprised at the ease with which she homed in on the strangeness of this room.

'Why do you ask?

'The old lady living in here doesn't like your taste,' she replied. I smiled, struggling to come to terms with what she'd said. Again Dawn said, 'Nothing here': the old lady was to be left in peace.

She checked the back bedroom and the bathroom and then continued up the narrow stairs to the double guest bedroom. Many times I had rushed up to this room when we had guests, having smelt smoke. The Old Saddlery was a no-smoking building.

Dawn looked towards the wide street window and smiled. 'Just a man smoking his pipe,' she said. 'Harmless.'

'We have a house full of spirits!' Anne whispered to me.

When Dawn walked into the small bedroom, she stopped. Within seconds she was curled up on the bed, just as I had done so many times. Sue warned us that it was all starting. Anne backed away a little down the landing, and my heart began to race. I was mesmerised.

Dawn began to sob, and I felt I was watching myself. The sobbing continued for a few minutes until out of Dawn's mouth came the faint, frightened voice of a female child. The child repeatedly asked for her mother. It was fascinating.

Still crying, the child said, 'It's so dark in here.' She described the room, how dirty it was — her mattress on the floor and thin bars at the tiny window. In reality the room was clean and bright, with clear glass and curtains at the window.

Dawn put her hands to her face and started to shake. Again the child spoke, this time to Sue, asking where her mother was. Sue indicated the window and down towards the kitchen doorway. The child became more distressed, 'Why won't Mummy help me?' she cried. Over and over again she repeated, 'Why won't Mummy help me?'

Dawn left the bed and crouched in a far corner, still crying. It was distressing to watch. She became agitated, saying, 'He's coming, he's coming. Don't let him beat me again. Why won't Mummy help me?'

Sue bent down and took Dawn by the arm. Helping her up, she led her from the room. Anne and I glanced at one another nervously, wondering what was going to happen next. Sue tried to encourage Dawn up the narrow stairs to the attic, but Dawn stopped outside the roof room.

God, what is going to happen now? I wondered, as my mind went reeling back to my sister telling me a young girl had hung herself in this room. Dawn sank down onto the staircase outside, crying.

The child spoke again. 'Where is Judy? I am not going to leave her.' I was speechless. She looked at me through Dawn's eyes. 'Where are the birds? Where are the beads with pretty colours? I've been hiding things from you.' The mystery of my missing miniatures was solved.

The child read my thoughts. In a low voice, she spoke directly to me, telling me something no-one knew, *no-one*. She described me alone at night lying in bed and a dreadful loneliness would come and a tear would run down my face. 'Judy needs me.' This child knew me. 'You are walking parallel with spirit,' Dawn had told me. I finally accepted that I was.

Without warning the atmosphere changed and a violent energy came as the child described her death by strangulation. She had not committed suicide; she had been murdered by her father. I was filled with anger and before I could recover, the mood changed and the child was calm. 'I can't leave Judy,' she said, 'she is not happy. Judy needs someone of her own. I am not going to leave her.'

Sue looked at me and in a firm, stern voice directed me to help Dawn climb the remaining stairs to the attic. Anne was asked to help too. In the attic, Sue directed Anne to sit behind me and she sat behind Dawn. Sue informed me that the mother was there, in the far corner. I could see nothing, but the room gradually became icy-cold. Sue spoke in a gentle voice to the child, explaining that her mother was present and wanted her to go with her. But the child continued to say over and over again, 'I am not leaving Judy.'

I was anxious, torn between solving the situation and handing the child over to an unknown — the mother who had not helped her child when she had been so desperate. As far as I could see, handing the girl over was not going to be the solution. Sue was prepared for my reaction and reminded me I had given my word to cooperate. She explained that the mother would soon fade and the opportunity would be lost.

I looked at the child, remembering everything that had happened, until I found the words. 'I don't want you here.' Immediately there was a ghastly, wrenching feeling in my chest, I leaned back and Anne held me. It went on and on — a loss of energy from my insides out. It was scary. I held on until I lost consciousness.

When I came to, Dawn was Dawn and I was myself. The rescue had worked. Returning to the restaurant, more than a little shaken, I told Dawn I thought she was a brave woman. I could not thank her enough. It had been a dreadful strain, and Dawn and I found we needed to drink lots of water.

She told me the child's name was Julie and that she was about eleven or twelve years old. Earlier, Pat had given me that name and Acora had described the child. Dawn explained that I had been experiencing the emotions of the child and the father: the fear and distress of the child and the anger of the father. She warned us the father would walk the house again just to make his presence felt. Sue played the tape recording of the rescue and we could hear the ticking clock. Dr Bampty had been proved correct without doubt, and I felt a great sense of relief that the distressing past-life issue for the spirit child Julie was resolved and she was now safe.

But we were to discover the trauma was not completely over. Two days later I found Anne standing in the small bedroom by the window and, not realising anything was wrong, spoke to her about an issue regarding David. To my dismay, she turned on me with such fury that I had to back away. I felt sure this was the emotion I had felt, and encouraged David away from the house until Anne calmed down. Several days later I went down to the kitchen to help her with the pre-opening routine. I spoke to her, but was met by silence. Then she began to verbally abuse me. I moved away, saying I was going to open the restaurant. As I went to the restaurant door a large piece of china crashed into the door frame by my head. I looked around just in time to see another large plate flying my way. Anne was shouting a mass of jumbled sentences.

When she picked up a long kitchen knife, I dived at her and managed to hold her firmly against the bench. She started sobbing as David bounded through the door from the stairs, having heard the commotion. Slowly, very slowly, Anne released her grip on the knife and a wave of relief swept through me as she collapsed onto the floor. David and I agreed we had to get his mother out of the house. She was distressed and agitated as I drove the three of us to Pat Densham's home.

Pat told us that, although the rescue of the child had been a success, the father was still a problem. She advised us to contact Dawn. In some ways it was a comfort for me to see Anne affected — I had dealt for so long with it all on my own — but her physical violence towards me was concerning.

Dawn and Sue came to see us and we sat in the restaurant. Dawn said the child was gone, but the father was angry and for some reason was using Anne to demonstrate his anger. We had to find out why and deal with it before I was put at risk again.

'The father stays in the passageway,' she said. 'He was disturbed when you went to open the restaurant and used Anne to stop you.' As Dawn explained, she and Sue exchanged glances. They both said, 'The clock is ticking again.' They looked towards the entrance to the passageway. 'He is here,' they said in unison.

I went cold inside and apprehension flowed through me as I moved closer to Anne, as if to protect her. Anne was rigid. Dawn stood and began pacing up and down, up and down. She had taken on Fred's persona, thrusting her shoulders back, seeming to grow to his size. He began to knock over the restaurant chairs. The violent atmosphere in the room was almost unbearable. Sue, totally calm, said Fred was drunk. 'It is his intention to intimidate.'

'Well, it is working,' I replied.

Through Dawn, Fred began to speak. He strode towards Anne and towered over her. Nose to nose, he said, 'You remind me of my wife.' I became tense. All the times I had asked Anne for help she had given none, only criticism or silence. The child had asked her mother for help, over and over, but received none. For a moment I felt in accord with this man but then the feeling left me.

Dawn became herself again and sat down. It was amazing to watch the transformation. She explained the father was seeking the child but could not find her. He was not able to 'cross over' to the next existence because his wife would not forgive him. As she spoke, Dawn changed again, this time appearing slight and fragile. She began to speak in a timid voice, the voice of a frightened woman, the persona of the mother. She explained how she could not forgive herself for not protecting her daughter, and was adamant that she would not forgive the father. She was making a stand.

How complex it was! I was relating to the issues and emotions as if watching a play. When the mother left, Dawn told Anne she must forgive the father. I recognised this was also a present-day situation for Anne regarding her own father. Anne's response was that she was not prepared to do this. Dawn took on the stance of Fred, becoming aggressive and pacing, as before, but Anne sat silently with a blank face. Fred started to use abusive language so I gently touched Anne's arm in an effort to break her silence. I felt I had to do something or the situation might not be contained. Sue spoke to Anne very firmly. 'Do it now. Do you forgive him?'

Anne replied in a quiet, timid voice, 'Yes.'

This filled me with apprehension: it was not a sincere reply. When I had released the child, Julie, I had done so with love, but this was not happening here. This present situation was all too personal for Anne. Sue asked again, 'Do you forgive him?'

Anne spat out the word, 'Yes.'

Fred walked towards the passageway. Dawn stopped, and he must have continued on as Dawn returned to the table as herself, but very shaken. We must have all shared the same thoughts. Had it worked? Was Anne free? Was Fred free to completely pass over? I only knew I had played my part and the spirit child, Julie, was free.

Our lives should have been peaceful now, but tensions began to grow again, not because of spiritual problems, but on account of a very human one: money. Anne had been forced to take David out of private school: competing with his father and her other son, she had been providing a private education that was draining our resources.

Four years before, Anne had applied to immigrate to Australia with David after her divorce, and sought approval from the Family Court in Bristol. But in January 1982 her application failed, partly due to her ex-husband objecting but mainly because she had never been to Australia. Anne accompanied me on my brief return visit to Australia a few months later, leaving David with her parents in England, in order to appeal the Judge's decision. In the expectation of a divorce settlement, she borrowed the funds for the journey. Her appeal failed, the Judge ordering that she wait another three years.

As an Australian resident I was required to return to the country at regular intervals to renew my residency visa. I booked to return to Australia in February 1985 with the aim of being back in Ashburton prior to my birthday in early March.

The previous year my birthday had been marred by an unpleasant incident. My mother and I had seen a framed Japanese silk print of wild geese flying in formation in the shop next door and had admired it. On our return to the restaurant, Anne overheard Mum offer to buy it for my birthday, and immediately went to the gift shop and bought it for me instead! I was embarrassed and Mum was upset; there was an undercurrent between the three of us. Breakfast on my birthday was filled with tension when I opened the present. On the back of the framed print Anne had written in bold lettering: 'Judy. No you can't fly away. Love and best wishes for a Happy Birthday. The Old Saddlery 1984. Anne.'

Now, a year later, I was planning to take that flight, and it was decided that while in Australia I would look for a sponsorship for Anne and David to assist them with their renewed application before the judge. We researched the best way for me to travel and I decided to purchase a Capital City airfare ticket. I spent my entire visit flying between Adelaide, Melbourne, Sydney, Brisbane and Sydney once again, before flying to Hobart. When I returned to Adelaide I reconnected with two friends who had opened a café at the Art Gallery of South Australia. They were interested when I told them Anne had taken a *Cordon Verte* course. I obtained the necessary forms from Immigration. I'd secured a job sponsorship for Anne.

When I arrived back in Ashburton we began to plan Anne and David's move to Australia. Our bank manager, Geoff Coyte, advised us not to sell the Old Saddlery until after summer trading and to keep trading right up to any sale. We obtained quotes from several overseas removalists and took David to Bristol to engage his own solicitor for representation in the Family Court. David and Anne were very excited at the prospect of moving to the other side of the world.

Weeks passed and then we received a phone call from our café friends in Adelaide — their sponsorship application had failed. As usual, Anne's reaction was long bouts of silence and David expressed his disappointment with difficult behaviour. While sorry for them, it was difficult for me to deal with the customers while tension reigned in the background. Soon I started dreading opening hours, but dreaded even more the hours when we were closed and all alone together. The words *Visit Dawn*, repeated in my mind, so I went to visit her at her home.

'One day,' she said, 'you will understand what symbols mean and then you will understand the meaning of life. You are opening up. One day you will be truly psychic.' We spoke of the atmosphere at the Old Saddlery and of my feelings. Dawn asked me what I would really like to do, and without having to think, I said, 'Get on a plane.'

Her reply was, 'Well, do it.'

On my return to the Old Saddlery, I confronted Anne about her attitude. We were business partners and something had to be decided.

We discussed the possibility of my sponsoring Anne myself, involving yet another trip for me Down Under.

Once again, we looked at flights and prices and a knowing began inside me that I must visit specific places. A sense of trust preceded these detailed directions and the route for me to follow led to New Delhi in India, where I would take the popular Triangle Tour to Agra and the Taj Mahal, then on to Jaipur and the Pink City, and back to New Delhi. Next, I must fly to Kathmandu in Nepal, and directions were given as to the places to visit. On a stated day, I was to fly to Bangkok and visit the Grand Palace before flying to Australia. The push for me to visit these places was so strong it left me both nervous and excited. The airlines were chosen for me, along with a departure date from Heathrow airport. I assumed I would be away for six months. The Old Saddlery was back on the market.

I went to see Acora, knowing he would be pleased I was leaving the building, even though I had not been disturbed since the rescue of the child. Anne insisted on coming with me. Acora told us both not to accept the first offer. 'There will be a second offer.' He was adamant about this and so we agreed. As we were leaving, Acora took me aside. 'Is Anne going with you?'

'No,' I replied, and he seemed pleased.

My friend Herm visited the restaurant and I confided about my travel plans and the directions regarding the routes and destinations. She was fascinated. I told her I felt it was my father insisting I take this trip, requiring me to pack twenty-eight boxes, to include: china from the restaurant overflow stock, the Willow Pattern miniature chamber pots, bedding and other items, and clothing, all in preparation for my rented home in Australia. Through my hockey club in Adelaide, I had arranged to rent a friend's beach shack in Middleton, South Australia. The boxes were already on their way by sea.

'It sounds as if you will be in Australia longer than six months,' Herm replied.

My sister Barbara was involved with a local theatre group and rarely came to the restaurant, so I was unaware of a situation that was building between her and my mother. It would be so traumatic it would dramatically change all of our lives forever. The first hint of change was when Mum rang and told me she was thinking of selling her apartment. I was shocked. Her home was ideal and she was very happy there.

I discovered later that Barbara had taken a high-flier from the theatre world to Mum's apartment for afternoon tea and he had taken a fancy to the place. There was talk of an offer to purchase. Barbara had told him I was returning to Australia to live and it would be better for Mum to live closer to her. I couldn't understand her reasoning, as there was no intention on my part to reside permanently in Australia at this time and Barbara lived just a ten-minute drive from Mum. I had an uncomfortable feeling about the whole suggestion.

Mum said, 'A nice little house had been found near Barbara's', and she asked me to drive to see it. It was part of an estate and I felt it would be a security nightmare. The street was at the bottom of a steep hill, no shops or post office. At present, Mum could just walk to her local shops and draw her pension, and the bus to Torquay stopped outside her apartment. She was on the first floor in a very upmarket area, and she was friendly with the owner of the apartment below hers. It was a very safe environment.

Mum was being swept along by Barbara and her second husband, Eric, and I was aware of the hard-sell tactics they were both using. There are times when your own gut instinct tells you something is not quite right, and for me this was one of those times. The high-flier usually stayed in an expensive serviced apartment when he visited Torquay, but preferred to purchase a residence. Barbara had involved herself in this decision and so Mum's apartment had been visited. A price was mentioned, but Mum refused, the offer was a thousand pounds below her asking price, if she did agreed to sell. Barbara returned with a new offer. She told Mum she was acting as this man's agent and he was willing to raise the offer a thousand pounds but he wanted the apartment to be left fully furnished.

Mum responded by saying she wanted to keep certain pieces of her furniture, but would replace anything that she decided to take with her. If she had sought independent advice, she would have been shown this new offer left her even worse off. To refurnish would cost more than a thousand pounds. As his agent, Barbara would be earning a fee, so it was now in her interest to encourage Mum to move.

Anne and I visited Mum to talk about our plans regarding Australia and while we were there Barbara and Eric arrived. We were to witness the next stage of the saga. They began to walk around Mum's home, discussing the furnishings. In the dining room, they commented that the furniture would look nice in *their* home. They then expressed interest in the handmade telephone table in the hallway. Mum had to step forward and literally prevent them from taking the table then and there as they left.

The next day Barbara rang to invite me to meet her for coffee in Wellswood, a very exclusive area of Torquay. We had never in all our lifetime had coffee out together before. I drove to meet her at the café. She was between cleaning jobs, one of several casual occupations in which she was engaged to support herself and her four children, and, as always, was in a hurry. One of her jobs was cleaning the home of a solicitor. I was aware of how tired and stressed Barbara was. Being overweight, she was breathless and her bleach-blonde hair was flattened by perspiration. We ordered coffee.

She told me the high-flier now wanted to buy Mum's apartment in the name of his nephew. He wanted Mum to change her solicitor to the man who employed her. 'This will make the sale go through more easily,' she said. The fact that she was talking to me behind Mum's back gave me real cause for concern. My concern increased when she said I had more influence with her. She asked me to put it to Mum that changing solicitors was a good idea. When I asked why, her reply was, 'Mum's solicitor might query the sale.'

That convinced me all was not well, and when I told her I was not happy about the whole thing she got up and walked out. I drove to Mum's apartment and told her what had happened. She was confused and I was very anxious. I advised her not to change our family solicitor and then drove home. I was only home a short time when the phone rang. It was Mum. She was excited and was ringing to tell me Barbara had suggested she travel with me to Australia for a six-month holiday. I was taken aback. I knew Mum had only a small amount in the bank. I asked how she was going to pay for her trip, as I had no extra cash. Mum explained Barbara was going to ask the high-flier for a deposit of a thousand pounds to ensure the sale progressed. All this was making me very uneasy, but I was struggling to cope with the tensions in the Old Saddlery and negotiating an involved overseas trip, and I didn't have a clear enough head to express my concerns to Mum in a forthright way.

Why was Barbara encouraging Mum to use the deposit to go away with me? She needed all of her capital, not less. Each offer was making her less financially secure. This latest development threw me into turmoil. It was now just weeks to my departure and I had to change a complex trip booked for one into a trip for two. I drove Mum to London to obtain her visa for Australia, and put through visa applications for the other countries to be visited. Unknown to me, the promised one thousand pounds deposit had not arrived and Mum was forced to draw from her savings to pay for the visas and her air tickets. In London she was issued with an Australian extended multiple-entry visa.

Anne's reaction to the news my mother would be in Australia with me for six months was first shock, then aggression, then long bouts of silence. Barbara and her high-flyer were creating havoc in all of our lives, but worse was to come. As his agent, it was Barbara's responsibility to ensure the payment of the deposit. Instead, on the pretext of taking Mum for a drive, she drove Mum to her own bank. She had made an appointment with her bank manager for Mum to switch her bank account to Barbara's branch. Mum refused to keep the appointment as her bank manager had served her well for almost a lifetime. Ignoring the tension, Barbara then drove Mum to her employing solicitor, to yet another pre-arranged appointment. This time Barbara persuaded her to go inside.

Once inside the solicitor's office, Mum was told she was there to sign an already prepared document. It was to hand over her power of attorney to Barbara, so she could act for Mum regarding the sale of her apartment while Mum was in Australia. There had been no prior discussion with Mum and she did not know what was happening. Barbara's solicitor explained, that — giving 'power of attorney' to someone — meant giving away all her rights to control her financial affairs and assets. There was an embarrassing silence as Mum grasped the seriousness of the matter. 'Surely you can trust your own daughter?' the solicitor asked. It was embarrassing with Barbara standing in the room, so Mum signed. Then Barbara made herself scarce.

Rather than say anything to me about the circumstances regarding her signing the power of attorney, Mum continued to draw from her savings. Anne and I visited her to talk about the travel arrangements. By now we knew Barbara had Mum's power of attorney to handle the sale of the apartment, but not how it had been obtained. Barbara was there when we arrived, and when Mum and Anne left the room she spoke to me about handing over my power of attorney to ensure an easy sale of the Old Saddlery. Having made it clear over the years that she disliked Anne, I wondered how they would work together. Barbara was insistent, so I reluctantly agreed. I thought it was strange how quickly the necessary papers were presented to me for my signature, but I was hugely distracted by the dramas at home and trying to organise Mum's travel, and so allowed the niggling thoughts to move to the back of my mind.

Time was running out for Mum to pay for all her travel bookings. She confronted Barbara about the deposit and was told the sale was off, the high-flier having decided he no longer wanted to buy. Mum was now committed financially and emotionally to the trip, and so was forced to withdraw all her savings. I was still in the dark about the dubious means by which Mum's power of attorney had been obtained. We discussed whether to cancel the sale of the apartment, but Mum said she wanted the little house, having been convinced by Barbara and Eric the move was a good thing.

The evening before we were to leave for London and Heathrow airport, Barbara came to Mum's apartment. Anne and David were also there. They were going to drive us to the airport the next day. Barbara spent the evening looking through the 'Properties for Sale' column in the local newspaper while I watched, thinking how odd it was. She mentioned other properties for sale, but Mum was adamant — there would be no sale unless it was to buy the specific little house. The phone rang and it was my nephew Tim, calling to say he loved me and goodbye. Barbara used this distraction to leave.

At Heathrow, we were met by a former school friend, Dianne, who had come to see us off. Dianne gave me a St Christopher medallion. 'To keep you safe,' she said.

As I accepted Dianne's gift, Acora's words, spoken prior to Anne re-entering my life, came into my mind, 'A woman with the initial "A" is coming into your life. But keep in touch with all your friends, because one day you are going to need them.'

Our plane landed in New Delhi on 27 October 1985. The airport was like a huge shed — the new airport in memory of Mrs Ghandi had not yet been built — and the luggage from all flights was piled high in a corner. It took a while to find our suitcases and we were exhausted when we walked from the airport. From around a corner came the smiling dark face of our tour guide. He knew us from photographs we had provided. 'Judy, all night I dream of you,' he said, and I laughed.

We walked from a poorly air-conditioned building into another world. The noise struck me first: bicycle bells constantly ringing and the blaring of taxi horns. I watched an elephant slowly kneel as several tourists struggled into the *howdah* on its back to make themselves comfortable. The guide explained this was the complimentary taxi to their hotel. Fortunately, our guide found us a normal taxi and bargained with the driver over the price to take us to our luxurious hotel.

Our first excursion involved the famous Red Fort. There was some sort of festival taking place and there appeared to be thousands of people. A snake charmer cornered my mother and asked for two rupees. I rescued her by handing him the money. This made Mum a little nervous, but most people we encountered were taken with her tall, elegant stance and thick, wavy, white hair, treating her with great respect.

The following day we set off by coach for Agra where I would fulfil a dream of visiting the Taj Mahal. But I was aware I had not chosen this route and wondered at its importance. This incredible monument was built by the Emperor Shah Jehan in memory of his third wife, Mumtaz Mahal. His intention was to build a mausoleum in black marble on the other side of the river, but his son Aurangzeb took power and imprisoned the emperor in a fort in Agra. As I read the story, the words *Taken power* repeated in my mind and I experienced an inexplicable feeling of loss.

Later, a young boy approached Mum, spoke his name and then said, 'Remember my name; that is all I have.' I watched my mother falter as she reached out to him, but he was soon lost again in the crowd. I had observed a seller of wares before entering the Taj Mahal and was drawn to an elaborately decorated soapstone box. I spotted him again and bought the box, handing it to my mother as a gift. As she accepted, I felt compelled to say to her, 'This box connects you to this place and a child.' The words *taken power* and *a child* repeated in my mind. I had the feeling of loss as I wrote the words in my notes.

Our tour continued on to Jaipur and the Hotel Bissau Palace. Later, we were driven out of the city to the 17th-century mogul Amber Fort, passing the Water Palace on the way. The palace is built in a lake, and its reflection on the surface of the water creates the charming impression that it is floating. At the base of the hill leading up to the fort we were helped on to one of sixty beautiful elephants to be carried there. There were spectacular views and interesting buildings to explore before returning to our hotel in Jaipur. Later, we returned to Delhi by rail. The

Pink Express was packed but we had seat reservations so could travel in comparative comfort.

We flew from Delhi to Kathmandu with Air India, and the views of the Himalayas were breathtaking. Nepal was covered by a network of terraces, for this was how families farmed the land, each generation creating new terraces. Kathmandu Valley is its historical centre of culture. I thought about our visit to India, the emotion of loss and the message *taken power* and *a child*, and wondered what we were to absorb in Nepal.

Following the awesome experience of witnessing sunrise in the Himalayas, our guide took us to Durbar Square in Bodhanacs, to a temple with five pagodas — the highest temple in Nepal. As I climbed the massive staircase I felt an incredible pull towards the huge statues that lined each side of the stone staircase. I headed for one of the stone elephants but found myself held fast beside the huge figure of a seated man holding a cylindrical container in his right hand. *Manuscript* repeated in my mind, and then the direction *Ask your mother to capture this image of you with this statue*.

Later we were driven to another Durbar Square in Patan, and the Temple of Ten Thousand Buddhas. I was drawn to touch one of Buddha's images when a strong sense of *familiarity* came and the confirmation, *Yes, this is a part of you*.

Our last temple of the day was on a hill on the outskirts of the town, the Stupa of Swayambunath, the oldest sacral building of Buddhism, built 2500 years ago. The all-seeing eyes of Buddha were enormous and featured on all its four faces. On its east side, 365 steps led to the top. A shaven-headed female Buddhist monk was turning the prayer wheels and Mum and I joined her. There was a *familiarity* about this and Mum and I exchanged excited smiles. Our young male guide explained that the coloured eyes were the wisdom eyes of Buddha and the dot between them was the mark of the third eye. *Third eye* repeated in my mind, until I added this information to my notes.

Another day was spent at the temple district of Pashupatinath, the most sacred and divine Hindu temple in a gorge of the Bagmati River. Again I experienced a sense of *familiarity* and belonging as I marvelled at the golden roofs. I was drawn to stand by a row of beggars, many crippled, and our guide explained these people had undertaken a hard karmic lesson, everyone helping as best they could. I was only then able to walk away. The words *a hard karmic lesson* repeated in my mind, and I felt apprehensive.

Durbar Square, Bodhanacs, Nepal

The flight to Bangkok provided the opportunity to re-read the messages. We were booked to spend time at the Grand Palace and visit the Chapel Royal to see the Emerald Buddha. Inside the chapel, the direction came for me to learn the origins of the Buddhist faith. The Emerald Buddha is a one-piece jade, an object of national veneration. I started to walk away but was held until I looked at the *Guide to the Grand Palace* and read:

> ... life-story of the Buddha commencing with the south-west corner on the right of the high altar where is depicted his birth, childhood, youth, and renunciation in search of Truth. On the east wall fronting the high altar the temptation and enlightenment, the figure underneath the Buddha's seat being that of Mother Earth ...

The words *in search of Truth* and *Mother* repeated again and again, until I was freed to join Mum outside. Later, on the flight to Australia, I set aside a page to re-record the messages. As I wrote them down, a sense of deep grief came and I was made aware that The Lovers pots and the Wild Geese print from Ashburton were on their way to Australia.

> Highlighted words 1985: The Lovers – a rescue – Taj Mahal – taken power – a child – a feeling of loss – manuscript – Buddha's image – Yes, this is a part of you – third eye – a hard karmic lesson – in search of Truth – Mother.

On 9 November we landed in Sydney and flew on to Adelaide. Jan, the friend who owned the beach shack, was waiting with another hockey friend, Julia. Mum and Julia had first forged a close friendship when Mum had flown to Adelaide in December 1975 to spend Christmas with me. We stayed two nights with Julia; then I hired a car in order to follow Jan to the beach shack in Middleton, near Victor Harbor. The shack was a holiday home on the edge of the beach. There was no telephone, just miles of sand with low surf. Its location presented problems: when I returned the car we would be without transport, and I could not find work without a car. It was a beautiful place but we were cut off. I rang Anne from the local telephone box and we agreed I should buy a second-hand car. My share of the funds from the sale of the Old Saddlery would clear this debt. As a result, I found work as a trainee manager with a motel in nearby Goolwa.

Mum wrote letters to her sisters and Barbara about our travels and asked Barbara to withdraw all her recent pension payments and send Mum a banker's draft, having left signed cheques for this purpose. Barbara replied, but ignored Mum's request, offering no explanation. Her letter contained only family news and a ten-pound note. Annoyed, Mum replied by return post, requesting the several hundred pounds. Barbara ignored Mum's request yet again, sending another ten-pound note and offering no explanation. Mum was being left in Australia with no personal money.

It was only then that Mum told me the story of her handing over the power of attorney to Barbara. When she finished, the atmosphere was heavy with our silence, the unspoken words hanging in the air between us. Against my better judgement, we decided to give Barbara the benefit of the doubt.

I opened a joint account for Anne and me with the ANZ Bank to receive my share of my capital input and profit share from the sale of the Old Saddlery. She sent over her signature in a letter but wrote that she was planning to close the restaurant before Christmas. I replied by return, reminding her that our bank manager, Geoff Coyte, had said she must continue to trade right up to any sale. It had to be sold as a going concern.

Anne's letter held a shock: she wrote that the house Mum wanted to buy had been sold *before* we left. So that was why Barbara had looked at real estate advertisements the evening of our departure. But why had she not told Mum? There was no reason for her to hold on to Mum's power of attorney, so why hadn't she admitted that?

Christmas came and went without any contact from Barbara, only letters from my twin nephews, Tim and Mark. Mum and I celebrated Christmas with Julia and a friend as our guests. On New Year's Eve we walked the beach and sat and watched the last sunset of the year, wondering what 1986 would bring.

At last, a letter arrived from Anne to tell me she had kept the restaurant open right up until Christmas. I was relieved — the business loan repayments had to be paid — but then surprised when she wrote she had spent Christmas with Barbara.

Mum wrote in response, offering her apartment to Anne and David if a buyer was found for the Old Saddlery. Before she sealed the envelope, Mum enclosed a copy of the letter to Barbara. We were waiting for Barbara to admit the little house had been sold.

Anne replied, thanking Mum for her offer. Barbara replied, telling Mum the house was sold, but giving the false impression it was a recent event. She wrote of a new plan to continue to try and sell Mum's apartment, an idea she said was put forward by her daughter and my niece Debby. By combining funds, three families could buy a house to share. A home for Debby and her children, Barbara and whoever, and Mum would have her own room.

'Debby would never suggest this,' I said. 'This is Barbara's idea.'

My mother's written response was a swift and absolute 'No'.

Barbara rang Mum at Julia's on 27 January, Mum's seventieth birthday, having been told by Mum in a letter that she would be calling into Julia's before a celebration lunch in Adelaide. Barbara spent the entire phone call crying, and I wondered why. It was a day of celebration and Barbara herself had been the one who had encouraged Mum away from home to travel to Australia. Mum was not able to confront Barbara regarding her odd behaviour concerning the bank draft requests, or the suggested plan to use her capital to buy a large home and put Mum in a single room.

While all this was happening, I was drawn to an advertisement regarding one of the historic buildings in Victor Harbor. There was a plan to convert the property into a retreat for businessmen. Applications for caterers and management were being sought, so I applied, and following an interview, was successful. There was a requirement to invest. I rang Anne, as this would be an ideal means to obtain a sponsorship for her. I rang the Old Saddlery throughout the day but there was no reply. There was a limit on the time allowed to provide the funds, so out of frustration I rang Barbara, explaining the urgency to contact Anne, and arrange the transfer of two thousand Australian dollars to our joint account. Barbara said she did not know where Anne was. As my sister held my power of attorney, I asked her to arrange the transfer, and wrote by express mail to tell Anne. Anne replied immediately, and to my amazement she was annoyed I had transferred the funds. I assumed that there must be a misunderstanding, so went ahead, obtaining the sponsorship documents for her from Immigration.

Mum and I walked the beach each day, gradually becoming more apprehensive. She still had not received her bank draft; it had been months now. She wrote to her English bank manager to arrange for the transfer of her pensions and all payments were transferred. We were thankful Mum had not changed to Barbara's bank manager.

I experienced strong urges compelling me to walk along the beach to the stone mill, a feature of Middleton, and then to visit the local estate agent and ask for permission to enter the empty mill and take photographs. It was not for sale, but he held the key and allowed me entry. During the early hours of the following day, I woke up with a start, my mind filled with images and information. I reached for my notebook and started writing everything down at speed, the information given being centred on the mill as a place for healing. Conversion of the mill was described in detail.

It all began with the practitioners and how they would operate financially. There would be a restaurant serving organic food — seafood, wholefood and vegetarian cuisine — and a health shop for organic supplies. Accommodation would be comfortable but sparse. There were to be youth counselling services, welfare and drug abuse programs, counselling for victims of child abuse and battered wives, Alcoholics Anonymous and cancer support groups. Young people were to be encouraged to take part in community work according to the theme 'the encouragement of deeds to be done without payment'. Educational courses, a health salon with swimming pool and sauna, and walking and nature trails were to be developed. The many levels of the mill were highlighted by individual colours to encourage harmony, the emphasis being on including the entire family unit as part of the overall healing process.

Once I had written this final statement, my mind cleared and I was exhausted. I shared this with Mum when she awoke and she read through the detailed notes. The direction *Speak to the owner* repeated in my mind. Later I rang him at his home to make an appointment. When we met, he loved the idea but said it was impossible. 'You are way ahead of your time,' he exclaimed.

I left feeling frustrated until the assurance *All is in order* entered my mind.

My job had ended and I began designing health programs for clients following my having dowsed programs for friends. The clients would send their signatures by post, which I touched. Then in combination with the pendulum, I was able to bring through information concerning their wellbeing. One morning, the pendulum took on a life of its own. I had been mulling over finances when thoughts came of my friend and bank manager, Geoff. The energy was strong and the clockwise *Yes* response unmistakeable. A letter formed in my mind.

I instructed him that my share of the proceeds and profit upon any future sale of the Old Saddlery must be forwarded to me here in Australia. After posting the letter, I opened an account with the local building society. The directions came into my mind so forcefully that I did exactly what was asked of me. I wrote to my friend Herm in England, requesting she visit the Old Saddlery. The restaurant was closed, she said, the business no longer operating. A lodger was renting a room, and Anne was attending a massage course with Barbara.

'The Old Saddlery's not open! How is the business loan being paid?' I said. I struggled with Anne's neglect of our business and Barbara's strange attitude towards Mum, regarding her requests for funds.

Walk the beach.

I noticed lines of shells shaped like butterfly wings at the water's edge. I bent to pick up a pair and the direction came, *Yes, collect them.* A calming energy was pushing through my turmoil. I used my pendulum to select thirty-nine shells over several days. Mum and I drove to Victor Harbor to buy a sheet of hardboard cut in a circle. Pink material covered one side. Daily, as the shells were brought in from the beach they were glued to the material in precise positions. Early on the morning of 8 March, my fortieth birthday, Mum went to the beach alone to find the fortieth shell. Then the understanding followed, *Butterfly Circle to be framed with jarrah*, a very heavy hardwood found only in the South West of Western Australia. Dawn Davies' words came to mind: 'One day when you understand symbols you will understand the meaning of life.'

The ending of a phase and a new phase is about to begin.

I touched the glass covering the forty shells and the heavy reddish jarrah frame. I opened the fortieth birthday card from Barbara, then the card from Anne, who had encouraged my mother's family to sign her large card. Each contained a single ten-pound note and the same message, 'Have a drink on me.' I was surprised Anne had visited all of Mum's family. Normally I would have thought this a novel idea, but I felt nervous. Neither Barbara nor Anne rang me on my birthday, breaking a long-standing tradition. They knew I was being given a birthday party by Julia, at a friend's home in nearby Victor Harbor, and they had Julia's friend's telephone number. Something was wrong.

Three days later Mum received a letter from Barbara to say that she now wanted to let Mum's apartment, and Anne and David were moving in with her for a few weeks. Confused, Mum rang Barbara from Julia's home and asked Barbara if the Old Saddlery had a buyer and if Anne and David were going to live in the apartment, as she disagreed about the renting option. Barbara kept saying it was not her affair, that she knew nothing. Anne did not answer the phone at the Old Saddlery. We left Julia's house still confused. Looking at Barbara's letter again we noticed that it had taken nine days to reach us.

Late the following night, we were disturbed by Julia's friend from Victor Harbor banging on the kitchen window of the shack. There had been an urgent phone call from England for me and the person was going to ring back. Mum and I dressed quickly, filled with trepidation, concerned something had happened to the twins, as they had written at Christmas telling us they now had motorbikes. We decided that if either or both were hurt we would go back to England.

The phone rang, it was Anne and she was crying and repeating she was letting me down. I asked her to calm down and tell me what was happening.

Through her tears she said, 'I'm taking all the money. I have sold the business and I am buying another home here. David needs a home. I must have all the money.'

Anger began to build in me as I realised Anne must have signed a contract. 'Then why are you ringing me?' I replied calmly, hiding my anger.

'You must ring Geoff Coyte. He is refusing to allow the transfer,' she replied. Barbara must have used my power of attorney for this to be happening.

Shocked, I understood that Barbara had misled Mum yesterday. My apprehension increased as I understood Mum and I had been strung along for months. What had brought about this collusion between them? Anne was crying only out of sheer frustration at being stopped. I took a deep breath and paused for a moment to recover. I now understood the reasoning behind the urgent direction for me to write to Geoff, requesting my share of the proceeds of any future sale to be sent to Australia. Was it my father who was aware of the happenings in England and determined to protect Mum and me?

I informed Anne I would speak to our bank manager. She was silenced by the tone of my voice.

I asked her about the sponsorship and she replied, 'I've changed my mind.'

'How do you think I will manage without my capital?' I asked her. 'How am I going to pay for the car we agreed I buy so I could work over here?'

She replied, 'You have your mother with you, which is all you wanted.'

'What on earth are you talking about? You know very well Barbara arranged for Mum to travel with me to Australia at the very last minute,' I replied.

Anne continued to plead. I warned her I was ending the phone call and put down the phone. I felt violently sick. I told Mum what was happening and informed her I was going to ring Geoff. He was relieved to hear from me. He had read my letter requesting the transfer to me of my share of any sale funds and realised I knew nothing of what was happening. He explained that the purchasing solicitor had stopped the sale after querying Barbara's signature. The solicitor asked to see the power of attorney held by Barbara and said that it did not cover the sale of a home and business, only a home. So everything was stopped. Geoff had been informed that Anne needed to buy herself a home because my mother wouldn't let her use the apartment because of our two dogs. I asked where he thought my mother was.

'In her apartment in Torquay, of course.'

'She's here with me. Anne has permission to live in Mum's apartment.' Annoyed at being misled, Geoff said, 'Return immediately, before you lose everything.' I turned to speak to Mum and was appalled to discover she was visibly shaking, her face pale and eyes brimming with tears. I bent down and took her hands to calm her.

'We've been led by the nose, haven't we?' she whispered.

I helped her up and asked Julia's friend to drive us back to the shack. The next day I drove Mum to Adelaide to organise her stay with Julia while I was away in England. The building society approved a loan and when I approached an airline I was granted compassionate status for an early flight. Mum and I sent letters to Barbara's solicitor cancelling our individual powers of attorney.

On 13 March Mum answered Julia's telephone. It was Anne trying to encourage me to ring the solicitor. Mum told Anne how dishonourable she was. Anne fired back, saying that I knew she wasn't coming to Australia before I left and I had stolen the two thousand dollars by forcing Barbara to transfer the money from the business.

'Barbara and Anne know that is not true,' I said. The next day Mum rang Barbara's home and asked to speak to one of the twins first. Mark came to the phone and she told him I had not stolen any money and had spent months seeking a sponsorship for Anne and David with Anne's encouragement.

Mum then asked to speak to Barbara.

'She's asleep Nan, and I can't wake her,' Mark replied.

Mum responded by asking Mark to write down a message for Barbara. He was to write that she was ashamed of Barbara and that our powers of attorney had been cancelled. Mum waited a few minutes then rang again, determined to speak to Barbara, not accepting she was asleep. Barbara answered the phone. She started crying, saying, 'I signed nothing. Judy must ring the solicitor.'

Mum told Barbara she knew the truth and that Barbara's signature was queried by the purchasing solicitor and everything was stopped. Barbara ignored this, telling Mum she had tried to let her apartment and the woman on her way to view had just been killed on the motorway. Before Mum could respond to this news, Barbara spoke again.

'Judy has to phone the solicitor,' she demanded, and rang off.

'How are Barbara and Anne going to live with themselves after that?' I said. 'Barbara was bound by law to act in my interest. If the sale had gone through there would have been serious legal consequences and I would have been forced to take legal action against her personally, which could have involved criminal charges.'

'What are you going to do?' Mum asked.

'Go back to England and sort this mess out.'

A letter was on its way to Australia from Barbara's solicitor, acting for Anne. It was to inform me our business partnership was being cancelled and all assets transferred to Anne. Our letters cancelling our individual powers of attorney were on their way to England. It was now impossible for Anne and Barbara to attempt to cancel the partnership or continue the sale of the Old Saddlery.

I flew out of Adelaide heading for London. Mum had come to see me off, her face strained and full of sorrow. I sat in shock during the flight, not able to absorb the unbelievable situation that had developed in my family. I not only felt angry and betrayed but foolish for having been so gullible. It felt like I was being drawn into a whirlpool of manipulation, lies and deception.

In London I collected a hired car, drove straight to Devon and booked into a hotel. Next, I drove to Cornwall, to the bank where Geoff changed our bank account authority to ensure both Anne and I had to sign further cheques. I was informed that the business loan repayments were behind and the bank would foreclose if the sale did not go through.

Driving to the Old Saddlery, I felt sick inside. I parked down the street, observing it was closed with the curtains drawn. I walked the back lane and entered the garden. A young man emerged from the kitchen, surprised to see me. I explained I was a friend of Anne's. He told me he did not know where she was and that she only rang occasionally about her post. He added that he wanted to buy the property and had been allowed to move in prior to the sale. 'Some woman in Australia has stopped it,' he complained.

'I know Judy well,' I replied. 'If she has stopped anything it must be for a reason.'

Anne had been living elsewhere for some time. I left, driving straight to Torquay and Barbara's home. Parking some distance away, I watched and waited. Later, Anne drove into the driveway, David with her. The car Anne was driving was not ours, so I drove to the local car dealer and found it on display. The dealer was nervous because the car had been registered and insured in my name.

Caught like rats in a trap, Anne and Barbara must have rushed around changing everything as Mum made requests and I fulfilled my promise to find a sponsorship, trying to delay, as the date for the sale drew nearer and nearer. To my surprise, I hadn't received any phone calls on my fortieth birthday. Really, it was no wonder with completion imminent.

I began to feel overwhelmed. The now-familiar calming energy came through the turmoil of my emotions and the direction, *Drive to Acora.*

He allowed me in without an appointment. Taking one look at me, he told me to sit. 'It is all black, totally black,' was his opening statement. 'But you're going to win. I don't know how, but you will win in the end. Judy, everyone has been poisoned against you, and I mean everyone.'

I drove to Mum's apartment, where I discovered the dining room table scattered with her bank statements and paperwork. A disruptive anger had erupted in this room. A small white envelope was placed against a vase in the middle of the chaos with its flap open and held securely in position by the handle of the vase. Protruding from it was a photograph placed upside down. I tried to control the feeling of dismay as I removed the photograph. It was our mother, smiling, unlike my last memory of her when I left Adelaide. Mum's life had indeed been turned upside down, as was the motive here, and I wondered how Barbara could do something like this with our mother's image. What was wrong with her?

I put Mum's photograph inside my suitcase, then rang her to tell her what I had found. She wanted me to tell her everything, agreeing that Barbara placing her photograph upside down was sinister and disturbing. In her opinion, Barbara must be having some kind of brainstorm. We both agreed that while Anne was going around the whole family with my fortieth birthday card, she was trying to dissolve the business partnership and sell the Old Saddlery, with Barbara's help. Mum was angry. 'They tried to strip you of everything.'

A solicitor's aide met me in the driveway the next day to serve me documents. The legal battle had begun.

My hire car had to be returned, so I drove to the local agency and walked back to Mum's place. A neighbour stopped to warn me that Barbara had called in. I had locked my suitcase inside Mum's bedroom, so it was safe, but Barbara had left the garage door half open and black garbage bags had been thrown around inside. They contained some of my clothes and personal items from the Old Saddlery. But Barbara was too late: I had found Mum's upside down photograph. Here was more evidence of Barbara's out-of-control temper.

I rang a locksmith who changed the garage and front door locks. I went to Mum's bedroom, opened my suitcase and held Mum's photograph. A rush of emotion came, and I was compelled to say aloud, 'You will be under my protection from now on.'

A friend, Paula, came to visit me. She had stayed at the Old Saddlery for bed and breakfast and lived nearby. I told her what had happened and she offered to stay the night, as I was distressed. It was late and we were up talking when a car entered the driveway. Then the letterbox lid flapped in the front door and the car drove away. A small white envelope, identical to the one that had held Mum's upside down photograph, lay on the mat. The note inside read, 'You are greedy and stupid. I am taking my children away from you. You will be a lonely old woman.' It was not signed, but I recognised Barbara's handwriting. I struggled with my emotions as I tried to read the contents of the note aloud to Paula, but tears finally forced me to hand the note to her. 'What's with your sister Barbara?' she asked.

The contents of this note and the written intention of Barbara to deprive me of the children shocked me in the same way as her turning Mum's photograph upside down and placing it in an envelope to ensure the photograph stayed that way. I was apprehensive now not only for Mum and myself, but for Barbara herself and the family. I wrote to Mum and enclosed a copy of Barbara's note. I returned the original to its sender through Anne, by post. I did not want that ill-wishing energy anywhere near me, and enclosed a note to Anne requesting access to the dogs and stating when I would collect them.

I spoke to a new solicitor, but I was not impressed by his reaction to what was happening. All the same, I applied for legal aid, which was granted because I remained a British citizen although an Australian resident. I rang and spoke to Geoff, who was anxious. Both the purchasing and selling solicitors were also anxious.

I drove to Ashburton in Paula's car in order to speak to the prospective buyer. It was strange, knocking on the passageway door and seeking admittance to my own home. The man to whom I had previously spoken in the back garden opened the door.

'Hello, Miss Roach,' he said.

I started to apologise for not identifying myself earlier, but he stopped me, telling me he now knew the solicitors had stopped the sale. He invited me in and I was stunned to see the restaurant piled high with boxes, packing cases and furniture. The removal van had arrived but departed empty, accounting for Anne's distressed calls urging me to agree to the sale. I assured the man that I would do my best to resolve the dilemma.

When I went to Barbara's home to collect the dogs the following week, I was met at the front door by Anne. She looked dreadful: unkempt and strained. When the dogs came out they were excited to see me, but Anne was standing in Barbara's doorway and I was not welcome. It was not only very odd but very hurtful, especially being aware that Anne would have read the contents of Barbara's returned note. 'You are one of my oldest friends. How can you live with yourself?' I asked, as she avoided eye contact. 'That's my family in there, not yours. What is wrong with you?' She continued to avoid eye contact. 'I have returned to sort this mess out.'

'I know, Judy,' she replied. It was a startling response in the circumstances.

When I returned the dogs, I was met by a different Anne. She had changed her clothes, brushed her short dark hair and looked more like her old self. All the same, she slammed the door after telling me it would be the last time I'd see the dogs.

I rang the solicitor handling the sale and he agreed to see me. The atmosphere was fraught with tension. I told him I had no intention of signing any sale contract until a new document was drafted, which ensured the remaining capital, after clearance of all business debts, was held in trust, until a decision was made in a court, or between Anne and myself. He knew I meant it. The document was drafted quickly and completion date for the sale of the Old Saddlery set for three days time, 27 March 1986. I reminded him that he was obligated not to discuss this with any other person. If he did, I would not sign.

I rang Geoff about the proposed sale date and he was relieved. Later, I rang the purchaser, and he too was relieved. I returned to the Old Saddlery and in the presence of the prospective buyer, I searched through the packed boxes to retrieve my belongings, noticing a personal folder was missing, including confirmation I was David's godmother. On top of a box was the gift card for the Wild Geese print Anne had given me two years before. I recalled the atmosphere when I opened this gift, remembering my mother had wanted to buy it for me and Anne had rushed to buy it instead. There was something *familiar* about this print with its flying geese, and the unease I felt then I felt again.

The arrangements for David to be represented in the Bristol Family Court had not been cancelled. Keeping my promise to him, I passed on the sponsorship I had received from Canberra, Australia, a few days before my birthday, to his solicitor in Bristol. When legal aid forms came for David, I redirected them onto Anne at Barbara's address.

The sale of the Old Saddlery was to be finalised on David's birthday. Anne and I had arranged to have a discussion beforehand. I was waiting for her to collect me in her car to ensure that we would arrive at the solicitors together, when the phone rang stirring me from my thoughts.

'Why are you not going to the solicitors?' Geoff demanded.

'What do you mean? Of course I'm going. I am waiting for Anne.'

'Barbara has phoned me and told me you are not willing to sign.'

'That is not true,' I replied.

Geoff told me to wait while he sorted everything out. The phone rang again. 'I've spoken to Anne,' Geoff said.

'Is everything all right now?'

'Yes, but what is going on with your sister? When I was talking to Anne I heard her shouting in the background, urging Anne not to be alone with you.'

Anne arrived, shaking with nervous apprehension. On the drive to the solicitor she asked me about the sponsorship. I told her I had posted the documents to Debby Steele. I had kept my promise to David, but thought it strange she had not cancelled David's solicitor.

She waited then asked, 'What are you offering me?'

'Absolutely nothing,' I replied, 'you have encouraged my family to think I am a thief and a liar.' Anne's hands began shaking slightly as she gripped the steering wheel. 'Did you and Barbara consider how I would cope financially and emotionally if your plan had worked?'

With a defiant tone she responded. 'We thought you would just disappear.'

'Well,' I said, 'you and Barbara were both wrong — *very, very* wrong.'

At the solicitors we were each given a pen, and Anne was handed my document. She began to shake visibly. She looked at the solicitor, but he said nothing. I waited. She waited. Then she signed both my document and the sale contract. The words about Anne spoken by the gypsy in the Old Saddlery came to mind: 'I want you to know the character of this person.' Well, I knew now, but Barbara's extreme behaviour remained a mystery.

For a few days I was too stressed to leave the apartment. It was late evening and my mental and emotional exhaustion was overwhelming. I was aware I had managed to uncover only a small part of what had been happening while Mum and I had been sent to the other side of the world, together. To discover the whole truth would be more difficult. A despondent feeling swept through me as I accepted that it would be difficult to uncover what was behind this appalling situation.

I wandered into the kitchen and sat on the floor, my back against the kitchen bench. The glow of the street lights filtered in through the dining room. I had turned off the lights in the front of Mum's apartment, trying to gain some peace — only the light in Mum's bedroom remained on. The phone had not stopped ringing for days, but when I answered, there was silence. I needed to create an impression I was not at home.

I felt as if I had run a long race, and now it was time to hand over the baton to someone else. I had nothing left to give. From deep inside came words that I was forced to speak out loud, 'Now, it is your turn.' I was aware of inviting *another* to complete the course and then more words came up and out from deep inside me, 'to get to the truth'.

I slept well and awoke to find my mind was filled with a different energy that was superimposing itself over my thoughts, in the form of clear, precise, abrupt instructions. I sensed it was not my father, but my gut instinct told me this new energy of *another* came from a safe and loving source. It was *familiar,* bringing a sense of wellbeing, and I made the conscious decision to follow the instructions.

On the first day of April Anne came to see me at Mum's apartment. Her opening remark was, 'You must care: you have travelled all this way'. What was she up to now? She followed me to the dining table. Then I understood it was the sponsorship, so I waited until she had signed the cheques for all our outstanding bills.

'No, Anne, I did not return for you — our friendship ceased the moment you rang me in Australia and confessed your actions. I came back to sort out the legal mess you and Barbara have created.' She stared at me, then turned and left.

Paula had mentioned a woman called Mu Woolvett who, she had heard, was special, and I was directed to make an appointment to see her on 2 April. I hired a car and drove the forty minutes to Staverton Bridge and Herb Cottage. I was greeted warmly by a very slim woman in her mid-thirties with shoulder-length straight brown hair, wearing a multicoloured flowing skirt and top.

'I have been waiting a very long time for you, but you are finally here,' she said. Before I could ask her what she meant, she ushered me inside. I was offered tea and invited to sit down at the kitchen table, where a white candle flickered. 'I am tuning into your Akashic Records,' she said, explaining how every action, thought and emotion in our lifetimes is recorded in a universal library, and she was able to access and read these records. She told me spirit had been waiting ten years for me to listen. Now that all my material wealth had been taken, I was ready to listen.

'Everything that is happening now has a past-life connection. The woman, Anne, is obsessed with a mother figure; do you understand what I mean?'

She knew Anne's name! I was floored.

'Yes,' I replied. 'There was a spiritual imbalance in the very old home where we worked as business partners: a dispute over a female child between the mother and father, over the abuse and eventual murder of the child, centuries ago, by the child's father.'

'Anne's obsession with her children is part of that. You and her son David have shared many past lives and you are more his mother than she. Whilst she is obsessed, she will envy you for that. You were married in a past life and she let you down then and now she is repeating it,'

Mu explained. This helped me understand why Anne had removed the certificate naming David as my godson from my personal file left behind at the Old Saddlery.

'You have been an Australian Aboriginal many times,' she said. 'Your destiny is Australia and you are ready to meet your spirit guide. You will see her. Judy, you are part of the New Age of Aquarius, the healing spiritual age. Souls trapped in their unresolved past lives are being left behind, resentful. You are being prepared to be a great healer.'

A man in his early thirties came into the room and greeted me, then told me my auric shield needed cleansing. He asked me to stand and ran his hands around my body several inches away from it, flicking his fingers, as though clearing them of negativity. He said he was freeing my energy source. 'You have great physical and spiritual powers, and you are nearly ready for the hard work ahead,' he told me. 'You must stay away from your sister as she will drain you of energy at this important time. You must not worry about your mother. Tell her not to worry about her future. Her aura is clear, light and happy. Your sister is re-living a past-life situation.'

Mu explained about Masters who trained people, adding that I was higher than the spiritual plane and had been here many times in preparation for this stage. I had suffered severe emotional turmoil during many past lives, but this time I was in control of myself and causing no auric ripples. I was to trust events, and if it was Anne's course to go on with the conflict then that was how it must be. I was not to interfere in her destiny.

Mu gave me more tea. 'A good drink when working with spirit,' she said. I was told I had a job to do, a project. 'You are my last student. Now I can stop.' I was confused by her statement, but the word *project* repeated in my mind.

She looked into the candle flame and asked me whether I saw anything. I looked but saw nothing. As I was leaving she told me I would need her soon, and I was to phone her. I left without giving her my address or telephone number. My meeting with her had been too strange. When I arrived home I was so tired I slept for twenty-four hours.

Paula and I spent time together and I shared everything with her.

Travel to Exeter now. The instruction was clear and insistent in my mind. I arrived in Exeter by coach and waited.

Walk down the street. I found myself outside a solicitor's office. When I went in my attention was drawn immediately to the name of a female solicitor, and I engaged her to handle the pending legal negotiations. I spent hours with her, explaining all the details.

I was distressed when I arrived back at Mum's apartment and soon developed a raging headache. I lay down on her bed, but sat up when I could stand the pain no longer. By the bedside light was Mu's telephone number and I rang her. She said she would come straight away. I replaced the phone, realising I hadn't given her my address. I went downstairs to unlock the front door, thinking I would ring her back. There was a shadow waiting outside and I could see someone through the clouded glass. I opened the door and Mu was standing there!

Confused, I asked, 'How did you do that? This is impossible.'

Reassuring me everything was all right, Mu helped me upstairs and back to bed. She started talking to me in a calm voice as she produced a small object. 'This particular crystal is not from the Earth plane,' she said, as she placed it in the centre of my forehead, 'although it is clear quartz.'

Within seconds the colour blue came, then waves of blue, as the pain receded. I had experienced this before, in the Old Saddlery. When the pain was gone, Mu removed the crystal from my forehead and placed it in my right palm, closing my hand around it.

'A gift,' she said. 'One day you will use it for healing.'

She asked how I felt, and a sharp pain vibrated in my right shoulder. My response was instant: 'The distress for me is that I feel my sister has stabbed me in the back.' Mu asked me to imagine a pink bubble and I became aware of a calming energy around me.

'Now what do you see?' she asked. I felt as though I was floating in a safe place. It was as if I were in the womb. From a distance a face began to form. It was Barbara's expressionless face staring blankly at me. I saw a dark, ugly umbilical cord connecting us, much larger than in real life, and I felt overpowered by its size. Mu asked me if I wanted to cut the cord and I had no hesitation agreeing. She suggested I bring through a pair of scissors in my mind. I was not sure I could do this, but then it happened. I had the means to cut the cord.

'This is forever,' she warned, but I didn't hesitate. I cut the cord and Barbara drifted away and disappeared. I had no feeling of loss and the pain in my shoulder soon left. A huge weight had been lifted from me.

Mu lit a candle and asked me to look into its flame. As I did so a vibrant energy surrounded me and I surrendered myself to its rainbow of colours. After Mu left I slept for another twenty-four hours. When I awoke, the clear quartz was still there, confirming the experience. It was a relief to know that Barbara and I would *never ever* return as siblings.

Paula asked if I knew anyone who could give her a reading. I was drawn to the local paper, then to a tarot reader's advertisement, living in the nearby village of Brixham. When we got there Paula encouraged me to have the first reading. I selected my cards and waited.

'I see Australia. You have a strong connection there,' the elderly woman began. 'You think you will settle there, but I believe you will end your days in New Zealand. When it is over, someone will come into your life, a soulmate. All will be good then. You are just going through an emotionally draining time.'

She waited and moved her hands across my cards then looked up at me. 'There is a man in spirit in a naval uniform that stands behind you at night,' she said. 'There is another man on the Earth plane, older, from India, with a moustache and beard, and he needs your help. You are to trust him, as he is a warm man with a fatherly outlook, and he will become very fond of you, Judy. You will go back to Australia in a little while. There will be conflict and a cancelling of a will.'

I enquired what the reasons were behind this present situation. She replied, 'Past lives, greed, and sibling rivalry. The dark-haired lady wants all the money, and your sister envies your lifestyle, freedom and abilities. There is a very young man you are close to, in fact much closer than his real mother. If he doesn't make it to Australia this time, he will later. He will eventually write and keep in contact, and when he makes it to Australia he will not want to return to the UK. This young man has a keen mind and this dark-haired lady could lose both her sons, as the other boy has no regard for her. You reap what you sow.'

She glanced down at the cards. 'You will come out of this a better person, Judy. In Australia you will eventually be successful and content for the first time in your life.' She looked up and smiled. 'This is all to do with your soulmate.' *Soulmate* repeated several times in my mind.

Paula was so intimidated by my reading that she declined to have one.

I posted a copy of the reading and the details of my amazing experience with Mu to Mum for her to read and record in her notebook. Once this was done I felt I must visit Acora, so two days later I sat with him on the Barbican in Plymouth. He was pleased to see me. He waited, as if listening, then told me that my situation had gone from all black to grey now. He saw Anne as a personality who never reached her goals, always the one left behind. Living alone in the Old Saddlery over the winter had destroyed her faith, and she and Barbara had decided through our letters that we were doing all right, didn't need them, and formulated a plan. Anne could not see me obtaining the sponsorship and Barbara felt she had lost the two people who had provided for her and her children for years.

'You are not going to lose out,' he said. 'You will return to Australia soon, as it is your destiny to be there. In the next three years you will become a respected member of the Australian world, a successful businesswoman. Bad luck was around you from the time you set foot in the Old Saddlery until the minute you left. Anne watched you come and go and could not escape, and when you left this last time it was the end for her.'

Acora said it was a good thing I returned to protect Mum's flat. I was to tell her she was not to return yet, as she would heal in Australia. He saw Mum living in Australia and visiting England and relatives. He said David needed my strength and that we had an unusual tie.

I sent Mum a copy of Acora's reading for her notebook. Mum replied, telling me that she wanted her grandson, my eldest nephew, to have her record player for his birthday on 30 April. He attended a special-needs school twenty minutes' walk away. I took the gift to him and he rushed to meet me with a smile, hugged me and asked me to come home with him. I told him I was not able to. It wrenched at my heart to see his disappointment.

Days later I received a legal letter from Barbara and Anne's solicitor ordering me to stay away from my eldest nephew. Barbara was making good on her threat to take her children away. I posted the letter immediately to Mum, knowing not to allow Barbara's reactive past-life energy near me. A week later I posted a request to Anne, asking if I could see David on 10 May for a few hours. In response, and late at night, a note from Barbara's second husband, Eric, was furtively pushed through the letterbox lid in Mum's front door. Inside a small white envelope was written 'No access. Keep away.'

'Who does he think he is? He is a stranger to the family,' I said.

I walked to Barbara's home on 10 May and knocked on the front door, but no-one answered. I knew everyone was inside. What can I do to get past this? I wondered. Then I walked back to Mum's apartment. *Give the clock to Barbara.* It was the answer to my question. The mantle clock had belonged to our father and it was to be a gift from him to

Barbara. I rang Anne to warn her I was coming and Paula drove me to Barbara's home. As we parked, I looked up and saw Barbara staring at me from the first floor window. We held each other's gaze. It was the first time I had seen her since the evening before Mum and I left for Australia the previous year. *Taken power,* was the warning given to me at the Taj Mahal. There was a look of triumph on Barbara's face. I held her stare knowing it was important to do so. As I absorbed the brief moment in time, I knew we had lived this moment before. Barbara had taken my family away from me before in a past life.

Paula said, 'Judy, you can't go in there'.

'That's my family in there,' I replied, and got out of the car.

The front door was opened by Eric, with a thunderous look on his face. He'd obviously been sent to intimidate me, but I was unmoved. I handed him the clock and he shouted, 'Don't darken our door again,' then slammed the door in my face. I remembered Dawn had heard the spiritual clock ticking prior to the rescue of the child in the Old Saddlery and I understood there was another child to be rescued — our father's elder daughter.

Mu's warning came to mind: 'All souls left behind in their unresolved past lives are being left behind resentful.' I was to record the date, 11 May, and remember this was Aunty Val's birthday. She was one of Mum's sisters and I wondered at the connection.

At Mum's request her apartment was to be sold, so I went to the local real estate agent. Later I was encouraged to open the top drawer by Mum's bed and found an oblong metal box. It contained my father's war medals, dress medals, certificates and old photographs. I was directed to take these to Mum in Australia. I packed and headed for Heathrow airport. On the flight back to Australia I felt a little relief that I had gained some answers as to why Barbara and Anne were acting as they were — negative past-life issues. Anne had forced us both to sell at fifteen thousand pounds below market value. However, having been restored, the Old Saddlery had realised a profit of twenty-three thousand pounds. I re-read a page in my notebook:

Highlighted words 1985: The Lovers – a rescue – Taj Mahal – taken power – a child – a feeling of loss – manuscript – Buddha's image – Yes, this is a part of you – third eye – a hard karmic lesson – in search of Truth – Mother.

I allowed my mind to re-live the events surrounding these words. The Lovers pots were in Australia. The trapped spirit child in the Old Saddlery had been rescued. In India, the story regarding the Taj Mahal was a warning that Barbara had taken power over Mum and my assets. The child by the Taj Mahal who had approached Mum saying, 'Remember my name; that is all I have' was a cry for help. I marvelled at the unique circumstances that had revealed these messages. Mum and her elder daughter, Barbara, were now separated and I wondered if they were lost to one another forever.

When visiting Nepal I had been drawn to a statue of a scribe holding a scroll and the word *manuscript* had come. I had no understanding of this, but had felt a sense of familiarity when I touched Buddha's image at the Temple of a Thousand Buddhas, and I had not been surprised by the confirmation, *Yes, this is a part of you*. Mum and I had felt the sense of familiarity and excitement when turning the prayer wheels at the Stupa of Swayambunath. Then I knew Mum and I had been moved on from the past lives spoken of by Pat in Ashburton, by undertaking this journey to specific places in India, Nepal and Bangkok, to experience the images of past-life memories we had shared. Mum and I had been close then, as we were now, and I couldn't wait to tell her.

Mu had placed the clear quartz — not from the Earth plane — on my third eye, providing healing. A hard karmic lesson lay ahead, but I would continue in search of Truth and protect my mother at all times. I was encouraged to review more:

Highlighted words 1986: Alternative place for healing – Butterfly Circle – 40 – the ending of a phase and a new phase is about to begin – project – soulmates.

I contemplated these words. An alternative place for healing would play its part in my future. The Butterfly Circle framed with jarrah from the South West of Western Australia, with its forty shells enclosed, had been packed and was waiting in Adelaide. *The ending of a phase* ... was clearly the traumatic finish to the life familiar to Mum and me with Anne's phone call after my fortieth birthday ... *and a new phase is about to begin* — the new phase *had* begun. The word *project* was highlighted along with Mu's words, 'You have a job to do, a project.' The elderly tarot-card reader in Brixham had forecast that, when all this was over, there would enter my life a soulmate with whom I would be both successful and content.

Mum was relieved to see me. I could see in her eyes that the past months had been hard for her. As I drove us back to the shack at Middleton, I told her about the handing over of Daddy's mantle clock to Barbara, via Eric, and that Barbara would be helped by means of a rescue, although I did not know when or how. Mum was quiet for a while, then told me she had received unpleasant letters from all three of her sisters while I was away. I stopped the car and asked her to tell me everything. Her youngest sister, Pat, had demanded Mum return to England; and all three sisters were of the opinion that I was to blame for everything that was happening. I stared back at Mum in shock. Mum knew the truth and had been distressed by her sisters' reactions. Acora's warning came to mind: 'Judy, everyone has been poisoned against you, and I mean everyone.' I was outraged that Barbara and Anne had created friction between Mum and her sisters.

I found work as a waitress in a newly opened restaurant in Middleton. Early in July Mum and I went to what turned out to be an interesting social event in Adelaide. What made it more interesting for me was that at one stage a middle-aged woman I'd never seen before took me to one side and asked me if I was a nurse. When I replied that I was not, she looked at me and said, 'Well one day you are going to be involved with the heart.' I was thinking about this on the way home when I needed to turn right. I checked the reversing mirror and saw that the road was clear. I indicated, and moved right, stopping to allow oncoming traffic to pass. Then out of the blue there was an almighty thud as we were hit from behind and propelled forward into several other cars. It all seemed to happen in slow motion.

At first I was in shock, then I turned to Mum to discover with relief that she wasn't hurt, though she was shaken. I smelt petrol and broke out of our car and stumbled to the vehicle behind, my neck and right leg quite painful. No-one came to help — they just stood and stared. I shouted to them to phone for an ambulance, but no-one moved. I helped the woman who had caused the accident get out of her car. She was crying but unhurt. She said her foot had been forced to press the accelerator.

Still no-one came to assist, everyone standing still and staring. What on earth was happening? I was reminded of the occasion in the Old

Saddlery when the tray of cream teas had been forced out of my hands and no-one had reacted. It felt like I was in a time warp then and now it was happening all over again.

I limped into the nearest shop to use their phone and requested ambulances, police and the fire service. Mum and I were taken to the Adelaide Hospital. X-rays and tests revealed nothing was broken but I had a whiplash and a severely bruised leg and ankle. However, the worst pain was in my lower back. The police interviewed us at the hospital and advised us to employ a solicitor for insurance and compensation claims.

The effects of shock lasted for many weeks and I had to stay still in bed for days while my back recovered. Julia took us in once again and the car was taken away to be repaired. A few days after the accident I received a letter from my solicitor in Exeter informing me Anne had bought the house she wanted. The solicitor arranging the sale of the Old Saddlery had allowed her to take the capital to buy the home from the proceeds of the sale before freezing the balance, contrary to my legal document. 'He must have found a legal loophole to help Anne,' I said.

Days later I received a typed letter from Anne, from Barbara's address. Although she had recovered her investment, she still wanted it all, including my share of the profits. She accused me of stealing the two thousand dollar transfer and falsely stated I had used business money to travel to Australia many times. She wrote that I had taken Mum away from her family and would no doubt spend all her money when the apartment sold. Anne had chosen the path of conflict. The letter had been written on the day of our accident.

Dawn Davie had told us that, when she drove to the Old Saddlery for the rescue of the child, her steering wheel had been interfered with, trying to force her off the road; now the woman who had crashed into us said her foot had been forced to press the accelerator. I had been warned by Mu that Anne was obsessed with a mother figure. I had confirmed this would be from our time at the Old Saddlery. Memories came of Anne throwing china at me before picking up a knife; then Dawn, having taken on Fred's persona, bending over Anne saying, 'You remind me of my wife'. The rescue of Fred had not been successful.

I replied to Anne's typed letter with a curt response. Mum and I had been put at risk.

I was to learn years later that Barbara misrepresented my response to Mum's three sisters as being an attack on them, ensuring a rift between us for years. Mum and I spent the day writing the true extent of my investment. I watched with fascination when Mum picked up Anne's letter and beside each paragraph printed in red biro 'A lie' and at the bottom she signed it. I posted a copy of Anne's letter, my financial input and Mum's comments to my solicitor in England.

A few days later, when I was able to walk, Mum said she wanted to make a will, so I arranged for her to see a local solicitor. He asked Mum if she had children and who her beneficiaries were. I was dumbfounded when she told him she only had one daughter, Judith Ann Roach. Then she turned to me and said, 'You will never be homeless again'.

After several months there was still no news from the estate agent regarding Mum's apartment, and one morning in early September she handed me her return air ticket. Mum and I were still staying with Julia so I could return to England for three weeks to pack all her belongings and sell her furniture. Before leaving, I was directed to visit India, Nepal and Bangkok on my return trip. I understood this was important.

I arrived in England on 19 September and soon discovered Barbara had taken Mum's apartment off the market. I spoke to the estate agent who then rang Mum to confirm the apartment was still for sale. I spent time packing and arranging the sale of the furniture. I had received a letter from Barbara and Anne's solicitor before leaving Australia, complaining I was unavailable due to my residing in Australia. I had replied, giving him the dates of my visit to England, but he did not contact me.

On 21 September I remembered that it was Barbara's birthday. Three years before, Mum and I had paid for her to fly to Guernsey, and my father's spiritual personality had superimposed itself over my face at the airport when Mum cried as Barbara's plane took off. I had reassured Mum that Daddy was looking after Barbara. So much had happened since then. Barbara and Mum were now lost to one another and I wondered how it would be possible to rescue Barbara from reacting to a negative past-life issue. In response, I was reminded that my father's mantle clock was in her home.

Directions came to ring my friend Herm, who had told me about Anne closing down the Old Saddlery in 1986. Herm asked me to go with her to see a woman called Veronica. My life was filled with clairvoyants, but I felt comfortable with them and their remarkable gifts were providing me with brief insights as to what was happening.

Veronica spoke of India, and I was taken aback, having been instructed to travel there on my way back to Australia. She saw an elderly Indian man showing me carpets, clothing and jewellery. 'A very successful businessman,' she said. 'He thinks of you as another daughter. You will travel all through Australia. Does this mean anything to you?' I replied that it did.

During our stay in Delhi in 1985, Mum and I had spent time with the owner of the hotel's gift shop, Pal Sethi, and he and I had exchanged letters since. I had been directed to visit him again — it was important.

'Your spirit Guide was a Catholic nun,' Veronica said. 'She comes from a hot country. She is dark-skinned and wears a white habit, but is no longer limited by her Catholicism. The ideas she gives you now are from a broader reality. This lady is with you all the time. There is a dark-haired woman who has crossed your path. There is a lot of bad feeling to do with a property. A young man who is fond of you is caught up in this too. I see you walking down a corridor to an aeroplane with yet another young man with a wonderful smile and sense of humour. A companion will come into your life — a teacher — and children will be involved. I see you involved in alternative things.' She waited. 'You will become well known for something to do with the heart. You will also write a book; I see it on the shelves. People will read this book and it will affect their lives.'

Again, the mention of the heart. I recalled that, prior to our car accident, I had been told I would work with the heart. My writing a book solved the message *manuscript* and my being stood by the scribe statue in Nepal. I left Veronica knowing the source of my guidance. Mu had said I was ready to see my Guide and I wondered how this would be possible.

My Guide requested that I write to Dianne, who had been at Heathrow when Mum and I left England in 1985. I relayed all that had taken place since saying goodbye. I paid the monies from the sale of the furniture into Mum's bank account, locked the garage holding her packed boxes, and left for Heathrow airport. Again I was on a flight to India, this time alone, but I was not alone and never would be. I now knew about my Guide.

I revisited the Taj Mahal and sat where Mum and I had sat together. I marvelled at the Taj Mahal's reflection in the long pool, creating the illusion of two symbols of love.

Remember this moment, my Guide instructed.

In Delhi, I visited Pal Sethi and he invited me to dine at his home. He wanted to expand into the Australian market and asked whether I would be interested in organising the outlets. I told him I would make enquiries for him. Before I left Delhi, he gave me several gifts, including a beautiful silk print of Lord Buddha.

I flew on to Nepal and was given instructions to go into Durbur Square. I found a medicine man waiting near the flight of stone steps where I had stood alongside the scribe statue during my last visit. His forehead was painted with white paint, three semicircles of orange paint, and two red dots, one marking his third eye. I gestured I wanted to take his photograph and he seemed pleased. His image was to be taken back to Australia. Again, the third eye was being highlighted and I pondered its importance.

During our visit to Kathmandu, Mum and I had visited a carpet factory employing Tibetan refugees. My Guide directed me to send them Pal Sethi's Buddha painting. 'You are a woman after my own heart,' I said. 'You reach out to all peoples and all cultures.'

Visit the palace now, my Guide urged. I joined the large crowd outside the Palace of Kumari. They were looking up at a small window, waiting for something. Then a young girl appeared, her hair piled high and adorned with a golden headdress. The publication *Travel in Nepal* reads:

> The Living Goddess Kumari is revered as the living daughter of the Goddess Kali and the patron Goddess of the Valley. A four-year-old girl belonging to the goldsmiths' caste is chosen ... The conflict of her personality follows the widely-held notion that out of destruction comes rebirth.

At this time, the overwhelming concern for me was that the tapestry of my family unit was being destroyed and I seemed powerless to stop it. The words 'out of destruction comes rebirth' were being highlighted and used as a message to give me comfort and hope.

I returned to my hotel in awe of the ancient customs and unbending faith of these people, knowing I had learnt an important lesson. When directed to go somewhere, even though I did not understand why, it was important to go. My Guide was working with me and teaching me, and I sensed it was part of a bigger plan. I thought how different the world was for the Living Goddess at her tiny window as compared with the child in the Old Saddlery who had looked out of her tiny window for centuries, crying out for help.

When I arrived back in Australia, Mum and I accepted that we had to get on with our new life. I was drawn to contact a real estate agency in Port Elliot. Later that day, we were shown a furnished log cabin in Goolwa, near Middleton. *Yes, this one*, my Guide confirmed. We loved it and moved in right away. The cabin was set among trees, it had its own private garden, and it was within walking distance of the sea. The first items to be unpacked were the Butterfly Circle and Wild Geese print.

Nothing Mum wrote to her sisters wast believed. Barbara had convinced them she had not signed a contract and had no underhand involvement with Anne. All three replied, saying they did not want to discuss Barbara and only wanted Mum to write about her adventures. Hurt, Mum wanted to end all communication with them, but I advised her not to allow Barbara's influence to come between them and reminded her past lives were in play and that Daddy was with Barbara and we had my Guide. Mum decided to consult the clairvoyant Veronica in England, by post. Veronica requested a tissue Mum had handled.

By return post came a letter: 'As I held the tissue, Tess, I saw a middle-aged fair-haired lady and a man in spirit who wore a naval uniform.' Veronica asked Mum if she was in Perth, Western Australia, which struck us as very strange at the time, considering her letter was sent to our address in South Australia. My attention was drawn to the Butterfly Circle with its frame of jarrah — found only in Western Australia — and I wondered if she was providing an insight into the future for Mum and me. She went on to say that Mum was with the fair-haired lady, and there was a link with a property in England that needed to be sold. The fair-haired person was a daughter. The property would be sold and Mum would buy a place in Australia. Veronica said she had seen a dark-haired woman, then the name Anne came. There was disharmony around this woman, none of which was Mum's doing. This woman only wants to cause hurt, but she would not achieve what she wanted. This tied in with a property, money and a legacy. 'Tess,' she wrote, 'I feel you will live permanently in Australia … But you will return to England for visits. There is a gap between your daughters that has come about through jealousy. The woman Anne has turned the elder against the younger, but she will not win. In time the elder daughter will realise she has been wrong and all will be reconciled. A long time away and she will need her mother and sister again. This is an understanding you are to hold onto.'

Mum's visa required her to leave Australia at the end of twelve months. We had to find a way for her to leave the country and then re-enter for a further twelve months. I was encouraged by my Guide to drive to Adelaide with Mum, and there I was directed to a particular travel agency, then to an advertisement for P&O Cruise 401. This took in five ports over thirteen days, and was scheduled to leave Sydney at 5 pm on 6 November, within days of her visa's deadline. My Guide was adamant Mum was to take this cruise. Money was tight — there were car repayments to make and rent to pay, and I had not found work — but Mum was able to pay for the cruise with the money raised from the sale of her furniture in Torquay. I checked that she'd paid the $20 departure tax and verified that her passport would be stamped as having left the country and stamped on her return, in order to comply with her visa requirements.

On 19 November Mum flew back to Adelaide, full of the trip and the wonderful people she had met. She looked happy and well. As I started to drive back to Goolwa and our log cabin, Mum remarked, 'They didn't stamp my passport.'

I stopped the car and checked her passport. It was true. Mum explained that she had gone straight to the purser's office and was told that on this particular cruise one did not officially leave Australia. She was overdue and here illegally. We drove to the Adelaide Department of Immigration, where we were taken into an office. While Mum was questioned, a young woman stood quietly in the background listening. I sensed she would be the one to decide if we were genuine or not. The point I stressed was that we had paid the $20 departure tax and therefore truly believed Mum was leaving the country.

A decision was made to issue her with a temporary resident visa under the Aged Parent Scheme, upon application for permanent residency. I could not believe it! Mum left clutching these precious forms, understanding a successful application depended on me having a job and her supporting herself for a minimum of ten years, with no Australian pension. Mum and I marvelled at the sequence of events in order to achieve this outcome.

I had spent hours seeking information from Pal Sethi, as he had assured employment for me if his application to have a franchise in Australia went through. I wrote to him. He replied and confirmed his offer and Mum's application for residency was submitted. I had been directed to India a second time, and now I understood the huge importance of that visit.

There had been no news from the estate agent in England regarding the sale of Mum's apartment or any decision from Immigration, but we trusted guidance and wrote to an English removalist requesting collection of the boxes from the apartment's garage and their shipment to Australia. With the nun as my Guide, I was to learn that there would be future acts of faith. My confidence was increasing in my ability to work alongside this special person and my commitment and trust became total.

I received instructions to drive to Sydney and to encourage Mum to start writing to a friend she had met on the cruise who lived near the Blue Mountains. We booked into a motel, but I was soon lost in the busy Sydney traffic. Mum could see I was becoming tense and suggested I dowse my way to the motel. I thought the idea strange, but followed the left and right indications of the swing of my pendulum and was bowled over when the motel sign appeared. We were sent out to look for accommodation to rent, but found nothing.

I was to learn it was a reconnaissance trip.

Mum wrote letters to her three sisters telling them she had applied for Australian residency, but there was no response. Three Christmas cards arrived for Mum only; there was no Christmas post for Mum or myself from Barbara and the children. Regardless, Mum and I enjoyed the three days, visiting special places in the area. We did receive a letter from my friend Dianne in England, who had responded to my letter written from Mum's apartment in September. She was concerned for our wellbeing and began to correspond regularly with me and then independently with Mum. This was to be of great comfort to her for years and of great spiritual importance to me later.

The New Year of 1987 brought a legal letter from Barbara and Anne's solicitor containing a cheque for three thousand pounds. 'Full and final settlement,' it stated. The sum didn't even cover a fraction of what I had spent on renovating the Old Saddlery, let alone my investment and a half share of the sale profit. I returned the cheque, posting it back to England with a letter declining their offer.

There was no family birthday post for Mum in January or for me in March.

I was sent to a map of Sydney and told, *Move there*. Then the post brought a letter from Mum's cruise friend, inviting us to stay with her if we ever came to Sydney. I was told again, *Move there*.

The car payments were a drain, but then I realised that in Sydney I could manage without a car. Before I could gather my thoughts, I was directed to drive to Victor Harbor and stand outside the office window of the garage. The salesman came out and began talking to me. In response, out of my mouth came the statement, 'I am considering selling my car.' Later, at home, my Guide requested I go for a walk; I did, leaving Mum alone at the cabin. When I returned, the salesman had taken the car for cleaning, having obtained the keys from Mum. All the car documents were in the glove box. I rang the salesman, who told me he had sold the car. 'But the car was on terms,' I told him. I wrote quickly to the finance company telling them what had happened. Again, a remarkable sequence of events was brought into play by my Guide, this time to free me of the costs of the car.

It was late April when we boarded the coach to Sydney, having arranged with Mum's cruise friend to stay with her. Accommodation was cramped, but our hostess loved having us there.

On 7 May I awoke filled with enthusiasm, and my Guide directed me to hire a car and drive to Springwood in the Blue Mountains to a particular real estate agency. An agent mentioned a property at 30 Rickard Road, Warrimoo, that had recently been withdrawn from sale. *Yes, this one*, she confirmed.

Even though the house had been withdrawn from sale, I asked the agent to ring the owners and request we be allowed to view it. Much to his surprise, the very elderly owners agreed. The cottage was basic, but had an incredible garden planted with flowers such that some were in bloom all year round. It provided a spectacular view of the mountains and a small gorge. We were amazed by the blue haze in the distance, created by evaporating eucalyptus oil from the trees, which gave the Blue Mountains their name. There was a bird-stand in the garden with two sulphur-crested cockatoos feeding. *You must live here*, my Guide said.

The agent was taken to one side by the couple and returned smiling. He confirmed that the cottage was again for sale and encouraged Mum to make an offer, which she did, making the purchase subject to the sale of her apartment in England. Veronica was right: Mum was buying a place in Australia, but it was not in Western Australia.

Mum's passport was returned to her from the Immigration Office in Adelaide on 11 May. It was exactly a year since I had delivered my father's mantle clock to Barbara's home the previous year and her face had been so full of triumph. Two days later, a letter arrived from Immigration and Ethnic Affairs. 'Dear Mrs Roach, I am pleased to inform you that your application for resident status in Australia has now been approved.'

We were elated, then wondered when Mum's apartment would be sold. A week later, on returning from a walk, we found all the outdoor letterboxes in Mum's friend's street had been vandalised. Post had been thrown around as if in a fit of temper, and my mind was taken back to Mum's apartment in the previous March, when I had found her dining table in disarray. Letters had been destroyed, but next to our friend's box was a white envelope addressed to Mum and inside was the contract for the purchase of her apartment. The completion date was 19 June. Thanks to my Guide's instructions, Mum's belongings were already *en route* to Australia and scheduled to arrive in Melbourne on 5 June. *Now move to Windsor*, she instructed, which was a surprise, but I began making enquiries.

Windsor is near the base of the Blue Mountains, on the edge of the Hawkesbury River. Knowing our stay there would be for just a short time, I booked a caravan, even though it had the distinct disadvantage of being many kilometres away from the Windsor post office, which I would have to walk each day. Taking Mum with me by taxi one morning for an outing, I was drawn to a pine furniture factory display shop. Inside, I found myself ordering furniture for a four-bedroom house. Our cottage had only two bedrooms and we had not yet moved in, but I continued ordering three double beds, a Welsh dresser, wardrobes, bedside tables and more. The furniture for the cottage was to be made first. Mum stared at me, but I understood that, once a decision had been made and followed through on, my Guide would move on to the next stage, well in advance of it happening.

Handover of the cottage was delayed until 24 July. I was encouraged to hire a car and drive us to Broken Hill.

The next morning we were to drive 130 kilometres from Broken Hill to Mootwingee National Park, Mum recording the events in her notes while I took photographs. This would be the first Aboriginal area Mum and I visited together. I recalled Pat Densham, back in Ashburton, telling me I had been an Australian Aboriginal many, many times. In the 12th century, born in Ashburton in the same street as the Old Saddlery, one of two sisters, I had died in a fire at the age of sixteen years. Following this death, I chose to return as a male Aboriginal in Australia and was killed by a spear during a tribal war. Mum and I were in awe of the fact that once again I had moved from North Street in Ashburton to live in Australia following traumatic circumstances. *Killed with a spear during a tribal war*: the words sent a searing pain through my right leg below the knee. We walked the dry creek bed near a rugged formation that featured Aboriginal paintings. Galahs surrounded us, flying low, forcing us to stand by a waterhole. Instinctively, we dipped our hands into the water to absorb the energy of this element, aware that something unusual was happening.

Just as we were moving into our Blue Mountains cottage, our belongings from South Australia arrived, then our handmade pine furniture from Windsor, followed by Mum's belongings from her apartment in England. The first item unpacked was the Butterfly Circle, which was placed under Mum's bed; later the Wild Geese print was hung in my bedroom.

Decorate, my Guide insisted. I was sent off by train down the mountain to Penrith to buy decorating materials. On the second of three trips I was instructed to buy a metal ladder. It caused chaos on the train and I was not amused. When at home again, I complained that the journey had been embarrassing. I waited. There was no response. I went to walk away but was held fast. The sensation of laughter filled my being and I laughed. I was being encouraged to see the funny side of the trip.

The wallpaper had to be soaked in the bath, then carried across the sitting room to the bedrooms. High walls meant long pieces. One piece fell off the wall. I was annoyed and impatient, but before I could express my frustration, a gentle energy filled my being and out of my mouth a soft, calm, feminine voice said, 'Oh dear. Oh dear'. Mum looked up at me in astonishment: I had spoken with my Guide's voice. Her words had moved through me like a gentle wave and we sat for a while in wonder at the experience.

I obtained employment as a night security officer with a Sydney newspaper. Each evening I travelled the hour and a half by train to the city to work the twelve-hour night shift, arriving home again at dawn, exhausted. The pay was excellent and I was guided to save everything I could. I wondered what was ahead.

News came from my Indian friend, Pal Sethi. For personal reasons he'd decided not to branch out into Australia. I replied, telling him of the important role he had played in ensuring my mother could stay with me in Australia as a resident. Mum and I had been sent to Delhi to meet him, and I had been sent again to organise a possible business connection with him. The old lady in Brixham last year had said he had a fatherly outlook towards me, and the clairvoyant Veronica had told me he thought of me as a daughter. I had no doubt that he, Mum and I shared a past-life connection.

Early one morning when I was not required to work in Sydney, I was woken, pushed out of bed and instructed to travel by train down the mountain. I left a note for Mum and walked to the station. After several stops, I was to alight and walk, before being stopped to note the street name of Martin Place. I was directed to take the same journey to the same street three times within a fortnight.

Early in September a legal letter came advising of a court action to unfreeze the remaining assets from the sale of the Old Saddlery. I was required to attend court in Torquay, England, at the end of the month. I had saved enough. My flight allowed me a stopover in Germany, where I caught up with Erika and her family, and then rented a flat in Paignton, England, within walking distance of the court at Torquay.

Realising I was back and ready for court, Barbara and Anne's solicitor changed the date of the hearing to 23 December. If I stayed, I would lose my job in Australia and I didn't want to leave Mum alone for long. Then came a shock: My solicitor rang to advise that my legal aid entitlement had been withdrawn. Anne had signed a sworn affidavit to the effect that I was an Australian citizen and therefore not entitled to legal aid. It required an enormous effort by my solicitor to convince the legal aid department this was untrue. My aid was reinstated, and when Barbara and Anne's solicitor discovered this, he again changed the court date — to January 1988.

Mum and I spoke on the phone. Although it was distressing, we agreed I had to stay. What was Barbara and Anne's solicitor so afraid of? My question was answered when I met Acora later. 'You are entitled to half of everything because you were on the deeds,' he said. 'There is something they are hiding and I do not know what it is, but you will find out in good time.'

I replied, 'I don't want half, I have only requested my capital and profit share.'

As I was leaving he caught hold of my arm. 'Judy,' he said, 'I want you to be aware that everyone has been poisoned against you, and I mean everyone. I see you involved in some sort of centre in Australia. You'll start it off and then your partner will join you there. Something to do with a key. You'll turn the key and it will go on working for you. God bless.'

No-one in the family attempted to contact me during my extended stay, although my address was known due to the legal contact. I was distressed that I would not be with my mother for Christmas or for her birthday in January. One day I hired a car and drove to Dartmoor; on another I walked the seafront at Torquay, wondering if I would catch a glimpse of the children. The distress was combined with anger and frustration as Barbara's written words echoed through my mind, 'You are greedy and stupid. I am taking my children away from you. You will be a lonely old woman.' I could not find any comfort in the words of the Living Goddess in Nepal: 'Out of destruction comes rebirth.'

Early in January Erika flew to England to spend time with me following a phone call when I told her about reconnecting with Jim, a retired police colleague, who had invited me for afternoon tea at his home. There was a person of interest who lived near me and he asked me to keep an eye on her activities, handing me an old charge sheet. Some time later I was glad that Erika had been with me when a plain-clothes officer came to my rented flat to talk to me. This potentially dangerous task kept me occupied while Barbara and Anne's solicitor kept delaying. I wrote to Mum about the involvement with Jim and sent her a copy of the charge sheet. I was certainly sticking my neck out in doing this — just as Jim was going against police policy in giving it to me — but I wanted to share my situation with Mum and had in mind also that her having the charge sheet might afford me some protection if things went wrong. This situation would soon become a point of conflict for me and would be used years later by two of Mum's sisters to humiliate her.

My Guide requested me to visit my father's family in Exeter. I spent time with a cousin, who arranged a visit with Uncle Dick, my father's brother, who was blind. He described how my father, a Chief Petty Officer, had won the Distinguished Service Medal in the war while serving aboard a British L-class Destroyer. My parents had attended a Presentation of Medals by the King at Buckingham Palace on 20 March

1945. Uncle Dick asked if I looked like my father. When I replied that I did, he asked me to look at the wall behind me.

I turned, and on the wall was an old faded photograph. 'Your grandmother was a spiritualist,' he said. 'She was a well-known medium in her day. She would speak out in front of folks in Dawlish.' I wondered why my father had never told me this. I stared at this woman, studying her face, and the word *Medium* repeated. 'You will do that one day,' Uncle Dick said.

I replied quickly, 'No, I won't', but he just smiled.

He gave me a parting gift: a small book entitled *At the Feet of the Master*, printed in India. As a boy, J. Krishnamurti had written down the precepts for right living as given to him by his guru. These were now a source of inspiration and guidance for thousands of people in India. As I read the words 'At the Feet of the Master' I recalled Mu Woolvett telling me in 1986 about Masters who trained spiritual people.

Spend time with Dawn, my Guide requested. 'You don't like it here,' she said. 'Your thoughts are always across the water. You will be going back soon to Australia.'

I asked her what she saw, and she spoke of the legal tangle. 'It will be a while before it is resolved. Things will not work out as you expect and there will be personal loss. You have more to do in Australia than here. You only feel emptiness in England.' She waited for me to absorb this. 'There is a man in spirit with one eye blocked. He says you often think of a place in Australia that gives you peace. You must go there.' My father had one eye covered due to failing sight.

Dawn mentioned New Zealand. 'Mountains,' she said. 'I see you going to and fro until you settle there. A Bible is being placed on a desk. You will be guided towards healing.' Again, she waited for me to absorb this. 'A man with reading spectacles is giving out birthday greetings to you and a firm handshake to give you strength.' I thought of my father again.

Dawn asked if my voice had been taken over and I told her what had happened in the Blue Mountains. 'This will happen from time to time over a period of five years,' she said. 'With this is the colour royal blue, the link to spiritual protection, but it links you to the Roman Catholic Church. Do you understand what this means to you?'

I explained that two years ago the clairvoyant Veronica told me my spirit Guide was a Catholic nun. 'Sister of Mercy,' my Guide announced, her soft, gentle voice coming out through my mouth once again.

Dawn stared at me for a moment and then continued in a quieter, more respectful tone. 'Let it slip into your mind that all roads lead to the same place, and that because she was a Catholic nun does not mean she is going to impress Roman Catholic teachings. She has left that behind. The word I see is 'discipline'. That is what she will encourage you in, discipline. Self-discipline and discipline with others around you.'

Dawn waited for me to absorb this. 'You have memorable links with India,' she said. 'You are going to return again with another person, to a particular spot.' I left with the confirmation that I was being trained.

On my return to the flat I found a letter from Australia, requesting me to attend a medical examination regarding Mum's and my car accident claims. I rang my solicitor to explain I was returning to Australia. We agreed to say nothing to Barbara and Anne's solicitor, who was still delaying the actual arrangement of any court date.

I had a shock when I alighted from the Blue Mountains train and saw Mum on the platform. Her glasses were broken and her false teeth were damaged. She had taken a bad fall and had stitches in her chin. I felt anger towards Anne and Barbara for separating us and putting Mum in harm's way. It was a relief for us to be together and we celebrated my birthday on 8 March. From that moment on, at precisely 4 am each day, I was woken with the push to finish decorating. There seemed to be a great urgency.

Within weeks of my return, a threatening letter arrived at the cottage using letters cut out from a newspaper: 'I only have to be lucky once. You have to be lucky always.' Then the phone rang and it was the voice of the person who Jim had asked me to keep an eye on, in England. 'I know it was you,' she said, and then rang off.

On 18 May a letter arrived from my solicitor in England to inform me that a court hearing had been held in my absence and Anne had been awarded the remaining assets. Someone had told Anne I was back in Australia, so she'd arranged a quick hearing. My solicitor wrote that she had tried to contact me, but I had received no letter or phone call. Neither was there any proof of her posting any letter.

Appeal, my Guide urged. My solicitor replied by return, enclosing an appeal form and a request for the sum of ten pounds to lodge the appeal. Mum wrote a cheque on her English bank account. I was aware there was a time limit with regard to lodging any appeal. *Send a copy to the Case Registrar*, my Guide instructed. I pointed out to the Torquay Registrar that my solicitor had failed to inform me of my right to appeal. What was going on in the legal system in England to allow this to happen? In the letter, I asked for time to continue with our accident compensation claim here in Australia and to allow this I suggested a court date be set for the end of August.

My Guide had specifically chosen this solicitor. *Trust the process and all will be revealed.*

Mum and I were sent to Penrith on the train. We were walking by a tourist outlet when I was stopped, then sent inside. I returned with a brochure on a place called 'Nelson Bay — a blue water paradise'. I was guided to book accommodation and then hire a car. Two days later we drove north. We were sent to Salamander Sales and soon found ourselves looking at blocks of land at the Port Stephens Tree Top development. We were shown Lot 74, Lampton Close, and Mum agreed to purchase. We drove home not knowing what to think, as neither of us had ever been involved in house building.

Back at the cottage it was full steam ahead with the decorating, the final touch being the hanging of a print of an English hunting scene. As I hung it I received the message, *Ring the Springwood agent.* I heard myself telling him Mum wanted to sell the cottage. The property market had soared in Sydney and the Blue Mountains. Later that afternoon, the agent rang to say he was bringing a young man to view the property. The young man had walked into his office minutes after my phone call. He loved everything about the cottage, especially the wallpaper. Before Mum had time to sign the agreement to sell she was accepting an offer to purchase. We were left shell-shocked. The phone rang and it was the agent from Salamander Sales requesting a completion date on the block of land, which of course we were now able to provide.

'That was amazing,' I said to Mum. *Keep trusting the process,* my Guide replied.

On completion of the sale of the cottage, Mum and I stored all our belongings and rented a home at Soldiers Point, within walking distance of her block in Lambton Close. We decided to have a silent telephone number and a post box at the nearest post office from now on because of the anonymous note and the threatening phone call from England. We became involved with a particular building company and were kept busy with plans and applications. It was here Mum was encouraged to join a craft group and work with long-stitch tapestries. My interest in traditional tapestry was encouraged.

The Port Stephens council rejected our building plans for Lot 74. The builder began to argue with the council, having never been refused before. But my Guide sent me to Richardson & Wrench Real Estate in Soldiers Point. On display there was an advertisement for an auction to be held on 5 November. I submitted Mum's block for auction. It was a nerve-racking time, and Mum and I walked by the sea to calm our nerves.

When nothing had been received by the end of September from the Torquay Court or from my solicitor in Exeter, I wrote to the Case Registrar. A reply arrived by return:

Torquay County Court to Miss J. Roach: Date 7 October 1988:
With reference to your letter of 30 September, the Court has never received an Appeal or fee in this matter. If your solicitor was instructed to lodge an Appeal, then you should take the matter up with him. Signed Chief Clerk.

The time frame for an Appeal had now lapsed. The next day a letter arrived from Legal Aid advising me that my legal aid had been cancelled. My solicitor had closed the case. When I read this I was furious, 'What is it with these people? The law is meant to work for everyone.' I was not comforted by my Guide's response, *Trust the process.*

On 18 October I was encouraged to write to another firm of solicitors in Bristol, concerning my former solicitor's failed actions and Barbara's attempted misuse of my power of attorney. Legal Aid responded by suggesting I reapply, while the firm in Bristol asked for further details regarding the sale of the Old Saddlery.

The next day my Guide directed me to hire a car for four days, starting 23 October. We drove 177 kilometres north to the Barrington Tops National Park along the Mount Carson Trail to our accommodation. The narrow road wound its way along the edge of the plateau, with sheer drops to one side. Mum and I were exhausted when we arrived. Early the following day we drove 78 kilometres east to the township of Gloucester. On entering Gloucester I was forced to stop the car when a pain went through my right leg below the knee. I barely managed to open the car door before I was sick.

'What's wrong?' Mum asked.

'I'm not sure,' I replied, remembering that I had felt the pain the previous year when we were at Mootwingee National Park. When I'd recovered, we visited the local real estate agency.

An agent showed us a spacious modern four-bedroom brick-and-tile home on the outskirts of town. *Yes, this one,* my Guide said. Mum made an offer to purchase, which was accepted. She insisted I be the joint owner. The pine furniture I had ordered for a four-bedroom home was waiting in Windsor. I returned the hire car only to arrange to rent it again in November. Through the Gloucester estate agent I had asked that we be allowed to rent our new home, at 59 Dawson Crescent, from early December until completion day.

On the first day of November my Guide requested me to drive 150 kilometres north to the Community of St Clare at Stroud. We sat inside the chapel to absorb the essence of this unusual place. I was encouraged to buy the Prayer of St Francis of Assisi for myself and one for Mum's eldest sister, Audrey. The brochure told how this son of a wealthy merchant had devoted his life to God. In 1210, Pope Innocent III had sent him and eleven followers to preach under the name Friars Minor. His work was balanced by the life of prayer of his friend St Clare and her Sisters. We were in the monastery of the Blessed Virgin Mary.

I had mixed feelings about Mary, questioning the importance given to her by the Roman Catholic Church. I walked for a while near the chapel thinking about my Guide's request to post the prayer to Aunty Audrey in England before being instructed to read the Prayer of St Francis aloud. 'Lord, make me an instrument of Your peace; where there is hatred, let me sow love; where there is injury, pardon; where there is doubt, faith; where there is despair, hope; where there is darkness, light; and where there is sadness, joy.'

The following day, my Guide insisted we drive 150 kilometres north to the Green Cathedral Tiona Park within the Booti Booti National Park and make a special note of the day. The Green Cathedral was an unusual place, with logs for seats and a wooden pulpit all within a grove of trees. An information board explained the concept: 'The groves were God's first temples.' On leaving the Green Cathedral we were encouraged to visit a coastal village an hour and a half's drive away along a narrow dirt road. On arriving at the village, which was only a few homes, Mum complained about her ankle. I saw her leg had ballooned, and realised she must have been bitten by something.

'I feel hot and a little nauseous,' Mum said. I turned the car around, anxious by now, and set off back along the dirt road. We looked at our watches, knowing it would be an hour and a half before we even reached the highway, after which we had to drive to find medical help.

'Try and stay calm,' I said. 'I can't drive faster because it's a dirt road.' Twenty minutes later, the highway came into view. 'Not possible,' I said, looking at Mum as she checked her watch.

I drove down the highway until we found an open chemist. Thankfully, the bite was not serious. Later we spoke about what had happened, especially as I had driven at normal speed but had covered the journey in twenty minutes. The only explanation was the urgency to find help must have triggered some kind of 'time warp'. We did not have to make a special note of this day as it would always stay in our minds. This was a first-hand example of what Mu Woolvett had experienced on the day she came to help me at Mum's apartment in 1986, when I had rung about my headache and she had arrived in minutes, having covered a distance that should have taken her thirty or forty minutes.

When we returned to Soldiers Point, the contracts for the purchase of our home in Gloucester and the sale of the block of land in Tree Tops were waiting in our post box. At 11 am on Saturday 5 November, the block was sold by auction. It was only then that we comprehended that the sale of Mum's cottage in the Blue Mountains and of her block at Port Stephens, each having made a profit, ensured Mum had recovered her losses from the under-value sale of her apartment and furnishings in England. We had trusted the process and were thrilled with the outcome. I was at a loss as to why there was legal conflict with England, but my Guide was a determined woman and I was happy to leave it in her capable hands.

People were still sending their signatures through the post, requesting advice. I developed a program called 'Pendulum Analysis', including references to past lives. The information would come through from my Guide, and I would confirm this by using my pendulum. During one program, the pendulum indicated *Yes*. I waited. *Buy a magazine*. I walked quickly to the newsagency, where I was instructed to buy *Australian Wellbeing*, No. 29, 1988. Days later I was encouraged to read the article 'Soulmates: The quest for your perfect mate' by Denise Linn:

> Although the term 'soulmates' is commonly used to describe the one passionate love of your life, soulmates can be described as all of those individuals that you have been with, time after time, in past lives. This idea is based on the reincarnation theory that you incarnate lifetime after lifetime with other like-minded individuals. These souls can be likened to a great flock of birds that travels to

distant countries, yet always flies together. I have found consistently, based on information gathered in my reincarnation seminars, that individuals often incarnate as a group and tend to be drawn together lifetime after lifetime. (2)

Dr Bampty, in England, had shared her theory that many people returned to villages and townships to put to rights unresolved past-life issues for others or for themselves.

I was then sent by my Guide to the packing box that had accompanied us from the Blue Mountains. When I opened the required parcel I discovered it was the Wild Geese print Anne had given me for my 38th birthday at the Old Saddlery. On the back of the framed print Anne had written: 'Judy. No you can't fly away …' One year later Mum and I did fly away, to Australia. I looked at the flying geese and then re-read the article: 'These souls can be likened to a great flock of birds …' I understood that the print symbolised a group of souls. I hung the Wild Geese / Soul Group print in my bedroom, and then read on:

> There is a tendency to think that our soulmates are only those individuals whom we meet and have an instant affinity for in this life. However, I have found in my regression work that soulmates can also be those people whom we have difficulties with in our present lives. In fact, those very challenging individuals often are those with whom we have had the most intimate past-life connections. (2)

Anne, Barbara and Mum's three sisters were certainly challenging at this time. In 1986, Mu Woolvett had told me Anne and I had been unhappily married in a past life. I read on:

> Understanding the concept of karma can make these seemingly negative soulmates more understandable. Karma is the idea that what you sow, you reap. Your harvest is not necessarily dictated by a governing deity but rather by your own sense of integrity … Hence we reap according to our own inner sense of right or wrong … This idea of karma applies to past lives … How do you recognise a soulmate? … If there has been a sexual liaison in a past-life, there will be a tendency for a physical attraction to occur in the present life, sometimes almost explosively intense … Soulmates can be our parents, children, business associates, friends and lovers. (2)

I was surprised to learn soulmates can be parents, children, business associates, friends and lovers. The Lovers pots from Ashburton had accompanied Mum and me from the Blue Mountains. When Anne and I moved to the Old Saddlery in 1983, my attention had been drawn to these two miniature pots and 'The Lovers' design. The Old Saddlery had been a 'doorway' to unresolved past lives and the issues in play involved jealousy, resentment, sibling rivalry, money, property, relatives and children. My love for my mother's sisters and my sister's children had been a focal point in my life. While their loss was terrible, their behaviour was now quite foreign, as if a black, negative cloud had engulfed them. I recalled the warning of the gypsy who had sat with me in the restaurant: 'There is a black cloud over this house, lots of bad luck and misfortune.'

That night I had a vivid dream of a young, slim woman with dark eyes. There was a regal stance about her. Her large brown eyes held an intense emotion and came closer, then faded. I woke with a feeling of deep grief and loss that stayed with me all day.

On 18 November a letter arrived from the solicitors' firm in England with details of a solicitor, Martha Street of Bristol, who was prepared to review my case. I replied enclosing copies of everything that had occurred before and since Mum and I left England, in October 1985.

Five days later a letter arrived for Mum from her sister Audrey in response to her receiving the 'Prayer of St Francis'. I was not mentioned, which hurt, but it was progress. Mum replied with a newsy letter and then sent Christmas cards to her three sisters.

We moved to Gloucester early in December, having booked a hire car. Our belongings from the Blue Mountains were delivered as the extra furniture for a four-bedroom home arrived from Windsor. We watched in fascination as the two deliverymen unloaded the pine furniture, not once seeking our directions, placing Mum's double bed and mine in bedrooms at the front of the house and the third double bed in the room leading from the enclosed sunroom. The single bed, along with my office furniture, was placed in the fourth bedroom. When they had departed we wandered around our home, enjoying the feeling of comfort. The Butterfly Circle was placed under Mum's bed, the Wild Geese / Soul Group print hung on my office wall and The Lovers pots were on display in the kitchen window as they had been at the Old Saddlery.

On Christmas morning Mum handed me a tapestry of four rainbow lorikeets for me to work. The importance of the gift would be revealed later.

We were sent by my Guide to the Rose Garden Restaurant at Port Stephens, where I was instructed to buy two postcards of yellow roses. We were then encouraged to drive to and walk the grounds of the Community of St Clare at Stroud. I pondered the breakthrough for Mum with regard to her three sisters, following my sending the Prayer of St Francis to Aunty Audrey. On our return home, I handed one postcard of yellow roses to Mum for her diary. The other postcard, my Guide insisted, must be placed beside the Soulmates article in the office. Then the Wild Geese / Soul Group print was to be taken down from the wall to rest with the article and the yellow roses postcard, highlighting a connection between them. Later, my notes regarding the dream of the regal young woman with dark brown eyes were to be added to the formation. I was then encouraged to record these highlighted words on a page in my notebook:

Highlighted words 1988: Soulmate – yellow roses – soul group – dream – regal young woman with dark brown eyes.

Who is this regal young woman and why has she come to me in a dream? I wondered.

The first post to arrive in 1989 was a copy of a Torquay County Court Ruling. It had been posted four months earlier, in September 1988, and sent via sea mail to our home address at Soldiers Point before being redirected to Gloucester. The ruling stated that there had been an appeal hearing on 1 September 1988 and, because neither I nor my solicitor had attended, the money being held had been released to the applicant.

On 30 September 1988 I had written to the Case Registrar requesting that I be informed of the appeal hearing date; the Chief Clerk replied on 7 October, stating he had received no appeal or fee in my name. He omitted to inform me an appeal hearing had been heard on 1 September. On re-examining the Chief Clerk's letter and its envelope, I noticed his reply had been sent to our address and not to our box number. The address was known only to my solicitor: when the decision was made to have a post box, my Guide had said, *apart from your solicitor*. The Chief

Clerk and my solicitor had been in contact, so why was my appeal not lodged and the fee not paid? Why did the Chief Clerk fail to mention an appeal hearing had taken place? Fortunately, I had responded to my Guide's instructions to seek out a firm of solicitors in England and the solicitor Martha Street was already reviewing my case and seeking another suitable solicitor to represent me. I sent Martha the recently received letters regarding my former solicitor's failure to lodge my appeal and to cash Mum's cheque, and the Chief Clerk's failure to mention an appeal hearing had already been heard.

Think ahead, my Guide requested.

I wrote to my cousin in Exeter, whom I had met the previous year prior to visiting Uncle Dick, and asked her to go to the Exeter post office and check the records of registered letters. Specifically I asked her to find the entry for the registered letter I sent to my former solicitor with the completed appeal form and ten-pound fee. My cousin replied by return, telling me my former solicitor had signed in person for it. I sent this information to Martha in Bristol and she replied recommending a solicitor called Alison Wynell-Mayow, who requested funding until legal aid could be arranged. I obtained a bank draft and walked to the post office to send it off.

I returned home carrying a letter for Mum from John, Barbara's first husband and father of her grandchildren. He had written a newsy letter, providing Mum with details of her grandchildren's lives and addresses. The twins, Tim and Mark, were in Guernsey, working as chefs with Jan, a friend of Barbara's. He told us Barbara was engaged to be married for a third time and I wondered what had happened to Eric.

Early on 6 February my Guide insisted that I walk to a tourist outlet to pick up a brochure on Western Australia, read it the next day and make special note of the date, 7 February. I was taken to a page featuring Geraldton and the Bill Sewell Complex, and encouraged to write to the Complex requesting names of estate agents, and then post the letter. Standing outside the post office was a woman who had served me at a local shop. She asked if I was involved with craft. 'Tapestry,' I replied. She spoke of a craft morning and offered to drive me there the following week. *You must go*, my Guide urged.

I walked home thinking about Geraldton in Western Australia and looked it up on the map. It was on the opposite side of the continent. This was too huge a move for me to contemplate. But I remembered that the Butterfly Circle, with its Western Australian jarrah frame, was still under Mum's bed, and that in 1986 Veronica, the clairvoyant, had asked Mum in her reading if she lived in Perth. Geraldton is north of Perth.

On 14 February, Valentine's Day, I was driven to the craft morning and continued to work the rainbow lorikeet tapestry. Sitting next to me was a petite woman in her mid-thirties with shoulder-length straight brown hair, who spoke to no-one. We were offered a hot drink, but the young woman asked for hot water as she had her own herbal tea bag. I missed a stitch, in surprise, when she started speaking to me about herbal teas. Her name was Cathy and she invited me to visit her at her home in two days' time.

She appeared nervous and distressed when Mum and I arrived, but still invited us in. We talked about alternative theories and she asked me to complete a pendulum analysis for her. As we were walking home Mum said, 'What a ghastly atmosphere in that house. You could cut it with a knife.'

A trip to Sydney, my Guide predicted. Then Cathy rang to say she was off to Sydney for the day and whether we wanted a lift. 'Yes please,' I replied.

During the drive I asked Cathy for her signature, explaining it was necessary for her pendulum analysis. I could sense the cogs of her brain processing this. In Sydney, Mum and I were led to the Garden of Friendship at Darling Harbour — a Chinese Garden with the Clear View Pavilion and the Twin Pavilion symbolising the friendship between Australia and China. *Clear View* and *Twin,* repeated until I understood my nephew Tim would one day see through the smokescreen created by Barbara and Anne to hide their actions.

At home later I started painting the sunroom and its attached double bedroom with the view to converting this very private area into guest accommodation.

Around-the-world ticket, my Guide predicted.

A letter arrived from Alison, my solicitor in Bristol, to warn me there might be an appeal hearing in England regarding legal negligence on the part of my former solicitor.

For my birthday in March, gifts and cards arrived from friends, but nothing from family. Erika's gift created a surge of grief-like emotions that were hard to control. It was a painting on papyrus of the Egyptian Sun God Re — the Creator God — from her recent trip to Egypt. I was drawn to touch the figure before placing it by the Soulmates article, the postcard of yellow roses and details of my dream of the regal young woman with brown eyes. I was so shaken by these unexplained emotions that I was forced to rest. Later, my Guide requested I update my notes regarding the woman in my dream to include *Egypt*.

Cathy rang requesting a pendulum analysis for her husband, then again wanting three more for her three children. I began to feel pressured, particularly when the request included a wish to watch me use the pendulum. She sat with me as I worked on her analysis, moving to one side her requests in relation to her other family members. I asked her about a connection she had with a ring belonging to someone departed, to which she replied a ring belonging to her grandmother's sister had created a family upset. I told her the ring was significant and there would be a strong connection between Cathy and her grandmother once her Nanna had passed over also. The passing would be soon.

I became tense as I tried to dowse the food items for Cathy and my pendulum took control by giving the anticlockwise swinging response *No* each time. I fetched my set of psychic cards and turned the pack face down. The pendulum responded with *Yes* to certain cards. I handed these cards to Cathy to turn over and read, one advising her to consult her doctor urgently. She looked at me in surprise, explaining there was a problem only she and her husband knew about.

I asked Cathy what she owned that had belonged to a grandmother who had died some time ago. Cathy said she had pressed maidenhair ferns that had been taken from the family Bible. With a look of guilt she admitted she took them without permission and her father had become irritated because they had marked chosen pages.

'They came from page twenty,' I said. 'Find the Bible and look it up. The reading of the page will give you comfort in the future.'

Cathy spent the day trying to work out how to borrow the Bible from her parents, who were Catholics. In the end she admitted everything to her mother and was told there were three pages with the number twenty, References, the Old Testament and the New Testament. The latter included St Matthew's account of the Transfiguration. Cathy had recently read a book regarding incarnation that made reference to the same account.

Within days of Cathy watching me work, my Guide sent me to the newsagency to stand by its window. I saw a notice in which she was advertising that she could now dowse, along with her skills as a herbalist. I took a copy of the notice home. I was annoyed, because this was not a tool to be played with. It took practice over some years to become neutral and allow the information and guidance from your higher self, or your Guide, to flow.

She rang to tell me a story about her mother. Having been told by Cathy of our session, her mother had been unable to sleep, concerned about the use of the pendulum, and prayed for guidance on 19 March. At 2 o'clock the following morning she had been compelled to record a message, *I am behind this. Put your heart in my heart and I will guide you.* Cathy's mother asked about dowsing, so Mum and I arranged to spend time with her and her husband and share some of our experiences. We liked them and a friendship was soon to develop between the four of us.

The next morning I found a book on our doorstep about a place called Findhorn, a spiritual community in Scotland. I did not know who had left it, but suspected it was Cathy. It concerned three people: Eileen Caddy, her partner, Peter, and a friend, Dorothy. Eileen left her husband and several children to work with Peter, creating a strong spiritual connection and later founding Findhorn, a place of learning. Cathy collected the book a few days later. After she had gone, Mum and I agreed that neither of us felt comfortable in her presence, though we could not explain why. We sensed there was something hidden deep in Cathy's personality, but could not pinpoint what it was.

Early on 11 May, Aunty Val's birthday, I was woken and told to drive 128 kilometres south-east to Nelson Bay. Not having a car, I had no option but to contact Cathy to ask her to drive me. I was taken to a jewellery shop to buy a silver bracelet featuring seven dolphins linked head-to-fin and an accompanying silver necklace featuring a larger dolphin. I was instructed to wear both. On the return trip back to Gloucester, I remembered 11 May 1986 when I handed my father's mantle clock into Barbara's home. The handing over of the clock indicated that the rescue of Barbara was a task required of my mother and me by my father. Now a huge effort had been made by Cathy and me to buy a silver set of jewellery featuring eight dolphins.

'What is so important about dolphins?' Cathy enquired.

'I have no idea.'

Later, I was encouraged to update my notes regarding the regal young woman in the dream, recording 'dolphin' next to 'Egypt'.

Mum had been told about a clairvoyant named Bruce, and we wrote to him for a reading:

Tess — what an unusual lady, God gave you a very difficult life, but he always protected you ... A long time ago you came to the realisation that you had a special task in life and I want to say, 'You did well.' Theresa, you must not blame yourself for anything that has happened. You did have to make decisions that had to be made ... you are going to see special things happen in the future that will make you very happy ... travel overseas to see family. Are there two properties? I feel one is going to be sold. As I wrote that message an older lady came through, a grandmother, and said, 'You will do the right thing.' This lady was stern but loving to those who knew her. There is spiritual activity around both you and Judith and it means a happier future in there for you both.

Judith, with you I get excited about your future. I see you with greater love in your life, greater balance. Whatever this love is in your future, it comes with the word 'soulmate'. As I wrote this, a tall man came from spirit and showed me a future for you as birds. He smiled when he showed me, and said, 'Happiness beyond belief.' As I said, 'Keep an open mind.' Judith, you are very psychic yourself and you feel, see and talk to spirit. You have always known that you will achieve something special and you have the potential to do this. Judith, something was missing from your childhood that stops you from showing people the real you. I feel the real Judith within is trying hard to emerge. I also know there is a loneliness you have within you that you cannot share with others, also sometimes a tear at night for some reason? You, I feel, are a special person who has been hurt and in some way is cynical about life and also very fragile. So what, many people are like that. Legal advice — papers to be signed. I feel you will write a book and have a hand in producing one. Your plans, they will come to fruition.

By mid-year Cathy had moved to the Blue Mountains with her children, telling us life at home had become intolerable. But her children wanted their father and their home. *Spend time in the mountains*, my Guide said. I travelled by train to visit Cathy for the weekend. The atmosphere between Cathy and her three children was dreadful, and I wondered why I had been sent to visit. That evening I was sitting in Cathy's lounge room when I became aware of being lifted higher in my mind. I was awake and aware of my surroundings. Up I went into the universe, higher and higher, until the Earth formed, and moved away from me. I moved higher still until the Earth was a distant planet. It began to revolve on its axis. As I watched, small moving pictures appeared in a band around it, each a cameo of time. I was observing my past lives. I was not able to view the scenes clearly, but I described what I saw to Cathy. *Karma clearing issues ahead*, my Guide warned.

Within weeks Cathy's children had returned to Gloucester and Cathy moved into our guest accommodation. Mum and I accepted that she was to stay with us, but felt pressured.

Ten days later Cathy and I were instructed to drive to a place near the Blue Mountains called Oberon, to search for a place called Iona Sanctuary. We found it in a valley, but it was unoccupied. I was directed to stand away from Cathy and read my notes regarding the regal young woman who had come to me in a dream:

> Highlighted words 1988: Soulmate – yellow roses – soul group – dream –regal young woman with dark brown eyes – Egypt – dolphin.

A surge of grief-like emotions came, and I remembered they were the same emotions I'd felt when I opened Erika's birthday gift from Egypt. I then felt drawn to touch the seven-dolphin bracelet and take a photograph of Cathy standing in front of the Iona sign. I was being shown that the regal young woman in my dream, Egypt, Iona, Cathy, dolphins and I were all linked. At home later, I was guided to read further from the Soulmates article:

> Sometimes lovemates will be much older or younger than their match or they will have different races or socio-economic standing. Yet the urge to be together is stronger than society's values … However, when lovemates unite, for whatever duration, there is a true mating of the heart and the soul that is fathomless. (2)

The words 'mating of the heart' and 'the soul' were highlighted. I was instructed to change the heading regarding the young woman in my dream to read Heart Issue (1).

On 15 September I was encouraged to buy the *Sydney Morning Herald* and read the part entitled, 'Re-hearing Order … a man has won an appeal to have a re-hearing.' *Around-the-world ticket*, my Guide confirmed.

Communication came from Allison, enclosing legal aid forms for me to sign. I was taken by my Guide to my briefcase, the one I used in the police force. 'Justice,' I said. I was then sent to my hand luggage, where I discovered the *Sacre Coeur* — the Sacred Heart Medal — that I had bought in Paris with Mum when we visited the Notre Dame Cathedral at Easter 1974. We did not visit the Basilique du Sacre Coeur itself, but I was compelled to buy the medal. Mum and I lit candles to my father and sat inside the cathedral absorbing its atmosphere as I held the *Sacre Coeur*. This medal from Paris was to go with me on my around-the-world trip seeking justice. *French connection*, my Guide said.

My Guide organised the itinerary and I was wondering how I was going to pay for it when post arrived from Adelaide. The solicitor handling our 1986 car accident claims presented final offers and advised us to accept them. The sum offered to me would cover the cost of the trip. Cathy, who was negotiating a divorce settlement, said she wanted to come. I was not keen, but my Guide was firm: *She must go*. Then I recorded the following:

Around the World 1989: Justice – Sacred Heart – Notre Dame Cathedral.

At the beginning of October I received an urgent phone call from my legal firm in England, who had compiled a Statement of Facts and placed it before a barrister. The barrister had responded, saying a hearing should never have taken place and his enquiries had revealed that Anne had taken out a 36,000-pound mortgage on the Old Saddlery and purchased another home; then, when the Old Saddlery was sold, this debt was paid off and what was left declared to me and frozen. This would have required the assistance and signature of my power of attorney — Barbara. The barrister was now seeking an Appeal out of Time hearing.

Notification arrived to inform me the appeal hearing was scheduled for 6 December at the Plymouth County Court, Devon. I was instructed to visit the local estate agency and begin the process of selling our home in Gloucester. We had been moved to Gloucester to connect with Cathy, and now we must move yet again.

Cathy's parents came to see us and invited Mum to spend Christmas with them. Her mother handed me a package — a 'Miraculous Medal', with story attached — plus a card quoting Isaiah 49:15: 'See, I will not forget you. I have carved you on the palm of my hand.'

On 1 November Cathy and I flew out of Sydney and headed for Bangkok. I was aware that the previous year, on the same date, the young woman with dark brown eyes had come to me in a dream. Since then I had been given clues as to who she was: a soulmate, part of a soul group with a link to yellow roses, dolphins, Cathy, myself, the word Iona and Egypt. The clues were listed as Heart Issue (1) and I wondered if there were other soulmates with past-life heart issues. In 1986 Veronica had said, 'You will become well known for something to do with the heart.' Not long before, Cathy's mother had received the message: *I am behind this. Put your heart in my heart and I will guide you.*

During the flight I read the story about the Miraculous Medal. I knew little about Catholicism, but I was aware that if a seemingly miraculous event occurred it was strictly investigated. If the Church of Rome gave it their blessing, there was a possibility that it had happened. I was taken aback to learn that the medal was created in Paris in 1830. In my hand luggage was the Sacred Heart Medal, also from Paris — two very strong connections with France.

The leaflet explained that in the Mother House of the Sisters of Charity of Saint Vincent de Paul Paris, there lived a novice nun, Sister Catherine Labouré. She had a great devotion to Mary and, on the night of 18 July 1830, Mary's guardian angel, in the form of a child, summoned Sister Catherine to the chapel. Here she met with Mary and was told God had a mission for her. Four months later Mary came again to ask Catherine to reveal her vision and discuss the details of a medal in Mary's image for people to wear around their necks. I updated my Around the World 1989 notes, recording Miraculous Medal next to Notre Dame Cathedral.

We landed in Bangkok and were encouraged to visit the Temple of the Emerald Buddha. This is where *in search of Truth* had been highlighted in 1985, when Mum and I visited *en route* to Australia. I bought a postcard and posted it to Mum, wishing to share this with her. I recalled our journey to Australia: how we had been moved on from the past lives mentioned by Pat Densham in Ashburton by visiting specific places in India, Nepal and Bangkok. We had drawn on the energies of happy past-life memories. Mum and I had followed in the path of Buddha, experiencing the sense of familiarity when turning the prayer wheels at the Stupa of Swayambunath, Nepal. The son of a Nepalese rajah, Buddha was born in 563 BC in Kapiluastu in Nepal with the name of Siddhartha Gautama. He left his life of luxury at thirty to devote his life to contemplation and self-denial, and reached enlightenment sitting under a tree. Then known as Buddha, he spent the rest of his life teaching the Four Noble Truths and achieving the enlightened state of Nirvana. He died in 483 BC.

Cathy and I spent time with the people, observing them as they worked their crafts, creating scenes of busy hands and intense concentration. The following day we travelled to Chiang Mai and later walked through a Meao hill-tribe village. We watched a Mong family in their traditional dress — intricate costumes created in beautiful batik, their accordion-pleated skirts skilfully embellished with cross-stitch and appliqué. They wore silver jewellery created with tools at primitive forges. Silver is treasured by these people for its spiritual value as much as for its monetary value. I pointed towards my silver dolphin bracelet and the father smiled back at me knowingly.

Before leaving Thailand, Cathy and I were encouraged to visit the Wat Phra That Doi Suthep Temple, containing holy relics of Buddha. The entrance of this 14th-century building features gold leaf and colourful mosaics. I photographed two of the temple monks in their orange robes. As I captured their images, *monks* repeated in my mind.

It was cold and the sky was dark when we landed at Heathrow on 16 November. We picked up our hire car and drove into Wales, where we were to stay in Hay-on-Wye at the Old Black Lion, a comfortable 17th-century coaching inn. Wales was never a country that appealed to me, so I was interested to learn why we were directed to spend time there.

Early the next day we drove to an arched ruin. It was the 800-year-old archway of a monastery. A decorative board related the story of Gerald of Wales, who accompanied the Archbishop of Canterbury around Wales raising volunteers for the Third Crusade. Gerald had admired the hard-working life of the Cistercian community. The monastery was called *Ystrad Fflu* — Valley of Flowers. Cathy and I followed a ritual similar to what we'd done at the Iona Sanctuary by the Blue Mountains. I stood away from her, but this time read aloud the card given to me by her mother, with its quotation from Isaiah 49:15. 'See, I will not forget you. I have carved you on the palm of my hand.'

A surge of energy like flashes of lightning pulsated from the ground. *Cistercian monks*, repeated in my mind. My Guide instructed that the archway be photographed and I recorded how Gerald's party had journeyed north with the third son of Lord Rhys, Prince of South Wales. My Around the World 1989 notes were updated to include Cistercian monks, monastery and Prince of Wales next to Miraculous Medal. On our return to Hay-on-Wye, my Guide asked me to buy a second-hand book, the story of the spiritists of France (another French connection). I was required to read only the paragraph that described groups that would meet and access healing guides.

The following day we drove back to England and headed for Stonehenge on Salisbury Plain. I was guided to stand away from Cathy, but this time to read the paragraph describing the spiritists of France as the sun set over the ring of grey lintels. Many more than four metres high, they still bear the markings of the tools that shaped them more than 4000 years ago. Stonehenge is now famous for the Druid ceremonies held there, but I was to learn later that at least 1000 years separated the time of the megalith builders from the era when the Druids flourished. I photographed Stonehenge as the last, lingering, long rays of the sun disappeared. *Remember this moment*, my Guide said. A rush of familiarity filled my being, combined with an overwhelming need to walk within the circle. *Druid energy*, she explained. When I had recovered, my Around the World 1989 notes were updated further by adding Druid energy.

The next place to visit was the tower that rises 500 feet above the Vale of Avalon, the medieval chapel of St Michael at the top of Glastonbury Tor. According to local legend, the Holy Grail — reputedly the chalice used by Jesus at the Last Supper — had been buried at the foot of the Tor by Joseph of Arimathea. I was aware that Glastonbury is reputed to have passing through it one of the main ley-lines in England, the St Michael Ley, which is said to be aligned along the path of the sun on 8 May, the Spring Festival of St Michael. The theory is that the planet Earth has a meridian system made up of a planetary gridwork of subtle energy channels referred to as ley-lines. The Australian Aboriginals recognise these subtle energy channels as songlines.

I had been given instructions not to share note entries with anyone on this journey around the world, and I was reminded of it again as we climbed to the top of the Tor. While sheltering from the wind by the wall of the tower, a surge of royal blue moved across my vision, and Cathy said she saw the image of a monk. I was aware of standing on a ley-line and absorbing the familiar blue energy of spiritual protection. In 1986, Mu had used this energy combined with clear quartz — not from the Earth plane — to rid me of a headache.

At the base of the Tor I photographed the flow of spring water coming from a moulding with unusual markings. I was taken aback when, instead of standing away from Cathy, I found myself asking her to anoint me with water from the spring. I watched in fascination as she cupped her hands and then felt the mark of the cross being formed on my forehead. I washed my mouth and hands in the spring water — some form of cleansing. I was being moved on from the Buddhist past-life links I shared with Mum to walking in the footsteps of past-life links with ancient monks and Cathy. I updated my Around the World 1989 notes to include St Michaels Tower, Glastonbury Tor, and ley-line.

Free European return flights had been offered with our airline tickets, and we used them to visit Erika in Germany. When she drove us from Frankfurt to Maulbronn Monastery, built in 1147 by Cistercian monks, I shook my head in disbelief: Cathy and I had been sent to a ruined Cistercian monastery in Wales. While walking inside, I was aware of a double shaft of light coming at an angle from a small circular window through the semi-darkness. I was encouraged to stand in this twin shaft of light so that it touched my now-cleansed forehead — my third eye. Flashing white stars moved across my vision. I took a photograph before rejoining Erika and Cathy.

Two days later we were driven to Lake Constance, on the Swiss border. Erika drove past the Basilica of Birnau, a Cistercian priory dedicated to Mary, and I was guided to note that Erika had been drawn to take us to yet another Cistercian site. In the car she handed me a brochure, and I read that this was probably the earliest of many places of pilgrimage associated with Mary in southern Swabia. I updated my Around the World 1989 notes to include Mary:

Around the World 1989: Justice – Sacred Heart – Notre Dame Cathedral – Miraculous Medal – Cistercian monks – monastery – Prince of Wales – Stonehenge – Druid energy – St Michael's Tower – Glastonbury Tor – ley-line – third eye – Mary.

That evening, while viewing photographs of Erika's trip to Egypt, I started to feel a little distressed. The birthday gift of the papyrus painting of the Egyptian Sun God Re I had received from her the previous year, when placed by the Soulmates article, the yellow roses postcard and details of my dream of the regal young woman with brown eyes, had created a surge of grief-like emotions, and later the clue 'Egypt' had been added to Heart Issue (1).

I went to bed feeling disturbed and anxious, and awoke the next day with *Egypt* and *Switzerland* repeating over and over in my mind. Erika had driven near the Swiss border before showing us her Egyptian photographs. Later, I was encouraged to add these clues to Heart Issue (1) notes:

> Heart Issue (1): Soulmate – yellow roses – soul group – dream – regal young woman with dark brown eyes – Egypt – dolphin – Switzerland.

On 29 November we flew back to England and headed north to Newcastle by coach to visit Dianne. After a few days she decided to surprise us by driving us to Holy Island. The brochure *Lindisfarne Priory and Holy Island* read:

> Lindisfarne, later known as Holy Island, was the site of one of the most important early centres of Christianity in Anglo-Saxon England. Founded in 635 by St Aidan, the first bishop of northern Northumbrians, the monastery rapidly achieved international fame as a centre of learning and culture ...

Here was yet another story about the journeys of the monks from long ago. I was not surprised when Dianne wanted to take a photograph of Cathy and me standing under the Rainbow Arch — the ruined church's most remarkable feature and the last decorated rib of vaulting to be erected in the church. I read that St Aidan, the founder of Lindisfarne, came from the island monastery of Iona in Scotland, and I stood away from Dianne and Cathy to absorb this piece of information. As I held the dolphin bracelet and read the Iona sign, I recalled that Cathy and I had been sent to the Iona Sanctuary near the Blue Mountains to read the clues regarding the identity of the regal young woman in my dream. This revealed a link between the young woman, Iona, Cathy, dolphins and me. Today, Dianne had played her part and revealed the meaning of Iona. We left her and headed for Plymouth by coach.

On my day in court I was shocked to see Anne with long bleach-blonde hair — a younger version of Barbara. David was with her, but he looked at me with hatred. I had not expected this and it hurt. Of course Acora had warned me that everyone had been poisoned against me. I refused to allow David into the courtroom, while Anne refused to allow Cathy. There was a small elderly man with Anne who was also denied entry.

Having waited years for Anne to give an account of her influence within my family, I was disappointed at not being required to enter the witness box. The barristers spoke between themselves and the judge on all legalities. Anne was called and I listened to her with disbelief. At one point she was asked about the letter in which I had asked for the return of my capital input and profit share, but she denied receiving it, as did her legal team. Finally the decision: the judge would not allow my appeal, but granted an application to the House of Lords to appeal his decision, and to begin the process of suing my former solicitor. I watched Anne as she left the room with a look of triumph on her face. I sat for a while to come to terms with what had happened and realised I didn't feel anything. The search for justice was to make my former solicitor accountable.

My Guide directed me to spend time with a former police colleague who lived near St Ives, and I breathed in the fresh Cornish air. Days later, standing at Land's End, the most westerly point in Britain, the wind was so fierce we could barely open the car door. *Visit Sennen Cove*, my Guide said. It was just over a mile away. I walked the beach alone, allowing the last remnants of negativity from the unhappy past-life link with Anne, as my spouse, to be carried away by the sea breeze. As I went to leave the beach I was stopped by *another* holding my hand. I held my breath as relief flooded through me. *This is where you will meet a man with a mark on his forehead, a symbol. In the harbour, there will be a boat with a red stripe and a broken oar. Wait there and he will come. You will know him*, my Guide said.

I must be returning here again one day, I thought. Then the *person* let go of my hand and I left the beach.

I spent two days studying the Advice of Appeal from my barrister and wondered how much longer this conflict with my former solicitor would continue and what the outcome would be.

On 20 December Cathy and I flew to Toronto. It was so cold I thought I would not survive. We stayed in our hotel for days, trying to adjust to the freezing temperatures. She rang a friend in America, who invited us to spend Christmas with her and her family in Iowa. She drove us to the Ledgers National Park, 1200 acres of land dedicated in 1924. The American Indians had used this site for councils and pow-wows. According to legend, chiefs and warriors of the Sioux, and later the Sac, Fox and other tribes, gathered at this Indian Council Lodge to boast of their wars and other adventures. I walked alone to absorb the energy of the place. The next stage of our around-the-world trip was to fly on to Vancouver for a few days, where I was instructed to photograph a whale in the Vancouver Aquarium and walk Stanley Park.

In the New Year of 1990 we arrived back in Australia. During our stay in Iowa we had been introduced to 'Christmas Garlands', and we decided to create our own version, 'Decorative Garlands', invest in a van and drive through the Blue Mountains selling our craft. Subsequently Mum opened a shop under the name 'Fair Seasons' in the local arcade to display and sell our garlands. Meanwhile Cathy had the opportunity to spend time with her children and parents.

Although the Gloucester property had been placed on the market before I left the previous year, no-one had shown any interest. On 2 October my Guide requested that an eight-sided cardboard symbol 23 centimetres across be created and covered in fabric layers, each layer leaving a slim border of the previous colour. The first colour was yellow, the second blue, the third green and the final colour a central 12-centimetre circle of red. My Guide requested that I make note of the numbers 4 and 12, and then identified the symbol as being *The Four Core Colours*. On the back, Cathy wrote the version of the Lord's Prayer given to her by her mother: 'Forgive us the wrongs we have done, as we forgive the wrong others have done to us.' Within days of completing the Four Core Colours a buyer came to view the property.

I was instructed to travel to South Australia to buy a home. An estate agent in Victor Harbor showed me a new two-bedroom brick-and-tile unit in a courtyard in Acraman Street. *Yes, this one*, my Guide said. Within weeks Mum and I found ourselves living in Victor Harbor within walking distance of the beach. Our extra furnishings were placed in storage. The Butterfly Circle, with its 40 butterfly shells, was stored under Mum's bed, the Wild Geese / Soul Group print hung in my bedroom, and The Lovers pots were on display in the kitchen. Cathy followed, working in Adelaide itself and renting a townhouse.

Mum and I sat on the beach on the last evening of 1990, recalling how we had sat on nearby Middleton beach on the last day of 1985 wondering what lay ahead, aware that we had completed five years together in Australia. On Mum's birthday in January, gifts arrived from her sisters Pat and Val — an attempt, we assumed, to maintain contact with her. That evening I was guided to write the words *Entwining of Souls* and place them on top of my diaries from 1985 to 1990. Inside them were the details of our happenings since leaving England in October 1985. Requests for pendulum analysis arrived in the post and soon I was completely occupied working through them.

On my birthday in March I opened a handwritten card from Dianne. She had written, 'Love bears all things, believes all things, and hopes all things. Love never fails.' I was directed to go to the arcade and search for tours of Europe. There was nothing happening with regard to my former solicitor, so I had no idea what this trip was about.

On 8 April I was watching a television program on the plight of the Kurds in Iraq when I found myself saying aloud, 'Something has to be done.' I was pushed out of my chair and sent to the box I had bought in India for Mum, into which she had placed a silver capsule with a silver figure inside it that had been carried by my father through the war years. When I held the figure my Guide said *Something will be done*. To my surprise I saw that the figure was Mary. Then I placed the capsule containing the figurine on the centre of the Four Core Colours. Later, the Kurds were helped by the English and the Americans.

Tours of Europe were highlighted again, and I was encouraged to write to Rene Vaillant, who lived in Brittany, France. He was a dowser and herbalist. My English friend Herm had introduced me to him years ago and he had helped Mum with a health issue. He and I had written occasionally over the years, and I could think of no reason why I needed to contact Rene. But, as requested, I wrote a letter to renew my contact with him. Once my letter was posted, I sought information regarding flights with British Airways, American visas and arrangement of Youth Hostel Association memberships. *Buy a large backpack*, my Guide instructed.

Cathy moved out of her rented townhouse and booked to stay at the Adelaide YHA, from where she visited us at weekends.

Neither of us knew how we were going to pay for the now booked trip until I received the direction *Sell the van by auction*. I had been told *Fly 15 August*. Auction day was scheduled for the day prior to the deadline for paying for our flights and accommodation. The van sold and I walked from the auction to the travel agency and paid for everything.

A friend loaned me her car, enabling me to work for much-needed funds gardening at an empty holiday cottage near Middleton. On 26 July I was sent by my Guide to the wall calendar inside the cottage and told to turn the page to the month of August, which featured snow-capped mountains in Switzerland. *Mary* repeated in my mind, and later at home I was guided to add this new clue to Heart Issue (1) next to 'Switzerland'.

On 3 August I was encouraged to find a new white candle and my notebook. I lit the candle and Mum and I wondered what was going to happen. Then a flow of words entered my mind, *Rene, concentrate on Rene. Time spent in France and more time will be spent in England than first thought. Necessary you spend this time in England, a spiritual journey. Your time is now. Tuesday morning at six you are both to walk on the beach.* 'Wow!' I said. 'That was different and interesting.'

We arrived on the beach three days later at 5.45 am. Mum felt compelled to write her name, 'Tess', in the wet sand. Then she wrote her name three times and three times we watched as the waves took the words out to sea.

Three overseas trips for Tess, my Guide predicted. I shared this with Mum. We understood that the very simple but powerful ceremony we performed that day would ensure that every time Mum left Australia she would return safely, no matter what.

Sell the unit, my Guide urged. My reaction was the same as it had been two years before when I was about to leave her alone for the trip around the world and was told to place our home in Gloucester on the market to sell. 'Why now, when I am about to leave?' I asked.

Mum reminded me that, when we lived in Gloucester, the clairvoyant Bruce had mentioned in his reading our selling of two properties. My Grandmother Lilian had come through to tell us that we would do the right thing.

We had sold our home in Gloucester and moved to Victor Harbour; now we must sell our unit and move again. Six days later we placed it on the market.

Cathy and I flew out of Adelaide on 15 August and headed for Los Angeles. I had been directed to book into the Santa Monica Youth Hostel — a huge ugly stone building. While we were there all the lockers were broken into, but Cathy and I wore body belts so had nothing precious stolen. We caught a bus to Hollywood to see the Walk of Fame and visit Disneyland. Everywhere we went I was acutely aware of an undercurrent of tension and possible violence. I was relieved when we boarded the flight for England.

When we arrived at Heathrow on 19 August I rang Herm, and she invited us down to Plymouth to stay at her place. It was good to see them: Herm, her husband, Alan, and their children, but I quickly sensed an undertone. Within days I knew we would be staying longer to assist the family unit through a personal crisis, and this would take time. I registered with the Plymouth unemployment office as I needed to support both Cathy and myself. Of course I had been warned there would be more time spent in England than first thought.

While dowsing through employment advertisements, I was taken to a firm called Securewest, in Kingsbridge, who employed only former British police officers. The pendulum indicated *Yes*, so I posted off my resume.

Alan asked me what the word 'walk-in' meant to me. He said he felt it applied to me. Alan also used the pendulum and said he had been taken to this word with regard to me. I relayed the story of my visit to a Spiritualist church in the Blue Mountains with Cathy two years before. Inside the church I had been drawn to read part of a book that related the theory of a 'walk-in': an agreement made by two individuals prior to the birth of one. Both were aware that the issues to be resolved on Earth would become so traumatic that the incarnated individual would seek assistance from the individual in spirit. The spirit entity would walk in and reside permanently within the incarnated individual. The task of both was to resolve the traumatic issues and bring a new understanding through to Earth by completing a project. I had mentioned this theory to Cathy at the time and she'd replied, 'Sounds like you.'

Alan asked if I thought Cathy was right, so I shared what happened in my mother's apartment in 1986. Alan knew only part of the story surrounding the family drama. I described my anguish following the discovery that everyone had been poisoned against me and the realisation that I was confronting issues beyond my understanding. I described sitting exhausted on the kitchen floor in semi-darkness, as if I had run a race and it was time to hand the baton to someone else, when words had come that I was forced to speak aloud: 'Now it is your turn ...' I was aware of inviting *another* to complete the course, and then more words came from deep inside me: '... to get to the truth.'

I described how I had awoken the next day filled with an energy that superimposed itself over my thoughts in the form of clear, precise and abrupt instructions. I knew this energy came from a safe and loving source and was *familiar*; I made the conscious decision to follow the directions. Later I was sent to visit Mu, who had told me I had a job to do, a project.

Alan interrupted to ask if I knew what the project was. I told him I had no idea, but many clairvoyants had said I would be involved with the heart in the future. I went on to tell him that, months later, I'd returned to England to put Mum's apartment on the market and was guided to ring Herm, who invited me to visit the clairvoyant Veronica. It was she, I said, who told me I had a Guide, a Catholic nun, who was with me all the time. 'Is that who you let walk in?' he asked.

'Yes. My Guide is helping me and others, including Mum, safely through negative past-life issues and entanglements, to personal and spiritual freedom.'

On 12 September Mum rang to tell me there was a possible buyer for the unit.

Spiritual elevation in Brittany. Travel to France eighteenth of September, my Guide said.

On that day Herm drove us to Plymouth Sound, where we caught the Roscoff ferry. We left her waving until both she and the coastline of England disappeared in the thick early-morning mist.

Cathy was disturbed by the movement of the ship, but I was only excited at the thought of spiritual elevation in Brittany. When we walked away from the ferry we were greeted by a sign that read 'France'. In my money pouch was the Miraculous Medal handed to me by Cathy's mother in 1989, prior to Cathy and me setting off on our around-the-world trip to walk in the footsteps of monks of long ago. *French connection*, my Guide said.

It was a tiring walk through Roscoff to the railway station, with me pulling my trolley case and Cathy carrying the backpack. For the first leg of our journey we had to travel to Morlaix, and opted to go by bus after staying the night at the YHA. I rang Rene before we caught a train from Morlaix, and he met us in Lorient late in the afternoon. Rene was in his sixties, slim, with grey wavy hair, and he spoke English. Cathy and I squeezed into the front seat of his Mercedes van. After a few minutes he stopped outside a health shop run by his son and emerged with three kinds of organic bread, then set off for the farm — or centre, as he called it. We drove for half an hour, passing his home on the right, until we went though the village of La Faouet, then turned right beyond a bridge over a flowing river into an area of green woodlands and fir trees. We turned down a lane and stopped outside three old stone buildings, all joined together. One of them had a new roof. Other buildings were scattered around in overgrown fields littered with farming machinery and masses of blackberries. 'It is going to be a centre for alternative studies,' Rene explained.

The well had dried up, so there was no inside running water, and there were only two globes for lighting. A very unstable wooden ladder led up to a loft that had been renovated with a new floor. There was no electricity there, but assorted mattresses were scattered around. Rene led us outside to show us the toilet and back inside to the kitchen, with its open fireplace. He explained he had wanted us to see the centre before we decided where to stay: here or in the village. *No* was my Guide's reply to the notion of us staying in the village.

The only source of running water was a stream that ran through the property. In the kitchen, Rene explained the workings of the gas stove and gave us olive oil for cooking. There was an ample supply of mineral water for drinking and we were shown the organic vegetable garden. Rene told us he worked at the centre every day, even though he had an alternative practice. He was part of a circle of six men with a female medium. They had rented the farm and land for four years with a view to buying. After he left we gathered tomatoes and zucchini from the garden, soaked them in the oil and made sandwiches using the bread.

We lit the kitchen fire with logs from a pile outside and, when Rene returned in the evening with bottles of cider, we sat and talked. He explained his group were biodynamic farmers — a method of farming initiated by Rudolph Steiner in the 1920s. It was a revelation from spirit based on the theory that man is seen to be the junction between the Earth and the Cosmos. Earth vibrated at a different level to other planets, and the biodynamic farmer was the meeting-point of these two vibrations.

His plan was to make the farm biodynamic and repair the buildings so people could stay there. The aim was to teach visitors how to stop pollution by ceasing to use pesticides and to be in tune with themselves and nature. Rene explained how the group worked. The female medium would meditate and the male members would encourage her to bring information from spirit. *Remember Wales,* my Guide said. I had been asked to buy a book describing the spiritists in France and how groups of people accessed healing guides. Now I was in Brittany speaking to a member of one such group.

Before he left, Rene brought in an electric cable so that we would have light in the loft. There was no glass in the front door, so to lock the door would have been futile. Up in the loft, a small square window overlooked the meadow, the stream and Rene's vegetable garden. I awoke to a shaft of light coming through the window. Morning mist hung heavy over the valley, creating patterns on the trees. I sat outside to start a letter to Mum, describing everything. I would post it at the end of our visit.

I washed in the stream, enjoying the cold water. Cathy waited a few hours until it was warmer, then we walked the two kilometres to La Faouet, a 16th-century village with an open-sided market in its central square. Later we helped Rene harvest his potato crop. That evening, Rene used his pendulum to dowse over our hands. He asked spirit the steps Cathy and I should take to increase the spiritual awareness of our mental bodies. We were to say a prayer, after 4 pm but before sunset, and ask only what God wanted to give us in order for us to achieve: 'I ask only what you want of me, the power, wisdom, cosmic love and energy, in order to be able to achieve those things.' Rene demonstrated how we were to place our hands, not in the traditional way, but with palms lifted upwards, fingertips touching, thumbs stretched outwards and held below the navel. Once the prayer was spoken, we rubbed our hands together to cut the contact with the ray of energy.

Rene talked about the chakras in the human body and their function. He explained chakras as being vortex energy, moving quickly in all directions in the physical body and the ethereal body, and as the energy of the nerves, forming the whole. The mental body is further out again, bigger, and can be seen by animals. There are seven major chakras and twenty-one minor chakras, and this energy flows to forty-nine smaller chakras, then to two hundred mini-chakras over the acupuncture points. Gold and silver needles are used for plus and minus meridians. The energy returns to the seven major chakras and out again to the

Cosmos. If the energy does not return to the Cosmos, then disturbance, congestion, blockages and illness result. Rene specialised in the removal of such blockages.

The word *chakras* repeated in my mind. Rene then spoke about spiritual healing, 'Energy is given to people who need it through the healer,' he said. 'The healer receives energy from the Cosmos through the mind chakra and passes this energy into the patient. The energy is then returned from the patient to the healer and back to the Cosmos. If healers are not skilled, and use their own energy and not the energy of the Cosmos, they become exhausted.'

Rene explained that we all have a life number. He told me mine was six.

The next day, 21 September, he came early and used his pendulum to dowse where he was to work. His pendulum had a slow movement because of its long chain, whereas mine was rapid due to it being much shorter, and I was able to respond to instant directions. I used my pendulum as my link between the human and spirit realms, but he and I were both accessing the same energy. Rene told us that a man had handed him a pendulum fifteen years before when he was at an exhibition in London. He showed Rene how to use it. One is encouraged by another to start using a pendulum, just as I was by Jack Temple in 1983. I was distracted when I remembered it was Barbara's birthday.

Cathy asked Rene about his religion. Rene said he was born a Catholic, but as a seven-year-old something had happened that had changed his ideas. He was standing at a crossroads between his mother's and grandmother's homes when a black shadow and then the form of a man with a hood appeared on the wall of the stable. Frightened, he ran to his grandmother, who told him the shadow had been seen by others in the village. Eighteen years previously the same man appeared, but this time he spoke Rene's name. Not knowing what this meant he went to a clairvoyant friend, who told him the man was Rene's Guide, a Druid monk. His Guide wanted him to seek out the history of Brittany, the Celts and Druids. He learnt that Catholics had brought Christianity to Brittany by force, murdering those who would not follow their religion. The Bretons, like the Welsh and Cornish, were Celts. The Druids (Celtic priests) were astrologers, mathematicians, judges and lawmakers, who also led religious ceremonies and settled legal disputes. They followed the Law of Nature and sought to discover ancient principles.

'Cosmic energy and spiritual energy: how are they measured?' I asked.

He spoke of Anders Angstrom, a Swedish man born in 1814, who became a physicist and discovered how to measure energy. Rene drew the scale used to measure Angstroms, starting at 8-9-10,000 and up to 40-50-60,000, explaining most people are below 8,000 and that an Angstrom is a 1/100,000th part of a 100th part of an atom. He used his pendulum to dowse along the scale to take my measurement. It was 46,000. 'This will continue to increase,' he said. 'You are very much attuned, Judy.' I placed the drawing of Rene's Angstrom scale in my notes.

Rene told us that in Druid times the one with the highest energy was the leader of a group. There were seven in a group and, if one more wished to join, the leader had to move on and form a new group. I found myself touching the silver bracelet of seven dolphins joined head-to-fin on my wrist and then the single dolphin at my throat. There was something *familiar* about this story. Rene said there were various types of Druids. The Ceremonial Druid is strict and hierarchical, and concentrates on rituals such as those held at Stonehenge at solstice and equinox. The Healing Druids, artists and harp players are called Ovates.

I had been sent to Stonehenge to take a photograph as the sun set on our around-the-world trip, in the footsteps of the early monks. My Guide requested I remember the moment. A rush of familiarity had come then, as now, and this was explained by my Guide as being, *Druid energy*. Now, I was in Brittany, talking to Rene about Druids and his Druid Guide. Rene nodded, as if reading my mind. I understood he was a member of my soul group. He waited as I absorbed this understanding; then, smiling, he continued.

'Before Atlantis sank, three groups escaped: one group to Mexico, one group to Egypt and the other to Brittany. Egyptian Atlanteans built the Pyramids and Brittany Druids erected monoliths in large triangles to bring energy through from the Cosmos.'

Rene drove us to Langonnet to a ruined hillside farmhouse surrounded by trees. He used his pendulum to find what he termed 'death spots' in the ground in the ley-line energy. He asked me to go inside the ruin and, as I went, I received the word *Death*. Immediately I had a feeling of fear and sorrow, but these strong feelings were not mine. I had learnt the difference at the Old Saddlery. These were the emotions of people long gone. The ruin gradually became a home in my mind as it had been in the past. I stood outside with Rene, and he asked me to allow the feelings to happen. I did, and felt fear for the family. I knew what the fear was — the approach of the German army during the occupation.

I told him the family had escaped through a tunnel and showed him where it was, using my pendulum. Rene knew the history of the farm and he was pleased with me. The underground tunnel was an old stream that, like the well, had run dry. The Germans had not checked the well, assuming it was full of water.

We then walked down the lane into a field in a distant corner of which was a monolith about 25 feet high. Rene said it was a Standing Stone, a source of cosmic energy and one of three that created an equilateral triangle. They were placed there by the Druids and were 159 kilometres apart. There were two such triangles in France, both in Brittany.

Move closer, my Guide urged. I was aware I was standing by something used in ancient times to bring through energy from the Cosmos. Rene explained with sadness that the other equilateral triangles had been destroyed by the Catholics. Opposite the Standing Stone was a small granite cross placed to defy the existence of the monolith and what it represented. Rene spoke about the stone itself. Standing Stones contain healing rays, he began. Twenty-four visible and invisible colours emanate from them, set on a spring of waves coming from the Cosmos but reflected at the Earth's magma, jumping from the ground. The Earth's magma is the molten, semi-fluid matter below its crust. From this spring of energy, he continued, two ley-lines have to join two other springs, forming a triangle of energy, the sun-side being the positive and the shade-side the negative. All colours of the spectrum are represented within the stones. Between the two monoliths are dolmens — Standing Stones with flat tops — creating a neutral area that disperses energy from the triangles. The dolmens have no energy, and the Druids would sleep under them or on top of them to relax. A Druid would direct a person to touch a specific area of the Standing Stone that would cater for their needs. Healing Druids, he said, could see the healing colours.

I moved closer, placing both my hands on its surface. My heart began to race and I became emotional. Rene told me I had chosen the area for the heart, our feeling centre. The words *Standing Stone* and *heart* repeated in my mind.

Rene explained later that the Celts had dominated Europe throughout the Bronze Age to about 450 AD, when the Romans began to conquer Celtic areas. The Celts were conquered physically and spiritually, he said, and the Church of Rome's influence spread.

The next day my Guide urged me to walk in the woods to the Chapel of Sainte Barbe, who was reputed to have performed many miracles.

Deep green moss had formed on the granite under lush tall ferns and trees. It was a steady climb on a narrow granite footpath to the chapel, with its stained-glass windows.

I could see the large granite chapel at the bottom of a flight of steps. The caretaker and his wife were friendly, so Cathy and I bought a glass of wine each. I was drawn to buy a postcard of the headless Sainte Barbe statue and her spring; I was then drawn outside to the bell tower to pull on the rope until the swinging clapper made contact. The caretaker ran out when there was another thunderous ring of the bell, and he shouted and gesticulated that I was to stop. Cathy was embarrassed, but I kept pulling the rope. I turned to the caretaker and gestured towards the chapel to indicate that I wanted to go down into the grounds. He relented and let us through the locked gate.

'What was that all about?' Cathy asked.

'I have no idea.'

We discovered that the Chapelle Sainte Barbe du Faouet was built in the 16th century. The entrance to the chapel was locked, so I walked around the huge building until I came to a flight of stone steps. I was about to walk towards them when I was drawn to look to my left. There was a grotto in the wall with a statue of Mary inside it. I walked to the grotto and stared at the statue, but Cathy held back. This was the first time I had stood in front of a grotto. 'Why is your name constantly featuring in my life?' I asked.

A sense of elevation filled my being, and I told Cathy something was happening; she told me to go with it. I didn't have much choice. I wasn't lifted off the ground, but the sensation of floating turned my body and walked me gently down the pathway deeper into the wooded area, which gradually filled with a silvery mist.

'I feel as if I am walking on the moon,' I shouted back to Cathy.

'Keep going,' she shouted, as she raced after me.

At the bottom of the pathway I was turned to the left onto another pathway; then the feeling of floating left me but I knew I was to walk on. At the end was an open space that held a small headless statue inside a grotto, partly covered in moss. This was the Sainte Barbe statue and spring. Small steps led down to the spring at the base of the statue.

SAINTE BARBE
et les jeunes filles à marier

Sainte Barbe, née sur les bords de la mer de Marmara, est invoquée au Faouët pour protéger de la foudre et des incendies. Mais des jeunes filles se rendent à la fontaine; Sainte Barbe les aidera à trouver un mari. Il suffit de jeter une épingle sur l'eau de la source sacrée. Si l'épingle surnage, elles trouveront un mari dans l'année. Si elle coule, il leur faudra attendre un an.

Postcard image of the headless Sainte Barbe statue and spring, Brittany

I was directed to take a photograph of the grotto, statue and spring, with no idea of how important this photograph would become. We walked back along the pathway, but instead of turning right in the direction of the Mary Grotto we walked on until we reached the road again. Later I told Rene about my experience, to which he replied, 'The Saint Barbe spring is a source of cosmic energy.' I asked him what had happened to the Druids. 'They were forced to live in the forests for generations,' he said. 'Many became Catholic to survive, but still held their pagan rites.'

The next day we walked to the village for bread, but on the way back were sent to the Sainte Barbe spring again. When we reached it, Cathy and I stood for a while to absorb the atmosphere. The air around us became thick and heavy and we had to take deep breaths. She said afterwards that she saw a white light and had the feeling of weightlessness. I bent down and put my left hand in the small pool of water in front of the statue. When I removed my hand from the water, it and my arm up to the elbow were a luminous green. My heart pounded as I looked up at the headless statue of Sainte Barbe; then the colour in my arm faded. I was encouraged to update my notes later:

Around the World 1991: Druid energy – chakras – Standing Stone – heart – Mary Grotto – spring of Sainte Barbe – luminous green.

The following afternoon Rene arrived to take us to a church outside La Faouet: the church of La Chapelle Saint Fiacre, built in 1480. Its main feature, the jube or choir loft, was intricately carved and painted with vegetable dyes of red, blue and green. Rene moved within the church using his pendulum, and then stopped by the jube. He said, 'Judy, you have travelled all this way across the world because of the colour blue.' He continued with a message for me from his Druid Guide, 'In order for Judy to achieve spiritual elevation, she must imagine a blue circle, surround herself with this blue circle at midday on the new moon and pray for five minutes.'

We walked down a track to dense woodland, with beech, oak and chestnut trees, to a hollow. Inside the hollow were two pools, one square and the other oblong, lined with natural granite. There was granite seating around the larger, square pool. The small oblong pool contained the spring, and a granite channel carried the water to the square pool with the seating formation. The water then trickled into the trees, forming a small stream.

'People were immersed, naked, in these pools in ancient times,' Rene said. 'They were used by the Druids at the time of the solstice and equinox for purification purposes. Much later, Saint Fiacre used them to heal skin diseases.'

He said there were two ley-lines running diagonally to the spring and stream; one was 8,000 and the other 11,000 Angstroms. They joined, then flowed into the smaller, oblong pool.

I sensed this was a sacred place, but it did not have the same power as the Sainte Barbe spring. Yet I felt honoured to be there. Rene asked us to move to a low bridge over the stream, where we sat either side of him. It was glorious, with the trees swaying in the breeze. I fell into a meditation. I jumped when Rene asked, 'What do you feel?'

'Tree energy,' I replied.

'Yes,' he said. 'Today we have only the dryads or spirits of the trees. If you come early in the morning, you will see devas. Nature spirits encourage and maintain the plant kingdom; they work with the devas.'

Cathy spoke of Findhorn in Scotland. Dorothy, close friend of Eileen Caddy, one of the founders, was reputed to be able to both see and communicate with the devas. 'Findhorn,' she said, 'refers to the devas as archetypal spiritual intelligences and the group soul of a species.'

'One's third eye has to be open to be able to see devas,' Rene responded. I wanted to ask him about the third eye, but my Guide said *No* to this thought.

That night, Rene spoke to me of making a commitment to spirit. I explained that I had been told I had a project ahead. He then told me I had come to Brittany, not only because of the colour blue, but because I was to take that step to total commitment. Taken aback, I replied that I did not think there was anything else I could be doing to be more committed.

Rene waited and then said, 'You must say the prayer I have taught you.' He repeated the Celtic prayer for me: 'I ask only what you want of me, the power, wisdom, cosmic love and energy, in order to be able to achieve those things.'

I could not make the commitment at that moment. But later, as I watched the stars in the night sky through the loft window, I knew I would say the prayer. I wanted to make that total commitment and at sunrise I did.

Visit Mary's Grotto, my Guide requested.

Druid purification pools, La Chapelle Sainte Fiacre, Brittany

I followed the pathway and stood in front of Mary's statue and said, 'Thank you.' I walked away confused, wondering about the connection between Mary and me.

Rene took me out to a large field and asked what I felt. 'I think there is a stream running to the right, underground,' I replied.

'You think it is a stream, or you know?' he asked.

'I know it is a stream,' I replied.

He was stern, and this caught me off guard when he asked if I was sure — he knew it was running to the left, he said. I stood my ground, telling him it was definitely running to the right. He continued to look at me sternly and then he smiled. 'Now you are ready. It runs to the right,' he confirmed. I breathed a deep sigh of relief and returned his smile.

Early the next day Rene came to drive us to the bus for Roscoff to catch the ferry back to England. A few days later I collected the many photographs taken on our trip to Brittany and discovered with amazement that my snapshot of the headless Sainte Barbe statue, taken on 22 September, had captured the image of the figure intact — with the head! Present in the photograph as well, above the grotto, is the date 1708, also not visible at the site. *Cosmic energy*, my Guide explained.

During the next few days Cathy became tense and cried a lot — then would fly off the handle when approached, affecting everyone around her. One of her daughters had written from Australia to say she was missing her, and Cathy was trying to find a way of replying. I seemed to be on hold — and it was a while before I accepted that it was a time for rest. I went to the local woodlands.

The tenth of October is important, my Guide said.

A letter arrived from Securewest in Kingsbridge requesting me to attend an interview on 10 October. It went well and I was given time to let them know when I could start. Mum rang a few days later to confirm we had a buyer for our unit in Victor Harbor.

Travel to Australia eighth of November, my Guide requested.

I was to return to Australia to help Mum and then bring her back to England. Before I could absorb this, I was instructed to ask Alan to help me find accommodation. He drove me to Torr Farm Cottages at

My photograph of the statue of St Barbe with head mysteriously present and the date 1708 restored

Yealmpton, near Plymouth, to meet a friend who rented out holiday cottages. I was shown 'Spark Cottage'. *Yes, this one*, my Guide confirmed.

'Interesting,' I said to Alan. 'Mum's youngest sister, Pat, lives in Yealmpton.' I had a job, a rental cottage, and Mum waiting to join me.

Cathy said she also wanted to return to Australia on 8 November.

During all this activity I was encouraged to take notes from a page of a book at a friend's home — *Vibrational Medicine* by R. Gerber:

> Seventh Chakra ... the crown chakra or seventh chakra, which is considered one of the highest vibrational centers in the subtle body, is associated with deep inner searching: the so-called spiritual quest. This chakra is most active when individuals are involved in religious and spiritual quests for the meaning of life and the inner search for their origins as conscious evolving beings. (3)

At the time I was being encouraged by my Guide to take part in religious and spiritual quests, so it didn't surprise me that I was being urged to buy this book. She insisted I did not read further until directed to do so in the future.

In the beginning of November Cathy and I travelled to Staverton Bridge to visit Mu Woolvett. The last time I'd seen her was in 1986, when she'd come to Mum's apartment in Torquay and used the clear quartz — not from the Earth plane — to dispel my headache and help me cut the umbilical cord with Barbara. We met her at the front door as she was balancing several pot plants.

She smiled warmly at me and said, 'You've come a long way in your quest. But oh, haven't you been through a lot. You have just caught me, as I'm moving to that cottage over there today. Come and have a look at my new home. I've got a message for you.'

Mu offered us tea, lit a candle and then sat opposite me at the table. 'Brotherhood,' she said, 'a coming-together for you and others. You will all sit in a horseshoe shape, like the spiritual government. The horseshoe shape is in preference to a circle. A circle is closed and goes on the same. A horseshoe is open to everyone. The horseshoe points upward towards the ethers.'

She looked at me, then said, 'Your aura is silver and shiny. You are able to give energy to others. Your job is to travel to places to distribute this energy.' When I left I understood she had played her part within the soul group.

The next day I received a letter from Securewest informing me I was required to start work on 7 December. I had time to return to Australia, sort out the unit, and bring Mum back. Cathy and I were booked to fly out in three days. Alison, my solicitor, rang to say she was moving to the next stage regarding me suing my former solicitor. Then Alan's friend rang to tell me Spark Cottage would be available on 7 December. 'That was awesome timing,' I said to my Guide.

Keep trusting the process, she replied.

We flew out of Heathrow on 8 November, heading for Adelaide. Cathy flew on to Sydney to her family. Mum and I had to be back in the air by 30 November.

Invest your capital, my Guide said, sending us to a local estate agent, who quickly took us to view a newly built cottage in Thomas Street, Middleton. *Yes, this one*, my Guide said. We agreed to buy it on completion of the sale of our Victor Harbour unit.

Fly to Frankfurt twenty-fourth of November, my Guide said. We booked one-way flights to London via Frankfurt. I rang Erika and she was thrilled that she would be welcoming Mum to her home in Germany for the very first time.

During the packing of our possessions and the organising of the garden at our recently purchased cottage I was encouraged by my Guide to ask Mum to write to Barbara's friend Jan in Guernsey, then buy Christmas cards for Barbara, the grandchildren and her sisters. These were to be posted right away and were to include details of our return to England and the Yealmpton address. I was instructed to post a gift for Aunty Pat for her birthday in December.

We were due to arrive on 1 December, but would not be able to take possession of Spark Cottage until 7 December. We were relieved when Alan invited us to stay with his family in the interim. Cathy rang to say she was flying to London via Japan, and had booked a return ticket from Sydney. Mum and I wondered why we had been guided to book one-way flights to England.

We flew out of Adelaide on 24 November, as instructed, and Erika met us at the Frankfurt airport. Mum and I were suffering jet lag — she'd been unwell before we left and I hadn't recovered from the return trip to Australia — so we slept in for several days. Then Erika drove us to the medieval city of Rothenburg ob der Tauber, Germany's best-preserved walled city, and invited us to explore the Christmas shops of Kathe Wohlfahrt, where we discovered a world filled with Christmas cheer. We flew out of Frankfurt on 1 December.

Six years had passed since Mum and I left England, flying to India *en route* for Australia. As the plane was landing at Heathrow Mum experienced a moment of apprehension followed by several minutes of breathlessness, and then asked if we would be returning to Australia. I reassured her we would, reminding her of the ceremony we had performed on 6 August at Victor Harbor, when she wrote 'Tess' in the sand three times and three times the waves had taken her name out to sea. My Guide had said *Three overseas trips for Tess*. There would be two more, but each time she would return safely to Australia.

It was odd having Cathy welcome us, and again we felt pressured. The three of us travelled to Plymouth by coach. I couldn't relax, as I was to be fitted for a Securewest uniform before starting work for a group of stores. Meanwhile, Mum and Cathy prepared for the three of us to move into Spark Cottage. Any spare time was spent in consultation with my barrister, preparing for the proceedings against my former solicitor.

Then another contract was negotiated by Securewest. The IRA had made threats against shipping. The Royal Navy was protected by military police and we were given the task of protecting the merchant shipping. I was to partner a Cornishman called George, a keen historian who had spent years visiting battlefields. Our shifts were long and cold as we patrolled the ships at night. I wondered at the contrasts in my life: spiritual elevation in Brittany, house-moving in Australia, early Christmas in Germany and on patrol in England in case of terrorist activity. My Celtic partner and I shared stories as we drove to and from the ships, working twenty-four hour shifts — six hours on and six hours off. George wore a Celtic cross and told me he lived near Tintagel in Cornwall, King Arthur country. *You must go there*, my Guide insisted.

Spark Cottage was about to live up to its name: sparks were soon to fly. Mum rang her sister Pat on her birthday, 12 December, but there was no reply. She rang Audrey, and again there was no reply. Finally, she rang Val, and they talked and arranged to meet the following week. Mum's health became a worry, so I took her to the doctor, who assured us her blood pressure was fine. I was finding the long hours with Securewest a problem and Cathy was stressed over not wanting to return to Australia when her holiday visa expired.

On 16 December I returned after a tiring twelve-hour shift to discover that Aunty Pat and her husband had visited the cottage and banged on the door until Cathy answered. They suggested to Mum that she was being held prisoner and, although floored by this, she managed to calm them both by assuring them that it was not so. They left after inviting Mum to their home on the outskirts of town in two days' time. Aunty Val rang asking if she could visit, and was clearly tense when she arrived with her husband. Mum had literally to stop Aunty Val pacing around the sitting room by assuring her that all was indeed well and that she was not being held a prisoner. She was collected two days later by Aunty Pat's husband in his car and then walked back to the end of the lane by Aunty Pat, who refused to come any further.

'What is this nonsense about you being held a prisoner?' I said.

'Barbara has created an unnecessary atmosphere of drama,' Mum replied.

I was told by Securewest that I would be working in Harwich over Christmas after completing a twelve-hour shift, which did not amuse me. It was three days before Christmas and I was exhausted. We decided to have Christmas the next day, and so opened our cards and presents. When I rang Mum on Christmas day she had received invitations to visit from Aunty Pat and Aunty Val. I arrived back at the cottage at midnight on 27 December and got up early to prepare her for her visit with Aunty Val. Then Aunty Audrey rang saying she wanted to pop in, but only if I was not there. I was too tired to take in the fact that I was not being included in any visits. On New Year's Eve, however, when I returned home to discover Aunty Audrey had called in while I was out, I erupted. I was feeling really hurt by all this. Mum said she was going to confront her sisters as to why I was being rejected.

The year 1992 began with my returning to work in Harwich with George. On 7 January I was busy getting ready to meet up with him when I discovered we had no milk. I walked to the village and found myself heading towards Aunty Pat. She saw me, faltered and moved on to the road to avoid me. I stepped out in front of her and said, 'Nice to see you, Aunty Pat,' and kissed her on the cheek. Her eyes filled with tears. I walked on, but she called after me. I turned and she said, 'Look after yourself.'

I replied, 'Yes I will,' and carried on walking with Acora's warning in my mind: *Everyone has been poisoned against you, and I mean everyone.*

That evening I was sitting quietly with Cathy and Mum when I was forced to walk out into the dining area of the kitchen. The kitchen had a glass door, and as I walked towards it a face appeared on the other side. It was Barbara. But before I'd really grasped that it was her standing there, I opened the door. The cottage filled with angry tension.

Barbara spoke in a tense, controlled voice. 'May I come in?'

'Of course,' I said, opening the door wider for her. She was followed in by an elderly man with glasses. As he walked past me I wondered where I had seen him before. I turned to Barbara. 'Who is this?'

'This is my fiancé.'

I shook hands with the elderly man and a long awkward pause followed. His face was so familiar. Was he a solicitor or something? They both waited, so I said, 'Would you like to see Mum?'

Barbara's reply was terse. 'If I am allowed.' This is the source of the nonsense about Mum being my prisoner, I thought. There was an atmosphere of drama and intimidation surrounding this unexpected visit. 'Of course', I said.

All three of us walked towards the drawn curtains dividing the dining area from the sitting room. I realised this was going to be a huge shock for Mum, so I went in first, telling her Barbara was here. As I spoke, the two of them entered. I went protectively towards Mum, but she got up from the couch and faced Barbara. Both made a slight forward motion, but touched arms only.

Mum spoke first, 'What a surprise.'

Barbara pulled away. 'Well, it is a surprise that you've not contacted me before this,' she complained.

As instructed, Mum had sent her a Christmas card telling her of our planned visit to England and our new address, but she was giving her fiancé the impression Mum had ignored her. I understood this visit was just for his benefit. Barbara's manner became aggressive, so I reached for Mum, indicating she should sit down. I then asked Barbara and her fiancé to sit down. Barbara's response was instant. 'We are *not* staying.'

I was determined to keep the mood civil. 'We are having a hot drink, would you like one?'

Barbara again repeated that she was not staying. I thought I'd try something else. 'Have you met Cathy?' I asked.

'I don't need to meet Cathy, thank you,' Barbara replied. She and her fiancé remained standing. I studied the man until I recognised him. Three years before he had accompanied Anne to the Plymouth Court. Barbara had lacked the courage to attend, but she was here now and I was going to ensure we gained some answers before she disappeared yet again.

Before I was able to act upon these thoughts her attention was turned on Mum. She towered over her, her tone very aggressive. 'I thought you would have contacted me,' she repeated. Mum's Christmas card was obviously going to be ignored.

I stepped in and said, 'For God's sake, Mum has had a stroke.' Mum had suffered a mini-stroke while living in Gloucester in 1989, when a scrap of paper arrived from Barbara with the words 'Come home to those that love you.'

I turned to Mum. 'This is a shock for you. Take your time.' I reminded Barbara she was in our home and any issues were to be addressed to me.

Mum intervened, saying, 'I told you I would not write to you until you came to me with an explanation.' She was referring to Barbara's attempted misuse of my power of attorney to sell the Old Saddlery in 1986. 'Can you tell me why you didn't act in Judy's interests with your …' Mum stopped mid-sentence and I realised she was struggling for breath.

I added, '… power of attorney.' I took over. 'You signed the original contract. You were attempting to sell without my knowledge or consent. You misused my power of attorney.'

Barbara glared at me and shouted, 'I signed nothing.'

I pushed on. 'Not true. The sale was stopped on the day of completion when your signature was queried by the purchasing solicitors.'

My sister turned to her fiancé and rolled her eyes. 'You can see now how she has poisoned my mother against me, can't you?' She glared down at Mum before turning to me. 'Anyway, you had no money in the business.'

'That is not true. My financial input was considerable, but, regardless of whether it was or not, you were legally obligated to act in my interests. Mortgaging my home and business and handing the funds to Anne was not acting in my interests. Is this why you said I was stupid in the note you had put through Mum's letterbox in 1986? You were assuming I wouldn't find out?' She glared back at me as I continued. 'I trusted you. But you housed Anne and you misled Mum when she rang you from Australia. You told her you were not involved and that it was not your affair, yet when I returned to England days later I found Anne living with you in your home, and she had been there for some time.'

'She was ill,' Barbara replied.

Mum suddenly spoke: 'You didn't even like Anne when we left,'

My sister confirmed this. 'No I did not.'

'Well,' Mum said, 'when Judy returned home Anne was living with you.'

'She was homeless,' Barbara replied.

'Which is it?' I said. 'Was she ill or was she homeless? Neither is true,' I said before she could answer. 'The plan was that once the Old Saddlery was sold, Anne was to move to Mum's apartment. You knew that. Geoff Coyte, our bank manager, had been told Anne was not allowed to move into Mum's apartment because of our dogs, giving the impression Mum was still in England, which was not true either.'

'I had all the dealings with the bank,' she responded.

'So it was you who misled Geoff.' I continued to push. 'I know you were party to the first contract because Anne rang me crying, saying she was letting me down.'

Barbara retorted, 'I had the wrong power of attorney.' She looked down at Mum and said, 'I was here,' meaning she knew all the facts and Mum didn't.

I drew her attention away from Mum. 'I know what really went on because I spoke to everyone involved — the purchaser, the bank manager, Anne — and I have written it all down.'

'Well you would,' she threw back at me.

'What about the six years of silence?' Mum asked.

Barbara glared down at Mum. 'How could I write when you said you wouldn't even live in the same town as me?'

Mum's reply was immediate. 'I didn't use those words.'

Barbara stormed back, 'Yes you did.'

'No,' I said, 'Mum did not write that. Everything we write is read by the other.'

A much calmer reply came: 'I can see that.' All I saw was a family torn apart and in pain and I had no idea how to resolve it. I was jolted from these thoughts by Barbara demanding, 'What about the note sent to me, with newspaper cuttings used as threatening words? I had to go to the police.' I tried telling her we also received a similar note in the Blue Mountains, but she announced, 'There is no more to discuss.'

I heard her whisper to her fiancé, 'I have really tried.' Then she looked down at Mum and shouted, 'Goodbye mother,' and flounced out of the room with fiancé in tow.

To calm our nerves, I encouraged everyone to remember the conversation word for word, and we recorded everything. We signed the notes as being a true account. Mum and I sat alone in the sitting room by the lit fire, her heartbeat having returned to normal. She said, 'What is really going on?' I suggested we work through the clues, starting at the beginning in 1985, when Barbara tried to sell Mum's apartment to a high-flier and asked me to try and convince her to change her solicitor to Barbara's.

'I refused,' Mum said.

'Yes, but when that failed,' I said, 'you were driven to Barbara's bank to switch your account there, and when you refused she drove you to her solicitors where there was a prepared power of attorney document waiting for you to sign.'

'I was embarrassed into signing.'

'I know you were. Then she encouraged you to fly to Australia with me, leaving her in control of your assets. Asking me to sign a power of attorney was an afterthought.'

We recalled the evening before we drove to Heathrow — Barbara searching for homes for sale and failing to tell Mum the house she wanted to buy was sold. 'There was no need for Barbara to keep your power of attorney, as you'd made it clear it was that house or nothing,'

I reminded Mum of what had happened later, in Australia. She had asked for several hundred pounds to be sent over, and Barbara had sent a ten-pound note. That had happened twice, leaving Mum in Australia with no money, until we organised the transfer of her monthly pensions. It was the beginning of 1986 by then, and Barbara was working with Anne to sell the Old Saddlery without my knowledge. Barbara wrote suggesting she continue to sell your apartment and for you to buy a home to house Debby and the children, Barbara and whoever, where she would have her own room.

'I said no to that suggestion,' Mum responded forcibly.

'Barbara then tried to let your apartment, ignoring your letter offering it to Anne. Then to help Anne she misled Geoff Coyte, telling him you didn't want her to live in your home and she had to buy one, taking all our joint assets,' I said.

'A woman died before or after viewing my home,' Mum replied sadly.

'Not in Barbara's wildest dreams did she imagine I would return and find your upside-down photograph placed in an envelope.'

'That was a shock to me.'

'But our most important clue,' I said. 'I just couldn't understand what was happening. I prayed that Daddy would help us, then turned you upright and said you would be under my protection from then on.'

'Your father heard you.'

'Then Barbara sent that note saying she was taking her children away.'

'I was horrified,' Mum said.

'Both actions showed us an extreme need to control. Obtaining our powers of attorney was a step in that direction. She's furious because you and I now live in Australia. The plan was to make me penniless and helpless and you would have been forced to return to England, having only a holiday visa, and made to live in a room in her house, under her control, which you would have paid for.'

'Well, I sold the apartment and transferred the funds,' Mum responded.

'Yes, it all backfired, thank goodness.'

I reminded Mum we had been warned at the Taj Mahal, *en route* to Australia, with the words, *Taken power*. This famous ancient story surrounding the Taj Mahal told of a son who had imprisoned his father and taken power over the family inheritance. We had been sent there together and later I had been sent to visit alone. It was these two visits to India that ensured I connected with Pal Sethi, as it was he who later ensured Mum would become an Australian resident.

'Thank God for Pal Sethi,' Mum said.

'I will free you and me of this past-life trauma.'

A seventh and final attempt to resolve this issue, my Guide said. I shared the message with Mum. We were to understand that Barbara was here for the seventh time to free herself of an ongoing past-life issue that involved family assets and control. I was not able to say how we would resolve it, but believed it would be so. This was the rescue my father was determined would occur, this one last time.

Later I sent our signed notes to my barrister. He told me that if I had attended the court hearing on 10 May 1988 I would have won. This visit by Barbara would provide new evidence in the suit against my former solicitor for negligence. My Guide asked Mum to send Barbara a card. She sat down and wrote:

> Dear Barbara, you entered our home a stranger, full of anger. When you find the courage to face what you have done, and admit the truth to both yourself and others, then and only then will you be welcome in our home as family. Mum and Judy.

She rang her sister Audrey, as confirmation was needed for an arrangement made for them to meet in Plymouth. When Mum sought confirmation of Barbara's address, a heated discussion erupted. Aunty Audrey's son rang and cancelled the meeting. The next day, Aunty Pat cancelled Mum's visit to her home, offering no explanation. In the middle of this drama, John, the grandchildren's father, rang Mum. I became distressed when told about the tension between the sisters, but my Guide assured me *This was all part of the healing process*, so I passed this information on to Mum.

On 21 January I returned home in time to meet John and his wife, who stopped their car to tell me they were taking Mum out to lunch. I was sent off to Harwich the next morning, and returned several days later, exhausted. Mum wrote to Aunty Pat confronting her with the fact that she was allowing herself to be influenced by others.

I was looking forward to 27 January, Mum's birthday, and arranged for her to spend time with Acora the clairvoyant. A card arrived from John, then cards from friends; gifts came from Pat and Val. Aunty Pat rang to say she had received Mum's letter and appreciated how much she had hurt her, and invited her to visit her at home. This was followed by a phone call from Aunty Val. Mum and I caught the bus to Plymouth, walked the Barbican and enjoyed lunch before keeping our appointment with Acora.

'Tess,' he said. 'You and Judy will return to Australia very soon and be involved in a business venture. It is important you keep your distance from Barbara at this time because animosity coming from within her will be the cause of serious health problems for you later. Barbara is after something,' he warned, 'but I don't know what it is.'

A contract in Harwich was postponed and I was to work locally. On 30 January Alan visited and asked me if I knew *who* my Guide was tuning into. When I replied that I sensed it was from a loving source, he suggested I ask her.

Look out of the window at twenty minutes past nine, my Guide responded.

I stood by the kitchen window looking out into the night. It was cold and clear. I was drawn to the Plough, with its seven brilliant stars, when a single star to the right of that constellation began to move. I thought it was a shooting star, but it started scribing circles, and moving from left to right, before assuming its original position in the night sky. 'Mum, Cathy,' I shouted. 'Come and look at this.'

'Look over there,' I said, pointing out into the darkness. 'See that star?'

The star started moving, tracing its original pattern in the night sky once again. As the three of us stood watching in awe, I realised it was not my imagination. This was my Guide's response to Alan's question.

On 1 February Mum was driven to Aunty Pat's home and was surprised to find her sister Val there as well. Mum was shocked when they tried to discredit me and humiliate her. They confronted her about what they said was my 'so-called' involvement with Jim in 1988 — when Mum was in the Blue Mountains and I was in England trying to resolve the legal issues between Anne and myself — telling Mum it was a lie and my vivid imagination. I had lied to Mum then; therefore I was lying about Barbara and everything else now. Aunty Val rang Jim, who was waiting, and handed the phone to Mum. He denied meeting with and speaking to me about someone of interest he wanted me to observe. There was a look of triumph on Aunty Val's face when Mum replaced the receiver. But Mum had read the charge sheet and knew the name of the plain-clothes officer. Knowing the truth, she was frustrated with Jim and annoyed with her sisters. She told me later that she did not show any emotion, merely saying she would speak with me. Mum knew it was confidential and she understood that Jim was attempting to deny everything.

'How on earth did they find out?' I asked.

Then I remembered the anonymous letter we had received in the Blue Mountains after I had returned. Somehow, the person of interest had discovered I had helped Jim and turned it around to implicate me trying to cause strife for them. This was how Barbara and Anne's solicitor found out I was in Australia and Anne went to court and gained access to all our outstanding funds.

'There is no coming together now,' Mum said sadly.

Acora's warning in 1986 came to mind. *It is all black, but you're going to win. I don't know how, but you will win in the end. Judy, everyone has been poisoned against you, and I mean everyone.*

'Don't give up. I will write out the truth for you to send to them,' I said.

Six days later I was working when Cathy rang to say Jim had now admitted to seeing me, but told Aunty Val I'd left for Australia before meeting any plain-clothes officer. He was still not revealing the whole truth, but at least they were checking. What is driving Aunty Val to discredit me in support of Barbara and against Mum? I wondered.

Trust the process, my Guide replied.

'This is all part of a much bigger picture,' I told Mum.

Access to the children, my Guide said. Mum wrote to Barbara requesting access to her four grandchildren.

Resign and leave sixth of March, my Guide said. I handed in my notice to Securewest. Mum wrote to her sister Pat telling her I had handed in my notice and we would be leaving for Australia some time after 8 March. Aunty Val's husband rang in reply, asking her to visit them the next day. She returned in a happier frame of mind, having told them about the many issues regarding Barbara and her apartment, and Barbara obtaining her power of attorney. She also told them she had asked for access to her four grandchildren.

We booked Cathy's flight back to Sydney via Japan for 9 March.

I was sent away to work, and gave Mum the funds to take her grandchildren out for lunch. After travelling on the bus to Torquay with Cathy on 15 February, she met up with them and also with her great-grandchildren. Afterwards Tim drove Mum and Cathy back to Spark Cottage. He wanted to see me, but of course I was working. I felt a sense of relief when I heard he'd told Mum he only remembered how much I had done for them in the past. I sensed he was not comfortable with now being told that I was a bad person, and I sent love to him in my thoughts.

John rang inviting Mum to spend a few days at his home in St Agnes, Cornwall, and she went down by train on 25 February. Meanwhile I was directed to hire a car and tour Dartmoor. Cathy asked to come with me.

Dartmoor is the place of my birth and where I spent most of my life before moving to Australia — roaming its wild open spaces and climbing its granite tors. I drove to Ashburton and stood opposite the Old Saddlery, now a flower shop. I was starting yet another journey back in time — to where I did not know. I drove to Widecombe and bought a tartan car rug. Our accommodation at The Plume of Feathers in Princetown was sparse but clean, and later we climbed Haytor, where I consciously breathed in the wonderful atmosphere and vibrant energy of Dartmoor.

On 26 February, Tim's birthday, I drove to Mortonhampstead and felt compelled to dance around the Dancing Tree near the town centre. A sense of celebration came and I laughed, while Cathy watched in fascination. I held this wonderful feeling *en route* to Gidleigh, where we visited the Church of the Holy Trinity and then walked Mariners Way through the pine forest and over the Teign River onto the moor. I stood alone as the dense mist slowly lifted, waiting to see the view. The words from my visit to the Garden of Friendship in Sydney in 1989 came to mind: *Clear View* and *Twin*. I felt again the knowing that one day Tim would see through the smokescreen that had been placed by Barbara and Anne to hide their actions.

The next stop was Scorhill Farm. We were to walk to the Tor until Scorhill Circle came into view. I walked to the outer ring of this ancient Druid site, consisting today of only twenty-three Standing Stones and eleven fallen stones. I was aware only of a sense of loss, and I thought of Tim. The original circle would have contained sixty or maybe seventy tall Standing Stones. *Walk the circle seven times clockwise*, my Guide requested.

As I did so, the feeling of loss increased; the loss of Tim had been awful. *Stand by the triangular stone*, my Guide said. I positioned my hands according to Rene's instructions and repeated the Celtic prayer aloud: 'I ask only what you want of me, the power, wisdom, cosmic love and energy to be able to achieve those things.' *Wash away the loss of Tim*, my Guide urged. I walked to the stream nearby to wash my hands in its icy-cold water. Within the ripples of the water I saw an image of Tim walking the outer rim of the circle.

I drove to Peter Tavy, a pretty village on the western flank of Dartmoor, and then moved on to nearby Churchtown, where we booked into a B&B.

Early the next day we set off for Brentor and the 13th-century Church of St Michael de Rupe. I was aware this church was on the ley-line that ran through St Michaels Mount in Cornwall and Glastonbury Tor. Cathy and I had been sent to Glastonbury Tor as part of our journey back in time to walk in the pathway of ancient monks. The church was at the top of a small tor and featured a bell tower made of granite blocks.

As I walked the tor towards the church I felt Tim's energy beside me. Inside I was drawn to a spectacular leadlight window displaying Michael the Archangel and his Sword of Justice. I stood in front of this image and found myself longing with all my heart for justice and the revealing of the truth. The longing came from deep within and was so intense that I felt light-headed. *Again* I felt Tim's energy standing beside me.

Michael the Archangel and Sword of Justice were added to my Around the World 1991/1992 notes.

I rang Mum and was happy to learn she had enjoyed her visit with John. The next morning we woke to a sunny day after overnight frost. I drove to Mortonhampstead — and stood by their Dancing Tree, sensing something I could not capture — then on to Dunsford and Drewsteignton to admire their many thatched cottages.

Send a postcard to Tim, my Guide instructed. A message formed in my mind, and I wrote that Mum and I would be in the car park at Cockington, Torquay, at 2 pm on 29 February.

Michael the Archangel, Brentor, Devon, England

Celebrate, my Guide insisted. We drove to Fingle Bridge to eat a celebration lunch at The Anglers Rest, neither of us having any idea what we were celebrating but enjoying our delicious meal anyway.

The last place my Guide required me to visit was Spinsters Rock: I was to stand near this dolmen. On Dartmoor, dolmens were burial chambers erected above ground and this was the only one still standing in Devon. I remembered Rene and his explanation that dolmens in Brittany were neutral areas between Standing Stones. The Druids would lie underneath or on top of them to relax, and I was encouraged to do this. I sat under the great flat granite stone supported by upright stones and wrapped the rug from Widecombe around me. A silver mist moved across my vision and I had to concentrate to shift it. I saw Tim reading my postcard. Dolmen was added to my Around the World 1991/1992 notes. I returned to Spark Cottage with instructions to keep the car.

On 29 February I tried to book Mum and me on a flight to Adelaide on 10 March, but instead found myself booking for Perth, Western Australia. I told Mum before we set off to meet Tim at Cockington. 'This is the reason why we flew one way from Adelaide,' Mum said. Cathy was quiet: this sudden turn of events was a shock.

At 1.45 pm I stood in the car park of Cockington village while Mum and Cathy waited in the car. A car sped into the car park, squealed to a halt, and out climbed Tim. He was wearing faded blue jeans and a blue jacket with brown trim on each shoulder. He rushed over and gave me a long hug. I was aware of the love pounding in his heart and the fact that he now towered above me. We all shared a celebration drink at the Cockington pub and then walked the grounds near the 11th-century church. Barbara and the conflict were not mentioned.

Cathy took a photograph of the three of us: Mum, Tim and me. I felt good for the first time in a long while. I understood that by visiting Druid sites on Dartmoor I had turned back time, just as I had done with Mum in 1985 when we walked in Buddha's footsteps to past-life energy and memories of when Tim and I were together in harmony.

It was wet and windy when we crossed the Tamar Bridge into Cornwall the following day. Mum and I sent postcards to friends to tell them we were flying to Perth. I drove to Tintagel, the country of King Arthur and his Knights of the Round Table. Mum stayed in the car while Cathy and I walked to Arthur's castle. The sky was bright blue and the waves crashed against the cliff's face. After walking the cliff pathway to the stone where the famous Sword of Excalibur was reputed to have been held, and where Arthur spent time with Merlin, Cathy took the final photograph of me — standing under the archway of the ruined castle. I stood apart from her to update my notes:

> Around the World 1991/1992: Druid energy – chakras – Standing Stone – heart – Mary Grotto – spring of Sainte Barbe – luminous green – Michael the Archangel / Sword of Justice – dolmen – Arthur and Merlin – Sword of Excalibur.

I was encouraged by my Guide to buy a compass and then an ordinance survey map of Dartmoor and post them to Tim. In my mind there came the knowing that one day he would learn everything his nan and I had experienced since leaving England in 1985 and that we would visit Scorhill Circle on Dartmoor together to rekindle our harmonious past-life link and draw on its unique Druid energy.

Mum and I flew out of Heathrow very early on 10 March, several sealed boxes of our belongings having been stored by Alan. The three sisters arranged to meet Mum before she left, reluctantly accepting her return to Australia with me. Mum gave each a tapestry she had completed in Australia. On the flight I mentioned her sisters and their odd reactions.

'I don't understand how they can believe all the nonsense they have been told by Barbara and Anne,' I said. 'Their common sense seems to have flown out the window. It is almost as if they need to believe ill of me, and I find that very disturbing.'

Our plane landed in Perth twenty-four hours later, in the early hours. We sat inside the airport waiting patiently for guidance. No accommodation had been booked and the taxi drivers watched us with interest when we were the only people left sitting in the airport lounge. There was an 'Accommodation Board' but I was not to read it; then after several hours I was sent to stand in front of it. *The Regency Hotel*, my Guide said.

This hotel sent a courtesy taxi. On arrival the desk clerk explained that as it was after a certain time we could stay the rest of the night and the following night for the price of one. We had limited funds, so the long wait had been worthwhile. The task of finding permanent accommodation began later that day. I was encouraged to buy a newspaper and ring a number and was told about an apartment in Hurlingham Road, South Perth. I travelled by bus to view it. *Yes, this one,* my Guide confirmed.

The apartment was furnished and I arranged for us to move in the next day. South Perth is on the opposite side of the Swan River to Perth City. At night the city lights were spectacular, and we stood on the river's edge marvelling at the sight, not quite believing we were there. Cathy wrote of her distress regarding family issues and her wish to join us. Mum and I did not want this. I replied saying that we were seeking peace from conflicts and needed quiet time. Cathy replied saying she would sleep on the floor if necessary, and we felt pressured. In April Cathy flew over, so the search for a larger home began in earnest. I discovered a three-bedroom unfurnished villa apartment near the river and arranged for our furniture to travel across the Nullabor Plain from South Australia.

In mid-April I was instructed to light a white candle and hold a jade necklace I had bought for Mum at Singapore airport *en route* to Perth. A message came through for Mum, which I wrote down:

> *Several journeys to be taken across the water. Entanglements and complicated personal issues still to be resolved. Great thought and decision-making. This will take a lot of courage, a big step. You have a fear of breaking sentimental ties. Don't just step forward, jump.*

I handed the message to Mum for her notes.

On 26 April I was sent across the river by ferry to the Perth Library to read a passage from a book concerning the Taj Mahal. The story explained patterns of behaviour passed down in families. One brother had killed another; until then the law regarding bloodline inheritance had been obeyed, but following the crime a curse seemed to fall on the family and the law of karma came into being. Mum and I had been sent to the Taj Mahal and, unknown to me, Barbara had gained Mum's power of attorney by stealth, taking control of the family inheritance. But I recovered the inheritance with my Guide's help and Mum's trust. Barbara's actions, and the reactions of Mum's three sisters, were being confirmed as a karmic pattern of behaviour passed down in families. *Tim will play his part. He has a strong love for you,* my Guide said.

Cathy spent time in the Perth Library trying to trace her grandfather's arrival in Australia from England. If she could prove the connection she could apply for a British passport and work in England. She did not want to go back to her family in Gloucester.

On Aunty Val's birthday, 11 May, I was encouraged to hire a car and drive to the Pinnacles, north of Perth. Cathy asked to come with me. This date had been highlighted as being important by my Guide. The Pinnacles, in Nambung National Park, were awesome — yellow sand with tall wind-shaped limestone pillars, giving the appearance of another planet. I was pulled towards a group of pillars to walk clockwise around them six times.

Draw on her energy, my Guide insisted. Whose energy? I wondered. In response, I was taken to yet another pillar and stunned to see its formation was reminiscent of Mary's hooded figure, and the name Tess — my mother's name — written in the sand. I took photographs to give to Mum. On the drive back to Perth I wondered why Mary was featuring in our lives and why Aunty Val was determined to undermine me. Suppressing the truth would not help Barbara resolve her past-life issues regarding family inheritance and control. *Trust the process and all will be revealed*, my Guide said.

Later, I was guided to buy a newspaper and read about land sales in Geraldton. Geraldton had been highlighted on 7 February 1989 in Gloucester, when I had been asked to note this date and then write to the Bill Sewell Complex requesting names of estate agents. Mid-June, I flew to Adelaide to prepare our cottage to be offered for sale. On my return I was encouraged to visit the Perth Library to read two quotes from Gandhi:

> I have learnt one thing, and it is this, that if we take care of the facts of a case, the law will take care of itself. Let us dive deeper into the facts of this case ... Whatever a man sows, that shall he reap, the law of karma is inexorable and impossible of evasion. There is thus hardly any need for God to interfere. He laid down the law, and, as it were, retired.

A ten-page letter arrived from my barrister David Spens proposing a claim against my former solicitor and I thought about the two quotes from Gandhi.

Travel to Geraldton twentieth of July, my Guide insisted. I booked seats and the coach stopped outside the Bill Sewell Complex. We had been moved from one side of the continent to the other as predicted and were seeking the assistance of an estate agent who showed us a new duplex in Solomon Circle. *Yes, this one*, my Guide confirmed.

We put in an offer to purchase, subject to the sale of our cottage in Middleton. I arranged for Mum and me to rent the duplex in September prior to any settlement date. It was out of town, but the bus stopped right outside.

Visit the building society, my Guide requested. An odd request, as there would be no mortgage on the duplex, but I spoke to the manager of a building society regarding mortgages, still not knowing why.

The owner of the guesthouse where we were staying offered to drive us to the Greenough Flats National Trust Village, an historical village with original buildings. Historically, Western Australia is termed a Free State, having been settled by free settlers, although convict labour was brought in later. I sensed a negative atmosphere as we entered the old courthouse and the long, narrow cell block. There were four individual cells for white offenders and a larger cell for holding as many as fifteen Aboriginals, crowded together and chained to a metal bar along the back wall. The historical notes told us prisoners were allowed to exercise outside for an hour a day, but the Aboriginals were not. I cringed inside — I could feel their suffering. It was too much for me and I walked outside, filled with anger, and sat under a tree. Aboriginals charged with serious offences were walked to Perth — a journey that took three weeks. On our return to Perth by coach, I thought of the Aboriginals forced to walk all that way, and felt only disgust at the authorities who obviously both allowed and encouraged it.

Cathy burst into the apartment one day in August, after spending the whole day at the library, with the news that she had traced her grandfather. He had arrived in Sydney on 8 July 1886, aboard the *Port Arthur*. She could now apply for a British passport. Her excitement was soon crushed, however, by a letter from her ex-husband. She had asked for one of their three children to visit at Christmas, but was told *not one of them* wished to come. She rang her son, and he confirmed what his father had written. Her dark mood continued for months. This rejection was a turning point in her life.

Mum and I travelled to Geraldton ahead of the removal van and, as with our other moves, my Guide instructed that The Lovers pots be placed in the kitchen window. The Wild Geese / Soul Group print was to be hung by the single bed and the Butterfly Circle with its jarrah surround placed under Mum's bed. The Four Core Colours symbol created in Gloucester was placed by my bed on a side table. The extra furnishings were put into storage.

After two weeks I was forced back to Perth. Cathy was not coping following her children's rejection. When I returned to Geraldton three weeks later, Cathy came too. She asked to stay with us until she could find a home to rent. Having Cathy with us created tension, but my Guide was insistent that Cathy was meant to be with us at this time.

Legal action, my Guide warned.

At the end of November I was encouraged to open a joint building society account with Cathy. The feeling of apprehension became so powerful that it kept me awake at night. I shared my concerns with Mum and she said she felt the same – it was the feeling we'd experienced in Gloucester when we first met her: something troublesome and unpleasant was hidden deep within her personality.

We hired a car for Christmas. When I was arranging the table for Christmas lunch I was instructed to place a copy of *The Universal Druid Prayer*, which had been sent to me by a friend, at Cathy's place for her to read out loud, which she agreed to do:

> Grant, O God, Thy protection;
> And in protection, strength;
> And in strength, understanding;
> And in understanding, knowledge;
> And in knowledge, the knowledge of justice;
> And in the knowledge of justice, the love of it;
> And in that love, the love of all existences;
> And in the love of all existences, the love of God;
> God and all goodness.

As I listened to Cathy's voice the feeling of apprehension returned, and my mind went reeling back to earlier in the year when we'd walked inside the Church of St Michael de Rupe at Brentor, on Dartmoor, and I stood in front of the leadlight window of Michael the Archangel, holding his Sword of Justice. *Legal action*, my Guide had warned.

The apprehension increased even further when she encouraged me to update my notes with this new clue:

Heart Issue (2): Cathy – soulmate – legal action.

By my standing in front of the Archangel Michael in Cathy's presence, longing for justice and the revealing of the truth, I understood that the process had begun.

Boxing Day morning we all headed north to the Kalbarri National Park, which was full of wildflowers. Low purple shrubs were overpowered by tall, elegant, white-flowering plants that stooped over the road. We drove to Kalbarri itself, booked into the caravan park and then went to the beach for a swim. Jack Temple had restored this ability for me in Austria years before. I watched from the water as Mum walked the beach alone, to sit at Pelican Point. I sensed her grief — the loss of the comradeship of her three sisters — and felt a moment of deep sadness and overwhelming helplessness.

Kalbarri was settled by Cornish miners whose leases were in what is now the National Park. It was the abundance of fresh water that had attracted them. The river, described as only a few million years young, had carved a deep gorge through the ancient Tumblagooda sandstone, and the contrast of brownish-red and purple against bands of white was spectacular. We were told by the local fishermen that whales came near the entrance and dolphins would play in its lower reaches. When I heard this I touched my seven-dolphin bracelet and the feeling of apprehension returned for a fleeting moment. I was already aware that for some reason — yet to be revealed — Cathy, myself and the regal young woman in my dream of 1988 were linked by the symbol of dolphins.

On the first day of 1993 I was encouraged to write to the Findhorn Community in Scotland regarding their workshop program and to highlight 'Findhorn' in my notes with regard to Cathy and her heart issue. When I posted the letter I found another one waiting from my barrister requesting the Transfer of Deeds document for the Old Saddlery, which I sent. I was guided to update my notes regarding Cathy, recording the clue 'the transfer of deeds'. Cathy's past-life heart issue was gradually being revealed in the same remarkable fashion as the identity and past-life heart issue of the regal young woman.

> Heart Issue: Cathy – soulmate – legal action – Findhorn – the transfer of deeds.

Prior to Mum's birthday in January, a card arrived from Tim's twin brother, Mark, telling Mum he missed her. This brought tears to her eyes. He asked her what it was like in Australia and she sent back a long, newsy letter by return. This was followed by a letter from Aunty Pat asking for our telephone number and then gifts arrived from the sisters.

Sadly, Mark never replied to Mum's letter.

In mid-February Cathy was successful in her application to work at the Geraldton Art Gallery — a venue that provided a busy and entertaining social life for Mum. On 26 February, Tim's birthday, Cathy and I hired a car and drove north to Shark Bay Marine Park to spend time with Monkey Mia dolphins. We stopped *en route* late evening at the Nanga Holiday Resort, a former sheep station, and my mind went back to the previous year when I had been sent to Scorhill Circle on Tim's birthday to connect with him, accessing Druid energy. Three days later he had driven to Cockington to see me, giving me a warm hug.

Early the next day we drove to Shell Beach Conservation Park, with its millions of tiny white shells heaped into ridges almost 10 metres high, unique because the shells are from only one type of animal. I was to note that Scorhill Circle on Dartmoor and Shark Bay in Western Australia held a past-life connection for Tim and me.

Arriving at Monkey Mia, we were thrilled to discover our cabin was opposite the shore where the dolphins visited. A small crowd had gathered at the water's edge, so I leapt out of the car and ran to join them, gradually moving through the silent group, absorbing the atmosphere of intense anticipation of the people awaiting the arrival of the dolphins. For half an hour these graceful silver-grey mammals swam in front of us seeking the fish being held by the ranger, who carefully ensured no-one touched the dolphins. Instinctively, I moved away from the crowd and stood alone watching and enjoying the scene.

My heart began to race when one of the larger dolphins broke away, swam in a circle to avoid all the others, and headed in my direction. It approached me at speed, and for a moment I was tempted to step out of the shallow water onto the sand; but I held my ground as it approached. The dolphin dived, leaving only its fin above water and then resurfaced in front of me, side-on, revealing one eye. Time stood still as I searched into the depths of that one dark eye, requesting the answer to the dolphin link between myself, Cathy and the regal young woman in my dream.

I was woken at 6 am the next morning. *Follow the pendulum*, my Guide insisted. The movements of the pendulum soon took Cathy and me into the nearby bush, where we saw numerous tiny animal markings in the sand and were taken to a grave. There was no headstone — just a raised brass plaque that said the buried child had died at the age of three. The plaque was surrounded by dead branches bound together by thin strands of rusting wire, creating a triangle effect. Modern pole fencing had been erected to protect the place. *Remember this grave, this is the link with Tim*, my Guide said. I stood beside the grave for a while, contemplating how devastating it must be to lose a child, and moreover to lose them at such a young age.

That evening at 9.20 pm Cathy and I were guided to sit on the pier. The sky was clear and full of stars, and I realised it was the same time as 30 January the previous year, when I had been directed to look out at the night sky at Spark Cottage. A path of white light flashed across the sky and then a bright star moved in circles from left to right.

'There is that same star,' I said to Cathy.

We returned excitedly to our cabin. My Guide requested I light a white candle and a lengthy message came, which I recorded in my notes:

Judy. Travel imminent. Long-term results. Peace out of the situation. Select times for spiritual development. Monetary gain will bring long-term security. Place your faith in my instructions. There will be new concepts coming through which will broaden your horizons. Less security will be necessary. Tomorrow travel on the boat to the Pearl Farm. Leave with hope in your heart. A long life leading into a stage now in your life when you will be asked to help resolve health problems; it will come about by a meeting with a spirit guide. Look for signs of magic. Sentimental senses will increase. Turn around and watch the result of your actions. Look at the people you have been related to and move on; their influence is over. Put aside all forms of duty, responsibility and guilt. This is not how life is meant to be. People mature quickly when made responsible. Two spirits entwined, searching for God. We brought you here to watch the exchange between the human mammal and the sea mammal, the dolphin. Both are interdependent. Look at how the human stares. The dolphin is free to come and go, as you are free to come and go. Visit Hamelin Pool. People who want to see you will seek you out.

The message *You are free to come and go* highlighted the necessity for me to remain attachment-free and I was comfortable with this — comfortable working with just Mum as a team. The past-life heart issues of soulmates and the rescue of Barbara were to be resolved within the aspects of my being an observer and not a participant.

I went to the water's edge early on 1 March, and sent love across the sea. I was assured I would be surprised at the result. At 10.30 am we boarded the boat to take us out to the Pearl Farm. I was fascinated by the dugongs in the shallows, and took photographs to complement an earlier shot of two large dolphins swimming together. We went to Hamelin Pool before driving home to walk out over the still, clear water on the walkway.

My Guide requested that the photographs of the two dolphins and the dugong be enlarged four times and then framed together. A third symbol to join the Butterfly Circle and the Four Core Colours. About a week later I was standing in front of this symbol, remembering having sent love across the sea, when the phone rang. It was Aunty Audrey, requesting — through Cathy — to speak to Mum, only to Mum. A few days later, Aunty Val rang requesting to speak only to Mum — hurtful for me and disturbing for Mum, but progress.

On my birthday, 8 March, I discovered, with delight, that Mum had taken her Christmas gift to me — *Kimberley Dreaming to Diamonds* by Hugh Edwards — to a book-signing by the author, and had rewrapped it. Inside I found the words 'For Judy, with my best wishes. Hugh Edwards 1993'. The author relates the story of Lieutenant George Grey, who was commissioned by the British Government to lead an expedition to the North West of Western Australia in 1837, and his experiences with the Aboriginals. As with other books that had drawn my attention, I was under strict instructions not to read their content, only to make note of particular sections under guidance. Mum and I lit a white candle and noted sections of page 25:

> The miracle when it appeared on March 26th, in the vicinity of the river was totally unexpected. Grey wrote: *'Looking over some bushes, at the sandstone rocks which were above us, I suddenly saw a most extraordinary large figure peering down upon me ...'* It was a large painting at the entrance to a cave ... Grey was the first European to gaze on the striking 'Wandjina' paintings of the Kimberley ... (4)

My Guide highlighted 'Wandjina', then the words 'Kimberley' and 'diamond' from the title of the book. I was guided to update the clues regarding the regal young woman of my dream:

> Heart Issue (1): Soulmate – yellow roses – soul group – dream – regal young woman with dark brown eyes – Egypt – dolphin – Switzerland – Mary – Wandjina – Kimberley diamond.

Dianne sent me *The Findhorn Garden Story* by The Findhorn Community, and inside the book she had written, 'Truth is when you know what is right and what is wrong. It comes from deep within our souls and the inner strength to do the right thing.' Again, I was not to read the book until later guided to note particular pages or words.

For Christmas 1988 Mum had given me the tapestry of four rainbow lorikeets, and the purchase of all tapestries since had been supervised by my Guide. Now, in 1993, I had just completed one of gum-nuts with their seven faces peeping out from behind gum leaves. I was being encouraged by Dianne's gift to remember that Dorothy at Findhorn accessed the devas and nature spirits. This fourth symbol was referred to as the gum-nuts tapestry / nature spirits.

I recorded the clues 'tapestry', '7', 'garden' and 'devas' in my notes.

Days later I received a job offer from the Icarus Safety and Securities Services. I worked in uniform and plain clothes for the business community, and at lunchtime I would walk to the beach and listen to the local Aboriginals and their stories, and a feeling of helplessness would come. The struggling Aboriginal communities lived on the fringes of Geraldton.

Following Mum's departure to visit Monkey Mia with a travel group and Cathy's departure to attend a family wedding in Sydney, I was given the prediction *An energy centre ahead for you*. Was this the predicted project mentioned by Mu in England?

On 11 May Mum and I were at home in Geraldton discussing family issues, aware that this was Aunty Val's birthday and that for an unknown reason she was supporting Barbara. My Guide requested I find my notes regarding our trip to England the previous year – in particular Barbara's visit to Spark Cottage – and to read aloud the message 'A seventh and final attempt to resolve this issue.' Then I was requested to go to Mum's bedroom, open the Indian box that held my father's silver capsule and take from it the silver figure of Mary. I was to place it on my notes beside a lit white candle. A message followed, which I recorded:

> *There are great expectations of your success here. There have been six attempts in life experiences to bring Barbara's soul back to the Light. She will forever be in your debt as a soul participant in future growth.*

Mary, my Guide and my father were highlighting the requirement for the rescue of Barbara, and Aunty Val was part of that rescue. But how, I wondered. In response, I was sent back to Mum's bedroom. I replaced the box with the capsule and returned figurine and found myself drawn to pick up another Indian box and take it to the lit candle. Mum watched as I went to my office and returned with the framed gum-nuts tapestry / nature spirits symbol. I was guided to put the Indian box on the tapestry, then open it to discover two New Zealand coins. My father, while serving in the navy, had collected coins from around the world, but they were in a sealed bag, so how these two found their way into this box was a mystery. I updated my notes accordingly:

Heart Issue (3): Tapestry – 7 – garden – devas – New Zealand – coins.

Are there any more soulmates with heart issues? I wondered. *No*, my Guide replied.

We were being told that this third soulmate with a heart issue was going to help us bring Barbara's soul back to the Light and there was great expectation of our success. I had tried to reach into Barbara's conscience the previous month by writing to her and pointing out that, no matter what she had thought about the situation between Anne and me, she had been legally and morally obliged to act in my best interests. There had been no response, and a copy of my letter to Barbara was added to Mum's ever-increasing file.

Cathy and I were instructed to travel to Rottnest Island aboard the ferry *Star Flyte* on 7 June. This would involve a coach trip to Perth, then a train to Fremantle, on the coast south-west of Perth, followed by the 19-kilometre ferry trip to the island. The first recorded landing on Rottnest was by the Dutch explorer Willem de Vlamingh in 1696. He saw the marsupials we call quokkas and thought they were rats, hence *Rottnest*, Dutch for 'rat's nest'. Settled by the British in 1829, the island was used as an Aboriginal prison from 1838 to 1931 except for the years 1849 to 1855. Two thousand died there, I read. I felt sick.

As I stepped from the ferry I recalled that the penal colony in Van Dieman's Land — Tasmania — was established around the same time. In 1834 Commandant Charles O'Hara Booth created a juvenile prison on a peninsular across the bay from Port Arthur. Boys between the ages of 13 and 19 were sent to Hobart to train in various trades. I remembered Pat telling me, back in Ashburton, that I had committed suicide after being transported from Cornwall to Van Dieman's Land as a young boy. I walked away from the ferry feeling a little anxious.

We explored Rottnest by bicycle, and enjoyed the rugged coastline and the turquoise sea. Late in the afternoon Cathy asked me to stop cycling, stand still inside a circle of trees and listen as she read aloud something she had written. 'I choose you to be my lifelong companion,' she began. 'I am making that choice. I symbolically leave behind my father and mother, my children and friends to walk the path beside you. In doing this I am putting God first in my life. You are His gift to me. His gift to you is my promise to be your friend through eternity.' I was embarrassed, wondering where those intense sentiments had come from. Looking into her eyes, I saw she was staring at me with a blank look as if far, far away, and I understood she was experiencing a past-life flashback. I walked away, not sure what to say, so I said nothing. Later I placed her written declaration inside my notes.

Back in our Perth hotel I showered and was dressing when a pain shot across my shoulders. I shouted out and Cathy came running. She then described markings like whiplashes across my shoulders. They began to fade when she told me what she was seeing. I had been disturbed by the deaths of the two thousand Aboriginals imprisoned on Rottnest.

In July a letter arrived from Alison, my solicitor in England, with a compensation offer from my former solicitor. I rejected it. Later she wrote again, this time requesting my authority for the release of documents from the solicitor who had completed the sale of the Old Saddlery. He had allowed Anne to buy a home contrary to our agreement. This lost capital was to be taken into account in the present compensation claim.

Cathy found herself a large furnished rental home by the sea and moved out. We had not discussed the declaration she had felt driven to make on Rottnest Island, but her words 'my lifelong companion' had been added to her past-life heart issue:

Heart Issue: Cathy – soulmate – legal action – Findhorn – the transfer of deeds – my lifelong companion.

Cathy's employer at the Geraldton Art Gallery, Bev, spoke to her about their reception evenings and the need to find a caterer. When Cathy mentioned I had run a restaurant in England I was approached regarding a part-time catering opportunity. I came up with an idea of specialised finger foods. Cathy and I were given the contract to cater for the next event and were thrilled when later offered more contracts.

One night Mum woke me — distressed — having woken from a vivid dream about John, the father of her four grandchildren. Over and over she repeated, 'He can't breathe. He can't breathe.' John was writing regularly, calling her 'Mum', and had confided not long before that he had a serious heart condition. I wondered at Mum's link with John and was told they were soulmates and he was part of our soul group. This was to be the first of many happenings for Mum.

Sail on the Leeuwin, my Guide said. We boarded the sailing ship for a day's excursion on 12 September. Mum was fine until the ship headed back towards Geraldton, when she became disturbed. 'A strong sense of familiarity,' she said. She expressed her relief when we were back on dry land. I enjoyed the trip and felt admiration for the sailors who had circumnavigated the globe in such vessels. A few days later Mum rang while I was with Cathy at her place preparing for a catering contract. She had something to share so I went home, and she told me what had happened the night after our trip on the *Leeuwin*.

She had woken from a deep sleep to find a young man sitting a few feet away by her cheval mirror — a visitor from spirit, but she was not afraid. 'He was sitting with his legs crossed, relaxed and smiling,' she said. 'He was in his mid-twenties, with a small fair beard and lovely blue eyes.' By the way he was dressed Mum knew he was from the era of the sailing ship. The energy coming from him was of love and protection. She felt safe so went back to sleep. Later she woke up again and saw the image of a huge man in front of the window. Still feeling safe, she went back to sleep.

My Guide had asked us to sail on the *Leeuwin*, so I lit a white candle and waited. She confirmed that Mum had sailed here before in a past life, arriving in Western Australia with a young husband who had died soon afterwards. She had been taken in by a baker and his wife and later married a soldier, the very large man she had seen.

Early in November I was referred once again to the book *Kimberley Dreaming to Diamonds* by Hugh Edwards, to record a small section on page 26:

> It was dangerous to annoy a Wandjina, a being with lightning, storm and flood at his disposal … The Aborigines saw the Wandjina as supernatural beings. They had individual names like Bundjinmoro, at Manning Creek; Pindjuari, the crocodile Wandjina of the Oscar Ranges; and the Kaiara, the sea Wandjinas, of Bigge Island and other sea caves. (4)

When the words 'disposal' and 'crocodile' were highlighted, a feeling of intense panic swept through my being. My Guide's calming energy quickly followed, bringing relief to my body and calming my severely jarred emotions. *There is a higher purpose in your life. A special contribution you can make*, she said. But I was dismayed when she encouraged me to add these clues to a soulmate's past-life heart issue notes:

> Heart Issue (1): Soulmate – yellow roses – soul group – dream – regal young woman with dark brown eyes – Egypt – dolphin – Switzerland – Mary – Wandjina – Kimberley diamond – disposal – crocodile.

Just before Christmas I was given the message to prepare the duplex for sale; then a letter arrived from Alison in England telling me my former solicitor in Exeter had tried to say she was bankrupt; but, as we were suing the firm and not her as an individual, this ploy failed. The compensation claim was continuing.

Cathy invited Mum and me to celebrate the three days of Christmas at her place. On Christmas morning I opened the first of two gifts from Cathy and discovered it was a knife — a Swiss Army knife. As I held it I filled with alarm and accidentally cut my finger. In stark contrast, her other gift was breathtaking. A square frame held the life-like image of a turtle in an ocean of turquoise and blue, all hand-cut from leather. Under the turtle were four squares with nine orange, yellow, white and pale blue fish. The eye of the turtle also reflected these colours. It was titled, 'The Chase' and was one of only four to have been made.

On Boxing Day my Guide requested Mum, Cathy and me travel to Kalbarri in a hire car. A repeat of last year, but only for the day this time. I was instructed to buy a shark's tooth for Tim. *A symbol of Tim's repressed emotions*, my Guide said. Later, at home in Geraldton, I was directed to have an oval silver link fitted to the tooth by a jeweller. Then it was placed on one of my father's heavy triangular copper paperweights for a few days. The words *I will not forget you* accompanied this action. Then the shark's tooth was gift-wrapped and sent to Tim as a present from my father, his maternal grandfather.

On the first day of 1994 I was encouraged to write a set of words in my notes: *Self help healing centre. New partnership. Money coming. Legal situation.* Then to place the page with these words on top of two photographs. Two years before, when Mum and I were living in South Perth, Cathy had flown over to join us. She'd handed me these photographs as a gift from her sister Liz to me. A friend of a friend had spent time in Medjugorje, Bosnia-Herzegovina, where Mary had first appeared as a beautiful woman in 'golden splendour' in June of 1981. While there, the friend took photographs of the setting sun and, when they were developed later in Sydney, one had superimposed upon the sunset image a young Jewish female face (page 138). The second photograph revealed the figure of the same woman, dressed in white and pale blue with a long set of rosary beads running through her hands. In her hair she wore a circular crown of roses and three symbols hung at her waist (page 390). The friend took them back to the developer, who showed her the negatives to prove they were indeed her photographs. In the close-up photograph of Mary she has her eyes cast downwards. There is a blue haze around her throat and on the right side of her face.

The sets of words remained on top of these photographs for days, until I was asked by my Guide to have the close-up photograph placed in a blue frame and the message written again and sealed with clear tape onto the back of Mary's image — a clear indication that the self help healing centre and Mary were connected.

Weeks later, at 8.30 pm on 21 January, I was sitting in Cathy's home when I was taken to look at Mary's image, which I had been instructed to carry with me, and to concentrate on her downcast eyes. My mind went back five years to 1989 and the twin shaft of light in the Maulbronn Cistercian Monastery in Germany. The monastery had been in semi-darkness then, as this room was now. The twin shaft of light at the monastery had moved through my forehead and star formations had appeared. Now a half-arch of triangles similar in shape to the moon in its final quarter appeared. The triangles were blue and black, or just blue, flashing independently, with a bright yellow glow around each one. I closed my eyes but the image stayed, the arch gradually filling with deep yellow. I sat engrossed for about ten minutes until I was told to go and lie down in one of the bedrooms in darkness.

The arch and triangles reappeared, the flashing becoming small, gentle waves as the arch moved inwards, reducing in size. It moved towards me and I held my breath as it entered my right eye. Both my eyes ached afterwards for several minutes. I awoke the next morning with a headache that gradually faded during the day. I looked at Mary's image and my right eye ached as a reminder of what had happened the evening before. *The Mary Ray*, my Guide explained.

'What on earth is the Mary Ray?' I asked.

Divine energy.

Later I was reminded of my first arrival in Geraldton when I took home an abandoned blue heeler puppy. I called her Jessie. Researching her breed, I discovered that the founding stock was the smooth-haired Blue Merle Collie, imported from Scotland. It had a strong instinct for working stock, an obedient nature and, when crossed with the native dingoes, a silent method of working. Plus qualities of exceptional hardiness and endurance. *All qualities in you*, my Guide explained.

Cathy's parents flew across to celebrate Mum's birthday on 27 January. Then Cathy and I hired a car and took them to Kalbarri, where we ate lunch by a waterhole once used by the Aboriginal Yamatji people, beside the Murchison River. The following day we visited Shark Bay Marine Park, spending time with the dolphins. On our way back we took them to see Shell Beach Conservation Park then south to Perth and Margaret River and on to the southern forests. I was wondering what this trip was about when I was taken to touch a jarrah tree. I remembered the Butterfly Circle, in its jarrah frame, lying under Mum's bed — waiting. We visited the quaint timber town of Pemberton, where it rained and the fresh smell of the surrounding forests was unbelievable. I sensed I would return to this region one day. On arriving in Balingup we were encouraged to visit the Cheese Factory gift shop. I was sent into a room filled with jarrah pieces. *Dowse*, my Guide said. The pendulum located a large heart-shaped piece of jarrah. *A tool for healing*, she said.

Before taking Cathy's parents to Perth airport we were to visit New Norcia, the only monastery town in Australia, built by Benedictine monks 150 years before. Cathy's mum bought the Lady of Good Counsel Medal in the gift shop and handed it to me. Now I had two medals from her: the Miraculous Medal and the Lady of Good Counsel Medal. The painting *The Lady of Good Counsel* was given to the founder of New Norcia, Bishop Salvado, by St Vincent Palotti, in Rome in 1845.

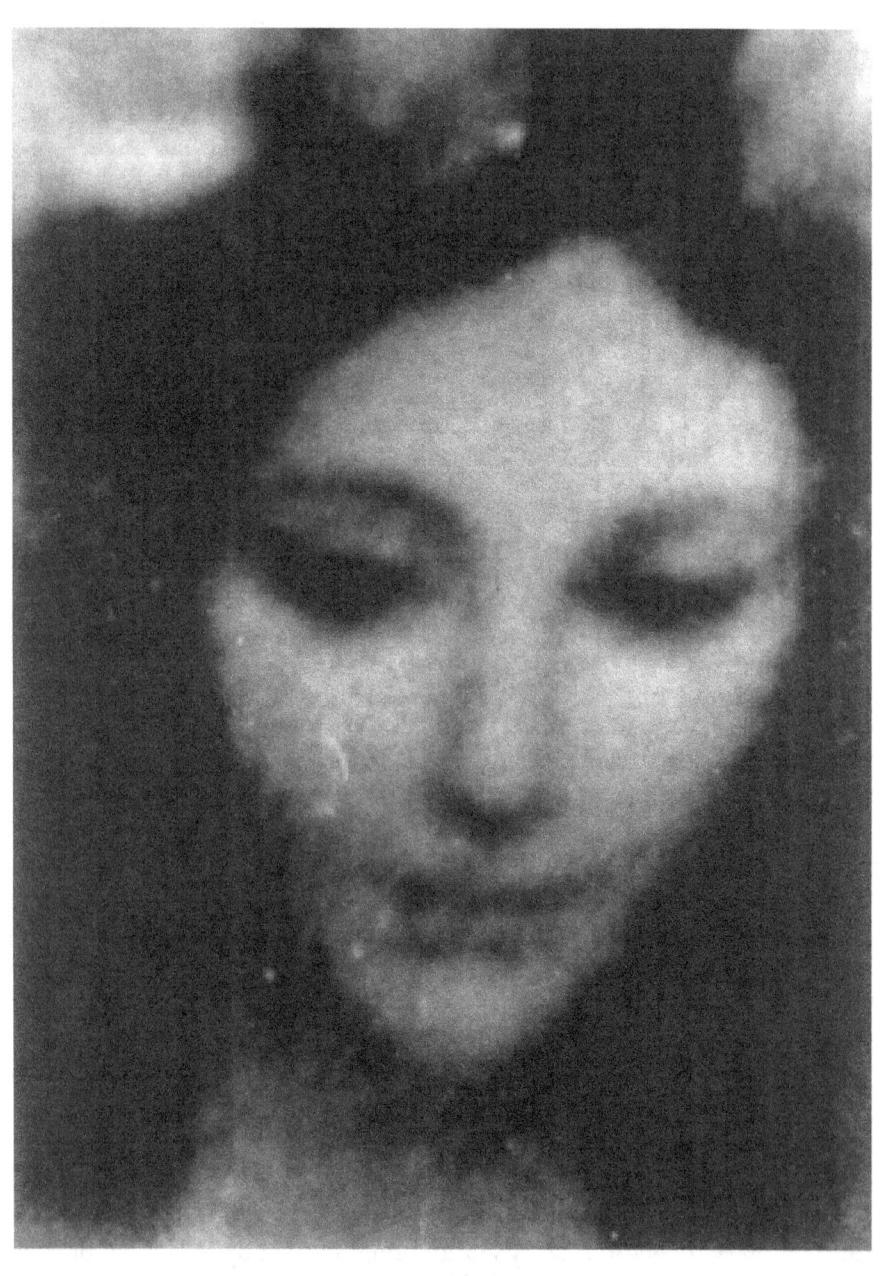

Image of Mary captured at Medjugorje, Bosnia-Herzegovina

On the way back to Geraldton our coach stopped in Dongara and I was given the message, *Dongara. Self help healing centre. The Lady of Good Counsel. Retreat. Four Core Colours* and the numbers 4 and 12 connected with this symbol were also highlighted. I was guided to record in my notes the following:

Energy (1): The Four Core Colours – yellow – blue – green – red – 4 – 12 – Dongara – self help healing centre – The Lady of Good Counsel – retreat.

When we reached Geraldton Cathy had a temper fit. Something had been said to her by her parents regarding the children. Frustration and hurt poured out of her for hours. Then we went to the beach at sunset and walked along the water's edge with Jessie the dog. The sea was calm and the sun was setting in a sky of orange and gold. A thin golden ray remained on the surface of the water, and when it vanished the sea became dark blue. I encouraged Cathy to walk in the water to release the anguish until she was calm again.

Mum's health was becoming a worry: there was an ongoing bowel problem. It became so serious that she had to see a specialist. Three days after my birthday, on 11 March, I was instructed to resign from the security firm. I was pleased, as I needed time to ensure Mum could attend her hospital appointments. It became necessary for me to borrow a car. I needed to buy a car, but had no idea how.

Cathy and I were still involved with our casual catering, and in mid-March we received a request to cater for a two-day conference. I felt we could do it, but Cathy did not, and a heated discussion followed. Having put out thoughts concerning a car, I was determined not to let this opportunity slip by me.

I submitted a quote that was accepted. I wrote out the menus, having approached specific places that could provide top-quality food. I booked taxis to collect the food over the two-day period and hired the equipment needed; including china and tables. I brought in a waitress to help me on both days. Now all I had to do was bring everything together. The midday meal would be the hardest, with various main dishes to be collected from the restaurants and cafés I had chosen. But both days went well and my waitress and I were very pleased with ourselves. I was able to buy the much-needed second-hand car.

A letter arrived from my solicitor in England with a compensation offer. *Reject the offer*, my Guide insisted. People were coming to view our duplex, and my Guide instructed that all sale proceeds be placed in Mum's building society account and then we must rent a newly built home in Sovereign Waters, within walking distance of the sea.

While I was worried about Mum's health, Cathy was concerned about family and lack of communication. Combining a job and casual catering was proving to be stressful for her. A sense of relief came when Mum's tests came back clear just as Cathy's children wrote to her. The vehicle I'd purchased was an estate car, which enabled me to move us into the rental home in Sovereign Waters.

Create a garden, my Guide insisted. With the owners' consent, plants were delivered and I began the huge task of creating a garden there. On 23 May I was to stop working to read a part of the book *The Findhorn Garden Story*:

> I was unemployed with no prospects of a job … However the arduous spiritual training Eileen, Dorothy and I had undergone in our lives enabled us to accept this extraordinary state of affairs. We learnt to surrender everything, including our wills, to God … When the guidance told us not only to live in the moment but to enjoy it, that is what we set out to do. (5)

Visit Dongara fourth of June, my Guide said. I was drawn to a feature in *The Dongara Rag* on 'The Old East End' just outside the town — a modernised 100-year-old farmhouse — and I booked to stay in their bed-and-breakfast overnight. Cathy asked to come with me and my Guide insisted I allow this. Once I had booked, I was instructed to drive to the Geraldton Library, where I was sent to a book on Egypt and then to a specific god:

> The Papyrus of Khonsu Wanderer (Upper Egypt), the Moon God, recognised from at least 2500 BC, a deity at Thebes. There is a Khonsu Precinct as part of the Temple of Amun in the Karnak complex.

The god was wearing a crown comprising a crescent moon subtending a full moon orb. An ankh, the Egyptian cross, was hanging from the horizon. As I studied the image of the Egyptian Moon God, I recalled my experience on 21 January, when I had been taken to Mary's image.

Half-arched triangles similar in shape to the moon in its final quarter had appeared and I remembered holding my breath when they entered my right eye. My Guide explained this as being the Mary Ray and divine energy. The words 'Dongara', 'Egypt' and 'ankh' were highlighted by my Guide, and these clues were added to my notes regarding the three soulmates with past-life heart issues. I had been moved back in time to past-life issues involving ancient Egypt and the cray-fishing township of Dongara.

Cathy and I enjoyed staying at the Old East End in Dongara. Both the farmhouse and the cottage had been beautifully restored. In the gift shop I was drawn to buy a square-framed mirror, the wood having come from the original timbers of the roof of the flour mill outside Dongara, beside the highway. It was wired in only one corner, so when the mirror was hung it had a diamond effect. The word *Diamond* repeated again and again, until I remembered Kimberley diamond was one of the clues with regard to the identity and past-life heart issue of the regal young woman in my dream.

The mirror was wrapped, not to be reopened again until Christmas Day.

Within days of our visit to Dongara, Cathy erupted over an issue at her new workplace, having recently left the Art Gallery. Following this outburst I was taken to a book Cathy herself had borrowed, titled *The Tibetan Book of Living and Dying* by Sogyal Rinpoche. Karma was highlighted and then words spoken by Padmasambhava:

> If you want to know your past life, look into present conditions; if you want to know your future life, look at your present actions. (6)

The words 'karma' and 'past life' were highlighted by my Guide. I closed the book and updated the clues regarding soulmates with past-life heart issues. When I tried to absorb these clues, my mind was taken back to my conversation with Alan in England. He had asked me what the word 'walk-in' meant to me, and I'd explained that the issues to be resolved on the Earth plane would become so traumatic the incarnated individual would seek assistance from the individual in spirit. The spirit individual would walk in and reside within the incarnated individual. The task of both entities was to resolve the issues and bring through a new understanding to Earth by completing a project. The project ahead of me somehow involved the heart and was part of the agreement between my Guide and myself to bring through a higher understanding. Days later she insisted I ask for a reading by a clairvoyant visiting Geraldton.

'Bouts of sadness. It is time you stopped the sadness to change the memories and your life would be easier. Soon there will be something to totally engross your mind, but even then you are to take time out,' she said, and waited for me to absorb this. 'There is the influence of a son around you and you will eventually spend time with this son.'

I thought of Tim, and to my surprise the clairvoyant nodded.

'You hold strong beliefs and will soon be helping others. Your Guide is a woman. She is wrapped in an off-white robe and is dark-skinned. You are to stop worrying about people's opinions, or that they may change their feelings for you. You are to remember that disruptions are sometimes a blessing in disguise. Legal situation is coming. You will win, a necessary experience for your growth.' Again she waited for me to absorb this.

'The son, you must pray for him. He is in a complex situation and has mixed feelings, as three other people are involved.'

I remembered the gypsy in the Old Saddlery telling me Tim had reincarnated as my nephew just to be near me. The clairvoyant smiled and said, 'You were not destined to have children this lifetime so he came through your sister.'

I stared at her trying to come to terms with what she had just said. 'You are definite, adamant and truthful,' she went on. 'Your sister has loneliness and feels depressed at times, but she is strong and clear-minded. She listens only to herself. You will be opening more spiritual doors soon.'

Later at home I was instructed to create a nook area, with comfortable cushions tucked away beside the passage leading to the bedrooms. Mum and I would sit in there in the evenings to talk and relax.

Another offer arrived from my solicitor and once more I refused it.

In mid-August Mum collapsed onto the floor in the dining room. Thankfully, I was home at the time. She reached for my hand and held it tight while we waited for the ambulance to arrive.

'Don't leave me. Do something,' she urged. I rang Aunty Pat, and later flowers were delivered to the ward from Mum's sisters. She was allowed to go home the following week.

On 21 September, Barbara's birthday, I woke up with a jolt. *Do something*, my Guide urged. Of course Mum had said the same thing after her collapse.

'Do what?' When I walked towards Mum's bedroom the understanding came that she was to ring Barbara. She was surprised, but rang her, wishing her a happy birthday and thus breaking the silence between them. Slowly, very slowly, Mum's health began to improve. Acora's warning on her birthday two years before in England was proving to be correct. He had warned her that future health problems would result from the strong animosity coming from deep within Barbara. The phone call was the means to ward off the animosity and allow Mum to return to good health.

Early in October Cathy and I attended a spiritual group meeting in Geraldton and met Marg Parker — a woman in her early fifties with short wavy dark hair and a warm smile. We discussed attending a meditation workshop in Northampton. I'd passed through the township on my way to Kalbarri and recalled seeing the Convent of St Mary and the Church of St Mary in Ara Coeli. *You must go*, my Guide said.

At home later I was sent by my Guide to *The Tibetan Book of Living and Dying* and was encouraged to read aloud, 'The Spiritual Path — Help me, inspire me to purify all my karma and negative emotions, and to realize the true nature of my mind.' (6)

We drove to the Convent of St Mary on 7 October and discovered our accommodation was within the convent itself. Meditation group sessions took place in the large annex room near the kitchen, but I was restless, not wanting to be part of anything. I wandered off as a pushing energy kept me moving. The next day I tried to be a part of the group but the restlessness grew even stronger, until I gave in and absorbed it into my being. The words from *The Tibetan Book of Living and Dying* repeated in my mind. Once I had accepted the energy I rejoined the group.

Marg watched me sit and then announced a flower reading. We all walked outside to select a flower, and then on returning placed it in the centre of the circle. No-one knew to whom each flower belonged. My flower, a violet, was selected by Eileen, the woman sitting next to me. As soon as she held it, she said. 'I see a dreadful situation surrounding this person. Soon you are going to be given an opportunity to remove this blockage. You must get rid of it, or it will dry you up, and it could last forever. A nice clean-cut situation is coming and you are to seize it.' She then spoke of 'A flat tyre on a car holding good vibrations.'

I left when another meditation session began, being drawn to walk outside into the rose garden by the church and towards its Mary Grotto. A surge of energy passed through me and the same feeling of elevation came that I had experienced in Brittany when I stood in front of the Mary Grotto at Chapelle Sainte Barbe. Mary was wearing all white with a blue sash around her waist. A girl knelt to the right, near a small pool of water in a tiny well-like shape in the rock. I was directed to pick a purple wildflower and place it at Mary's feet. I felt embarrassed: this felt odd to me.

I was encouraged to walk inside the church. At first I felt uncomfortable being inside a Catholic church, but soon found myself requesting that my mother and sister Barbara be reunited, and the negativity removed from my family. When I returned to the meditation group it had grown even larger. Marg watched as I sat between Eileen — who had given my flower reading — and Cathy. She selected a tape and soft music began to play. When we were all settled she began to speak in a voice that was *familiar* to me. I closed my eyes and in the distance a small, oblong object formed, which soon became the entrance of a swirling tunnel, which I entered. From within the centre of the tunnel came a bronze Celtic cross with a purple gemstone. It came closer, growing bigger and bigger, until it bowled me over and I came out of the meditation with a start.

I was shaken and stared across at Marg, who was already observing me. I looked around and everyone was watching her and me. Then I sensed *another* behind me and heard a loud buzzing noise. Marg moved slowly towards me and sat down in front of me. I was held fast within a hot energy field, unable to move. Marg spoke softly. 'Are you religious, Judy?'

'No, not really. Why?' Marg told me there was a man — possibly a bishop — standing behind me, an Anglican maybe. He was swinging a large incense burner. He was not wearing a typical Catholic robe, rather the colours of someone very high within the church.

'He means you no harm; he is protecting you,' she said.

'Get rid of him Marg: the heat is ghastly,' I replied, trying to move.

Marg smiled, telling me the man had a message for me and suggested I pass the heat to the people on either side of me. This took a lot of concentration on my part, but I managed to do it and Cathy burst into tears. The group waited in silence. I felt a rush of emotions and then found myself telling my story to a room full of strangers, and how I saw

Barbara's actions as a dreadful betrayal. I spoke for a long time until I was empty.

No-one moved or spoke.

Again a rush of emotions and I began to cry. I looked around at the silent faces. 'I can forgive her now but I know I will never forget,' I said.

A middle-aged woman called Mary spoke. 'Thank you for sharing, Judy.'

'You took the opportunity,' said Eileen. 'You have removed the blockage and you are now free.'

I remembered I had been encouraged by my Guide to speak aloud the words from *The Tibetan Book of Living and Dying*: 'Help me, inspire me to purify all my karma and negative emotions and to realize the true nature of my mind.' This was the energy I had allowed into my being on arriving in Northampton. I returned to Mary's Grotto and, as in Brittany, felt compelled to say, 'Thank you.'

The wildflower I had been guided to place at Mary's feet was the same colour as the gemstone I saw in the Celtic cross during the meditation. As it was being placed in my diary the words 'Celtic cross' and 'gemstone' were highlighted by my Guide. When I updated my notes I was given the understanding that the soul energy of the three soulmates with past-life heart issues was being encouraged in order for them to make their intentions clear:

Soul Energy (1): The Four Core Colours – yellow – blue – green – red – 4 – 12 – Dongara – self help healing centre – The Lady of Good Counsel – retreat – Celtic cross – gemstone.

Next day I took Marg to one side and asked her to describe what she had seen. She told me the spiritual man was tall, with a solid build, wearing a white robe with gold trim. 'He was not a priest,' she said, 'but a man of authority.' She had felt this in his energy as he swung incense in a golden container, creating billowing clouds. 'He stood behind you with an arch of protection. The feeling was that everything would be all right. His message to you was *Follow the path you have chosen and all will be well.*' I was to learn years later that this person was referred to as an 'Ancient' — a holder of the knowledge of one's destiny, from whom one seeks guidance and protection.

I rejoined the final meditation session and as soon as I closed my eyes and heard Marg's voice a human eye formed in front of me. It became two eyes and then a face, then a series of faces, and with each change of face came a different culture, until all the cultures of the Earth presented themselves, both female and male. I came out of the meditation with a start, not sure what to think. To have the cultures of the world present themselves to me was mind-blowing and I felt humbled by the experience.

I was drawn to talk to Norm, a member of the group who was a Reiki healer, and he offered to visit Sovereign Waters to give Mum healing. He was in his seventies, with white hair and a goatee beard. My Guide confirmed this was to be, so I agreed. At home later I was referred to *The Findhorn Garden Story*, where I read: 'Faith comes with practice. Live by Faith until it becomes rocklike and unshakeable, and find the True Freedom of the Spirit.' (5)

Focus on Dongara, my Guide insisted. Mum and I drove to Dongara, where I was guided to buy a postcard of the Royal Steam Roller Flour Mill. At home was the wrapped parcel of the mirror from the Old East End gift shop, with its frame made from original timbers that supported the roof of this mill. I was sent to the second-hand shop to buy a tall brass candleholder. *The Dongara candleholder*, my Guide said.

Cathy started spiritual counselling sessions with Marg to relieve her stress.

The librarian at the Geraldton Library, who we'd met through our catering work, drove to Sovereign Waters simply to hand me an Aboriginal painting on a flat stone of two wild geese, entitled *Birds Flying*, by the Aboriginal artist Duk Duk. My Guide requested that I place it in the nook area where Mum and I relaxed. In my mind I could see the framed Wild Geese / Soul Group print still packed in the garage. *Soulmate on their way*, my Guide warned.

Several days later Cathy tried ringing her children in Gloucester only to discover, with dismay, that their phone had been disconnected. After frantic telephone calls to family, Cathy learnt they were now living in Queensland. Resentment built up in her again.

During this tense time I was encouraged by my Guide to visit a garden nursery to buy a slim white Buddha statue — symbol of the Four Noble Truths — and place it in the nook with Mary's image from Medjugorje; the Dongara candleholder with its red candle; a large amazonite gemstone; a cream candle in a brass holder; my father's silver capsule containing Mary's silver figure; an old Christmas card from England; and shells from the Shell Beach Conservation Park near Shark Bay.

Create a Jappamala, my Guide said. A *Jappamala* was used for prayers by the American Indians and was made with 108 coloured stones. *Dark blue beads*, my Guide insisted. Cathy offered to create this for me. She bought the beads and strung all one hundred and eight together.

An early Christmas card arrived for Mum from Barbara, following Mum breaking the silence between them on Barbara's birthday in mid-September. The first Christmas card in eight years. As with her sisters and their communications, my name was not mentioned. Mum watched me carefully as I opened Barbara's card.

She will come from the British Isles, my Guide warned. I dropped the card. 'If Barbara places one foot on Australian soil I will leave,' I said. 'Sorry, but that is how I feel right now.'

Mum held both my hands until they stopped shaking and then touched my face. 'My dear girl, I understand perfectly.'

I struggled to overcome the emotion of hurt as I picked up the card. 'Barbara would never make such a journey,' I said with confidence.

After the meditation weekend at Northampton Marg asked me to do a pendulum analysis for her, which helped her to work through old hurtful emotions. Following this I was inundated with signatures from her group to such a degree that Cathy suggested I buy a computer.

Mum wanted to send her sisters something different for Christmas, so I ordered huge poinsettias to be delivered. Within hours all three sisters rang to wish Mum (and only Mum) a Happy Christmas. Mum and I attended a champagne breakfast at the Geraldton Art Gallery Christmas Eve, after being given the instruction by my Guide to *celebrate*. On Christmas Day we were up at 6 am to take Jessie for a walk on the beach before opening our gifts and the parcel from the Old East End, Dongara. I hung the mirror in my bedroom. *Focus on Dongara*, my Guide insisted.

On 27 December at 8 am Cathy and I were together at Sovereign Waters, as I had been directed to meditate in the nook while holding the *Jappamala* necklace. The colour royal blue dominated the meditation. A lit red candle was held in the Dongara candleholder, with beside it a lit sandalwood incense stick. The lit cream candle reflected Mary's image and the old Christmas card from England. The sea shells from Shell Beach were placed around the painted stone *Birds Flying* by Duk Duk. My father's silver capsule containing Mary's silver figure was at the base of the amazonite gemstone. I came out of the meditation with my mind filled with information, which Cathy recorded:

Ten Year Mary Project. The symbols represent the following. The incense and red candle: 'See I will not forget you. I have carved you on the palm of my hand.' The Duk Duk birds: Two independent souls doing God's work. Freedom of flight: Flights there will be. Money provided to cater for this. Christmas card: A new child in your life. Christmas means a new child. A lot of contact. She is specially chosen. There is a double meaning for her being in your life. Mary's image: Peace, sincerity, a long life with spirit. You will work closely with her for ten years. You will feel Mary's presence during this time. Amazonite: Truth, clear understanding and solid foundation. You will stand at the foot of a mountain. Number fifty-one: A hard climb with many rests, but the view from the top will be worthwhile. As from the first of January next year spirit's requirements are an older building, much larger and on two levels; a garden with trees and more trees to follow, on a slope; the sea nearby and mice in an outer building; to be a secret location until the month of March. Many people will be drawn there. You, Judy, will see it grow to completion. The end product of your journey. Lots of tables, chairs, writing material, crayons, music and rebirthing. Start now.

'At last the predicted project,' I said with relief. I asked Cathy to draw a long line across the page from left to right, ending in a spearhead. A pain shot through my right leg as Cathy drew the image.

There was no doubt in my mind that I would complete this project from 27 December 1994 through to 27 December 2004. Mum came into the nook and I read the message to her, but before we could discuss its content Norm knocked on the front door. He had come to give Mum her first healing session.

The next day my rental agent came to tell me the owners now wished to sell the property. She assured us she would find another rental home.

On 30 December my Guide insisted I drive Mum and myself to Dongara, but only for four hours. Including as it did a drive north of the township to Seven Mile Beach, this required precise timing. On our return we found a message on our answering machine from the rental agent to say she had found a home in Dolphin Street, available next year. *Yes, this one*, my Guide confirmed.

I was taken to the file that held the notes taken in 1986 when Mum and I were living in South Australia. I had woken in the night after taking photographs of the Old Mill at Middleton with my head full of information, which I wrote down. These notes, along with the Mary Project 1994 notes, were to be shown to Marg. The Ten Year Mary Project 1994 had begun. We met on 3 January 1995, and I read aloud the details I had been given in 1986 regarding a Middleton Mill development and then the Ten Year Mary Project 1994 notes. The vision for Middleton had not been a prefiguration as such of what was now being envisaged for Dongara, but it had brought firmly into my consciousness the notion of being involved in the channelling and development of an Energy Centre.

When I returned home I found that the new manager at the Geraldton Art Gallery had rung to offer me work as a receptionist and a security presence during exhibitions. I accepted this position, thrilled to be part of an atmosphere of such talent and creativity.

On 8 January I was resting in my bedroom at Sovereign Waters when I looked at the clock. It was 2 pm. I became aware of a movement by the window. The luminous shape of a female appeared, standing with her left side towards me. She was wearing a white nun's habit with a high collar. She glided towards me but I could not see her face.

Bending, she spoke into my right ear, 'Around the world,' and then the image faded. The room filled with a deep blue haze and I tried to stay within its energy, but this faded also. I lay there for several minutes trying to grasp that I had seen my Guide.

'To actually see her means everything to me,' I said to Mum later.

'What does her message mean?'

'The answer to your question may be in my notes.'

Around the World 1989: Justice – Sacred Heart – Notre Dame Cathedral – Miraculous Medal – Cistercian monks – monastery – Prince of Wales – Stonehenge – Druid energy – St Michael's Tower – Glastonbury Tor – ley-line – third eye – Mary.

Around the World 1991/1992: Druid energy – chakras – Standing Stone – heart – Mary Grotto – spring of Sainte Barbe – luminous green – Michael the Archangel / Sword of Justice – dolmen – Arthur and Merlin – Sword of Excalibur.

'Maybe your Guide is asking you to draw on all these energies and experiences for what lies ahead,' Mum said.

Mum's seventy-ninth birthday on 27 January was to be extra special. I had bought a garnet necklace while in India alone nine years before and was told *This is for Tess*. Mum smiled when she opened my gift. She told me garnets were her birthstone and her mother had given her a garnet ring for her twenty-first birthday. Mum had lost the ring so this necklace was special. My Grandmother Lilian had come through with my father when I met the medium Dawn Davie in England, and years later in Gloucester through the clairvoyant Bruce, and I sensed she was here again today, enjoying Mum's birthday.

The next day I was taken to a magazine called *Calm* and the words 'Rebuilding the Cathedral'. The words were highlighted by my Guide to be recorded in my notes.

On 3 February another member of Marg's group came into my life: I drove to see Christina Ross following her request for a pendulum analysis. She was in her thirties with long straight brown hair. I liked her immediately, feeling relaxed in her company.

Visit the Blue Mountains, my Guide insisted. Six days later Cathy and I were on a flight to Sydney and collecting a hire car. We were booked to stay in Waratah Cottage, Wentworth Falls. I loved being back in the Blue Mountains, as the gardens were spectacular: so much rain produced so much growth. The next day we drove to meet one of Cathy's sisters, Liz. This was the sister who, three years before, had asked Cathy to hand me the two Mary photographs taken at Medjugorje when Mum and I lived in South Perth. I had met Liz before, and liked her, but soon there was a tense atmosphere between the two sisters and, after spending the night at Waratah Cottage, Liz departed.

My Guide requested Cathy and me to drive to Springwood and attend the Spiritualist church. There was a round basket left at the entrance in which to place jewellery for the circuit medium to hold and relay messages. I put in a silver bracelet Cathy had given me.

'Don't resist,' the medium said, when she held my bracelet. 'An opportunity has come and you are resisting; the opportunity will come again. You must change your nationality.'

This indicated that I would eventually become an Australian citizen; the legal situation in England with regard to me suing my former solicitor must have been drawing to a conclusion.

Before leaving Western Australia my Guide had requested that we contact World Vision in Perth, but the organiser, Michael, was abroad. When we returned to the cottage there was a message to say he would be meeting us at Perth airport on our return.

The following evening I was guided to light a candle and note a message:

A big trust issue is coming up, that you are to go with. Guidance will be precise, clear and very long lasting. Look now at the day and date.

The next day would be 14 February — the same date I had been sent by my Guide to meet Cathy, six years before, in Gloucester. This time I was directed to drive us to Glenbrook in the Blue Mountains, taking six matches, a rose quartz, a white candle and a leaf from a red-flowering plant. I parked the car. *Walk for one and half hours,* my Guide said.

We followed the pathway, winding its way through the undergrowth. Rain was falling; there was an atmosphere of fresh air, water and vibrant green. After an hour and half, we arrived at 'Red Hand Aboriginal Cave'. As soon as I saw the sign, a sharp pain shot through my right leg once again and I fell forward, just managing to hold on to a tree. This was of course the pain that had come in the Mootwingee National Park in 1987, before Mum and I walked near Aboriginal paintings, and again one year later on our arrival in Gloucester. In February the following year I had been sent to meet Cathy at a tapestry morning. The pain had come again following the recent channelling of the Ten Year Mary Project 1994.

My Guide requested me to light the white candle and place the rose quartz at its base on the red leaf of the red-flowering plant. I used only the one match to light the candle, and smoke filled the cave as I repeated the Celtic prayer out loud: 'I ask only what you want of me, the power, wisdom, cosmic love and energy in order to be able to achieve those things.' I was conscious of starting yet another journey back in time when a rush of energy moved through me from the ground as another doorway to the past was opened. Cathy and I had a past-life link involving Ancient Egypt, and I was being made aware that we had a past-life Aboriginal issue. As we walked back I wondered about the five matches left in the cave. *Five good years, last year not so good,* my Guide said.

The next day Cathy's parents arrived late afternoon, and things became tense when her mother mentioned her children. Four days later her two sisters joined us for the day. When the family were together the tension increased, with embarrassing silences.

Zig Zag Railway, my Guide said, so I drove there. The station shop had a stand for postcards. *Look at row three,* my Guide requested. On its own was a postcard of a kookaburra, with the heading, 'Australian Citizen'.

'This is really going to happen. I am going to change nationality,' I said to myself.

That evening my Guide insisted Cathy and I attend the Springwood Spiritualist church, regardless of the fact that her parents were still with us. A sense of urgency came as I put an aquamarine gemstone into the basket. The medium selected my gemstone. 'No smoke without fire,' she said. 'A lot of talk is going on about you. Someone is appearing to give out love and caring, but in fact is saying bad things about you in the background.' When I lit the candle in the Red Hand Aboriginal Cave it had filled with smoke.

Cathy became uncomfortable, moving around in her chair. 'There are twins around you,' the medium said. 'These boys will stand either side of you for a photograph and you will give a special kiss on the cheek for just one. There are lots of changes in the next few months. There is a wheelbarrow with a special link to the past. You will work long hours soon.'

When Cathy and I flew back to Perth, Michael from World Vision was waiting at the airport and took us to his office to speak about a campaign in Geraldton. That evening in our hotel, my Guide requested I light a candle and write down the letters M.A.R.Y. An explanation followed:

> M – *Many months work with World Vision.*
> A – *April campaign.*
> R – *Reasons will create success.*
> Y – *Your future lies within this organisation.*
> *Marg Parker will be a major player in your life.*
> *Leave the month of March clear.*

On my return to Geraldton I was overwhelmed with requests for the pendulum analyses, and Cathy became impatient when typing them into the computer for me. I was uncomfortable being near her since the warning in Springwood. She decided to spend more time with Marg. The atmosphere between us had changed since our visit to the Red Hand Aboriginal Cave, with Cathy seeking any opportunity to create arguments.

During the first week of March Cathy and I were invited to Perth by World Vision and Michael took us out to lunch. We decided to meet at the start of April to discuss a campaign, confirming my Guide's message, *A – April campaign.* Later, in our Perth hotel room during my meditation, the colour blue featured.

Go to Busselton, my Guide said. We drove the 220 kilometres south to Busselton and were guided to St Mary's Church — the oldest Anglican stone church in Western Australia. Inside on the right I discovered, to my astonishment, a leadlight window depicting Mother Mary wearing a cloak the same blue colour that had appeared during my meditation. Beside her was Mary Magdalene wearing gold. Outside the church I was led to a tombstone upon which was engraved 'In Thy light shall we see light'.

On my forty-ninth birthday, in March, the post brought yet another offer from the solicitor in England. *Accept the offer*, my Guide said. Nine years to the day, the legal entanglement in England was resolved, and I stood patiently in the post office waiting as my acceptance was faxed back to England. *Apply for citizenship*, my Guide insisted. I collected the necessary papers before driving home.

Marg asked Cathy and me to go with her to visit Yilgarn Permaculture Farm just outside Geraldton. We spent time with the owner, Julie Firth, a New Zealander. She was slim, in her early thirties, full of life and enthusiasm. I listened as she walked around her self-supporting farm, sensing that the concept meant everything to her. *New partnership*, my Guide said.

Michael rang from World Vision regarding a project for Zambia and explained his idea to sponsor forty children in one village. I soon discovered how much time and effort this sort of project involved. Cathy helped, along with many volunteers.

At the beginning of April we moved to Dolphin Street and a two-storey rental home. *Celestial Dolphin Centre*, my Guide said. She requested that I create a meditation room on the ground floor, and days later I stood inside the room waiting, until I was taken to a framed postcard of Stonehenge that hung on the wall. In 1989 I had stood and watched the sunset at Stonehenge and received the words *Remember this moment*. I went to leave the room but was held fast until I re-lived the memory of Stonehenge in my mind. *Druid energy*, my Guide said.

Later, she highlighted my dolphin necklace and seven-dolphin bracelet. That night I had a terrifying dream of a huge shark's fin moving towards me through clear blue water. I referred to a dream book and read 'Shark — danger, dishonesty'. *Shark amongst the dolphins*, my Guide warned. *Celestial Dolphin Centre*, she repeated.

Who are the Celestial Dolphins? I wondered. But, more importantly, who is the shark amongst the dolphins?

I registered the Celestial Dolphin Centre as a small business. *The heart's journey*, my Guide said, and instructed that the notes regarding the three soulmates with past-life heart issues be updated with this latest clue.

When the Celestial Dolphin Centre business certificate arrived in the post, I was sent by my Guide into the meditation room carrying the certificate to the framed print of St Michael's and All Angels Church, Cornwood, England. During the Second World War, families were moved inland away from the ports and coastal areas for their safety. I was born after the war in, 1946, in this Dartmoor village, in the nursery wing of the local manor — Delamore House — and christened in that church. The print was to be hung at the entrance to the Celestial Dolphin Centre. *Druid energy*, my Guide said. The information underneath the drawing of the church was highlighted:

> The parish of Cornwood was largely classified as wasteland in the Domesday Survey, it was then colonised by free peasants in the 12th and 13th centuries. The parish contains dozens of prehistoric hut circles, several Bronze Age burial mounds and the longest known stone in the world. The church itself dates from the 14th century.

I was being reminded that I was born and christened within this ancient parish.

When I was in Brittany, Rene Vaillant had described Druids as being priests, people of ancient Europe, judges and lawmakers, who led religious ceremonies and settled legal disputes. The Druids of Brittany, he said, had come from Atlantis, one of three groups to escape before the island sank: one to Mexico, one to Egypt and one to Brittany.

The words 'Druid energy' and 'settled legal disputes' were highlighted by my Guide, and the soul energy within which the three soulmates with past-life heart issues were being encouraged to identify themselves was updated. With 'disputes' being highlighted, I understood that, having settled the legal dispute surrounding the Old Saddlery, I was headed for another:

> Soul Energy (1): The Four Core Colours – yellow – blue – green – red – 4 – 12 – Dongara – self help healing centre – The Lady of Good

Counsel – retreat – Celtic cross – gemstone – Druid energy – settled legal disputes.

At the end of April Cathy and I were directed to drive to Wooleen Station, north of Geraldton. The approaching dirt roads were very rough, as was our accommodation in the shearers' quarters. We spent a sleepless night under our mosquito nets, listening to the determined creatures buzzing around outside trying to force their way in. The next morning we were instructed to take a three-hour four-wheel-drive tour, stopping at various Aboriginal cave sites. One featured a Rainbow Serpent incised into the rock, and my Guide requested I take a photograph to capture its image. The painting was an arch, similar to a horseshoe, with a small open square at the top and small circles at each end. In the car I was carrying the book *Dreamtime Heritage: Australian Aboriginal Myths* by A. Roberts and M.J. Roberts:

> In the mythology of the Australian Aborigines, the most widespread of their beliefs was in the existence of a huge serpent which lived in water holes, swamps and lakes … In some myths, Rainbow-serpents appear as Ancestral Creators. Their bodies contained not only the first Aboriginals, but all the natural features … the Rainbow-serpent was an awesome creature of power and importance. (7)

We were exhausted when we returned to the shearers' quarters. I watched from a distance and felt a sense of concern as Cathy wandered off to sit in the centre of a dry river bed. She had been withdrawn all day, standing apart from me and the tour guide.

That evening we sat by an open fire, gazing up at the Milky Way. I became lost in its vastness. Then I came out of my relaxed state with a jolt. *Rainbow Serpent, power, importance, Aboriginal link*, my Guide had warned. My mind went reeling back to our recent trip to the Blue Mountains: the Red Hand Aboriginal Cave filling with smoke, and later the medium warning me of someone appearing to give out love but in fact saying bad things about me. I had opened the doorway to an Aboriginal past life with Cathy on exactly the same date six years after being guided to meet her in Gloucester. Today we had been sent to another Aboriginal site and we had both touched the Rainbow Serpent, an awesome creature of power and importance. *Conflict*, my Guide warned. These clues were added to notes on Cathy and her past-life heart issue:

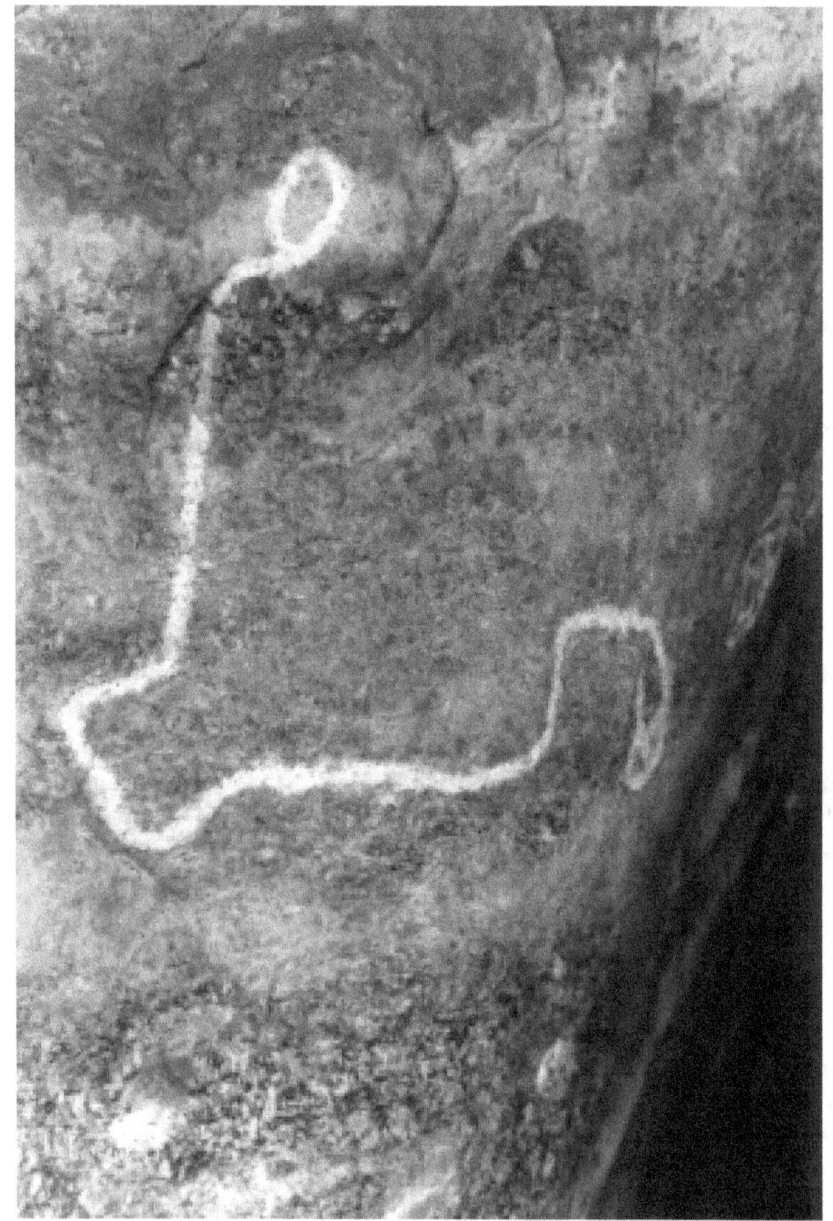

Aboriginal cave painting, Wooleen Station, Western Australia

Heart Issue: Cathy – soulmate – legal action – Findhorn – the transfer of deeds – my lifelong companion – Dongara – Egypt/ankh – karma / past life – heart's journey – Rainbow Serpent – power – importance – Aboriginal link – conflict.

On the last day of May the compensation draft regarding the case against my solicitor in England arrived. I had recovered a fraction of my losses from nine years before. The $30,000 was deposited with the building society in Geraldton. In the same post was a letter advising me that my application for Australian citizenship had been accepted and the ceremony was due to be held at Greenough on 6 June. When I held the legal documents I recalled how I felt during my visit to the Port Arthur Penal Colony in Tasmania in 1976. Standing on the cliff edge and being drawn to jump, I had stepped back quickly. Pat's past-life reading in Ashburton years later had provided the explanation. Although innocent, I had been deported from England as a boy for stealing money in the 19th century and committed suicide. Today I had received compensation from England and a future as an Australian citizen. *These matters have been put to rest*, my Guide confirmed.

Three days later Cathy and I were encouraged to drive to Dongara, where I parked the car and walked straight into Roy Weston Real Estate Agency. John, the agent, offered us both chairs. He asked what he could do for me and there was a long, embarrassed pause while I waited for my Guide's response to come. 'I am looking for a property to buy,' I told him, then sat back in shock. Cathy looked at me in bewilderment when John turned to his filing cabinet and then placed a file on his desk. *Buy the third one*, my Guide insisted.

John drove us to a unit by the sea and a home in the township itself, then towards a property north of the flour mill. As we drove past the mill I knew I was to buy the next place we viewed. We entered the six-acre property via a dirt road and parked in front of a three-bay tractor shed as high as a two-storey building. We followed John down a gravel pathway to a shed, then through a small gate surrounded by tall shrubs to a large home. I felt nervous and excited as we walked through a covered outdoor area to a wide glass sliding door. A young, slim woman came out to greet us. 'Hello, Anne, can we come in?' John asked. My heart missed a beat: I had just settled a dispute involving that name.

The house was spacious, with a large sitting room and enclosed wood fire, four bedrooms, a roomy kitchen with walk-in pantry, a laundry and a bathroom. There were corridors with high ceilings and half-wall jarrah panels, and wide verandas at the back and on one side. The land itself was a mass of high grass, wild turnips and lupins. Tuart trees lined the dirt road and grew by the house. The sea was nearby at Port Denison, and without doubt there would be mice in the tractor shed.

'The Ten Year Mary Project,' I said to Cathy. *Yes*, my Guide said.

On 4 June the manager of the building society came to Dolphin Street to take me through a mortgage application. I had the deposit, so put in an offer. But I was not earning enough. Only with a joint application with Cathy could I purchase it, but I did not want a joint title and said so. I began to feel nervous when Cathy and I argued later. She was adamant she wanted to commit and be a part of the Mary Project 1994.

Mum wanted to use her capital, but my instructions were firm. I read the message I had brought through in the Blue Mountains to her: 'A big trust issue is coming up, that you are to go with. Guidance will be precise, clear and very long lasting.'

Neither of us wanted to be involved financially with Cathy, but I was being given no alternative by my Guide. The joint application was processed. My insides filled with dread.

Our offer was accepted and I drove Mum to the property. She didn't like it. 'Too wild and too far out of town,' she complained. This was indeed a big trust issue.

We drove to Greenough for my Citizenship Ceremony on 6 June. When I swore the Australian Citizen Pledge I looked at Mum and became emotional. It was a moving moment when I saw a combination of love and pride in her eyes. She was the only person I wanted with me on this special day. I was handed my certificate and a bunch of Australian native flowers and we left walking arm-in-arm back to the car.

The building society rang to say the mortgage application was approved. I paid the deposit, using all the compensation settlement. The property was to be known as the Celestial Dolphin Centre and the house as Iona Lodge. Cathy had been photographed in front of an Iona sign near the Blue Mountains six years before. I knew then that Iona, Cathy, dolphins and I were linked, as was the regal young woman in my dream. Excitement replaced apprehension when I accepted that the property required by spirit in order for me to complete the Ten Year Mary Project had been purchased.

Rebuilding the cathedral, my Guide said. This message had first come on 28 January, when I had been sent to a *Calm* magazine to read these words and record them. How do I rebuild a cathedral, and why? I wondered. *French connection*, my Guide replied.

I was encouraged to update the notes regarding the required soul energy, to enable the three soulmates with past-life heart issues to make their issues known.

Focus on Dongara, my Guide said. I resigned as coordinator for World Vision.

Mum asked me to organise for her to see a solicitor, as she wished to amend her will. In the solicitor's office she produced her former will and requested that Barbara be included. She being a daughter, Mum now wished to bequeath her a string of pearls that had been given to her by Daddy. Marg and her husband witnessed the document later.

We discussed the building of a self-contained extension for Mum, using her capital, on the same day that an offer was made on our duplex and we agreed to sell. We approached builders in Dongara for quotes, and Mum's mind became full of ideas for her needs. To protect her I arranged for a legal document to be drawn up, keeping her capital separate from my joint title with Cathy and our mortgage.

On 7 July, settlement day, the Celestial Dolphin Centre in Dongara came into being. Cathy was planning workshops while I was guided to make an 'Iona Lodge' sign with 'Highland Green' background and black Celtic lettering.

Six days later my Guide instructed me to take the Dongara brass candle-holder to Iona Lodge and place it at the centre of the large oval English oak table in the kitchen, its white candle to be lit whenever I visited the property. The lodge filled with the atmosphere of teamwork, with Mum cooking our meals, Cathy making curtains for each room and me painting the kitchen, bathroom and hallways. Norm visited and offered his services as a handyman.

On 18 July my Guide directed that Mary's image be taken to Iona Lodge and placed by the lit Dongara candle, her face reflecting the bright orange in its flame. This date was *familiar*, but I was unable to bring this knowing to my conscious mind. I was encouraged to return to the lodge towing a trailer filled with boxes and the packed turtle picture given to me by Cathy two years before. As I unpacked what was to be the first picture to be hung inside Iona Lodge, I marvelled at the breathtaking beauty of the leather-carved turtle, but when I read the title *The Chase*, I became breathless, as if running, so much so that I had to sit. My Guide insisted I hang the picture in the sitting room and

Cathy's clues regarding her past-life heart issue were updated to include the clue 'The Chase'.

The heavy Old Saddlery legal file had been sealed, the legal situation had been resolved, but the emotional impact within the family was yet to be healed. The hurt was still there and the family divided; only the revealing of the truth would resolve this now silent conflict.

Three days later I was alone at the property, having lit the Dongara candle by Mary's image. I walked into the eastern paddock with the completed Iona Lodge sign and felt compelled to hold it aloft towards the rising sun. I looked down at the acres and acres of dense undergrowth and became overwhelmed, then distressed. 'Nine years of my life waiting for this!' I shouted out to the universe.

The next day was the Opening Day Ceremony of Iona Lodge. I watched with fascination as Christina and Norm, working together, attached the Iona Lodge sign to star pickets. At 4 pm they carried the sign down the eastern paddock towards the Brand Highway, walking a pathway I had cleared earlier through the dense growth. Six of us followed. I dowsed to discover where the sign must be erected; then seven of us (Norm, Christina, Marg, Cathy, Audrey, Mum and I) were photographed, standing behind the now-erected Iona Lodge sign, by a young woman from Dongara called Terri.

Celtic Seven, my Guide said. Marg was the one who had brought us together. Norm, Audrey and Christina were part of her meditation group, which Cathy and I had joined. Mum had become involved through Norm and his healing sessions, and Christina and Audrey were now friends and very caring of Mum and me.

Inside the lodge I set out goblets of wine on the oak table by Mary's image and lit the Dongara candle. The atmosphere was of excitement and great achievement. Then a connection I hadn't seen before hit me: the Iona Lodge sign was painted Highland Green and Iona is in Scotland. Norm raised his goblet. 'To Iona,' he shouted, with much gusto.

'To Iona,' we responded.

Past lives, karma clearing, my Guide warned.

Norm produced a bouquet of tiny pink rosebuds and handed them to Mum. The *familiarity* of the moment was so overpowering I left the room to contemplate the seven of us having been monks together on the island monastery of Iona. I recalled also that Cathy and I had been sent to the Iona Sanctuary near the Blue Mountains for me to take a photograph of her standing by its sign. Today a photograph was taken by another Iona sign. *Another past-life image captured*, my Guide explained. I updated my notes detailing a second emerging soul-energy influence:

Soul Energy (2): Celtic Seven – pink rose energy – past lives / karma clearing.

In 1989 Cathy and I had walked in the footsteps of the Cistercian monks, commencing in Wales with the 800-year-old ruined monastery, then sheltering by St Michael's Tower on top of Glastonbury Tor, where Cathy saw the image of a monk. In Germany we had visited Maulbronn Monastery, built by Cistercian monks, and then driven near the Basilica of Birnau, a Cistercian Priory. Later, Dianne in England had ensured we understood the meaning of 'Iona' by taking us to Holy Island and the Lindisfarne Priory founded in 635 by St Aidan, who had sailed there from the island monastery of Iona. I now understood why there was an overpowering feeling of *familiarity* as the Celtic Seven stood together around the oak table. When Norm raised his goblet and shouted, 'To Iona' and we all responded to his call, we had acknowledged our past-life connection.

Our time as monks together was obviously a time of teamwork and achievement. But the fact that we were referred to as the Celtic Seven, and my Guide's warning regarding past-life karma clearing, indicated that a doorway to our distant past had been opened. When Cathy and I spent time with Rene in Brittany, he had explained that in Druid times the one with the highest angstrom measurement was the group leader. There were seven in a group, and if one more person joined the group the leader would have to move on to form another group. I touched my bracelet of seven dolphins and then the dolphin at my throat realising there had been eight of us walking with the Iona Lodge sign earlier in the day, the eighth one being a stranger to the group.

Norm donated a second-hand lawnmower and I mowed the grass from the main entrance through to the tractor shed and then the lodge itself. In the meantime, finding a builder for Mum's self-contained extension was proving to be a frustrating task. *The lodge*, my Guide insisted, *was not to be disturbed*, and this was the dilemma.

I was hanging the Wild Geese / Soul Group print, with its five flying geese, when Christina rang offering me five live geese. This was the beginning of a friendship in which we would communicate telepathically at times. *Blue Celestial Dolphin*, my Guide said. I had wondered who the Celestial Dolphins were, and this new information from my Guide not only identified Christina as being a Celestial Dolphin but attached a colour to the title. It also revealed a link between Christina and the Celtic Seven.

On 29 July we held a workshop at Iona lodge: 'Earth Changes / Mind Changes'. A good number attended, and the sitting room proved an ideal location.

Shortly after, a young man called Terry came into our lives. He was a carpenter, and he built a double robe in one of the bedrooms. My Guide had instructed us to move to Dongara on 4 August and we needed storage space. Cathy continued to work at the mining company and I continued to work at the Geraldton Art Gallery.

Days after the move, I was standing alone in the eastern paddock when I became filled with rage. The feelings were not mine. I spoke the angry words out loud, 'Go on and leave me.' I was trying to cope when a young man drove in through the main entrance. He walked straight up to me, asking if I was all right. I was taken by surprise, and before I could answer he spoke again.

'Anne was not happy here,' he said. He had spent time with the previous owners. I tried talking to Cathy about this later, but she quickly changed the subject. She had a solution to the building of Mum's extension and suggested it could be added to the other side of the breezeway. The breezeway was a covered outdoor seating area attached to the lodge next to the double shed. The extension could be built around the double shed, turning it into an independent room and leaving the lodge untouched. Mum was happy with the idea. An architect drew up plans for the local council, and it gave the go-ahead for Cathy and me to become owner builders. Meanwhile, Mum was made comfortable in the bedroom on the north side of the lodge. This large room accommodated her double bed and furniture, creating a spacious bedsitter.

Early one morning I went to see Mum and found her sitting on her couch. As I stood in the doorway she startled me by staring with wide eyes. She explained that a jagged bolt of luminous green light — *like lightning* — had appeared above my head, passed through my body and gone out the side windows. 'The effect was a gentle, jagged ray of colour,' she said.

Green Celestial Dolphin, my Guide said. Two Celestial Dolphins had now been identified: Christina and I. The Four Core Colours symbol was placed in my bedroom on display, my Guide indicating there was a link between its four colours of yellow, blue, green and red and the Celestial Dolphins.

Create a guest bedroom, my Guide urged. Then the phone rang. It was Bev Cox, the former manager of the Geraldton Regional Art Gallery, wanting to stay and attend the next workshop. She arrived on the day before it started. Marg was the speaker, and gave all who attended a healing. She told me she saw power coming from my navel and heart chakras more than she had seen before.

'There is a type of casing all around you,' Marg said. 'You are operating on a different vibrational level to the rest of us.'

Following the workshop, Bev gave me a gift of a Double Dolphin candle-holder made from bronze, and I was guided to unpack the heart-shaped jarrah piece I had purchased in Balingup a year before. I put it on the oak table with the candle-holder in its centre, Mary's image having been moved prior to our first workshop.

Cathy's sister Liz rang. She was planning to fly over to Perth in the near future and asked to stay with us.

My Guide encouraged me to walk in the eastern paddock with its feeling of rage. I tried speaking to Cathy later, but she would not discuss it. The tension between us increased further when a young woman from Dongara rang Cathy regarding a pendulum analysis. Cathy was not the one who had brought through the analyses, and when the woman arrived I waited to see what would happen. The situation was embarrassing for everyone.

Later Cathy told me the workshops were too much for her to organise. 'This is a ten-year project and we have only been here a few weeks,' I said. Cathy shrugged her shoulders and walked away, but I followed her. 'What is really going on Cathy?' I asked. Again she shrugged her shoulders and walked on.

On 22 August I received the first instruction regarding the eastern paddock. I was sent out with the second-hand lawnmower to stand between two horsetail sheoak trees with the engine running. In front of me were high grass and wild turnips. Then we were off — I followed the machine as it carved its way towards the double row of six tuart trees. The lawnmower came to a halt by the Iona Lodge sign. It was a strenuous experience, but a narrow pathway had been cut following the route walked by the Celtic Seven and the stranger a month before, 22 July. *Pathway to the past*, my Guide said.

Days later I was sent to the double row of six tuart trees to cut a pathway through their centre — another difficult task, which took days. *The Tuart Walk*, my Guide said.

Mum was drawn to an article in *The West Australian* dated 11 August entitled 'No worries with sporty ash' by John Banks. It described a batch of Australian desert ash trees that had 'sported' during propagation in 1910: instead of fading to butter yellow, their leaves turned deep red in the autumn. The name for the new variety became claret ash, and this particular tree was to be the first we would plant. It was exciting when it arrived, and I dowsed for its planting position and began to dig. Cathy said it must be planted elsewhere. At first I thought she was joking, but she wasn't. Mum remained quiet as I carried on digging the hole. Cathy walked away angry, but the tension did not destroy my pleasure in planting the tree between the tractor shed and the main entrance.

'What is wrong with her?' I said to Mum. Before she could comment we were distracted by a pair of nankeen kestrels, flying low and calling out. They spent time in the tractor shed during the day and rested in the tuart trees at night. Each morning I watched as they absorbed the first rays of the rising sun flooding the tractor shed.

Terry, our carpenter, came forward with a plan: He would team up with a friend and build Mum's extension. He soon set about organising tradesmen for a quote and early in September we shook hands on the agreement. I asked him if he knew anyone who could help me move nine concrete pavers within twenty-four hours. A wiry, middle-aged man appeared in the breezeway and announced he was here to help. We created a square according to my Guide's instructions under the tuart trees within the lodge garden itself.

I was up early and waiting on 14 September when Terry drove in, ready to work. The thought of building Mum's extension was thrilling, but within hours we came up against a problem. A limestone reef ran throughout the district and a section of it was at ground level where we planned to build. A digger was required to shift the limestone.

Three days later in the middle of the night I was forcibly shaken awake. I dressed and walked to the main entrance and waited in the darkness. My Guide requested me to take ten strides towards the claret ash and mark a small 'x' on the ground with my right boot. *Standing Stone*, my Guide said. How on earth am I going to find a Standing Stone? I wondered.

I returned to bed and slept until woken by Terry's arrival. We did not speak as he went to the bobcat inside Mum's building site and began to dig. My Guide insisted I walk to the main entrance and wait. Minutes later Terry drove out of the site with a large stone inside the bobcat's bucket and came towards me.

'Where do you want this Standing Stone?' he shouted. I stared back at him in disbelief. He in turn shook his head in bewilderment at what he had said. *Do not interfere*, my Guide warned. I shrugged my shoulders, indicating I had no opinion, leaving it with him.

Terry drove closer and then stopped near where I had drawn the 'x' during the night. I watched with fascination and wonder as he manoeuvred the heavy stone upright, placing it above the faint 'x' using the bobcat's bucket for support. He walked around the stone until satisfied and climbed back into the bobcat and drove back to the building site. I was reminded by my Guide that it was 18 September and five years to the day since Cathy and I had landed in France and were later taken to a Standing Stone in Brittany. Now I had a Standing Stone at the Celestial Dolphin Centre in Dongara.

'That was amazing,' I said. *Druid energy*, my Guide replied.

'Timing and dates are everything to my Guide,' I said to Mum later.

'Then you must never be distracted or allow any distractions.'

My thoughts were turned back to the Celtic Seven. We had been in harmony when we erected the Iona Lodge sign, but the time of the Celts had been Bronze Age through to about 450 AD, earlier than 635 AD, when St Aidan left Iona to establish a community of monks at Lindisfarne.

I now felt resentment coming from within Cathy, which had revealed itself after the lighting of the white candle in the bronze Double Dolphin candle-holder. I was encouraged to read the notes I'd made regarding Dolphin Street when I registered the Celestial Dolphin Centre as a business and the clue 'heart's journey' was added to the notes of all three soulmates with past-life heart issues. I was being warned that the revealing of Cathy's past-life heart issue was on schedule. The precise placement of the claret ash and Standing Stone were all part of the Heart's Journey.

Cathy had been relaxed in Brittany until 20 September, when Rene had measured my spiritual energy. He said most people were below 8,000 Angstroms, mine was 46,000 and rising. Cathy had asked him to measure hers. He told her it was 26,000, which was high, but when I smiled at her, she had looked away. From then on Cathy had sought to separate herself, but seemed driven to follow Mum and me after every move.

Standing Stone, Celestial Dolphin Centre, Dongara

Mum was fascinated when I showed her the Standing Stone. 'It has an unusual shape,' she commented. 'Can I touch it?'

'Of course, and when you feel upset about Barbara or anything, just walk to this stone and you will know where to place your hands for comfort and healing.'

I told her it was five years to the day since Rene had taken me to a Standing Stone in Brittany and I had felt drawn to touch the area for the heart, our feeling centre. *French connection*, my Guide said. *Now you must encourage the release of its healing energy*. Mum and I walked — then we danced around the Standing Stone seven times clockwise, laughing and enjoying the moment. Terry and his fellow workers watched in amusement.

'My Guide has amazing timing,' I said.

'Her timing is only made possible because you trust her guidance.' *We are one*, my Guide confirmed.

We were distracted by a discussion between our plumber and the council engineer over the two long leach drains for Mum's extension. The engineer insisted they should go across the eastern paddock. *Stop this*, my Guide urged. I negotiated a compromise with him. The leach drains would run along the fence on the northern boundary.

In mid-October Cathy's sister Liz arrived and helped me move Mum into her new extension. Liz created a garden for her and worked in the lodge garden. I thanked her for sending me, through Cathy, the two photographs taken of Mary at Medjugorje.

During the night of 20 October I heard a humming noise and went out onto the veranda that faced east, overlooking the eastern paddock. The sky was different, with a mass of stars to my left. I called to Liz and Cathy to join me on the veranda. A huge glow of yellow light formed in the centre of the horizon, then two smaller yellow glows side by side. One of the smaller glows faded, appearing minutes later by the Tuart Walk, to our right. Our attention was drawn back to the mass of stars on our left when one bright star began to flash and change colour while moving around the sky in small circles. It changed its colour from red to green, then green to red again. On our right came another star just as bright. It also moved in circles and changed colour, but from red to blue and blue to red. Both the stars moved into formation with other stars to form two triangles. The second triangle faded in a burst of orange. Then the first triangle faded in a similar burst of colour.

The Mary Display, my Guide explained.

'The Mary Display,' I repeated aloud.

'I have heard about this,' Liz said.

'My God,' I said, 'that was the Four Core Colours.' I rushed inside and returned with the Four Core Colours symbol. 'I channelled this in Gloucester five years ago.'

Sealed on the back was the modern version of the Lord's Prayer written by Cathy: 'Forgive us the wrongs we have done as we forgive the wrongs others have done to us.' The eight-sided symbol held the colours of green, blue, red and yellow. I walked to the eastern end of the Tuart Walk in the darkness, wondering at its significance, as this was where a yellow glow had appeared after moving from its position, highlighting this area.

Liz helped the plumber and me carry the huge jarrah table used during our work for catering contracts into Mum's former bed-sitting room. It was a massive effort to manoeuvre it from the garage in Mum's extension to the lodge and through the bedroom's French doors. The Butterfly Circle was again placed under Mum's bed.

Two days went by; then I was guided to write down a message for Mum: *Ten years is a long time, the beginning was most painful.*

Three more days passed. On 26 October, ten years to the day since we were with Barbara in Mum's apartment in Torquay before flying to Australia, a letter arrived for Mum from Barbara. It contained only family news; there was no enquiry as to the wellbeing of either Mum or myself. *Ten years of a cycle completed*, my Guide said.

The Butterfly Circle under Mum's bed had been completed on the morning of my fortieth birthday with the addition of the fortieth shell. Within days Mum and I had discovered Barbara's actions regarding the sale of the Old Saddlery. How many more years were held in this cycle between the three of us before its completion? I wondered.

I resigned from my employment with the Geraldton Regional Art Gallery in late October. Before leaving I was drawn to a book in the gallery shop, in which I found the drawing of a Judicial Druid and understood it was to be photocopied twelve times. The number 12 had featured in October 1990 with the creation of the Four Core Colours, and was now being highlighted five years later. These Druids settled legal disputes, and I felt a moment of apprehension as I later filed the photocopies at the lodge.

While working at the Art Gallery I had been guided to buy an original watercolour titled *Dolphin Dreaming*, by Tracey J Taylor. The painting featured three dolphins swimming in the same direction. I thought it was to be an eightieth birthday present for Mum in January, but instead I hung it in the newly converted meditation room, and Taylor's name was highlighted. The sitting room had originally functioned as a workshop area but was now the meditation room. Huge cushions were scattered around in front of the log fire and two Indian cloths hung along one wall, creating a unique atmosphere.

By November I was so concerned over Cathy's attitude that I asked her to tell me what was going on, as I could no longer cope with the undercurrents. Cathy was adamant it was her family, but I did not believe her. In contrast, Mum's extension was completed mid-November with the installation of rainwater tanks. She loved its open plan and expressed her happiness with living at the centre and being part of the Mary Project 1994.

On 21 December I was shaken awake and directed outside into the darkness, to the area between Mum's extension and the tractor shed, and told to dig with a spade. I uncovered a large natural pond-like formation within the solid limestone reef with a seat formation at its centre. *Crystal pool*, my Guide explained.

Regardless of the fact that I had been digging and was tired, I was instructed to write a letter to the Findhorn Community in Scotland, announcing the existence of the Celestial Dolphin Centre in Western Australia, describing it as 'a centre which encourages new awareness through ancient wisdom and energies.' Why Findhorn? I wondered.

With the dawning of 1996 I started planning the celebrations for Mum's eightieth birthday, 27 January. On 10 January an early pink birthday envelope arrived for Mum from Barbara. Again, the number ten featured between them. In August 1985, while living in Ashburton, I had bought *A Dictionary of Symbols* by Tom Chetwynd. I was referred to this book by my Guide and asked to read one line:

Ten – The end of one cycle begins another. (8)

Was I being warned there would be ten years to wait before the resolution of issues between Barbara and Mum — which had started our journey? Mum would be ninety.

Post came from Rene Vaillant in Brittany with information concerning Jesus. He felt I had to know that Jesus was born in the spring. This was the second time he'd felt compelled to tell me Jesus was not born on 25 December. *French connection*, my Guide said.

Claire, a woman who I had met briefly, agreed to hold a workshop at the centre. She was in her early fifties with short black hair, and had spent eighteen months working at Findhorn in Scotland. She suggested 2 March for her Findhorn Workshop, which was the month mentioned in the Mary Project 1994 channelled message.

More birthday cards arrived for Mum, and I really enjoyed the build-up, secretly planning a party with live music, friends, good food, great wine and a magnificent cake. Gifts began to arrive from friends and family overseas, and I hid them. Cathy was taking my car to Geraldton to work, so I was forced to walk to and from Dongara along the Brand Highway to collect our mail. Two days before the big event, words repeated in my mind during this walk, *Pink roses for the Lady of Iona*. Norm arrived later with another bouquet of pink rosebuds for Mum, and I watched with fascination as he handed them to her, saying 'For the Lady of Iona'.

On the morning of Mum's eightieth birthday her phone rang on and off for hours. Her three sisters rang, then John — the father of her grandchildren — and friends from overseas. Then Barbara rang: this was her birthday gift, she said. She told Mum she was planning to visit Australia. Once I recovered from the initial shock I reasoned with myself that maybe Barbara was travelling all this way to bring peace back into the family and we would not have to wait another ten years after all.

The party was a great success. 'That was the most remarkable day — thank you,' Mum said. We sat in the meditation room after everyone had left. 'How do you feel about Barbara's news?' she asked.

'First shock, but my Guide did warn me she would be coming over.' I looked across at her. 'Hopefully, she wishes to make amends.'

The next day apprehension began building inside me, so I went to the Tuart Walk in the eastern paddock. I did this when I felt disturbed. As I walked I understood that the emotion was about Cathy. I sensed she was about to make an announcement, and on 4 February she dropped her bombshell. She spoke to Mum first, indicating she wanted to leave for a few months — to find herself. I was concerned, as she hated living alone. I rang someone with a flat for rent in Geraldton. The next concern was the car, but she said I must keep it; she would be able to get to work from her new home. When I asked what her true reason was for leaving, she replied, 'Spirit is guiding me to do this.' I accepted her explanation with a sense of unease. The evening prior to Cathy's departure I asked her again her reason for leaving. She looked at me and said, 'To find myself'.

The next day I drove her to her new home. On my return to the centre the phone was ringing. It was Selva, a clairvoyant, who had visited many times. 'Has she gone?' she said. I was stunned.

'Yes, but how did you know? She only left this morning.'

'My Guide says you must be told that Cathy is misleading you,' she said.

'If that is true then I require proof.'

At sunrise the next day I walked to the eastern paddock with Jessie at my heels, as usual, but felt compelled to shout out to the universe, 'Spirit, shine on this place and give it life.' My Guide encouraged me to return to the lodge and remove Cathy's belongings, packing everything into boxes and placing them in the now enclosed shed.

'If Cathy is planning to return, why do I have to do this?' My Guide responded by asking me to unpack the Aboriginal spear given to me by an elder when I spent time on a reserve in South Australia in May 1979. I took it to the room with the jarrah table and hung it from a cord below Mary's image. This was the room in which Mum had seen the bolt of green light appear above my head and pass through my body, identifying me as the Green Celestial Dolphin.

Dolphins Healing Room, my Guide announced.

I recalled Cathy drawing a spear at my Guide's request when the Ten Year Mary Project 1994 had come through, and I looked up at the spear on the wall. *Remove the Iona sign now*, my Guide urged.

I removed the Iona Lodge sign and carried it up the paddock to its entrance. *The time of harmony has ended*, my Guide warned. The clue 'Aboriginal spear' was added to Cathy's past-life heart issue.

Following Cathy's departure my Guide ensured that I spent three whole days clearing the Tuart Walk, making the pathway much wider. But each day I was sent inside the lodge to stand in front of Cathy's large empty wardrobe. The top shelves were too high for me to reach. The third time, I was taken to a ladder so I carried it into the bedroom.

'Okay, what is it you want me to do?' I asked. I was encouraged to climb the ladder and look into the top shelf. I nearly missed it. There was a notebook right at the back. The cover gave no indication of what the book contained, so I opened it and started to read. Cathy's thoughts before signing the joint title with me were recorded in detail. She described how she was only tolerating Mum and me and had no intention of staying and working in Dongara. Selva's Guide was right: I had been misled. I found myself sitting on the tiled floor in the bathroom vomiting.

I gained control of myself, drove to Dongara and photocopied the relevant pages, then went on to Geraldton to Cathy's place of employment, where I placed the notebook on the desk in front of her. She looked up at me in surprise and then saw her notebook.

'Oh, my God,' she said, putting her hands to her face.

I left her and waited outside until she eventually came and joined me. I told her calmly that her belongings were packed, requesting she arrange for their collection. As I drove home, outrage filled my being. I sought help inside the Dolphins Healing Room, where I looked at the Aboriginal spear under Mary's image, allowing the soothing energy of my Guide to steady me before I told Mum what had happened.

'This is all part of a much bigger picture,' I explained.

I had met Cathy on 14 February 1989.

We had visited the Red Hand Aboriginal Cave on 14 February 1995.

Today was 14 February 1996.

The Heart's Journey was on schedule.

I had been guided to include Cathy on the title, and now I had to protect the Mary Project 1994. I drove to a settlement agent in Geraldton and obtained a Transfer of Land document to transfer the title to me. I rang the Art Gallery to cancel the celebrations Cathy had planned for my fiftieth birthday on 8 March.

My Guide insisted that The Lovers pots from Ashburton be placed on display in the kitchen and the Wild Geese / Soul Group print be taken to the Dolphins Healing Room and hung by the window. I was then to carry a newly purchased square green Maori totem candle to the Healing Room and place it on the jarrah heart symbol on the table. As I watched its flame, the feeling of reaching out to someone was strong. This person held the totem energy of the soul group; this new clue was added to the notes of the third soulmate with a past-life heart issue.

Three days later I took the Transfer of Land document to Cathy at her office. I was required to pay her a sum of money to make it legal, and we agreed on one dollar. The title would be transferred to my name and Mum and I would assume responsibility for the mortgage repayments. Cathy signed and her receptionist witnessed our signatures.

I handed Cathy her dollar. 'My lucky dollar,' she said, smiling.

Later, my Guide sent me to a jacket in Mum's wardrobe to read its label, — 'Virgo'. I was encouraged to add this clue to Soul Energy (1) and the notes of the third soulmate with a past-life heart issue:

Soul Energy (1): The Four Core Colours – yellow – blue – green – red – 4 – 12 – Dongara – self help healing centre – The Lady of Good Counsel – retreat – Celtic cross – gemstone – Druid energy – settled legal disputes – Celestial Dolphin Centre – Iona Lodge – rebuilding the cathedral – Virgo.

Heart Issue (3): Tapestry – 7 – garden – devas – New Zealand – coins – Dongara – Egypt/ankh – karma / past life – heart's journey – totem energy – Virgo.

This person's energy held the Four Core Colours and they were therefore a Celestial Dolphin, and I wondered which colour they represented — red or yellow — and why?

Liz, Cathy's sister, rang from New South Wales. 'You must now sell shares in the centre for fifteen thousand dollars each to pay Cathy compensation for the loss of her home,' she said.

'What home, what compensation? All the funds for the purchase of the property and the building of Mum's extension were paid for by Mum and me. I found Cathy's notebook after she left, and it revealed she had no intention to remain at the centre.'

Liz was silent for a moment; I sensed she was shocked by this information. 'I am flying over to Perth even though your birthday celebrations are cancelled, and would like to see you,' she said. Liz's phone call left me disturbed. Cathy's name was on the title, so her cooperation was important. I had not yet processed the Transfer of Land document.

My Guide encouraged me to re-light the Maori totem candle. *Friends through time, soulmate,* she said. This clue was added to the third soulmates notes.

I was sent outside to create an 'entrance' to the eastern paddock in preparation for the arrival of this soulmate. The new entrance was to be created with large stones from a pile left on the sand dunes near the property; the Iona Lodge sign was to remain on the ground nearby. Mum helped me with the loading and unloading of our trailer until we had created two piles of stones connected at the top by a long thick branch.

It was basic but effective. My Guide insisted I pour water over the stones in a simple ceremony and then the entrance was photographed. An image had been captured and another door to the past was opened in the heart's journey.

It was time to send out the invitations for Claire's workshop:

Findhorn Workshop

> The Findhorn Community — A Personal Perspective — will be held at the Celestial Dolphin Centre, Dongara.
> Saturday, 2 March 1996 between 9.30am and 4.00pm.
>
> The Findhorn Foundation, a charitable trust, is part of an international spiritual community of about 350 people living, studying and working together in the north-east of Scotland. It was founded in 1962 by Peter and Eileen Caddy and Dorothy MacLean in a caravan park about a mile away from the village of Findhorn. The format of the day will include: an opening meditation; a history of Findhorn; Claire's personal experience of Findhorn, and what it has meant in her life; the latest video from The Foundation; Findhorn Today; and a closing meditation.

I began the day by welcoming everyone to the centre. 'By the end of this year there will be a working community here — quite unique in its own way. We will create a small but necessary cog within the world's spiritual wheel.' I welcomed Claire to Dongara. 'It is her day of sharing and our day of learning.'

Following the meditation Marg approached me with a box, explaining it was from Cathy. I took it to the Dolphins Healing Room. I was reluctant to open it. When I did, it contained a red rose. I was confused. 'Why would Cathy give me this?' I said. *Red rose energy*, my Guide replied. I handed the box and rose back to Marg to return to Cathy. I was then taken aback when guided to update the notes regarding the soulmates with past-life heart issues and the second soul energy to include red rose energy.

Part of the day included a walking meditation. Claire led us down through the eastern paddock, up through the Tuart Walk and out again to the main entrance. The meditation ended by encircling the Standing Stone, and Claire took us through a Findhorn blessing.

Claire was staying in the guest room. During the night I was woken with a start. She had requested to be included if anything happened, so I knocked on her door and took her to the eastern paddock, where we walked to its southern corner.

Mark the ground, my Guide said. I drew a long thin line with my boot, in front of a purple globe tree, and then I marked out a larger area in a square.

'Do you know what this is all about?' Claire asked.

'I have no idea,' I said. *The Mary Area,* my Guide said.

Later my Guide insisted we drive to Dongara to the garden nursery to buy a large white ceramic dolphin, to be displayed on the wooden fence at the main entrance. When Claire left for Perth I was guided to touch the White Dolphin as I read the clues regarding the three soulmates with past-life heart issues, aware of drawing them to me. The Celestial Dolphin Centre was highlighted by a white dolphin and the centre's stationery headed with a symbolic 'Leaping Dolphin' and the insight: 'Dolphins — their healing traditions aimed at restoring the integrity of mind, body and spirit.' Cathy's name was removed from the centre's business registration.

The evening before my birthday I was directed to drive into Dongara and hire the video of *King Arthur*, featuring Sean Connery, and watch it for a set number of minutes. I set my watch accordingly. As the moment approached, King Arthur and his knights rose to their feet with goblets in their hands — just as the Celtic Seven had on 21 July, when Norm shouted, 'To Iona'. Arthur shouted at the precise moment I had been encouraged to make note, 'In serving each other we become free.'

This was to be the Celestial Dolphin Centre's motto.

All references highlighted by my Guide featured the same form of communication, where I would be sent to a brochure, magazine or book, for example, and, at the moment prior to opening, the page number would be highlighted in my mind, then a paragraph or line, or even a word. This ensured I read only what was required.

Early on my birthday, sitting alone in the meditation room, my mind went back ten years to my fortieth birthday — to the intense feeling of apprehension upon opening my birthday cards, with their ten-pound notes, from Anne and Barbara. Days later, I was to learn of their actions regarding the Old Saddlery and its title. Ten years later I discovered Cathy's actions regarding the Celestial Dolphin Centre and its title.

What was it about my fortieth and fiftieth birthdays? I wondered. *St Michael and All Angels*, my Guide replied. This was the name of the church in the village of Cornwood, the place where I was born and christened. I was encouraged to find the print of the church and hang it above where I had been sitting. When I stood in front of it I found myself creating a circle around my body with my right hand, fingers pointed outwards — asking for the protection of St Michael. This action was *familiar*, and in my mind I could see Archangel Michael in the leadlight window of the Brentor Church. I re-lived the feeling I had experienced then — how I had longed with all my heart for justice and the revealing of the truth. I understood this had been my intent prior to my birth in this lifetime, and to achieve this I would need the protection of St Michael and all the angels. This repeat situation with Cathy was part of the process to reveal a truth concerning a past life and free us from a karmic attachment. *In serving each other we become free*, my Guide said.

Mum came into the meditation room singing the birthday song. Then I opened the many gifts from her and friends. Dianne's gift was an Ogham stone bearing the symbol for March. The oval stone had been handmade by *St Justin of Cornwall*. Its leaflet read:

> The ancient Celts celebrated months of the year with certain trees, not astrologically.

The Celtic tree for March was the ash. I realised that the planting of the claret ash at the centre had come about because it was my Celtic birth month tree. I read that the ash tree symbolised:

> ... the inner and outer worlds linked, with macrocosm and microcosm, drawing forces together and being a focus for energy.

Two days later I was walking towards the tractor shed when a huge barn owl in full flight came from inside it. My Guide insisted I go to the Standing Stone and concentrate until I saw it had the side-on outline of an owl. *Wisdom*, my Guide said.

As arranged, I drove to Cathy's flat to meet her sister Liz. Cathy stood back as Liz gave me a hug before handing me her birthday gift. When I opened it I was taken aback by its beauty. It was a solid glass dolphin with muted rippling shades of green and blue, my and Christina's Celestial Dolphin colours. Liz had been at the centre the night of 20 October the year before, when we watched the awesome Mary Display. On my return to Dongara I placed the dolphin on the jarrah table.

On 15 March I stood by the lawnmower, started its engine and moved into the eastern paddock, where it suddenly took on a life of its own, pulling me behind it. Around and around we went, creating long pathways, until we had created an unusual shape. It was huge, with three closed areas and one open. *Heart,* was shouted at me over the noise of the engine, but the shape was not a human heart. 'So this is the heart so many people predicted,' I said.

My own heart was racing with all the physical effort. As I tried to recover, a horse calmly trotted past the new entrance to the paddock and towards the Crystal Pool. I found it standing over the Crystal Pool seeking to drink. I approached it with caution, having had no experience with horses. I rang my neighbour Maria and she came to put a rope around his neck and walk him back to her place. The horse must have trotted along the highway and up the gravel road to the main entrance before heading to the Crystal Pool.

Dianne's birthday gift included information regarding the Celts. To them the horse meant Sovereignty and Supreme Power. My Guide then referred me to *A Dictionary of Symbols* by Tom Chetwynd:

> Energy is either in harmony or in conflict, so horses may be symbols of harmony and right relationship, or of war. (8)

I had just completed the outline of a huge symbolic Heart in the eastern paddock when this stallion appeared. I hoped his visit symbolised harmony and not the opposite. The next day he was again at the Crystal Pool — *waiting.* As Maria walked him out of the property I woke up to the fact that she was Greek, so I looked up my Greek mythology and was directed to go outside and read the information standing by the Crystal Pool:

> The Sea God Poseidon created the horse, which indicates a strong association with the passions … The horse was sacred to him.

As I read the word 'passions' a searing pain shot through my heart, forcing me to sit. The horse being a stallion indicated male passions. *Crystal pool, supreme power, male passions, heart pain, conflict and loss,* my Guide repeated again and again until the heart pain eased and I could breathe normally. I walked away from the Crystal Pool, drained by the turbulent masculine emotions it held. *Egypt,* my Guide warned.

I understood that my heart passions, as well as those of another, were involved.

I photographed both the Crystal Pool and the stallion, and placed their images beside my notes regarding the three soulmates with past-life heart issues. Egypt featured within all three, and now this disclosure of male passions, heart pain, conflict and loss, held in the Crystal Pool energy — and its area — filled me with alarm. I updated the three soulmate notes with this new clue of 'male passions' next to 'red rose energy'.

My emotions were so overwhelming that I asked for help. I was taken to my fiftieth birthday card from Christina. She had written, 'Move into the Light.' I lit a new white candle and sat for a while in the Dolphins Healing Room to recover.

Claire drove up from Perth for the weekend and it felt really good to be working with someone who had experience with guidance. We began clearing masses of lupins and wild turnips in one of the enclosed areas of the Heart within the eastern paddock. It was a huge undertaking, but the more we worked the more information I was given.

Mary Area and Tuart Walk are the throat chakra, my Guide said. *Mary Area and Heart are the heart chakra.*

The next day Terry drove in. We watched him pick up a long piece of timber left over from a previous task and walk into what we now called the Healing Garden (eastern paddock). He did not look at us or make any attempt to speak. He placed the piece of timber on the ground in the Mary Area, where I had marked a line on 3 March. Still not speaking, he returned to his truck many times to fetch a variety of tools, a spade and a bag of cement, and to collect more timber. By 10 am he had created a bench seat. The line I had made would have disappeared after a few days and it was now twenty-two days later. Terry had created the Mary Seat. When I suggested he send me a bill for his work, he replied, 'This is a love job.'

'Is that how it happened with the Standing Stone?' Claire asked.

'Amazing, isn't it. He is obviously tuning into the energy here.'

When Claire had gone I continued to work each day in the Heart area by the Mary Seat, freeing it of its choking wild growth. Late one evening I was forced to stop and sit on the bench, when I became filled with emotions so intense that I found it difficult to breathe.

Celestial Dolphin on her way, Egyptian link, my Guide said. My hard work was paying off, drawing another Celestial Dolphin to the centre. Would this dolphin with an Egyptian link have a colour code? I wondered.

The centre was being discussed in Dongara and in Geraldton. Everyone had the impression it was to be a full-time centre for practitioners and workshops, but I sensed it was something else. When visitors came I gave them all the information I could. One day a young man asked why I had a dolphin on the gate, a strange looking stone, a small ash tree and this bench. He had summed up these four symbols in simple terms. As I went through their individual symbolic meanings he studied me and then smiled. I returned his smile upon realising these symbols were linked to the Celtic prayer Rene had taught me. 'I ask only what you want of me, the power, wisdom, cosmic love and energy, in order to be able to achieve those things.' The dolphin symbolised healing powers; the Standing Stone symbolised wisdom; the Mary Seat symbolised cosmic love and the claret ash was the focus for energy. From then on I sat on the Mary Seat at 4 pm every day with Jessie, the atmosphere around us dense and powerful as I repeated the Celtic prayer.

On 8 April, unannounced and very distressed, Cathy arrived in a friend's car asking to stay overnight, having argued with her boyfriend. A woman from Dongara had booked the centre for an Egyptian Evening and all present were given readings using Egyptian cards.

'Judy,' she began. 'There will be delays regarding money. It will be frustrating. Those who deserve it will get it in the end. Someone is not doing the right thing by you, causing problems over money. This will be overcome, but make sure you have everything in writing. You are being encouraged in self-discipline. There will be a positive outcome — although it will be delayed — something to do with a home.'

Cathy was sitting next to me and I became aware she was uncomfortable with the message. There had been no further mention of the $15,000 compensation for her.

The woman continued. 'A testing time, Judy, but a lot of loyalty around you to keep you going. Loyalty will keep the embers burning when you are discouraged. The trusted person you can rely on, stable, close relationship, lots of stability. Finances, joint skill to deal with it. The nature of the problem is karmic. An older woman is helping you, a strong woman with motherly qualities, and she will help with the establishment.'

Early the next morning I made Cathy a cup of tea and found her sitting up in bed crying. As I listened to her tale of woe, a gold and jewelled necklace formed around her neck. It was Egyptian: I recognised it from pictures I had seen. The gemstones were lapis lazuli and turquoise, the gold dull and fine. It faded, and once again I heard Cathy's voice. She was annoyed, having grasped I was not listening. She left after I told her she must speak to her boyfriend about their issues, not me. I understood the sighting of the necklace indicated that the doorway to Ancient Egypt, for Cathy and me, had been opened.

Terry, the carpenter, arrived within minutes of Cathy's departure. The shed within Mum's extension was being converted into an office, leaving another bedroom free in the lodge. In mid-April, when the work was finished, I applied for a bed-and-breakfast licence to supplement our income, as Mum and I were finding the mortgage repayments a drain. The task of painting the office began and Audrey, a member of the Celtic Seven, arrived to help, bringing all the furniture and office equipment. Once the office was completed I was directed to go out into the Heart and begin clearing the second enclosed area of weed growth — these areas now being referred to by my Guide as *chambers*.

Hold a Mary May Day, my Guide insisted.

'Wow! What is this?' I said.

I found Mum to tell her that we were to hold a Mary May Day. May Day, a Celtic celebration, was being linked with Mary, and Mum was as excited as I was. When I was a police officer in England I had volunteered for duty during the Helston Flora Day celebrations in the county of Cornwall. This day began with the gentlemen in coat and tails, accompanied by partners dressed in flowing gowns, followed by the children dressed all in white dancing the Furry Dance through the streets. The Furry Song makes references to St George and the Dragon, Robin Hood and St Michael, all part of the remnants of a pagan spring celebration, the dance being used to fight away the influence of the devil — according to legend.

I would advertise Mary May Day '96 as an Open Day. I watched the woman's look of surprise, followed by confusion, at *The Dongara Rag* office, when I handed her my advertisement. Having a Mary May Day / Open Day was going to raise eyebrows. Audrey arrived with furniture for the Dolphins Healing Room for Mary May Day: two comfortable jarrah chairs and a folding massage/healing table Norm had made for her. 'My gift for the centre,' she explained.

The centre's Soul Energy notes were updated to include Mary May Day '96.

Late on the evening before Mary May Day '96 / Open Day, I sat down exhausted, thinking I had accomplished everything. But no, I was guided to go to the tractor shed to collect pieces of timber left over from Terry creating the new main entrance. Despite the darkness I wheelbarrowed the timber into a cleared area by the fence in the southern corner of the lodge garden. I was sent to find a round stone from within the Heart, then create a cross on the ground and place this stone in the centre. I had created a Celtic cross in direct line with the Mary Seat. I started to walk to the lodge but was veered off towards the tractor shed, and was waiting outside when out flew a barn owl, forcing me to duck, and for the first time I experienced the emotion of *exhilaration* — a feeling of joy combined with relief — so powerful that it made my head reel.

Earlier, during the month of April, I had been instructed to write to Julie Firth at her permaculture farm in Geraldton concerning plants for the Healing Garden. Now I felt I must speak to her on the telephone. I'd first met Julie in March the previous year when Marg invited Cathy and me to go with her to tour Julie's self-supporting property. Still filled with the feeling of exhilaration, I asked Julie to visit the Celestial Dolphin Centre and we agreed on the date of 14 May. As our telephone conversation ended, Claire drove in and I showed her the Celtic cross.

On Mary May Day '96, four of us stood at the four points of the Celtic cross waiting for the sun — Claire, Mum, Christina and myself. I repeated the Celtic prayer as the rays moved across the Heart, and the other three repeated the prayer in unison. The exhilaration returned as I pondered Julie's pending visit. Norm arrived to join Christina to provide healing, while Claire and I talked to the many visitors.

A group of women decided to organise a weekly meditation evening at the centre, Terri, the stranger who had taken the photograph of the Celtic Seven, was part of this group. The librarian from the Geraldton Library donated tea towels, her gift featuring the Aboriginal design *Bundiyarra* — dolphins. As I was handed her gift, the warning *Shark amongst the dolphins* came. I looked at the group with a feeling of unease.

Days later I was directed to the Dongara Crystal Shop, where I discovered that the woman with the Egyptian cards was there providing readings. I was encouraged by my Guide to *ask for a reading* and the woman took a long, deep breath before speaking.

'I see you surrounded by protection but personal growth with sacrifice, something you are giving up in exchange for something to do with a baby, a child. Do what feels right in your heart. Past lives are coming through strongly. A personal testing time and you will come out stronger. You and your mother will communicate in a lovely way. I see you giving up an old for a new relationship.' The woman leaned across the table and held my hands. 'Be careful,' she said.

Warning. This is a message from Ancient Egypt, my Guide said.

Later I was encouraged to update the notes of the first soulmate with a past-life heart issue to include the clues 'Warning. This is a message from Ancient Egypt' and 'a child'.

I was guided to a letter received from a visitor, and then to read a small part:

> … each chakra vibrates at an increasingly higher energy and colour rate and corresponds to a different physical, mental, emotional, spiritual attribute.

I was fascinated to learn that chakras vibrated with energy and colour, and I wondered if this was in any way connected to the colour coding of the Celestial Dolphins. *Yes,* my Guide said.

Later the clue 'chakras' was added to the notes of the third soulmate with a past-life heart issue next to 'male passions'. Once I had written this I was instructed to work in the lodge garden where the nine cement pavers had been placed the previous September. My Guide requested I create a small inner rim and larger outer rim outside the pavers, both of which must be of limestone rocks. It took a lot of effort to cart these stones and I was allowed a limited time to complete this work in between clearing the second chamber of the Heart of dense weed growth.

On 11 May my Guide highlighted the date, and I was taken to my 1986 diary to be reminded that on this day, ten years before in England, I had passed my father's mantle clock into Barbara's home to begin the process of rescuing Barbara and bring about the revealing of the truth.

The next day I went to Dongara to collect our post and found an envelope from Dianne, enclosing a diagram from a Celtic book. She asked me if it meant anything, and I was floored to see it was the symbol of three squares I had spent time creating — a Celtic Triple Enclosure, symbol for the Human Consciousness:

> The outer square was the part of the mind that relates to the physical world of the senses. The inner square was the unconscious mind

through which visions are received of gods and other worlds. The middle square was the part of the mind receptive to both physical worlds and spirit.

Two days passed and I was still trying to come to terms with Dianne's accurate communication when Julie drove in through the main entrance. She came with a wwoofer — a member of a loose network of 'Willing Workers On Organic Farms' who travel the world staying in places like Julie's and working for their accommodation and meals.

The Light of Iona, my Guide said, as Julie walked towards me. Trying to comprehend the message, I stumbled through my welcome to Julie; then highlighted words from *The Findhorn Garden Story*, 'Converting the annex for Dorothy', (5) repeated in my mind. Dorothy's role at the Findhorn Community was to communicate with nature spirits. Julie was at the centre to make that connection for me and the reason the double shed had been converted to an office. I had converted the annex for Julie. She studied me with curiosity as I processed this information. It was embarrassing listening to my Guide and trying to speak to Julie at the same time.

Julie was full of energy, walking around the property at a great rate, making notes and talking to her co-worker. The Healing Garden itself was where she was meant to be, but I was not to make any suggestions. She walked into the lodge garden and towards the Celtic cross, recording plants that were growing there. She was not as aware of the Celtic cross as I was but, as we stood there talking, a shot of energy flashed between our elbows. I jumped and Julie looked at me, then asked regarding the Healing Garden, 'What is out there?' I walked her slowly through the new entrance, smiling to myself: the shot of energy from the Celtic cross had moved her in the right direction. Julie informed me windbreaks had to be planted and swales dug to catch the rain. She explained in detail, but soon lost me. I knew she would be the centre's planting consultant.

After Julie left, my Guide sent me to the Dolphins Healing Room to light the Maori totem candle and update the notes of the third soulmate to include 'The Light of Iona'. Julie had been born in New Zealand. Was she the one I had reached out to when lighting this candle and a soulmate who was seeking to resolve a past-life heart issue? *Yes*, my Guide replied. This was the new partner and a Celestial Dolphin with an Egyptian link:

Heart Issue: Julie – tapestry – 7 – garden – devas – New Zealand – coins – Dongara – Egypt/ankh – karma / past life – heart's journey

– totem energy – Virgo – friends through time / soulmate – red rose energy – male passions – chakras – The Light of Iona.

During May of 1993, in Geraldton, Mum and I had been discussing Barbara's seventh attempt to resolve an ongoing past-life issue regarding family inheritance and control when I was sent to find an Indian box and place it near my gum-nuts tapestry / nature spirits. Inside the box I found two New Zealand coins and I had amended my notes accordingly:

Heart Issue (3): Tapestry – 7 – garden – devas – New Zealand – coins.

Mum and I understood that this soulmate was going to help bring Barbara's soul back to the Light. As I watched the flame of the totem candle, I understood that Julie being *The Light of Iona* meant she had been a monk on the island monastery of Iona and was also the soulmate holding the totem energy of the soul group — the Dolphin.

My Guide directed that the wooden dolphin given to me by Norm the previous year be placed beside the lit Maori totem candle. This was followed by the silver dolphin Christina had given me for my fiftieth birthday and the glass dolphin from Cathy's sister Liz. Later, members of the newly formed meditation group were attracted to the idea of placing dolphins in a group formation and added their own dolphins to the table.

Shark amongst the dolphins, my Guide warned. *Trust the process and all will be revealed.* I understood that, by encouraging this group to contribute their dolphins, this would help reveal who was the shark amongst the dolphins.

On the last day of May I was standing by the water tanks near Mum's extension checking their water level when I was hit by something on my right shoulder. Turning, I saw a huge black moth fluttering around, reeling from the impact. Before I could recover, one of the kestrels that visited the tractor shed daily swooped down towards me, its claws extended. It grabbed the moth, flew back to its perch and tore the moth to pieces while looking at me. Its mate flew down to a branch beside me and the first bird joined it. Although everything happened quickly, it was as though I was watching in slow motion. I remained very still, just taking it all in. The two birds followed me in the garden all day, leaving me in no doubt that I was and would be protected, but from what I did not know.

The month of June brought donations of plants: Australian lavender, three yellow-flowering gums, which were planted between the Standing Stone and the main entrance, and nine Chinese peppercorn trees, which were put aside until Claire arrived for the weekend. Claire and I were directed to the fence line by the Brand Highway where the nine peppercorns were to be planted, leaving a pathway between the trees and the fence. The ground was a limestone reef with little soil and we wondered how we could go about it. *Use your pendulum*, my Guide said.

I paced the fence line until the pendulum indicated that we dig — each time we discovered a space between the boulders. We enjoyed the task, cheering when we found a space, and planted six trees. Then I was stopped. I was amazed when I saw a yellow form like a mist behind the six planted trees, and then it was gone. The three remaining trees were to be planted leaving a required space between the sixth and the last three trees. We started at the southern end, working northwards, and after lunch we returned. I was encouraged to walk towards the end of the fence line, stopping five paces from the end.

Dig seven hand widths down, my Guide said. I used my pendulum and found a circle of soil, enabling us to dig to the required depth. We walked the property selecting the stones that were to be placed inside this hole in a spiral-like coil up to the surface and above. A huge central stone was placed on top with eight large stones surrounding it in a complete circle. We both stood back, tired after our efforts, wondering what we had created and why. The next day, before dawn, I was woken and sent out with a bucket to the garden's bore tap, close to the new symbol, to fill the bucket with water.

Beacon, my Guide explained, as the sun's rays slowly appeared over the horizon. I poured the water over the Beacon. *Love and Light to this property, Australia and the world*, my Guide said.

Claire walked into the Healing Garden, and I was thrilled to share with her what had happened. We enjoyed a celebration lunch with Mum: it was 3 June, twelve months to the day since I'd been sent to Dongara and instructed to buy this place. I was on schedule. My Guide then referred me to the book *Vibrational Medicine* by R. Gerber and to *make note of seven specific chakra colours*:

Crown Chakra (Violet) – Third-Eye Chakra (Indigo) – Throat Chakra (Blue) – Heart Chakra (Green) – Solar Plexus Chakra (Yellow) – Spleen Chakra (Orange) – Root Chakra (Red) (3)

My Guide had confirmed earlier that the colour codings of the Celestial Dolphins were linked to these chakras. As the Green Dolphin I was linked to the heart vibration within the Mary Area with its Mary Seat and the Heart. Christina, as the Blue Dolphin, was linked to the throat chakra vibration held within the Mary Area and the Tuart Walk.

On 7 June 1996 I walked into the Healing Garden to an established coastal mort tree. Under the canopy of this tree I found an opening on one side that enabled one to walk under it to an open space. *The Love Tree*, my Guide said. Inside I found two identical black-and-white feathers on the ground. *Dolphins Healing Room*, my Guide said. I placed the feathers at the base of the Double Dolphin candle-holder by Julie's name. I was referred to the book *A Dictionary of Symbols* by Tom Chetwynd:

> *A feather of a bird* is sufficient to symbolize the entire creature. (8)

Identical feathers were placed with the identical dolphins and Julie's name. Were Julie and I one of a pair?

When people sent me notes or letters in the post I filed them, for a word or a sentence might be important in the future. Claire sent me information regarding the number forty:

> Forty is the number of waiting, of preparation, testing and punishment. The emphasis was often placed upon testing rather than punishment. The number forty marks the completion of a circle ... a passing on to a fresh level of activity ... Lord Buddha and the Prophet Mohammed began their mission at the age of forty ... forty-ninth year is the end of a journey.

My fortieth birthday had been highlighted with the completion of the Butterfly Circle at Middleton in March 1986 and the beginning of a new way of life. The last few months of my forty-ninth year had been turmoil until Cathy walked out.

I had just finished the exhausting task of clearing the second Heart chamber of weed growth and was about to walk into the third and largest chamber when I was approached by a woman wanting to book a Reiki Weekend Workshop. We agreed on 21–23 June. I joined the closing ceremony, when the Reiki Master gave each person, including me, several turquoise gemstones. I had a round Indian box with two identical silver dolphins on its lid that my Guide had instructed me to buy when Mum and I were in India, and I placed in it these gemstones and the Miraculous Medal given to me by Cathy's mother in 1989. Buddha had used turquoise gemstones to call upon spiritual help. I was being warned of something pending, but assured of spiritual help. The next day Christina arrived and asked to be part of a candle reading. We sat at the oak table in the kitchen and I lit a new white candle and handed her paper and pencil. She wrote the date, 24 June 1996, and waited for me to speak aloud my Guide's words:

For Judy, the mind that knows and cares. Adversities coming but have no fear. You have learned one of life's important lessons. Appearances are deceiving. Be very cautious. You will need all your courage to survive the next attack. During meditation, ask whoever comes for protection with the word loyalty. A word of warning: You are entering dangerous territory, Egyptian times. You have the chance to withdraw if you so desire. If you brave the danger, you will overcome it. It is all to do with a mastery of minds. Cathy has to go her chosen path. There will be many symbols of compassion and concern. Pay special attention to a bright star; this will be confirmation the journey has begun. It will take energy, but afterwards you will feel euphoria, like a second awakening. Cathy will feel like she has walked out of a tunnel and into the Light.

I could agree or not agree. I agreed.

The karma clearing will begin, my Guide said. I felt apprehensive until she directed me to the silver dolphins box, where I was to hold the turquoise gemstones and the Miraculous Medal. I was protected. The phone rang; it was Cathy demanding my notes for *Entwining of Souls*. Having received the warning — *entering dangerous territory, Egyptian times* — I was on my guard and told her that the notes were mine and she had no claim on them whatsoever. I looked inside the manuscript file and discovered Cathy had typed the title on a blank page and underneath her name as the author. I was confused and annoyed as to why she would have done this. The phone rang again as I was studying the file.

It was Selva the clairvoyant. I was dumbfounded when she spoke about a book. 'This book *must* be published,' she said. 'You *must* publish the book.' She continued, 'You *must* protect yourself and *believe* in the law of karma. The book will be your journey of spiritual growth.'

During the next meditation evening I asked the group for protection, as previously instructed by my Guide, using the word 'loyalty' and explaining that I was moving back in time to a past-life situation. I offered no explanation, as I felt apprehensive about trusting this group. The warning *Shark amongst the dolphins* applied to someone within it.

Cathy contacted me again following her outrageous claim to the ownership of my manuscript notes, but this time she wanted out of the mortgage. Although she had made no repayments, the debt was still recorded against her name, hampering any credit applications. I began the process of transferring the title to my name by visiting the building society and completing an application form, but days later a reply came to say they would not allow the transfer unless I applied for a single mortgage. With my income that was going to be difficult.

I was instructed to begin to clear the third Heart chamber of its wild growth. While working there I was thinking about the tense situation regarding Cathy when a middle-aged man walked in. He asked if this was the place with the Celtic cross. I said it was. He asked to see it. He neither introduced himself nor asked who I was; he was only intent on seeing the cross. I walked him into the lodge garden, where he spent time measuring the cross, taking angle markings. At last he smiled. 'This is the right place,' he said – then left!

The next day I found a dead barn owl in the Heart. I was confused, as there were no signs of injury. As I carried it to the Celtic cross for burial, I felt uneasy. My Guide was adamant that it must be buried at the southern end of the cross. I was then sent inside to light the Double Dolphin candle and play the *Call of the Dolphin* tape, which had been given to me on my fiftieth birthday by a regular visitor to the centre. Christina rang within minutes and I told her about the owl. She explained that, according to Aboriginal *Dreaming*, birds would sacrifice themselves to impart their energy. Had the barn owl sacrificed itself to give of its wisdom? A feather would have been enough. However, I did not miss the fact that when I lit the Double Dolphin candle and played the *Call of the Dolphin*, Christina — the Blue Celestial Dolphin — responded.

Mum and Dianne had been corresponding, and I was resting when Mum handed me a copy of her latest letter to Dianne, concerning life at the centre:

Dear Dianne,

Some time, way back, I went to see a clairvoyant and she told me I would hear the Angels sing. Recently, Marg Parker came once a week for six weeks to hold a meditation evening at the centre. During one of these evenings, we were taken on a journey to meet an Angel. Marg said, 'Maybe the Angel has a message for you.' I heard a whisper, You have done well.

In the same meditation, we met an Archangel, and Marg said, 'Maybe there is a message for you.' I heard a whisper, Only a little longer.

Dianne, in my last letter I told you about the present I brought back with me from a meditation evening, carrying in both hands a shining light which my higher self had told me was Love. Someone else organises our evenings now, and last week she asked me if I would do an Angel Meditation for the group as she knows I have a message for them. I said that I would sometime later when I had the inspiration.

Our evenings here have developed beautifully and after the meditations we all adjourn to the kitchen and refreshments are served. I went to bed one night thinking of things to say. Anyway, the next morning I wrote a meditation on faith, hope, compassion and love. Ours is a young group, very enthusiastic, and sometimes we are asked to provide a segment towards the evening. There were three segments for the last session. Then it was my turn to read my segment. There were twelve people sitting around and I read out my thoughts, and it felt good to be myself at last. All my life, I have been very reserved in company, always fine with a one-to-one conversation, but not wanting to speak up in a group, and here I was quite relaxed. So Dianne, my dear, I feel that I have grown over the past few months. Both Judy and I send you and yours love, Tess.

By the end of July I was providing healing sessions. Mu, in England, had said I would do this. Christina would visit the Dolphins Healing Room and I would access, from my Guide, which crystals, Bach flower remedy or other healing method was needed to bring up an emotion. I was attuned to emotional distresses and able to ask the right questions to open doors that released emotional blockages.

I was approached by two practitioners requesting to work at the centre: a massage therapist and a reflexologist. Their request was followed by a note sent through the post from a recent visitor to the Healing Garden:

> There are seven great streams of energy. Every form of nature is to be found upon one ray or another. As these rays interact with one another, this reproduces the 'forms' we see in the world.

I was instructed to file the note and go outside to sit on the Mary Seat and from there to go back to the office to unwrap the white Buddha that had been placed inside the nook in the house in Sovereign Waters. The nook was where I had channelled the Ten Year Mary Project 1994. I had wondered at the time why the Buddha had been placed there and what connection — if any — there was between Buddha and Mary.

During my visit to the Emerald Buddha in Bangkok, the words *in search of Truth* and *Mother* had been highlighted. Many times on my journeys Buddha had featured; now this Buddha was highlighted. I was referred to photocopied pages from a book sent to me in the post: *Chakras: Rays and Radionics* by David V. Tansley:

> The Seven Great Builders ... There are seven rays, but it is important to realise that the seven rays that are our concern are the sub-rays of the 2nd ray. We live in a 2nd ray system, a system in which Love and Wisdom are being developed and expressed. Christ and Buddha are the main exponents of this ray ... (9)

The link between Buddha and Mary was Jesus and the second ray system. I read on:

> The Second Ray: The Ray of Love – Wisdom. This is the ray of universal love, intuition, insight, cooperation, philanthropy and wisdom. Upon this stream of energy emerge the sages, teachers, healers and reformers of humanity ... (9)

In late July, Julie Firth, the planting consultant, sent through her recommendations for windbreak plantings. Large growing trees were to be planted outside the property to protect the Healing Garden from the winter winds and later the heat-carrying winds. In early August, twelve two-metre swamp sheoaks were delivered to be planted outside along the Brand Highway, parallel with the nine peppercorns on the inside of the fence line. Mum and I carried the trees to the fence line in readiness for being instructed when to plant them, aware again of the number twelve.

I had finished planting the swamp sheoaks two weeks later when it poured with rain. I sat in the meditation room listening to the rain when a forceful pushing motion sent me to the Dolphins Healing Room to light the Double Dolphin candle and play the *Call of the Dolphin* tape. My expectation was that Christina would ring as before — but nothing happened. The candle remained alight and the music continued to play. I returned to the meditation room. Half an hour later there was a knocking sound on the glass sliding doors of the room. I looked and saw Julie's face. She was soaked through. I opened the door and then saw her boyfriend, who was also soaked through. They had been driving from Perth to Geraldton when they had a flat tyre.

I gave them each a warm towel and a hot drink before ringing for assistance. It was still pouring with rain when I drove them back to their abandoned vehicle to wait for help to arrive. As I drove home I realised that Julie had responded to the *Call of the Dolphin* in the same way as Christina. They'd had the flat tyre at the time of my lighting the candle and playing the tape. I recalled the flower reading at the meditation weekend at Northampton on 7 October 1994, when Eileen had said, 'A flat tyre on a car holding good vibrations.'

Weeding of the three Heart chambers occupied all my time for the next three days. Then Julie arrived at the centre to stay overnight, prior to holding a permaculture workshop the following day in response to a number of people showing an interest in the subject. She brought twelve Rottnest Island tea trees to plant in between the twelve swamp sheoaks on the Brand Highway fence line.

Julie had booked an evening massage in the lodge, so I left and walked out into the darkness. I was taken by my Guide to stand under the canopy of the Love Tree. This was the second time this tree and Julie had been linked. The first time had been a couple of months earlier, when I'd found under its canopy identical black-and-white feathers that were still at the base of the Double Dolphin candle. I was drawn to look upwards, and a spectacular shooting star flashed across the night sky and the words of 24 June repeated: *A word of warning. You are entering dangerous territory, Egyptian times. Pay special attention to a bright star. This will be the confirmation the journey has begun.* I stood enclosed by the Love Tree and requested protection.

The workshop was a success. Julie had brought plants to be sold and I took a photograph of her with them. This image would become a focal point later. After I had planted the eastern boundary along the Brand

Highway, I was instructed to buy plants for the southern boundary. As Julie was leaving she turned and walked to the Healing Garden and stood for a moment facing the Heart. 'I can now see it will all happen,' she said, smiling.

Cathy rang, wanting to stay for the weekend. We were still trying to find a way to have the mortgage transferred. I had tried to obtain a bank loan to replace the mortgage, but failed, and I soon became apprehensive. Mum and I had been honouring the payments for six months, but with difficulty. I decided to present a revised set of figures to the building society.

When I took a cup of tea into Cathy's room the next day, an Egyptian necklace slowly appeared around her throat. This time the gemstones were in a swirling setting, I described it to her. *Two necklaces, two women, two situations*, my Guide warned.

Julie sent me information in the post concerning an International Permaculture Conference to be held in Perth at the end of September. Early in the month I drove to her place to collect plants, and we discussed the conference. I had been given instructions to attend and, trusting the funds would become available, I'd signed the booking forms. As we talked I was drawn to a metal figure holding a crystal in each hand, standing on a large amethyst gemstone base. Julie suggested I take it with me. The figure was Merlin; later I placed it on the jarrah table in the Dolphins Healing Room.

On 3 September my Guide instructed me to go to the Crystal Shop in Dongara, where I was drawn to buy a card featuring an Egyptian god. Later, I placed it beside Merlin, and as I did so a surge of multicoloured energy went through me. The card read:

> Anubis – Egyptian Mortuary God, period of worship 2700BC–400AD. The God of Mortuaries, he takes the form of a jackal or black dog. The Egyptian Book of the Dead has him standing by scales in which the heart is weighed in the Hall of the Two Truths. He is sometimes referred to as the 'claimer of hearts' ...

When I read the words 'claimer of hearts' a pain shot through my chest creating a rapid heart rhythm, and I looked up at Mary's image on the wall seeking help. *Ripped from your side in Egypt*, my Guide said. Was this Julie's past-life heart issue?

The post brought a surprise tax refund that covered the cost of my attending the permaculture conference. I was invited to Julie's farm for a pre-conference workshop to welcome the organisers. It was 23 September, the same date on which I had been sent to the Sainte Barbe spring in Brittany in 1991. As I drove to her place I remembered putting my left hand in the pool and, when I had withdrawn it, seeing that my arm was luminous green up to my elbow. My heart had pounded then, and later Rene had confirmed that the Sainte Barbe spring was a source of cosmic energy.

Julie held an interesting workshop. I studied her as she presented her lecture, feeling the oddness of knowing we had been together in Ancient Egypt. *Ripped from your side*, could indicate a parent and child, husband and wife or even lovers. Julie, in turn, watched me as I moved around after the lecture. She approached me but was forced to veer off when a woman in her mid-twenties approached me directly. She introduced herself as Tatia, from South Africa, and we talked for a long time before going into the tent for something to eat. Later, with everyone standing around the outdoor fire singing songs and talking, Julie walked away and indicated I should follow her. We sat on a stone wall in the silent darkness.

'Why didn't you come into my life a week earlier?' she asked. I felt the sharp pain in my chest again and flinched, unable to ask what she meant. She took my hand for a second, asking if I was all right. I didn't mention the past-life message, but I understood that the past-life male passion energy held within the Crystal Pool at the centre was mine. We returned to the group in silence.

Tatia asked me if she could visit the centre the next day. When she came, *en route* for Perth and the conference, we sat on the Mary Seat. I told her what had happened regarding my family and why Mum and I were now living in Dongara. We walked the Healing Garden, then later ate lunch with Mum.

I was encouraged to join in the meditation group on 25 September, and during the session I saw Mary's image, on this occasion with her eyes open. As I came out of the meditation a woman in the group was looking across at me. It transpired that she had seen Mary also, her head surrounded by a golden halo and that she had spoken my name, Judy. We hugged briefly and she said she was afraid of my power. I told her, 'I have no power. I am here to create a Healing Garden.'

When I arrived at the conference in Perth, Tatia handed me a gift for the centre — a beautiful African cloth of gold, black and green. That night Julie introduced me to Hudda, an Arabian woman from Palestine. It was good for me to talk with her, as I was pro-Jewish.

The next day my Guide insisted I visit the church within the grounds of the Swanleigh Convention Centre. As I walked towards it I was not surprised to read the sign 'St Mary's Church'. I sat inside for a while before being taken to a grave with the name Gardner on the headstone. I was then instructed to walk to the edge of the grounds, where I came to a rosebush. I was told to pick two red buds: one to be left on Gardner's grave, the other to be placed in Julie's room with a note thanking her for encouraging me to attend the conference. The word 'rose' had been appearing in my notes often, and now this gesture towards Julie, the name 'Gardner' and 'Mary's Church' were highlighted and my notes updated:

Heart Issue: Julie – tapestry – 7 – garden – devas – New Zealand – coins – Dongara – Egypt/ankh – karma / past life – heart's journey – totem energy – Virgo – friends through time/soulmate – red rose energy – male passions – chakras – The Light of Iona – Gardner – Mary's Church.

Soul Energy (1): The Four Core Colours – yellow – blue – green – red – 4 – 12 – Dongara – self help healing centre – The Lady of Good Counsel – retreat – Celtic cross – gemstone – Druid energy – settled legal disputes – Celestial Dolphin Centre – Iona Lodge – rebuilding the cathedral – Virgo – St Michael – Mary May Day '96 – Gardner – Mary's Church.

I found myself drawn to the words 'rebuilding the cathedral', 'Virgo' and 'Gardner' within the combinations, and the feeling of exhilaration came, as it had when I'd first rung Julie, on the evening before Mary May Day '96, and arranged to meet at the centre on 14 May. *French connection*, my Guide explained.

I talked to a woman called Sam from the University of Sydney who was completing a survey on the theory of permaculture. She and Hudda were booked to travel on the coach to work at Julie's farm for a while, and Hudda asked if they could stay at the centre. That evening they joined our meditation group. Sam confided that she had felt attracted to a young man at the conference, and I suggested she follow her heart and ring him. John represented the Findhorn Community at the conference.

Sam's visit highlighted the fact that Findhorn was constantly making its presence felt: Cathy's urge to visit and Findhorn being part of her past-life heart issue, Claire opening the centre on 2 March 1996 with a workshop using Findhorn principles, and the references highlighted by my Guide from *The Findhorn Garden Story*, given to me by Dianne. I had no doubt Sam would visit Findhorn one day and continue to play a part in my life and the Celestial Dolphin Centre.

At times I found the work in the Healing Garden heavy going. I cleared the outer edge of growth by the southern fence line and the dirt road, and planted boobialla and native hibiscus Julie had provided; then I created a new wider pathway within the garden itself to a coastal mort to be known as the Children's Tree.

I was not able to lift the heavier limestone boulders, but, knowing they had to be moved, I left them for several minutes until a sensation came flooding through me where I felt much taller and stronger. The feeling of being taller meant I had to adjust and walk carefully. (During one of her visits I had told Christina I felt as if I took on *another* form, that of a male.) A Reiki healer called Keitha called in and asked to give me a healing. We were surprised when given the go-ahead, as until that moment I had not been given consent by my Guide to allow any healer to enter the vibrations of my auric shield. As I lay on the massage/healing table in the Dolphins Healing Room, she saw the energy of a male superimposed over my body, like another aura. 'The man has a large build and is dressed in Celtic clothing,' she said. I had not told her about lifting the boulders.

The meditation group began to flex its muscles, with some wanting to move on to more advanced meditation. The majority preferred the enjoyable basic evenings. I tried to stand back, but the situation became a conflict and I was drawn in. I was uncomfortable with the proposed new direction, and said so. 'This group will break down,' I told Mum. *Shark amongst the dolphins*, my Guide said.

Julie visited briefly to take measurements of the garden in order to create diagrams on her computer. When we had finished I suggested she take Merlin home with her. She did, but a few days later returned the figure to me on her way to Perth.

Expect the unexpected, my Guide said. Mum received a letter from Barbara to say she and two friends would be arriving in Perth on 6 November, after stopping over in Bali for two nights. They would be hiring a car and driving to Dongara, then flying out of Perth on 15 November. I had commented once that if my sister ever set foot in Australia I would leave; but I had progressed emotionally since then and offered her my home, the lodge. Christina came for lunch and I shared my apprehension regarding Barbara's visit.

Christina and I had been brought together for the warning, on 24 June, of Egyptian times. Now we were to create Seven Healing Bands using coloured three-inch squares, each with a twenty-centimetre light blue band bearing a specific runic symbol, according to the *St Justin of Cornwall* information sheet. I recorded the instructions for her:

> *Gold with light blue band and runic symbol Mystic.*
> *Dark blue with light blue band and runic symbol Gebo.*
> *Orange with light blue band and runic symbol Ansuz.*
> *Red with light blue band and runic symbol Hagalaz.*
> *Yellow with light blue band and runic symbol Berkana.*
> *Green with light blue band and runic symbol Algiz.*
> *Purple with light blue band and runic symbol Perth.*

Combining colour and runic energy, my Guide said. *To be used during healing sessions.* I was taken to my father's *Simplified Dictionary – Encyclopedic Edition*:

> Rune – a character in one of the alphabets of the ancient nations of northern Europe, especially of the Anglo-Saxons and Scandinavians ... a secret or magical mark or sign.

I wrote down the details in my diary and my notes. *A marriage of minds*, my Guide said. This was in reference to Christina and me.

Two days later Barbara rang from Perth. Two years prior to that I had asked spirit that Mum and Barbara be reunited and all negativity removed from my family. This had been inside the church of St Mary at Northampton during the meditation weekend in 1994. Hopefully *this* would be achieved during the visit. Any issue I had with Barbara would be kept on hold.

Barbara said she and her friends wanted to visit the Pinnacles at Cervantes on their way to Dongara. I found it interesting that she was drawn to a place where, four years before, I had photographed our mother's name, Tess, written in the sand by a pillar that was reminiscent of Mary's hooded figure. Also interesting was the fact that Barbara would arrive at the centre eleven years to the day after Mum and I arrived in Australia in November 1985.

I did not wish to be at the centre when Barbara drove in. That moment was for her and Mum, so I arranged to visit Julie's farm. I was restless when I arrived there, so went walking along its boundaries. I was confronted by a huge eagle. It dived in front of me, repeatedly calling out. Its call held a warning, but also protection. After watching the sun disappear I returned to Dongara. I felt nauseous as I approached Mum's extension: I was about to meet the person who had changed our lives. But she was also a person who had travelled across the world to visit her mother.

Everyone was sitting at the table enjoying a meal when this large woman I did not recognise stood up and put her arms around me, giving me a tepid hug. I was shocked at Barbara's size. She handed me a gift. I moved away, placing the kitchen bench between us. I felt vulnerable because I had loved this person, but I would never allow her to hurt me or our mother again. I opened the gift; it was a dolphin aromatherapy candle-holder. *A dolphin that has lost her way*, my Guide said.

Our guests spent the next two days visiting Dongara and Port Denison, walking the beach with Mum. They planned to visit Kalbarri and hoped to take Mum with them, but she had been short of breath for days prior to Barbara's arrival and was not well enough to make the trip. When they set off we watched them drive away, realising Barbara was not here to resolve any issues, or to accept responsibility. Her friends had remained close, ensuring all conversations remained neutral. So why had she come? Acora had warned Mum in 1992, when I had taken her to see him for her birthday, that Barbara was after something, but he did not know what.

Meanwhile, the post brought a gift for me from Sam in Sydney: a silver dolphin. John from Findhorn had communicated and they were now close. She planned to visit him in Findhorn at Christmas, and go to the island monastery of Iona. Sam's gift of a dolphin and her intention to visit Iona confirmed she was part of the soul group.

Two days later Barbara and her friends returned, and the evening they were to leave for Perth we ate out in Dongara. Everyone discussed their impressions of Australia, but Barbara and I would not allow eye contact, let alone converse. I watched with disappointment and sadness as she hugged Mum the next day and said goodbye. *Until she faces the issues they will remain an unresolved heart wound*, my Guide warned.

Julie arrived with her boyfriend to resume measuring the property and the creation of Levels of Planting. He unpacked a computer from her truck, setting it up in my office ready for use the following day. Julie would stay for two days and a friend from Dongara would come to help us. The first level was to be the outline of the whole property and plants already present, the second level Julie's recommended planting. As all the data was fed into the computer, diagrams were printed to enable me to explain the garden concept to visitors.

An urgent phone call from England disturbed Mum: her sister Val was unwell and in hospital. I watched her reaction with concern. Aunty Val and Mum had been close companions before the conflict.

A young man named Steve asked to work with Christina during her weekly visits to the centre, offering Reiki. Christina had a husband and a young family, and time spent at the centre with Steve recharged her batteries.

On 21 November Julie arrived with her computer and we walked through the garden in the late evening and stood by the Beacon. We discussed how she was to be paid for her work, and later drew up an agreement. She insisted it was an investment. While she and Mum talked I was sent to the leaflet *Iona – Mother of Lindisfarne*. My Guide's message *The Light of Iona* highlighted Julie's connection. The leaflet read:

> So in 563 Columba left Ireland and eventually landed on Iona ... Then he and his monks buried their boat on the beach and set about building their monastery ... Iona has become a centre for inspiration, unity and healing.

The Dongara Iona did not have that feeling of unity. Within the meditation group there was still tension, and within the Celtic Seven tension was growing also. We saw considerably less of Norm and Marg as they saw more and more of Cathy in Geraldton.

The next day Julie and I started our day with the Beacon. I explained how it came into being following the planting of nine peppercorn trees and then digging a hole seven hand-widths deep and creating a spiral-like coil inside with stones — a central stone surrounded by eight smaller stones. As I spoke, my mind went to Rene Vaillant and

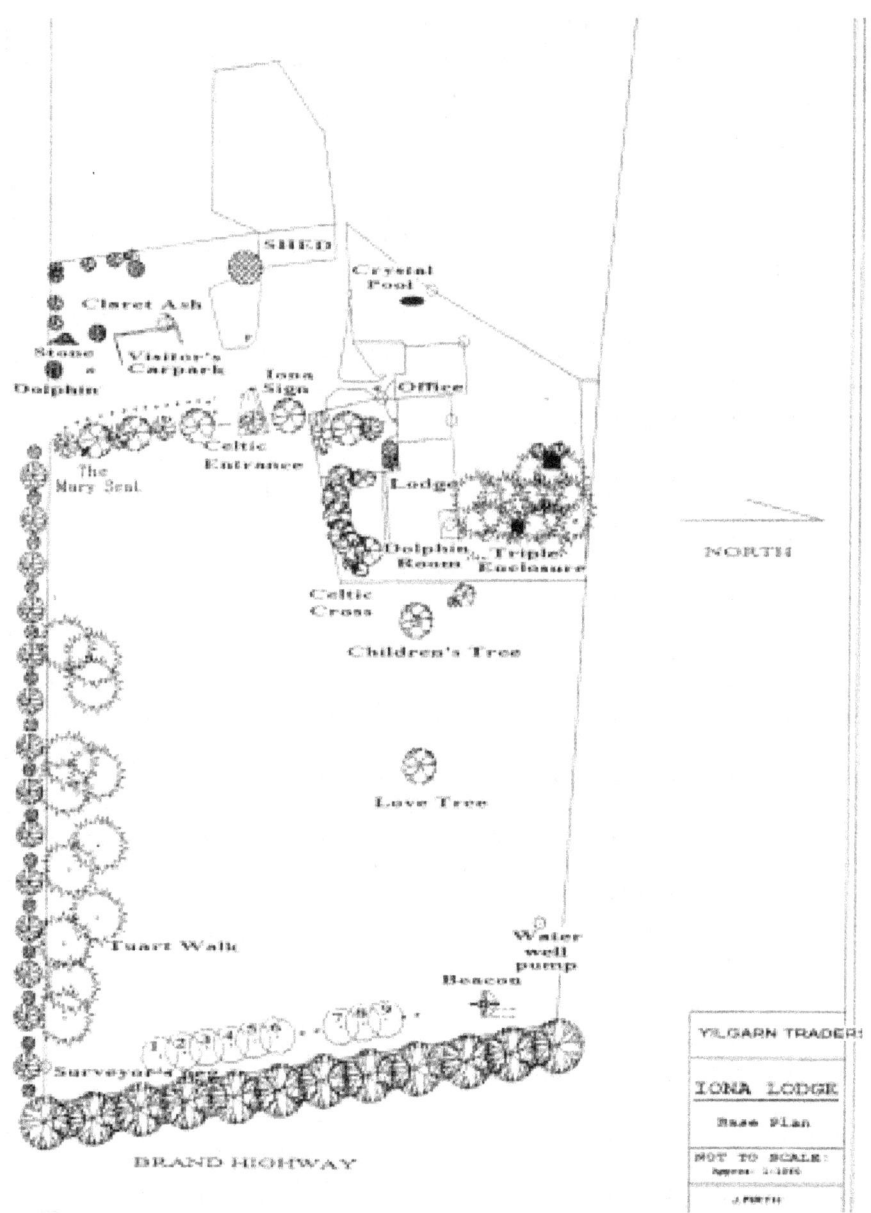

First level of the property and plants

his story regarding the Celtic crosses of Brittany. In order to survive the persecution, the Celts removed the axes of their crosses, leaving the central stone as a beacon. We returned to my office and I asked Julie to create a diagram to explain the Beacon, to be referred to now as the *Celtic Beacon*, showing both axes of a Celtic cross, which was not visible in the garden. As she did this, my mind filled with numbers. Julie fed this data into her computer as it was being given to me:

Vertical axis 1 – 2 – 3 – 4 and 1 – 2 – 3 – 4 – 5.
Horizontal axis 1 – 2 – 3 and 1 – 2 – 3.
Creating the numbers 1 – 2 – 3 – 4 – 5.
The first six peppercorn trees to be marked 1 – 6.
Creating the number 6.
The numbers closest to the Beacon centre $1 + 1 + 4 + 1 = 7$.
Creating the number 7.
The central stone is surrounded by eight smaller stones.
Creating the number 8.
The inclusion of all the peppercorn trees to be marked 1 – 9.
Creating the number 9.
Both axes hold the number 1 combined with the central stone 0.
Creating the number 10.
The third layer of numbers radiating from the centre $3 + 3 + 2 + 3 = 11$.
Creating the number 11.
The outer numbers of both axes $5 + 3 + 1 + 3 = 12$.
Creating the number 12.
The central stone holds the seven–stone spiral beneath its surface = 7.
The surface numbers closest to the central stone $1 + 1 + 4 + 1 = 7$.
A Celtic cross to be created around the Beacon with a two-metre surround.

I was encouraged to find a letter sent to me by a visitor to the centre who had mentioned the symbolic meaning of the number 7:

Seven – the sum of the number of Divinity (3) and of Mankind (4).

The influence of the core group of twelve Celestial Dolphins, my Guide explained. 'So there are twelve Celestial Dolphins,' I said.
Core Group, Core Colours, my Guide confirmed.

22 November 1996

This area represents the influence of the 'core group' of the twelve Celestial Dolphins.

The Beacon is 7 layers deep with a circumference of 8 stones and a central solar stone. A Celtic Cross will be made from the Beacon with a 2 meter surround

1,2,3,4,5	- Contained in the arms of the cross
6	- Peppercorn Grove has two areas, area one has six trees
7	- Numbers closest to the Beacon centre = 1 + 1 + 4 + 1 = 7
8	- Beacon core is surrounded by 8 stones
9	- The whole Peppercorn Grove has 9 trees
10	- The 1 is contained in the arms of the cross and the centre circle is the 0
11	- The third layer of numbers radiating from the centre = 3 + 3 + 2 + 3 = 11
12	- The outer numbers of the Cross = 5 + 3 + 1 + 3 = 12

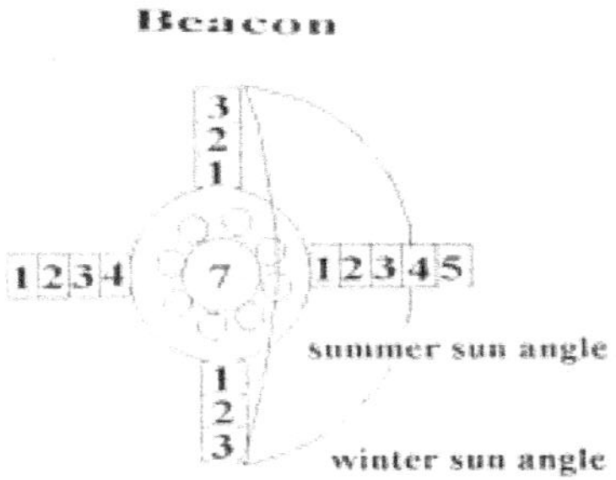

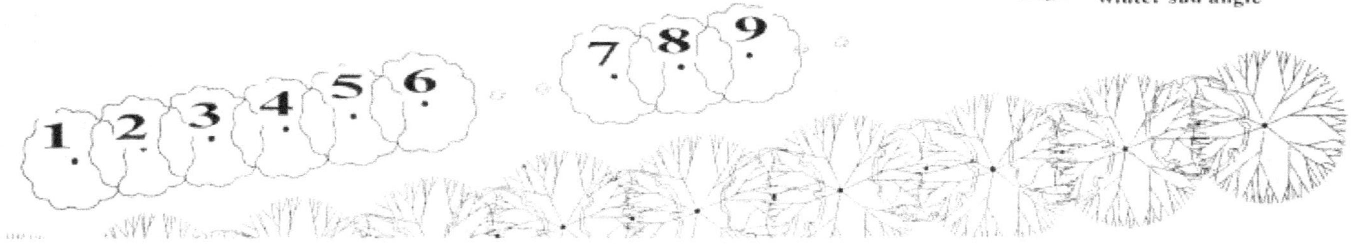

Celtic Beacon, core group of twelve Celestial Dolphins

On 2 October 1990 I had been instructed to create an eight-sided symbol now known as the Four Core Colours — featuring the colours of yellow, blue, green and red. *Core Group, Core Colours*, my Guide repeated several times.

The Celestial Dolphin Centre Core Group comprised three people: Christina, the Blue Dolphin; myself the Green Dolphin; and no doubt Julie was the third. I had been guided to give Julie a red rose in Perth; could this indicate she was the Red Dolphin? There was one member yet to be identified: the Yellow Dolphin. Now I understood the numbers (12) and (4) being linked to this symbol: the Twelve Celestial Dolphins and Four Core Group. Julie printed the diagram and we walked to the Celtic Beacon, standing either side of its circumference and touching its central stone — symbolic of Divinity (3) and Mankind (4) — before returning to the office computer, where Julie displayed her diagram and notes revealing the Seven Major Chakras to be created within the property:

Red: Base Root – Linked with the solar plexus chakra and Celtic Beacon.
Orange: Navel – Part of the Love Tree, linked with the brow chakra.
Yellow: Solar Plexus – Linked with the base root chakra and Love Tree.
Green: Heart – Linked with throat, crown and navel chakras and Mary Area.
Blue: Throat – Tuart Walk, linked with the heart chakra and Mary Area.
Indigo: Brow – Triple Enclosure, linked with the crown and navel chakras.
Violet: Crown – Lodge, Dolphins Healing Room, linked with the brow chakra.

Influence of the Red Dolphin, my Guide confirmed.

When Julie left I sat on the Mary Seat to ponder her past-life heart issue. 'Why didn't you come into my life a week earlier?' she had asked as we sat on the wall at her workshop. I remembered 7 June, the date by Julie's name, when I was sent to the Love Tree to find identical feathers. These were placed at the base of the Double Dolphin candle-holder. Identical feathers and identical dolphins — we were identical twins. Male, because the past-life heart issues of all three soulmates involved male passions. The Egyptian Mortuary God Anubis had been highlighted the previous month along with the words 'claimer of hearts', which upon my reading them had created a disturbingly rapid heartbeat. When I sought help, my Guide had explained my distress at Julie having been *ripped from your side in Egypt*. I understood that he (Julie) had died under violent circumstances and I was a week too late in finding him. This would be a past-life heart issue until we found one another again, explaining my feeling of exhilaration when Julie agreed to come to the centre.

Cathy made an appointment for us to see an accountant, the idea being that he would help me approach the building society again. Cathy paid for the meeting, wanting out of the mortgage. She said she had received a message, *Judy will be sole proprietor,* and was determined to achieve this. She asked to buy our computer and had taken it, which was why Julie was forced to bring her own.

Buddha was highlighted by my Guide, and I was sent to place the Buddha statue in Mum's garden near the Crystal Pool. As instructed, I positioned twelve bricks in rows of two, creating thirteen units with Buddha's statue at one end. *Sacred thirteen,* my Guide explained. The Celtic Beacon held the numbers 1–12. I dowsed my files and was taken to a photocopied page from *Eagle's Wings*, Volume 4, No. 5, *Understanding our Sacred Symbols*:

> ... sacred symbol, the cross of Christianity, you can count 12 inner and outer corners. These represent the 12 disciples. In the centre of the 12 disciples was Jesus, so the centre of the cross is counted as 13. There is the sacred number 13! (10)

My Guide had revealed another Sacred 13 that featured Buddha.

On 28 November Julie came to stay overnight, bringing her computer. I did not mention our past-life, twin-sibling connection. We were up early the next day and sitting with the computer switched on when a Level of the garden appeared without our prompting. This level contained all the symbols within the property, including Buddha's Sacred 13. 'That's impossible,' I said, 'I've not shared with anyone about my creating Buddha's sacred symbol.' Julie shook her head in response, unable to offer any explanation.

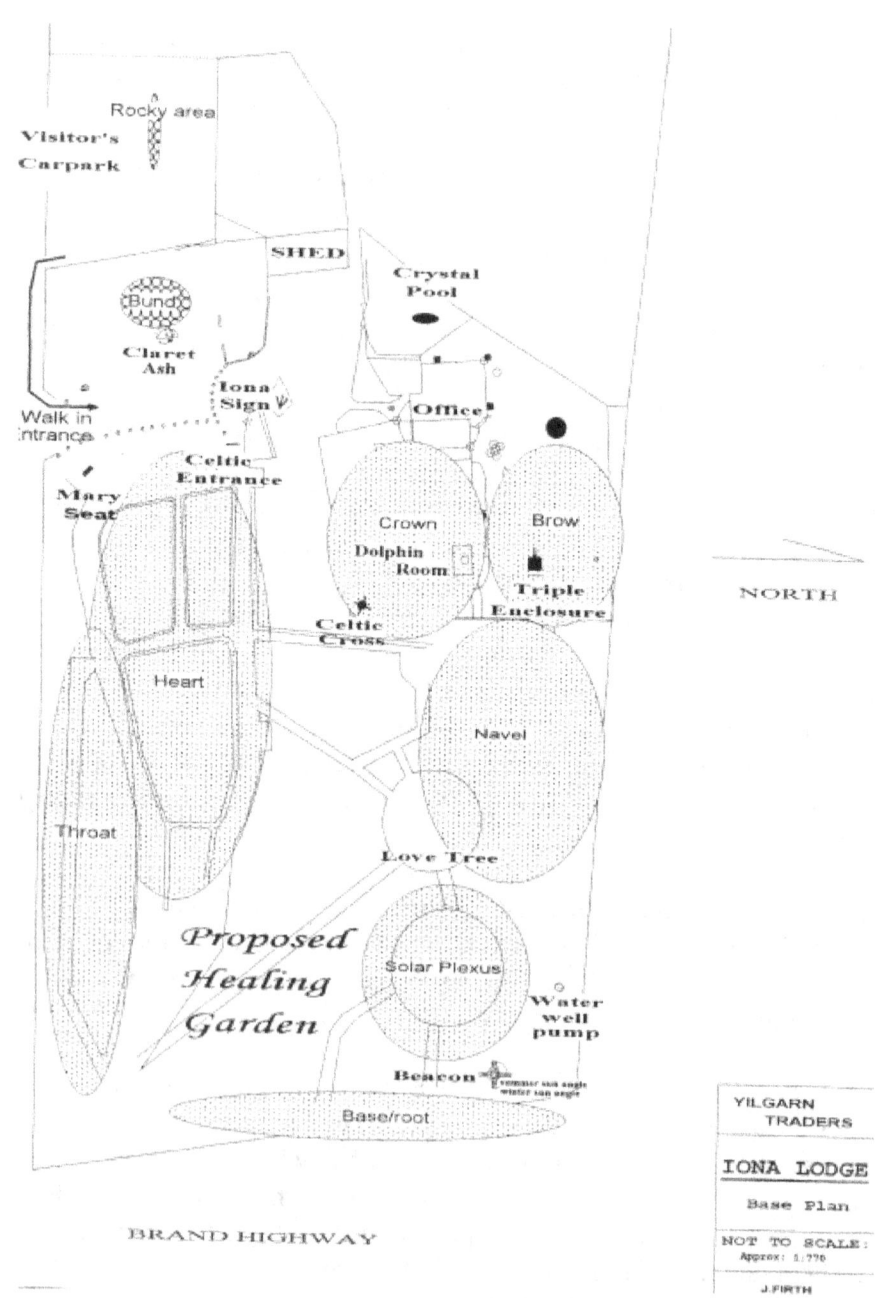

Seven Major Chakras, Healing Garden

Entwining of Souls

My Guide asked Julie to join three sets of symbols, one at a time, in order to reveal the Seven Healing Triangles held within the energy of the property. As I directed her where to place the lines on the computer screen, I could feel my Guide's enthusiasm:

Dolphin – Claret Ash – Mary Seat: *Mystic – Gold*.
Dolphin – Crystal Pool – Celtic Entrance: *Gebo – Blue*.
Dolphin – Dolphins Healing Room – Sacred 13: *Ansuz – Orange*.
Mary Seat – Iona Celtic Cross – Tuart Walk: *Hagalaz – Red*.
Mary Seat – Celtic Beacon – Love Tree: *Berkana – Yellow*.
Mary Seat – Claret Ash – Triple Enclosure: *Algiz – Green*.
Crystal Pool – Triple Enclosure – Garden Water Well: *Perth – Purple*.

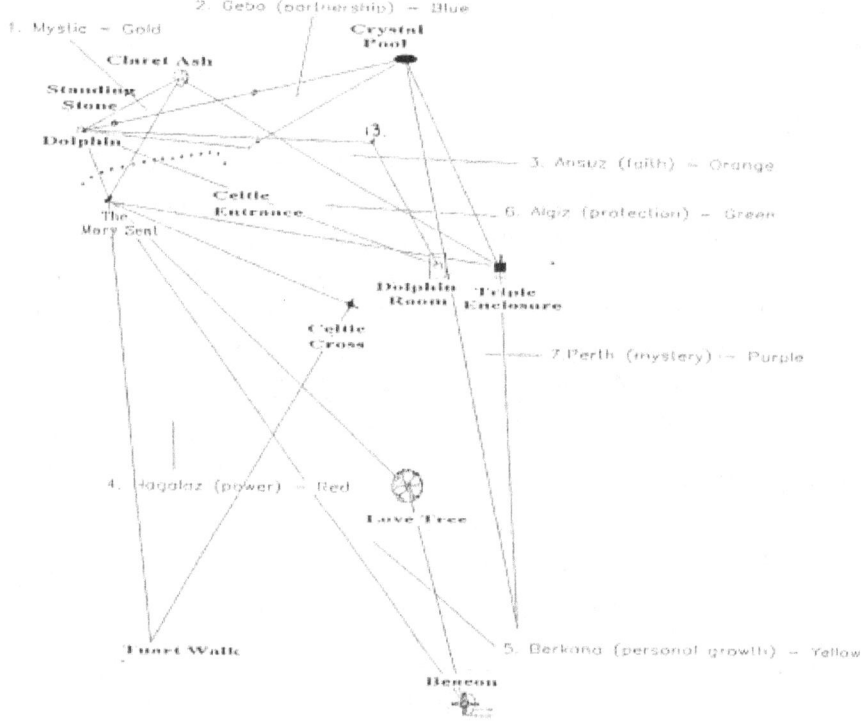

Seven Healing Triangles

There were Seven Healing Triangles with the same colours and runic influence as the Seven Healing Bands. By creating Buddha's Sacred 13 in Mum's garden, the Seven Healing Triangles had been activated. My Guide instructed the Soul Energy (2) notes be updated to include the clues '7 chakras', 'Buddha', 'Sacred 13', 'runic energy' and '7 Healing Triangles', and that the entrance to the Healing Garden created by Mum and me in preparation for Julie — with its two piles of stones and a long branch — to be referred to now as the *Celtic Entrance*.

Mum received an urgent phone call from England to say her sister Val was ill yet again, and there were serious concerns for her wellbeing. Mum became distressed, so I asked her if she wanted to go back to England and she replied that she did. There was a belief in Mum that her sister would recover if they rekindled their companionship in person. I arranged a loan with the bank and booked Mum on a flight leaving Perth early in December, aware that we would be parted for Christmas. I shared this development with Julie and a letter arrived from her the next day:

Dear Judy,
If people think you will instantly respond to their needs, you will be used beyond your capabilities. Use this 'time' wisely, Judy, your Mum will be back in two months and you'll lose your pure focus. You are the Key to this project, we must not lose you. It is very important to prioritise things and to ground yourself. I would like to be there for you – now is not the time. You must do it yourself. I know you can. Thanks for the wonderful few days. I am going to hijack you one day and run away on a magic holiday. Julie.

Mum and I were driving to Geraldton to pay for her flight tickets when the car stopped with a grinding noise. A passer-by gave me a lift to a phone and Julie collected us, and the car was towed to her place with a damaged big end. With a pending car bill and the loan for Mum's trip, I was unexpectedly in financial difficulty.

Julie drove us to Perth airport. It was hard for me to part with Mum, not least because I was concerned that she was now in her eighties and flying to England. I reminded her this was the second of her three predicted trips back to England and that she would return safely to Australia and me.

On returning to the centre I found another blow waiting. The building society had again rejected my application for a single mortgage. I sat on the Mary Seat with Jessie at my feet, alone and wondering if I would cope emotionally.

Barbara rang later to say Mum had arrived safely. We had not spoken since her visit to Dongara, and the air between us was filled with tension. I was violently sick afterwards. I calmed myself by writing the first of what would be daily letters to Mum: we had agreed to keep connected.

The Geraldton Guardian rang wanting to write a feature on the centre. I asked Julie to be part of this, as the centre's planting consultant. On 18 December the reporter and a photographer arrived — both women. I told them the story of Julie's proposed redevelopment of the Healing Garden and we showed them the diagrams. Then we walked around the property. Both appeared enthusiastic. I gave them the photograph I had taken of Julie on the day of her permaculture workshop, and we watched them drive away.

On Christmas Eve Julie visited the centre, handing me a pink Mexican rose to plant by the Celtic Entrance. The word 'pink' was highlighted in my mind. Norm, the Reiki healer and one of the Celtic Seven, had given Mum pink roses twice, and the second Soul Energy contained the clue 'pink rose energy'. There was a link between pink, male energy and the Celtic Entrance, and now Julie was introducing this energy in plant form:

> Soul Energy (2): Celtic Seven – pink rose energy – past lives / karma clearing – red rose energy – St Michael – Mary May Day '96 – 7 chakras – Buddha – Sacred 13 – runic energy – 7 Healing Triangles – pink – male energy – Celtic Entrance.

Julie came again on Christmas morning, and I gave her a surprise Christmas stocking full of gifts. She was like a child when she saw it, and I thought about us having been siblings long ago. Julie handed me a red rosebush; it was not from her permaculture farm, as she grew only native plants. She said it was a rose with a fantastic perfume. She spent time creating a Living Enclosure between the lodge and the Celtic Entrance, using arched black plastic piping, before leaving to celebrate Christmas lunch with her boyfriend and their friends.

At the permaculture conference in Perth my Guide had instructed me to place a red rosebud on the headstone of a person named Gardner, in the grounds of St Mary's Church, and to give a second red rosebud to Julie. The name 'Gardner' and 'Mary's Church' were highlighted and added to Soul Energy (1) and Julie's past-life heart issue notes. I was being shown now that there was a connection between red roses, Gardner, Mary's Church, Julie and me.

Mum had left behind her Christmas gift for me — a tapestry named *The Three Musicians*. It featured three young Egyptian women, two with their foreheads touching. I recognised the necklaces around these women's throats: they had appeared around Cathy's neck. *Two necklaces, two women, two situations,* my Guide said. As I studied the tapestry I was filled with deep sadness. I left it and went into the Dolphins Healing Room to light a candle and recover. The clues *Warning, This is a message from ancient Egypt* and *A child* repeated over and over in my mind.

Early on 2 January 1997 I was disturbed by the ringing of the telephone. It was Julie. 'Have you seen the newspaper?' she shouted. I replied that I hadn't. 'The centre is on the front page!'

I walked to Dongara to buy *The Geraldton Guardian*. There it was: my photograph of Julie under the heading, 'Creating a wave of excitement':

> A small farmlet near Dongara is creating a wave of excitement amongst some of the world's most highly respected healers. The Celestial Dolphin Centre is described as a 'unique Celtic energy centre' and already operates as a healing clinic where Mid-West people and visitors world-wide have begun arriving to use the property's energies for self-awareness and healers for relief. However the centre has not yet reached its full potential — an almost inconceivable planting project will create healing gardens. The project is the brainchild of Judy Roach who has enlisted permaculture designer Julie Firth (above) to help create her vision. Full story page 12. (11)

The article on page 12 explained a little of my background as the founder, and my being a healer with a Celtic background who had spent time learning about energies. Earth energies — ley-lines — ran throughout the six-acre property and I had accessed them to create healing triangles within the garden designs. These gardens would represent the body's seven chakras — crown, brow, throat, heart, solar plexus, navel and root — in physical shape, colour, element, touch and smell. Thus a different atmosphere would be created within each chakra area, evoking feelings in people that relate to their body zones. The gardens would include paths, seating areas and shade. I closed the page and walked back to the centre, then read further.

The article explained that, while my focus was on energy fields, I had sought the assistance of Julie Firth, a local garden architect and international dryland permaculture designer, to create my vision, and this was the first time she had designed gardens for a healing centre. Julie described the project as a challenge, as she had to create my vision of all-year-round colour and chakra qualities, while contending with the Mid West's lack of water, high limestone table and highly alkaline soil. Australian plants flowered all year round and WA natives would be given priority. The reporter tried to gauge the magnitude of the project by quoting my vision for the heart chakra as being the energy zone for blood circulation — energising the blood and the physical body with the life force, its vibrational colours being green and pink, the latter colour associated with one of the four elements — 'air'. Julie's intention was to create the heart chakra garden to look like the human heart pumping blood, and this would be achieved by creating a 'pulsing effect' using subtle plant colour changes. She would recommend the plants with the smell and aesthetic qualities to evoke the feeling of this body zone.

I was drawn to look up at Mary's image on the wall, with the Aboriginal spear still hanging underneath, before continuing to read the article. I had shown the reporter and the photographer Mary's image and was interested to read their comments on this aspect. The Dolphins Healing Room was described as being filled with gifts from people who had experienced the property's energies, including a psychic photograph of what was believed to be Mother Mary. The photograph, they wrote, was taken of a sunset at Medjugorje, where Mary is said to have appeared to children, and when it was developed it revealed Mary's face. The reporter referred to this as 'an astounding gift', and went on to write that the centre had created a Mary Seat in honour of this woman and her remarkable photograph. I was quoted as saying that, although I appreciated this Christian icon, the centre did not focus on one religious denomination but was a place for everyone. The article ended with the centre's King Arthur motto: 'In serving each other we become free.'

Cathy rang. She was having my car collected from Julie's property for repair by a contact of hers. Julie had returned to working on her own property but remained the centre's planting consultant.

The heart is to beat, my Guide said. Julie was given the task of choosing the plants to symbolise the 'flow of life' within the Heart Chakra. This was a challenge, as there was no fresh water in the Healing Garden, only salty bore water from the well. The other issues were high winds, long periods of intense sunshine and the limestone reef.

Foundation Day twenty-fifth January, my Guide said, so I began to consider how the centre's Foundation Day '97 might be celebrated.

Julie came up with the inspired idea of featuring sunflowers: these beautiful flowers would be in season. She would supply them for Foundation Day / Sunflower Fest '97. My Guide requested that I contact the supplier of the *St Justin of Cornwall* Celtic jewellery. *For Tess*, she explained. Other stallholders were encouraged to participate, and they would be located in the three-bay tractor shed. All the local churches were invited to provide cream teas. Terri, the photographer of the Celtic Seven and now leader of the meditation group, would be my helper and Julie would bring plants for sale. A Reiki Master and an astrologer were invited to participate and the pending event grew larger and larger.

I was set the task of creating a large symbol outside the main entrance under the White Dolphin, its shape to resemble the crest formation used in heraldry above the shield of a coat of arms. I marked the outline with boulders and selected smaller stones. I was instructed to paint the smaller stones white and use them to spell out 'One and All', the Cornish motto. Before I could create these words, a white horse came trotting down from the sand dunes. He came straight to me, and I steered him back up the dirt road to the paddock next door. I rang the ranger and he collected him. As I placed the white stones in a triangle inside the Crest, I wondered if there was a connection between a white horse and white stones.

On the day Mum's flight was due to arrive in Australia I was encouraged to stand inside the Living Enclosure that had been created by Julie on Christmas morning. It was 4 pm, the time Mum's plane was scheduled to land. I was instructed to collect four long thick logs from our store of wood to create a symbol within the enclosure itself. I placed the longest of the logs at the western end using three smaller logs as prongs; it was somehow a *familiar* formation, but I could not bring the connection to my conscious mind. The phone rang: It was Mum, in Perth.

It rang again: This time it was my nephew Tim, who wanted to tell me he loved me lots and I was able to tell him his nan had arrived safely. Claire had met Mum at the airport and taken her home. The next day my very exhausted but relieved mother arrived back in Dongara by coach. Her effort had been worthwhile — her sister Val had rallied.

When Mum had recovered from her jet lag, we talked. Aunty Val was still unwell, but her recovery was anticipated, although it would take time. She told me that her sister had decided she was too old and of no further use to anyone. She'd had no self-worth and had been living on past hurts and betrayals. But when they talked she accepted that she had allowed herself to get into this low state and that with a positive outlook she could change her life. Mum was told she was everyone's Christmas surprise and was made welcome. She told me also of how Barbara was rushed into hospital with a suspected heart attack as she was due to leave, but numerous tests revealed nothing. My niece Debby told Barbara in no uncertain terms that Nanny was returning to Australia, and Barbara was sent home.

Preparations continued ahead of Foundation Day / Sunflower Fest '97. Terry, our carpenter, erected white panels in the tractor shed for Healing Garden information. The electrician fitted floodlights there to highlight the Standing Stone and the makeshift car park in the back paddock. I cleared pathways inside the Healing Garden and maintained the three enclosed Heart chambers, a never-ending task.

I ordered circle dancing music and asked Cathy to organise a meditation evening. I was planning my first public speech to thank Mum for her support and loyalty, to thank Cathy for ensuring the property could be purchased and to thank Julie for her huge effort. On the morning of the big day I noticed that Julie's rosebush, planted in the breezeway, had produced a long-stemmed red rosebud overnight.

Hundreds of people came. Although nervous, I plucked up the courage to speak to the crowd. I asked Julie to join me on the stage and told everyone how she had taken time from her own project to help with mine. I had wondered what to give someone with such a unique rapport with the plant kingdom, and my only flowering plant had produced a perfect rose overnight. I handed it to her. *Red rose energy*, my Guide said.

Working with Julie had been a life-changing experience. A surge of emotion so powerful moved through me that I was forced to stop speaking. I asked Julie to speak as I stood back trying to recover. She looked at me with concern but I indicated that I was all right. I also handed her a pair of silver earrings: two Spears of Epona, the Celtic goddess. As I did so, a sharp chest pain came and I just managed to leave the stage. I walked to the Love Tree to recover, and was able to rejoin the crowd within minutes. Julie found me and handed me her planting diagram for the heart chakra and pathways. She had named it the 'Pulse of Life'. I watched her drive away, aware that she was wearing my gift, the Spear of Epona earrings. I was sent into the Dolphins Healing Room by my Guide to read Julie's past-life heart issue notes:

> Heart Issue: Julie – tapestry – 7 – garden – devas – New Zealand – coins – Dongara – Egypt/ankh – karma / past life – heart's journey – totem energy – Virgo – friends through time / soulmate – red rose energy – male passions – chakras – The Light of Iona – Gardner – Mary's Church.

Many clues had been revealed, but there were soul elements yet to be disclosed — Egypt/ankh, Virgo, Gardner and Mary's Church — which I would carry forward in my notes until all had been revealed. I was then encouraged to study Julie's diagram of the Pulse of Life and her proposed planting to encourage the Heart to beat.

Julie suggested the outer rim be planted with vetiver grass to introduce the colour green, the heart chakra's primary vibrational colour. The Heart itself was to be planted with a 'pulse' created by a flow effect of plants ranging from pale pink to mid-pink to dark pink, the heart chakra's secondary vibrational colour. This flow would move through the three enclosed chambers. The fourth chamber was to be open at its eastern end, and an Indian siris tree planted inside for shade and to produce yellow and white flowers. The entrance to the Heart Chakra / Pulse of Life would be a wide pathway between Chambers One and Two and featuring a Judas tree, chosen for its green heart-shaped leaves and pink flowers. On either side of the Judas tree was to be a desert kurrajong tree, also producing yellow and white flowers. The largest enclosed chamber, Chamber Three, was to include the element of Air, with a wind wheel to add to the movement and flow. Julie suggested that the pathways outside the Pulse of Life be edged with pink tamarisks, pink Geraldton wax, rosea and *Eucalyptus leucoxylon*. As soon as I read this, I knew it was not correct. *All white-flowering plants*, my Guide insisted.

Within the Heart Chakra there was a squared area near Chamber Three. This was missing in Julie's diagram. I spoke to her on the phone,

explaining that the outer pathways and the squared area near the curve must have white-flowering plants, and thanked her for her patience. I was then encouraged to *make a note of the colour white*. There were white-painted stones in the Crest and a White Dolphin at the main entrance; now my Guide was insisting on white-flowering plants around the Heart Chakra / Pulse of Life. A white horse had arrived as I was creating the Crest. When the stallion visited the Crystal Pool it indicated Supreme Power. What is the power held within the colour white? I wondered.

Julie's rosebush produced another long-stemmed red rose overnight! 'How do you do that?' I asked my Guide.

Red rose energy, she replied, *all petals to be left to dry and stored*. I cut the rose and carried it into the Dolphins Healing Room.

The *Midwest Times* featured the enjoyable events of Foundation Day / Sunflower Fest '97 from my summation, under the heading 'All Roads Lead to Dongara':

> Sunflowers helped celebrate a new concept which has just become available in the Mid-West. There was an air of excitement as busy people set about preparing for the first ever Sunflower Fest '97 at the Healing Energy Centre in Dongara. Stalls, local craft, Celtic jewellery, hand-crafted and sent from Cornwall; crystals, jumble and food stalls were complemented with tarot readings; palm reading; visiting clairvoyants, both local and from Perth; plants, herbs, folk singing – all creating the atmosphere of fun and learning ... The founder, Judy Roach, has a Celtic background; this has a strong influence on the centre's overall theme. Since March 1996 the lodge and six-acre limestone property north of Dongara has been undergoing a major transformation. Ley-lines, healing triangles and a healing garden project that will have areas designated to reflect the human body's chakra centres ... The next celebration will be Mary Day on 3 May. Though the centre is nondenominational this event will feature children dancing the Cornish Furry Dance and circle dancing, and the event is named after Mary – the Universal Mother...(12)

February brought the news that Cathy's father had died. She did not wish to attend his funeral and was upset as she rang me from the airport, not wanting to board the flight. I was booked to spend a weekend alone at Kalbarri and, to ensure she missed the flight, she offered to drive me there herself. Two years before, on 14 February 1995, Cathy and I had been encouraged by my Guide to visit the Red Hand Aboriginal Cave in the Blue Mountains; later the circuit medium at the Springwood Spiritualist church had warned me by saying, 'Someone is saying bad things about you ...' *Accept her offer then withdraw from her*, my Guide said.

When Cathy had left, my Guide encouraged me to read part of an article in an old magazine handed to me by a visitor, *The National Geographic* May 1977:

> ... *Druids exercised great political influence, forecasting the future, fixing auspicious times for enterprises, educating the young nobility and conserving traditions* ... Once a year they met in *solemn assembly* in Chartres, tribal centre of the Carnutes, in Gaul ... (13)

The word 'Chartres' was highlighted and my notes updated:

> Soul Energy (1): The Four Core Colours – yellow – blue – green – red – 4 – 12 – Dongara – self help healing centre – The Lady of Good Counsel – retreat – Celtic cross – gemstone – Druid energy – settled legal disputes – Celestial Dolphin Centre – Iona Lodge – rebuilding the cathedral – Virgo – St Michael – Mary May Day '96 – Gardner – Mary's Church – Chartres.

French connection, my Guide said.

Many clues had been revealed but there were energy elements yet to be disclosed, such as yellow, The Lady of Good Counsel, rebuilding the cathedral, Virgo, Gardner, Mary's Church and Chartres, which I would carry forward in my notes until all had been revealed. I was encouraged to continue reading:

> Horses were in the Celts' blood. In their religion too. Epona the horse goddess is represented more widely than any other Celtic deity. (13)

I wondered if Julie was wearing the Spear of Epona earrings.

On 14 February I was instructed to walk into Dongara to the Crystal Shop and buy a silver locket and chain. My Guide requested that I cut in half one of the dried petals from Julie's red rose and place one half in each of the half sections of the locket. I closed the locket and placed it on the jarrah table at the base of the Double Dolphin candle-holder. I lit a new white candle and played the *Call of the Dolphin* tape.

Eight years, our time is now, an unknown female whispered.

'Who are you?' I asked.

There was no reply, only silence.

It was eight years since I had been sent by my Guide to meet Cathy at a tapestry morning on 14 February. The soulmate who had been waiting eight years to enter my life and the life and energy of the centre was requesting to do so now. Three days later I was guided to buy a frame in order to work the Egyptian tapestry featuring the three women. On this day a year before I had driven to Geraldton with the Transfer of Land document for Cathy to sign. I felt apprehensive as I compared these two dates. The two women in the tapestry whose brow chakras were touching wore the necklaces that had appeared at Cathy's throat. I saw that the title was written in German: *Drei Musikanitennen*.

Two necklaces, two women, two situations, my Guide warned.

Three days later I was sent to the Dolphins Healing Room, specifically to the dolphins that had been placed on the jarrah table by the meditation group and others who wished to express their support for the centre. I placed among them a gold dolphin I had purchased not long before at the shop where I'd bought the silver locket. As I did so, I received the words *Golden Dolphin*. I was drawn to a box I had purchased in India and called the Taj Mahal box, where I now kept the silver locket with the two dried halves of a rose petal and other dried rose petals. My Guide requested that I place a red rose petal on the nose of the golden painted dolphin. *Golden Rose Dolphin*, she explained. When I took the locket out of the box I received the word *Marriage* and was requested to place a rose petal by the silver locket. *Healing*, my Guide said. An hour later I was encouraged to take out another petal and this time received the message *Jumping for joy*. I was drawn to look at Merlin and for the first time noticed a blue oblong crystal in the front of his hooded hat. A shaft of sunlight coming through the window was refracted by the crystal to shine a blue ray across the room. *The blue light*, my Guide said. I updated my notes with regard to the first soulmate with a past-life heart issue:

Heart Issue (1): Golden Rose Dolphin – soulmate – yellow roses – soul group – dream – regal young woman with dark brown eyes

– Egypt – dolphin – Switzerland – Mary – Wandjina – Kimberley diamond – disposal – crocodile – Dongara – Egypt/ankh – karma / past life – heart's journey – red rose energy – male passions – Warning. This is a message from ancient Egypt – a child – Taj Mahal – the blue light.

A dolphin in need of healing, my Guide explained.

I was instructed to walk into Dongara and buy a set of *Sacred Path Cards: The Discovery of Self Through Native Teachings* by Jamie Sams. On my return I was guided to dowse for a card, and the one I was given was the Hour of Power. The accompanying book explained:

> Hour of Power – Ritual of Joy ... each person also has an Hour of Power during a day's cycle ... it may be just before sunrise when the world is still and quiet ... it may be 3:00 or 4:00am when the stirrings of life are totally quiet and Entering the Silence is easier. For some it may be high noon ... it may be sunset ... For all people, their special time of the day or evening is their Hour of Power. (14)

My Hour of Power is 4 am: the time when I am usually wide awake and ready to start the day.

Days later a woman called Hanna held a moon meditation in the meditation room, the astrological signs involved being Scorpio, Cancer and Pisces. The music *Whales of the Pacific* was played. A leaflet read: 'It is described as a mystical journey to a magical place where mermaids sing forever in harmonious reprise with whales. Dugongs were once thought by sailors to be mermaids.' In a guest bedroom, here at the lodge, was the framed photograph from Monkey Mia of a dugong swimming with two dolphins.

Moon, my Guide said, and I was taken to my diary for June 1995: 'I was sent to the library to read about the Papyrus of Khonsu Wanderer, the Moon God. An ankh, the Egyptian cross, hung above the horizon, and *Egypt* and *ankh* were added to the clues regarding the three soulmates with heart issues.'

Cathy said she was organising a party for my birthday to make up for the previous year. I sensed there was a moment of truth to come between us, and my anxiety increased when I was referred to Chetwynd's *A Dictionary of Symbols*:

> Betrayal is the dark side of trust which it shatters. And also the dark side of forgiveness to which it may lead. Without coming to grips with the dark side of nature there is no possibility of development. But unless it can be related to the wider symbolic context of meaning and value, betrayal is simply brutal … (8)

On 1 March, the day I started to work on the Egyptian tapestry, a Cornish water diviner visited the centre. With his rods in his hands, he walked towards the Celtic Entrance and stopped by Julie's Living Enclosure. He had discovered a watercourse. He found that it ran through the back paddock, beneath the tractor shed and through the Living Enclosure into the Healing Garden — where it ran beside the Heart Chakra / Pulse of Life. I posted this information to Julie, asking her to complete a diagram including this new underground watercourse, and a separate diagram of the Seven Major Chakras combined with the Seven Healing Triangles, to reveal the healing energy here — seen and unseen.

She, in the meantime, had posted an amended diagram of the Heart Chakra / Pulse of Life, to be handed out on Mary May Day '97 / Open Day. In her diagram the Heart Chakra / Pulse of Life was surrounded by white-flowering mulla mulla, Dongara mallee and Geraldton wax. The small squared area that had been missing previously was now included.

Julie to open the Healing Garden, my Guide requested. As I wondered how this would be possible, as Julie was so busy, part of an article taken from an unknown magazine arrived from Sam, now living at Findhorn:

> Iona — such a tiny Hebridean isle! A mere satellite of the much larger island of Mull! Yet its history and religious importance is out of all proportion. The monastery here, founded by the Irish monk, Columba (the dove), became the first of a whole family of monasteries in Scotland, Ireland and Northumbria …

Sam had enclosed a photograph of MacLean's Cross on Iona Island. Julie held the title of *The Light of Iona*. I was pondering my Guide's insistence that Julie open the Healing Garden on Mary May Day when I was taken to the photograph of MacLean's Cross. I was guided to remove from the Taj Mahal box the silver locket containing two halves of one of Julie's dried rose petals, and hold it in my left hand. I was instructed to select a dried rose petal from the box and carefully placed the locket and the petal on top of the photograph. *Julie will come*, my Guide said. *Maypole*, she insisted. Where on earth was I going to find a maypole? In response to my question I was encouraged to complete the outline of a woman in the Egyptian tapestry, indicating there was a link between this woman, a maypole and Mary May Day '97. My Guide requested that I update the notes regarding the Golden Rose Dolphin with the clues 'maypole' and 'Mary May Day '97', and then walk into Dongara.

There I was instructed to buy *Medicine Cards: The Discovery of Power Through the Ways of Animals* by Jamie Sams and David Carson. On returning to the centre I was taken to study a picture of a whale while playing the *Whales of the Pacific* tape given to me by Hanna at her moon meditation, then to *dowse for a card*. When I turned the card over, it was the Whale. The accompanying book explained:

> Whale – Record Keeper … If you have pulled Whale card, you are being asked to tap into these records and allow yourself to be sung to by those who have the original language … This will open your personal records so that you may further explore your soul's history … (15).

Further explore your soul's history, my Guide said. I sat listening to the music while I updated the notes regarding the Golden Rose Dolphin with the clues 'silver locket' and 'soul's history'.

On 4 March Carol Hope, a local tarot card reader who I had met previously, pre-booked an evening for a meditation group. Then students from a Perth university arrived, seeking to tour the Healing Garden. A woman on holiday from Switzerland who ran a successful dance academy booked for one night's bed and breakfast. We were sitting on the Mary Seat when she said, 'I see Julie Firth's left hand in the Healing Garden and a luminous green light is moving up her left arm. But Julie is tied by ropes, by people's opinions. She will break free and cross that bridge. I see a pole with coloured ribbons attached; people will come from around the world to visit this place. Clairvoyants will hold a world conference here and healers will come to recharge.'

Four days later Mum came to the lodge, inviting me to her extension for my birthday breakfast. Her theme this year was pink: a rose-pink tablecloth and a tall pink candle. In the evening the meditation group came and I was entertained with singing and storytelling. Hanna brought a herbal medicine stick, which she lit, then moved around those present, skirting each person's body, cleansing their aura.

A large envelope arrived in the post from Julie. It contained the diagram with the underground aquifer plus a second diagram highlighting the aquifer within the Seven Major Chakras Healing Garden design — emphasising the energy running beneath the Iona Lodge sign by the Celtic Entrance, through the Healing Garden beside the Heart Chakra / Pulse of Life, beneath the place where the 'Iona Lodge' sign had been erected the previous year by the Celtic Seven and exiting the property via the base root chakra.

'Ley-line energy,' I said to Mum, when I showed her Julie's diagram.

In a third diagram, Julie had superimposed the Seven Healing Triangles upon the proposed Seven Major Chakras within the property. Although the Standing Stone was not named, it was recorded as a small circle between the main entrance and the claret ash.

I rang Julie about opening the Healing Garden on Mary May Day and was not surprised when she said she was too busy. We discussed the outer rim planting of the heart chakra and how I was going to need three hundred vetiver grass plants at a dollar each. Julie went silent, then said she would bring them down with other plants to sell on Mary May Day '97 / Open Day. Following our conversation I was guided to remove the silver locket from the MacLean's Cross photograph. Julie Firth — The Light of Iona — was coming to the centre to open the Healing Garden as forecast by my Guide.

On 19 March I asked Carol Hope, the tarot card reader, to share her experience of the evening's meditation with the group, but she was reluctant. However, she asked to see me the next day and shared what she had experienced.

'During the meditation,' she said, 'I was taken into the garden to the Tuart Walk, where a spirit figure wearing a cream nun's habit with a brown trim was waiting. It was Mary, and she had her arms held out and was smiling. She repeated your name, Judy, several times.' She thought the nun's habit was of the order of the Sisters of Mercy.

Carol was guided to look up towards the Love Tree and saw a spirit child waiting under its canopy. 'She was dressed in the same habit and smiling, young and free. I asked her what I should say to you, and she said I must tell you that you will know when you have to leave. You will not follow anyone else or listen to anyone else. You will always follow the guidance.'

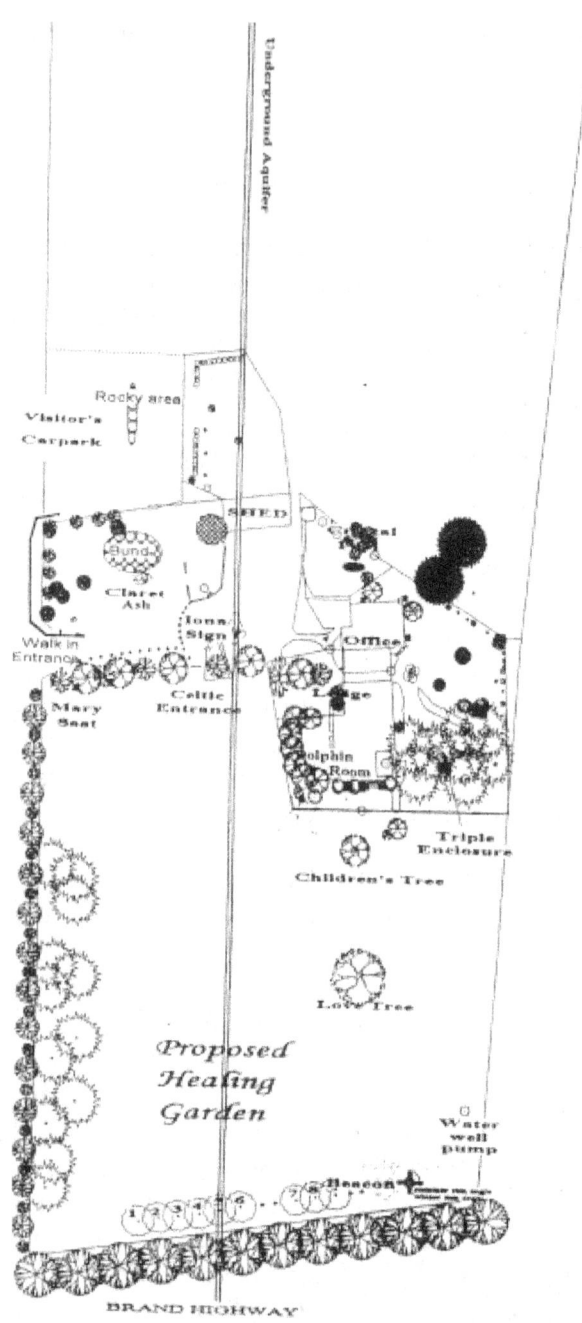

Underground aquifer, ley-line energy

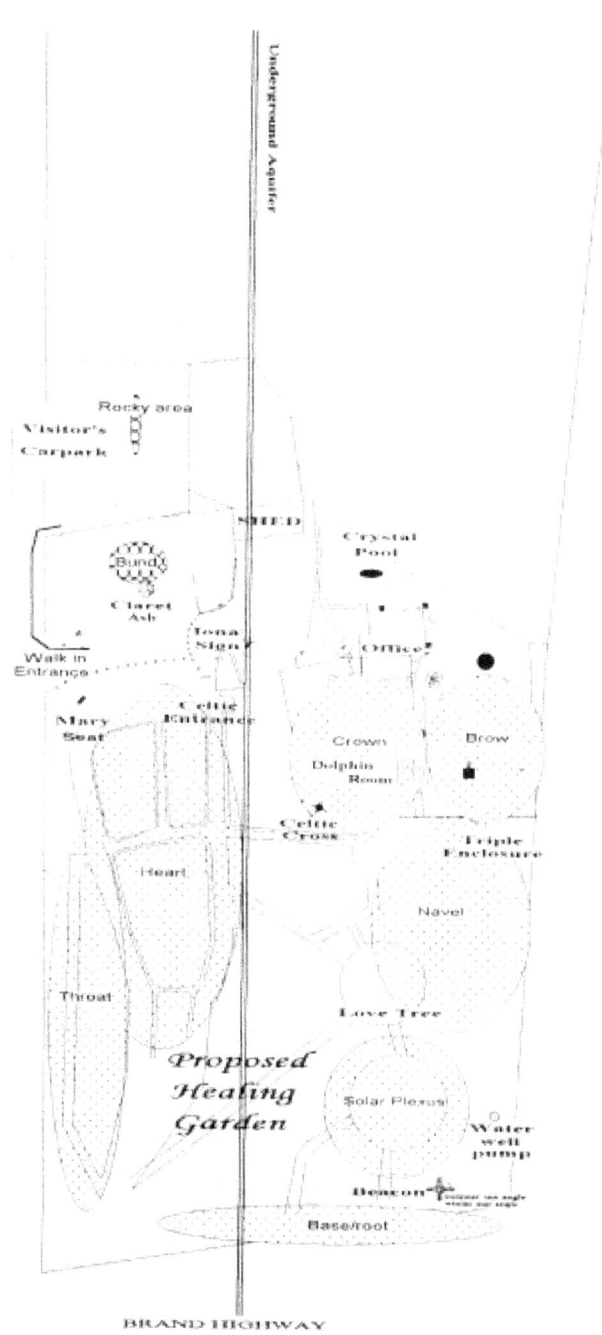

Underground aquifer, ley-line energy, Seven Major Chakras

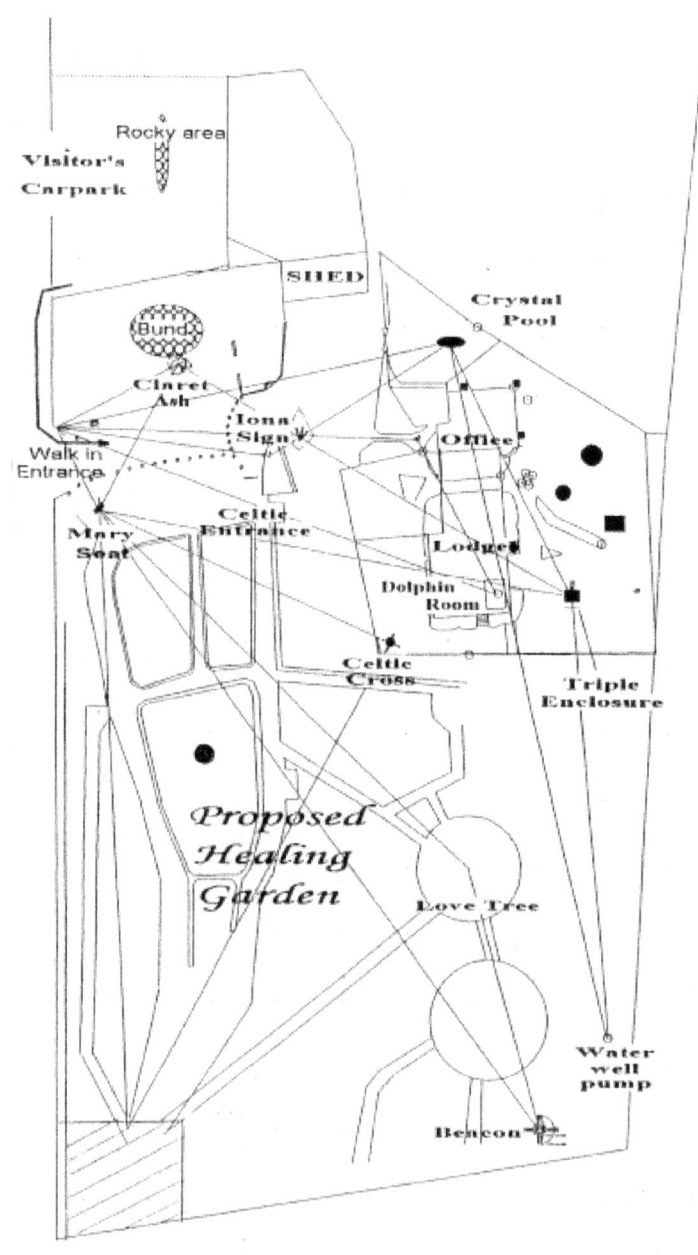

Seven Healing Triangles, Seven Major Chakras

I waited until Carol had finished, then told her I had not seen Mary but I had been visited by my Guide, a dark-skinned Catholic nun. Carol asked if I had asked to see Mary and I replied, 'No, I do not feel the need.'

I found it interesting that Mary appeared to Carol at the Tuart Walk entrance, the area highlighted by a yellow glow during the Mary Display in 1995. Mary wearing a cream nun's habit reminded me of 27 December 1994, when I had been guided to light a cream candle to highlight her image in order to bring through the Ten Year Mary Project.

My Guide encouraged me to arrange for the Cornish Furry Dance to be performed by local schoolchildren on Mary May Day — dressed all in white as in Helston, Cornwall. But what about the music? I wrote to the Cornish Community in South Australia and my friend Jill in Cornwall, England. Pam O'Grady from South Australia sent a tape after confirming it was a genuine Celtic Day. She included the music for maypole dancing and the dancing steps, and Jill sent a video, *Helston Flora*, which featured the Furry Dance steps and the music. I smiled when I read her note, which began 'Hey Jude', a term of affection that only she used. A disused electricity supply pole was donated by the meditation group for use as the maypole, but I had not comprehended how technical it all was. Terry was considering how to erect it and how to secure the sixteen ribbons to the top, but was not finding it straightforward. The pale blue and deep gold ribbons were being made in Sydney.

The workshops included Reiki, aromatherapy, colour therapy, stress management, meditation, permaculture and astrology. The tractor shed would be filled with stalls, and a Gypsy Row would feature tarot card readers and soothsayers in their tents. My Guide had required an oak tree, sacred to the Celts and the month of May, and Julie had a small oak tree in her nursery that she would plant on the day.

April brought rain and Julie gave direction for the construction of swales, V-shaped trenches to catch the rain, these to be dug within the Heart Chakra / Pulse of Life. I rang Tatia, the South African woman I'd met at Julie's workshop the previous year, and she agreed to ask the permaculture community in Perth to assist me with installation. Within days I had a volunteer. Ginna agreed to be my wwoofer, and we created a 'spirit level' with two clear plastic tubes connected to either end of a garden hose. The tubes were marked to show the various levels and then filled with water and sealed at both ends. We placed the hose across stretches of ground until our levels were the same and then used the pendulum to learn where each swale was to begin. We dug four swales before Ginna left three days later. Now I needed mini bridges where the swales dissected the Heart. Along came Roger, husband of Mary in the meditation group, and he found wooden pallets at the tip that did the job perfectly.

When the Healing Garden was in its early stage of development and I had a car, I was sent by my Guide to the tip to collect cray-pot slats dumped by fishermen and store them in the tractor shed. She directed me to place straw, cardboard and carpet inside the three cleared Heart chambers to prevent weed growth, and to put the cray slats on the top to stop everything blowing away. This would allow the breakdown of these materials to form soil. Roger volunteered to visit the tip daily with his trailer to get the materials.

A visitor named Irene helped me with this work, and it took us all day to complete a small section of one chamber. When we sat on the Mary Seat to recover, she asked if she could have a copy of the Heart Chakra / Pulse of Life diagram. Two days later the phone rang and it was Irene wanting to bring a friend to meet me. The friend turned out to be a middle-aged male with a beard and longish unkempt hair who she introduced as Martin. My heart missed a beat. Three times in the Blue Mountains in 1987 I had been sent to a street sign, Martin Place; ten years later in Dongara I was being introduced to Martin. He was carrying the Heart Chakra / Pulse of Life diagram and asked me where the design had come from. 'It came from my mind,' I said.

He told me that when he was shown the diagram by Irene he knew he had seen it before, so he hunted through his pile of old magazines until he found *Nexus* magazine for October/November 1996. I had not heard of this publication. He turned to page thirty-nine and an illustration of the Egyptian Goddess Nut. (16)

'This is your Heart Chakra / Pulse of Life,' he declared. I compared the two diagrams.

The flow effect was the same, and both contained two circles and their shape and form were similar. The Egyptian goddess was protected by women with sistrums and the Heart Chakra / Pulse of Life by white-flowering plants. The heart of the goddess in circular form was represented in the Heart Chakra / Pulse of Life by the wind wheel, while her navel chakra, also in circular form, was represented in it by the Open Chamber.

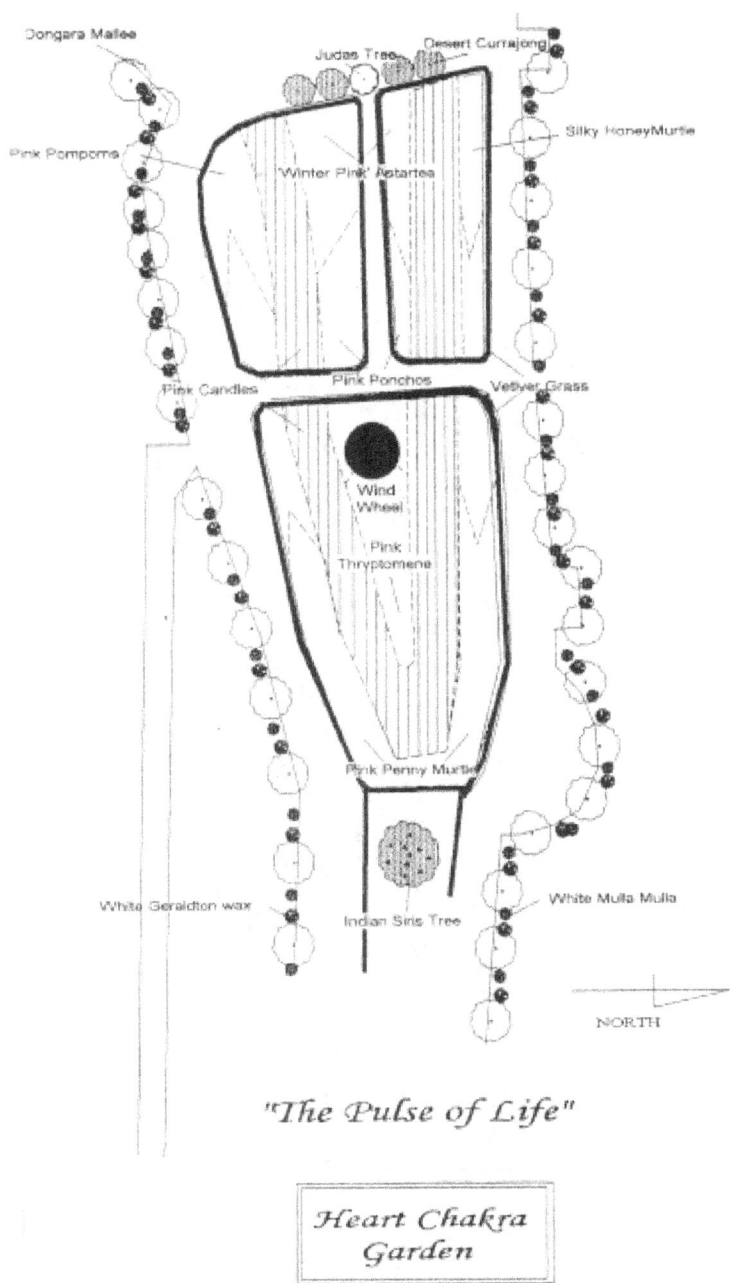

The Pulse of Life, Heart Chakra Garden

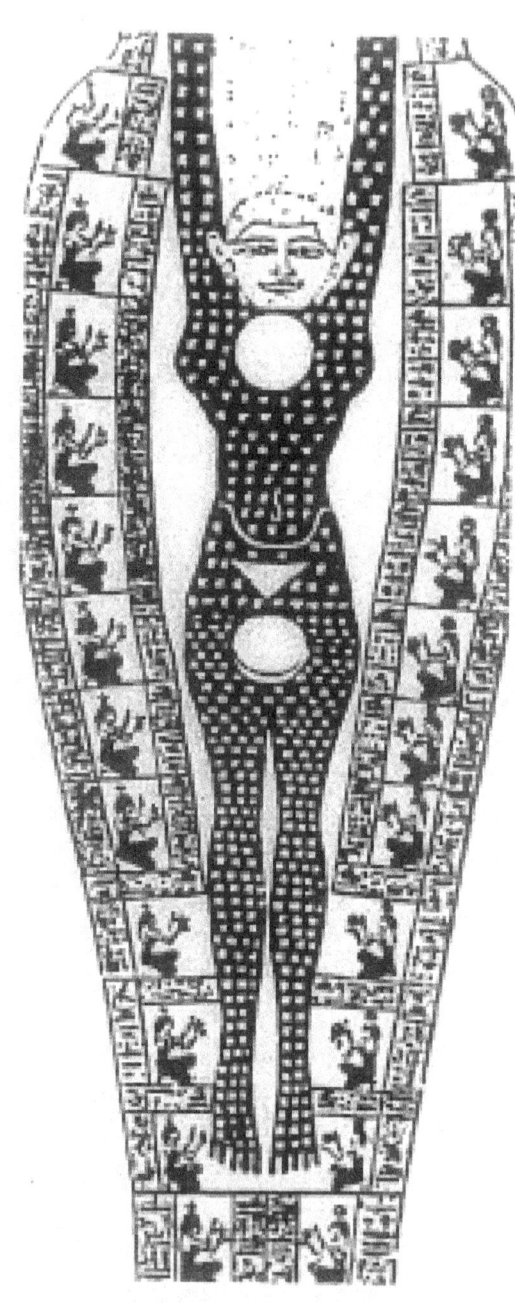

The Egyptian Goddess Nut

Martin told me his father used to make maypoles. Wow, I thought. When I explained the problem Terry was experiencing with ours, he said he would get help from his father and return with the information.

Later, I showed Martin's diagram of the Egyptian Goddess Nut to Mum. 'What do you think?' she asked.

'I'm not sure what to think.'

The next day, 14 April, I received the message *A search of secret Egypt* while standing in the Dolphins Healing Room. My Guide directed that the silver locket was to be placed at the base of the Double Dolphin candle-holder, replacing the identical feathers that linked me to Julie, and the candle lit while the *Call of the Dolphin* was played. *A search of secret Egypt to begin*, my Guide said. I sensed it was a warning.

I was working in Chamber Three when Martin drove into the car park. He had the guidelines regarding the maypole stand and photocopies of the image of the Egyptian Goddess Nut. My Guide had not allowed me to research this goddess, but later encouraged me to place her illustration beside the silver locket, highlighting a link between the maypole, silver locket, Nut and the Golden Rose Dolphin. I was instructed to update the Golden Rose Dolphin and Soul Energy (2) notes accordingly.

A week later Hanna, who had held the moon meditation, invited Mum and me to dinner. She had offered to make the 'Healing Garden' sign for the Celtic Entrance for Mary May Day '97 and I was guided to show her the Heart Chakra / Pulse of Life diagram and the Egyptian Goddess Nut illustration. In her lounge I was drawn to the bookcase and the book *Goddesses for Every Season* by Nancy Blair:

Nut – Egyptian Sky Queen. Egyptian Goddess of the turquoise day sky and the royal-blue night. Nut arches over the Earth, animating all things with Her cosmic regenerative energy. In Egypt, heaven was the body of a woman. (17)

Hanna handed me her Egyptian ankh — the Egyptian cross – suggesting I borrow it. *Beware*, my Guide warned.

When Mum and I returned to the centre, the Egyptian tapestry was highlighted and Hanna's ankh and a lapis lazuli placed on the brow chakra of the Egyptian woman, linked with the clues 'maypole' and 'Mary May Day '97' — the Golden Rose Dolphin.

Someone is thinking about you, Libra, my Guide said.

Next day Roger drove in to ask if I needed any further help. He was drawn to protect Julie's Living Enclosure and began to search for star pickets and fencing at the tip. Roger, who was in his fifties with thin greying hair and a solid build, wore short shorts and a sleeveless top regardless of the weather. He and his wife, Mary, enjoyed the weekly meditation sessions at the centre. Roger also discovered, with joy, that when he and I worked together in the garden he gained temporary relief from the constant movement in his weakened right arm, caused by an aggressive form of Parkinson's disease.

Days later Terry drove in with the maypole and left again with the instructions from Martin. My Guide insisted the maypole be erected near the Celtic Entrance. Children were practising the Furry Dance and the 'Healing Garden' sign was completed. The practitioners were aware of their workshop times and venues. There would be a one-dollar entrance fee to cover the cost of the vetiver grass that was to enclose the Heart and the white-flowering Dongara mallee trees to outline the Heart's outer pathways. Hanna called in, carrying the completed 'Healing Garden' sign:

> Healing Garden opened by Julie Firth.
> A designer with vision, 3 May 1997.

My Guide insisted that I return Hanna's ankh as she handed me the sign — as this was not the ankh that related to the identity of the Golden Rose Dolphin.

Tess to make a pink ceremonial curtain, my Guide requested. Julie was to draw this curtain aside in a ceremony on Open Day. Pink — the secondary vibrational heart colour — was being introduced. I was referred to a section of a page in a pile of loose papers:

> Pink is a healing colour and represents love and romance ... It belongs to the fire and the earth elements, depending on the shade, and it is good to use in the relationship and knowledge areas.

My Guide instructed that the pink curtain feature at its centre the Ogham symbol for the oak — two short vertical lines meeting a longer horizontal line — and I was taken to a reel of black-and-gold ribbon containing the Greek symbol of eternity. I handed this to Mum. The *St Justin of Cornwall* information read:

May – Oak ... Solid protection ... doorway to mysteries.

Mum was also given the task of completing two long-stitch tapestries — a Parisian scene for Cathy's birthday, 1 May, and a bunch of red poppies for Julie's birthday, 5 May. On 30 April I awoke to find myself held fast within a swirling circle of intense golden energy. *The Golden Rose Dolphin of Egypt*, my Guide explained. At 4 am the next day this message was repeated; then it was repeated throughout the day.

On 2 May Mum completed the pink curtain and proudly handed it to me. *Something ending, something to begin*, my Guide warned.

I recalled my fortieth birthday in South Australia in March 1986, when Mum found the fortieth shell and we secured it inside the Butterfly Circle. A message had come through warning of an ending of a phase and a new phase. I updated the Soul Energy (2) notes, the energy required to encourage the Golden Rose Dolphin to reveal their identity:

Soul Energy (2): Celtic 7 – pink rose energy – past lives/karma clearing – red rose energy – St Michael – Mary May Day '96 – 7 chakras – Buddha – Sacred 13 – runic energy – 7 Healing Triangles – pink – male energy – Celtic Entrance – maypole – Mary May Day '97 – Egyptian Goddess Nut – silver locket – Golden Rose Dolphin.

At 6 am on Mary May Day '97 / Open Day, I carried the pink curtain to the 'Healing Garden' sign and repeated the Celtic prayer as the sun rose and its orange rays moved through the Heart Chakra / Pulse of Life. As I held the pink curtain aloft, showing it to the universe, I proclaimed, 'I have fulfilled my promise: the Healing Garden opens today.' I threaded the curtain through the cord and covered the sign. Only Julie could push this to one side and I was given the understanding that, as she did so, she was giving her consent for me to move on from our past-life connection and open yet another doorway to ancient Egypt.

Light the Dongara candle, my Guide instructed. I went to the Dolphins Healing Room and lit the candle, watching the glow of its flame reflect on the silver locket, now at its base, and Mary's image on the wall.

As Julie drove in through the crowd I understood that this would be her last visit. At 2 pm we stood across from the maypole, with its sixteen ribbons of blue and gold. *Blue Mary Ray and Golden Rose*, my Guide said.

The music began to play and the crowd watched in anticipation as the Queen of the May entered the property through the main entrance, followed by children dressed all in white and dancing the Cornish Furry Dance. I smiled as I watched Julie's face fill with wonder at the unfolding scene. The Queen of the May stopped in front of Julie to hand her Australian wildflowers; then Julie walked between the dancers standing in two rows beside the maypole and waited a moment before looking back at me. She then drew the pink curtain aside. Everyone cheered and my heart filled with pride. I looked at my mother and she smiled; Julie entered the Healing Garden and planted her oak tree.

I began my speech, but soon found myself rambling. The crowd became a blur of faces, when the shooting star — the one that had appeared in the sky when Julie had stayed the previous year — moved across my vision and I heard the message of 24 June, *A word of warning. You are entering dangerous territory. Egyptian times.* I tried to focus on Julie, but she looked away. Then I discovered Marg's face — smiling with encouragement — in the waiting crowd and found my rhythm, enabling me to finish my speech.

I looked at Julie again but she looked away: I had been moved on. I was alone standing by the maypole, following the successful exhibition of the intricacies of maypole dancing, when a woman in her early forties, tall and slim with shoulder-length dark wavy hair and intense brown eyes walked up to me and gave me a hug.

'I thought your speech was very good,' she said.

'I'm sorry, but do I know you?' I replied, confused by her personal approach.

'Yes, I have been coming to your meditation nights since February.' English was not her first language but she was easy to understand.

'I'm sorry but I can't place you,' I replied.

'My name is Greta,' she said, 'you helped me once with a kind remark.'

'That's good,' I replied, 'but I talk to many people on a daily basis.' Greta did not appear to be offended by my comment.

'I am leaving Dongara soon,' she said, 'and wanted to say goodbye to you.' She explained she was leaving to sail around the world with her husband and two children.

'Really!' I said. 'What an adventure; you must send me a postcard.' I wondered why I would ask a stranger to send me a postcard.

Greta walked away when a middle-aged man asked me to share my Cornish background, as he was from Cornwall. I told him my maternal great-grandfather was believed to have been a Cornish wrestler. I strolled away from the maypole unaware that my exchange with Greta would soon turn out to be a life-changing event.

The clairvoyants in Gypsy Row had been busy all day, and I waited for the crowd to leave before visiting Carol. The last time she and I had spoken she had told me about seeing Mary in the garden. Now, during a tarot-card reading, she warned me of a situation concerning me and a tall fair-haired person with a determined character. I must be on my guard, she said, as I could be hurt. This was not what I wanted to hear. I left her tent to stand beneath the canopy of the Love Tree, staying there for several minutes before leaving to find Julie, to show her the comparison, handed to me by Martin, between the Heart Chakra / Pulse of Life and the Egyptian Goddess Nut.

Julie left with a copy of the Nut sketch and her gift from Mum — the red poppies tapestry. I watched her drive away, accepting that she and I were parting of our own free will and our past-life heart issue of being forcibly separated was resolved.

In serving each other we become free, my Guide said.

A practitioner who stayed overnight was sulky the next morning, and I wondered what or who had upset her. I rang Terri, the meditation group leader, with whom she had arranged to be picked up, then walked her to the Mary Seat, where she said she wanted to sit for a while. A few minutes later I discovered she had left the seat and was now standing outside the main entrance. Then Terri arrived and they drove off together.

Cathy wanted to see me the following day. I gave her Mum's gift of the tapestry. She was restless, wanting to go abroad, but I was only half listening to what she said. My mind was full of Carol's warning about my interaction with a determined person.

During the evening of 5 May I was alone when Hanna phoned wanting to see me. It was urgent she said. When she arrived I took her into the kitchen to make tea, not connecting her visit with Carol's warning. I became very uncomfortable when she began to express an attraction to me. I walked into the meditation room, a step nearer the door through which she would soon be leaving. She followed me, talking in a soft, controlled voice, wanting me to listen to the story of her life. 'I do not want this and you would know that,' I said to her.

Within minutes I was walking Hanna to her car. Where on earth did all that come from, and why? *Trust the process and all will be revealed,* my Guide said. I was encouraged by her to share all this with Terri, the meditation group leader. I rang her and was floored when she said she was aware of Hanna's attraction. Terri, to my horror, had decided that I had encouraged Hanna, and I was filled with a dreadful sinking feeling. Within days I was faced with conflicting responses. Hanna rang warning me not to trust anyone in the meditation group. Then Terri visited, accusing me of betraying Hanna's confidence; the conflict spread and I was judged by her group. I returned to work, unaware of the simmering situation within the town. Soon the people who came to the centre on a daily basis no longer visited. Only a young woman and her daughter, new to Dongara, came to help with planting the vetiver grass. The meditation evenings continued, but few attended. When Hanna rang for the last time, I informed her I had shared everything with my mother, because of tension coming from the meditation group and Terri.

Changes coming, my Guide warned. I wondered how many more changes I could cope with.

Early the next day I was confronted by Terri regarding the practitioner who stayed overnight on Mary May Day / Open Day. I was accused of throwing the woman out. I didn't realise at the time that this was also being discussed within her meditation group. I told Terri she knew very well that I would do no such thing and, whoever had upset the woman, it certainly wasn't me. Following this confrontation my Guide sent me to the jarrah table, where I removed Terri's meditation group's dolphins, *to be returned*.

Shark amongst the dolphins, my Guide explained.

The predicted situation had come to a head, having simmered for a long time. I could see Terri was using the circumstance regarding Hanna to her advantage, needing to be the focal point. She was taking this opportunity to undermine me, regardless of the fact that there was no truth in the gossip she was spreading. The shark amongst the dolphins was revealed, and I recalled the day the 'Iona Lodge' sign had been put in place the previous year, when Terri had photographed the Celtic Seven and stood with us when Norm shouted, 'To Iona'. She was part of our past life together and the predicted karma-clearing process. *Trust the process*, my Guide said.

Soon Terri was openly running me down, and all meditation group evenings were cancelled. Although this hurt, it was a relief to have this negativity removed from the centre. The hurt was similar to losing a family unit, and a constant reminder of the hurtful circumstances surrounding the loss of my own family. I spent time in the Dolphins Healing Room, allowing all hurts to surface and be released.

I had been working hard all day on 15 May when unexpectedly my Guide sent me inside to shower and change. A few minutes later there was a knock on the glass sliding doors. It was Greta, the woman who had said goodbye at the maypole on Mary May Day '97.

'Hello,' she said, 'remember me?'

She was on her way to see a theatrical show in Dongara and asked me to go with her. *You must go*, my Guide insisted. When she'd driven me back to the centre afterwards, I asked her why she had invited me to go to the show. 'To say goodbye.'

'But you already said goodbye when we were by the maypole.'

'Did I? Are you going to invite me in for coffee before I drive back to Geraldton?'

Take her to the office, my Guide said. I made coffee, then walked Greta into my office, and soon found myself explaining the Healing Garden concept using the diagrams, which had been enlarged to six times their normal size and laminated for display on Open Day. Greta came across as a private person who would not share easily. I wondered if her need to approach me — a virtual stranger — twice, with the word *goodbye*, was maybe a cry for help. She studied me for a few moments when I had finished explaining the diagrams. 'This means everything to you, doesn't it?' she said.

'Yes it does, which is a good thing as it is a ten-year project.' I walked with her to her car and was about to walk away when she held my arm.

'I am not a very nice person and I have no real friends,' she said. What an odd thing to say, I thought, while watching her drive away.

Greta rang early next morning offering to work in the Healing Garden later in the week, but before ending the conversation she said, 'I can't stop thinking about you and it is most inconvenient.' I thought it was odd that she should be thinking about me at all. She rang the following day complaining of a stomach problem and asked to delay her visit until 22 May. Following her phone call I was sent to the Open Chamber of the Heart Chakra / Pulse of Life to place the pots containing the vetiver grass that Greta would be planting. With this done, the green outer rim of the Heart Chakra would be planted.

Late in the afternoon of 22 May, while standing in the Open Chamber, I watched as Greta drove into the car park. She ran into the garden smiling and I received the message, *Jumping for joy*. As Greta hugged me I received the words, *Marriage* and *Healing*. I remembered that in mid-February, when I was guided to remove the silver locket from the Taj Mahal box, these three sets of words had featured when I touched the dried red rose petals. Earlier that day I had placed one of the petals at the nose of the gold-painted dolphin in the Dolphins Healing Room. While Greta and I were planting the vetiver grass I looked at her and wondered if she was the Golden Rose Dolphin.

As I set my camera to capture her image, she looked up at me and announced, 'I'm staying overnight, is that all right with you?' I could only nod in agreement. What is wrong with me? I wondered. We worked until dark to ensure she planted all her plants and then ate a late meal in Mum's extension before retiring. Early the next morning Greta drove back to Geraldton and the boat, which was now the family home.

The following Thursday she came to work again and the next day drove me to Geraldton to spend half an hour on the boat and meet her husband and children, then to collect the Indian siris tree from Julie's farm. I returned to Dongara on the coach with the tree. There was something *familiar* about the parting from Greta and her daughter that I could not bring forward into my conscious mind.

She was due to sail away soon, and on the last Thursday in May she visited to work, then gave me a goodbye gift to open after she had sailed. The next morning she took it back again! On the last day of May she rang, very distressed, because there had been heated discussions between her and her husband concerning their proposed trip. She asked if she could visit the centre. Mum was completing a long-stitch tapestry featuring a bouquet of pink roses as a thank-you gift to Greta for working in the garden, when she walked into Mum's extension carrying a bunch of yellow roses for her. I watched with fascination as they exchanged their gifts of roses.

Greta was distressed and struggling to swallow. I was drawn to her throat, seeing for the first time that she wore a gold necklace with a tiny gemstone held in its centre. I asked her what it was. 'A Kimberley diamond; my husband gave it to me.' After she left, I looked in my notes for any reference to a diamond.

It had been four years before on my birthday, 8 March, when I'd been encouraged to read a page from my mother's gift *Kimberley Dreaming to Diamonds* by Hugh Edwards. The words described the Wandjina paintings and the word 'Wandjina' was highlighted in my mind, as were

'Kimberley' and 'diamond'. Then I added these clues to the notes of the first soulmate with a past-life heart issue, the Golden Rose Dolphin. Greta was wearing a Kimberley diamond that held negative vibrations.

On 5 June I was sent by my Guide to the Mary Seat to pour water over the bench, requesting that everyone involved in the first meditation group situation be protected, and for Greta to be helped. I began to walk back to the lodge when she arrived. Again she was distressed, telling me she was separating from her husband, leaving the boat and taking her children. She had already found accommodation in Geraldton. I was shocked. She explained that she had not wanted to sail around Australia — let alone the world — and had been too afraid to say so until now. I was sent into the Dolphins Healing Room to the silver locket with its two dried half red rose petals. I stood waiting, not sure what to do. *Give it to her*, my Guide urged.

Greta looked surprised as I gave her the locket, but without speaking she removed the Kimberley diamond necklace. Once the silver locket was at her throat, she asked if she could plant the siris tree in the Open Chamber of the Heart Chakra / Pulse of Life. The next day a friend brought a gift from Greta to replace the one she had taken back. Was the 'Goodbye' conflict in the Golden Rose Dolphin resolved?

I went to the Open Chamber to stand inside this now completed area. As I studied the vetiver grass, I wondered at Julie's reasoning for its planting. My Guide referred me to the book *The Directory of Essential Oils* by Wanda Sellar:

> Vetivert Grass/Root ... Known as 'the oil of tranquillity' ... Calming oil and a reputed panacea for stress and tension ... It revitalises the body by fortifying the red blood corpuscles crucial in transporting oxygen to all parts of the system. (18)

This plant complemented the Heart Chakra / Pulse of Life and Julie's proposed planting of pink-flowering plants of all shades from pale to dark pink, the flow of the life force.

Carol Hope visited with a friend to ask what had happened regarding Terri and her meditation group. I told her the story, and remarked on how accurate her prediction on Mary May Day '97 had been. She said she felt compelled to tell me something else. 'Judy, you have experienced a great love in a past life, a love the rest of us only dream about. It will come to light and there will be great turmoil in your life.'

When she left I returned to my task of digging holes and planting the thirty white-flowering Dongara mallee trees around the pathways of the Heart Chakra / Pulse of Life itself.

On 17 June I received a phone call from Switzerland for Greta – she was Swiss, it had transpired – and I gave them her Geraldton number. My mind went back to my travels with Erika in Germany in November 1989, when we'd spent time near the Swiss-German border, and of how, subsequently, I had felt unease when shown photographs of her trip to Egypt. Had something happened in Greta's life in that same month? Had she put out strong feelings for help? I did not share my thoughts, as she was far too stressed.

Early next day I sat on the Mary Seat knowing that Greta's husband was sailing away. I recalled my birthday in Gloucester in March 1989, when Erika sent me the Egyptian papyrus of the sun god Re. This gift had to be placed by the Soulmate article, a postcard of yellow roses, and details of the dream of a regal young woman with dark brown eyes. At the time I had been so shaken by the surge of emotion that I had to rest. Greta had recently given Mum a bunch of yellow roses. Was she the woman in my dream, and how could that be possible?

Meditation evenings started again but with a more mature group of men and women. Roger and his wife, Mary, were part of it, and Mum was writing weekly meditations and running this successful, harmonious and enjoyable weekly evening.

Roger arrived carrying a long bench he had made from logs, and we placed it inside the Open Chamber near the newly planted siris tree. A feeling of *familiarity* came as I sat on the bench the next day with the early-morning sun on my back. Its orange rays touched the tree before moving onto the Heart Chakra / Pulse of Life. My heart began to beat at a fast rate and I tried to breathe slowly. By this time the sun's light was everywhere, highlighting the horse-tailed sheoak trees at the western end of the Healing Garden. A mist of silver light appeared around these trees, creating a formation symbolic of the Taj Mahal. In 1986 I had taken time to admire the reflection of the Taj in water nearby, and the message *Remember this moment* had come.

I thought of the Taj Mahal being a symbol of a great love story, and Carol's words repeated: 'Judy, you have experienced a great love in a past life, a love the rest of us only dream about. It will come to light and there will be great turmoil in your life.'

The next day Greta arrived unannounced and handed me a bunch of yellow roses in the Open Chamber. I nearly said something, but my Guide warned me not to. *Karmic truths*, she said. I updated the Crystal Pool Energy and Greta's past-life heart issue notes with this new clue:

Crystal Pool Energy: Supreme power – male passions – heart pain – conflict and loss – Egypt – heart's journey – Golden Rose Dolphin – karmic truths.

Heart Issue: Greta – Golden Rose Dolphin – soulmate – yellow roses – soul group – dream – regal young woman with dark brown eyes – Egypt – dolphin – Switzerland – Mary – Wandjina – Kimberley diamond – disposal – crocodile – Dongara – Egypt/ankh – karma / past life – heart's journey – red rose energy – male passions – Warning. This is a message from ancient Egypt – a child – Taj Mahal – the blue light – maypole – Mary May Day '97 – silver locket – soul's history – Egyptian Goddess Nut – karmic truths.

Many clues had been revealed, but there were elements yet to be disclosed that I would carry forward in my notes until all had been revealed. *Eight years, our time is now*, the unknown female whispered. It had been eight years since I'd received the gift of the Egyptian sun god Re from Erika. Greta's Egyptian past-life heart issue was gradually being disclosed, and the Crystal Pool Energy was involved. *For Sale sign*, my Guide said.

I understood any action I took could be cancelled when the required outcome or truth had been revealed, so I stored my concern and spoke to the local estate agent with the awareness in the back of my mind that the Celestial Dolphin Centre was a ten-year project. The next day the post brought a card from Sam in Findhorn, Scotland, asking if I was still as focused. I nodded when I read her card and admired the cover displaying a dolphin. It filled me with encouragement to follow this new path.

Greta asked me to assist with an access commitment that involved a drive north to Shark Bay, or further, depending on where her husband's boat was moored. As I drove her car my mind went back to April, when I was taken to the Egyptian tapestry to place Hanna's ankh and a lapis lazuli on the brow chakra of the woman linked with a maypole, and my Guide had said *Someone is thinking of you, Libra*. I looked at Greta, who was resting with her eyes closed. I was stunned when *another's* profile covered her face, complementing her features. I looked again, seeing only a young, beautiful Egyptian face. Greta opened her eyes and smiled through this profile, which disappeared.

Further explore your soul's history, a search of secret Egypt, my Guide said. I nervously returned Greta's smile. I glanced back at her again and saw she was still watching me.

'This may seem a strange question but what is your birth sign?' I asked.

'Libra.'

We had to go as far as Coral Bay to meet the boat, and I walked on the beach there while waiting for Greta to drive her children to their father. Before travelling I had been instructed to create a large triangle with logs and limestones inside Julie's Living Enclosure to be referred to as 'Merlin's Triangle'. The word 'Triangle' bothered me. Greta returned alone, and we drove back to Dongara in silence. I understood it was hard to part with children and respected her need to be quiet.

Julie arranged delivery of white-flowering mulla mulla and Geraldton wax, and I began to plant in order to complete the outer pathways of the Heart Chakra / Pulse of Life. Greta worked alongside me at times, having moved from Geraldton to a rental home in Dongara. I was stopped in the middle of planting by the arrival of the Judas tree and the desert kurrajong trees. The limestone reef was solid by the entrance to the Heart Chakra / Pulse of Life, and I was forced to dig with a pickaxe before I found soil. As I planted the Judas tree, a negative emotion went through me and I wondered if it was my Anglican background reacting to the name Judas.

I was encouraged by my Guide to work in the Curve, within the outer pathway, by Chamber Three, and soon found myself being moved around the garden. I would wake with the intention to work in one area but quickly be sent to another. If I wandered I was given a push until I was back again in the required place. The Curve played on my mind: it was hard work clearing this area. I stood back and recognised that I had created a boomerang shape. Upon this realisation, my Guide directed me towards the Love Tree, where I was to stand and wait. *Love is karma is growth*, she explained.

I was encouraged to gather mulch from under the Love Tree and place it around the mulla mulla and Geraldton wax, edging the Boomerang. *The boomerang returns, you reap what you sow, the law of karma*, my Guide said. *Love is karma is growth*.

Within days of the Boomerang/Karma area being cleared, severe tensions developed between Greta and me. She had a sarcastic manner when stressed. Her issues centred on the children and access, and I suggested she speak to their father and not to take her anxiety out on me. I developed a headache and then vomited. I had been feeling fine until I had expressed my feelings.

Cathy rang to say she felt bogged down with her partner and his four children.

I was guided to walk to the Dongara Library and was drawn to a book and the required page. It read, 'Every day of the year the procession to the Taj begins with the long shadows of sunrise and ends in the fading light.' I had experienced this in the Open Chamber of the Heart Chakra, with shadows and mist creating something like a representation of the Taj Mahal. I tried to let go of the book but was held fast by the image of a blurred female face, blurred apart from her brown eyes. Back at the lodge I was telling Mum about this when Greta arrived, and I was distracted. Then, when she and I were talking later, I realised it was her eyes I had seen.

Ask her how to say brown eyes in her native tongue, my Guide said. Although my pronunciation was not good, I was able to imitate her words and say 'brunni Auge'. I confided to Mum that Greta's eyes were the last memory I had at the moment of her death in a past life. Eyes filled with great sadness and deep love.

Greta announced she was considering working again for Swissair, being a former employee. I needed time alone and said I thought the idea sounded great. I drove to the beach in my neighbour's car to watch the sun go down over the sea, and sensed a presence behind me. It was Greta. She had searched for me, leaving the children, who had recently returned from spending time with their father, in the nearby sand dunes. I turned, only aware of her angry brown eyes. I confirmed I wanted to stand back from her and work in peace, and she pointed angrily at the children. 'I am *not* going to allow that,' she shouted. I was taken aback by the implications of her words. She pointed again at the children. 'Can you really give them up?' I was lost for words as I stared at someone I no longer recognised, until her features lost their anger.

'These are *not* my children,' I said, trying to get through to her. 'It must be scary being a single parent but they have you and they have a father.' I took her arm and we walked to the sand dunes and the waiting children. Later at home I shared what had happened with Mum. 'Greta's behaviour was intimidating,' I said, 'she must have experienced a past-life flashback similar to mine, when I saw her eyes at the moment of her death.'

Greta rejoined Swissair, planning to leave Australia in October for seven weeks. This was an opportunity for her and the children to spend time with their Swiss family. I offered to drive them to the airport in her car, and to look after her house in Dongara.

Cathy rang to tell me she was travelling overseas in October. I was surprised, as she had complained about having no money. Greta and Cathy were both leaving Australia in October and I felt concern as the thought entered my mind that their soul energies were running parallel. *Two necklaces, two women, two situations*, my Guide warned.

In August Greta suggested a trip to the South West while her son visited his father in Darwin. We drove to Yallingup, where she'd arranged an interview at the Steiner School. She wanted to move south, and this school was in her mind for the children. We stayed in the caravan park and I took her little daughter Cindy for a walk while Greta attended her interview. In the evening the three of us went to the beach and I built sandcastles with Cindy at the water's edge while Greta watched from a distance. There was a strong bond between this intelligent, determined child and me.

At the end of the month I was instructed to clear Chamber Three ready for the placement there of hay, cardboard and carpet. Greta arrived as I started the task. 'Are you going to spend your life pulling weeds?' she asked. 'What is the point?'

Her sarcastic remark indicated the Ten Year Mary Project 1994 was an issue, and I decided to explain yet again the importance of this place to me. The next time she visited we sat on the Mary Seat and I explained to her how her sarcastic energy disturbed me. I was aware this area held the unseen runic Healing Triangle Mystic — the path of karma. Greta got up and walked away. *She will leave*, my Guide said.

Cathy rang to tell me she was booked to fly to Findhorn and that she'd found an engine for my car.

Greta returned with a positive attitude and we spent time with the children. I took slides of Cindy with the vetiver grass and we went inside the Children's Tree to introduce the energy of a child to the Healing Garden. At the end of September I was invited to join Greta and her children on a camping trip to Kalbarri. I did not enjoy the experience, longing to be back at the centre. She asked if I could switch off from the spiritual link and live a normal life. I smiled and told her it was a way of life for me now.

A man named George rang from Perth to book overnight bed and breakfast. I was busy preparing for his arrival when Greta drove in and handed me a bunch of yellow roses. I knew she was trying to understand something foreign to her. I was directed to place her roses in the single guest room. My guest arrived and commented on the lodge being called Iona, as his wife was in Iona, Scotland, and he was very taken with this. He had no knowledge of the Healing Garden, only that I had a bed-and-breakfast licence.

George was enjoying breakfast with Mum in her extension next time we met, and he asked me why I had placed roses in his bedroom. I had been guided to put them in the guest room after another unpleasant exchange with Greta. Not wanting to go into all that, I said I thought the roses would look nice, but he gave me a questioning look. After breakfast George took me to one side and asked whether I had been *told* to put the roses there. I accepted that something was happening, so I affirmed I had. He then said that he was a retired minister of the Church of England and had spent time in Egypt last year.

'I want to show you something,' George said, and walked into his room. In turn, I was sent to my office, where I was taken to the copies of the Heart Chakra / Pulse of Life diagram and the Egyptian Goddess Nut, and guided to take them to George. I found him searching through a photo album. I placed my two diagrams on his bed as he turned around holding a single photograph that he placed beside them.

'I took this photograph in the Valley of the Kings,' he said. The photograph was of Nut. He looked at my diagrams and I looked at his photograph. We both stared at one another. 'They are the same!' he exclaimed. I had to sit down.

Out of all Egypt and all his photographs he had been drawn to show me this one. I asked why he had questioned me about the roses, and he said that in his Egyptian hotel room there had been roses. When drawn to stay here, he had felt compelled to bring his album. When he discovered the roses in his room, he knew he was meant to show me this photograph. I asked him about Nut and he said she was known as the 'Cycle of Life'. I stared back at him in disbelief. Julie had named her diagram the 'Pulse of Life'. George pointed to the women featured in the Egyptian goddess illustration.

'They are all holding sistrums,' he said. 'These are containers used for incense to protect and purify the human soul.'

I told him Julie had selected all pink plants for the pathways around the Heart Chakra / Pulse of Life, but my Guide insisted that they had to be white-flowering. George said in ancient times incense was used as a protection, but in modern times we white-light ourselves for protection.

'This is why there have to be only white-flowering plants around the Pulse of Life,' he said. 'You have brought an ancient Egyptian concept into the modern day, for access by everyone. A garden is the perfect place to reach all and everyone.'

George relayed the story of the sky Goddess Nut being the consort of the earth god Geb. In the ancient Egyptian belief, the sun and soul were swallowed by Nut at night and passed through her body for rebirth in the morning, giving her the name the 'Cycle of Life and Rebirth'. He had seen, in a tomb, the symbol of Nut's body showing the sun rising on wings. He said there was an awesome silence there.

Greta's gift of roses had been a vital component of the situation, revealing that there was more to her than being a Celestial Dolphin — she was the Golden Rose Dolphin.

Mum and I walked the outer pathways of the Heart within the Pulse of Life to the place where the 'Iona Lodge' sign had been placed by the Celtic Seven. We turned as one to take in the view of the Heart Chakra / Pulse of Life as the first rays of the sun moved through the symbol, the Heart itself enclosed by vetiver grass and the outer pathways made apparent by the planting of the white-flowering native shrubs.

'Martin was right,' I said, 'this is the Egyptian Goddess Nut.'

'It's wonderful!'

I told her George had said that in ancient Egyptian belief the sun and soul were swallowed by Nut at night and passed through her body for rebirth in the morning, giving her the name the Cycle of Life and Rebirth. 'Look!' Mum exclaimed. 'It's happening here.' The Heart Chakra / Pulse of Life / Goddess Nut glowed in the bright orange sunlight.

Greta and her children visited to spend the evening at the lodge, and as we began to prepare the meal she handed me a wrapped gift. When I opened it, I was taken aback to discover it was a cassette titled *Windjana Spirit of the Kimberley* by Tony O'Connor. Inside she had written '7/10/97. To Judy, one step closer to your dream of experiencing the Windjana. Greta.'

Earlier, she had been drawn to the book Mum had given me for my birthday in 1993 – *Kimberley Dreaming to Diamonds* by Hugh Edwards – and I remarked that I would like to tour the Kimberley region and visit the Windjana National Park. When I re-read the title *Windjana Spirit of the Kimberley* and Greta's written words 'experiencing the Windjana', fear swept through my body. Windjana Gorge is famous for its crocodiles, and Greta's past-life heart issue held the clues 'disposal' and 'crocodile'.

I was directed inside the walk-in pantry and stood there not sure what to do. I was given the message *Ten days*, and sensed a masculine energy around me. Before I had time to question the meaning of this message I found myself asking Greta if she planned to visit her father's place of memorial in Switzerland, and if so to place ten roses there, not a dozen. A long silence followed while Greta studied me intently. I waited, but she did not further the conversation. *Ten days, ten roses*, my Guide warned through the now weakening male energy.

This would be Greta's last day at the centre for seven weeks. I was encouraged to speak to her concerning her taking the children out of the country, as soon-to-be ex-husbands would rarely agree to such a thing. She shrugged her shoulders in response. I asked for her husband's address, to enable me to forward his mail, still being delivered to Dongara, and she handed me an address in Darwin. I suggested the children would miss him, but she shrugged her shoulders. I accepted it was a not-to-be-discussed subject and let it go.

I lit a white candle for the table during our meal together and later I put the same lit candle in my bedroom. In the morning there was a huge wax spill beneath the candle, dark in colour. A feeling of dread came. Trying to push it aside, I helped pack Greta's car. As we headed for Perth the feeling stayed. I was quiet on the trip. There was a knowing in me that something was wrong, very wrong.

Before we left Dongara, Greta had handed me an envelope with a note and a gold key on a gold chain; her parents had given it to her for her twenty-first birthday. I was shaken by the responsibility of its contents. The note read:

Dear Judy,
This is the Key to my Heart. Please hold it until I return. You are responsible for opening my Feeling-Centre. Thank you, Greta.

This was accompanied by her jewellery box, which she left with me for safekeeping. I walked away when the flight was called, too disturbed to see the plane take off.

It wasn't many days before Greta rang from Zurich sounding depressed and saying she was not happy being away from Dongara and staying with her mother. I had been guided to return an anchor brooch to Cathy, which she'd sent to me with a note saying 'I will be your anchor.' Greta and Cathy were flying overseas within a few weeks of each other, and notes from both of them had expressed unusual sentiments.

I bought a computer, and Cathy offered to take me through the basics before she, too, left for Europe. She said she would be down at the weekend, so I invited her to lunch. I learnt then that she had sold my car, taking all the proceeds to cover the cost of fitting a new engine and paying for her trip to Findhorn. I was livid, but given directions to wait. *Trust the process*, my Guide said.

As I was writing down Cathy's instructions for using the computer, I looked up to discover she was staring at the cutting from *The Geraldton Guardian* featuring Julie's photograph, and I wondered what she was thinking. She became flummoxed when she saw I was watching her, and started a conversation about something irrelevant. *This moment is to register*, my Guide said.

During lunch Cathy spoke of my plan to sell, having driven past the 'For Sale' sign on her way in. I shared my concern that Mum and I would lose financially if we sold, because we had overcapitalised with building her extension. I would lose my deposit, creating a financial loss. I had explained this to Cathy's sister Liz when Liz had rung suggesting I compensate Cathy with a $15,000 cash payment. I changed the subject but Cathy brought it back again, asking about all the things we would leave behind. I looked at Mum; it was an odd thing for Cathy to say. When you sold you took everything with you, I thought. Cathy knew this, but she commented that if it was sold as a centre it must be left as it was.

On 21 October Cathy rang to say she was off to Perth airport.

Four days later a distraught Greta rang from Zurich to tell me her husband was very upset. I wondered how she knew he was distressed and asked her to explain. She explained he had become upset before boarding the plane.

'What plane? Where?' I responded, totally confused.

'In Zurich.'

'Zurich! I have been sending his post to Darwin!' There was a strained pause; then Greta said he had been with them for ten days.

'Why did you lie, allowing me to think he was in Darwin?' I asked. She didn't respond. 'What games are you playing? For some reason you are trying to create a false impression that I would mind him being with you and the children. Why would you need to do that?' She hung up.

The appearance of the dark wax on the morning Greta left had been a warning, along with *Ten days, ten roses*. I was sent by my Guide to a quote by John Ruskin, a prominent 19th-Century social thinker, that Mum had copied into her notebook:

> The essence of lying is in deception, not in words; a lie may be told by silence, by equivocation, by the accent on a syllable, by a glance of the eye attaching a peculiar significance to a sentence; and all these kinds of lies are worse and baser by many degrees than a lie plainly worded; so that no form of blinded conscience is so far sunk as that which comforts itself for having deceived, because the deception was by gesture or silence, instead of utterance.

Greta had written earlier to tell me she had visited her father's memorial, and on the way a florist was selling bargain bunches of ten roses instead of a dozen. *Ten days, ten roses*, my Guide said.

Vivid memories of Greta's shoulder-shrugging and silence — when I asked about her husband allowing her children to leave the country — made me annoyed. A triangle involving Greta, her husband and me was being created by her. 'Why is this happening?' I asked. *The lesson of unconditional love*, my Guide replied. 'Well, it's going to be a long lesson — I want no part of her.'

Three days later I was shaken awake and sent out into the Healing Garden. Sitting on top of the maypole was a diamond dove. *Think*, my Guide said, so I sat on the Mary Seat to think. Maypole and diamond — what did they have in common? Greta had hugged me at the maypole and removed the Kimberley diamond. It was all too stressful; I wanted out. *There is no way out*, my Guide warned.

As I walked towards the lodge a huge brown snake crossed my path. *Union of opposites*, my Guide explained. I waited until it slithered back into the undergrowth, pondering the message that there was no way out. I wrote and told Greta how I felt. Several phone calls later she and I had reached a mutual understanding.

On 29 October I awoke early feeling edgy, still not happy about the situation. A photograph of Greta was highlighted by my Guide. It was to be placed inside a blue frame with a section from one of Julie's dried red rose petals attached to the frame alongside Greta's left shoulder and the picture to be hung in the Dolphins Healing Room opposite Mary's image.

Two days later I was guided to drive urgently to Clark's Estate Agents office in Dongara, which I did using Greta's car. I walked inside to find a staff member holding a pile of magazines. I was drawn to the one on top, *The Bulletin With Newsweek*, 2 September 1997, featuring the headline 'Visions of Mary. Australia's "Miracle" Town: A New Lourdes?' I was allowed to borrow it.

Back at the centre, and standing in front of Mary's image, I was encouraged to read a part of the article, by Helen Chryssides, 'Visions of Mary. Off the wall: The Anglican Church's first heavenly apparition has put Yankalilla on the miracle map.' In part it read:

> The approach by road into Yankalilla gives little indication that you are nearing what may become the Lourdes of Australia, if Father Andrew Nutter's predictions prove accurate … On July 24, 1994, a new parishioner, Susan Fehlberg, was sitting in a pew when she 'saw what looked like a Christmas card image of the Madonna and child' on the back wall, to the right of the altar. 'I had not had a religious upbringing that included Mary and so I did not realize the importance or significance of this,' admits [a] theologian from Victor Harbor, not far from Yankalilla … Thousands have since visited the church — declared a Marian shrine in December 1996 by the local Bishop … As for the apparition itself, now protected by an electronic security zone, its outline is defined by a crude iron frame which may soon be removed because the shape has now changed, expanding to that of a mother with a toddler, and a rose — Mary's 'signature' … To the best of Nutter's knowledge, this is the first known apparition in an Anglican church … [It] has filled the church with the scent of roses — 'Mary's symbol' … Confirmation: This year

Nutter was the first Anglican priest to lead a tour to Medjugorje in Bosnia-Herzegovina where Mary has been appearing almost daily since 1981 to a group of seven visionaries ... (37)

I shook my head, trying to grasp that a rose petal — Mary's 'signature' — was by Greta's left shoulder, opposite the image of Mary that came from Medjugorje. *Golden Rose Dolphin*, my Guide said. I updated Greta's past-life heart issue with the clue 'ten days, ten roses' and then reviewed the highlighted connections between Mary and the Anglican Church.

In March 1995 Cathy and I had been sent to St Mary's Anglican Church, Busselton, to view one of its leadlight windows with its representations of Mother Mary and Mary Magdalene.

After reading the *Bulletin* article about the apparition at Yankalilla, I was encouraged to further update the outstanding elements within the first soul group notes:

Soul Energy (1): Yellow – The Lady of Good Counsel – gemstone – settled legal disputes – rebuilding the cathedral – Virgo – Gardner – Mary's Church – Chartres – church of Yankalilla – a rose – Mary's signature – Medjugorje, Bosnia-Herzegovina.

As I updated my notes, *The Geraldton Guardian* newspaper cutting featuring Julie's photograph fell from the office wall! Cathy had stared at this before leaving for Findhorn.

I was encouraged by my Guide to read part of the information that had been given to me along with the Miraculous Medal. A sense of enthusiasm came as I read the story regarding the novice nun Catherine Laboure, born in Paris in 1806, the ninth of eleven children. At nine years old, when her mother died, this lonely child clasped a statue of Mary, saying, 'Now you will be my mother.' Years later, Catherine met Mary and was given the design of the medal. *French connection*, my Guide said.

The next day a gold page-marker from the Wailing Wall in Jerusalem arrived from Greta, and I placed it beside the Miraculous Medal information. The message *lonely child* repeated in my mind. The clue 'a child' featured in Greta's past-life heart issue, and I amended her notes with the addition of the words 'lonely child'. My mind went back to the lonely spirit child Julie in the Old Saddlery who had waited for centuries to be rescued.

'There is another lonely child seeking protection,' I told Mum.

'Is the child in spirit?'

'I don't know, but the child is part of Greta's past-life heart issue.'

On 9 November, twelve years to the day after Mum and I had landed in Adelaide, a letter from Cathy arrived from Findhorn, and I read it with disbelief. She wanted to discuss her taking over the Celestial Dolphin Centre, but could not conceive how to make it work financially. She said that if we cooperated to keep the place functioning it would all happen. I was to seek spiritual advice and let her know the outcome. She was willing to do whatever *they* wanted. 'I have no idea of creating another Findhorn,' she wrote. 'I feel in some ways I have gone beyond them in experiencing the reality of living our faith in the real world. Let me know what you think. Yesterday they emphasised that I needed to be very open-minded about what lies ahead of me and that there will be no money worries. Today, they tell me that I am to take over the running of the centre.'

I didn't believe this. I had observed the moment when Cathy had decided to take over the centre, and her presence at Findhorn was being used as a means to an end. The idea for Julie to assist her had formed as she stared at her picture in *The Geraldton Guardian* cutting, not at Findhorn. And the discussion regarding the sale of the centre had taken place after lunch before she left, not at Findhorn. Mum and I recalled how uncomfortable she had been when I pointed out that any sale would be a financial loss and there would be no $15,000 for her. When I changed the subject, she had steered it back, wanting to know what we were leaving behind. Her letter was just a ploy to gain ownership of the centre instead of the money she felt she was owed. My Guide's direction to put up a 'For Sale' sign had revealed Cathy's motives. *Mastery of minds,* my Guide warned. *Keep trusting the process.*

I wrote a reply to her sister Liz's address in Sydney, where Cathy would be staying on her return. I was polite, saying that I had no indication she was to take over the centre, and reminded her that she had been given the message that I would be the sole proprietor. I would know soon enough whether she accepted my having sought advice or, if I was correct, whether this was another attempt to mislead me. I thought about Findhorn, and discovered in my notes that in 1993 I had been guided to write a letter to that community requesting their workshop program for Cathy. The same day I had received a letter from my solicitor requesting a copy of the transfer of the deeds for the Old

Saddlery, and this clue was included in her past-life heart issue. Four years later I receive this letter from Cathy, now staying at Findhorn, suggesting the transfer of deeds of the Celestial Dolphin Centre.

I drove into Dongara to post my letter and found another parcel from Greta. It contained three reels of gold thread she had bought in New York for the Egyptian tapestry. Now I had no doubt — Greta, Cathy and I were the women featured in the tapestry. The outline of the women with touching brow chakras was now to be worked; I knew which one of them symbolically represented Greta's soul energy, but was left to wonder which one of us was the other. Their foreheads touching could mean they were in accord, but I did not feel in accord with either woman at this time.

A letter arrived with a parcel of photographs of Greta in uniform. Her next trip with the airline would be to Cairo on 11 November. I was referred to Gerber's *Vibrational Medicine*:

> Colour therapy is not new to the twentieth century. This unique art was applied in ancient time in the healing temples of light and colour at Heliopolis in Egypt ... The green ray resonates most vibrantly with the heart chakra ... The heart chakra stands as a midpoint between the two worlds of spirit and matter. (3)

This must be why the heart chakra dominates the Healing Garden, I thought. My Guide instructed me to write to Greta urgently:

> Dear Greta,
> Request Ceremony Cairo '97: At 10.00 pm Egyptian time on 24 November, you are to light a candle in your hotel room, open the silver locket containing the two halves of a dried, red rose petal and repeat out loud: 'I ask that the place known as the Celestial Dolphin Centre, Dongara, Western Australia is free to become what it is meant to be.' Please wear the silver locket until you return from Egypt and back to Dongara itself. Thank you, Judy.

I was careful to ensure Greta understood the importance of the time: 10.00 pm in Egypt. She would receive this letter in Zurich after flying back from Cairo. I did not know if she would be sent to Egypt again but I followed the guidance.

Two days later, a letter arrived for Greta's husband. She had warned me to expect it, and asked me to redirect it to Darwin, now that he was back in Australia. The address included 'G', Greta's initial. My Guide asked me to cross out the G — I had no idea why. During the night I was woken, forced out of bed and taken to the wardrobe, to Greta's jewellery box. I was instructed to *open it*, but was uncomfortable with this and so waited until asked again. The Kimberley diamond necklace was on top, and the knowing that this necklace held negative vibrations came to mind. I closed the box. My Guide requested that the box be placed on the pillow where Cindy had slept on her last night at the lodge before leaving for Switzerland.

This is forbidden, an unknown male voice shouted angrily.

I was shaken by this sudden outburst, but my Guide's calming energy soon moved through me. The necklace was a gift from Greta's husband and Cindy's father. I was directed to place one of my kestrel feathers on top of the Kimberley diamond itself. *Protection*, my Guide explained.

Hours later I wrote an aerogram to Greta to tell her what had happened. It was unusual for me to share, but thought I should tell her I had opened her jewellery box. I did not know who I was protecting, I said, and did not want to be any part of a triangle with her and her husband. I did not share with her that I sensed there was danger for Cindy in the words *This is forbidden*.

At noon a headache began that became unbearable, and I was sent to sit and hold the now-sealed letter to Greta, linking it with my headache. I concentrated on the blue of the aerogram. A battle of minds began with the angry energy, as I was determined to post my letter to Greta. *This is forbidden*, the unknown male shouted. Every effort was made to force me to let go, but I would not. Drawing on all my resources, I was able to speak to him and assure him Cindy was safe — safe from what I did not know — and the throbbing pain stopped. What had happened to cause such anguish? I sensed the answer was held in the energy of the Kimberley diamond.

I drove to Dongara and posted the letter. Later I was taken to my notes for the previous year, in particular for the few days after Mary May Day '96, when I'd been sent to the Dongara Crystal Shop to find the woman with the Egyptian Cards. *This is a message from Ancient Egypt*, my Guide had warned. The woman had spoken of personal growth with sacrifice — something that I was giving up to do with a baby, a child, and that past lives were coming through strongly.

A card arrived from Greta, posted in Egypt. It featured *The Dancers of Nakhte*. She wrote, 'Judy, aren't these the three ladies on your tapestry? I have bought a special Egyptian gift for you. Love G.'

My Guide instructed me to take the card into the Dolphins Healing Room and place it by a lit white candle in the Dongara candle-holder. A doorway to the past was being encouraged to open. I waited:

Transfer of energy to be made from Cairo to Dongara at four in the morning on the twenty-fifth of November.

How do I do that? I wondered.

I drove to Dongara to collect the post and found a letter from Greta with her updated flight schedule. On 24 and 25 November she would be in Egypt again. I was thrilled when I read the dates, and drove back to the centre to read the instructions I had already sent her. I had asked her to light a candle and open the silver locket at 10.00 pm Egyptian time on 24 November — she was scheduled to arrive in Cairo earlier in the evening. I didn't know what time that corresponded to in Dongara so I rang the operator, who informed me that 10 pm in Egypt on 24 November was 4 am in Dongara on 25 November — my 'Hour of Power'! I ran across the breezeway to tell Mum about this exciting development.

Greta rang from Geneva and I told her there was a letter on its way concerning her next trip to Egypt and asked her to follow my request. She agreed, but made a sarcastic comment about everything to do with the centre being of such importance to me — but I didn't mind. It was exciting to know that, from 4 am on 25 November, the Celestial Dolphin Centre in Dongara would be free to become what it was meant to be.

My Guide sent me to Dongara again, and this time I was taken to a greeting card with kookaburras featured on its cover. I bought the card and wrote inside, 'Not to fail again in the current challenge. Not to make the same mistakes again.' I displayed the card on a shelf in my office as a constant reminder during future challenges.

Mum and I worked until late evening of the 24th and sealed all the notes taken during these preparations in a white envelope. I woke at 3.30 am the next morning. The transfer of energy would take place within the Dolphins Healing Room. I performed the required pre-transfer ritual at 4 am. My heartbeat slowed as the candle burning in front of Mary's image, now on the healing table, struggled to stay alight. It slowed even more and I felt a moment of panic — but stared at Mary's image, willing

The Dancers of Nakhte

the energy to arrive — then the bright orange flame grew stronger, until it was taller than the candle. A bright blue swirling energy surrounded Mary's image, the candle's flame gradually reduced and my heartbeat returned to normal, in harmony with the flame. Greta had played her part for the soul group — the energy from Cairo had been transferred. *The blue light*, my Guide explained.

I received a note from the El Salam Hotel, Cairo, to confirm that Greta had followed my instructions and to tell me that later she had found a pink rose in her bathroom. This was now pressed so she could bring it back to Australia. On 3 December she and the children arrived back in Perth. I noticed, with relief, that she was wearing the locket as my Guide had requested.

I spent time in the Dolphins Healing Room on the massage/healing table with a crystal in one or both hands, the *Call of the Dolphin* playing. The blue light from Egypt would surround the healing table as the music lulled me into a relaxed state and I would move into its energy. I understood how unresolved issues stayed in the body. My Guide referred me again to Gerber's *Vibrational Medicine*:

> The chakras are the energy repositories of karma. One might say that the chakras are like batteries which store 'karmic energy charges'. Chakras absorb the subtle energies which relate to the development of the soul in previous lives, and assist in the transformation of the physical body to express unlearned spiritual lessons in the form of physical illnesses. (3)

During several incarnations heart issues had remained unresolved within me and certain soulmates. I re-read the words 'The chakras are the energy repositories of karma.' Cathy and I had an unresolved heart issue from an Aboriginal past life. Julie and I had resolved our past-life heart issue from Egyptian times, but Greta's heart issue — which involved a lonely child — was unresolved. Barbara's repeat past-life issue regarding family inheritance and control was yet to be resolved. The revealing of the truth was still to be achieved. I had protected the family inheritance and I, the rejected sibling, had not disappeared, as was the stated wish of Barbara and Anne: my father required the rescue of his eldest daughter.

On 5 December Greta arrived at the centre with Cindy, bearing gifts for me from her travels. There was a wind chime from Jerusalem — her second gift from the Holy Land. The first had been the page marker from the Wailing Wall, which was still with the Miraculous Medal information. 'Page marker' and 'Jerusalem' had been highlighted and added to Greta's past-life heart issue and the Crystal Pool Energy notes. Greta also handed me a wrapped gift that turned out to be a silver Egyptian ankh. This was a clue held within the notes relating to all three soulmates with past-life heart issues. Greta watched me with coldness in her eyes, but this changed when I hugged her and thanked her for her gifts. My Guide insisted the ankh was to be placed in the silver dolphins Indian box with the turquoise gemstones and Miraculous Medal. When Greta left, I walked to the Heart Chakra / Pulse of Life / Goddess Nut. I understood the heart chakra related to our ability to express love: self-love and love towards others.

Greta flew with her children to Queensland to hand them over to their father for Christmas. My Guide instructed me to hang her Jerusalem wind chime in my bedroom and highlight the three doves, the three hearts and the central hand with a quartz crystal that hung on four strands containing fifty amethysts. I worked the three women in the Egyptian tapestry, stitching golden thread through their clothing and heart chakras. *Egypt, Jerusalem, three Egyptian women*, my Guide said. I understood that the connection between these women would unfold in the present day as I gradually worked to complete the tapestry over a set period of time under instruction. I was encouraged to *touch each amethyst*, and then was referred to the book *Stone Power* by Dorothee L. Mella:

> Amethyst ... A very popular stone amongst the Egyptians ... Jewish priests wore it to symbolize spiritual power ... center stone of their identity breastplate ... (19)

The clues 'Egypt' and 'priests' were added to Greta's notes and the Crystal Pool Energy notes, highlighting once again the energy link between them both. Many clues had been revealed, and I would carry forward others yet to be disclosed within Greta's, Cathy's and Julie's past-life heart-issue notes:

Heart Issue: Greta – dream – regal young woman with dark brown eyes – disposal – crocodile – karma / past life – male passions – lonely child – karmic truths – ten days, ten roses – page marker / Jerusalem – Egypt and priests.

Heart Issue: Cathy – legal action – karma / past life – Rainbow Serpent – power – importance – Aboriginal link – conflict – the chase – Aboriginal spear – male passions.

Heart Issue: Julie – Virgo – Gardner – Mary's Church.

An invitation came for Mum to visit England for six months, as her sister Val would be celebrating her golden wedding anniversary. Barbara and Aunty Val would pay Mum's fare one way and I would save for her return fare. We booked her to fly out of Perth for England on 27 February. This was her predicted third overseas trip.

The next year, 1998, began with a warning from my Guide: *Greta. Gauntlet. Challenge.*

Cindy's third birthday was on 2 January, and Greta, on a brief visit to the lodge, rang her in Queensland, where she was spending time with her father.

A young woman from Germany came to visit. I asked her if she would like to join us for lunch and, after she had eaten, she walked within the garden. When she returned she handed me her lapis lazuli necklace. The round stone was held by a bronze claw clasp on a black leather strap. This was important, she said, so I accepted her gift. She told me when she entered the Heart Chakra / Pulse of Life / Goddess Nut, she burst into tears as memories came of her mother, who had died when she was twelve years old. Heika was now twenty-seven. She had walked into the Love Tree, where she felt her mother's love for the first time since her death. The necklace was her gift for the Dolphins Healing Room.

The clairvoyant Selva rang to ask if I was planning to move. I told her I felt the 'For Sale' was a situation within a situation. She said I would live at the centre for a long time, and when I did move it would be to a home I would lovingly restore.

'In a valley, another centre,' she said. 'People will come just because you are the energy there.'

The more time I spent with Greta, the more my stress level increased, leaving me feeling drained. On my own, or with other people, I was fine.

I tried to speak to her, but she pushed the idea to one side. A friend I contacted said I was doing the right thing — self-healing and speaking to Greta. I tried again to speak to her, but she walked away, returning later with a large tapestry/long-stitch 'The Dolphin Family', featuring smaller dolphins swimming near a large dolphin. *The Dolphin Family*, my Guide said. We decided to give the tapestry/long-stitch to Mum for her birthday.

When we grew tense — there was no common ground — Greta left, returning with a gift or roses. We were both frustrated over trying to understand one another and remain friends.

She and I spent a week planting black wattle and illyarrie trees on the southern side of the gravel road, leading to the main entrance —forty-nine trees in total. It was a massive effort, but we enjoyed the challenge. I needed to ensure these trees had enough water, and made regular runs to Greta's house in her car to fill empty plastic containers.

On 21 January Greta drove to Perth to collect her children from their father, who had brought them back from Queensland. I had been wearing her ankh on a silver chain but was instructed to remove it after she left. She rang next day and I told her I had removed it. This upset her, so I replaced it. Within half an hour I was vomiting: her ankh held negative vibrations harmful to my wellbeing. When she returned I told her what had happened, but she dismissed it. I asked what time she had made contact with her husband. 'Half an hour after talking to you,' she replied.

Early on Mum's birthday I went to her extension singing the birthday song, then asked her to put on her dressing gown and a pair of shoes. We walked out into the cool of the morning to the bottom of the garden by the Brand Highway in time to watch the sun rise. The temperature changed dramatically with the warmth of the rising sun as it moved slowly through the Heart Chakra / Pulse of Life / Goddess Nut. I watched Mum close her eyes, taking in this moment, then took her back to the lodge for breakfast. When the phone rang, Mum learnt that the temperature in Devon, England, was minus 2 degrees. 'I am so fortunate to be here,' she said.

I planned a day of surprises for Mum, and Greta lent me her car to achieve this. I drove her to Julie's permaculture farm near Geraldton, where she introduced us to her new emu pets and we sat in the shade as they raced around under sprays of water. Julie talked to them and stroked their long necks. I had her Merlin with me, but Julie insisted I keep it, saying, 'Make him work for you.'

I drove her to the Rose Café in Geraldton, where Christina joined us for lunch. She gave Mum a birthday card featuring Merlin on horseback with the Celtic goddess Epona also riding a horse. Above them in the sky was the faint image of Michael the Archangel. Michael held his sword of Justice within the enlarged circle of the letter P in Epona. On the back was written, 'When we travel in Her company our journey is greatly blessed' by John Kyle. (36) Inside the card Christina had written, 'To dear Tess, may your journey be fruitful. Thank you for your friendship and meditations. Love, Christina.'

We had left Julie (the Red Celestial Dolphin holding Merlin) to meet with Christina (the Blue Celestial Dolphin and her card featuring Merlin). Julie had lent me Merlin in 1996, and I'd handed her the Epona earrings on Mary May Day '97. Christina's card featured Epona and Merlin riding together. Julie's words came to mind: 'Make him work for you.' I drove back to Dongara wondering how I was going to make Merlin work for me. *Goddess energy*, my Guide replied. The first soul energy notes were given the new heading 'Goddess Energy':

Goddess Energy: Yellow – The Lady of Good Counsel – gemstone – settled legal disputes – rebuilding the cathedral – Virgo – Gardner – Mary's Church – Chartres – Church of Yankalilla – a rose – Mary's signature – Medjugorje, Bosnia-Herzegovina – goddess energy – Merlin.

While Mum and I were sitting on the lodge back veranda for our afternoon tea she asked me why she had to go back to England for the third time. She would have preferred to stay with me at the centre. We lit a candle and the message came: *Tess has a job to do — to assist family unity.* I was not happy either — with Barbara and Aunty Val only paying for Mum's travel one way — but I assured Mum I would save the money for her journey back to Dongara. I returned the car to Greta, who insisted she and her children visit Mum, and I watched as she handed her yellow roses and the children sang the birthday song. *Yellow*, my Guide said.

When Greta had gone I walked to where Mum had stood to watch the sunrise that morning. It was the area in Julie's diagram where the solar plexus chakra was yet to be developed, the area where I had seen the colour yellow when planting the peppercorn trees with Claire. *Yellow Dolphin*, my Guide said, and I realised that Mum was the fourth Core Group Dolphin, the Yellow Celestial Dolphin. Mum was *thrilled* when

I shared this with her, and understood that the delay in being told was somehow connected to the introduction and revealing of the goddess energy.

I was guided to sit in the Dolphins Healing Room and hold Heika's lapis lazuli. The previous year I had placed a lapis lazuli and ankh on the forehead of the woman in the Egyptian tapestry symbolising Greta. I pondered our past-life Egyptian connection, and in response I was taken to 15 and 16 March in my 1996 diary and the stallion's two visits to the Crystal Pool. The answer regarding Greta, Egypt and me was held in this area and its developing energy:

> Crystal Pool Energy: Supreme power – male passions – heart pain – conflict and loss – Egypt – heart's journey – Golden Rose Dolphin – karmic truths – page marker / Jerusalem – Egypt and priests.

When I returned to working in the garden the next day I was bitten on my ankle by a bull ant and, due to the pain and swelling, I was not able to work again until 13 February. On this day a legal letter arrived from Cathy, demanding $15,000 for her signature. I spoke to Greta about Cathy's letter.

'Cut your losses and move south to be near and available to me,' she said. I stared at her in disbelief.

Seek legal advice, my Guide urged. Armed with the Transfer of Land document, and my efforts to execute the transfer, I borrowed Greta's car and drove to Geraldton, handing everything to my solicitor. He was not able to see me until 17 February, the day Cathy had signed the Transfer of Land document two years before, in 1996. When I returned to the centre I was sent to touch the Aboriginal spear on the wall under Mary's image. *Aboriginal link, conflict, karma clearing*, my Guide predicted.

I spent time wondering about how Greta's ankh was adversely affecting my wellbeing. Having asked for help during my next personal healing session, I was given the message *1993*. I went to my 1993 diary, read about Mum's birthday gift to me of the book *Kimberley Dreaming to Diamonds* by Hugh Edwards and the reference to a Kimberley diamond.

The Kimberley diamond had been a gift from Greta's husband prior to the arrival of their first child, a boy. A female child, born in Egypt, had stirred male passions. *This is forbidden* came when I placed Greta's jewellery box, containing the Kimberley diamond, onto the pillow where Cindy had slept the night before she left with her mother for Switzerland the previous year. I had been part of a negative relationship triangle with Greta in an Egyptian past life and the angry energy from that time had revealed itself. I was as determined to discover the truth as the angry male energy was determined to stop me.

Would Greta speak only truth to me in the future? *Ten days, ten roses*, my Guide replied. This message had come through prior to Greta's leaving for Switzerland and visiting her father's memorial place. *Father figure*, my Guide said. The angry male energy was a father figure. The clue 'This is forbidden' was added to Greta's past-life heart issue and the Crystal Pool Energy notes next to 'Egypt' and 'priests'.

When I had discovered Greta's ten-day deception, I remembered with a jolt her leaving with me the gold key necklace and the note 'This is the Key to my Heart. Please hold it, until I return …' Under guidance I posted the necklace to her in Switzerland, understanding that in doing so I was rejecting her. There were moments of indifference towards me surfacing in Greta. I had felt it when she handed me the ankh on her return from Cairo and insisted I accept the gold necklace. I had rejected her before in Egypt, and this was part of her past-life heart issue — and it involved a lonely child. Carol, the tarot card reader from Dongara, had warned, 'Judy, you have experienced a great love in a past life, a love the rest of us only dream about. It will come to light and there will be great turmoil in your life.'

I drove Mum to Perth airport in Greta's car on 27 February.

A few days before she was due to depart, Mum had become breathless and her right knee had begun to swell. She was taken aboard her *Royal Brunei* flight in a wheelchair. We were very distressed — both finding it hard to be parted. I rang Barbara and told her Mum was unwell and to ensure someone was at Heathrow to meet her. After hearing Barbara's voice I was again violently sick.

Days later Greta visited and departed under a cloud of friction. When she left, a headache started that got continually worse until I could no longer cope. I rang my neighbour Maria, who drove me to the Dongara Medical Centre. This was two days before my birthday. Mum rang from Barbara's early in the morning; I did not tell her I was unwell. I thanked her for her gifts of three framed long-stitch tapestries of cottages — Australian miners' or loggers' homes — surrounded by dense forest. On the back of each frame Mum had written, 'So happy that you chose me as your Mum. Love to you.' Everyone with her ignored my birthday and I understood why Mum sounded strained, having to be there with them and coping with all this family tension.

Greta called in with the children all singing, 'Happy birthday, Judy.' I was handed a gift of a delightful dolphin wraparound skirt, several colourful balloons and a card. My birthday was spent on the beach and sharing a late evening meal with Greta. It was a wonderful relief from the many previous tense moments between us.

By now back in South Africa, Tatia sent a dead spider inside her birthday card. It was bright orange and huge, and made me jump as it fell out of the card to the floor. I was directed to place it on top of Greta's gift of the dolphin skirt. *Orange Dolphin*, my Guide explained. So Tatia is the Orange Celestial Dolphin, explaining our rapport at Julie's workshop prior to the permaculture conference in 1996. Inside her card Tatia had written the warning 'Look after your Heart, it is precious like rain.'

My solicitor, Tom, rang to say Section 127 of the Transfer of Land Act stated that if the Land Title Transfer Document was signed and both parties agreed, as Cathy and I had previously done, the document must be processed. The building society had no authority to insist that I become a single mortgagee and the Transfer of Land should have gone through. If it had I would not now be in this legal dilemma with Cathy. When Tom came down to visit not long after this my Guide said *He has been especially chosen.*

I had been given a substantial cash donation by Steve, who worked with Christina. I wrote to inform him of the legal situation and asked him if I could use the money for legal fees to protect the project. He rang later to say 'Yes'.

On 17 March my Guide sent me into the Healing Garden to place a circle of large limestones around the siris tree in the Open Chamber of the Heart Chakra itself. *Encouraging cycle of events*, my Guide explained.

I wrote asking Tom how I could represent myself, and a response came back to say the land transfer was being processed, but this was followed by another call to inform me Cathy's solicitors had been warned by the building society that the transfer was to be processed. I was annoyed by their interference, as Mum and I had paid the mortgage for two years. I was unable to understand why they would want to stop the transfer taking place. *Trust the process and all will be revealed*, my Guide said.

The post brought an Iona scarf from Sam in Scotland and seven chakra-balancing scarves from Dianne in England. I placed both gifts on the Jarrah Heart in the Dolphins Healing Room. *Iona, chakra balancing, jarrah heart, truth,* my Guide said. I touched these healing tools, marvelling at Sam and Dianne's coordination.

Eight days later Cathy's barrister placed a caveat on the Celestial Dolphin Centre, preventing the transfer to my sole name. I was taken to the Miraculous Medal inside the silver dolphins Indian box and instructed to place it inside the building society mortgage repayment book. Cathy's message came to mind: *Judy will be sole proprietor.* Her actions were placing her in conflict with her own guidance. She had twenty-one days to explain to the court her reasons for placing the caveat. What could she say, having invested no funds and made no mortgage repayments — and having walked out? She had signed the Transfer of Land document two years before and had tried to help me process the document many times since.

On 29 March my Guide encouraged me to go to the maypole, then walk six paces left and place four large stones on the ground. The stones were to be the circle of a Celtic cross. I completed the cross using timber from the tractor shed. The maypole was the Egyptian link with Greta, and I understood our Celtic link would soon be revealed, enabling us to return further back in time to ancient Egypt and the lonely child.

I had been encouraged to clear a large triangular garden between the Love Tree and the Children's Tree, with adjoining pathways. I was looking at the Celtic cross by the maypole thinking about the child in Egypt when Cindy walked along into the Healing Garden. I went to see what she was doing and found her watering this huge newly-cleared area with a tiny watering can. She moved along the pathways and stood under the canopy of the Children's Tree, watering this enormous tree with the last drops of water. *Area of relationships,* my Guide said, as Cindy walked back towards me. *Influence of the child,* she explained, as I gave her a hug. It was Cindy's obvious determination that made an impression and I sensed, then felt, the bond between us. Future development of the Relationship Area would encourage the angry, disruptive male energy from the past to reveal itself, and Cindy's action was encouraging this.

When I first started the Area of Relationships, Roger had brought his sickle and helped me clear the land. Now we worked together for weeks developing the area into an amazing and complex symbol. He searched the tip for mulching materials and brought wooden cray slats that we placed into precise patterns on top of a mass of carpeting. There were long designs and small circular designs, and red plastic cray-pot holders were used in specific areas. Once the design was completed, another pathway was created to the Love Tree. Here there was to be a smaller area, but covered with similar materials. Roger happened to bring a circular carpet on the day I needed one. This often occurred between us — a type of telepathy — as I had experienced also with Christina and Julie.

When Roger placed the circular carpet in the centre of this small area, I received the words *Encouraging cycle of events*. We then created a design using red plastic cray-pot holders placed row upon row to form inner circles. *To ward off negativity*, my Guide explained. We were fascinated by her use of the most basic of materials.

Roger never questioned what we were doing as we worked. He was as driven as I was to follow the guidance, arriving at the crack of dawn each morning with a trailer-full of materials for me to use during the day. I was acutely aware that the creation of the Healing Garden would not have been possible without his physical input and energy. Late each evening before retiring, I walked the property with Jessie at my heels to absorb its atmosphere as the garden was being transformed.

A young couple from Dongara visited wanting to buy the property, and their estate agent followed later with an offer. If I sold now and had to pay Cathy $15,000, Mum's capital investment would be involved and that was not to happen. I voiced my concerns to Greta, but she pushed them aside saying I should move south, live near her, and give Cathy what she wanted. The project was of no value as far as Greta was concerned. The couple later backed out of the offer, but I now knew Greta's driving force was for me to leave the centre. 'I require you to be near and available to me when I move,' she said.

There was a daily flow of visitors through the garden, and I needed to find a way of explaining the concept to them. So I got Terry to make a board on which to display information regarding the Standing Stone, Living Enclosure / Merlin's Triangle, Crystal Pool, Celtic Entrance, Celtic Triple Enclosure, Heart Chakra / Pulse of Life / Goddess Nut, Celtic Beacon, Mary Seat, Boomerang/Karma, Area of Relationships, Love Tree / Children's Tree and Tuart Walk.

On 8 April I was sent out to the main entrance to take down the White Dolphin. Roger made a large wooden box and I placed it safely inside. This was a shock for us both. Greta rang during this time, asking to see me: she was distressed. So I walked into Dongara to her home. We had both been placed in a kind of crisis state and it was *familiar*. We spoke of moving south but I was apprehensive about this and told her so. As I walked home my apprehension lifted and a feeling of freedom flooded my being along with the words *She will leave*. I realised Greta and I had experienced a crisis like this once before, long ago, and I had walked away from her then, as now.

The next day I agreed to drive south with Greta after Easter to look for a rental home for her and the children. Easter arrived and Greta offered her Dongara home to her husband, enabling him to have time with their children. Four days later Greta and I drove to Busselton. We visited St Mary's Church; I remembered being sent there by my Guide in 1995 and photographing the leadlight window featuring Mary and Mary Magdalene.

Greta wanted to drive to Nannup the following day, and spoke of us finding my valley. I became nervous. I had not brought this message through: it had been told to me by Selva the clairvoyant. Selva had forecast I would live at the centre in Dongara for a long time then move to a home, which I would restore — 'in a valley, another centre,' she had said.

The next morning we drove to Margaret River, and I longed to stay there. The yearning was so strong that I could not converse. Greta understood that I wanted to be alone and walked away. There was a positive energy here that I found comforting. The following day as we drove through Busselton on our way to Dongara, I noticed a bright-blue-painted house for rent. We talked about its possibilities for Greta and then drove on.

Back at the centre, my Guide referred me to a pamphlet given to Mum by Cathy's mother, *The Holy Child Jesus of Prague*. It stated, 'The more you honour me, the more I bless you.' It explained the history of a waxen statue of the Infant Jesus, an heirloom of the Spanish royal family. At the turn of the 17th century the statue was presented as a wedding gift to the soon-to-become Countess Polyxena. The Countess became a benefactress to the Carmelite Fathers when Ferdinand II of the Hapsburg dynasty gave them the Church of the Holy Trinity in Prague, a former Protestant church renamed Our Lady of Victory. After the death of her husband, the Countess presented the statue to the Carmelites. *Our Lady of Victory* ran through my mind all day.

On 21 April I was shaken awake with the instruction to change the name of the Celestial Dolphin Centre to the Healing Garden of

Dongara. Early the next day I received the instruction to remove the 'Healing Garden' sign Julie had unveiled on Mary May Day / Open Day '97 and ring Christina to discuss a new brochure. Later I was guided to return the White Dolphin to the main entrance. I was content as I walked the Healing Garden of Dongara. Greta had made the request during the Request Ceremony Cairo '97 for the centre to become what it was meant to be and this was taking place.

My solicitor, Tom, rang to tell me the twenty-one days for Cathy to justify her caveat had not begun as there was a technicality regarding her signature. This would mean more costs for me, but I agreed to carry on.

I was taken to *The Holy Child Jesus of Prague* pamphlet to speak aloud part of the prayer: 'Almighty Infant, lift Thy little hand and bless our temporal possessions, take them under Thy powerful protection and keep them from misfortune and loss.' Then my Guide encouraged me to go to the area designed *to ward off negativity*, and stand at its centre and repeat the prayer. It was only then that I could comprehend the huge part Cathy's mother was playing in the soul group. Several times she'd handed me symbols of her faith, and the Miraculous Medal was inside the building society mortgage repayment book. She had now provided the means (the prayer) by which I could protect the centre and the project to keep it safe from her daughter Cathy's past-life negative influence.

The next day I was sent to Dongara to buy paint. 'Meadow Green' was highlighted and my Guide informed me that this was for the Information Board. When I had finished painting, I was encouraged to find the amazonite crystal that had featured during the channelling of the Ten Year Mary Project 1994, and compare it with the paint: they were the same colour. I was referred to my notes and read, 'Amazonite represents truth, clear understanding and solid foundations.'

I had removed the 'Healing Garden' sign unveiled by Julie and was now to remove the 'Iona Lodge' sign. Maria, my neighbour, had loaned me her car while she was away on holiday, and the next day I took the signs to the tip. When I returned I took my cassette player into the tractor shed and *The Cornish Furry Dance* soon vibrated across the property. As I danced around the maypole and the Celtic cross on the ground near it, the feeling of freedom came. I was encouraging truth, clear understanding and solid foundation through this dance of celebration.

I painted the maypole stand with Green of Amazonite, a term now used by my Guide in reference to the Meadow Green paint and the healing potential of the amazonite crystal.

Drive to Seven Mile Beach, my Guide requested. Four years before, on 30 December 1994, while living in Geraldton, Mum and I had been guided to drive to Dongara and nearby Seven Mile Beach to spend just four hours away from home. The realisation came that those four hours represented four years, which would be completed on the coming 30 December. On this day my Guide asked me to wear a red chequered shirt, blue denim shorts, blue socks and my gardening boots. On our arrival at Seven Mile Beach Jessie ran straight to a pile of clothing placed high in the sand dunes away from the water. The clothes were all neatly folded. There was a red chequered shirt, blue denim shorts, blue socks and pair of Rossi boots. There was no-one in the sea or walking the beach and it was as if I had removed my own clothing and walked away. *The feeling of freedom*, my Guide explained. I took off my boots and socks and walked in the water. *You are a survivor, take heart*, she said.

Four days later, a visitor flew into the Healing Garden — a kookaburra. Its joyful laughter made me smile. I remembered the card in the office with the kookaburras and the message *Not to fail in the current challenge. Not to make the same mistakes again.*

Terry arrived to put the final touches to the information board as Roger drove in with a pile of carpeting for the Heart. I watched him drag the heavy carpets one by one from his trailer into Chamber One and I wondered at our past-life connection. He was as driven as I was to complete and maintain the garden, especially the Heart itself. *Power in your garden*, my Guide said.

Roger made Seats of Reflection from recycled materials. The first was to be placed opposite the entrance to the Heart Chakra / Pulse of Life / Goddess Nut by the Judas tree and another by the Celtic Entrance and Julie's pink Mexican rose. He was busy placing the seats when I returned from collecting the post. Christina had sent an updated brochure for the Healing Garden in which she mentioned Seats of Reflection. This unspoken coordination between the three of us was to happen more and more.

My Guide sent me to the lodge to remove the Aboriginal spear from under Mary's image and take it to the office. As I hung it on the office wall I heard the word *Justice*. In Aboriginal law, an offender would be speared and left in the desert. If they survived, they were taken back into the group. *You are a survivor, take heart*, my Guide said.

Mum had tried to work the dolphin family tapestry handed to me by Greta and given to her for her birthday before she left for England, but could not get to grips with the stitches and so asked me to try. I secured the tapestry onto a standing frame and was working the dolphin family tapestry when I glanced across to the Egyptian tapestry. *I had a dream and the dream was you*, whispered an unknown female. 'Who are you?' I asked. There was no response, only silence.

I was drawn to the woman in the Egyptian tapestry symbolically representing Greta, and the dream I'd experienced in 1988 came to mind. It had featured a young woman with a regal stance. Her brown eyes had held an emotion I did not understand and I had woken with a sense of great loss. As I re-lived the dream, the words repeated again, *I had a dream and the dream was you*.

Greta made the grand announcement that she was moving south, but then became ill. I spent days catering for her and the children, driving to and from the centre daily.

On 14 May my solicitor served the Twenty-One Day Notice on Cathy. There had been no effort to justify her placement of the caveat. Two days later I finished the white-light planting of the Heart Chakra / Pulse of Life / Goddess Nut. The Heart was now protected. Julie's red rosebush died overnight. *The heart is protected*, my Guide said. Roger took the dead rosebush to the tip.

My Guide sent me to an article in a folder, but only to the author's name — Jude Priest. The clue 'Jude Priest' was added to Greta's past-life heart issue and the Crystal Pool Energy notes beside the sentiments *This is forbidden*. As I recorded Jude Priest, Greta strolled into the office carrying a rose plant inside a pot. The label read 'Barossa Dream Rose'. I had not mentioned that Julie's red rose had died overnight. She said it was a gift for me. When I accepted her rose an overwhelming sense of loss forced me to walk away. I was being moved on from a red rose to a dream rose.

I had a dream and the dream was you, whispered the unknown female.

How can Greta be the woman in my dream? I wondered. In response, I was to note a fourth soulmate with a past-life heart issue — me:

Heart Issue: Judy – Jude Priest – I had a dream and the dream was you.

The clue 'I had a dream and the dream was you' was added to the Crystal Pool Energy notes next to 'Jude Priest'.

I was warned by my solicitor that a summons was going to be served on me but he was far from ready. He did not actually advise me to leave, but the message was clear. I quickly packed a bag and caught a coach heading south. This was an opportunity for me to check on the blue-painted home in Busselton on Greta's behalf, and I returned on 6 June with the rental forms for her to sign. While I was there I also organised a post-office box for her. I was told by my Guide to hold on to the keys and hand them over to her only when her move was organised.

I discovered the Love Tree had split in half while I was away, but was greatly relieved to find it remained alive. Greta had worked in Chamber Two, attempting to place paper and hay, but it had blown around in the wind. She spent considerable time trying to repair it, but failed. I watched her, knowing it was too late. She had remained silent the previous year when I had asked about taking the children out of the country. I was encouraged away from these reflections to thoughts of creating an enlarged area for the Celtic Entrance, enabling visitors to read the information on the information board. Roger used the fencing from Julie's Living Enclosure / Merlin's Triangle. Julie's Mexican rose was replacing the thrown-out 'Iona Lodge' sign by being encouraged to grow to its full pink potential. I sensed a soul energy change within Greta, and was encouraged to read the influence of the second Soul Energy at the centre:

> Soul Energy (2): Celtic 7 – pink rose energy – past lives / karma clearing – red rose energy – St Michael – Mary May Day '96 – 7 chakras – Buddha – Sacred 13 – runic energy – 7 Healing Triangles – pink – male energy – Celtic Entrance – maypole – Mary May Day '97 – Egyptian Goddess Nut – silver locket – Golden Rose Dolphin.

Influence of the Pink Dolphin, my Guide said. Who is the Pink Dolphin? I wondered.

Julie's Living Enclosure was dismantled and Merlin's Triangle moved to the Celtic Entrance, but not inside the Healing Garden area itself. I was fascinated by these movements, understanding they were linked with Greta's plan to leave. She began to pack her belongings, and once I knew this I took the property off the market. I had trusted the situation within a situation and had seen the reactions and learnt the agendas of both Greta and Cathy.

Cathy said her reason for placing the caveat had been because of the Transfer of Land document. She suggested that I had obtained her signature under duress. Cathy was determined to get her hands on some money, but the money was not mine to give. A court date was to be arranged and I was not sure if I could afford to employ a barrister for the appearance in Perth. I asked for the papers to represent myself and they were processed in Perth at the Supreme Court. Years before, I had not been allowed to speak in the Plymouth County Court; this time I would speak. I recalled standing in front of the leadlight image of Archangel Michael in Brentor Church, Dartmoor, longing with all my heart for justice and revealing of the truth. Here was an opportunity to achieve that.

Late that night I was visited by a very angry Greta demanding to know what was happening. She was aware I had taken the property off the market. I explained the legal events of the day, but she ignored everything I said, announcing that it was my fault she was leaving without me. She didn't want to go, but when she did, maybe then I would follow. I stared at her, speechless. I had told her I was not moving south and would fight to keep Mum's capital and secure our home. The warning I received at the beginning of the year came again, *Greta. Gauntlet. Challenge.* This was happening now. Greta stormed out, reacting again to a past-life flashback and the turmoil of our past-life separation crisis.

I went to the office, where I was taken to a meditation from Findhorn. It was from Findhorn that Cathy had written saying she had been told by the devas she was to have the centre. This was after meeting Dorothy, the woman famous for her communication with the nature kingdom. We now had a set of comparisons between Dorothy, the spirit devas and the letter written by Cathy. The meditation included the warning 'Ensure that deva substance will not stimulate your desires in a selfish or sensational way.' A desire had started in Cathy when she discovered I had placed the centre on the market to sell.

Two necklaces, two women, two situations, my Guide warned.

A calm Greta came to see me days later asking me to help her design something for the leadlight evening classes she was now attending. I drew a Celtic cross for her. This was to be completed over the next few weeks and given to me as another farewell gift before she left. I did not get drawn into any further discussion with her. As she was leaving I spoke to her about allowing people to be themselves; otherwise she would end up pushing them away.

I was ready for the court on 22 June when a last-minute notice arrived: there was a delay, as more documentation was needed. All correspondence was coming to me, while Cathy would be incurring legal fees. A new date was set for 29 July and I received a copy of Cathy's sworn statement regarding the duress. The circumstances surrounding the signing of the transfer document were vague in the extreme. The receptionist who had witnessed our signatures would discount any accusation of Cathy being under duress.

Two days later Greta brought the completed leadlight Celtic cross to the centre. It was a beautiful small rectangle. The cross was granite grey with a bright blue diamond at its centre. There were four sections within the circle itself, of red and yellow with a green background. She was understandably proud of her work. We were beside the maypole and I pondered the completed cycle of events. Our friendship had started with her hug and a goodbye by the maypole the previous year, and now she was giving me a goodbye gift in the same place. I carefully placed the leadlight Celtic cross on the ground beside the wooden Celtic cross formation and took a photograph to capture its image and the moment.

In exchange I handed her photographs of herself and the children in the garden. One featured Cindy sitting on a pile of hay in the wheelbarrow. I remembered being told by a medium in the Blue Mountains that a wheelbarrow held a past-life connection for me. I was very fond of Cindy and would miss her terribly. It was on this day, 24 June 1996, in company with Christina, that I had been given a lengthy message, part of which said *A word of warning. You are entering dangerous territory, Egyptian times …*

As Greta was about to leave for Busselton I gave her the keys to the post-office box. I told her once again that I would be staying in Dongara to complete the project. Days later the white flowers opened on the Geraldton wax and the mulla mulla on the northern and southern pathways of the Heart Chakra / Pulse of Life / Goddess Nut.

She departed on 1 July, leaving behind the Barossa Dream rose and the leadlight Celtic cross. I watched the furniture van depart and returned to the centre with a sense of relief.

My Guide encouraged me to dismantle the Celtic cross I had created on the ground by the maypole and place Greta's leadlight Celtic cross on the windowsill of the Dolphins Healing Room. I was aware its colours were the Four Core Colours of yellow, green, blue and red, but, unlike the handmade cloth symbol, where the centre was red, Greta's leadlight had a central shape of a blue diamond. *Blue Mary Ray Diamond Centre*, my Guide said.

I stood at the Mary Seat after 4 pm and repeated the Celtic prayer, confirming my willingness to trust the process and complete the Ten Year Mary Project 1994.

Mum wrote to say she was missing me, our home and our way of life.

The first week of July brought a series of rainbows. A rainbow arched over the western side of the property, then a day later over the far eastern corner, and the following day over the southern area. Soon after this I noticed a van parked on the highway outside the centre bearing the logo of Telstra, the telephone company. It turned out that they were discussing an ominous plan to lay cables through the garden up to the lodge. I had a row of trees to protect outside the eastern border and two rows along the southern border, and there was no way a digger was going to carve its way through my Healing Garden.

I stayed with the man and his machine as he dug a wide trench along the eastern boundary, protecting the swamp sheoaks and Rottnest Island tea trees. I gave him a drink and asked if he was interested to know why I had planted these trees outside the property. As he drank his tea, he listened intently while I identified the trees, explaining their purpose as both wind and heat breaks. We spent the week together ensuring not one of the trees was damaged while he dug his trench, laid cables and re-covered the trench. Round one was won; now for round two: I had to protect the two rows of trees lining the property to the south along the dirt road. I had not responded to the written request to enter my land, so all work stopped and I was able to relax. I found it interesting that there had been just three rainbows: the northern side of the property had not been protected by a rainbow's arch.

I was invited to spend a weekend with Greta in Busselton. As I did not have a car, this would involve a twelve-hour journey on two coaches. I became apprehensive and walked to the Mary Seat to sit and wait for directions. *You must go*, my Guide insisted. I had only been sitting a moment when a golden fox strolled through the Celtic Entrance. It looked across at me before continuing on down to the Tuart Walk / Throat Chakra, where it stood sniffing the air. Every few minutes it lifted its head to see if I was watching. I was referred to the book *Medicine Cards* by Sams and Carson:

The Fox – Camouflage ... it is a sign that you are to become like the wind, which is unseen yet is able to weave into and through any location or situation. You would be wise to observe the acts of others rather than their words at this time. (15)

With this in mind I booked to travel south. Roger arrived and we worked together fencing the edge of the Healing Garden from the main entrance to the Celtic Entrance, ensuring visitors passed by the information board. The visit by the fox went through my mind. The colour gold had featured in different forms — the gold and black ribbon used for the Oak Ogham symbol on the pink curtain for Julie to open the Healing Garden, the reference to Greta as Golden Rose Dolphin, the gold Egyptian necklaces that appeared around Cathy's throat, the Egyptian tapestry on which gold thread was being stitched in the women's clothing. Today a golden fox had walked through the Healing Garden. *Atlantis*, my Guide said. I was referred again to the book *Vibrational Medicine* by R. Gerber:

> During its last 30,000 or more years, the technology and sciences of Atlantis evolved to a high degree of sophistication. At its peak, sometimes referred to as the Golden Age of Atlantis, the Atlanteans had grown to become a race of highly developed individuals who were skilled in all manner of architecture, engineering, astronomy, agriculture, and especially the healing arts. (3)

The words 'healing arts' were highlighted and then I recalled giving Greta a healing one morning when the message came *This person has enough love to heal the planet*. I had wondered then how this love and healing potential had been overtaken by scepticism. *Misuse of power*, my Guide said.

On 11 July I began my journey south, arriving late in the evening. Greta met me at the coach, but I couldn't bring myself to enter the house until I had spent time alone walking the beach. It was dark, but the moon's rays reflected on the surface of the sea. I visualised Greta's leadlight Celtic cross in the window of the Dolphins Healing Room and the moon's rays shining through its diamond centre of blue. *Blue Mary Ray Diamond Centre*, my Guide said.

Greta and I were up early the next day intending to spend time walking the coast. Cindy wanted to come with us, but Greta would not allow it. We sat on a high ledge above the rough sea, the coastline spreading away for miles — both silent. I turned to speak, but no words came. I was drawn to lean towards her, touching her forehead with mine, a *familiar* sign of affection. Why did I do that? I wondered. I was aware that our brow chakras had touched as with two of the Egyptian women in the tapestry.

I was due to stay until 17 July, but two days later I had an anxiety attack. I know now it was an anxiety attack, but at the time I did not recognise it as such. It followed a cutting remark from Greta concerning my enthusiasm for working in the Healing Garden that came without any justification. It was like a body blow. The sarcasm continued, but I no longer heard the words, only felt the negativity. I went to my trolley case and began to pack, but then unpacked. I did not know where to place my emotions with any safety. I packed and unpacked, packed and unpacked for more than half an hour. A complete loss of control and the most ghastly feeling I have ever experienced. I had touched Greta's forehead and this was the result. Cindy became so anxious that she shouted, 'Leave Judy alone'.

I was still shaken the following day when I went to see a doctor. I described what had happened. He said it was a panic attack and wanted to prescribe medicine. I had been fine until I touched Greta's forehead with mine and drugs would not solve the problem. I had experienced at first hand the past-life turmoil stored within Greta's brow chakra. Greta appeared unmoved by the incident, but I was encouraged by my Guide to walk the beach to rationalise what had happened.

I was invited to morning tea with a group of Greta's friends. She did not want to discuss what had happened. I stood back while everyone talked about the business of the day, then above the noise one person asked me about my life in Dongara. Everyone stopped speaking to enable me to answer, but as I went to speak, Greta stretched across in front of me asking an irrelevant question of another person. Her action was rude, creating a hushed, embarrassed silence. But she carried on speaking, regardless, and I left the room. She had publicly displayed her displeasure with my involvement in the Healing Garden and we drove back to her home in silence. The golden fox had warned me to observe the actions of others.

I was encouraged by my Guide to walk the beach at sunset. *Egyptian wife*, the unknown male shouted angrily. Whose wife? I wondered.

I was instructed to update my own past-life heart issue notes with this new clue. As I left the beach the thought came to phone my Dongara answering machine, and I discovered Mum had left a message to say she would be home on 11 September. I prepared to leave Busselton as planned on 17 July.

Greta stood behind me as the coach pulled in and I wondered what she was doing when I heard the words 'Trust me.' A shiver ran up and down my spine; the voice was the same whisper, *I had a dream and the dream was you.* I turned but saw only Greta. I was to board the coach when Greta handed me a bunch of wildflowers. This had become Greta's pattern: to hurt, then give me a gift. It was a relief when the coach pulled away. It arrived in Dongara late in the evening.

I was given no time even to empty my case on arriving home, but was sent by my Guide into the Dolphins Healing Room to light a new long white candle and place it in the Dongara candle-holder in the centre of the jarrah table. I was worn out, but followed the request. It was a few minutes past 11 pm. I stood looking into the candle flame as it rose higher, then the phone rang. It was Greta, saying 'goodnight,' on my answering machine. Her leadlight Celtic cross reflected the Four Core Colours in the candle's light. *Blue Mary Ray Diamond Centre*, my Guide said. At last I was allowed to go to bed.

Roger arrived early the next day with materials for the garden. I worked until 1 pm, until directed to leave the garden and go to the Dolphins Healing Room to turn the leadlight Celtic cross around. I wondered at this request, but carried it out. I was then guided to go into the office and remove the Miraculous Medal from within the building society mortgage repayment book and take it to the Dolphins Healing Room and place it at the base of the Dongara candle-holder. I was not to relight the candle, but say aloud, 'What we need is a miracle regarding Cathy.'

I returned to the garden to work until I was sent back to the lodge. Fifty minutes had elapsed between my visits. I picked up the box of matches to light the candle but it was gone! Assuming it must have fallen on the floor I looked, but found nothing. The Dongara candle-holder was empty, the Miraculous Medal still at its base. It was the first time something like this had happened. My Guide referred me to my 1995 diary and I read, '18 July, Mary's image was taken to Iona Lodge and placed by the Dongara candle-holder. A candle was lit and the orange light from its flame shone on Mary's face.'

Three years before to the very day.

I was woken at 7 am the following morning to discover the candle had not been returned. I was instructed to read a part of the information regarding the Miraculous Medal. It revealed that at 11.30 pm on the night of 18 July 1830, in Paris, Sister Catherine Laboure was approached by a guardian angel in the form of a little child who summoned her to the chapel where a few minutes after midnight she met Mary. The same dates, but 168 years apart.

At 10 am I was taken back to the information again to make a note: 'It is a little token of love designed and bestowed upon you ...'

I looked at Mary's image and felt compelled to say, 'Thank you.' *French connection*, my Guide said. I was then guided to fetch the mortgage repayment book and place it at the base of the Dongara candle-holder by the medal, indicating a miracle with regard to Cathy.

The 20th of July began for me at 3 am. I was encouraged to work white wool stitches around the heart of the two women with touching foreheads within the Egyptian tapestry — *protective white-lighting stitches*, my Guide explained — and then to put a white stitch within each brow chakra. I removed the tapestry from its frame and rolled it up ready for storage.

Roger brought two wooden donation boxes and stands with covers he had made at home, and these were positioned at the Celtic Entrance for donations towards the cost of printing the handout brochures now on display on the Information Board.

Seven days later my Guide requested seven white-painted stones to be taken from the words 'One and All' within the Cornish Crest at the main entrance and placed inside Merlin's Triangle. The next day I worked from dawn till dusk, eating only once. I mulched around the oak tree and painted the two donation boxes Green of Amazonite. I cleared the weeds in the Mary Seat area, understanding a change of energy was coming.

The day of the Supreme Court action regarding Cathy's placement of the caveat, 29 July, was a stressful day. I walked into the breezeway and was amazed to discover the Barossa Dream rose had produced two beautiful long-stemmed rosebuds overnight. I heard soft words coming from within the rosebush. *Valuing honesty and commitment, softly let go of the past, enabling others to change.* I was distracted by the phone — it was my solicitor to tell me the judge was allowing Cathy to move to a Trial Hearing.

I walked into the Dolphins Healing Room holding the two rosebuds and touched the Miraculous Medal beside the building society mortgage payment book. *Softly let go of the past, enabling others to change*, came from deep within me. It was a difficult request as I struggled with the possibility of a trial. Within days of the court hearing I received a shock letter with the news that Cathy was demanding $45,000, plus legal fees. I replied by return saying I would not even consider her ridiculous demand.

At 2 am on 7 August, a full moon was overhead as I walked to the main entrance with my wheelbarrow to remove more white-painted stones, leaving eight in a pile. I wheeled this load to the maypole to join the seven inside Merlin's Triangle. I was guided to take four heavy intact cray pots, with their red pots included, from Heart Chamber Two to Chamber Three. The positioning was precise, with the pots placed on top of one another.

Four years of conflict, my Guide warned.

This area was to be the Heart Element, to include a wind wheel. The heart chakras of the two Egyptian women with touching brow chakras had recently been protected by white lighting in the tapestry; now the Heart Element symbol of four years of conflict was to be erected in the Heart Chakra / Pulse of Life / Goddess Nut, encouraging the revelation of the truth and protecting all those involved.

Roger arrived early and we discussed the Heart Element and him creating something that would spin there, complementing the element of air. After saying he'd follow up on it, he asked about the legal situation with Cathy. He was shocked at the latest developments. I felt relaxed talking with him about it. *Pink Dolphin*, my Guide explained. So Roger was the Pink Celestial Dolphin, representing the second vibrational colour of the Heart! No wonder he was as driven as I was to maintain the Heart.

After Roger left, my Guide asked me to take the Barossa Dream rose from the breezeway to the Healing Garden where, still in its pot, I placed it in the Open Chamber beside the siris tree. Greta rang and we had a heated discussion, both of us deciding our friendship was not working. I walked back to the Open Chamber and sat on the bench by the Barossa Dream Rose. *Four years of conflict*, my Guide warned.

My attention was centred on Julie's oak tree, and I marked a spot midway between the oak and the Relationship Area, indicating where the Barossa Dream rose would be planted. I placed the last eight white-painted stones from the main entrance on this spot. *Rose energy*, my Guide said.

Two nights later I was woken and told to put the Miraculous Medal on a chain and wear it. I tried to leave the room but was held fast and forced to take deep breaths, as the swirling energy around me was so intense. I was encouraged by my Guide to read more concerning the Miraculous Medal. I read that Bernadette at Lourdes in France was wearing the medal when she saw the Lady of the Grotto and was recorded as saying Mary appeared as she was featured in the medal. The amended goddess energy notes — formerly Soul Energy (1) notes — through which Julie and I had worked were updated with these latest clues:

Goddess Energy: Yellow – The Lady of Good Counsel – gemstone – settled legal disputes – rebuilding the cathedral – Virgo – Gardner – Mary's Church – Chartres – Church of Yankalilla – a rose – Mary's signature – Medjugorje, Bosnia-Herzegovina – goddess energy – Merlin – Miraculous Medal – Lady of the Grotto.

French connection, my Guide said.

My Guide insisted on an updated Healing Garden brochure being placed on the jarrah table and the Miraculous Medal information put inside. I was sent to find a business card from a settlement agent in Geraldton, and this was also placed within the brochure. I was being reassured of a positive outcome regarding the legal dispute with Cathy.

I spent time the next day pacing the position for the Heart Element in Chamber Three in preparation for Roger. The circumference of the base was to be seven paces north and seven paces south of the chamber's central point. When I returned to the lodge after finishing this the phone was ringing. It was Greta; she was distressed and asked me to meet her in Perth. I was reluctant; then a friend rang to say she was driving to Perth and asked if I wanted a lift. *The care of the soul sees another reality*, my Guide insisted. We booked into accommodation in South Perth and spent time walking by the river. I returned to Dongara on 21 August.

The next day my Guide directed that the Barossa Dream rose be planted near the pile of eight stones. As I carried the plant, the words *Change of heart* repeated three times. After planting the rose, I placed the eight white stones around it. *A protective circle of white*, my Guide said. I took one stone from near the Mexican rose and placed it by the white circle, creating a group of nine. *Relationships*, she said. I removed two stones from Merlin's Triangle and placed them in the circle, creating a group of eleven. *Eleven dolphins and a rose*, my Guide said. I sat by the Barossa Dream rose to try and grasp this new information. As the Golden Rose Dolphin, Greta had accessed the Rose Energy for the Celestial Dolphins. There had been an indication that gold/golden, was connected with Atlantis. Atlantis was before Ancient Egypt.

I sat on the Mary Seat to ponder the Dolphins. Was the separation of the Dolphin Family the loneliness inside me the same as the spirit child Julie had felt in the Old Saddlery? I was being moved back through past lives and karmic issues to the Dolphin Family. This would explain my close relationship with my mother, the Yellow Dolphin, and the ease I shared with Christina, the Blue Dolphin, Roger, the Pink Dolphin and Tatia, the Orange Dolphin. There was the pull Julie — the Red Dolphin — and I had felt to work together to bring through the Heart Chakra / Pulse of Life / Goddess Nut concept, in order for me to journey back through our past lives. Greta, the Golden Rose Dolphin, had been unable to say goodbye, being drawn back to the centre. The Ten Year Mary Project 1994 was to heal our hurts, karmic attachments and separations, and bring through a new understanding. One of these separations involved a lonely child who was in great need of my protection.

Two days later, on 24 August, I tried to walk through the meditation room but was stopped and drawn towards the print of St Michael's and All Angels Church in Cornwood, Devon, place of my birth, and encouraged by my Guide to form a protective circle around myself and repeat, 'I ask for the protection of Michael the Archangel.'

Roger arrived carrying the Celtic Quadrant Knot under his arm: a large round base painted Green of Amazonite with pieces of trellis attached, creating the four sections of the symbolic knot. My Guide had asked for this to be made before the arrival of a couple from Balingup. Roger took the symbol to the main entrance and attached it opposite the White Dolphin. An hour later Shirley and Keith drove in. I walked them around the Heart Chakra / Pulse of Life / Goddess Nut; then we sat on the Mary Seat in order for me to explain the chakra concept. Later, we walked to the main entrance and the Quadrant Knot where Keith asked if I knew the history of this symbol. I said it was a hedgerow design used by early British monks to surround their herb and healing gardens.

'Do you work with Merlin?' Keith enquired. We had walked passed Merlin's Triangle within the Celtic Entrance. I had been aware of this but had not mentioned it.

'Why would you ask me that?'

'Because I felt his energy by the Pulse of Life.'

'I have a symbol there described as Merlin's Triangle,' I replied.

Keith smiled and nodded in response, and in my mind I could see Julie when she handed Merlin back to me on my mother's birthday saying, 'Make him work for you.'

Late evening on the following day Greta rang, spending the entire phone call putting me down. Her husband had returned from an overseas trip and there had been tension between them. The ghastly feeling I had experienced in July after touching her forehead came flooding back, and I tried to contain the anxiety but couldn't. Struggling to control the nausea, I rang Roger and Mary, who took me to the Dongara Medical Centre. Mary drove me back home the next day after collecting my post on the way and handed me an envelope from Greta. Inside I found a Friendship Card telling me how important I was to her. That night my Guide insisted that I place Greta's card near the phone. As I did so the phone rang — it was Greta. I thanked her for the card and she started again, telling me how I let her down and I was never there when she needed me. The feeling of anxiety began to surface and a throbbing headache started, so I quickly ended the conversation. *Egyptian wife*, the unknown male shouted angrily. *This is forbidden.*

The phone rang again and Greta left a message on the answering machine. 'What is happening to me?' she sobbed. 'Please help me. You must help me.' My Guide told me not to respond and instead sent me into the Dolphins Healing Room to the magazine *Insight*, January 1998, to the article 'Aura — the extended body' by Jude Priest — highlighting again the author's name. This was the second time Jude Priest had been drawn to my attention. I went to my diary and read, '16 May, Jude Priest was highlighted and as I wrote this new clue in my notes, Greta strolled into my office carrying a Barossa Dream rose plant in a pot.'

I was jolted back to the present by the phone ringing, and again it was Greta. I was half afraid to speak as she was reacting to a traumatic past-life separation situation while I was desperately trying to understand the past for both of us. She was calm, warm and friendly. I did not tell her I had spent the night at the Dongara Medical Centre. 'Would you please come down on Monday and spend time with me?' You would never have known it was the same person whose energy had caused me to go from being relaxed to being so disturbed that I needed help. There were two personalities within Greta, one caring, the other hurtful. I said I needed time to think, but I would respond. *You must go*, my Guide insisted, *this is the next stage.*

I went into the meditation room to recover and heard a droning noise. It grew louder. I looked outside and saw a massive dark cloud hovering over the lodge, getting bigger and bigger, noisier and noisier. A vast swarm of bees. I had never witnessed such an event before. The queen found a crack in the southern corner of the cavity wall in the room and the swarm quickly disappeared inside. My Guide again referred me to the book *A Dictionary of Symbols* by Tom Chetwynd:

> Bee ... bees are the sacred attributes of many goddesses ... (8)

The wording 'the sacred attributes of many goddesses' was highlighted.

I rang and booked a coach seat for a return journey to Busselton, and told Greta I would be down to see her. The children were away visiting with their father, so we drove to the Porongurups, near the Stirling Ranges — a beautiful area. I searched for tiny trigger orchids in the bush. My enthusiasm soon died when Greta's bouts of sarcasm began. We walked the Mountain of Many Moods in silence. In the local café the subject of my sister was brought up. Greta would often encourage me to talk about an issue that made me feel vulnerable; then her sarcasm would come at full force and I would lose confidence. This time I kept the hurt of Barbara's actions under control. Greta became restless. I did venture to say that if anything became too stressful I would say 'Stop!'

In our chalet I became aware of Greta looking at me with a coldness in her eyes that was becoming a *familiar* feature. I braced myself, seeing the hurtful and angry person, and then it came — another put-down. The feeling of nausea started — but I held it fast inside me. I returned Greta's stare and said 'Stop!' She got up and walked away.

She became so agitated that we decided to leave, but as we drove away her car began to make a noise. While the car was taken to a garage we went back to the café and I tried to share a few of the messages I received from my Guide. There was a long pause and then Greta gave a condescending smile, got up and paid the bill. I felt like a child who had spoken out of turn and was now to be ignored — another ghastly experience. We spent that evening with German friends of hers in

Busselton. The couple conversed in English for my benefit, but Greta replied in German. Again, the friends conversed in English. Greta persisted, taking the husband to one side to maintain their conversation in German. The wife was embarrassed. Greta had found yet another way to humiliate me.

'Tell me about the Healing Garden,' Margo said. Greta left the husband and crossed the room, placing herself between Margo and me. I let Greta stand there until she became uncomfortable and then I answered Margo's question and explained the concept. I looked up at Greta, wondering what had happened centuries ago to turn her away from being the spiritual channel for the Celestial Dolphins and soul group to being this hurtful reactive person. What had happened that left her so unforgiving towards me? *Egyptian wife*, the unknown male responded angrily.

Later, Greta drove us to the beach and we walked by the water's edge. Although it was a beautiful night, there was a tense silence between us.

'Why does my mind fill with hate towards you sometimes?' she asked.

'I don't know, but until I find out neither of us will be free,' I replied.

Try again and speak to her from your heart, my Guide urged. 'We are part of an amazing past-life healing process to rid ourselves and others of hurtful negative karmic attachments,' I said.

Greta faltered as she heard my words, then I saw her shrug them off again. I left the next day, and returned to Dongara to find the lodge full of dead, dying and angry bees. I had to pay someone to smoke out the hive and was informed *five* queen bees had set up home within the lodge walls. *Sacred attributes of many goddesses*, my Guide explained. *Ending of a friendship in October*, she warned later.

At 5 am on 8 September I removed Greta's ankh from around my neck. I had offered an explanation of our intentions to Greta and I placed her ankh on the jarrah table. I had a sore throat for several days, but understood this was part of a healing process for my throat chakra as I worked to clear my heart of stored traumatic past-life karma. I received an emotional card from Greta saying that I was in her thoughts. The ongoing struggle between the distant past and the present was affecting us both in different ways.

Mum was scheduled to arrive on 11 September. I was filled with excitement when I set off at 3.15 am on the Greyhound coach to meet her, but was shocked when I saw her. She was limping badly and struggling with her luggage. I helped her to a nearby seat. Her knee was so swollen that I could not touch it, so I went to find a wet cloth to wrap around the swelling. Mum was very emotional as she had endured a twelve-hour stopover at the closed Bangkok airport with only a male stranger for company. This was a scheduled stopover, but no arrangements had been made by the family member who booked her return flights to ensure she was catered for and protected. I found a taxi and we made our way to the coach terminal to begin our journey home. 'It's *disgraceful* you were put at risk,' I said angrily.

Mum did not recover for days — I waited until she was well to ask her about her time in England. Her sisters had treated her with love and she had spent a lot of time with them. The grandchildren were loving and attentive. However, staying with Barbara had been filled with embarrassing moments. One day when the conversation turned to me having received compensation from my English solicitor, Barbara had exploded, adamant that this was not possible, and Mum was not believed. When the conversation progressed to the sale process of the Old Saddlery, Barbara again said she had signed nothing. Mum chose not to argue. Barbara's third husband had taken every opportunity to make her feel uncomfortable. I was upset that Mum had been in such a difficult position as a guest in Barbara's home. We took comfort in the fact this was her last overseas trip.

Telstra arrived to dig through my Healing Garden and I refused them entry. The contractor went back to the highway and followed the new cable along the eastern border. He returned, having decided to enter the property next door, and dig all along our mutual fence line before connecting with my cable to the lodge. The north had not been protected by a rainbow in July, as this boundary had not needed protecting from Telstra.

I was informed by post that there was to be a Supreme Court hearing in Perth on 21 September. Cathy was not going to gain access to Mum's capital. Barbara had failed and so would she. The court session was to be held in an office block, away from the Supreme Court. This time I would speak to the Registrar, unlike the last time in Torquay when the case was heard in my absence. I sat with others waiting their turn, but my time passed and I had not been called. Gut instinct told me to open the courtroom door and when I did, I heard Cathy's solicitor speaking. I walked in and the Registrar looked at me, annoyed. I introduced myself and she waved me to the front. No-one had called me — I had nearly missed out yet again. I spoke only when requested, standing and giving my responses. I knew everyone found it disturbing that I was representing myself. I sensed the undercurrent, but didn't mind: I was going to protect Mum's capital. What was happening was wrong, and I said so, and then I spoke of the ridiculous so-called duress accusation.

'With respect, ma'am, this is a farce,' I said, as stunned silence filled the court room. The Registrar leaned forward and looked at me as I held her stare, then gave me until the twenty-fifth to lodge a sworn statement for her consideration. I had stopped the conflict progressing to a trial situation. I had four days to present my statement so I rang Greta and we agreed I should stay with her. I caught a coach to Busselton and spent two days putting the facts together. I returned to Perth and filed the witnessed document at the Supreme Court.

Back at the centre, Mum and I began to relax until the post brought a shock. I was going to be charged Cathy's legal costs. I sent a letter to the Costing Registrar explaining my financial situation and received an immediate response agreeing to a delay if Cathy and her barrister approved. A lot of money was involved and I began to feel nervous. The post brought a response from Cathy's solicitors — there would be no delay, and the review hearing would go ahead. *Trust the process*, my Guide said. 'I am trying, but sometimes it's hard,' I replied.

My attention was drawn to Julie's diagram of the Heart Chakra / Pulse of Life and I was sent to stand inside the Open Chamber to study Chamber Three. It was minutes before I saw that the flow (life force) indicated by cray slats was not the same as in Julie's diagram. This had to be altered, and it involved the moving of hundreds of cray slats. I went to start the work, but was told to rest. Much later, I worked by moonlight and was given the insight as to the necessary changes within the Heart Chakra to ensure the success of the Heart's Journey.

I was resting when my Guide referred me to a book given to me by Cathy titled *River God*, by Wilbur Smith. On the back was a brief explanation of the story regarding ancient Egypt and the Land of the Pharaohs, describing a legend shattered by greed and drained of its lifeblood as weak men inherited the crown. Cathy had written, 'Pages to transport you into another world, or maybe another lifetime.' Then 'Ancient Egypt' and 'greed' were highlighted and Cathy's past-life heart issue notes updated with these clues:

Heart Issue: Cathy – legal action – karma / past life – Rainbow Serpent – power – importance – Aboriginal link – conflict – the chase – Aboriginal spear – male passions – ancient Egypt – greed.

Once these words had been recorded, I was sent into the Dolphins Healing Room to pick up Greta's ankh, but this time I did not feel nauseous. I held the ankh for several minutes before being guided to place it on one of Julie's dried rose petals, beside the rose quartz. I was referred to the book *The Crystal Workbook* by Sheril Berkovitch:

> Rose Quartz … helps to clear stored anger, resentment, guilt, fear, jealousy. (20)

I had been invited to Busselton for Greta's birthday later in the month, but felt it would be better if I was not there. Her husband and mother were both visiting, and they were going out and about together as one family. I wondered if she was trying to reunite her family, so I sent her a note expressing that very positive thought. I bought gifts to make up a parcel for her and several times requested to post it, but was told to wait.

On 7 October, a week before Greta's birthday, the same date that the previous year I had been given the warning *Ten days, ten roses* before Greta flew to Switzerland, I was allowed to post her birthday parcel, but only after Roger had finished erecting the three large sections of trellis onto three sides of the square formation near Chamber Three of the Heart Chakra.

'The area of no secrets,' came from Roger's mouth. He stared at me in dismay then completed the task. *Revealing of more secrets*, my Guide warned.

After receiving this warning regarding secrets and posting Greta's parcel, I worked the dolphin family tapestry combining long stitch, tapestry stitch, wool and silk thread. As I started the stitches around the lower edge, Roger drove in, but this time with his trailer full of mini pavers to create the horizontal and vertical axis to transform the Celtic Beacon into the Celtic cross, as channelled on 22 November 1996.

Powerful heart vibrations like spasms moved within my chest as I worked on the tapestry and later as I carted the pavers down to the Celtic Beacon in the wheelbarrow. Next day, Roger brought the wind wheel for the Heart Element — symbol of four years of conflict. As soon as it was in place, its three white and three blue blades began to spin and I was sent indoors by my Guide. The phone was ringing. It was Greta.

'Please Judy, come down for my birthday,' she pleaded. *You must go,* my Guide insisted, *this is the next stage.*

I awoke on 13 October filled with apprehension. I packed and unpacked again. I was travelling under instructions to take the coach to Perth and the train to Bunbury, instead of the coaches to Busselton, forcing Greta to drive to Bunbury. I was nervous, wondering what lay ahead. The next morning we all lit candles and sang the birthday song for Greta. We were enjoying the beach when a stern remark in Swiss German, from her mother, sent Greta into turmoil. Of course I had no idea what had been said, but it had upset Greta and she turned on me, starting the put-downs. Annoyed, I went to leave the beach, but Cindy held my hand tight. *Influence of the child*, my Guide said.

The next day, at Bunbury rail station, I sat inside my carriage waiting for the train to pull away and looked at Greta. She walked up to the carriage window and both of us instinctively put our hands against the glass. An invisible barrier; no matter how much we tried there was something dividing us. A look of helplessness appeared on Greta's face and a feeling of helplessness formed inside me. As the train pulled away, I wondered how much longer we would be held by this traumatic past-life attachment and separation issue.

I returned to Dongara to discover, with disbelief, that a Telstra contractor had begun to dig a cable trench leading from the highway up towards the main entrance. There was no room for this trench beside my fence line, and the now-exposed roots of my plants were damaged. I waited until digger and driver returned, then asked what the sense was in battling with the roots of my shrubs when there was more than enough room on the other side of the road, behind the black wattle. The driver left. Early the next day he was back digging, but on the other side, admitting he had misunderstood his firm's directions. Roger and I began the enormous task of repairing the damage. I felt distressed and Roger was upset. The native hibiscus had to be secured and huge boulders moved.

Together we lifted the boulders over the fence line and into the Tuart Walk. Later, when we worked to complete the Heart Element, these massive boulders were included in the structure of the element itself. My Guide assured me all was in order: the damage, my challenging the cause of the damage and our repairing the effects of the damage. This energy was part of the Heart Element and its wind wheel. I returned to the lodge to rest and discovered three messages from Greta waiting on the answering machine — asking me to meet her in Perth on 26 October. An attempt, she said, to repair the damage caused by her mother and herself to our friendship. The energy of repair was part of the four years of conflict spinning within the Heart Element.

Early the next day my Guide insisted that the small stones from the damaged area be placed around Merlin's Triangle. Roger drove in with a trailer load of cardboard and carpets and we dragged it all to the Relationship Area near the Children's Tree and Love Tree. It was an exhausting job to ensure the Relationship Area was maintained and repaired. *There will be an investment,* my Guide said.

On 23 October, a Welsh woman named Michelle who was staying in the Dongara Youth Hostel volunteered to work as a wwoofer. She had felt drawn to the garden and wished to contribute. She was young and fit, and I was thrilled to let her help me with a circular bale of hay that was to be spread in Chamber Three. A job that would have taken me days to accomplish was completed in just two hours with her help.

Then we had a visit from Rita, a middle-aged woman from Holland. She spent time in the garden, then left. The next day she returned, explaining that she was working locally for a while and asked to spend time with Mum. She continued to visit with Mum to talk, watch a video or take her out for a drive in her car.

A Maori woman from New Zealand drove in a few days later. She felt a need to share her labyrinth and displayed her design in the tractor shed — a black design printed on a huge white sheet. She invited me to walk the labyrinth and I did. She questioned why I called the lodge Iona. The name had drawn her to visit. She explained that in her native language, the words *Io* and *Na* meant 'All Encompassing. Supreme One,'

I had agreed to meet Greta in Perth on 26 October only after sharing my concerns with my Guide, who assured me this was a necessary part of the Heart's Journey. I went to the tourist bureau to book the coach and discovered in my post box a card from Greta: 'The words we most want to say are difficult to find sometimes, their journey begins far, far away in the heart.' The words 'far, far away in the heart' caught my attention.

Damage, challenge, repair, my Guide said. The Heart Element / Four Years of Conflict held the energy of repair.

Greta's words were describing the difficulty we were to face in order to reveal our past-life heart issues. Another card arrived from her. Prior to opening it, I lit a white candle and said the Celtic prayer. Inside the card she had written, 'I have the same candle and I light it every evening for a few minutes. Maybe you would like to do the same and our thoughts can come together.' A part of her was as determined as I was to seek out the truth. *Her soul and the universe want to be free of this*, my Guide confirmed.

I was met on 26 October at the Perth Coach Terminal by a moody and irritable Greta, and we soon argued over my need to develop the Healing Garden. I walked out of our accommodation in South Perth requesting that she drive me back to the coach terminal. She became upset and kept repeating, 'It is not right that you are leaving.'

On my return home, I was sent into the Dolphins Healing Room and to the seven chakra-balancing scarves given to me by Dianne for my birthday, arriving later in the month and in the same post as Sam's scarf from Iona. They were still on the Jarrah Heart. *Iona, chakra balancing, jarrah heart, truth*, my Guide said. I was encouraged to place Greta's ankh on the green scarf / Heart Chakra, and then hold the ankh and read aloud the words, 'The words we most want to say are difficult sometimes, their journey begins far, far away in the heart.' I had been sent to Perth to hear Greta say, 'It is not right that you are leaving.' This was the hurt from long ago, and she was holding me accountable for leaving: another past-life flashback providing another clue. I had been guided to give Greta a *St Justin of Cornwall* Love Rune pendant for her birthday, and she had worn it when we met in Perth. The introduction of runic energy had caused the eruption, and I was encouraged to read again the accompanying card: 'Love Rune ... awakening the *lover* within.'

A miniature pressed-flower pansy card arrived from Greta and I was directed to place it within the diagram of the Seven Healing Triangles, inside Hagalaz — the great Awakener, which dominated the Heart Chakra / Pulse of Life / Goddess Nut in the Healing Garden. I was shaken by a surge of emotions and then referred to the article 'The Language of Flowers':

Pansies are dedicated to St Valentine, the Patron Saint of *lovers*.

There was now a reference to lover and lovers. The silver locket containing two dried half-red rose petals, given to Greta, had been purchased on 14 February 1997, a day for lovers. Greta had replaced the locket temporarily with the Love Rune. My Guide instructed me to hold a Hagalaz Rune:

Hagalaz – Elemental Power. Hagalaz is the great Awakener, a Rune that causes change, freedom, invention, disruption of events that seem beyond our control ... Hagalaz releases the energy you need to accept changes and grow with them.

Greta had worn the Love Rune, revealing that we had been lovers long ago and I was on notice that our lives were to have disruptions beyond our control. The clue 'lovers' was added to Greta's and my past-life heart-issue notes. The clue 'Egyptian wife' was added to the Crystal Pool Energy.

I worked all night moving the flow of cray slats within Chambers One and Two to correspond with Julie's diagram. Later, the Healing Garden brochure from Christina was highlighted for me to study the Healing Triangle Hagalaz — the great Awakener — the vibrating energy within the Mary Seat, Tuart Walk and the Iona Celtic cross areas (within the lodge garden). I was being reminded that Greta's Barossa Dream rose had been planted within the energy of this Healing Triangle.

I recalled being taken to the Dongara sand dunes by Greta the previous year, when she had asked me to stand where she had stood many years before after discovering she had been deceived, an experience that had changed her. As I listened, there had been a moment of *familiarity*, but I had not been able to grasp its meaning. That moment came again, and it centred on the birth of a child and a partner's deception. My past-life heart issue notes were updated to include the clues 'birth of a child' and 'deception' next to 'lovers'.

The month of November began with two messages. *The solar plexus chakra is your wisdom chakra*, my Guide said. *Merlin is only a prayer away*, she added. Merlin's Triangle was still outside the entrance to the Healing Garden.

My Guide encouraged me to place large limestone boulders in circles around each black wattle and illyarrie that Greta and I had planted the previous year along the dirt road leading to the main entrance and White Dolphin. There were forty-nine trees in total, and the task she set me was overwhelming, so I sat by the wheelbarrow and pondered it. Roger drove up, and I told him what I had to do next. He smiled and began moving large boulders from within the car park and we worked for two days until we finished.

I was taking photographs in the garden when I was stopped with a start. I rushed to the lodge, unsure of the urgency, and in the meditation room I discovered a snake. It reared up at me, forcing me to grab a brick from the breezeway and drop it on its head. I lifted its dead body with a stick, revealing its green markings. My Guide encouraged me to take it to the Crystal Pool and bury it. As I buried the snake, a message from the angry, disruptive male energy came through with force: *Male passions*.

These events had shaken me. I had killed something. My Guide took me to a diagram 'Buddhist Wheel of Life' to the symbols at its centre, representing the three delusions that keep humans on the Wheel of Life and out of Nirvana: the red cockerel or lust, the green snake or hatred, the black pig or ignorance. Although I had killed the symbol of hate, I remained distressed. The next day I was instructed to move the buried snake to another place, but when I dug there was no snake — it had vanished! I sat on the ground with a feeling of relief. The fact that the snake was not where I had buried it, nor were there any signs of it having been removed, helped me understand that the emotion of hatred had been dealt with, or was about to be dealt with. There were negative emotions coming from the past involving male passions and hatred. I was taken to the Crystal Pool notes to add the clue 'male passions' and to read the other clues held within this area:

> Crystal Pool Energy: Supreme power – male passions – heart pain – conflict and loss – Egypt – heart's journey – Golden Rose Dolphin – karmic truths – page marker / Jerusalem – Egypt and priests – This is forbidden – Jude Priest – I had a dream and the dream was you – Egyptian wife.

I worked the dolphin family tapestry and completed the brow and crown chakras of the largest dolphin; then I carefully stitched the outline of three dolphins closest to the large dolphin, symbolically representing the Four Core Group Dolphins.

On 5 November I found Michelle asleep in her campervan in the car park. While working with us as a wwoofer for three months, she lived in her van in the tractor shed.

Travel south again, my Guide said. Shortly afterwards Greta rang, asking me to visit her. So I went to Busselton the next day. While she and I spent time on the beach, I noticed Cindy would hang back and sit on her own. *Lonely child*, my Guide explained.

The next day was peaceful, and I felt confident I could stay the week. Then we went for a drive, and out of nowhere came the angry energy again. She was rude, once again mocking my commitment to working for spirit. She meant to hurt and she did. I left the car, walked back to her home, packed and left. I understood I had been sent to reconnect with Cindy, and that was all that mattered. The angry, disruptive, masculine energy from the past was not going to stop me from discovering the truth and protecting Cindy. Mum was waiting for me when I returned late in the evening. 'What happened?' she said.

'The aggressive energy came through Greta again.'

'Are you all right?' She sounded concerned.

'Yes I am. I am stronger and able to move in and out of its energy and influence.' I went on to say that the requirement was for me to reconnect with Cindy and, as she well knew, if there is a child involved who needs protection, nothing and no-one would stop me.

A letter arrived from Julie suggesting I plant a black-berried mulberry in the Base Root Chakra. I had completed the black outline of the Four Core Group Dolphins in the dolphin family tapestry; now Julie was suggesting I plant a black-berried mulberry tree in her chakra. Having recently flown over the property, she wanted me to know that the Heart Chakra / Pulse of Life / Goddess Nut could be seen clearly from the air.

On 11 November my Guide insisted that Michelle should move Merlin's Triangle inside the Healing Garden itself. Roger and I watched as she dismantled the triangle and reassembled it inside the garden, between the Celtic Entrance and the pathway leading to the Judas tree — entrance to the Heart Chakra / Pulse of Life / Goddess Nut. She was obviously very proud to be doing this. I explained to Roger that Michelle was from Wales and that, according to her, Merlin was the son of a Prince of Wales.

The Telstra contractor visited, asking if I wanted a load of large limestone rocks. I was thrilled with this offer and gift. He drove them to the Brand Highway and unloaded them over my fence line. We had enough to build a wall and create an entrance into the Base Root Chakra, where Julie's mulberry was to be planted. Michelle said she would build a Welsh dry wall. My Guide insisted that the wall feature the Celtic symbol of three entwined circles, with the mulberry tree planted within the middle circle. To the Celts the number three was sacred — the most important number in their culture. In that tradition important things occurred in threes, such as the Cycle of Life reflected in birth, death and reincarnation. *Influence of Merlin and Red Dolphin*, my Guide said. Julie's words regarding Merlin came to mind: 'Make him work for you.'

Michelle came rushing into the lodge later, excited and agitated. She had walked towards the site for the dry wall when a red-tailed snake with a green head crossed her path. As she relayed her story, I was given the words *Love is a rose*. I went to the site and then walked between the nine peppercorn trees and the fence towards the Celtic Beacon. The knowing came to me that this was the Celtic Walk. All remaining limestones were to be used to create an entrance/exit for the Celtic Walk and Solar Plexus Chakra.

A series of pathways connected the Base Root Chakra, the yet-to-be-developed Solar Plexus and the Heart and Throat Chakras, and in time would connect the yet-to-be-developed Navel Chakra, which circled the Love Tree. The Brow (Third Eye) and Crown Chakras were held within the lodge and its garden, away from the general public.

My Guide encouraged me to place my hands on the Central Solar Stone of the Celtic Beacon and ask for protection, referring to it as the *Negativity Beacon* and explaining that its energy would enable visitors to clear and balance their own auric shields.

In the post I received from Greta a remedy consisting of bergamot, lavender and geranium in an almond oil base. 'To help with your anxiety and apprehension,' she wrote, instructing me to rub the oil on my temples. I felt uneasy: although on the surface the note was filled with kind suggestions, underneath was an element of control. 'You need help,' was her message. There was a determination about Greta that I had not seen before, and this was confirmed when she wrote again saying that it was a shame I had such important things to do, working for spirit, that I had no time for either her or the children. Somewhere down the track there would be glory in it for me, while she was only able to offer me her friendship. She wrote that she must appear like a temptress trying to lure me away from my spiritual path.

I went to the Mary Seat to think, holding her letter. There was an element of truth hidden in her written words. It was not the Healing Garden that was the issue: it was my working for spirit. Greta invited me to come down and try to be more able to cope this time. My unease grew: she was using another form of taunting. I read her words again, trying to see past the taunting to the true meaning. I had the feeling this was how she had communicated in Egypt when we were lovers. Greta was revealing yet another important past-life flashback.

I was required to attend a mediation conference in Perth on 25 November and Mum came also: I wanted her to be with me, and her capital was involved. The Case Registrar made his decision after reading my sworn statement. We were shown into the mediation room, where Cathy and her barrister were seated. Mum and I stared at this person who had travelled with us for seven years. The Case Registrar attempted to sit us opposite Cathy and her barrister, but I refused. Her barrister outdid himself with legal jargon. Finally, when I was allowed to speak, I repeated my argument against the duress accusation, as per my statement. There was a lot of huffing and puffing from Cathy's barrister followed by a barrage of legal wording he knew I would not understand. The Case Registrar asked them to leave the room; he was going to negotiate between us.

The last, ridiculous, demand from Cathy had been for $45,000 plus legal costs, but it was not mentioned. Any settlement would be subject to the title being transferred to my name. The Case Registrar returned, suggesting the original sum of $15,000, to include Cathy's costs of $5,000. She would receive $10,000 and the caveat would be removed, the title transferred. But, if I failed to raise the money there would be a penalty of $5,000, to be in place for twelve months. Cathy knew I did not have $15,000.

Her barrister said, 'I am going to take your land away from you.'

I returned his glare, shaking my head, 'You won't.'

He insisted: 'I will.'

He won't, my Guide confirmed.

I said again, 'You won't.'

There it was out in the open: 'I am going to take your land away from you.' Greta had admitted to being a temptress and Cathy wanted to take our land.

Mum and I left and walked to a shopping area where she bought me a three-strand silver bracelet to provide protection at this traumatic time. On returning home I discovered three phone messages from Greta on my answering machine demanding to know the outcome of the mediation meeting. Before responding, my Guide insisted I update Cathy's past-life heart issue notes with the clue 'land dispute' next to 'greed'.

I rang Greta and explained that I had to find $15,000 and did not feel confident about that. I did not know what would happen if I failed, except for the $5,000 penalty. I was taken aback when Greta arrived at the lodge late that night. She had driven non-stop. We walked the Seven Mile Beach the next evening and sat in the sand dunes. She said she just wanted me in her life and that was all, no more arguments. I was not sure what to think. *Mastery of the minds*, my Guide warned.

During the afternoon a woman from Alaska who was hitch-hiking her way to Melbourne came to visit. During our conversation, she indicated that she and her friend Justin, who had heard about the garden, might wish to invest. Later, I received a phone call from another friend of hers, David, who wanted to come and stay in the near future.

Michelle completed the Welsh dry wall — the entrance to the Base Root Chakra — and I planted the black-berried mulberry tree and the two red-flowering cockies tongues chosen by Julie to complement the two vibrational colours of this particular chakra. My Guide referred me to Gerber's *Vibrational Medicine*:

> The first chakra is known as the coccygeal, base, or root chakra … The amount of energy flow through the root chakra is a reflection of one's ability to link with the Earth … It is connected with primal feelings of fear from physical injury and is the prime mover behind the so-called fight-or-flight response … (3)

On 1 December David arrived with his wife, and the next day I walked around the garden with them and they spoke of Merlin. According to them, Merlin's Triangle was a symbol of 'letting go of one's ego'. Merlin had been a teacher and philosopher, they said, encouraging his students to leave their egos outside in order to take in what he had to say. He was depicted as a wizard because of his healing skills, and the Catholic Church needed to discredit him. It was said that he had spent time meditating in a cave that contained crystals, but that was a misrepresentation. In fact, he had lived in a lodge in the grounds of King Arthur's residence.

David's wife gave me a small bottle of water from the well at Glastonbury Tor in England. This brought back memories of the cleansing ceremony I had performed at the base of the Tor nine years before. David wanted to interview me in a video. No-one was to take advantage of this place for financial gain, so I insisted I keep the video.

He then drew an Egyptian ankh. 'This was the original cross,' he said, 'then came the Celtic cross containing the Wheel of Life, and finally the Christian cross came into being.'

He mentioned that the Michael Ley-Line was named after the Archangel Michael. 'Recent discoveries have revealed another ley-line weaving itself around this energy, a feminine energy being referred to as the Mary Line. These two energies merge here also at the centre within the Healing Garden,' he said, 'but in a very unique form.'

Roger and I worked through the month of December creating a huge Celtic cross around the Negativity Beacon / Wheel of Life. He brought trailer loads of pavers and yellow sand from the tip for the base, and altogether put in a major effort. We worked long hours to have the cross completed before Christmas. It had been two years since Julie and I created a diagram, when my mind filled with numbers and an explanation that the area represented the influence of the Core Group of Four Celestial Dolphins. I was told a Celtic cross would be made with a two-metre surround, and now this would be achieved.

At the moment of our completing this task, Michelle arrived with a parcel from Greta. Inside I discovered a small Wheel of Life, handmade with tiny sea shells and dried seaweed from our beach in Busselton. It was truly beautiful. I had not shared with Greta that Roger and I were creating a cross around the Negativity Beacon / Wheel of Life, as the topic of my developing the Healing Garden was taboo. To hold the gift, and read her words 'Wheel of Life', made me realise Roger and I were on schedule with the Heart's Journey. *Influence of the Golden Rose Dolphin*, my Guide said.

At times Greta allowed me brief glimpses of the Golden Rose Dolphin. This gift gave me renewed hope that I would find her and the Dolphin Family would find peace. But first I had to heal the hurt and angry past-life lover personality emerging within her. Having been told by my Guide that there was spiritual enlightenment to be gained, I travelled to Greta again. There was the brief excitement of meeting, followed by unease, but I managed to keep us both calm. I did not want to miss the reason for us being together.

We went to a wildlife park and walked near a cage containing a wedge-tailed eagle. Greta kept on walking, but I noticed that the bird was tugging at a tail feather. It plucked the feather out and dropped it at the edge of the cage next to me. I poked at it with a stick until I could reach it. *This is a gift*, my Guide said. I looked up at Greta, who had now joined me, and handed the feather to her. She smiled and then handed it back. At that moment there was complete understanding between us. Something had happened and it was connected to this feather.

It was 22 December, and I wanted to be back in Dongara for Christmas Eve. Greta asked to borrow the feather, which she placed under her American Indian dream catcher beside her bed. I noticed it the next day when I took her a tray of tea, and the whispered words of the unknown female, *I had a dream and the dream was you*, ran through my mind. When I arrived back at Dongara I asked my Guide to explain the eagle's unique gift and was referred to the book *Medicine Cards*:

> Eagle – Spirit … power of the Great Spirit … The feathers of Eagle are considered to be the most sacred of healing tools. They have been used for centuries by shamans to cleanse the auras of patients coming to them for healing … (15)

I now had two means of cleansing the human auric shield: the Negativity Beacon / Wheel of Life and the eagle feather. Greta rang that evening and I told her of the importance of the eagle feather. I asked her to return it to me, as I wished to use it during my ever-increasing healing sessions — releasing emotional blockages, chakra balancing and so on. She was reluctant, saying she wanted to keep it. 'It may heal me,' she said.

'The eagle gave it to me. I must use it,' I insisted. Reluctantly, she agreed to post it to me in the New Year. As I walked away from the phone, the unknown female whispered *I hold you in my heart, I hold you in my arms, I hold you.*

Michelle planned to move on, and when she came to lunch on Christmas Day she handed Mum and me a huge rose quartz for the Healing Garden. Christina had sent me a diopside crystal shaped like a dolphin and there was a surprise gift for me from Barbara — two miniature books regarding Celtic Wisdom and Buddhist Wisdom.

'Why would Barbara send me gifts, and these in particular?'

'Only time will reveal her reason,' Mum replied.

As I held the Black Dolphin / Diopside from Christina, I felt sadness and a sharp pain surged through my heart. The familiar words came again, *I hold you in my heart, I hold you in my arms, I hold you.* The overwhelming sadness grew to such intensity that I was forced to place the Black Dolphin on the jarrah table in the Dolphins Healing Room. I was sent into the office to find an enlarged Heart Chakra / Pulse of Life / Goddess Nut diagram and place it on the jarrah table with the Black Dolphin / Diopside in the Open Chamber of the Heart. This was the area where only Greta had been allowed to plant the vetiver grass and later the Indian siris tree. Greta had asked to plant the tree after replacing her Kimberley diamond necklace with the silver locket.

On Boxing Day Roger brought four cabinet doors to create information boards for the garden. They would make the Healing Garden more self-sufficient. We used the doors as lids on hinges to enclose four boxes and stood them on poles. I spent time on the computer typing out the information to go inside the first box. It would contain information regarding the vetiver grass and how this hedge was to protect, nourish and heal the individual within the subtle energy of its vibrations. Roger and I had created Pulpit Board One.

The Black Dolphin / Diopside remained in the Open Chamber on the diagram of the Heart Chakra. When I touched it Greta's words came to mind: 'It may heal me.' My Guide referred me to the booklet *The Crystal Workbook* by Sheril Berkovitch:

> Diopside is light to dark green in colour, and also occurs in black which, when polished en cabochon, shows a cat's eye or star. It is therefore sometimes referred to as Black Star … *Chakra*: Green for Heart, Black for Base. Assists one in remaining detached and objective … clears blocked emotions. (20)

Earlier that year Julie the Red Dolphin had written a note suggesting I introduce the secondary vibrational colour of black in the Base Root Chakra with the planting of a black-berried mulberry. Now Christina the Blue Dolphin had sent me a Black Dolphin / Diopside as a Christmas gift, which still remained on the diagram within the Heart, my responsibility as the Green Dolphin. Three of the Four Core Group were now working in harmony in response to Greta's appeal, 'It may heal me.' I read further:

> Black Star: Used during the times of Atlantis and Lemuria as a scrying stone, Black Star will take you into the depths … Excellent for exploring past lives, taking you back slowly and carefully … (20)

Greta and I were being taken back slowly and carefully to our past life in Egypt — as lovers. I had an understanding of Atlantis, but what was this place Lemuria?

My Guide encouraged me to place Michelle's large rose quartz and the Black Dolphin / Diopside together and light a white candle, its flame reflecting on both gemstones. *A healer of the heart and for exploring past lives*, my Guide said.

In the early hours of the following day I placed both on the windowsill in the Dolphins Healing Room to catch the moon's rays by Greta's leadlight Celtic cross. The next day a woman called Ray rang; she was visiting Dongara and wanted to see me at 5 pm. When she arrived we sat on the Seat of Reflection by the entrance to the Heart Chakra / Pulse of Life / Goddess Nut and shared an intense conversation. I walked around with her until we sat on the bench inside the Open Chamber by the Indian siris tree, with its circle of stones. Ray was facing me, when she gasped as she looked up at the sky behind me. 'There is a cross in the sky,' she said.

I turned around, and in a clear blue sky saw a distinct cross created by a small formation of clouds. It held us both for several minutes. I did not know what to say, and Ray was stunned. She asked me to wait while she fetched something from her car. When she returned, she was holding a moonstone and asked if she could leave it in the garden. I said I would leave her, and she could bury it in the Indian siris tree circle if she wished.

As I sat on the Mary Seat and waited, my mind was taken back to when I had been woken in the early hours to move the rose quartz and Black Dolphin / Diopside into the moon's rays. Today I was with Ray, who had been inspired by a cross in the sky to bury a moonstone within the Open Chamber. This was where the Black Dolphin / Diopside had been placed in the diagram in the Dolphins Healing Room. Greta's words came again: 'This may heal me.' After Ray had gone, my Guide immediately referred me to *Crystals for Transformation, Healing and Spiritual Growth* by Soluntra King:

> Moonstone – Eliminates that which is not needed, gives only truth, no untruths. (21)

Ray had played her part, providing the crystal to ensure the careful process to open Greta's heart and eliminate that which is not needed, giving only truth, no untruths.

A new partnership at Iona, my Guide said. I was in my office and went to walk outside but was held until I noticed a faded rolled-up poster. When I unrolled it, I read, '1993 International Year of the World's Indigenous People. A New Partnership.' The reverse side read:

... depicts the diversity of Australian indigenous people (Aboriginal and Torres Strait Islanders) ... Snake, protector, provider; depicting harmony, the bringing together of 'a new partnership'.

A strong emphasis was made on the words 'a new partnership' and 'snake'.

The word snake reminded me of the Rainbow Serpent in the cave at Wooleen Station, where Cathy and I stayed in April 1995, and the warning *Conflict* had come after *Rainbow Serpent, power, importance, Aboriginal link*. I was being given an assurance that this present conflict over land from an Aboriginal past life with Cathy would result in a new partnership. My Guide's method of communication was a never-ending wonder to me.

Greta phoned as I finished reading this information, asking me to welcome the New Year of 1999 with her. I headed for Perth and again we booked into apartment-style accommodation in South Perth near the river. On this day, four years before, 30 December 1994, Mum and I had been sent by my Guide to Dongara and Seven Mile Beach for four hours. In May of this year, she had sent me to Seven Mile Beach again, where I had found a pile of clothing identical to my own and was told, *Yes, this is the feeling of freedom*. The understanding had come that 30 December 1994 was the start of a four-year cycle, and on 30 December 1998 Greta and I went to Northbridge in Perth and amid great excitement saw in the New Year of 1999 — completing this predicted cycle.

Cindy was celebrating her fourth birthday on 2 January and I asked to see her to give her my gift. She and her brother were in Perth with their father. That morning, in our apartment, I went to Greta holding a lighted candle and said, 'Today you brought a child into the world and this candle is a celebration for you as the mother of a new life.' The understanding came that this was something I had failed to do in our past life as lovers.

We went to see Cindy, the birthday girl, and I handed her a photograph album I had made from photographs of herself, her mother and brother. I had watched her looking at old photographs and thought new prints would help her to move on. Cindy was excited to see us and I concentrated on her. Greta was left struggling to make the conversation flow between herself, her husband and his latest girlfriend.

When I travelled by return coach to Dongara the next day, I thought over what had happened. I had given Greta the lit candle and spent time with a child, and felt something had been put right. Greta rang later to say she was seeking a divorce and buying a home.

Roger and I created a second board that we called the 'Egyptian Pulpit Board'. It was placed by the Open Chamber and would contain information regarding the Egyptian Goddess Nut, including a comparison between the illustration and my diagram of the Goddess Nut (Cycle of Life) and the Heart Chakra (Pulse of Life). The Egyptian Goddess Isis, daughter of Nut, was included and I updated the goddess energy notes.

Mum was holding a successful visualisation evening, and once a week Christina would call in to sit with Mum in her extension in order to be taken through the designated visualisation, prior to each evening session. Rita, the manager of the youth hostel, continued to visit Mum and they would spend hours sharing or going for trips to the local beauty spots.

Legal post arrived and two banks refused to grant me a loan of $15,000. I would be sent back to mediation and the $5,000 penalty imposed. I would have twelve months in which to sell the property or to find the increased sum of $20,000.

My Guide sent me back to work the dolphin family tapestry and to unpack and work the Egyptian tapestry. She gave me instructions as to which one to work and for how long. By 10 January I had finished the large dolphin and spent three hours stitching the ocean. I was working with the green and orange wool, stitching the coral reef beneath the large dolphin, when Justin, the friend of the hitch-hiker from Alaska, rang to book bed and breakfast for himself and two friends. When they arrived I took them into the lodge; then I was sent into the Healing Garden. In the south-east corner of the sky was a rainbow, not a complete arch, but a small section of an arch — a tiny picture frame. There were only two colours, green and orange, and I walked Mum into the garden to see it. I had been working on the dolphin family tapestry with green and orange wool; now this unusual symbol featured in the sky. *Influence of the Green and Orange Dolphins*, my Guide said.

I intended leaving Justin and his friends quietly to themselves, but they insisted I spend the entire evening with them. We sat in the meditation room as I related my story, explaining what it was like for me working here. Justin waited until I had finished, then said, 'You live in the void.' He explained how I had walked into this 'empty space' and was bringing through all my knowledge from my past lives into this present lifetime. 'This is creating the Healing Garden,' he said.

The next day my Guide sent me to the Heart, where I found a kestrel feather. I picked it up and returned inside to make Justin a bookmark with it. I did not want him to leave, but he had to return to Melbourne. Before he left, he helped Roger and me move a circular bale of hay from the Heart Chakra / Pulse of Life / Goddess Nut into the Area of Relationships. *Harvest*, my Guide explained.

'You will instinctively know who will care for this place,' Justin said.

The Area of Relationships had been identified and named in March the previous year when I found Cindy watering this huge area with a tiny watering can. I understood then that the development of this area would encourage the angry, disruptive masculine energy from the distant past to reveal itself, and Cindy's determined action encouraged this.

On 18 January I travelled to see Greta and we walked our beach. Although it was dark, Greta knew I needed to do this before I entered her home. The next day we walked the beach in the morning and again as the sun set. There was an energy building inside me and I understood that by walking the beach with Greta the words would surface. It was the third day when I stopped Greta and asked her to listen to what I had to say.

'There is a place for you in the universe that is yours. You are a unique human being, as we all are. There will be an end to all this drama and you will find peace. There will be a time when my Guide determines that I have completed my tasks in the Healing Garden and I too will leave with a peaceful heart.' I returned to Dongara feeling much calmer.

Roger brought another pulpit board and we placed it by the Mary Seat. It would contain a visualisation written by Mum in 1988 and an explanation of the Mary Ray.

Buddhist Wisdom / Four Parts of Truth featured on the first day of February, and I was encouraged to read the miniature book of Buddhist wisdom Barbara had given me for Christmas. Her past-life karmic issues involved truth, and I spent many hours on the computer putting information together for display within the Healing Garden.

'Barbara is appealing to you to help her,' Mum explained.

'Then she must continue to provide the answers as to how I do that.' *Truth and clear understanding*, my Guide confirmed.

Tension began to mount between Greta and me once again. She became evasive, and I sensed another moment of truth coming. Roger arrived with the fourth and final pulpit board and we placed it near Chamber Three of the Heart Chakra / Pulse of Life / Goddess Nut opposite the Place of No Secrets / Buddha's Four Parts of Truth. It contained details of the human energy field, the aura and the chakra system.

All pulpit boards were later painted Green of Amazonite. It was very satisfying when the work was completed.

A demanding letter arrived from Cathy's barrister insisting the property be sold in accordance with our Agreement, but this was not my understanding. I had twelve months, following a penalty, to produce $20,000. I sent a copy to the Case Registrar with a letter, questioning this claim. Cathy had held up a sale with her caveat, now she wanted a sale. Cathy's ever increasing legal costs would soon outweigh any financial gain she hoped to achieve. The property would be sold in spirit's timing, not Cathy's nor her barrister's.

I was taken to some folded cartons to tape one up ready for packing — I had no idea why — and the first thing I wrapped for inclusion was a gift from Greta: a hand-painted plate titled *The Dolphin's Dance*. This box was to be marked 'Dolphin Box' and the plate placed on top.

Two days later I travelled south to spend time with Greta in Perth. We went to an outdoor concert in the Supreme Court Gardens. The 1812 Overture was performed, ending with a fireworks display, and the effect was awesome. We'd been getting on reasonably well, but were both preoccupied: her divorce papers were being prepared and I was apprehensive about the pending legal situation with Cathy. The next day we walked to the Art Gallery of Western Australia, and found there were many colourful stalls in its forecourt. I noticed among them a booth where an Indian man was advertising himself as a tarot card reader. Greta listened as he told me what he saw. 'You have something very precious, Judy: your freedom.' He looked up at Greta, then at me again, 'You two must always live on opposite sides of any river.'

Greta and I spent 14 February together. I knew this would assist with my journey to reveal the trauma of our past-life relationship as lovers. On this day in 1997 I had been instructed to buy a silver locket; now, on 14 February 1999, she was wearing it. I was wondering what clue would be revealed, when, during breakfast in a café, she handed me a small teddy bear holding a dried golden rosebud from her garden. Why would she hand me a child's gift? *Influence of the Golden Rose Dolphin*, my Guide replied.

I arrived back in Dongara filled with the idea of placing an archway in the Healing Garden. Roger arrived and we discussed moving the wooden arch from the lodge garden and erecting it at the entrance to the Heart Chakra / Pulse of Life / Goddess Nut. The next day, between 3 and 4 pm, there would be a solar eclipse, and Roger and I must move the archway then. *Solar eclipse, a time of power and change*, my Guide explained. After transferring the arch I weeded the Base Root Chakra for the next two days. This was Julie's chakra, which was connected with the so-called fight-or-flight response. I was heading for a situation where I could fight, or take flight.

My Guide asked for a pyramid to be built alongside the Egyptian Pulpit / Open Chamber. *Marriage and truth*, she predicted.

Mum was busy entertaining her friend Rita, so I was not able to share with her my growing concern. At 6 am the next day my Guide sent me to the Egyptian Pulpit to create the pyramid, using bricks and pavers as its base. As I wheelbarrowed the materials from within the tractor shed, where Roger had left them, there was a stirring of emotions within me, and the message *Marriage and truth* repeated in my mind. I went to the Negativity Beacon / Wheel of Life to remove two large limestones to be used within the Pyramid Formation, and requested protection as I entered this moment of truth. *Allow the healing potential of this lesson*, my Guide insisted.

That evening Greta rang to say she had booked Mum and me to travel to her place for my birthday in March. As I listened to her plan I felt apprehension in my abdomen. I went to the Dolphins Healing Room to recover, aware only of the Black Dolphin / Diopside in the window and its meaning:

Diopside ... clears blocked emotions.

The next morning, following his own inner guidance, Roger walked to the Celtic cross surrounding the Negativity Beacon / Wheel of Life and dismantled it, leaving only the Beacon. When he left I poured water over the Beacon, encouraging all who touched its Solar Stone to gain access to their inner truth. That evening, a rainbow arched over the Negativity Beacon / Wheel of Life — an amazing sight. I was instructed to work the dolphin family tapestry, completing the coral reef with its many fishes.

I was referred by my Guide to *Crystals for Transformation, Healing and Spiritual Growth* by Soluntra King:

> Coral … Excellent Balancer and healer of the emotions and physical body … (21)

On the last day of February I was directed to look through a pile of handouts until I came across one that discussed the Star of David. I learnt this was also the Star of Melchizedek, the symbol adopted by the Jews upon leaving Egypt. I was aware of having past lives as a Jewish person and wondered what this connection would reveal. I was guided to speak to Roger on 4 March about us creating a large Star of David symbol for the Healing Garden.

I spent two days removing all the weeds in the Area of Relationships, as stress built up inside me in the form of breathlessness and severe agitation. As I walked by the lodge, the phone rang. It was Greta ringing me from a phone box. I asked why she was doing this and was told that she had thought about me and just wanted to chat. The next day she rang from another phone box. This time she said she was out walking and wanted to say hello. Mum and I were packed ready to travel south to Greta for my birthday, on 8 March, when she rang a third time and spoke in a hushed, guarded voice. 'What is really going on?' I asked impatiently. After a long silence Greta informed me her husband had been staying with her for the weekend and had recently left. *Marriage and truth*, my Guide confirmed.

'Tell me, why do you have this need to create a drama?' There was no response. 'Why can't you just tell me the truth?' I asked. Again, no response. I told Greta that, due to her continual need to mislead me, Mum and I would not be travelling to her place for my birthday. *Allow the healing potential of this lesson, past lives,* my Guide said.

That evening my Guide highlighted the dried golden rose Greta had handed to me on Valentine's Day and insisted I remove one petal and place it carefully in the hands of the Buddha statue outside in the Sacred 13 Formation. I was encouraged to read the notes I had taken from Barbara's Christmas gift regarding Buddhist wisdom and the Four Parts of Truth:

> The Truth of Suffering; to face the reality of our own suffering … Suffering in Buddhist terms means anguish, heartache, longing,

wishing, hoping for a person or object or a condition which is not present.

The Truth of the Cause of Suffering; to acknowledge the fact that we suffer because we don't like what we have; we desire things to be different from how they actually are. Desire itself is then seen to be the root cause of suffering, rather than the inability to achieve the objects of our desires.

The Truth of the Cessation of Suffering; to realize that, by resisting the pull to desire things, suffering ceases. To experience this is a reality called 'Nirvana'.

The Truth of The Way of Life That is Free of Suffering; to live in a manner which values the moment as it is, is free of desire and free of suffering itself. This is a totally harmless way of life and benefits all things.

I showed Mum this information, explaining I had taken it from Barbara's gift.
    'Barbara is appealing to you to help her.'
    'Buddhist wisdom also applies to Greta and her past-life issue,' I replied.
    Four days after my birthday I was encouraged to be up before sunrise to go to the Egyptian Pulpit / Pyramid Formation. I waited until sunrise, then picked a spray of purple bougainvillea from the lodge garden and walked to the Negativity Beacon / Wheel of Life and placed it on the Solar Stone.
    Two days later Christina arrived at the centre and my Guide instructed the three of us — Christina, Mum and me — to walk together through the Arch into the Heart. We were walking through the doorway to the past seeking the Dolphin Family. Christina said she could see and feel the vibrations of a family of dolphins swimming in the Heart.
    The next day I was shaken awake and encouraged to remove a petal from Greta's golden rose and place it in the Crown Chakra within the Healing Garden diagram along with a carnelian gemstone. My Guide referred me again to *Crystals for Transformation, Healing and Spiritual Growth*:

> Carnelian … Gives courage and fluency of speech. (21)

I was then given the enormous task of raking from the Negativity Beacon / Wheel of Life along the fence line to the Base Root Chakra entrance to the Throat Chakra / Tuart Walk and across to the Egyptian Pulpit / Pyramid Formation. It was a task that took all day — a walking meditation that was very *familiar*. As I created the lines in the sandy soil, encouraging a flow of energy, I understood I would be given the courage and fluency of speech for what was ahead, in particular for the opening of Greta's heart to reveal the hidden past.

My Guide directed me to wrap Mary's image in packing paper. Then I walked to Dongara to collect our post and was relieved to discover a notification from the Case Registrar that I was being given 60 days to attend yet another mediation conference. The attempt by Cathy and her barrister to force the sale of the property had been delayed.

When I found Mum to tell her, she was recording her thoughts. She had woken to a vivid memory of four years before, when she saw the flash of luminous green move through me at the doorway of the Dolphins Healing Room and out through the window.

On 19 March I made time to explain particular colours to Mum. Luminous green appears in visions in the early part of development to attract the attention of the medium. We talked about the rainbow that appeared when Justin visited from Melbourne and that it had held only two colours — green and orange. I explained that green indicates balance, to be brought into being in relation to any task. Orange indicates an awakening of compassion and brotherhood, a necessity for spiritual service to be undertaken, and constructive criticism. I watched as Mum highlighted the words 'task' and 'brotherhood'.

The day's date repeated in my mind and my 1989 diary was highlighted. On 19 March 1989 Cathy's mother had been worried about my use of the pendulum and prayed for guidance. At 2 am the next day she had been compelled to record the words from a spiritual being: *I am behind this. Put your heart in my heart and I will guide you.* Following this reminder, I unwrapped Mary's image and hung it opposite Greta's photograph with its rose petal — Mary's signature.

At 3.30 pm I was working in the garden when Mum walked down to the Tuart Walk / Throat Chakra. She stood in contemplation before approaching me to tell me that when she asked for a change in our circumstances a gold and brown butterfly fluttered across her path from right to left, and the understanding came that the entrance to the Tuart Walk was the Area of Goodwill and Prosperity. 'We will come through this awful time with Cathy,' she said, smiling.

The next day I was instructed to cleanse the auric shield of two dolphins. My attention was drawn to the red cotton cloth, handmade by Mum, and its runic symbol of Hagalaz, the great Awakener. It had been used during the transfer of energy from Cairo to Dongara in 1997. I placed the cloth on the jarrah table in the Dolphins Healing Room and positioned two wooden dolphins, facing one another, on the symbol. I rubbed onto the body of each dolphin the oil of bergamot, lavender and geranium that Greta had sent me, then placed a rose quartz touching both the dolphins and lit a white candle. The understanding came that the dolphins represented Greta and me.

When Roger arrived I handed him a circular hardwood board I had painted with Green of Amazonite. This was to be the base for the Star of David / Star of Melchizedek symbol. I walked to collect my post and found a parcel from Hudda in Palestine. Inside was a red-and-black cushion cover from Jerusalem. Julie had introduced me to Hudda at the permaculture conference in 1996 and she had stayed overnight at the centre.

Jerusalem featured in Greta's past-life heart issue and the Crystal Pool Energy. I added the clues 'truth of suffering' and 'Star of David / Melchizedek' to my past-life heart-issue notes next to 'birth of a child' and 'deception'. My Guide directed that the two wooden dolphins be moved from the symbol of Hagalaz and placed on the red-and-black cushion cover from Jerusalem. Apprehension filled my being when I updated my notes:

> Heart Issue: Judy – Jude Priest – I had a dream and the dream was you – Egyptian wife – lovers – birth of a child – deception – truth of suffering – Star of David / Melchizedek.

The following day I hung the Wild Geese / Soul Group print by Mary's image and was drawn to touch the two wooden dolphins. A warning came: *Your spiritual journey begins.* My heart missed a beat when the phone rang at that moment and Greta left an angry message demanding I speak to her — we had not spoken since my birthday. My Guide referred me to *Medicine Cards* by Sams and Carson:

> Crow – Law … Be willing to walk your talk, speak your truth … (15)

That night Greta rang. She was still upset about me cancelling my birthday trip. I was not to question her actions, she said. I was up all night with chest pains.

A terse legal letter arrived from Cathy's barrister demanding I sign an enclosed agreement for $20,000 or sell. There was no need for a mediation conference, he wrote. I replied by return, sending a copy to the Case Registrar. I was not signing any agreement.

The predicted year of turmoil had begun. *Two necklaces, two women, two situations*, my Guide warned. I was drawn to the women with touching foreheads in the Egyptian tapestry.

Before meeting with Greta in Perth on Valentine's Day I had been encouraged to find her gift of the Dolphin's Dance Plate and wrap it. Now I was guided to remove the wrapping paper, and for the first time I read its title: *Where the Dolphins Dance*. I placed this plate near the wooden dolphins in the Dolphins Healing Room.

On 24 March I was given the task of raking the sandy soil from the Mary Seat to the Judas tree, through the Arch of Life into the Heart itself. Then I was to rewrap *Where the Dolphins Dance*, write a note to Greta, and post the parcel. I wrote: 'Would you please hold this safe for me until I move south and live in Rose Cottage.' I stared at the words 'Rose Cottage' trying to absorb the fact that I was sharing a prediction with regard to moving south. I walked to Dongara to post the parcel. When I returned I sat on the Seat of Reflection near the Arch of Life and soon sensed a movement; then I saw a brown snake in Chamber One and lifted my feet while I watched it disturb my raked lines, and slither out of the garden. I was referred to *Medicine Cards* again:

> Snake – Transmutation ... Snake medicine people are very rare. Their initiation involves experiencing and living through multiple snake bites, which allows them to transmute all poisons, be they mental, physical, spiritual, or emotional. (15)

Within the Medicine Cards were nine blank shield cards, and my Guide requested that one of them be used to create an 'Ally card' for me. The instructions read:

> Ally card ... If you do shamanic work and have met your Ally on other levels of consciousness, you can create an Ally card for your personal use ... An Ally is your teacher and your guardian, a being that teaches the lessons of the physical and unseen worlds. (15)

I placed my Ally card on the jarrah table and was instructed to list my needs on a piece of white paper, attach it to the blank card and light a white candle. I wrote:

To be with people who have an interest in my work.
The opportunity to spend time with indigenous Australians.
Wisdom with regard to human contact.

Roger drove in with the Star of David / Melchizedek symbol, for which he had used trellis to create the triangles. He secured it to the centre of the Arch of Life / Heart Chakra, after which I experienced feelings of loss whenever I walked near it. I had been unaware that my and Greta's past-life heart issues were connected to this symbol. I went to Mum to tell her about the symbol and found her trying to complete a long-stitch tapestry, working with shades of violet. I was encouraged to light a white candle and then sit with her.

Following the prediction regarding Rose Cottage, we had wondered about a centre in a valley amongst the trees. The knowing came that the centre would vibrate to the colour violet and would be associated with deep inner searchings and the so-called inner quest.

Blue Mary Ray Diamond Centre, my Guide said. I repeated the message to Mum. 'I hope I am alive to see it develop,' she said.

When Roger and I had talked about a symbol for the Mary Area, I had drawn an oval shape for him that was *familiar*, and I had also seen violet energy in my mind, the colour of the Crown Chakra. The carnelian and the golden rose petal were still within the Crown Chakra in the diagram in the Dolphins Healing Room. The oval shape was marked with M (for Mary) at its base. When Roger and I walked towards the Mary Area discussing where to place this symbol, I recognised that I had drawn a Miraculous Medal. *Unselfish love and compassion*, my Guide said.

Roger arrived with the oval symbol, bringing a short metal post that he cemented in to hold it. I understood I was to paint this symbol the colour of lapis lazuli at a later date. The cement base would be a colour yet to be decided and the M to be made of jarrah. A lapis lazuli gemstone was placed at the base. Lapis lazuli — sacred stone of the Egyptians, Stone of the Heavens. When we stood back to observe our work I received the message *Travel south ninth April, important*.

A friend of Greta's delivered a parcel to me personally at the centre. I sat and stared at it, reluctant to find out what it contained. Eventually I opened it. There were Easter cards for Mum and me and a miniature book with a reference to a page. I walked away from the book, not wanting to read the page — but I felt the *pull* to open it, and struggled with this reaction. Greta had enclosed photographs of herself and the children, and the postcard *Sturt Desert Pea*, on which I had written the words 'Go with Greta, she is from the same source.' I had been encouraged to write this and give it to her in 1997, prior to her leaving for Switzerland.

The carefully considered contents of the parcel amounted to an appeal to me to continue the Heart's Journey. I walked outside and sat on the Mary Seat with Jessie curled up at my feet. Slowly, from deep inside, came an overwhelming feeling of loss. It was so overpowering that I was forced to hold the sides of the bench. My body shook with pain and I needed all my strength to remain seated. Once this reaction had passed, I returned to the lodge and cautiously opened the tiny book at the marked page. There I read words by Michael Drayton:

> So well I love thee as without thee I love nothing; if I might choose,
> I'd rather die than be one day debarred your company.

I showed Mum Greta's marked entry inside the miniature book and shared with her the intense feeling of loss and pain that I had endured when reading the quote. 'It is my belief that she was compelled to send this to me because it holds a past-life link between her and me.'

'Does she discuss them with you when you're together?'

'No, it is as if she forgets and reacts only to the energy involved.'

'Like pieces of a puzzle which you are expected to complete,' Mum said.

I walked to the Mary Seat to seek help. *Travel south ninth April, important*, my Guide said.

On returning to the lodge I was encouraged to stand in front of Greta's leadlight Celtic cross. Through its coloured glass I could see the blurred outline of the tuart trees in the lodge garden, with the sky bright red and orange filtering through the trees. *All this suffering must stop*, my

Guide urged. That evening the Healing Garden filled with the vibration of loss, and the Heart Chakra / Pulse of Life / Goddess Nut vibrated with so much anguish I could not stay. I was forced to retreat inside, hold the two wooden dolphins and cleanse their bodies with the essential oil. When I later ventured out into the garden the anguish was easier. I stood by the spinning Heart Element and requested help. The next day I wrote a note to Greta saying I was not withdrawing my friendship but I would not be involved in any further untruths. On 1 April the post delivered an Easter egg from Greta, with the words 'New beginnings — the egg'.

On Good Friday morning, during a celebration breakfast, Mum handed me her gift, a blue '50 Hour Dream Candle' — symbolic, she said, of how dramatically my life had changed since my fiftieth birthday. The lighting of this, she added, would highlight my dream to have a centre free of past-life karmic attachments and working with a team of healers. I handed Mum a Miraculous Medal for her purse. Later, I worked on the Egyptian tapestry before painting the Arch of Life / Heart Chakra with Amazonite Green. *New life, new beginning*, my Guide said.

I sensed energy vibrating from within the Star of David / Melchizedek as I painted the Arch, and was directed to stop, clean my brush, replace the lid and go to the Egyptian Pulpit / Pyramid Formation. I removed a large limestone from the pyramid at its base, and carried it to the Love Tree. There was an urgency to move quickly, as something was happening elsewhere and I was to keep pace with it here. I was sent from the Love Tree / Navel Chakra to the Negativity Beacon / Wheel of Life, to remove one large limestone and take it back to the Love Tree. So there was a movement of energy between an Egyptian and a Celtic symbol to the protection of the Love Tree / Navel Chakra — two past lives were running parallel at this moment in time. *'Two necklaces, two women, two situations,'* my Guide warned. *Love is karma is growth.*

I was urged to find the wheelbarrow and dismantle the Pyramid Formation. As I removed the first brick, a snake reared its head and I jumped back in shock. A few months before I had hurt my right hand on a star picket, leaving a scar; now I was aware of pain coming from within the scar. I held my hand as the pain increased to an intense throb.

I started barrowing loads of the pyramid's dismantled stones and bricks up to the tractor shed, which was where the star pickets were stored. I took one back with me. When I returned after the second load the snake was reared up, waiting. I killed it with the star picket and the throb in my scar stopped, but angry male words came up and out of me:

'You will *never hurt me again*,' I shouted, 'brown eyes, my Egyptian wife.' These were not my sentiments but those of *another*.

I returned after taking the third load to the shed to find the snake had disappeared; there was no sign of movement on the sandy soil, so again it was a symbolic killing — of the emotion of hatred. The previous year, when I'd received the message *Egyptian wife*, it was linked to Jude Priest. I went to walk away, but was held and forced to remember Greta's words, 'So well I love thee as without thee I Love nothing; if I might choose, I'd rather die than be one day debarred your company.' Strong emotions being expressed by two very distressed individuals.

I remembered that the Base Root Chakra was in place, connecting me with the primal feelings of fear from physical injury, and that it was the prime mover behind the so-called fight-or-flight response. There was no walking away; I would complete the Heart's Journey. I was referred by my Guide to Gerber's *Vibrational Medicine*.

> The second chakra has been variably referred to as the navel chakra, gonadal chakra, splenic chakra, or sacral chakra … sacral chakra is associated with the expression of sensual emotion and sexuality. The type and adequacy of energy flow through this center is reflective of the degree of involvement with emotional and sexual energy in an individual's life … (3)

The urgent movement in the Healing Garden involved the Love Tree, held within the yet-to-be-developed Navel Chakra. Sexual energy was involved with Greta's past-life heart issue and mine, and with the unknown angry male's. My mind was taken back to January, when I had been encouraged to work the dolphin family tapestry until I had finished the large dolphin, and then I was drawn to work with green and orange wool, stitching the coral reef. I had been sent outside to observe a section of an arch of a rainbow in the sky — a tiny picture frame containing just two colours, green and orange. *Influence of the Green and Orange Dolphins*, my Guide had said. Tatia in South Africa — the Orange Celestial Dolphin, the sexual chakra — was destined to play her part within the Heart's Journey.

The first post after the Easter holidays brought an invitation from Greta for me to join her at the Pinjarra Music Festival on 9 and 10 April. *Travel south ninth April, important*, my Guide had said.

As my train drew into Pinjarra station I watched Greta attempting to hide behind a post. A *familiar* feeling came of having seen her do this before, but behind pillars of gold. There was an air of triumph around her as she drove me to the festival grounds. She had drawn me back. Her tent was small, but had room enough for us both to sleep in comfort. I was coiled inside with tension. The words *Jude, priest, temple,* repeated in my mind. Greta lit a candle in an effort to ease the unspoken tension between us, but I was too drained to speak and soon fell asleep.

While browsing the stalls next day I was drawn to sets of Tibetan temple bells, *timsha,* and bought a set, thrilled with having another healing tool. An accompanying card explained the bells were cast from a mix of seven metals: gold, silver, mercury, iron, tin, lead and copper. The Tibetan Buddhists believed this compound produced a sound beneficial for purifying, healing, meditation and a ritual summons to the Buddha. I had another tool to assist with cleansing the Dolphin energy.

As I was buying the bells, Greta joined me, looking first at my purchase and then at me. I was forever searching, and this bothered her. Later, when we were sitting listening to the music, I drifted into a meditative state and saw a huge golden egg. The sound of applause brought me back with a start, and I found that Greta was studying me. Nothing was said and we drove to Busselton in silence. Greta sat rigid-faced in the car, trying to force me to converse, but I remained silent, aware she was seeking conflict. I borrowed her car the next day while she was at work, as I had been instructed to drive towards the township of Nannup. A sign 'Icon Studio' came into view. Inside the studio I marvelled at the artwork. While waiting to meet the artist, Marice Sariola, I read:

> Window Into Eternity ... Traditional icons are painted on solid wood ... coated with a mixture of rabbitskin glue and limestone powder ... Colours are made of mineral pigments, egg yolk and water by the painter. Background and halos are often of gold leaf ... God's eternal flame spreads into every corner of the painting, therefore no shadows exist. (22)

I remembered my vision at the festival, of the golden egg, and I was guided to buy a travel icon with a gold-leaf background entitled 'The Guardian Angel — Our Lady of Tenderness', two beautiful hand-painted images held within a folding jarrah frame.

As I drove back to Busselton I pondered the references to jarrah, a timber found only in the south-west of Western Australia. There were the Butterfly Circle with its jarrah surround under Mum's bed, the Jarrah Heart purchased in Balingup, the jarrah table in the Dolphins Healing Room and recently the direction to place a jarrah M on the symbolic Miraculous Medal within the Mary Area; now I had acquired this travel icon with its jarrah frame. I was given the understanding that Rose Cottage would be near a jarrah forest.

Many times there could have been an eruption, when sarcasm and put-downs were initiated by Greta, but I wove my way through the strained atmosphere. I showed the Tibetan bells to Cindy and, at her insistence, we walked around the house ringing them in each room. *Influence of the child*, my Guide said.

On my return to Dongara I discovered there had been rain in my absence and the grass pathways were out of control. I was directed to employ a gardener on a fortnightly basis to cut the grass both inside and outside the property. I was encouraged to add the clue 'temple' to Greta's outstanding past-life heart-issue notes, next to 'lovers', and then to my own past-life heart-issue notes next to 'Star of David / Melchizedek'. Later, the clue 'temple' was added to the Crystal Pool Energy next to 'Egyptian wife'. After writing the word in the Crystal Pool Energy notes, I was directed to walk through the Arch of Life / Heart Chakra under the Star of David / Melchizedek seven times, back and forth, back and forth. The image of Greta hiding at the Pinjarra railway station came to mind and then vivid images of her as a young Egyptian woman hiding behind temple pillars of gold. I was sent indoors to read sentences from a handout given to me by a visitor to the garden titled *The Star of Melchizedek*, from the University of Melchizedek in the USA:

> ... This star represents from ancient times, long before the Jewish religion was conceived ... This ancient symbol marks the great order of Melchizedek ... it is a language to the soul, an assurance that all will be gathered up into Perfection. (23)

Early on 20 April I was woken and instructed to walk to the Arch of Life / Heart Chakra and stand under the Star of David / Melchizedek symbol. I waited, and then walked to Greta's Barossa Dream rose, where I discovered two new blooms. A combination of words followed my touching the roses: *Two roses, two people, Order of Melchizedek, Mary*. I added these new clues to my past-life heart issue notes next to 'temple'.

Within hours the Case Registrar's office in Perth rang to inform me a mediation conference had been scheduled for 30 April. Then the office rang back to tell me Cathy did not want to attend. My response was to say that Cathy had started something and she must see it through. The mediation conference was subsequently deferred for a month.

I was set the mammoth task of widening the pathways within the Healing Garden, the work to be done at stated times. All rest times were to be spent working the Egyptian tapestry, for which I used the gold thread Greta had sent me from New York. On one occasion my Guide sent me, with the thread, to a purple blouse in Mum's wardrobe. I asked her what she thought when the gold thread and purple were put together. Her response was immediate: 'Royalty'.

My Guide insisted that the golden thread be incorporated into the clothing of the Egyptian female symbolic of Greta. *Royalty and power*, my Guide said as I stitched. Greta had been a royal personage in Egypt, and therefore a powerful woman. Once we had established this, I was told to put the Egyptian tapestry to one side and directed to read my notes of 12 March, when I had been sent to the Egyptian Pulpit to wait for sunrise before picking a spray of purple bougainvillea and placing it on the Negativity Beacon / Wheel of Life — indicating a link between Egypt, purple and wheel of life. 'Purple' was being highlighted again today in connection with Egypt, royalty and power.

On 29 April I travelled to Fremantle to meet with Tatia, the Orange Dolphin, who had returned from South Africa for a holiday. We walked the beach, and again I felt the connection I'd had when we first met at Julie's farm, in September 1996 prior to the permaculture conference in Perth. We shared memories of that day and how we had been drawn to speak. Tatia said she had seen the energy flow between Julie and myself.

'Do you believe in the theory of past lives?' I asked.

'Of course I do. Why?'

'Julie and I were identical twins in a past life in Ancient Egypt.'

'Are you able to tell me anything else?'

'No, it is important everyone involved uses their inner knowing.'

She said she agreed with this, adding that she knew her presence in Australia at that time was important on a spiritual level, and furthermore understood that I was not to influence her or anyone else. Then she asked me, 'What happened to the little girl Cindy I met two years ago in

Perth?' Greta, Cindy and I had stayed in Perth with Tatia overnight in August 1997 on our way back from Yallingup, when Greta had attended an interview at the Steiner School. 'Cindy and her mother now live in Busselton,' I said.

I arrived back in Dongara on 5 May to find the garden bathed in moonlight — just awesome. As I walked to the Mary Seat I noticed Roger had cemented in the base for the Miraculous Medal and painted it blue. When I saw the blue I was told to paint over it with dark green, and to attach the jarrah M later. The Star of David / Melchizedek stood out in the moonlight and I was told to go and touch it, which I had to stand on tiptoe to do. As I drifted towards sleep shortly afterwards, I received the message *Two roses, two people, Order of Melchizedek, Mary.* I was relaxed the next day until Greta rang to tell me she was planning to visit some time in the future and stay at the centre. *This is forbidden, she is my wife*, the unknown male shouted.

Roger visited two days later to attach the M to the base of the Miraculous Medal. *Influence of Pink Dolphin,* my Guide said.

I was guided to hand the dolphin family tapestry over to Mum for her to work the bullion knots in silk threads of light and dark orange to complete a starfish — orange, the vibrational colour for the Navel Chakra, expression of sensual emotion and sexuality.

Later I walked to Dongara to buy a plant, dowsing which one it was to be. Not until I was at home did I read its label: '*Hardenbergia violacea* Blushing Princess'. When I planted the purple-flowering native climber near my birth symbol — the claret ash — I received the words *princess, royalty, power, Egypt* with such force that I had to hold on to the fence to control my rapid heartbeat. Later I added the clues 'princess', 'royalty', 'power' and 'Egypt' to my past-life heart issue notes; then I was encouraged to compare these notes with the energy held within the Crystal Pool:

Heart Issue: Judy – Jude Priest – I had a dream and the dream was you – Egyptian wife – lovers – birth of a child – deception – truth of suffering – Star of David / Melchizedek – Temple – two roses – two people – Order of Melchizedek – Mary – princess – royalty – power – Egypt.

Crystal Pool Energy: Supreme power – male passions – heart pain – conflict and loss – Egypt – heart's journey – Golden Rose Dolphin –

karmic truths – page marker / Jerusalem – Egypt and priests – This is forbidden – Jude Priest – I had a dream and the dream was you – Egyptian wife – Temple.

The next two days I spent laying a single continuous row of larger and heavier cray slats, each containing a single large red pot, on top of the flat cray slats already in place in the three enclosed Heart chambers. An increased vibrational flow of red runic energy within the Healing Triangle Hagalaz — the great Awakener — which dominated the Heart Chakra / Pulse of Life / Goddess Nut, was being encouraged. Each day Roger brought trailer upon trailer load of these as I needed them. It was a demanding and exhausting experience for us both.

I stopped working to celebrate Mother's Day with Mum and provide a celebration breakfast with a table setting of orange bougainvillea. Before breakfast I went out to the Mary Area, where overnight I had left in a bowl of water some pink blooms from Julie's Mexican rose, in order to absorb the energy of this area. These were a gift for Mum.

'Pink is spiritual love from a spiritual brother and sent as a gift,' I explained, 'and a positive confirmation of their caring and attention to our quest.'

Mum shared with me that over the previous few days she had become aware of getting older and she felt great relief to have been given such a gift and message. I informed her I was being told she would be recharged and would soon get her second wind.

'I am so fortunate to be living here with you,' Mum responded.

'I feel the same about you,' I said, and gave her a hug.

Weeks drifted by as Roger and I worked in the area by the Heart Chakra / Pulse of Life / Goddess Nut, north of the Place of No Secrets / Buddha's Four Parts of Truth and the Boomerang/Karma area. More of the heavier slats, without their red pots attached, were stood in pairs and joined to create a chain-like formation that wound its way behind these areas. I had no idea what it represented.

A little later, while I was watering the Blushing Princess plant, a car drove in. It was Greta. I was confused, as she was not due for weeks. 'A last-minute decision,' she said, handing me a bottle of champagne. 'A celebration drink,' she added. *Meet the Blushing Princess*, my Guide warned.

What are we celebrating? I wondered as I followed her into the lodge, where she popped the cork and filled two glasses. When I accepted my glass of champagne a warning came to mind: *The answer to a more rewarding lifestyle is in your hands.*

Greta decided to walk the Healing Garden, and I watched as she disappeared, then reappeared looking angry. What could have happened? She asked me why the Star of David / Melchizedek was in the garden, as she did not feel it was right for it to be there. This symbol had disturbed me as well. I was so taken aback by the force of her words that I shut down, watching as her angry mouth spoke words I could no longer hear. The *familiarity* of having experienced this before came as Greta's face took on an Egyptian image. The princess was distressed, but I only heard *Order of Melchizedek*.

I was due in the Perth Mediation Court the next day, and realised the champagne was Greta's celebrating ahead of my being forced off the land by Cathy. It no longer tasted good. We drove to Perth in silence and booked into accommodation in South Perth, across the river from the Supreme Court. Greta asked if she could attend the mediation. Before I could say 'No' my Guide said *Yes*. It appeared I no longer had a year to find the $20,000; Cathy was backing out of our Agreement. The property must be placed on the market to be sold; if not, the next stage would be to auction. I felt sick.

Cathy and her barrister left the room while I had a heated discussion with the Case Registrar. Everything was contrary to the Agreement, but I remembered Cathy's barrister saying 'I am going to take your land away from you.' This was their intention, regardless of any agreements. Cathy's barrister returned with a proposal. Greta and Cathy stared at one another with Greta forcing Cathy to look away. The enormity of the situation came when I understood the three women in the Egyptian tapestry were in the room, two with the same intent. This was the link between the two Egyptian women with touching brow chakras; their individual desires were to remove me from the centre. *Two necklaces, two women, two situations*, my Guide confirmed.

I asked to be excused for a moment and left the room. *Sign the agreement*, my Guide urged. When I returned, I learnt to my utter dismay that a second caveat had been placed on the land. Cathy's barrister had arranged for this to cover his legal costs. Upon sale the $20,000 would be given to Cathy, and he would secure payment of his legal costs before the remaining balance would be paid to me. *You will be sole proprietor. You will not lose the land*, my Guide said.

If I raised the $20,000, it would be a full and final payment, Cathy's barrister would take out his legal costs and Cathy would be left with nothing. Cathy and he were certain that I would not raise the money and so would be forced to sell. I signed the Agreement regarding the $20,000, the time frame and the possibility of a sale and/or auction, after I was able to add the condition that the title would be transferred to my sole name upon payment of $20,000. As Greta and I left the building I watched Cathy hail a taxi, talking excitedly into her mobile phone, so sure of victory. *Trust the process*, my Guide said.

On my return to Dongara I was guided to remove the Star of David / Melchizedek symbol and place it in the tractor shed. I went with Mum to the Dolphins Healing Room to show her the Miraculous Medal information inside the Healing Garden brochure.

'Cathy will not take away our home and our land,' I assured her.

I placed the property on the market in accordance with the Agreement. Roger was annoyed when I told him what had happened. *A new partnership*, my Guide said.

Christina visited at the end of May, bringing yet another white Buddha statue. I placed this within the Place of No Secrets with the information the Four Parts of Truth. Several days later I was guided to place the Black Dolphin / Diopside Christina had given me on different chakras at varying times and on different days, within the Chakra Healing Garden diagram. I could recall the sadness I felt the first time I held this Dolphin and the message *I hold you in my heart, I hold you in my arms, I hold you*. Following its symbolic journey through the chakras, I placed the Black Dolphin / Diopside by the large rose quartz given to me by Michelle. *Strong healer of the heart*, my Guide said.

She stood me in front of the symbol I had created. Its paired, heavy cray slats, north of the Heart Chakra / Pulse of Life / Goddess Nut wound their way behind the Place of No Secrets / Buddha's Four Parts of Truth and the curved Boomerang/Karma; I recognised an Aboriginal Rainbow Serpent. Roger confirmed this when he brought two cray slats with red pots and red cages attached and placed them at the head of the serpent, symbolic of its eyes. The Rainbow Serpent wound its way eastwards thirteen metres, down towards the yet-to-be-created Solar Plexus Chakra.

I was working in the Heart on 15 June when Greta drove in. She approached me holding five red roses and the words *I hold you in my heart, I hold you in my arms, I hold you* filled my mind. Later I gave the roses to Mum. 'Mary's signature,' I reminded her, as she put them in a blue vase.

I was instructed to stand in front of the Wild Geese / Soul Group print hanging in the Dolphins Healing Room. I noted the correspondence between the five red roses and the five flying geese in the print. *Red rose energy and soulmates*, my Guide said.

Early the next day I was standing by the Heart when Greta joined me, walked straight to the Rainbow Serpent and stood near its head. 'Why is there a bucket of water nearby?' she asked.

'I don't know. There are many things here I do not understand.'

Greta pondered my response, then lifted the bucket and poured the water carefully over the serpent's head. Rainbow Serpent was held within Cathy's past-life heart issue as were legal action, Aboriginal link, conflict, the chase, Aboriginal spear and male passions. *Influence of the Golden Rose Dolphin*, my Guide said.

Aboriginals regarded the Rainbow Serpent as an awesome creature of power and great importance. Greta's actions had opened a doorway, releasing the energy to help me access Cathy's past-life heart issue secrets and resolve our Aboriginal karmic attachment.

To my surprise, Greta asked me to walk her around all the areas. As we walked to the Negativity Beacon / Wheel of Life, the feeling of *familiarity* came — we had walked together like this before. There was an air of interest about her that was pleasing, unlike the bouts of controlling authority that surfaced without warning. This was the personality I had worked with before the traumatic incarnations of Ancient Egypt. As we stood together by the Negativity Beacon / Wheel of Life, Greta touched its Central Stone. She was the link between 'Egypt', 'purple' and 'wheel of life'. I understood, by this action, that she had opened another doorway releasing the energy that would assist me to access our past-life heart issue secrets, and resolve our Egyptian karmic attachment.

My Guide encouraged me to walk Greta to the Iona cross in the lodge garden, the place where four of us had stood on the morning of Mary May Day '96. I relayed this to Greta and said the cross must now be moved inside the Healing Garden itself. 'Okay,' was her reply, 'let's do it this afternoon.' I was taken aback by her acceptance of the guidance.

During lunch Mum and I were very much aware of Greta's five red roses. After lunch she and I dismantled the Iona cross. Because I had buried a barn owl there in July 1996, I was careful, not wanting to disturb what would be a fragile skeleton. I removed the cloth that held the bird's body, but there were no bones — only a magnificent feather. The bird had left me its wisdom. Greta watched, wondering what had happened. I wanted to explain, but the words were lost. It was my experience and I was not to share it. My Guide asked me to take the brown-and-white owl feather to the Dolphins Healing Room and place it by the Black Dolphin / Diopside on the jarrah table. Greta and I dismantled the cross and placed the parts between Julie's oak tree and Greta's Barossa Dream rose. I stood back and watched as Greta put the pieces back together, spoke of her father having died eight years earlier and requested a healing.

When she was lying down on the massage/healing table, I placed the Black Dolphin / Diopside, the rose quartz and the owl feather on the Navel Chakra (sensual emotions and sexuality) in the Chakra Healing Garden diagram, then played the *Call of the Dolphin* tape and lit five white candles, placed in an arch by the diagram. I looked at Mary's image and the Wild Geese / Soul Group print, aware that Greta was the Golden Rose Dolphin, and requested instructions. I was directed to place the clear quartz — not from the Earth plane — on Greta's brow chakra. I had experienced a panic attack after briefly touching Greta's forehead with my own in Busselton, and I wondered what was going to happen now. She said she could see the colours purple and gold. I had not mentioned the gold thread and purple blouse. As soon as she mentioned these colours I heard, *Princess, royalty, power, Egypt* — the same message that had come when I planted the Blushing Princess.

My heart raced when the princess's profile appeared over Greta's face, revealing a young woman. The princess opened her eyes and smiled, and my being filled with love from long ago, so intense I was barely able to breathe as I looked into those brown eyes. This was the regal young woman in my dream. The profile disappeared and I found myself looking into Greta's questioning eyes. I did not share this past-life experience.

We worked on the Iona cross again the next day, surrounding it with grey gravel, delivered by Roger. The day after, we walked the Irwin River mouth and sat on the beach, watching the sea. Greta collected driftwood to take home with her. I enjoyed this rare moment of peace between us. Before she left, she bought pansies and planted them in a triangle outside the gate to the lodge: pansy — the flower of lovers. I sat on the Mary Seat aware that Greta and I had been lovers in ancient Egypt and the trauma of our affair was surfacing now with the permission of Greta — the Golden Rose Dolphin — in contrast to the emerging angry male energy held in the words *This is forbidden.*

The building society refused my application for a new mortgage.

At the beginning of July I was given two specific tasks to be worked on for an hour each, alternately. The first was within the Crystal Pool area itself — weeding — the other to work the dolphin family tapestry. Following my final hour by the Crystal Pool on the first day, I went inside the lodge to find a message on the answering machine. It was Greta, but not in her normal voice. She whispered the same words that I had heard in my mind many times: *I will never leave you*. Now they vibrated through my thoughts once again, and I felt compelled to sit within the Crystal Pool area on the seat-like formation. Energy engulfed me, arousing a series of emotions. First anger, then hurt, loss, grief and, finally, bliss. *I will never leave you*, the princess whispered. As I recovered, my mind went reeling back to the Old Saddlery and the trapped spirit child, who had expressed the same sentiment until I found the words to free us both.

On 5 July, after working outside in the Crystal Pool area for my set hour, I was guided to fill a tall glass with water and place it near Greta's leadlight Celtic cross. I was sent from the room for a few minutes, and when I returned there was a huge brown spider on the glass. I was guided to carry the glass and spider to the table where my music cassettes were stored. I waited. The spider crawled away from the glass and across the cassette player, and settled on a cassette set apart from all the others, *Gathering of the Shamans*. The dolphin family tapestry was highlighted; it was to be completed to the sound of this music. My Guide referred me to *Medicine Cards* by Sams and Carson:

> Spider – Weaving ... Spider is the female energy of the creative force that weaves the beautiful designs of life ... She can also be warning you that you are coming too close to an entangled situation. (15)

My Guide insisted I cut sprigs of lavender from Mum's garden for Greta.

On 7 July I was shaken awake in order to take Buddha's statue from the Place of No Secrets / Buddha's Four Parts of Truth, to stand at the head of the Sacred 13 Formation, and then to take the Buddha that was there back to the lodge — a movement of energy regarding Buddhist Wisdom / Four Parts of Truth. I laid several sprigs of freshly-cut lavender at Buddha's feet at the head of the Sacred 13 Formation. I was aware lavender oil promoted healing and prevented scarring, and on this day Greta would receive her sprigs of lavender.

I was referred to my 1995 diary, to be reminded that on 7 July four years earlier the Celestial Dolphin Centre had come into being.

Later that day I was bitten by bull ants through my thick gardening gloves. My hand swelled so much that I had to remove the dolphin ring Greta had bought in Zurich. I was struggling with the ring as I left the Healing Garden and walked into a large branch of a tuart tree. Struggling to free myself from the branch and the ring, the silver chain necklace I had bought during Greta's last visit fell apart and from my neck. I returned to the lodge distressed, aware only of the Buddha statue in the hallway — symbol of the Four Truths of Suffering. Before treating the bites I was directed to place the silver necklace and the dolphin ring in the gift box that had held the necklace. The Black Dolphin / Diopside was momentarily placed within the box. Shocked and apprehensive, I sat nursing my injured hand, when Greta walked in without prior warning. Gone was the Golden Rose Dolphin. The spider had warned that I was coming too close to an entangled situation. *I will never leave you*, the princess whispered.

People were coming to view the property and Greta wanted to see for herself how many. A sale would be welcome news to her, and I found it hard to be even near her as I understood the reason for the dramatic removal of the ring and necklace. The Golden Rose Dolphin personality had been forcibly pushed to the side once again.

Light relief came when Steve, the healer who worked with Christina, called in and we walked the Healing Garden. He talked about the Heart of Melchizedek, the theory being to work towards the healing of the heart. As I listened, I was aware that the princess who had reacted angrily at the Star of David / Melchizedek symbol was staying in my home.

Following Greta's departure I was encouraged by my Guide to look at the picture of St Michael's and All Angels Church, Cornwood, on the wall in the meditation room. I waited and received the message *Sword of justice*. A card arrived from an anonymous supporter who had written 'Love. Compassion. Justice'. There was also a postcard from Roger and Mary, who were on holiday near the Valley of the Kings in Luxor, Egypt — Roger, the Pink Dolphin, would be viewing the image of the Goddess Nut / Cycle of Life in a tomb there.

August found me travelling south to be with Greta. She was lodging her divorce papers and asked me to provide support. As I walked alone on the beach my mind was dominated by the message *I will never leave you. I will never leave you.* Early next morning I was woken by Greta carrying a tray with croissants and a vase of flowers. She said it was to make up for the hurtful drama on my birthday in March. She sat on the edge of the bed, and when I looked at her I saw the Golden Rose Dolphin. Out poured the hurts regarding my fortieth birthday, my family, Barbara and my business partner Anne. Greta listened, and when I thanked her she smiled and lit a white candle for me to blow out and make a wish. My silent wish was to return to England when the truth had been revealed.

Later, back in Dongara, the post brought a card from Greta: 'I'll steal your heart and set it free.' *I will never leave you*, the princess whispered. *Mastery of the mind*, my Guide warned.

I spent the next few weeks talking with the many people who visited the centre and spent my leisure time working the Egyptian tapestry with the gold thread. I went to Perth to lodge more legal papers and arranged to meet Greta. When we arrived at our accommodation, she handed me a small brown envelope marked 'Healing Heart Karma necklace'. Inside was a solid silver Heart with gold wire threaded throughout the left side and a leather cord. She had bought it in Nannup. I was aware that if I accepted the gift there would be consequences. I did accept, and took it back to Dongara and the centre, where my Guide directed me to place it on the Heart Chakra / Pulse of Life / Goddess Nut diagram in the Open Chamber with the Black Dolphin / Diopside and owl feather.

On the last day of August my Guide instructed that the Iona Cross that had been carefully reassembled by Greta between Julie's oak tree and the Barossa Dream rose be removed and the area raked. Now returned from Egypt, Roger took it to the tip.

September was a busy month, dealing with guests and updating the brochure. The visitors were keen to understand, and I found it all exhausting. Mum walked the property with Jessie and me each evening after our meal to help me relax and unwind.

My Guide instructed that the silver Healing Heart Karma necklace, the Black Dolphin / Diopside and the owl feather be joined by Greta's ankh from Cairo. As I positioned the ankh I received the word *Egypt*, and when I walked away *Rose Cottage*, and then *Travel south*.

During this required visit to the South West, Greta drove us to Nannup and to a Rose Cottage there that needed restoring. I knew this was not the Rose Cottage mentioned by my Guide, but I was aware Nannup was where Greta had purchased the Healing Heart Karma necklace.

When we walked our beach later, four dolphins swam by. *Rose Cottage and four dolphins*, my Guide said.

The next day was tense, due to a change in Greta: she was full of sarcasm once again. Although I did everything I could to move the conversation away from sensitive subjects when they came up, by the afternoon I had a terrible headache and lay down on a bed. Greta followed me, and I was soon overwhelmed by her put-downs. Feeling nauseous, I tried to get up to walk to the bathroom, but my legs were too shaky. When the vomiting started Greta stopped and took me straight to the hospital, where I was given injections and kept in emergency until I recovered. I was so shaken that I asked her to drive me to Perth the next day to connect with my coach. There was no apology from Greta, only silence. I felt as if I had been beaten. I ached from head to toe, my stomach was sore, my neck was stiff and I felt confused. When I boarded the coach at the station I did not say goodbye.

In Dongara I asked the taxi driver to take me to my post box before taking me to the centre. To add to my distress, there was a solicitor's letter informing me that Cathy intended to auction our home and land on 21 October. *Two necklaces, two women, two situations*, my Guide warned.

A friend told me that one of the plants growing in my breezeway was a Chinese Happy Plant. 'They flower every fifteen years,' she said. My plant was in flower; I would come through all of this and celebrate. I updated my past-life heart issue notes to include the new clues 'Healing Heart Karma' and 'celebration' next to 'Egypt'.

I shared with Mum the distressing event I'd experienced during my visit with Greta. 'I was not able to withstand the disruptive energy this time, and neither was Greta, but she drove me to a Rose Cottage in need of repair in Nannup near the river.'

'Was it our Rose Cottage?' Mum asked.

'No. But Nannup, it seems, is a place of importance.'

Post arrived from Nannup in the form of an envelope that held sixteen dried golden rose petals from Greta.

At 4 am on 6 October I was guided to place the large rose quartz crystal inside the Heart Element within the Heart Chakra / Pulse of Life / Goddess Nut. This enormous symbol looked spectacular under the red morning sky, surrounded by the green vetiver grass filled with hundreds of cray slats and the single row of large red cray pots marking the Flow of Life. The wind wheel within the Heart Element was forever spinning, symbol of Four Years of Conflict scheduled to end on 8 October 2002. Three more years of conflict, I thought.

The next evening I discovered the Barossa Dream rose had produced two blooms. I placed them on the M for Mary in the Miraculous Medal at the Mary Seat. Next morning they were gone: the issues between Greta and me were held in the hands of *another*.

Two roses, two people, Order of Melchizedek, Mary, my Guide confirmed. On 8 October she instructed me to remove the rose quartz within the Heart Element and take it to the Barossa Dream rose and leave it in the sun to be recharged. I returned the crystal after sunset and sealed it permanently inside, using huge boulders.

Remember the eighth of October. It is important, my Guide said.

Roger and I increased the overall length of the Rainbow Serpent, and each time I walked near its tail a pain would shoot through my right leg below the knee, a reminder of my karmic attachment to Cathy and our outstanding Aboriginal past-life heart issue.

A young woman named Mary moved to Dongara and needed a place to stay. We began to work as a team. As I worked the Egyptian tapestry indoors, she cleared the mass of growth by the Area of Relationships and the fence line to the Children's Tree.

Greta had rung, but before I returned her call I was guided to white-light the three crown chakras of the women in the Egyptian tapestry, using a stitch of white wool. Greta spoke, in the whispered tones of the princess, about nothing in particular. Her voice was the same as when she had stood behind me when I boarded the coach in Busselton and whispered, 'Trust me.' The same shiver as then ran through my spine as I listened to her.

A Barossa Dream rosebud blossomed overnight and I was guided to send it to Greta, to arrive the day before her birthday. When it arrived, it fell apart in her hands. She said she placed the petals in a blue bowl of water with added lavender. 'How many petals were there?' I asked.

'Sixteen,' she replied. It was the same number as the dried golden rose petals she had sent me from Nannup the previous month. I felt a great sense of relief: according to the Celts the number sixteen (Sigel) symbolised success.

When I'd replaced the receiver, my Guide sent me into the Dolphins Healing Room to remove Greta's ankh from beside the silver Healing

Heart Karma necklace, the Black Dolphin / Diopside and the owl feather, and place it at the centre of a ring of four dolphins on the jarrah table. The four dolphins were the brass dolphin from Mum, the silver dolphin from Christina, the blue/green glass dolphin from Liz and the blue/green Indian dolphin from Dianne. *Four dolphins, rose energy, goddess energy*, my Guide explained.

With the tape *Call of the Dolphin* playing, I placed the Amazonite crystal — representing truth, clear understanding and solid foundation — in a bowl of water and left it in the sun in the window beside Greta's leadlight Celtic cross. As I worked to finish the Egyptian tapestry, a queen bee and her swarm arrived at the lodge, taking residence in an eastern cavity of the room. The noise was deafening. *Goddess energy*, my Guide explained. *The goddess is alive*, she confirmed.

This was the energy in which I completed the tapestry. While holding it I was sent to the Egyptian Pulpit to read aloud the quote from the book *Goddesses for Every Season* by Nancy Blair: (17)

'Egyptian Sky Queen. Welcome Nut, Egyptian goddess,' I shouted.

Following this declaration to the Goddess Nut, the Heart Chakra / Pulse of Life / Goddess Nut was to be changed by filling in the four swales that ran through the Heart with soil and covering the area with paper, hay and cray slats. The bridges would be stored in the tractor shed until Roger could take them to the tip. The swales had served their purpose and were no longer required to deliver water to the Heart, now covered in carpeting and slats. The planting of the outer rim now absorbed any excess water.

I had sought legal advice regarding the Right of Residency that Cathy, Mum and I had signed to protect Mum's capital when buying the property. I drafted a statement, had it witnessed by a local magistrate, and sent it to the Supreme Court. The date arranged for the auction — 21 October — came and went. I had received an arrogant letter from Cathy's barrister ordering me to arrange an auction and pay the auctioneer. I had replied by return informing him this was not in our Agreement and if his client wished to hold an auction then she must pay for it. I heard nothing for weeks until a letter came in response asking me to speak to a specific local auctioneer and arrange a date for an auction and his fee would be paid. I did this and we agreed that a date would be set in January or February.

The child needs you, my Guide warned.

Having been guided to write to Greta, I paused with pen and paper ready, not sure what I was to say. Then it came to me that I should tell her I would be in her area soon and intended to book into a bed-and-breakfast place. She replied asking me to stay with her, assuring all would be calm.

On 14 November she was waiting for me. The next day she became unwell. I stayed five days, spending time on the beach playing with Cindy. She sat with me at home and when I became agitated and left, Cindy followed, insisting on giving me healing hugs. When I returned to Dongara the property was flooded by moonlight and I walked around enjoying the wonder of it all and appreciating the enormity of the concept.

At the beginning of December a letter arrived from Cathy's barrister, informing me an auction would take place on 15 January 2000. I was visited by the auctioneer, who wanted my agreement on a reserve price. I had no idea that this was unethical: a reserve price need not be known until minutes before an auction, but in my ignorance I allowed the process. I made it clear that Cathy's presence would not be welcome at the auction.

Mum had been diagnosed with angina. I took her to see a heart specialist in Geraldton, who referred her to Fremantle Hospital. Greta rang Mum from Busselton to tell her she was involved in a holiday house swap scheme in Fremantle and we must stay with her when attending the hospital for tests in the new year.

On the last day of the century Mum and I lit a new white candle and thought about Rose Cottage waiting for us down south. We stood together and watched the sun set for the last time in 1999 and were thrilled when luminous green light spread over the Healing Garden. As we smiled in wonder at one another I felt tremendous love for her. I was up at dawn to see in the beginning of the New Age — Age of Aquarius. My Guide's first request of the new century was for me to begin a project: a symbol to be created under the White Dolphin at the main entrance. As I worked, my thoughts turned to Cindy and the fact that the next day, 2 January, would be her fifth birthday.

I assumed I had finished the new project on the third day, but was informed by my Guide that a Solar Stone was required. A road grader had driven by, and I asked the driver to find me a boulder from the pile outside the property. He brought a huge circular stone and placed it carefully inside the symbol where the sun's rays would strike it at sunrise.

The next day I walked to the Dongara Library and visited their tourist section. I was taken to the brochure *Manjimup, Gateway to the Warren Valley*. Mum and I must visit Manjimup during our brief stay in Fremantle, I was told. This journey was important. I booked to stay in the Manjimup Caravan Park for two nights.

Days later, back in Dongara, I found a card from Greta in my post box featuring a silver heart. She had written 'A place in your heart.' I rushed back to the centre to the Healing Heart Karma necklace Greta had bought in Nannup and took it to the main entrance. The outline of the new project was the same as that of the necklace. While I had been creating it, thoughts of Cindy had come with the message *Powerful energy*. The energy of this symbol, with its Solar Stone, was a link between me, Cindy and the gift from her mother.

Greta rang to say she was in the process of buying a house in Busselton and I gave her details of our planned visits to Fremantle and Manjimup. She said she would meet us at the Perth Coach Station on 17 January.

But before that, on 15 January, there was the auction, and I woke up on that morning feeling very apprehensive. My Guide referred me to *Medicine Cards*:

Skunk – Reputation ... Project self-respect! (15)

The auction was at 11 am. Roger arrived with a swollen face, obviously upset by what was happening, and sat with his back to the auctioneer. Mum's group sat nearby. A German lady I'd never seen before asked me why I was trying to sell such a lovely place and I explained the situation to her. I was taken aback when, in an act of silent protest, no-one offered a bid. Then the German lady, whose name turned out to be Adelheid, asked me how much I would need to be able to stay. In front of the auctioneer I told her it was $20,000, and she surprised everyone by saying she wanted to make an investment. Christina gave me a hug when she heard what she was proposing, and when Roger did likewise he had tears of relief in his eyes. Adelheid asked me to wait for a few days while she contacted her bank in Germany.

Meanwhile, I would have to make sure her offer was acceptable, as my condition for making the $20,000 payment was the transfer of the title to my name. The building society would have to work in accord with everyone. Adelheid said she was travelling to New Zealand and would contact me on her return. The Agreement stated that, if the property did not sell by auction the first time, it would be put up for auction again. The pressure still remained.

At 5 am on the following Monday I was woken and sent to the main entrance to sit on the Solar Stone of the Healing Heart Karma and wait for the sun. When it came, it radiated its orange light over me and I found myself compelled to shout Greta's name. I was encouraged to shout it out a second time then enter the Healing Garden and stand under the Arch of Life / Heart Chakra and shout it for a third and final time. *Calling the Golden Rose Dolphin*, my Guide explained.

I waited before being encouraged to walk to the Egyptian Pulpit, where I was floored to see a golden light filling the Heart Chakra / Pulse of Life / Goddess Nut until it was bathed in it. I stood inside the Open Chamber unable to move, in awe of what I was seeing. The golden light faded and I returned to the lodge and placed the Miraculous Medal by Greta's leadlight Celtic cross on the windowsill of the Dolphins Healing Room. I was not to share any of this with Greta, my Guide said.

Greta was waiting near the Perth Coach Terminal when our coach pulled in. I was still full-to-bursting with what had happened at the centre, but I was not to share it with her so I gave her a warm hug instead. She stared back at me in surprise: it had been a long time since I'd done that. Greta's mother was visiting from Switzerland and the two mums got on well. We left the children with them and went for a walk around Fremantle. I was carrying in my purse the golden travel icon 'The Guardian Angel — Our Lady of Tenderness' that I had bought at the Icon Studio near Nannup.

We drove Mum to the hospital the next day for her tests. The following morning Greta tried to talk me out of going to the Manjimup area, and when I started to feel nauseous she became annoyed. Anyway she drove us to Perth to catch our coach. We spent time with Ray, the proprietor of the caravan park at Manjimup. He had been a timber worker and offered to take us to see places of interest. Next day he drove us to Donnelly Mill, with its workers' cottages, then to the Four Aces, a row of four giant karri trees, and finally to the Diamond Tree Fire Tower. I was beginning to wonder why Mum and I had been sent to this area when I was encouraged to stand back from the base of this enormous tree. I then received the message *Rose Cottage*.

Greta and Cindy met us in Perth when we returned the next day, but Greta did not want to hear anything about our adventure. I discovered she was furious that someone had offered to invest in the centre and I might be staying in Dongara. She took me into a bedroom and demanded I assure her I would be leaving Dongara and moving south to be near her and available to her.

Give her the card, my Guide said. What card? I wondered, trying to cope with the dreadful atmosphere. *Give her the card*, she insisted. I eventually grasped that she meant the information card regarding the golden travel icon, 'The Guardian Angel — Our Lady of Tenderness'. I fumbled in my purse to find it and handed it to Greta, but she tossed it down on the bed and shouted, 'I don't want this.' I had to hold onto the wall to stop myself falling, the feeling of vertigo was so intense. I picked up the card before lying down. I felt sick and asked Greta to find my medication. To me, the icon was precious, but Greta had rejected it. When she helped me off the bed, I looked into her angry face, understanding that she had rejected Our Lady of Tenderness before. She ushered me into her car with a gesture of disgust.

Cindy held my hand tight as we drove to the Fremantle Railway Station in silence. Every part of me was in turmoil. At the station Greta grabbed our cases and took Mum to one side, holding her arm with a gesture of affection. I was left standing by the car until Cindy came and took my hand. Without her help I would not have reached the platform. As the train pulled out I sat facing away from Greta. In my confusion Mum and I left the train at the wrong station and for a while took one going in the wrong direction. I struggled to recover, aware of Mum's distress. I was annoyed that she had witnessed my humiliation and had been steered away by Greta, leaving me alone and helpless. 'Judy, you cannot stay in this dreadful situation,' she said.

Back in Dongara, I wrote to Cathy's solicitor regarding the offer of investment. I requested his assurance that the two caveats would be removed and the title transferred to me upon payment of the $20,000. Cathy would remain on the mortgage but off the title. Later, I learnt Cathy's barrister was not available, and a more approachable solicitor contacted me. He pushed ahead for the offer to be accepted, but when the barrister returned I was told to ask the building society to remove Cathy's name from the mortgage. This was not in the Agreement: her barrister was creating drama and charging Cathy fees. I was referred to the book *Sacred Path Cards* by Jamie Sams:

> Moon Lodge – Retreat … Take a break. Your influence cannot be felt at this time because you are in need of replenishing your own energy … you need to be alone. (14)

Early on 24 January I was guided to walk through the Arch of Life in reverse then walk to the entrance of the Tuart Walk / Throat Chakra / Area of Goodwill and Prosperity. I waited until directed to return to the lodge and put the Miraculous Medal on the legal papers regarding Cathy. Then I was referred to the book *Medicine Cards* once again:

> Porcupine – Innocence … has many special qualities … the power of faith and trust. The power of faith contains within it the ability to move mountains. The power of trust in life involves trusting that the Great Spirit has a divine plan. (15)

Three days later, on Mum's birthday, we walked by the sea at Seven Mile Beach, aware she had a damaged heart. *The last day* repeated and filled my being with loss and grief. I learnt later that Mum had taken notes from a library book:

> There is always a Last Day. The Last Day you see a friend. The Last Day of your life. The Last Day of summer.

On 14 February I remembered the silver locket that Greta no longer wore. We had not spoken since my visit to Fremantle and her rejection of Our Lady of Tenderness.

The building society again refused to change the mortgage agreement as they had done since Cathy walked out of the centre four years previously, but the title transfer could take place if both parties agreed. At last they were going to allow the legal process. I received a letter from Cathy's barrister: my offer of settlement on the basis of Adelheid's offer of investment was being rejected. He insisted the property remain on the market and be sold. I knew Cathy's legal costs had been mounting and if I settled she would receive nothing.

Three days after my birthday, 11 March, I was guided to a file of letters and notes from the many visitors to the Healing Garden and to a specific letter:

> The evolution of the earth is arranged into ages, identified by the astrological symbols. Jesus came to herald the age of Pisces, and we

are now entering the Age of Aquarius. This is when we learn the oneness of everything. We are all the same, one consciousness at different levels of evolution.

I was directed to walk to Dongara, where I found a parcel from Dianne. Inside was my birthday gift of a miniature sword, 'The Excalibur'. On returning to the centre I was encouraged to hold the sword and read further from the same letter:

> The power that built the glory of Atlantis was switched off. The story of the Sword of Excalibur was symbolic of those energies being switched off. The Holy Grail is not an object, but levels of consciousness and spiritual awareness. This is what the Knights of the Round Table were searching for – known as the pursuit of the Holy Grail.

In March 1992 I had driven to Tintagel in Cornwall with Mum and Cathy to King Arthur and his Knights of the Round Table country and walked the cliff path to touch the stone where the Sword of Excalibur was said to have been held, and where Arthur spent time with Merlin. I was in wonder at the fact that I was holding a symbolic Excalibur Sword. Dianne had continually played a role in my life with regard to her gifts. *White Dolphin*, my Guide said. I was not surprised to learn that Dianne was a Celestial Dolphin.

If Jesus came to herald the Age of Pisces, who will herald the New Age of Aquarius? I wondered.

Make Merlin work for you, my Guide repeated.

I was encouraged to write to Shirley and Keith in Balingup and tell them about the information from a visitor regarding Merlin's friend King Arthur. Keith had felt Merlin's energy near the Heart Chakra / Pulse of Life during their visit in August two years before. They replied saying that on the day my letter arrived a friend, Norma from Bunbury, had visited. She spoke of having attended a lecture on the Merlin Factor. I was instructed to send them a postcard by return, asking them how I could make contact with Norma.

Notification arrived from Cathy's barrister to inform me he was arranging for the State Auctioneer to sell the property. I sat on the Mary

Seat awaiting directions and was guided to contact a local auctioneer and seek an appointment as soon as possible. The barrister's actions confirmed my earlier thoughts about Cathy having created legal costs greater than the settlement figure. He had placed a second caveat on the land to cover his costs and was spending at will. If the property was sold at auction, his costs would be taken from the proceeds before Cathy was given the $20,000 settlement. *Trust the process*, my Guide said.

I told the local auctioneer what was happening. He, in turn, explained the rules concerning any auction. 'Judy, you have more power in this than you realise,' he said. I left his office armed with the facts and my rights. *Keep fighting, you must win*, my Guide urged.

Trimming the vetiver grass around the Heart kept me busy for days. Then the post brought a response from Keith with details of Norma. I wrote to her requesting information about the Merlin Factor, enclosing diagrams regarding the centre and the Healing Garden. *Make Merlin work for you*, my Guide instructed again. *Now write to Greta*, she directed.

> Dear Greta, You will soon be linked to a group that will respect you as a woman, as a human being, as a soul and as an individual. Judy.

In response Greta sent me her new address, and my Guide instructed me to place it inside the ring of four dolphins from Mum, Christina, Liz and Dianne on the jarrah table near the Healing Heart Karma, Black Dolphin / Diopside and owl feather. I dowsed for a medicine card and when I turned it over saw it was the Owl. Then I turned to the reading in the book:

> Owl – Deception … you are being asked to use your powers of keen, silent observation to intuit some life situation. Owl is befriending you and aiding you in seeing the total truth … The truth always brings further enlightenment. (15)

Roger and I spent days placing trailer loads of carpets over the three enclosed chambers of the Heart, this continual maintenance being vital in the Heart's Journey.

A letter arrived from Cathy's barrister to say she had decided to accept my offer, but she was too late. Adelheid had found somewhere else to invest. I had no option but to put the property on the market. I posted the new contract to Cathy for her to sign.

Martin, the man who had revealed the similarity between the Heart Chakra / Pulse of Life and the Egyptian Goddess Nut, rang and asked to stay for a few days. Mum enjoyed catering for guests, and her breakfasts were gaining a reputation and drawing people to come and stay. As I replaced the phone, it rang again: it was Norma from Bunbury. She would make enquiries for me about the Merlin Factor. *Make Merlin work for you*, my Guide said again.

I was working in the Heart on 12 April when Martin arrived, bringing information photocopied from the *Nexus* magazine web page. I was floored when he told me the information was from a lecture by Sir Laurence Gardner, Kt St Gm, KCD, author of *Bloodline of the Holy Grail*, and that the lecture included many references to Merlin. Surprised, because I had never mentioned Merlin to Martin, I accepted the pages and went to the office, where I tried to recall the moment when the name 'Gardner' had been brought to my attention.

Searching through my notes, I discovered that four years before, in 1996, after I'd visited St Mary's Church during the permaculture conference, I had been guided to pick two red rosebuds and place one on the headstone of a person named Gardner and to give the other to Julie. The clues 'Gardner' and 'Mary's Church' had been added to Soul Energy (1) and to Julie's past-life heart issue notes. At the time I had been drawn to the clues 'rebuilding the cathedral', 'Virgo' and 'Gardner', and the feeling of *exhilaration* had come when I understood there was a link between red roses, Gardner, Mary's Church, Julie and me. I was instructed to read only part of what Martin had handed me:

> *The Hidden History of Jesus and the Holy Grail.* The early Christian Church leaders adopted scriptures and teachings that would obscure the truth about the royal bloodline of Jesus. (24)

I placed the lecture notes inside an envelope until guided to read further. I did not tell Martin about the Merlin's Triangle in the Healing Garden or about Norma from Bunbury enquiring about the Merlin Factor for me. It was two days before I was encouraged to read a paragraph from *The Hidden History of Jesus and the Holy Grail*, part 3, page 6:

> Jesus was born in 7 BC and his birthday was the equivalent of 1 March, with an 'official' royal birthday on 15 September to comply with dynastic regulations. But, when establishing the Roman High

> Church in the fourth century, Emperor Constantine ignored both of these dates and supplemented 25 December as the new Christ's Mass Day — to coincide with the pagan Sun Festival. (24)

Jesus' birth in March would explain his heralding the Age of Pisces, and I was aware that, in 553 AD, the Second Council had removed karma and reincarnation from the writings of the Church Fathers under instruction from Emperor Justinian. To read that Emperor Constantine had ignored the birth date of Jesus now revealed yet another untruth. I wondered how many more hidden truths my Guide would reveal. I returned the lecture notes to the envelope and worked in the garden for a while, trying to absorb these latest historical facts. Hours later my Guide referred me to page 8 of *The Hidden History of Jesus and the Holy Grail*, part 3.

> The sixth-century writings of Merlin were expressly banned by the Ecumenical Council, and the original Nazarene Church of Jesus became an 'underground stream' … But why should Grail lore and the writings of Merlin have posed such a problem for the High Church? Because, within the context of their adventurous texts, they told the descendant story of the Grail bloodline – a bloodline which had been ousted from its dynastic position by the Popes and Bishops of Rome who had elected to reign supreme by way of a contrived 'apostolic succession'. This apostolic succession was said to have been handed down from the first bishop, St Peter (and, indeed, this is still the promoted view). But one only has to study the Church's own Apostolic Constitution to discover that is simply not true. Peter was never a Bishop of Rome – nor of anywhere else, for that matter! The Vatican's Constitutions record that the first Bishop of Rome was Prince Linus of Britain, the son of Caractacus the Pendragon. He was installed by St Paul in AD 58, during Peter's own lifetime. From the 1100s, the powerful Knights Templars and their cathedrals posed an enormous threat to the 'male-only' Church by bringing the heritage of Jesus and Mary Magdalene to the fore in the public domain. (24)

Who were the Knights Templars and where were their cathedrals? I wondered. I returned the lecture notes to the envelope and sealed it. Acting on instructions, I posted the envelope and contents to Keith in Balingup.

Mum's friend Rita called in to say she was returning to Holland, and we organised a lunch for her — and for Martin, who was returning to Geraldton. The lunch turned into a surprise for Mum and me when Rita asked me to look after her car while she was in Holland. After she and Martin had gone, I drove it to Dongara to have it checked and was told the radiator required urgent replacement. I left it at the garage and walked home, a little inconvenienced but thrilled to have transport again.

Later, I walked by the Base Root Chakra and found a package in the grass inside the fence; it was a third Buddha left there by Christina. Buddha featured at the head of the Sacred 13 Formation. I placed this new Buddha in the Place of No Secrets / Buddha's Four Parts of Truth, and wrapped the one in the lodge for sending to Greta. Christina rang and I asked her to update the Healing Garden diagrams; along with my photographs, these would reveal and record the changes. I was instructed to send Christina the silver Celtic cross, one of the symbols used during the transfer of the blue light from Cairo in 1997. It was for her protection as I continued to seek the truth regarding past-life heart issues, and her chakra, the throat, would soon be activated.

The local estate agent handling the sale of the property rang to inform me that Cathy had refused to sign the new contract: she was forcing me into yet another auction. The following day details arrived from her barrister concerning the Perth auctioneer. I rang the auctioneer requesting that he visit the property, as there were conditions I wanted included and I wished to discuss the auction dates with him.

Mum and I received in the post a parcel from Greta containing Easter eggs. I was to rewrap the third Buddha and enclose a note, wishing Greta 'Wisdom and Truth. April 2000' and include information regarding the Four Parts of Truth. This parcel was not to be posted to Greta until after Easter — on 28 April.

On Easter Sunday Mum and I drove to the Greenough Fair to meet with Julie and buy two Greenough golden bottlebrush plants from her stall. Later, back at Dongara, I was taken to a *Pemberton Accommodation* brochure Mum and I had been given during our tour of Manjimup and told to place it in the car. More repairs were urgently required, so after Easter I returned the car to the garage. When it was roadworthy once again I wrote to Rita in Holland concerning the mounting costs.

To my delight, a parcel arrived from England containing all the items left behind with Alan when Mum and I vacated Spark Cottage in March 1992. The next day I was sent to Geraldton to return Cathy's possessions personally. I waited outside the health shop where she worked until I was told the moment to enter. She was alone. There was a look of shock, then panic, on her face when she saw me. I handed her the package, explaining that all its contents were hers. As I walked away I turned and looked at her for a moment before saying 'Goodbye'. It felt really good to be saying this, and a sense of freedom followed.

My Guide requested me to spend a day weeding the Tuart Walk / Throat Chakra. I stood in the middle of the now-cleared pathway with the understanding that I would be activating this chakra's energy, held in the twelve trees, as I read from *Crystals for Transforming, Healing and Spiritual Growth* by Soluntra King:

> Throat … The Real Self or the superficial, imitation being. To speak and be from your Truth. The Power of the Word and Sound. Communication, words reflect our whole being and can create great imbalance if negative. This chakra can hold a lot of suppressed anger and words unsaid. (21)

I requested the release of suppressed anger and words unsaid.

The Buddha parcel, including the Four Parts of Truth, was *en route* to Greta with the note 'Wisdom and Truth. April 2000.' On the last day of April, Martin arrived with a display board for the Place of No Secrets / Buddha's Four Parts of Truth, and on 1 May he installed it, further encouraging the energy of Truth held within this area.

The plants I bought from Julie were in the tractor shed and my Guide directed that one Greenough golden bottlebrush be planted by the Negativity Beacon / Wheel of Life. Vivid memories came of my visit to the Greenough Hamlet eight years before, when I felt the anguish of its former Aboriginal prisoners. *Aboriginal link, conflict, karma clearing*, my Guide warned.

An instruction to phone Greta surprised me. I thanked her for the Easter eggs and wished her 'Happy May Day'. On 2 May the Buddha parcel arrived in Busselton.

I sensed, and then felt, masculine energy in the Egyptian Pulpit. Two days later I placed the second Greenough golden bottlebrush nearby in its pot. Greta and I spoke on the phone; within minutes a pounding headache developed. The next day she rang and left a whispered message on my answering machine, 'Get off the fast train and onto the slow one and I will still be at the platform waiting for you.' I had no idea what she meant. After planting the Greenough golden bottlebrush, I created a protective circle around it with seven massive limestone boulders. My throat vibrated with a spiralling energy trying to force itself out of my being. I was encouraged to pick several vetiver flowers from the Open Chamber and place them in the circle. As I did so, I jumped back in apprehension and fell back on the hard ground at the force of the words that came blaring from my throat. 'You are Egypt,' I *shouted* in a deep, angry, male voice.

I took deep breaths until my heart rate returned to normal and I was able to walk. I shared with Mum what had happened and she made me a pot of tea and held my hands until I stopped shaking. I asked her to go to the office, as the image of the seven boulders ran through my mind, and locate the *Dictionary of Symbols* to find the explanation for seven:

Seven … Seven is often the last step before completion. (8)

The seventh and eighth of May were spent working with Roger fencing between the Solar Plexus Chakra and Rainbow Serpent, leaving an entrance for a wide pathway to and from the Love Tree / Navel Chakra. I would require help to clear the massive double-circular shapes in Julie's design of the Solar Plexus Chakra. Her words regarding Merlin repeated: *Make him work for you.* I thought about Gardner's lecture notes, with their Merlin information, and my Merlin connections with Keith in Balingup and Norma in Bunbury.

During this time of hard work, Cathy's barrister sent a completed contract from the State Auctioneer for me to sign and return. Enclosed was a bill for thousands of dollars for advance advertising. The auctioneer completely ignored my request for him to visit the property and there had been no discussion between us regarding any advertising or the contract. I sent an urgent letter of complaint to the President of State Auctioneers with a request that the actions of this auctioneer and Cathy's barrister be investigated. I then returned the contract to the auctioneer unsigned and wrote to the barrister outlining all my actions. I was not paying for any advertising and I would only take part in a legally prepared auction. Nor would I disclose the reserve price until just before any auction. I sent the Case Registrar an update of all these events.

A note arrived from Tatia the Orange Dolphin, still living in South Africa, following my sharing with her recent events in my life. It read, 'The stronger the Light, the more people and forces want to destroy it. Congratulations on holding the Light amidst all that! Tatia.' I was guided to place her positive note on top of my copies of the letters to the President of the State Auctioneers, the barrister and the Case Registrar. *Be prepared to travel to Perth*, my Guide said.

On 17 May I awoke with a jolt to the message *Visit Busselton*. At around this time three years before, Greta had entered my life.

I was instructed to go to the Crystal Pool to clear the area of its choking growth, but only after I had re-read the past-life energy held within this area and understood what I would be releasing:

> Crystal Pool Energy: Supreme power – male passions – heart pain – conflict and loss – Egypt – heart's journey – Golden Rose Dolphin – karmic truths – page marker / Jerusalem – Egypt and priests – This is forbidden – Jude Priest – I had a dream and the dream was you – Egyptian wife – Temple.

The day of the proposed auction came and went. But the relief was short-lived when a letter arrived from Cathy's barrister threatening me with court action if I did not pay the already-spent advertising fees. I replied, saying I had not agreed to any advertising and it was therefore his client's responsibility. That evening Greta rang to ask if we could meet in Perth on 27 May. My Guide insisted I go. After meeting her there as arranged, I drove to Busselton alone and used the street directory to find her new home. She followed later with the children. I found my gift of Buddha displayed on her mantelpiece and, although the anxiety of our past-life connection kept coming and going, I was able to stay on top of it and we spent quality time together. We visited new friends of Greta's from New Zealand, one of whom was a journalist named Kaite Hanson. She asked me about the Healing Garden. Greta walked away into the kitchen while I replied.

After the children had been sent to bed, Greta and I sat by the log fire. In the light of the flames I saw her as she had been in Egypt, many centuries before: her princess profile held that regal stance. She said I glowed in the firelight and I understood we had safely found that moment in time when we had been lovers. I was sure that the clearing of the Crystal Pool area and my accepting the release of its energy had brought this about.

Next day we were having breakfast when a loud crashing sound came from the lounge room. Cindy looked across at me with a face full of panic, I jumped up to find the Buddha had been knocked from the mantelpiece, its flame-like headdress, representing the light of supreme knowledge, snapped off. A picture on the wall had knocked the Buddha to the floor. The angry past-life energy had harmed the symbol of the Place of No Secrets / Buddha's Four Parts of Truth. The picture had been hanging above the fireplace where Greta and I had sat the evening before. *This is forbidden*, the unknown male shouted.

'Who gave you the picture?' I asked.

'My ex-husband.'

On my arrival back at the centre I discovered my blue-and-yellow plant pot on the veranda by my bedroom had been smashed into tiny pieces. It had been a gift from Greta. I wrote to her about the pot and what I believed to be the means by which Buddha had been damaged. She rang to say she had tried to repair it. I spoke about the angry past-life energy and my concern for Cindy, but she dismissed it all as nonsense.

My Guide sent me to Marg's spiritual circle in Geraldton. She said she saw a huge golden door with Celtic symbols, four golden bells and a graveyard around me. 'There will be the death of a situation, an ending,' she predicted. I asked for assistance on my return to the centre and was taken to a silver necklace, a gift from Cathy, and the silver ankh from Greta. I placed both within the cupped hands of the Buddha from the Sacred 13 Formation now in the lodge hallway.

Norma rang from Bunbury to say she was still trying to access information on the Merlin Factor for me. I said I would send her more information on the Healing Garden. In my letter I mentioned the lecture notes by Sir Laurence Gardner, now with her friends in Balingup, and Gardner's book *Bloodline of the Holy Grail*.

I began to work an 'Echidna and Campsites' Aboriginal tapestry under instruction from my Guide. The design held five symbolic circular campsites: a central one and one in each corner. These were joined by pathways, and an echidna walked across the top and across the bottom. The Australian echidna is an egg-laying insectivorous mammal with a covering of spines. I was given instructions when to work, completing half the central campsite before moving to work the third. My attention was drawn to the Seven Major Chakras information highlighting a connection between this tapestry and chakras. My Guide referred me again to Soluntra King's *Crystals for Transformation, Healing and Spiritual Growth* to note one chakra in particular:

> Causal – 3-4 inches behind the crown ... The colour is Turquoise. The power of the mind to create conscious forms. The Soul force into

the Mental Body. If the mind is disciplined, trained by meditation and self mastery it becomes receptive to these subtle frequencies ... As this chakra is activated by these practices, the old concepts, programmed belief systems and linear based concepts are released. ... (21)

Campsite, power place, my Guide explained.

In June Greta sent me a card featuring the *Aboriginal Dreamtime* story of the 'Fish Spirit — Barramundi Dreaming', without an explanation. On the back was printed:

> Dreaming paths are made through the warm estuary waters by the Barramundi Spirit Ancestors. Ceremonial songs are sung by the hunter to make peace with the Fish Spirit and ensure continuation of the species.

I added the clues 'campsite', 'power place' and 'hunter' to my past-life heart issue notes.

My Guide instructed me to work the echidna and campsites Aboriginal tapestry, and when I questioned the symbolic meaning of the echidna I was referred to the book *The Dawn of Time: Australian Aboriginal Myths* by A. Roberts and C.P. Mountford:

> Echidna was a very old man ... He was too old to hunt, yet in some way he prospered. Echidna actually lived on the flesh of young men whom he killed after coaxing them to his camp on some pretext. The Aboriginal men, horrified when they found out what was happening, surrounded Echidna and wounded him so many times that his back was a bristling mass of spears, and his legs and arms were broken and distorted ... Echidna, though badly wounded, had crawled into a hollow log, where he stayed until his wounds were healed. (25)

'Spears' and 'badly wounded' were highlighted when I looked at the Aboriginal spear hanging on the wall in the office and experienced a sharp pain below my right knee. The clues 'spear' and 'badly wounded' were added to my past-life heart issue notes next to 'hunter'.

Pack a suitcase for you and Tess, my Guide said. Several days passed before I was given the confirmation that a trip was pending and would involve our visiting an Aboriginal campsite — power place. I told Mum of this development and she was excited, as was I.

Twenty-four hours later I booked accommodation in Kalbarri for two nights and on 17 June we drove out of the centre. I turned to Mum and smiled. 'It is wonderful to be travelling with you and I wonder what we're going to achieve.'

In Northampton we visited the Mary Grotto and I placed a red geranium at Mary's feet. I scooped up water from the pool in front of her statue and touched her brow chakra, then mine. After I'd requested the revealing of more truths, Mum and I walked the grounds. Later, in Kalbarri, we were guided to the spring of the Yamatji people; this was the required Aboriginal campsite and power place. The waterhole was hidden under a tree, bowed by the winds of time, near the river. The site was neglected, so I spent time repairing the damaged flimsy mesh covering the waterhole and clearing the rubbish-clogged entry to the spring. Mum sat nearby and watched.

'We live on a continent where the oldest culture has walked for more than fifty thousand years, which is beyond my comprehension,' I said. 'I feel frustration and sadness when I see their culture being eroded and neglected.'

Mum and I ate lunch at a nearby café and were drawn to a gum-leaf bookmarker in the gift shop. We both said at once, 'We must buy this for Barbara's birthday.' *Out of fragile situations come miracles*, my Guide said.

I walked beside the river early the next morning watching the jumping fish.

Plant energy with specific colours from Kalbarri were chosen by my Guide for the Healing Garden and I bought the red-flowering Sea Spray grevillea to plant within the Healing Heart Karma Formation, a pink *Thyryptomene beackeaceae* and an orange and pink *Eremophila racemosa* to plant within the Crystal Pool area. Before leaving Kalbarri I visited the spring again and spoke aloud to the ancestors of the Yamatji people: 'I ask for your blessing for the next stage of my journey regarding Cathy.'

On 23 June I found a lengthy message on my answering machine from Norma in Bunbury. She was asking why I had used the constellation of Virgo for the placement of six symbols within the garden. I had no idea what she was talking about, so I rang her. She told me she had borrowed Gardner's *Bloodline of the Holy Grail* from the library, after Keith had mentioned the lecture notes I'd sent him and receiving the diagrams of the garden from me. She asked me to look at page 331, thinking I would have the book. I told her I had only read sections of Gardner's lecture notes. She promised to send me a copy of the page along with her tracing. I was totally mystified.

I was guided to organise the files containing diagrams and information regarding the garden, with five files set to one side. My Guide instructed me to post these to Greta in Busselton, Marg and Christina in Geraldton and Keith in Balingup. The fifth file was to be posted later to Kaite, the journalist in Busselton.

The phone rang. Greta had booked accommodation in Perth for 6 July. 'Will you join me?' she asked. *You must go*, my Guide urged, aware of my reluctance.

I rang and asked Martin if he could stay at the centre and keep an eye on Mum while I was away. I was concerned for her wellbeing as she was experiencing bouts of breathlessness. I would be with Greta on 7 July, the date five years before, in 1995, when the Celestial Dolphin Centre came into being. It was also the date in the previous year when Greta received the lavender sprigs that promote healing. *Peace and truth for the Dolphins*, my Guide said.

On 3 July I received a card from Norma with her tracing attached:

Dear Judy … Glimpsing through the book a few days later, I seemed to recognise the Virgo constellation as a shape I should remember. The next day, I pulled out your notes and the white page and pattern of planting seemed to be almost identical. I will photocopy pp. 330–335 and include them here with this card and tracing. What do you think? Best Wishes. Norma F.

I looked at her photocopy of page 331 from *Bloodline of the Holy Grail*, which featured 'The Virgo Constellation and Notre Dame Cathedrals. Based on a diagram by Louis Charpentier.' She had superimposed her tracing of the Virgo constellation from this page over one of my diagrams of the garden, and I was fascinated to see that the stars of the constellation sat over the Standing Stone, Crystal Pool, Triple Enclosure, Heart Element, Tuart Walk's lower entrance down to the Base Root Chakra Entrance and beyond. The Virgo constellation did indeed dominate the Healing Garden and property.

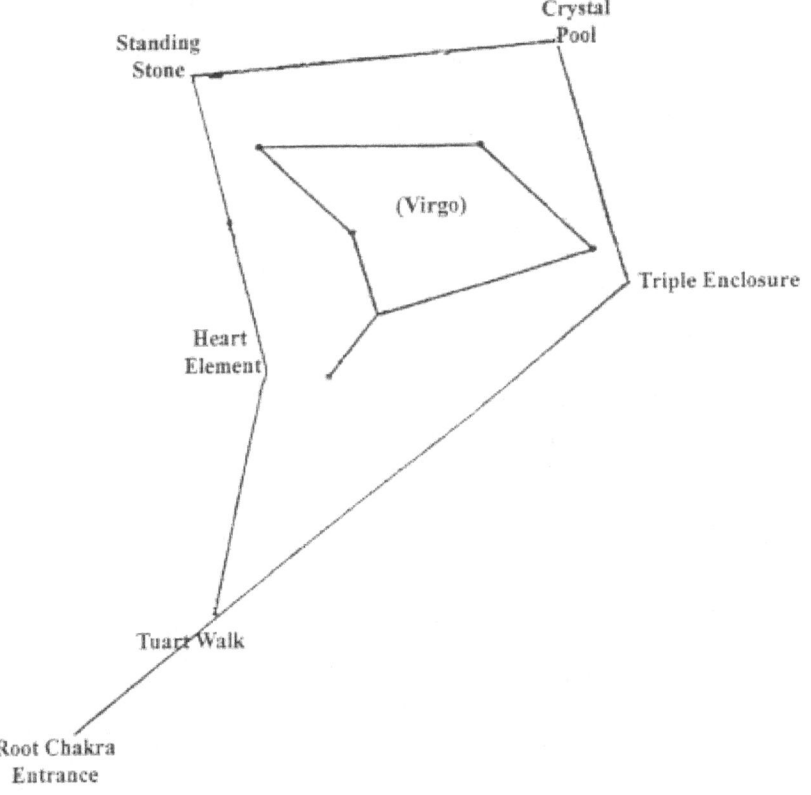

Tracing of the Virgo Constellation

My Guide encouraged me to read parts of two paragraphs on page 332:

> Then, within 25 years of the Council of Troyes, the Cistercians could boast more than 300 abbeys. But that was not the end of it, for the people of France then witnessed the most astounding result of the Templars' knowledge of the universal equation. City skylines began to change as the great *Notre Dame* cathedrals, with their majestic Gothic arches, rose from the earth ... By reference to the Tables of Testimony, the Cosmic Law and its sacred geometry were applied by the Templar masons to construct the finest holy monuments ever to grace the Christian world. (26)

In 1989 I had been directed around the world to follow in the ancient footsteps of the Cistercian monks and their monasteries, taking with me the Sacred Heart Medal acquired in Paris when Mum and I had visited Notre Dame shortly after my father's death in 1973. *French connection*, my Guide said. I was encouraged to read a line on page 332 and continue to page 333:

> In accordance with the Hermetic principle 'As above, so below', the combined ground-plan of the *Notre Dame* cathedrals replicates the Virgo constellation. Of all of these, the *Notre Dame* at Chartres is said to stand on the most sacred ground ... At Chartres the telluric earth currents are at their highest, and the site was recognized for its divine atmosphere even in Druidic times ... It was a pagan site, dedicated to the traditional Mother Goddess – a site to which pilgrims travelled long before the time of Jesus ... (26)

During February 1997 I had been sent on retreat to Kalbarri by my Guide and directed to read an article in the *National Geographic* of May 1977. This article featured the Celtic religion and highlighted the Druids (Celtic priests) and their meeting once a year in *solemn assembly* in Chartres, tribal centre of the Carnutes, in Gaul. 'Chartres' was highlighted and included as part of Soul Energy (1) now referred to as Goddess Energy. I was encouraged to read parts of another paragraph on page 334:

> On the basis of pre-Gospel writings which they found in Jerusalem, the Templars denied the Crucifixion sequence as described in the New Testament, and for that reason never depicted the scene. The 12th century window in the West front of Chartres includes a medallion of the Crucifixion, but this was transferred from elsewhere at a later date ... (26)

My mind went reeling back to my teens and Oberammergau, where the *Passion Play* is presented, and my creating a disturbance on seeing Jesus on the cross, and saying, 'This is not how it was, this is not how it is meant to be'. I was encouraged to read further:

> It was widely accepted that the Knights possessed an insight which eclipsed orthodox Christianity, an insight that permitted them the certainty that the Church had misinterpreted both the *Virgin Birth* and the *Resurrection*. They were nevertheless highly regarded as holy men, and were firmly attached to the Cistercian popes of the era. (26)

I was encouraged to read further to include page 335:

> In times to follow, however, the once revered knowledge of the Templars caused their persecution by the savage Dominicans of the 14th century Inquisition. It was at that point in the history of Christianity that the last vestige of free thinking disappeared. Neither special knowledge nor access to truths counted for anything against the hard new party line of Rome. So too did all traces of the female aspect disappear, with only Mary the mother of Jesus left to represent all womankind. In practice, her semi-divine Virgin-Madonna status was so far removed from any reality that she represented no-one. (26)

My heart began to race when I was encouraged to read more:

> But for all that, a ray of hope has prevailed through the centuries – for another female light shines from the cathedrals of *Notre Dame*. The age-old cult of Mary Magdalene ... the beautiful Magdalene window at Chartres has an inscription that reads, 'Dominated by the Water-carriers' (the Aquarians). Mary was the bearer of the Holy Grail, and she will undoubtedly become even more prominent as the great new 'Inspiration' of the Aquarian Age ... (26)

This was the answer to who would herald the New Age of Aquarius — Mary Magdalene. I was aware Mary Magdalene had been wrongly and shamefully depicted as a prostitute throughout the centuries, to undermine her in the eyes of the world. This would be a distressing past-life heart issue for her with regard to the Church of Rome.

Keith had returned Gardner's lecture notes and I was now encouraged to read *The Hidden History of Jesus and the Holy Grail*, Part 3, pages 7–8:

> But why the vengeful onset of the Inquisition? Because the Knights Templars had not only returned from the Holy Land with documents that undermined the Church's teachings, but they also established their own Cistercian churches in opposition to Rome ... They were the greatest religious monuments ever to grace the skylines of the western world: the Notre Dame cathedrals of France. Despite their present-day image, these impressive Gothic cathedrals had nothing whatever to do with the established Christian Church. They were funded and built by the Knights Templars, and they were dedicated

> to Mary Magdalene – Notre Dame, Our Lady – whom they called 'the Grail of the world' … Mary Magdalene … was being portrayed (by the world's greatest artists) wearing the red mantle of cardinal status or the black robe of a Nazarite High Priestess – and there was nothing the Church could do about it. The bishops' only option was to proclaim the practice sinful and heretical – because, in having previously elected to ignore Mary Magdalene and her heirs, she was outside their jurisdiction. (24)

Before I could take in the enormity of the presence of the Virgo constellation here within the property, I was instructed to move Mary's image to hang at the corner where the Queen bee had taken her swarm the year before, when I was working the final stitches of the Egyptian tapestry. My Guide's messages *Goddess energy* and *The goddess is alive*, had explained the queen bee's arrival and I had been sent to the Egyptian Pulpit to read aloud, 'Egyptian Sky Queen. Welcome Nut, Egyptian goddess.'

The phone rang twice, and I answered two separate calls from women in Perth both requesting urgent healing sessions with me for the following day. My mind was diverted away from the mind-blowing information from Norma regarding the presence of the Virgo constellation to thoughts of the healing sessions. My Guide insisted the clear quartz — not from the Earth plane — feature in both healings and be placed on their individual brow (third eye) chakras.

I recalled touching Mary's brow chakra at the Mary Grotto at Northampton, then mine, to encourage the revealing of more truths. My Guide referred me once more to Soluntra King's *Crystals for Transformation, Healing and Spiritual Growth*:

> Third Eye … The eye of the soul to see with Love … (21)

The first woman arrived at 10 am the next day. As she lay down on the massage/healing table she looked up at Mary's image hanging in the corner. 'I see you have Mary Magdalene here,' she said, smiling. I looked at the image as I tried to recover from the shock.

After the woman had left I sat alone in the Dolphins Healing Room. Norma revealing the presence of the Virgo constellation and my being encouraged to read Gardner's information regarding Mary Magdalene were all in preparation for me to learn the true identity of the image I had thought for years was Mother Mary.

I was directed to read my notes regarding the appearances of Mary prior to the capture of her image at Medjugorje. Several children had seen visions of a woman who they mistakenly assumed was Mother Mary in 1981, when she appeared as a young woman in golden splendour and calling herself the Queen of Peace. This was the golden light that had called to Greta three times in January, and had been rejected by her in Fremantle. I was honoured to know that the influence coming through my Guide was Mary Magdalene. I updated the goddess energy notes to include these clues:

> Goddess Energy: Yellow – The Lady of Good Counsel – gemstone – settled legal disputes – rebuilding the cathedral – Virgo – Gardner – Mary's Church – Chartres – Church of Yankalilla – a rose – Mary's signature – Medjugorje, Bosnia-Herzegovina – goddess energy – Merlin – Miraculous Medal – Lady of the Grotto – Goddess Isis / Goddess Nut – Notre Dame Cathedrals – Queen of Peace – Mary Magdalene.

I held Mary Magdalene's image and as I did so there came into my mind memories of bringing her to the centre on 18 July 1995 and placing her image by the lit Dongara candle.

Three years later, on 18 July 1998, I had been guided to place the Miraculous Medal at the base of the Dongara candle-holder and not to light the candle but instead go into the garden. When I returned, I went to light the candle, but it was missing. The next day I was guided to read part of the story of the Miraculous Medal, to learn that on the night of 18 July 1830, in Paris, Sister Catherine Laboure was approached by Mary's guardian angel, a child, who led her into the chapel, where Mary appeared. I looked at Mary Magdalene's image and understood that it was Mary Magdalene who summoned Catherine Laboure in Paris and to whom the design of the Miraculous Medal was given, and not Mother Mary as was assumed by the Church of Rome and eventually the world. *French connection*, my Guide confirmed.

At 2 pm the second woman arrived for her healing session. She quickly went into a deep meditative state, then opened her eyes with a start and smiled up at me. 'You have the Goddess Nut energy here,' she said, 'and I know her well.'

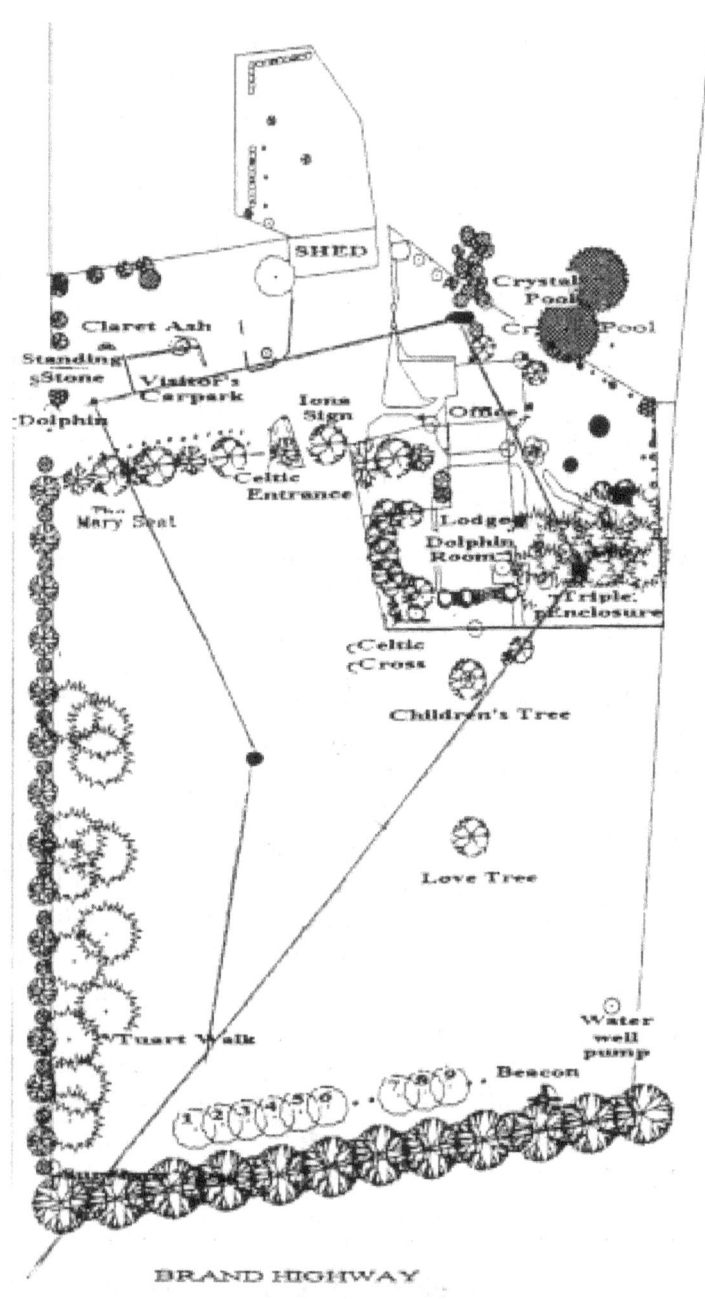

Virgo Constellation
Celestial Dolphin Centre, Dongara

On 9 July I was back in Dongara, having spent two days with Greta in Perth. The next day I was directed to stand in Chamber Three of the Heart, where I spoke out: 'I have fulfilled my promise. I was shown an old mill fifteen years ago in Middleton and told to create a place of healing. Dongara now has such a place.'

I received a phone call from Greta asking me to spend time in the South West. *You must go*, my Guide said. Due to Mum's declining health we had stopped taking in bed-and-breakfast guests and I was now registered as her carer. I arranged for her to be looked after in respite care and found it hard to leave her. I had shared my concerns with her and my reluctance to leave and it was only when my Guide assured me this was the next stage that we agreed this trip had to be taken.

Greta met me in Perth and drove us to her home. That night we argued about my commitment to the garden. I woke up the next day determined Greta's sarcasm would not get through. She drove us to a cottage in Denmark she had booked. Early the following morning we drove to the coast, where we discovered a wooden carving of two entwined dolphins. I took a photograph of our shadows as they appeared on the dolphins. *Time to be separated*, my Guide warned.

The following morning I awoke feeling peaceful, filled with the memories of my journey and how much I had learnt. I shared this with Greta at breakfast and her eyes became cold. Angry, disruptive energy emanated so intensely from her that I was only aware of her intention to hurt. The hurtful words were lost to me as I watched her angry distorted mouth. I left the cottage trying not to vomit and sat outside to recover.

'No, I do not want this,' I said. Greta did not argue, and we drove back to Perth. I was not able to absorb that I had taken a stand and Greta had not argued. Was it really over?

During the first week of August I wrote to Cathy's barrister, requesting that she sign the contract for sale now that the second auction had not taken place. I knew I had to abide by the Settlement Agreement and keep the property on the market. On 4 August Martin arrived to replace the Place of No Secrets / Buddha's Four Parts of Truth information board with another that he had designed to protect the board itself from the weather. I showed him the Virgo Constellation diagram. I was under instruction not to erect the board until 7 August, and Martin spent days preparing the base frame.

The post brought a letter from Greta detailing her arrangements for us to meet in September at her home in Busselton. There had been no communication between us since my taking a stand in Denmark. Earlier I had sent the file on the Healing Garden to her journalist friend Kaite in Busselton, and on 7 August, the day scheduled for the Buddha board to be installed, she phoned me. She wanted to make arrangements for herself and three of her friends to visit me and the Healing Garden in September. Greta wanted me away from the centre and Kaite wanted to meet me there. I was then permitted to erect the new Buddha board in the Area of No Secrets / Buddha's Four Parts of Truth. Greta rang several times while I was working on it but left no messages. By the end of the day I had a pounding headache that persisted for two days, forcing me to rest.

The post brought threats of court action and still no signed contract from Cathy. I wrote to the Case Registrar providing details of Cathy's refusal to sign a contract. Roger came, and I poured out everything to him. *Keep fighting, you must win*, my Guide insisted.

I was instructed to send details regarding the presence of the Virgo constellation within the property to Christina, before my Guide referred me to my father's *Simplified Dictionary – Encyclopaedic Edition*:

> Constellation ... a group of fixed stars, having a special name. Virgo ... the Virgin, a large constellation situated along the ecliptic and containing the bright star Spica ... the sixth sign of the zodiac.

My Guide encouraged me to clear the weed growth near the Rainbow Serpent and then to clear a pathway leading to the mass of growth inside the yet-to-be-created Solar Plexus Chakra. As I considered the work ahead, a young man arrived requesting permission to camp by the Standing Stone and work with me for a few days as a wwoofer. *We go to great lengths to find the right person for you*, my Guide said.

My right knee was painful and would lock at times, rendering me unable to move. It was of such concern that I installed an intercom between the lodge and Mum's extension so we could communicate. Mum came with me to Dongara when I bought the device so that she could post Barbara's birthday gift of the gum-leaf bookmarker. Birthdays and Christmas were the only link between Mum, her sisters and Barbara.

I had not agreed to Greta's arrangements for me to travel down to Busselton. Late one night she rang to tell me she had decided to go to

Uluru (Ayers Rock) instead of meeting with me, and her ex-husband would stay in her home to care for their children. She ended with the sarcastic comment, 'You can now look forward to the visit of your new friends from Busselton.' When she rang off, my Guide directed that I take down the framed Egyptian tapestry hanging in the hallway and retrieve Greta's Egyptian ankh from the cupped hands of Buddha and wrap them together in a parcel.

Over the next few days I felt violently ill with a headache and nausea, preventing me from leaving the lodge. The instruction came to *unwrap* the Egyptian tapestry and replace it on the wall. This was to ensure that I understood more past-life Egyptian issues were about to surface. Then I was to wear the ankh, and as soon as I placed it around my throat I felt apprehensive. I was sent outside to the Judas tree. It was in bloom — its first cluster of rose-pink pea-like flowers, bright amid their green heart-shaped leaves. When I touched the new delicate bloom, there was a sense of betrayal, followed by anger.

Greta flew out of Perth at 10.15 am on 16 September, heading for Alice Springs. At precisely the same time, Kaite and her three friends arrived at the centre. The five of us spent the day talking before they drove to their accommodation. The next day Kaite asked to interview me about the garden for publication in several newspapers. While we talked, her friend Chey found a pick and smashed the concrete base of the Crystal Pool that had been placed there by a well-meaning visitor, hoping it would fill with water. I watched in both apprehension and fascination, aware of the energy held within this area. *Egypt and male passions*, my Guide warned.

Christie walked around taking photographs while her other friend chose to clear along the Celtic Walk to the highway entrance of the Solar Plexus Chakra.

When the topic of Greta came up I struggled to explain how distressing it had been. Kaite suggested some people were vampires, in other words they stole your energy. Chey offered to take me through a Karmic Detachment Healing. My Guide insisted I allow this and I shared with her my concern regarding the triangle of Greta, her ex-husband and me. As I spoke, the ankh burned at my throat. I removed it, asking Chey to return it to Greta when they met again in Busselton.

The next day Mum said she did not feel well and her distress increased to such a level that I called an ambulance and she was taken to the Dongara Medical Centre. I left a message concerning Mum's wellbeing on Barbara's answering machine, and later there was a call from Mum's youngest sister, Pat. There was no response from Barbara. Flowers from Aunty Pat arrived and I gave them to Mum.

My Guide had urged me to ring Christina and ask her to research the Virgo constellation, and later that evening I was encouraged to study some information she had sent to me in the post:

> Virgo is the second largest constellation after Hydra. The constellation is a hard one to identify because most of its stars are fainter than third magnitude, excepting Spica, alpha Virginis. And its position is far away from the Milky Way ... The name Spica ... has the meaning 'ear of wheat' carried by the goddess ... the constellation for harvest. In antiquity, she may have been Isis, the Egyptian protectress of the living and dead and the principle mother goddess.

Isis featured within the goddess energy notes and within the Egyptian Pulpit. I was being shown that there was a link between the Heart Chakra / Pulse of Life / Goddess Nut and the Virgo Constellation / Goddess Isis. The Virgo constellation is the constellation for harvest, and this word had been highlighted by my Guide when Justin helped Roger and me to move a circular bale of hay from the Heart Chakra to the Area of Relationships in January the previous year.

Position in the healing garden, my Guide said. I studied the diagrams in Norma's photocopy of page 331 from *Bloodline of the Holy Grail*, which featured the constellation and Notre Dame. The bale of hay in the Area of Relationships was in the same position in the Virgo Constellation here as was the Notre Dame Cathedral within Gardner's Virgo Constellation. The request of 28 January 1995 regarding my 'rebuilding the cathedral' had been fulfilled by the placement of symbols that revealed the Virgo Constellation here at the centre.

This understanding had been given to me in the timing of the northern hemisphere, where the sun passes through Virgo in mid-September. It was mid-September here in the southern hemisphere. I shared all this information with Kaite before she left Dongara. Christie gave me a large diamond-shaped clear quartz for Merlin's Triangle, placing it within the triangle herself.

I shared all this with Mum in the medical centre. There had been silence from Barbara, so I spent time distracting Mum. When I returned to the centre I was able to cross through the final clues of 'Virgo', 'Gardner' and 'Mary's Church' held within Julie's past-life heart-issue notes, as all the clues held within her heart issue had now been revealed.

> Heart Issue: Julie – tapestry – 7 – garden – devas – New Zealand – coins – Dongara – Egypt/ankh – karma / past life – heart's journey – totem energy – Virgo – friends through time / soulmate – red rose energy – male passions – chakras – The Light of Iona – Gardner – Mary's Church.

I was then instructed to clear the weeds within the Brow Chakra / Triple Enclosure in the lodge garden. The last person to clear this area had been Cathy's sister Liz when she had stayed in 1995 and witnessed the Mary Display. Later, in 1996, she had given me the green-and-blue glass dolphin for my fiftieth birthday. Was there a link between her gift and this chakra area? *Yes, Indigo Dolphin,* my Guide replied. Liz is the Indigo Celestial Dolphin. I was referred again to *Crystals for Transformation, Healing and Spiritual Growth*:

> Third Eye ... The colour is Indigo ... When you have fully developed intuitive powers you are truly in command of the self. (21)

Emphasis was now being placed on the third eye and the red geraniums growing in the Triple Enclosure, taking my mind back to 17 June, when Mum and I had driven to Kalbarri to visit the spring of the Yamatji people. We had been guided to stop at the Mary Grotto in Northampton, where I placed a red geranium at Mary's feet before touching her brow chakra then mine, requesting the revealing of truths. Now I knew Mary's image was in fact Mary Magdalene and my Guide's energy source.

The twenty-first of September was Barbara's birthday. There had been no response to my message regarding Mum's health and no contact today, although Mum had sent a gift and a card. I brought Mum home five days later, collecting the post on the way. There was a package from Greta containing the ankh, a note expressing her frustration at my having returned it through Chey, and a sealed letter I did not open. I placed this letter on the jarrah table by a lit indigo-blue candle and Mary Magdalene's image.

A letter arrived requesting that Mum be admitted to Geraldton Hospital on 2 October for tests, and as we were driving there she expressed her hurt at Barbara's obvious lack of concern. *Damaging heart wound*, my Guide warned. I rang Barbara and left yet another message.

Write to Greta, my Guide said. I explained that I had not opened her letter and it would not be opened until 24 November. I wondered why my Guide had chosen the specific date of 24 November.

Early on 3 October I was looking at Greta's letter on the jarrah table when a magpie crashed into the window. The *pull* to open her letter was enormous and I had to drag myself outside to care for the bird. I felt sick inside with the surge of emotional turmoil. I brought Mum home from the hospital the following day and again felt the *pull* regarding Greta's letter. I thought of just touching the envelope but as I walked towards it there was a crashing sound in the kitchen and I rushed to investigate. Another dazed magpie hovered on the windowsill ... then fell out of sight. As I went to leave the room yet another magpie hit the window with a sickening thud. I raced outside to help both birds, but they were not there. I returned to the Dolphins Healing Room and spoke aloud: 'Okay. Okay. I will not open her letter.'

At that moment the phone rang. It was Barbara. When Mum answered on her extension I was relieved that the silence had been broken. In the post came a note from Greta: 'Strength and peace to you and Tess.' Kaite rang to tell me the centre and Healing Garden were to be featured in *The West Australian* newspaper some time in late October. *Prepare to say goodbye to Greta*, my Guide warned.

Late in the evening on 7 October, Greta rang. As soon as I heard her voice, a rush of emotion went through me. *Say goodbye*, was so overpowering I could not hear Greta's voice. The energy moved through me faster and faster and I remembered Greta's words, 'Get off the fast train and onto the slow one and I will still be at the platform waiting for you.' As I struggled with the memory of these words, my mind argued with her assurance that she would be waiting for me. Then it registered that she was telling me some inconsequential story about her ex-husband and a school function — but it was a story she'd told me before, *and this was a different version*. She was lying to me again! I had to sit down: my heart rate had increased to a disturbing level.

Only truth, no untruths, my Guide insisted, forcing me to question Greta on which version was true, which only increased her anger.

I struggled to calm us both, but the more I tried the more the energy flow increased, until I heard *Remember Ashburton*. This threw me completely, and I lost Greta's voice as I delved deep into my mind.

Memories came of sitting in the attic in the Old Saddlery with Anne, Dawn and Sue as we struggled to release the spirit child, Julie. The child kept saying she would never leave me and I had to find and speak the words that would make her go: 'I don't want you here.' The spirit child removed herself to rejoin her mother and gain spiritual freedom from the trauma of her violent death at the hands of her father. *Say goodbye*, my Guide urged. *Remember the ten days, ten roses.*

I had seen Greta shrugging her shoulders before leaving for Switzerland when I asked her about the children leaving the country, and realised she had intentionally placed me within a negative past-life triangle with herself and her husband, creating an ongoing drama. *Free yourself*, my Guide demanded. Greta was still arguing when I told her I did not believe her, and found the words to end our friendship, 'You will never humiliate me again.'

I replaced the phone and rushed to the bathroom to be sick. The phone began ringing and rang non-stop throughout the night. I sat on the floor in the Dolphins Healing Room until morning, my back pressed against the wall under Mary Magdalene's image, seeking protection. It was three years to the day since I'd received the warning *ten days, ten roses*. It was a year to the day since the large rose quartz had been sealed inside the Heart Element and my Guide said *Remember the eighth of October. It is important.* 'What about the lonely child and what about Cindy?' I asked. *Keep trusting the process and all will be revealed.*

An article titled 'Garden of Life' featured in *The West Australian* on 30 October. My photograph dominated the central page. The phone began to ring and people started to come, many travelling long distances to visit the Healing Garden or to have healings.

I was guided to the Dolphins Healing Room to stand in front of Greta's leadlight Celtic cross and to touch the central diamond of blue glass as the sun's rays poured through it. *Blue Mary Ray Diamond Centre*, my Guide said. I placed Greta's ankh with the Egyptian tapestry and sealed them in a box. Her sealed letter remained in the Dolphins Healing Room.

Kaite rang: there would be an article featuring myself and the Healing Garden in the *Acres Australia* newspaper in February 2001.

As a result of the article appearing in *The West Australian*, healing sessions were in great demand, each person making a donation towards the garden's development. These times were enlightening for me as I followed my Guide's directions regarding questions to ask. Sometimes I was given a specific date or a year and I would use crystals, Bach flower remedies and other healing tools to release emotional blockages. I placed the Four Core Colours, channelled on 2 November 1990 in Gloucester, on the jarrah table with the clear quartz — not from the Earth plane — at its centre. The person requiring help would see the blue light as it surrounded them with its vibrations.

The Dolphins Healing Room was cleaned after each session. All crystals were washed then placed in the sun or moon's rays. At times the eagle feather was used to clear auric shields to release emotions.

How can I protect the lonely child? I wondered. In response I was sent to the Dongara Library to bring home and read the series of novels *The Ramses Series*, Volumes 1–5 by Christian Jacq and other novels by the same author. This would be the first time I was allowed to read the content of any book rather than just a specific part.

I was required to read between the hours of 2 and 4 pm, and for these sessions I lit a white candle in the Double Dolphin candle-holder with dried Barossa Dream petals on its base. I was wondering if I was free of my past-life attachment with the Egyptian princess when I was instructed to drive to the tip in a hurry. There was a seagull trapped in a coil of fishing line, so I wore my thick gardening gloves to handle the bird and be protected from its sharp bill. As I released it, the words *Let nothing and no-one come between us* echoed within the cry of the bird as it took flight. The answer was *No*. I had said 'Goodbye' to Greta, but I was not free of our past-life link as lovers in Egypt.

On my return to the centre my Guide directed that the gold thread Greta had bought in New York for working the Egyptian tapestry be laid out on the jarrah table in three measured lengths, symbolic of a link. I created a gold triangle with them within the diagram of the Heart Chakra / Pulse of Life / Goddess Nut and an address card with the full names of Greta and her children in my handwriting. I put the card inside the gold triangle. I had heard the call from ancient Egypt within the cry of the seagull. Then I removed the address card from within the gold triangle and placed the *Call of the Dolphin* cassette inside it. I was going further back in time. *Courage*, my Guide said.

I posted Greta's twenty-first birthday golden key and chain back to her, and in a note wrote, 'I do not hold the key to your heart, you are free.' *She will have a change of heart*, my Guide said.

On 24 November I placed Greta's sealed letter — which had arrived in September and remained unopened — in a larger envelope, and returned it to her. I was now aware this was the date in 1997 when Greta transferred the blue light energy from Cairo. I was directed to burn Seashore incense to cleanse the Dolphins Healing Room of the negative energy of our past-life karmic attachment, which had accompanied the transfer of that energy. At 4 am the next morning 25 November the date in 1997 when I had received the blue energy from Cairo in Dongara I burned more Seashore incense.

On the first day of December I visited the Dongara Library to check my emails and found a brief message from Greta. 'I am hurt and not able to move on,' she wrote. I replied saying that she must. *In serving each other we become free*, my Guide said.

Three days later a woman called Suezi came and asked to camp near the Standing Stone and work as a wwoofer. This was the second time a willing worker had been drawn to camp by this symbol within the constellation of Virgo. She was eager to learn, and visited the tip with me to collect recycled materials, mainly single cray slats.

On 8 December I awoke to the message *The Dolphin energy must change*, and I was sent to Tatia's birthday message of March 1998: 'Look after your Heart, it is precious like rain.' I then placed her birthday card within the circle of four dolphins that had surrounded Greta's ankh on the jarrah table — the brass dolphin from Mum, the silver dolphin from Christina, the blue/green glass dolphin from Liz and the blue/green metal Indian dolphin from Dianne. Emotions of loss surfaced, followed by anger, then anguish. I sat on the Mary Seat with Jessie at my feet. Tatia's words repeated: 'Look after your Heart, it is precious like rain.'

I was encouraged to drive to the Dongara Library to find that Greta had sent another email telling me she was not coping. I was not to reply. At 2 pm I lit a white candle and watched it burn until 4 pm; I then blew it out and dismantled the golden thread triangle. I was on my way into the past alone. *Courage*, my Guide said.

Later that afternoon, while I was shopping in Dongara, the car came to a grinding halt by the garage. The engine block needed an overhaul, so I left the car there and walked home.

Eleven days later I was guided to move the dolphins surrounding Tatia's card and place one at each corner of the Seven Major Chakras Healing Garden diagram, and then place a moonstone — only truth, no untruths — on the Navel Chakra (sensual emotion and sexuality). *Absorbing this new energy*, my Guide said. I moved the Virgo Constellation diagram nearer to the Seven Major Chakras Healing Garden diagram and placed the four dolphins within the Virgo Constellation: Mum's on the Heart Element, Christina's on the Standing Stone, Dianne's on the Crystal Pool and Liz's on the Triple Enclosure.

When I collected the car I was sent for more materials. As I drove into the tip I was drawn to a large shield-shaped piece of chipboard. My instruction was to take it back to the centre and place it in the tractor shed beside the stored Star of David / Melchizedek symbol.

Before visiting Mum in her extension to celebrate Christmas breakfast, I was guided to place on the jarrah table the Christmas card I'd received from Greta beside a small silver circle divided into four sections that had been given to me by my father. A visitor had identified this as a Solar Cross — the most ancient spiritual symbol in the world. I had been sent to find this inside my father's war-medals tin. *Encouraging another cycle of events*, my Guide said.

I placed Greta's card and the Solar Cross by the Virgo Constellation diagram containing the four Celestial Dolphins; then I put inside it a photograph of Mary's Grotto at Northampton. *A partner for Greta*, my Guide predicted.

The New Year of 2001 began with three messages from my Guide. *Removal of both caveats. Concentrate on the heart. Repair the heart.* Roger intuitively arrived with materials to help me repair the Heart symbol.

My Guide sent me to the Crystal Pool to clear the weed growth and then mulch. *Work day and night until this area is finished*, she insisted. Completion was to be on Mum's birthday, 27 January. Feelings of distress and frustration began to surface as I worked. *Someone to bring you flowers*, my Guide said.

On 2 January, Cindy's sixth birthday, I lit a white candle and sent her thoughts of love and protection. I had already posted a gift and card. I was sidetracked from working in the Crystal Pool area to visit the Rainbow Serpent and repair the area with cardboard and cray slats. The word *Repair* was emphasised by my Guide.

I was confused by an instruction to send Greta slides of her input to the centre and a warning, *Keep your distance*. On my return from posting the slides I continued weeding the Crystal Pool and its surrounding area. After nine days emotions began to surface regarding Greta misleading me before leaving for Switzerland. The feelings became an overpowering eruption, forcing me to leave the Crystal Pool and walk the Healing Garden to calm down. *Male passions*, my Guide explained.

On 12 January a real estate agent and her niece arrived for the weekend. I was encouraged to honour this booking, although I was still recovering from the impact of yet another eruption. I found it difficult to talk when they arrived, but spent the evening discussing the Healing Garden concept with them.

Every time I walked into the Crystal Pool area, the issue of Greta's 'ten days, ten roses' deception surfaced. When I left the area I was able to control my emotions. It reminded me of leaving the Old Saddlery to recover from its negative energies. I soon became anxious about entering the Crystal Pool area, but I kept to the schedule.

I gave the estate agent my bedroom and her niece the guest bedroom and afforded them complete access to the lodge. I tried to sleep in Mum's extension on a camp bed, but all night I saw Greta's face at Perth airport in 1997 before she flew to Switzerland. I was being forced to see the moment she left. Over and over I visualised the scene until at last I saw it — the hidden knowing regarding the 'ten days' held within her brown eyes.

Two days later I was instructed to go to the tip, where my pendulum took me to an open book. When I picked it up I discovered it was a Bible with a reddish-brown leather cover and gold-edged pages. A red ribbon marked the open page, but I was not to read its content. I was dismayed that someone would throw away a Bible, and as I took it to the car memories came of Greta throwing aside the travel icon card of 'The Guardian Angel — Our Lady of Tenderness' and rejecting the golden light.

I escorted the estate agent on a tour of the whole property and when we returned I showed her the Bible. She wanted to open it at the marked pages but I explained it must only be read in my Guide's timing. I carried it into the office, where I made note of the numbers of the marked pages, 694 and 695, and closed it again.

The materials I was required to bring back from the tip changed to loads of paving bricks, which I piled near the Crystal Pool area. Mum and I were curious to know what the area would become. In the meantime I had written to Rita in Holland telling her about the expense incurred with her car. She replied by return telling me the car was not hers and I should contact the owner, a woman in Dongara. I did, and she decided it would be better just to transfer the registration to my name.

The purple flowers of an opal plant in the Brow Chakra / Triple Enclosure were highlighted. Purple was linked to the Egyptian princess, and again my Guide referred me to *Crystals for Transformation, Healing and Spiritual Growth* by Soluntra King:

> Opal is a crystal of the New Age – adapting to Earth changes and allowing inner balance to take place … Chakras: Soul Star, Crown, Heart and Earth Star. (21)

On 16 January I discovered an injured purple-black raven balancing on Mum's fence. I was immediately referred by my Guide to the book *Medicine Cards*:

> Raven – Magic … If you have chosen Raven, magic is in the air. Do not try to figure it out; you cannot … Something special is about to happen. (15)

The raven died hours later and I was encouraged to wrap it in a pink cotton cloth and bury it at the main entrance, using limestone boulders. *Something special is about to happen*, my Guide said, and I was guided to study the postcard featuring Our Lady of Good Counsel holding a toddler that Greta had sent me from the monastery of New Norcia on 21 January 1998. Our Lady of Good Counsel was highlighted, with the emphasis on a mother and child. I was instructed to play the cassette *In Touch* — a music tape we'd been playing during meditation sessions — and read from Gardner's lecture notes *The Hidden History of Jesus and the Holy Grail*, Part 3, pages 4–5:

> Prior to the birth of her second son in AD 44 Mary Magdalene was exiled from Judaea … She travelled (by arrangement with King Herod Agrippa II) to live at the Herodian estate near Lyon, in Gaul (which later became France). (24)

This explained the *French connection* and Mary Magdalene. I was encouraged to read further:

> Her life and work in France, especially in Provence and the Languedoc, appeared not only in works of European history but also in the Roman Church liturgy – until her story was suppressed by the Vatican ... It was in Gaul that the famous line of Jesus and Mary's immediate descendant heirs, the Fisher Kings, flourished for 300 years ... Mary Magdalene died in Provence in AD 63. In the very year, Joseph of Arimathea built the famous chapel at Glastonbury in England as a memorial to the Messianic Queen. This was the first 'above-ground' Christian church in the world, and in the following year Mary's son Jesus Justus dedicated it to his mother. Jesus the Younger had in fact been in England with Joseph before, at the age of twelve, in AD 49. It was this event which inspired William Blake's famous song, Jerusalem: 'And did those feet in ancient time walk upon England's mountains green.'(24)

Mary Magdalene and her son Jesus Justus — Jesus the Younger — were highlighted.

I was sent to the notes I had taken from the 1997 issue of *The Bulletin With Newsweek* that featured on its cover the words 'Visions of Mary, Australia's "Miracle" Town: A New Lourdes?' and told of the permanent appearance of a mother-and-toddler apparition on the wall of the Yankalilla church in South Australia — the Anglican Church's first ever heavenly apparition.

As I read my notes I held the postcard featuring our Lady of Good Counsel and a toddler, and Mary Magdalene's image taken at Medjugorje. My notes revealed that the church had been declared a Marian Shrine in 1996 and its priest was the first Anglican cleric to tour Medjugorje, where Mary had been appearing since 1981. Then it hit me. 'My God,' I said, 'it is Mary Magdalene and her son Jesus Justus on the wall in the Yankalilla church. She has chosen to appear in an Anglican church to highlight this.'

I was sent to my diary for 1994, the year Mary Magdalene and her son appeared in the Yankalilla church, to refresh my memory. The year had begun with the messages *Self help healing centre* and *New partnership* and my placing these messages on the two photographs sent to me by Liz, the Indigo Dolphin, of Mary Magdalene, taken at Medjugorje. Days later I framed Mary's image and attached the two messages to the back of the frame.

On 21 January 1994 I had been looking at Mary Magdalene's image when there appeared a half arch of flashing blue-black triangles with a yellow glow. I closed my eyes but the arch remained. I lay down in the darkness, and the arch reappeared, the flashings becoming waves as the arch moved towards me and I held my breath when it entered my right eye. My Guide explained this as *The Mary Ray* and *Divine energy*.

During February 1994, while touring with Cathy and her parents, I had been guided to drive to the monastery of New Norcia, where her mum handed me the Lady of Good Counsel Medal. On our way back to Geraldton the coach had stopped in Dongara and I was given the messages *Dongara Self help healing centre* and *Lady of Good Counsel*.

Around April–May 1994 Greta, the Golden Rose Dolphin, had conceived the child Cindy.

In May 1994 a book featuring Egypt was brought to my attention and the image of Khonsu — the Moon God with an ankh — with the Egyptian cross hanging from the horizon. The words 'Dongara', 'Egypt' and 'ankh' were highlighted. During June 1994 the words 'karma' and 'past life' were highlighted.

On 24 July 1994 Mary Magdalene and Jesus Justus had appeared in a small Anglican church near Victor Harbor, from where, in 1985, Mum, the Yellow Dolphin, and I, the Green Dolphin, had begun our journey to Dongara and the creation of the Celestial Dolphin Centre and Healing Garden.

On 7 October 1994 I had gone to Northampton, where Marg, the Violet Dolphin, was holding a meditation weekend. During a meditation, an Ancient visited me with the message that I was to follow the path I had chosen. During another meditation all the cultures of the Earth, both male and female, presented themselves to me.

At 8 am on 27 December 1994 I had channelled the Ten Year Mary Project, which spoke of my working closely with Mary, who I now knew to be Mary Magdalene.

All elements held within the goddess energy notes were now revealed, apart from 'settled legal disputes' and 'Lady of the Grotto':

Goddess Energy: Yellow – The Lady of Good Counsel – gemstone – settled legal disputes – rebuilding the cathedral – Virgo – Gardner – Mary's Church – Chartres – Church of Yankalilla – a rose – Mary's signature – Medjugorje, Bosnia–Herzegovina – goddess energy – Merlin – Miraculous Medal – Lady of the Grotto – Goddess Isis / Goddess Nut – Notre Dame Cathedrals – Queen of Peace – Mary Magdalene.

I was encouraged to make note of a part from the book *The Lady of Abu Simbel* in *The Ramses Series*, Volumes 1–5, by Christian Jacq:

> ... and the ritual tunic on which were painted blue-green wings that placed the sovereign under the protection of Isis, the female falcon, Ramses was radiant. (27)

In Egypt, Goddess Nut and Goddess Isis were mother and daughter. I updated the Crystal Pool Energy and my past-life heart issue to include the clues 'the protection of Isis' and 'mother and daughter'. Later, I trimmed the vetiver grass flowers around the Heart Chakra / Pulse of Life / Goddess Nut — Virgo Constellation / Goddess Isis and placed a few by the Barossa Dream rose. As I did so, I was given the knowing that Greta had held the Goddess Isis in high esteem during her Egyptian incarnation, but had rejected her. I was responsible, and part of her past-life heart issue was that I should make amends. The property held the Heart Chakra / Pulse of Life / Goddess Nut — Virgo Constellation / Goddess Isis in order to enable me to do so.

My Guide encouraged me to go to the Dolphins Healing Room and hold the clear quartz crystal — not from the Earth plane — and the realisation came that this was the crystal used by Greta to access the Rose Energy / Mary Magdalene for the soul group. In ancient Egypt she had rejected the goddess energy due to our having been lovers. In 1986 I had been handed the crystal by Mu in England after a healing session where I was taken within the energy of the rainbow of chakras, enabling my Guide to become part of me and allowing me direct access to the Rose Energy / Mary Magdalene for the soul group in the present day.

A tapestry 'Rainforest Frog' was drawn to my attention for me to buy and work. I was guided to record a sentence from the book *The Lady of Abu Simbel* by Christian Jacq:

> 'Observations of frogs' development had led the priests of the early dynasties to see in them the endless mutations of life; so the frog, in popular awareness, had become a symbol both of successful birth, at the end of the many stages from embryo to infant, and of eternity, which survived through time and beyond. (27)

I recorded the clue 'successful birth' in my past-life heart issue notes next to 'mother and daughter'.

Place the pavers, my Guide requested. This task was to be completed in just two days and I followed the instructions for their placement in the Crystal Pool area. That afternoon and into the night I was forced to lie down due to a headache, and all I could see were Greta's eyes filled with triumph. Next morning I continued working with the pavers, creating pathways and endings. I was guided to create an oval with forked ending; it was *familiar*, and a sense of unease came. Something was happening elsewhere with Greta, parallel with my working here.

A series of instructions from my Guide accompanied my apprehension:

At twelve noon request that you are healed of your karmic link with Greta.

I repeated the request out loud.

Request the Green Dolphin and Golden Rose Dolphin be set free.

I repeated the request out loud.

At four o'clock, light a candle and highlight the diagram of the property.

I followed this instruction, then prepared the Solar Cross to be worn.

New partner. I attached the Solar Cross to its chain. *Pass it through the flame three times.* I followed the instruction, then secured the necklace around my neck and went outside to the Brow Chakra / Triple Enclosure to turn three stones around. *Reversing the negativity*, my Guide explained.

Something was headed my way on a spiritual or personal level, or both, and I was referred by my Guide to the book *The Black Pharaoh*:

> Iunu, the city of Ra, the Divine Light; Iunu, the birthplace of Egyptian spiritual life. Iunu, where the pyramid texts had been conceived and written, texts devoted to the incessant transmutations of the royal soul in the hereafter. (28)

The words 'pyramid texts' were highlighted by my Guide.

Martin came carrying three pot plants, which he put beside the Crystal Pool. When I saw the lavender plants I recalled the message *Someone to bring you flowers*. He had brought the cuttings for Mum in advance of her birthday. He walked around the Healing Garden while I made a required trip to the tip, returning with a small metal triangle and a piece of turquoise cord. I wrapped the cord around the metal triangle and put it inside the large oval and forked symbol near the Crystal Pool.

Martin returned from his walk and pondered the Crystal Pool and its area. He indicated the pavers that I had laid in designs on the ground as instructed by my Guide. 'This is the internal floor plan of a pyramid and ankh burial chamber,' he said. He pointed out the entrance to the pyramid, the hidden chambers, the false wall and the burial chamber in the oval shape of an ankh. It was obvious after he had taken me through it, and I became emotional. He sat beside me listening as I spoke about Greta and the *ten days, ten roses* deception. He then asked me what I thought the turquoise triangle inside the oval of the Ankh Burial Chamber meant.

I was sent to my office by my Guide to review my notes for May of the previous year with regard to Power Place:

Causal – Chakra 3–4 inches behind the crown … The colour is Turquoise. The power of the mind to create conscious form. As this chakra is activated by these practices, the old concepts, programmed belief systems and linear based concepts are released.

The Crystal Pool and its surrounding area is the Causal Chakra. I returned to Martin and read aloud the information to him. He had been thinking about Greta and the 'ten-day' deception, and the fact that she had brought back an ankh for me from Cairo featuring here as an Ankh Burial Chamber. He felt the burial chamber I had been guided to create featured in a yet-to-be-discovered pyramid in Egypt. *Pyramid texts*, my Guide confirmed.

'This is the key that opened your past-life heart issue,' Martin said. 'It is your recognition of that *deception,* and deception in general, that you must look at now and change. The hurt is back in the past but you still carry the concept in your heart. Letting go will set you free.' After Martin had left I sat by the Ankh Burial Chamber and turquoise triangle. *Egypt and male passions*, my Guide warned. The triangle was positioned where a hurtful past-life attachment was stored.

A note arrived from Greta. She had posted it on 22 January, the day I had seen her brown eyes filled with triumph. The following day I had created the Ankh Burial Chamber and requested that we be healed of our karmic attachment. Her note announced that she was in a relationship and had no need of my friendship. It was written in a manner meant to hurt, and it did. This was the predicted new partner.

Then I felt relief — relief for both of us. I was instructed to take the note to the Healing Heart Karma Formation at the main entrance and read it aloud, and as I did so I was aware of a distressed energy coming from the symbol. This area linked me with Cindy. I recalled creating this symbol the previous year with her in mind and lighting a candle to her on her birthday, 2 January, putting her into the Light, and being sent into the lodge to the boxed Egyptian tapestry with Greta's ankh attached and told to post it to her. The ankh was the key — Greta's change of heart was setting us free of our past-life attachment, but the Egyptian link with Greta was to be maintained through the tapestry and the ankh in order for me to be able to protect Cindy. *Tess is to activate the Causal Chakra on her birthday*, my Guide said.

I arranged Mum's birthday table setting the evening before her birthday with her promising not to peep. She was waiting for me early on 27 January and I walked her into her kitchen/dining/sitting room and sat her in her armchair with her eyes closed. The blinds were closed, so it was only half light. On her kitchen bench I had arranged a dozen yellow balloons and a green leafy arrangement in a chrome pot, with unlit sparklers. The pot was surrounded by gifts and cards from friends, her sisters and me. On her kitchen table I'd placed a slim green candle in the centre of two glass dishes with red bougainvillea. I lit the sparklers and the candle and asked Mum to open her eyes. She glowed with the reflection of the sparklers and the candle and her eyes filled with delight. At 7 am she cut the wide yellow ribbon I had placed across the entrance to the Crystal Pool / Causal Chakra. She glanced over the area and said, 'To me it has the effect of the rays of the sun.' *Influence of the Yellow Dolphin*, my Guide responded.

I walked to the Crystal Pool / Causal Chakra and the turquoise triangle. *Male passions*, she warned.

The echidna and campsites tapestry was highlighted by my Guide. The Crystal Pool / Causal Chakra and campsites were power places within each of which was held unresolved issues of male passions. My past-life heart issue with Greta was as a lover in Egypt and it involved the birth of a child. My past-life heart issue with Cathy was as a male Aboriginal and involved a chase, conflict over land, a spear, and one of us being badly wounded.

Entwining of Souls

Let nothing and no-one come between us, the princess whispered.
I walked from the Crystal Pool / Causal Chakra and passed the Standing Stone to the Healing Heart Karma at the main entrance to sit on its Solar Stone and wait for the rising sun. As the sun's rays moved through the Heart I felt the distressed energy within Cindy.

On 30 January my Guide sent me to the tip to find materials to repair areas within the Area of Relationships. Once again there was an abandoned Bible, but this time it was plain and ordinary. Placed inside was a bookmark that read: 'For those that believe anything is possible.' I recycled the Bible by placing it on a table inside St Mary's Catholic Church in Dongara. The other Bible, with its brown leather cover and gold-edged pages, was still on a side table beside my computer. My mind went back to my visit, in early 1988, to Dawn Davie the clairvoyant and medium in England. During a reading she had mentioned seeing a Bible being placed on a desk.

As I woke the next morning I received the message *So Isaac was comforted after his mother's death*. That night I was guided to stand in Chamber Two of the Heart, where Greta had tried unsuccessfully to repair the damage caused by the strewn materials, following her visit to Switzerland in 1997 and her *ten days, ten roses* deception. I filled with intense hurt and anger at having been parted from Greta, but these emotions were from the distant past, and I found myself expressing sentiments beyond my understanding. 'It is happening again,' I shouted to the universe.

I knew I was experiencing a past-life flashback when I was compelled to fetch the Star of David / Melchizedek symbol from the tractor shed and place it in the car and drive to the tip. I left the symbol on the ground and drove away, wanting no part of it. I sat inside the Crystal Pool / Causal Chakra area on my return, distressed. My eruption was linked to this chakra, and there was urgency in me to contact Greta. An understanding came that the silver locket used to transfer energy from Cairo to Dongara in 1997 contained an oath, which had been transferred with our past-life heart issue attachment. *Let nothing and no-one come between us*, the princess whispered.

I sent Greta an urgent email suggesting she take the locket to our beach and throw it away into the depths of the ocean; I offered no explanation but trusted she would do so.

Having walked the Healing Garden most of the night, I was exhausted, angry and very hurt; the message *Adultery* repeated in my mind. These emotions increased until words burst out of me: 'This is happening again. You took her from me before.' These were my sentiments and anguish from the past. I was distressed the next day. On 3 February I was still trying to cope, not able to leave the lodge. The following day at 3.30 am, still upset, I went to the Dolphins Healing Room to light the Double Dolphin candle, play the *Call of the Dolphin* tape and wait for guidance. I was sent to the Bible that I had found at the tip on 14 January and asked to open it at the pages marked by its red ribbon:

Psalm 110
A Psalm of David ...
The Lord has sworn
And will not relent,
You are a priest forever
According to the order of
Melchizedek.

Jude Priest. You are a priest forever, my Guide said. The distress began to ease when I remembered how, when filled with hurt, I had removed the Star of David / Melchizedek symbol from the property. Was I being told Greta's and my negative reaction to this symbol, and my anguish at having parted with her before, were due to my being a priest of the order of Melchizedek? *Yes*, my Guide confirmed. 'What does this mean?' I asked. 'How can I be a priest forever?' There was no response.

The Ankh Burial Chamber held within the Crystal Pool / Causal Chakra held the secrets of our suffering and male passions from Ancient Egypt. As a priest I had been forced to part with the princess, rejecting her to remain within the priesthood. This would explain Greta's reactions in the present day to my working for and with spirit. But hidden in the Crystal Pool / Causal Chakra was the male sentiment *This is forbidden*. I felt real concern, as this meant danger for a mother and daughter. I touched the circular Solar Cross at my throat, understanding that this was the required cycle of events.

On 6 February the post brought a page Martin had copied from a web page 'The Afrocentric Experience. Ankh: The Original Cross.' I read and noted a specific section as I sat near the Pyramid / Ankh Burial Chamber:

The Ankh is defined as: *The symbolic representation of both Physical and Eternal life. It is known as the original cross, which is a powerful symbol that was first created by Africans in Ancient Egypt ... Commonly known to mean life in the language of Ancient Kemet (land of the Blacks) renamed Egypt by the Greeks ... An Ankh serves as an antenna or conduit for the divine power of life that permeates the universe ...* (38)

Greta holds the key, my Guide explained.

Greta had the silver ankh — her gift to me from Cairo — and the Egyptian tapestry in Busselton, and I had the Ankh Burial Chamber here in the Crystal Pool / Causal Chakra. I understood the ankh served as an antenna, and this would enable me to communicate on a soul level with Greta in order to seek out and resolve our past-life heart issues regarding the lonely child. My next task was to clear the pathway from the Negativity Beacon / Wheel of Life by the Base Root Chakra to the Solar Plexus Chakra (personal power).

The thought of being a priest played on my mind, and I was directed to spend time with Marg in Geraldton to relate the story of the Melchizedek saga. As I finished, her face glowed momentarily with the colour violet and I heard the message *Violet Dolphin*. I wanted to tell her she was the Violet Celestial Dolphin, but the words would not form. On my return to the centre, I was reminded that the meditation room and the Dolphins Healing Room were the Crown Chakra. I was referred once more to Soluntra King's *Crystals for Transformation, Healing and Spiritual Growth*:

Crown ... The colour is Violet. Pure Knowing, Inner Wisdom, Total Inspiration, open to Spirituality and Cosmic Truth. (21)

I was guided into the Dolphins Healing Room to Greta's leadlight Celtic cross, to touch its blue diamond centre and ask for the anger and hurt regarding the *ten days, ten roses* deception to leave Greta's heart and mine. I was set on a ten-day *Regime of purification* by my Guide, which was to commence on 11 February and which I recorded in my notes.

Day 1:
All the pathways around the lodge to be cleared. A new white candle to be lit and Greta's leadlight Celtic cross placed upside down for thirty minutes.

Day 2:
Chamber Three and the Heart Element to be cleared of weed growth. A new white candle to be lit and the Red Base Root chakra-balancing scarf and a rose quartz to be placed on the jarrah table.

Day 3:
The Brow Chakra and the Triple Enclosure to be cleared of weeds. A new white candle to be lit for thirty minutes beside the clear quartz — not from the Earth plane — placed on the jarrah table.

Day 4:
14 February, the day for lovers. All seven chakra-balancing scarves to be laid out on the jarrah table and a new white candle to be lit in the meditation room and Psalm 110 to be read aloud.

Day 5:
Work to be done with Roger within the Place of No Secrets / Buddha's Four Parts of Truth, placing nine blue tiles; 'nine — the divine number three multiplied by itself and the incorruptible number of completion and eternity.' A new white candle to be lit and the tape *Call of the Dolphin* to be played.

Day 6:
The message of 24 June 1996 regarding Egyptian times to be found and a part read aloud: 'For Judy. The mind that knows and cares. Adversities coming. Have no fear; you have learnt life's important lesson. Appearances are deceiving. Be cautious. You will need all your courage to survive the next attack. A word of warning, you are entering dangerous territory, Egyptian Times.' Then place the Black Dolphin / Diopside beside the Healing Heart Karma and the owl feather under a lit white candle beside the Egyptian times message to absorb the energy. The crystal to be placed in the ocean at a date to be revealed.

Day 7:
Roger to deliver two miniature wooden wheelbarrows for the Children's Tree. Clear this area of weeds and send love to Greta's two children.

Day 8:
At 5.30 am the Black Dolphin / Diopside to be cleansed with lavender oil, then the Place of No Secrets / Buddha's Four Parts of Truth mulched until the task is completed. The Black Dolphin / Diopside to be placed in a circle of turquoise gemstones and a new white candle lit for thirty minutes.

Day 9:
A section of *The Ramses Series*, Volumes 1–5, by Christian Jacq, *The Temple of a Million Years*, to be recorded in my notes: Two masked priests, one in the guise of a falcon, and the other an ibis, stood on either side of Ramses. They symbolised the gods Horus, protector of royalty, and Thoth, master of hieroglyphs and sacred learning. Pouring the contents of two tall vases over the prince's naked body, they cleansed him of his humanity. They remade him in the image of the gods, applying from head to toe nine different unguents that would open his energy centres and give him a perception of reality different from other men's. (29)
Day 10:
20 February — final day of purification. The Black Dolphin / Diopside, which had absorbed the negative energy of the 1996 Egyptian times warning, to be put in a large yellow envelope with a copy of the prediction highlighted on Day 6 and placed in the ocean at Busselton at 4 pm on 21 February.

At 8.30 am on the last day of purification, I discovered that the Blushing Princess plant had died and I was overwhelmed with grief. *The princess is dead*, my Guide said. *You saw her brown eyes at the moment of her death.* Greta's past-life sentiments of two years before returned to haunt me: 'So well I loved thee, as without thee love is nothing. If I might choose, I'd rather die than be one day debarred thy company.'

The Black Dolphin / Diopside had been given to me by Christina for Christmas 1998, and when I held the crystal for the first time a sadness and pain had surged around my heart accompanied by the words, *I hold you in my heart, I hold you in my arms, I hold you.* I understood these were my words to the princess when I held her at the moment of her death through suicide.

I went into Mum's extension holding my Guide's instruction. 'We have to take an important journey to Busselton,' I told her.

'Does it involve Greta?'

'Yes it does; it is to free our souls of our karmic attachment.'

'Then we must go. I will start to pack.'

Early the next day Mum and I drove south with the envelope containing the Black Dolphin / Diopside and the 1996 Egyptian times prediction. When we arrived in Busselton I walked slowly to the beach. Memories of my walks with Greta came flooding back. The sea was still, the beach empty of people. I removed the Black Dolphin / Diopside from the envelope and threw it into the sea; into my mind came the words I must speak aloud — 'I trust the princess can forgive all the hurts' — as the crystal, carrying the negative energy, vanished beneath the surface of the water. I stood alone knowing Greta was living a short distance away, but the invisible barrier of time was there, and I must not cross it. The feeling of aloneness was so acute that I found it hard to breathe. *This is your heart pain from long ago*, my Guide explained. When I recovered I sought out two butterfly shells before returning to the car and Mum. I drove to Margaret River and booked into a stone cottage for the night. I understood this visit would involve an ancient ritual to remove the remnants of vibrations of this ancient traumatic attachment. *New life for both of you*, my Guide said.

Early the following morning I was directed to walk a narrow path through the karri trees holding the photo of the Mary Grotto at Northampton. I remembered when it had been placed inside Greta's Christmas card on Christmas morning and the message *New partner* had come. I looked at the back of the picture and discovered the word 'soulmates' had been written there, but by whom I did not know. The two butterfly shells from the Busselton beach were attached to the Egyptian times warning of 1996 and I found myself standing close to a very large triangular stone slab, thinking about the word 'soulmates'. The next day I returned with the 1996 warning and the butterfly shells sealed inside an envelope. My Guide directed I walk the triangular stone slab seven times clockwise. The envelope with the butterfly shells was symbolic.

Two souls freed of the negative triangle, my Guide confirmed.

When I hid the envelope in this special place, from deep within my being words came that I was forced to speak aloud, 'To my beautiful lady, how I loved thee. This beacon dedicated to our love will forever be in the karri forest of Western Australia.' I photographed the slab, knowing Greta and I were free.

When we returned to the centre I was sent to my notes of 23 February 1999, where I had noted that Emperor Justinian had removed karma and reincarnation from the writings of the Church Fathers because he did not want the people to assume responsibility for their karmic destiny. Well, I had assumed my responsibility, and Greta and I were freed in a completed cycle of events: 23 February 1999 through to 23 February 2001.

According to Gardner's lecture notes *The Hidden History of Jesus and the Holy Grail*, 1 March was Jesus' birth date. This day revealed an unusual development in the Crystal Pool / Causal Chakra. I was sent by my Guide to sit there for a while as the sun rose, and then to the Brand Highway fence line. By the edge of the highway was a white shape — a dead barn owl. I found no sign of injury as I picked it up. I was directed back to the Crystal Pool / Causal Chakra and, as I sat holding this magnificent bird, I filled with apprehension. *Deception and wisdom*, my Guide warned. I assumed, for some unknown reason, that this barn owl was a male.

My Egyptian past-life male passions as a lover had been resolved, but there was *another* whose passions as a husband or father had yet to be identified. A plant had died overnight beside the entrance to the Ankh Burial Chamber. *Male passions*, my Guide said.

As I held the owl, I thought about this message. It was to be buried where the plant had died. A feather came away as I buried it. I placed it on the jarrah table with the Healing Heart Karma and the owl feather from the Iona cross. I became aware of faint, softly spoken words and waited until they were repeated. *This owl sacrificed itself to protect us forever*, the princess whispered.

I was then guided to weed the Negativity Beacon and the Solar Plexus Chakra. *This is your wisdom chakra*, my Guide said. *There will be a gathering of shamans*. A visitor to the garden had told me that shamans view illnesses as a kind of soul loss, which results in a depletion of energy. In order to remedy this, they often go on a journey into the hidden worlds in order to retrieve lost parts of their clients' souls.

Important journey for you and Tess, my Guide insisted. Mum and I drove north early on 7 March to be in Kalbarri to celebrate my fifty-fifth birthday. Years ago, prompted by a dream, a visitor to the garden had handed me two coins and now I must hand them on. We stopped at the Northampton Mary Grotto. *Place the coins at Mary's feet*, my Guide insisted. I made a request to Mary for the financial investment to save what I now knew to be the Ten Year Mary Magdalene Project 1994 and the sum of *$25,000* came to mind as I placed the coins.

On my birthday morning, Mum sang the birthday song as we sat at the breakfast table, which was decorated with silver hearts and stars. She handed me her gift: a ball of red jasper on a jarrah stand. Her card explained that jasper was the Mother of all Stones, bringing about the Love of all Mankind. I kissed her cheek and my heart filled with love for her.

Before we drove home I sought out two more butterfly shells. *Two more souls to be set free*, my Guide explained.

Barbara had sent me as a birthday gift a book titled *The Seat of the Soul: An Inspiring Vision of Humanity's Spiritual Destiny* by Gary Zukav. We had not heard from her since October the previous year, after my messages expressing concern regarding Mum's health. I put the book to one side without opening it, as directed by my Guide.

'Barbara's soul continues to appeal to you for help,' Mum said.

'The title of the book would seem to confirm that. But her incarnated personality seeks only to make me an outcast.' *Her soul and the universe want to be free of this need*, my Guide replied. I passed this on to Mum.

It had been ten days since I found the dead owl and, as I drove out of the main entrance and down to the Brand Highway, I looked to my left and saw to my dismay another white shape on the grass in the same place. *Ten days, ten roses*, my Guide said. I stopped the car, got out and walked to the white shape. It was another barn owl but lighter in weight, and I understood she was the female of the pair. I carried her to the Crystal Pool / Causal Chakra and sat on the bench holding her gently. The male — the priest — was buried at the entrance to the Ankh Burial Chamber. The female — the princess — was to be buried to the north of Greta's Barossa Dream rose.

Her suicide was the result of your ten-day affair, my Guide said. *Owl is befriending you, enabling you to see the truth.*

At the end of March, Roger and I were guided to create the Navel Chakra in the garden — Tatia the Orange Dolphin's chakra (life-producing energy, vitality and sexual energy). According to Julie's diagram the entrance was at the Love Tree. A lot of work lay ahead for us to create the outer edging near the Area of Relationships and the area around the Children's Tree.

With the creation of the Navel Chakra there began a new kind of communication with my Guide based on the Runes, beginning on 24 March when I was taken to brief references to them left behind by a visitor. The Seven Healing Triangles within the property held runic energy, and I was referred by my Guide to the Rune Nauthiz:

Nauthiz – Constraint. This is a difficult Rune: it puts you on notice that there will be holdups, reasons to reconsider your plans carefully.

I had written to Cathy asking her to visit, in an effort to resolve our differences, but the envelope came back marked 'Return to Sender'. It had been opened and then carefully resealed in an attempt to convince me she had not read it. During this time the sharp shooting pain below my right knee had returned and begun to linger.

With the arrival of April I was no nearer to understanding the energy within the Healing Heart Karma Formation and was referred by my Guide to a section of Barbara's birthday gift, *The Seat of the Soul* by Gary Zukav:

It can recognize, for example, a warm heart beneath a harsh and angry manner, and a cold heart beneath polished and pleasing words. (30)

Upon reading this I was sent outside to walk to the Barossa Dream rose and discovered an animal had tried to dig up the female barn owl — the princess. She was to be reburied at the base of the Egyptian Pulpit at the eastern end of the Heart Chakra / Pulse of Life / Goddess Nut. I was reminded the princess had chosen death by suicide, and then referred by my Guide once more to the book *Medicine Cards*:

Owl – deception … *Night Eagle* … Traditionally, Owl sits in the East, the place of illumination … If Owl is your personal medicine, no one can deceive you about what they are doing, no matter how hard they try to disguise or hide it from you. (15).

The symbol of the princess (female owl) was buried in the east, and the knowing came that the princess's death by suicide was part of the frightened energy in the Healing Heart Karma Formation along with something else I was not able to identify.

The next day I was guided to dig up the dead Indian siris tree planted by Greta and then directed by my Guide to the reference regarding the Rune Dagaz:

Dagaz – Breakthrough. Marking a major shift or breakthrough in the process of self-change, a complete transformation in attitude – a 180-degree turn.

I had dug up the tree without anger towards Greta regarding her many untruths.

Eight days later, when my right leg was not too painful, I was encouraged to use cray slats to create a formation around the Barossa Dream rose. When I had finished the task, I took a photograph and soon recognised the formation as being a Celtic Quadrant Knot. When the sun's rays shone on the formation, my Guide directed me to the reference regarding the Rune Sowelu:

> Sowelu – Wholeness. The sun's Energy Sowelu marks a time for recharging and regeneration right down to the cellular level. You may experience power surges, for the energy involved can be dramatic.

I returned to the Barossa Dream rose holding a prayer taken from the reference regarding the Rune that embodied the Spirit of Sowelu and addressed the sun by reading the prayer aloud. 'You, who hold the source of all power, whose rays illuminate the whole world, illuminate also my heart so that it too can do your work.'

In silent prayer I requested the emergence of the frightened energy of the nervous, lonely child from Ancient Egypt.

On Good Friday morning I was woken with a start. *Jerusalem, Salem, Capital of Melchizedek*, my Guide said. In 1997 Greta had sent me a gold page-marker from Jerusalem and in February 2001, a few months before this, I had been directed to read Psalm 110 through a red-ribbon page-marker in the Bible I found at the tip. This Psalm identified me as a priest forever, according to the order of Melchizedek.

A wwoofer named David arrived after Easter. He worked hard moving the heavy boulders from outside around the forty-nine trees to the Negativity Beacon / Wheel of Life area. Full of life and eager to learn, he insisted I tell him my story before he left.

I was taken aback when instructions came to drive to Pemberton a few weeks later, on 9 June. I rang the Pemberton Tourist Bureau to enquire about camping in the forest. *Andy*, my Guide said. *Something special is about to happen.* The staff at the bureau mentioned a man called Andy, and I rang him to discuss an itinerary. Then I drove to Geraldton to buy walking boots, socks, a raincoat, hat, scarf and gloves. Mum was happy to stay at the Dongara Medical Centre in their respite accommodation during my absence.

May began with a demanding phone message left on my answering machine by Cathy's barrister, threatening court action if I did not pay the $20,000. I wrote a letter in reply, keeping a copy for the Case Registrar. *Adversity*, my Guide warned. I was sure that the threatening attitude of Cathy's barrister had been provoked by my writing directly to her.

Committed to creating a place of healing, my Guide said. I would honour my ten-year commitment regardless of Cathy and her barrister. *The key words are pyramid and knowing*, my Guide confirmed.

On 3 May Mum held her visualisation evening, as it was Mary May Day at the centre. I was exhausted from talking to visitors all day, and spent the evening sitting in her extension while she was with her group inside the lodge. Afterwards Mum and I spoke for only a few minutes before she retired. Early the next morning she buzzed me on our intercom system so I went to check if she was all right. She told me she had just woken from a lovely dream. She was in Egypt, she said, in a sumptuous place with a high-born Egyptian lady — very beautiful. She was being treated as an honoured guest, spoiled and pandered to by this lady. She was enjoying every minute, and was surprised when she woke up to find it was a dream and not reality.

'You met the Egyptian princess; that's wonderful,' I said. 'I first met her in a dream years ago when we were living in Gloucester. This means you were there also during that incarnation. I wonder what role you played: you were in great favour.'

'Does this mean we will find the lonely child?' she asked.

'It would certainly indicate that we are making progress.'

At the end of May I arranged for Julie to supply another Indian siris tree.

During the first week of June a woman named Catherine Keogh rang asking to be a wwoofer for a few weeks in July. She was a Dunsborough artist, and she would park her campervan in the tractor shed and live there while working in the Healing Garden. In the meantime I was being sent south to Pemberton to meet Andy, and on 9 June, as instructed, I drove there. An itinerary for our adventure had been sent to me and I was excited about camping in the forest. He had arranged for me to stay at a B&B on my arrival and leave early the next morning. He set up two tents and proved he was an excellent cook. We ate and sat talking by the firelight until late; to be camping in the middle of nowhere held appeal.

Next day we were up early to walk in the karri forest, visiting Giblet Block, where groups of activists had made a stand to stop the logging of old-growth forests in the area. We walked the artistic circular pathway where these young people had created all sorts of natural sculptures while camped in the area until someone listened. There were a few prayer flags still there bearing symbols of the conflict and demonstration. I selected three to take back to the Healing Garden. I was seeing the forest through Andy's eyes, and it was the most relaxed I had felt in many years. Three days later he and I walked the 'Heartbreak Trail', where I was guided to bury under a triangle of stones the feather that I had been instructed to take with me from the male owl buried in the Crystal Pool / Causal Chakra. By doing this I was freeing myself of the trauma of having been part of a negative love triangle in Ancient Egypt.

After this we walked the Yeagarup Dunes, which were taking over a part of the forest. That night we exchanged ghost stories and I laughed so much I cried.

Early the following day we walked through a pristine jarrah forest. I had asked to do this because it was important to know there did exist areas that had not been logged. Before falling asleep I thought about the Butterfly Circle in its jarrah frame waiting in Dongara and the end of the predicted cycle of events between Barbara and Mum.

Back in Dongara my Guide instructed that Liz's green/blue glass dolphin on the Virgo Constellation diagram was to have a rose quartz placed under its heart area. She then referred me to Barbara's birthday gift, Zukav's *The Seat of the Soul*:

> Intuition – All the energy of the soul does not incarnate. To incarnate, the soul creates a personality from those parts of itself that it wants to heal in the physical environment, and from those parts that it lends to the process of healing in that lifetime. (30)

Greta had sought to heal her hurt and angry Egyptian princess personality, as I had sought to heal my grief-ridden priest personality. An Egyptian child personality was seeking help and healing. Julie and I were healed of our past-life forced separation. Cathy and I were seeking to resolve an Aboriginal past-life conflict over possession of land. Barbara was living her seventh attempt to resolve a past-life personality, which, in six previous lives, had rejected me as a sibling to control the family inheritance. Mum and I were seeking to reveal the truth in order for Barbara's soul to be turned to the Light. Barbara and her gift of the book regarding Buddhist wisdom contributed to my understanding of the Four Parts of Truth; now her gift *The Seat of the Soul* was ensuring that I would understand the soul.

On 23 June I was woken at sunrise and sent to the tractor shed to a pane of glass with a broken corner. I smashed the glass with my boot and took the pieces to the tip. I remembered the pane of glass in the Bunbury train when Greta and I had touched either side of the window. The invisible barrier was now smashed. *There are now no barriers*, my Guide said.

The massive boulders the wwoofer David had brought in from outside the property were in a pile beside the Negativity Beacon / Wheel of Life. They would be used to create an entrance from the yet-to-be-developed Solar Plexus Chakra to the Negativity Beacon / Wheel of Life. Roger volunteered to complete this enormous task.

At sunrise the next day I visited the Ankh Burial Chamber. The original mulch I had used contained seeds and weed growth, and the area needed to be cleared. I weeded and mulched again; then I enlarged the burial chamber. I was instructed to return indoors and play the *Call of the Dolphin* tape and read from the book *Sacred Path Cards* by Jamie Sams:

> Fire Medicine – Passion ... Any old fears of intimacy or commitment can act as limitations to relationships. If this applies to you, clear the fear. As the fear leaves, so will the coldness of past hurts, and you will be ready for more rewarding future relationships. (14)

Deep-rooted past-life emotions of loss, hurt and grief began to surface. *You are a priest forever*, my Guide warned. I understood that by working in this chakra past knowledge would surface. *The key words are pyramid and knowing*. This was followed by three days of work in the Heart Chakra / Pulse of Life / Goddess Nut. *You have always been mine*, the princess whispered. *This is forbidden*, the unknown male responded angrily.

Working in the Causal and Heart Chakra areas had been hard, and my right leg ached from the effort, but there was urgency in me and within the energy of the property, so much so that I was compelled to work regardless of the physical toll it was taking.

After a brief rest I was encouraged by my Guide to visit the Barossa Dream rose, where I discovered three buds. I placed these under a newly positioned blue rectangular ceramic plate inside the Ankh Burial Chamber / Causal Chakra. I moved the turquoise triangle from the oval of the ankh to allow for the blue plate and the three rosebuds. I understood these rosebuds symbolically represented Greta and her two children.

During the last night of June my Guide explained that the blue plate was a vibrational dial, and I moved it so that it pointed north–south rather than east–west, ensuring a change of direction for Greta and her children. *Passports and go,* my Guide said. Greta and her children were destined to live overseas for a while and this would ensure their safe return.

Catherine Keogh, the artist from Dunsborough, drove in on 3 July. We were up early the next day because she had been drawn to the Heart Chakra / Pulse of Life / Goddess Nut and wished to work within this area. I was talking to visitors in the lodge when Mum came in to tell me two women from Victoria had arrived. They had flown to Perth and driven to the centre, having been told about me by Justin. One of them had come for a healing, as she was bothered by a mysterious injury to her foot. During the healing sessions I used the eagle feather to remove karmic attachments, restoring mobility to her foot. In the meantime Catherine cleared Heart Chamber One of weed growth.

Mum received phone calls from Aunty Pat to inform her that Aunty Audrey, who was now living in a nursing home, was not eating. The staff said she had turned her face to the wall, which meant she had no will to live. It was a distressing time for Mum. She spoke to me of life with her eldest sister when they were young and how they were always together. I felt a moment of anger and frustration toward Barbara and Anne for creating the conflict that had divided the once-united sisters.

On 7 July I was instructed to paint with Green of Amazonite the shield-shaped piece of chipboard that I'd been guided to retrieve from the tip the previous December. This was the date the Celestial Dolphin Centre had come into being in 1995.

I understood Catherine was here to paint a single rose on this shield. *Mary Magdalene's signature,* my Guide confirmed.

The next day, prior to painting, Catherine drew a rose with seven leaves on the shield. The following morning I was guided to leave a leaflet on essential oils on the kitchen table, where Catherine was working. She chose 'Rose Otto — Queen of Flowers' for her inspiration, and drew a rose with forty-nine petals. My Guide asked for the rose to be painted in varying shades of blue to symbolise the Blue Mary Ray. Catherine needed five specific colours to complete the blue rose and its green leaves. At the Dongara Craft Shop they had in stock only these five colours in oil paint.

Algiz, top right corner, my Guide insisted. I drew in black paint the Algiz symbol at the top right-hand corner *Yellow glow*, my Guide requested, so I surrounded the black symbol with bright yellow paint. I was then directed to the reference regarding the Rune Algiz:

> Algiz – Protection – a mirror for the Spiritual Warrior. Remain mindful that timely action and correct conduct are the only true protection.

Catherine painted over my drawing, surrounding the Algiz symbol with a glowing, yellow auric effect.

On 10 July Aunty Audrey passed over to spirit. I sat with Mum after she received the news and we took comfort in the knowledge that she would now know the truth of what had happened. Mum decided to create a ring of fresh flowers and put it in the ocean at Port Denison on the day of the funeral.

On returning from shopping in Dongara I saw, walking by the lodge, a familiar woman carrying a child. It was Terri, the meditation group leader, and the *shark amongst the dolphins*. We walked to the Mary Seat to talk. She wanted to 'bring closure', explaining that, at the time of the upheaval in 1997 with regard to Hanna, she thought I had lost the plot. I felt this in no way justified her actions but remained silent, accepting that she was here to help herself, and I held no feelings of anger towards her. We walked into the Crystal Pool / Causal Chakra, where I explained a little of what was happening, finding it interesting that Terri had observed the beginnings of the creation of the Blue Rose Shield. After she left I found the jarrah Mary Seat had collapsed! It had absorbed the negativity of that time. I did not share the issues surrounding the *shark amongst the dolphins* with Catherine, and she did not ask why a jarrah bench seat had mysteriously collapsed.

The Dongara Library rang to tell me the book *Mary's Message to the World* was waiting for me. I had been directed to order it when Catherine arrived. I collected the book, but was only to look at the cover and make a note of the title. Rays of light were featured and my Guide sent me to the Barossa Dream rose. I understood that four rays made from cray slats had to be attached to its Celtic Quadrant Knot, and I completed the task.

Later, Mum studied the Barossa Dream rose with its four rays. 'Your book *Entwining of Souls* will be Mary Magdalene's message to the world,' she said. 'It's the new understanding you bring to Earth in partnership with your Guide.'

I was standing by the collapsed Mary Seat, wondering how I could raise the funds for a new bench, when a woman walked into the Healing Garden. She had driven up from Perth with her husband and child, and both adults wanted a healing the next day. I was up early to prepare the Dolphins Healing Room for my two visitors. Catherine was busy painting the Blue Rose Shield and I noticed she had brought a Barossa Dream rose from the Healing Garden and placed it on a shelf in the kitchen.

Following their healings, my visitors asked if they could weed the Mary Area. Catherine took a break from painting the shield and came outside to finish clearing yet another heart chamber of weeds. There was a surge of energy in the garden as everyone worked in harmony. As the couple left they handed me $120; my Guide told me to place it in an envelope.

During the night of 13 July I was woken and sent out to the pantry, where I kept an empty wine bottle with a 'Rose' label. I placed the bottle on the table with a white candle inside its neck and lit it before taking it into the Dolphins Healing Room, where I placed the Barossa Dream rose Catherine had picked beside it. *Celebrating the Mary Magdalene Project*, my Guide explained. I watched the candle's flame with a feeling of excitement.

The next day I was told by my Guide that the Navel Chakra / Love Tree and the yet-to-be-developed Solar Plexus Chakra must be linked, and I studied Julie's diagram of the garden, observing that she had mapped out a pathway not yet created. *You must create one now*, my Guide insisted.

On 15 July Catherine finished painting the Blue Rose Shield, then dated it 7.7.01 — the date when the message *Mary Magdalene's signature* had come from my Guide.

The date 7 July and Greta's address card were highlighted. *Integrity, a child*, my Guide said. *July seven, three years ago*. I was referred to my

1999 diary, where I read that the sprigs of lavender from Mum's garden had arrived at Greta's home in Busselton on that date. I had been directed to move the Buddha statue that stood at the head of the Sacred 13 Formation in Mum's garden to the lodge and replace it with the Buddha from the Place of No Secrets / Buddha's Four Parts of Truth with many sprigs of lavender placed at his feet. The message *Revealing of truths for the Dolphins* had featured. It was six years since the centre had come into being, and I had been encouraged to seek the truth regarding a past-life heart issue with Greta. But there was an unresolved issue surfacing, one that involved integrity and a child.

Tomorrow work in the Area of Relationships, my Guide requested. Catherine and I worked all morning clearing this area of weeds until I was sent to the newsagency in Dongara and used my pendulum to select and buy the first edition of a magazine, *The Glory of Ancient Egypt.* My Guide insisted that I place it on the left side of the photograph of Mary's Grotto at Northampton and surround it with dead petals from the Barossa Dream rose that had fallen overnight onto the jarrah table; highlighting Mary's Grotto and Rose Energy.

On 17 July Catherine varnished the Blue Rose Protective Shield before leaving to travel further north, and I realised she had been working on the shield for ten days. *Make note of the time and dates,* my Guide said.

On 18 July the *Call of the Dolphin* tape was playing as I carried the Blue Rose Protective Shield out into the Healing Garden. I held it up to the universe and shouted, 'I have done it.' I secured the shield at the main entrance above the Healing Heart Karma Formation, replacing the White Dolphin. Six years before, on 18 July 1995, Mary Magdalene's image had been brought to the Celestial Dolphin Centre, the same date that she had appeared in Paris in 1830: 18 July.

The Ten Year Mary Magdalene Project 1994 was on schedule.

The Blue Rose Protective Shield

Conflict, my Guide warned.

I washed the three prayer flags, symbols of conflict collected during my stay in the forest near Pemberton. They were very fragile, but I managed not to damage them and placed them between Julie's oak and Greta's Barossa Dream rose.

On 25 July I walked to where the 'Iona Lodge' sign had been placed by the Celtic Seven and received instructions to create a massive Star of Melchizedek symbol on the ground. This symbol would eventually dominate this area of the Healing Garden. *You are a priest of Melchizedek*, my Guide said.

I placed a large map of ancient Egypt taken from the magazine *The Glory of Ancient Egypt* on the jarrah table. *Living wisdom of Ancient Egypt*, my Guide said.

On my birthday in March 1996 I had been given a blue crystal ball on a three-pronged brass stand by Terri, the former meditation group leader, and had been guided to put it to one side. Six dolphins featured on its surface. My Guide now instructed me to put it in the meditation room with the Miraculous Medal. As I placed it there, Terry the carpenter drove in with materials for a new Mary Seat that would cost $140. Mum handed me the donation money from her visualisation evening to add to the $120 given to me by the couple following their healings. Exactly $140. A new Mary Seat had been created and the *shark amongst the dolphins* situation had been resolved, freeing me to use Terri's gift of the blue dolphins globe.

A journey ahead; use a coach ticket, my Guide said.

I received a letter from Cathy's barrister informing me he was going to enforce a court order regarding the Agreement. I faxed a copy to the Supreme Court, explaining that I had not been given the stipulated prior warning. I continued creating the Star of Melchizedek symbol, using materials brought by Roger, while I shared with him the latest legal news about Cathy. We covered this area with large carpets to stop weed growth before putting the cray slats in place. I understood that the energising of this symbol would encourage the revealing of the message *Integrity, a child*.

A woman arrived from Perth and asked to visit the Crystal Pool / Causal Chakra area, where she produced a tiger's eye gemstone and asked permission to leave it in the pool itself. I agreed and she left. My Guide referred me to Soluntra King's *Crystals for Transformation, Healing and Spiritual Growth*:

> Tigers Eye – Enhances our connection with our personal power and will. It helps to gain insight into our faults, and to perceive and think clearly ... Chakras: Causal, Third Eye and Throat. Astrologically: Taurus and Libra. (21)

'Whoever she was, she must be part of our soul group, to have driven all that way just to place a crystal in the Crystal Pool.'

'The right crystal for you at this time,' Mum replied.

The Crystal Pool / Causal Chakra linked me to past-life male passions regarding Cathy and Greta; now it held a new common factor — the tiger's eye and astrology: Cathy (Taurus) and Greta (Libra). My personal power and will were being encouraged to deal with both women. I was sent to a folder where I found a letter Cathy had written to me in 1994. She had tried to explain her reactive behaviour then and her battle with me as the means by which to bring her childhood apprehensions to the surface. This did not mean, however, that I was to allow her reactive behaviour to hurt Mum and me. The post brought a reply from the Supreme Court requesting I submit a statement putting my case. The situation with Cathy was coming to its conclusion. 'Cathy, then Greta and the child, and eventually Barbara,' I said.

Following this expressed intention, I was guided to go to the Tuart Walk / Throat Chakra with the poem *A Reason for Living* by G. Benton-Smith, which Mum had recently recorded in her notes and which I felt compelled to read aloud:

> I stood alone within the trees; alone I thought
> with all the world but rushing by, so lonely was I.
> Who in the world could know my Heart
> its aches, its hurts and striving to Thee?
> How lonely I was in Thee.
> But I stood there in the glade
> a peace unknown went whispering by;
> it looked at me a-standing there
> and saw the Heart in need of Thee, and stayed a while.

The ache of separation flooded my being. *A reason for living*, my Guide explained.

Walking the Tuart Walk / Throat Chakra, I wondered for whom it was that these sentiments held meaning and was taken aback when directed to send a copy to Greta. Then I remembered she had chosen death by suicide in Ancient Egypt.

On 4 August I awoke feeling emotional and walked to the new Indian siris tree in the Open Chamber. I could feel the thread linking me with Greta and the lonely child. It was 6.30 am and I waited for instructions until guided to walk around the tree seven times anticlockwise. I walked to the Star of Melchizedek and stood at its centre to say the Celtic Prayer 'I ask only what you want of me …' As I left, I realised that the Melchizedek symbol had provided somewhere for me to retreat. *Retreat*, my Guide confirmed. I had retreated to within the priesthood in Egypt and abandoned Greta.

Six days later a note arrived from Cindy saying she was missing me and enclosing a drawing of herself. She was flying to Switzerland with her mother, she said. This was Greta's response to my sending her the sentiments spoken in the Throat Chakra, and it confirmed the assurance I had been given in June when I moved the vibrational dial, and the words *Passports and go* predicted this trip and their safe return to Australia.

French connection, my Guide said. I was sitting in the Dolphins Healing Room looking at the photograph of Mary's Grotto at Northampton and holding notes written by Mum (source unknown) when I was encouraged to read a part describing the 'Miracle of Lourdes' in France:

> 11th February 1858, Bernadette Soubirous 14 years, a one-time shepherdess, had gone to the outskirts of the township of Lourdes … She was about to cross the mill canal near a Grotto, when she heard a distant murmur. She thought it to be a gust of wind. Later she would recall the moment as — 'I lost all power of speech and thought when, turning my head to the Grotto, I saw in an opening of the rock a 'rosebush', one only, moving as if it were in the wind. Almost at the same time there came out of the interior of the Grotto a golden coloured cloud. Soon after a Lady, young and beautiful, exceedingly beautiful, the like of whom I have never seen, came out, and placed herself at the entrance of the opening above the rosebush. The barefoot young Lady, draped in a white robe and a blue sash,

white veil, yellow rose on each foot, was carrying a rosary with white beads on a gold chain.' When Bernadette tried to make the sign of the cross she found her arm was paralysed. Instead the 'vaporous' Lady made the sign of the cross, and instantly Bernadette's stricken arm was well and mobile. Bernadette, who had been saying her rosary, was still on her knees when her sister and friend came back. She told them of her vision. They mocked her and called her an imbecile. Bernadette's sister reported the adventure to their mother who forbade Bernadette to return to the Grotto of Massabielle. But no restrictions could keep this fourteen year old from the Grotto. Nor could any imposition of secrecy keep word of the vision from the townsfolk. Soon they began to follow Bernadette to the Grotto. In that period the Lady in white appeared before Bernadette eighteen times, but did not speak to her until the third visit. In subsequent visits the Lady ordered Bernadette to drink from a fountain and bathe in it. Guided by the apparition, Bernadette dug a hole in the ground and finally water appeared. Then she later discovered a spring that gushed from the back of the Grotto. Three weeks later the Lady revealed her identity; 'I am the Immaculate Conception.' Shortly afterwards seven seriously ill persons praying at the Grotto enjoyed miracle ...

I was then taken to my notes of 11 August 1998, where I read: 'I was to wear the Miraculous Medal then I was held. When released I read about the Miraculous Medal. Bernadette at Lourdes was wearing the medal when she saw the Lady of the Grotto and said that Mary appeared as featured on the medal. The goddess energy notes were updated to include the clues Miraculous Medal and the Lady of the Grotto.' I stopped reading and looked at the photograph of the Northampton Mary Grotto and then at Mary Magdalene's image. Mary Magdalene had spent several hours with Sister Catherine Laboure in Paris 18 July 1830, and months later she gave her the design for the Miraculous Medal. Years later, at Lourdes, Bernadette Soubirous confirmed that the Lady who featured on the Miraculous Medal she was wearing was the Lady who appeared to her. The Lady of the Grotto and Mary Magdalene are one and the same. The Lady of the Grotto element here within the goddess energy was revealed.

French connection, my Guide said, and I recalled *The Bulletin With Newsweek*'s headline 'Visions of Mary. Australia's "Miracle" Town: A New Lourdes?' It was more accurate than the editor could ever have imagined. When is the world going to realise the apparition at Yankalilla in South Australia is Mary Magdalene and Jesus Justus? I wondered.

In response I was guided to remove the Miraculous Medal from the blue dolphins globe and take it to the Dolphins Healing Room and to the Virgo Constellation diagram, the astrological design used by the Knights Templars to build the Notre Dame cathedrals and whose constitutional oath supported a veneration of 'the Grail Mother', Queen Mary Magdalene. The Celestial Dolphins positioned on the diagram were highlighted: Mum on the Heart Element, Christina on the Standing Stone, Dianne on the Crystal Pool and Liz on the Triple Enclosure with the rose quartz. The Miraculous Medal / Mary Magdalene was now to be placed at the entrance to the Tuart Walk / Throat Chakra, and the rose quartz moved to the sixth symbol, the Base Root Chakra. I was then referred to *Crystals for Transformation, Healing and Spiritual Growth*:

Rose Quartz – Helps open the heart chakra ... (21)

Blue dolphins globe, my Guide said.

The story of the Miracle of Lourdes and the description of the Lady who appeared to Bernadette at Lourdes in 1858 were compared with the second, full-length image taken of Mary Magdalene at Medjugorje given to me by Liz, the Indigo Dolphin. *Blue dolphins globe*, my Guide repeated.

In 1992, when Mum and I were living in South Perth, Cathy had joined us, bringing two photographs for me from her sister Liz, taken of the sunset at Medjugorje in 1991. One of them was the psychic close-up image I now knew to be Mary Magdalene. The other revealed her full psychic figure, dressed in a white robe with a pale blue over-robe, and holding a long set of rosary beads running through her hands and down in front of her. In her hair she wore a circular crown of roses and three symbols hung at her chest and waist. Two of the symbols were made of what appeared to be gold; the other symbol caught my attention — a large blue globe.

Blue dolphins globe, my Guide said yet again.

I was encouraged to sit with Mum and re-read the story of the Miracle of Lourdes. Mum re-read it also, then handed it back. What were we missing? I read it again until I reached the part 'I am the Immaculate Conception'.

Image of Mary captured at Medjugorje, Bosnia-Herzegovina

'What do you think Mary Magdalene meant?'

'I have no idea,' Mum replied.

I was referred by my Guide to my father's *Simplified Dictionary – Encyclopedic Edition*:

> Immaculate Conception. *R.C.Ch.*, the dogma, officially proclaimed in 1854, that the Virgin Mary, though naturally begotten, was, through divine favor, preserved from all stain of original sin, from the moment when she was conceived in her mother's womb …

Mary Magdalene appeared to Bernadette Soubirous at Lourdes eighteen times in 1858, four years after the Roman Catholic Church proclaimed the Virgin Mary to be the Immaculate Conception. Mary Magdalene's appearances and declaration at Lourdes were to contradict the Roman Catholic Church's proclamation of 1854.

One hundred and forty years later, on 24 July 1994, Mary Magdalene appeared permanently on the wall at Yankalilla's Anglican Church in South Australia with Jesus Justus, the same year the Ten Year Mary Project 1994 was channelled in Geraldton — a very public and defiant move away from the Roman Catholic Church, as with the creation and dedication of the cathedrals of Notre Dame to Queen Mary Magdalene by the Knights Templars. *Only truth, no untruths*, my Guide said.

I spent the rest of August clearing a wide path between the Love Tree and the Star of Melchizedek symbol. On 4 September I received notification that Cathy was applying for a writ in order to take possession of the property and assets. Mum and I read the letter in silence. I rang a Perth hotel to book our accommodation and we packed our suitcases. I would attend the Supreme Court and represent myself. *Send a statement to the judge*, my Guide insisted. Master Sanderson would receive my statement only twenty-four hours before the hearing.

The next day I was taken to a heading in a newspaper, 'I Took on the Law and Won.' If I did not attend, our home, land and assets would be taken. I prepared the truth of the matter and all the facts I wished to relay to Master Sanderson.

Mum and I left Dongara on the morning of 6 September. The following day I walked along the Swan River to the Supreme Court. Would there be justice?

I felt apprehensive as I questioned a clerk and was sent to Courtroom 8. I told the legal clerk there I was going to speak for myself. She smiled and wished me luck. I found Courtroom 8 filled with barristers and solicitors, and listened with alarm as properties were either taken or returned. Cathy did not appear and neither did her barrister. When my case was called a man I'd never seen before approached the bench. I took it that he was Cathy's representative, so I joined him. He turned towards me with a look of surprise. I looked up at the legal clerk and she smiled.

The writ was read. It was based on the supposed fact that I had not allowed the second auction, which of course was not true. Master Sanderson looked down at me and waited. I lost my nerve as the enormity of what was happening registered and looked at the clerk, who nodded. I found my voice and for ten minutes went through the facts leading to my failure to hold an auction. I kept my eyes on Master Sanderson. I said I had not been able to sell the property because I did not have a signed contract, making it impossible for me to abide by the Settlement Agreement. The room filled with silence as I held his stare.

Master Sanderson read his notes and looked down at me. Then he looked at Cathy's representative and re-read his notes. The Ten Year Project's security depended on this man's decision.

He informed Cathy's representative that his application was rejected. I was speechless with relief. Master Sanderson went on to say I would not be paying their legal costs and the matter was to go back to mediation. I had to sit for a while in order to control the urge to give him a hug. I was then approached by Cathy's representative, who asked me in an appealing tone when it would be convenient to have a mediation conference. This was only a temporary stay of execution. Cathy could not stop now, as there would be no money for her if I were to find the $20,000 and settle.

I cried with relief when I found Mum waiting in our hotel room. 'You're the real thing, Judy, a genuine person, and he saw that,' she said.

As we drove up towards the centre, the Blue Rose Protective Shield stood out. I stopped to look up at the symbol of Algiz, conspicuous within its yellow glow. I pointed it out to Mum. 'Symbol for self preservation in the face of adversity,' I said.

A letter came from the Case Registrar advising that mediation was set for 8 November.

Barbara's birthday, 21 September, was drawing closer. She would be sixty. Although Mum hadn't heard from her since the previous year, she wanted to send her a gift.

Travel to Kalbarri, my Guide said. We set out on 23 September, stopping to visit the Northampton Mary Grotto. I now knew the girl kneeling at Mary Magdalene's feet was Bernadette Soubirous at Lourdes. I approached Mary Magdalene with the butterfly shells from a previous visit to Kalbarri and placed them at her feet, then I asked that Cathy and I be set free from our karmic attachment. *Remember Brittany*, my Guide responded.

It had been ten years to the day since 23 September 1991 when Cathy and I stood in front of the Sainte Barbe Spring in Brittany after visiting the Mary Grotto. Now I was in Northampton standing in front of another Mary Grotto and asking for freedom for us both. Six months before, I had stood at this very spot and made the request for $25,000 to release me from Cathy and save the Ten Year Mary Magdalene Project 1994.

Later that evening Mum and I sat on Kalbarri beach watching the spectacular orange-and-gold sunset. Both of us were exhausted. When I looked at her I filled with admiration. Her love and loyalty had enabled me to keep going all these years. We smiled at one another, sharing this understanding in our silence.

When we returned to the centre, Roger visited and I shared what had happened in the Supreme Court. He was as relieved as I was, but we understood this was not the end.

Catherine, my Guide said, and requested I stand by the Miraculous Medal symbol in the Healing Garden to ponder the history of this important symbol.

In July 1830 in Paris, Mary Magdalene met with Sister Catherine Laboure and they talked; months later they met again, and the design for the Miraculous Medal was discussed. In July 2001 in Dongara, Catherine Keogh and I discussed the Blue Rose Protective Shield, representing Mary Magdalene as the Miraculous Medal represented her in 1830.

I was sent to a file where there was a photocopied page with no author noted:

Aura – The spiritual body of the aura and Be-ing is goddess creation in all forms … The name of the 'divinity' does not matter. The woman may call it goddess or god, *Isis, Mary*, Mawu, Great Mother of Christ, call it energy, or her higher self, or the Intelligence of the Universe …

On 30 September I was encouraged to pick vetiver grass flowers from the Heart to place on the M of the Miraculous Medal symbol. As I did so, there came words that I was forced to speak aloud: 'The child was always held safely within my heart.'

My Guide encouraged me to stencil the initials of Greta's two children on each of the two wooden wheelbarrows brought to the Healing Garden by Roger. Three days later Roger brought a small block of jarrah and my Guide instructed that it be marked 'Rose Cottage' with a stencil and white paint. I remembered my note to Greta of two years before, when I sent her the plate *Where the Dolphins Dance*. The note had said, 'Would you please hold this safe for me until I move south and live at Rose Cottage. Judy'

During the night the blades of the Heart Element broke into pieces, though there had been no wind. Roger took them away, indicating he had three new blue blades at home. *A change of heart*, my Guide said.

I re-read Cindy's August letter in which she wrote that she was missing me and enclosed a drawing of herself. *Heart issue*, my Guide said. *I will always hold the key to your heart*, the princess whispered.

Confused energy had begun to build within the Healing Heart Karma Formation, my link with Cindy since 30 September, when I spoke with a voice coming from deep within, 'The child was always held safely within my heart.'

I had ended my friendship with Greta on 7 October of the previous year and, as this date approached, there was a movement of energy towards the child issue, involving Cindy or a lonely child from a past life in Ancient Egypt.

I sent Cindy a greeting card in the post with the words, 'Love is a Rose.' My Guide asked me to walk into the Heart Chakra / Pulse of Life / Goddess Nut on my return from Dongara and watch the new blue blades spinning within the Heart Element. *One more year of conflict*, she warned.

Days later I created a card with a white background and attached to its top left corner the information card for the golden travel icon Greta had rejected the previous year, the one that contained the wording

'The Guardian Angel — Our Lady of Tenderness'. I secured two dried Barossa Dream roses at the centre of the card and, beneath the golden icon information, a dried pansy — symbol of lovers. I was encouraged to record in my diary the date, 10 October.

My Guide sent me into the Healing Garden, where I found a massive hole in Chamber Three of the Heart. It was a dreadful mess, with various materials scattered all around. *Someone's heart felt the loss today,* my Guide explained. Cindy had received my greeting card, 'Love is a Rose.' *Golden Rose Dolphin will allow access,* my Guide added.

The Blue Rose Protective Shield was brought to my attention on the fourteenth, Greta's birthday, and my Guide directed that a 'Closed' sign be displayed at the main entrance. I booked coach tickets to Perth for the mediation conference on 8 November, in accordance with the instructions *A journey ahead, use a coach ticket.* I then removed the Blue Rose Protective Shield from the main entrance and hung it in the Dolphins Healing Room.

Post arrived from a visitor to the Healing Garden, who wrote:

> As the New Age vibrations affect more people, the spiritual awakening of thousands of sleeping minds will begin to kindle energies of love and healing.

On 25 October I returned the White Dolphin to the main entrance. *Symbol of Atlantis. Take courage in the changes,* my Guide said.

Erika sent me from Germany notes regarding Melchizedek:

> Melchizedek – Star of David: In Mesopotamia it was used by a Semite tribe. In old India it was used as a symbol for the heart chakra. The two triangles are said to mean a mutual penetration of the material and spiritual.

Four days later there came in the post a copy of a print of the Archangel Melchizedek from Herm in England. I placed it near Erika's Melchizedek information and 'The Guardian Angel — Our Lady of Tenderness' handmade card. The enclosed information read:

> The great priest-king of ancient Jerusalem was named after this angelic figure, which guides both men and angels on the seven steps to perfection and illumination. With light pouring from his

diamond-like robe, Melchizedek stands as a contemporary icon. Jesus was referred to as a 'High Priest after the order of Melchizedek'. Nanette Crist, Heritage Store, Box 444, Virginia Beach, VA 23458.

My Guide highlighted Mum's gift of the book *Bloodline of the Holy Grail* by Laurence Gardner. Inside she had written, 'Xmas 2000. Judy, you seek after truth. My love to you, Mum.' I was referred to page 225, 'Elements of Arthurian Lore':

> Fragments of the *Prince Melchizedek Document* found among the Dead Sea Scrolls indicate that Melchizedek and Michael were one and the same. It is this representation which features in the Revelation when the Archangel Michael (the descending Zadokite power of the Messiah) fights with the Roman dragon of oppression... (26)

The next day I lit a purple candle beside the Melchizedek letter from Erika, the Archangel Melchizedek poster from Herm and the 'The Guardian Angel — Our Lady of Tenderness' golden travel icon, then played the *Call of the Dolphin* tape. *We are tuning your senses*, my Guide explained.

The Dolphins Healing Room vibrated with purple energy and the colour purple was being highlighted as it had been two years before, in 1999, when I had been encouraged to work the Egyptian tapestry and then take a piece of gold thread to a purple blouse in Mum's extension. When I had asked her what she thought when the gold and purple were put together her response had been 'Royalty'.

On 3 November I awoke surrounded by the colour purple, and was encouraged to walk through this haze to the Dolphins Healing Room to hold the golden travel icon of 'The Guardian Angel — Our Lady of Tenderness' and touch the Archangel Melchizedek poster. The understanding came that I was being given the encouragement to make four requests. I was guided to play the *Gathering of the Shamans* tape, then go outside and stand in the Triple Enclosure / Brow Chakra and say the Celtic prayer. I waited until I was sent to the Healing Garden to sit on the Mary Seat and ponder. Later I went to the Dolphins Healing Room to light a white candle and read aloud my requests:

'I ask that the property always be protected.'
'I ask that the Healing Garden continue to function for healing.'

'I ask that I eventually be set free of my responsibilities here.'
'I ask my companion from Atlantis to start their journey so we can meet.'

In response, the Barossa Dream rose produced four blooms overnight!

I was encouraged to play the *Call of the Dolphin* tape for half an hour. *We are tuning your senses*, my Guide said again.

Four days later I took a coach to Perth for the mediation. I was sitting in the courtroom when Cathy arrived. She said, 'Hello'. I remained silent and she and I sat staring at one another as the Case Registrar and her barrister walked in. I was aware only of my Guide's instructions: *Allow two hours of talking, leave to catch the coach home. Sign nothing. Be patient during discussions and keep the vision of the Healing Garden in your mind*. I had my return ticket, and I made it clear I was on a time schedule. Cathy and her barrister left the room and the Registrar talked to me and then left. He returned with the request that I sign another document. I refused. I was firm in my refusal and the other two returned grim-faced. I was given more time to find the $20,000 and then they both walked out. I waited to thank the Registrar, who wished me 'good luck'. Outside, we could hear Cathy arguing with her barrister.

'That will be another five thousand dollars,' she said in a raised voice. They were arguing about the cost of yet more legal action.

A week later I was instructed by my Guide to write directly to Cathy to ask her to reconsider what she was doing. To post the letter, I walked to the Dongara post office, as I had every day since the car developed more problems. Two days later I was encouraged to play the *Call of the Dolphin* tape and light the purple candle by the now-opened golden travel icon and handmade card, with Greta's dried Barossa Dream roses and dried pansy. The gold leaf and the vibrant colours of the two hand-painted images featured inside the travel icon looked beautiful in the light of the candle flame.

Busselton, sister, ambulance, my Guide warned.

I wrote to Greta enclosing an explanation of the Heart Chakra. *Change of heart*, my Guide said.

By the time the repaired car was returned, my right knee had become so painful that I'd made an appointment to see the specialist in the Geraldton Regional Hospital.

At sunrise on 26 November Roger walked into the breezeway. I was pleased but surprised to see him, and even more surprised when he offered me $25,000 on a low interest loan to remove Cathy from my life and the life of the centre. I was nervous of accepting money from a friend, but it was the amount I had requested at the Northampton Mary Grotto. I required $5,000 above the $20,000 to cover the legal costs of transferring the title to my sole name. I explained Roger's offer to Mum later. 'We will have an agreement and I will make monthly interest payments,' I said.

Send a letter to Cathy's barrister, my Guide insisted. I wrote the letter quickly, explaining that I now had the settlement funds. I requested the necessary legal action to complete the Agreement and drove to Dongara to post it. In my post box I found a terse letter waiting from the barrister stating that yet another writ application had been made. The offer of the funds from Roger at this eleventh hour would stop this action, and I was in a position now to hire a solicitor. On my return to the centre I sat on the Mary Seat for a while, crying with relief, before going inside to be with Mum. 'Thank God it is all over,' I said.

'You and Roger are a team and he needed to do this,' she replied. *In serving each other we become free*, my Guide confirmed.

At the beginning of December, Suezi arrived to work as a wwoofer and quickly set about clearing the mass of weed growth in the Solar Plexus — Mum's chakra as the Yellow Dolphin. Roger and I walked in the now-cleared Solar Plexus Chakra and I was given instructions for him to erect large cray slats in a standing position like a triangle. This would create two circles, one within the other.

I visited the Ankh Burial Chamber, with its vibration dial linking me with Greta, and turned it a complete 360 degrees. Three days later I also turned Greta's leadlight Celtic cross 360 degrees and played the *Call of the Dolphin* tape.

A pair designed to be together, my Guide said. I thought of The Lovers pots from the Old Saddlery in Ashburton, which had been left behind by the former owner and later transported to Australia — one of the first items to be unpacked with our every move and placed in the kitchen window on display. Greta had one of the pair in Busselton and I had the other here on display.

I was moved on from these thoughts to holding several turquoise gemstones taken from the Silver Dolphin's Indian box, which had held the Miraculous Medal. *Brings lost souls back into harmony*, my Guide said.

I placed the gemstones on the diagram of the Virgo Constellation in the Open Chamber. I felt Greta's energy and understood that anger was surfacing. *A healthy part of the healing process*, my Guide said. *Truth is your protection; it does not matter what others think.* I sent an early Christmas parcel to Greta and her children enclosing the turquoise gemstones for Greta. Within days she returned the stones, having opened the parcel and searched its contents in advance of Christmas. *Truth is your protection; it does not matter what others think*, my Guide said again.

On Christmas Day I awoke to the message *Grow through an alternative route*. One of Mum's surprise gifts to me was an 'Isis Oracle Box' and I was referred by my Guide to my father's *Simplified Dictionary – Encyclopedic Edition*:

> Oracle – among the ancients, the reply of a deity or god, through an inspired priest, to some enquiry.

You are an inspired priest, my Guide said.

The Isis Oracle Box itself was an oblong orange box with the image of a kneeling Egyptian woman touching a glass ball similar to a clairvoyant's crystal ball. At her knees, beside the 'I' of Isis, were three blue scarab beetles. A fourth beetle featured at the end of the word Oracle. Above the words 'The Isis Oracle' was the All Seeing Eye of Horus (Sky Lord); under 'Oracle' was written, 'Invoke the spirit powers of Ancient Egypt to understand the present and foretell the future. David Taylor-Brown.' Inside the box were thirty Amulet Cards beside a pale blue sacred ankh, which separated the Amulet Cards from a pack of thirty Calendar Cards. There was also a book, *The Isis Oracle* by David Taylor-Brown, and, at the base of the box, a rolled Cairo calendar. The returned turquoise gemstones from Greta, which held the energy required for me to make the journey into the past, were placed on top of the Amulet Cards. *You are an inspired priest*, my Guide said again.

On 27 December I cleared my mind and used my pendulum to select a single card from the Amulet Cards pack, and the one chosen was Thoth. I was referred to notes I had taken from *The Isis Oracle*:

> There were other gods and goddesses in the Egyptian pantheon who were famed for their healing powers. Thoth, the god of wisdom, and Imhotep, the master architect ... were recognized to be healers because of their great wisdom. (31)

I wrapped in tissue paper Greta's turquoise gemstones, which she had touched and now held the vibrational energy of her soul, and placed them on top of the Thoth Amulet Card, then wrapped the closed box in the same paper. *Brings lost souls back into harmony*, my Guide said. *Her soul and the universe want to be free of this.* I wrote a note and attached it to the outside of the sealed box:

> Thoth. (6.30 am 27-12-01). Moon God – God of Reckoning and of Learning.
> Inventor of Writing. Scribe of the Gods. Protector of Isis. Husband of Ma'at.

Ancient methods to resolve ancient karma, my Guide explained.

On the last day of 2001 I took the Isis Oracle Box to the Dolphins Healing Room and placed it on the jarrah table.

During our time in Perth earlier in the year, attending the writ hearing at the Supreme Court, Mum and I had been instructed to visit the *Monet and Japan* exhibition at the Art Gallery of WA. In the gallery's gift shop I was sent to the Japanese display and bought a 'Play Handkerchief'. When unfolded it displayed the Japanese national costume. I posted it with a note to Cindy for her seventh birthday on 2 January 2002. On that day I was drawn to a sheet of gold paper and compelled to write the date '02-01-02'. *Sympathy and emergency*, my Guide warned.

I had received a similar message the previous year: *Busselton, sister, ambulance*. I felt concern for Cindy and was distressed, thinking how she had written that she missed me. I imagined her opening her Japanese birthday gift and reading my note:

> Dear Cindy, I bought this Play Handkerchief for you, just for you, to see and understand how people in Japan look in their traditional costume. In Japan there is Crown Prince Naruhito and his wife. They had a baby and they called her Princess Aiko. Maybe your mum can help you understand the enclosed newspaper story about the princess and her Naming Ceremony. Princess Aiko's symbol is a white flowered Asian azalea so she will have a pure heart like the pure white flower. Have a great day, Judy.

The words 'princess', 'baby girl' and 'naming ceremony' were highlighted. *Conceived out of wedlock*, my Guide said. She had provided more clues regarding the mother-and-daughter situation from Ancient Egypt: the princess gave birth to a girl as a result of our ten-day affair. The child's naming ceremony would have stirred complex emotions within three people — the princess, her husband and her lover, the priest.

I stood looking at the Isis Oracle Box, the Virgo Constellation turquoise gemstones rejected by Greta now inside it on top of Thoth, beside the Sacred Ankh. I was instructed to *change Greta's title from Golden Rose Dolphin to Rose Dolphin*, following her rejection of the gemstones. Then I placed on the Isis Oracle Box a metal key given to me on my twenty-first birthday. I thought of the golden key Greta had left with me before she flew to Switzerland in 1997 with the sentiments 'This is the key to my heart …' The key had been given to her on her twenty-first birthday. I was referred to 'The key' in Chetwynd's *A Dictionary of Symbols*:

> The secret of crossing into the unconscious is inextricably linked with sexuality. (8)

The princess and the priest were twenty-one when they had their ten-day affair. *Adultery, this is forbidden*, the unknown angry male confirmed.

I put the Isis Oracle Box beside a booklet titled *Meditations*, written by Theresa Roach. Christina had helped Mum put this together and had written, 'Theresa wrote these beautiful meditations over a period of 19 months — July 1996 to February 1998. These journeys and concepts were intended to relax the individual and assist with the first steps to self-awareness.' Christina and Mum selected twelve of her favourite meditations; I was taken to the one written on 25 July 1996 — 'Faith – Hope – Compassion – Love' — to read a part of it, with pauses for my own reflection, as I held the Isis Oracle Box:

> Angel of Love … For Love makes all things possible … For Love never changes … For Love forgives all … For Love seeks no rewards.

Mum and I drove to Geraldton to see my solicitors, where I was handed documents to sign to begin the process of removing the caveats. While we waited the clerk said, 'This would have cost Cathy a fortune.' Cathy's barrister would take the $20,000 and she would pay all outstanding costs. Later at home I was taken to the Rune Inguz:

New beginnings – complete a project the priority now.

On 8 January Cathy signed the documents to begin the first stages of the process towards a settlement, authorising the removal of both the caveats and the transfer of the land to me. This date was *familiar*; then I remembered 8 January seven years before. I was living at Sovereign Waters and at 2 pm the illuminated shape of a woman (my Guide) had appeared in a white nun's habit and whispered in my right ear 'Around the world'.

I underwent exploratory surgery to find out what was causing the pain in my right knee and was shocked later when the surgeon showed me the damaged knee joint on the X-ray. A healthy joint had been worn away by the work in the Healing Garden. Something inside told me it was meant to be, but I was distressed and not able to accept it.

The surgeon discussed my options. I was too young to have a knee replacement and he suggested I have the right leg realigned. This would involve removal of a wedge of bone from below the knee — the area where I felt pain when looking up at the Aboriginal spear — and the angle of the knee altered. The bone would be held in place by a metal plate until it re-knitted with the bone in the knee. The other knee was damaged, but this operation would serve until two knee replacements became unavoidable. His recommendations sounded ghastly, but I was directed to agree to this operation. I felt nauseous as I drove back to Dongara.

When I got back from Geraldton the Transfer of Land document had arrived in my post box and Roger witnessed it for me. I posted it to my solicitor on 11 January. When I'd done this the Dolphins Healing Room filled with the scent of roses — but there were no roses in the room. I remembered that the Anglican Church in Yankalilla filled with the smell of roses following the permanent appearance of the apparition of Mary Magdalene and her son Jesus Justus.

Three days later I was near the Mary Seat when I received the message *Your Atlantean companion's journey has begun.* I returned indoors with the instruction that the Isis Oracle Box was to be placed on a diagram of the property. As I did this a huge brown spider appeared and walked across the box, making me jump with shock. I was aware that to the Egyptians a spider meant 'Fate'. *See the messages and the omens coming your way*, my Guide said. Once again, the room filled with the scent of roses.

My right knee was so painful that I sat with Mum each day for twelve days working one of her long-stitch tapestries. Extensive X-rays were taken in preparation for surgery to my right leg. I was heading for radical surgery that would put me out of action for three or four months. The operation was to take place on 27 February. Roger said he would look out for Mum and me after the surgery.

On 14 February I was reminded that on this day in 1997 I had purchased the silver locket that I gave to Greta. I was guided to light a new white candle beside the statue of Merlin. *The priest and the rose*, my Guide said.

Travel to Toodyay on twenty-second February, my Guide urged. It took us four hours to get there. Our accommodation was in a caravan park, and that night a peacock landed on our veranda. It made a fuss before flying off, leaving behind a tail feather with an 'eye'. Why all this way for a feather? I wondered. When we returned home I was referred to the *Dictionary of Symbols* by Tom Chetwynd:

> The Peacock's Tail – These independent eyes (centres of consciousness) provide a vision which extends far beyond that of Ego-consciousness. It includes a blaze of vivid insight, comparable to the brightly coloured tail. (8)

See the messages and the omens coming your way, my Guide said. The words 'a blaze of vivid insight' were highlighted, and my Guide directed that the peacock's tail feather be placed under the Aboriginal spear in the office. *Aboriginal link, conflict, the chase*, my Guide warned.

On 27 February I awoke following my operation feeling helpless. I was attached to a morphine drip and my right leg was held fast. I became distressed when the nurse approached me with a reassuring smile. As I lay there, the rush of anger I had felt towards Cathy when I awoke the day of the auction came again. *Aboriginal link, conflict, the chase*, my Guide said through the haze of my distress, but I was in no mood to listen.

Later I sensed there was a person sitting by my bed; on opening my eyes I saw it was a religious minister in the chair watching me. I thought I was having a dream or hallucinating.

'Am I dying?'

'No, my dear,' he replied, 'I am merely on my hospital rounds.'

He moved closer. 'Do you live in Geraldton?'

'No, I live in Dongara.'

'I visit Dongara sometimes,' he said. 'Do you live in the town itself?'

'No, I live outside on six acres,' I said. 'I am creating the Healing Garden.' His kind smiling face changed as if I had offered him a glass of poison.

'*That garden*,' he *spat* at me. 'There is only one way and that is through Jesus.' I stared at him, taken aback at the force of his words.

'That is nonsense, absolute nonsense,' I said. 'You are leaving out two-thirds of the world's population, including Jews, Buddhists, Moslems and Hindus. We all come from one source and we all return to that same source. We are all one.'

He got up from the chair and stormed out of the ward. I lay back exhausted from the effort of challenging him. *You are a warrior monk*, my Guide explained. My mind went back to the time of the Knights Templar and their cathedrals.

It was another day before I could move from the bed and be helped to the bathroom, where the nurse assisted me onto a chair near the shower, then got me out of my hospital robe, and left. It was minutes before it dawned on me that I had to cope on my own. I started the shower, trying to enjoy the warm water, but began panicking when I struggled to turn the taps off. I stretched my body, struggling to hold the weight of my right leg until I stopped the flow of water. I began to cry with the shock and the pain. Outrage surged through my being, stopping the tears. I had lived this hell before, but not in the safety of a hospital. I had been abandoned and left to die. I saw and felt the searing pain of an Aboriginal spear held fast within my right leg below the knee where the wedge of bone had been removed. *Blaze of vivid insight*, my Guide said. I was experiencing a past-life flashback and its consequences. *Aboriginal link, conflict, the chase,* my Guide explained.

On 3 March I remembered the same date but a different year, when I had been sent to the Healing Garden to draw a line where Terry would place the Mary Seat. I spent hours walking the property in my mind, until I grasped that I would take the concept with me in my mind when I left the centre, along with the photographs, slides and notes. This had a steady, calming effect and I was walking with crutches three days later. Christina drove me home to Dongara, where Mum had arrived just minutes before after spending time in respite care.

I learnt later that on 27 February, the day of my operation, the land had been transferred to my sole name. I looked at the Aboriginal spear and the peacock feather and realised I had been given a vivid insight into the past-life heart issue with Cathy. During a tribal war and a chase in an Aboriginal past life I had been speared below the knee and Cathy had left me to die. At the moment of my death I had longed for justice. My right leg was injured again, but repaired on the day I recovered land in the 21st century. I had sought justice and I had achieved it.

I rang Cathy to explain that we had resolved an outstanding past-life karmic issue and she cried before saying, 'No more, Judy, please no more.' Later I remembered the prediction *Egyptian times* of 24 June 1996, when I was told *Cathy will feel like she has walked out of a tunnel and into the Light.*

> Heart Issue: Cathy – legal action – karma / past life – Rainbow Serpent – power – importance – Aboriginal link – conflict – the chase – Aboriginal spear – male passions – ancient Egypt – greed – land dispute.

All outstanding clues within Cathy's past-life heart issue were resolved; she was free. *In serving each other we become free,* my Guide confirmed.

Mum and I celebrated our freedom from Cathy and her barrister on my birthday, 8 March, with a special meal and a bottle of red wine. I was not able to move far but it felt wonderful to know there would be no more aggressive legal post.

On 19 March Roger arrived, proud to be the one handing me the envelope that contained the document 'Judith Roach — Title and Sole Proprietor'. When I gave him a hug, there were tears of joy in his eyes. Mum and I walked slowly to the Mary Seat after Roger left, as I struggled with the effort of using the crutches and balancing my right leg. We looked across the Healing Garden in silence.

Then I reminded her that 19 March had featured many times in our journey, but in particular four years before when Carol Hope visited for a meditation evening, 'It was obvious she'd had a profound experience, but she wouldn't share it. Anyway she returned the next day to tell me about it.'

'I remember. She saw Mary Magdalene by the Tuart Walk.'

'Yes, she was wearing a cream nun's habit with a brown trim and she gave Carol a message for me — that I would know when to leave and that I wouldn't follow or listen to anyone else but would always follow the guidance.'

'Your trust in your guidance has brought about today's outcome,' Mum said.

On Easter Sunday I was encouraged by my Guide to light a new purple candle after placing Mary Magdalene's image on the jarrah table in the Dolphins Healing Room, and then to read from a book given to me by my Uncle Dick in 1987, *At the Feet of the Master* by 'Alcyone' (J. Krishnamurti). I was referred to the section 'Discrimination':

> This is usually taken as the discrimination between the real and the unreal that leads men to enter the Path ... You enter the Path because you have learnt that on it alone can be found those things which are worth gaining. (32)

I read further as the candle flame shone on Mary Magdalene's image.

> When you become a pupil of the Master, you may always try the truth of your thought by laying it beside His. For the pupil is one with his Master, and he needs only to put back his thought into the Master's thought to see at once whether it agrees. If it does not it is wrong, and he changes it instantly, for the Master's thought is perfect, because He knows all. (32)

I looked up at Mary Magdalene's image, experiencing a sense of belonging. I was then encouraged to read part of the section 'Cheerfulness':

> You must bear your karma cheerfully, whatever it may be, taking it as an honour that suffering comes to you, because it shows the Lords of Karma think you worth helping. However hard it is, be thankful that it is no worse ... But in order to make the best out of it, you must bear it cheerfully, gladly. (32)

I tensed as I read this, as I had been far from cheerful regarding my right leg. *Read further*, my Guide said.

> You must give up all feeling of possession. Karma may take from you the things which you like the best – even the people whom you love most. Even then you must be cheerful – ready to part with anything

and everything. Often the Master needs to pour out His strength upon others through His servant; he cannot do that if the servant yields to depression. So cheerfulness must be the rule. (32)

My Guide then referred me to Barbara's birthday gift of the previous year, *The Seat of the Soul* by Gary Zukav:

Karma – The five-sensory personality is not aware of the many other incarnations of its soul. A multisensory personality may be conscious of these incarnations, or experience them, as its own past or future lives. They are in its family of lives, so to speak, but they are not lives that it, itself, has lived. They are experiences of its soul. From the point of view of the soul, all its incarnations are simultaneous. (30)

You are multisensory, my Guide explained. *Read further.*

Intuition – The central perception of the multisensory personality is that he or she is not alone. The multisensory human does not need to rely solely upon his or her perceptions and interpretations of events for guidance, because he or she is in conscious communication with other, more advanced intelligences … Higher self connecting to nonphysical teachers produces a level of truth that is true not just for you, but that would be true for anyone who came into contact with it. (30)

Light – Guides and Teachers assist the soul in every phase of its evolution. (30)

By mid-April I was able to walk around the property with the crutches, and I was guided to take a photograph of the Star of Melchizedek symbol in the Healing Garden. Words from *At the Feet of the Master* came to mind: 'Karma may take from you the things you like best — even the people whom you love most.'

Greta wrote asking me to return the spare key to her post box in Busselton. When I saw her writing I had a moment of panic, and I was guided not to open her letter until I'd read my diary entry of 17 April 1995, two years prior to meeting her. It described a dream of a dolphin swimming with its fin out of the water. Someone shouted, 'Shark!' but I knew it was a dolphin — although my body panicked then, as now.

On Mary May Day '02, I lit a white candle in the Double Dolphin candle-holder and watched as the flame went from weak to strong, accompanied by the word *Success*. I had responded to Greta's request, and my reply would arrive on this day, five years after she approached me at the maypole on Mary May Day '97. My letter read:

Dear Greta, (Mary May Day '97 – Mary May Day '02.)
I hope you found what you were then seeking, love and peace. Judy.

The travel icon 'The Guardian Angel — Our Lady of Tenderness' was highlighted, and later the garden symbol of the Star of Melchizedek. I was standing by this symbol when I felt Greta reaching out to me and it was to do with the lonely child of Ancient Egypt.

Two weeks later I was guided to remove the large diamond-shaped clear quartz crystal from inside Merlin's Triangle and take it to the Dolphins Healing Room. I placed a purple cloth on the jarrah table and the clear quartz on it in the middle. I put eight smaller crystals around its edge in a circle to protect the energy of this Central Quartz. I studied the dolphin family tapestry and saw there were seven dolphins swimming towards a large dolphin. So there were eight highlighted dolphins in the tapestry and eight crystals on the table. Six of the small clear quartz crystals had been used during healing sessions. The other two were the rose quartz and clear quartz — not from the Earth plane. I placed 'The Guardian Angel — Our Lady of Tenderness' alongside the Central Quartz. The understanding came that the rose quartz represented Greta the Rose Dolphin and the clear quartz — not from the Earth plane — represented me. All eight crystals were to be secured inside a leather pouch that Tatia had sent me from South Africa. *Atlantis group of eight*, my Guide explained.

Julie, myself, Liz, Dianne, Tatia, Mum, Christina and Greta were being referred to as the Atlantis Eight, our energy source being the Central Quartz and *Goddess Energy / Mary Magdalene*. Six held the colour keys of six chakras in combination with the runic energy within six of the Seven Healing Triangles. I recorded this in my notes:

Greta (Gold) – Triangle (1) – Rune Mystic – Path of Karma.
Christina (Blue) – Triangle (2) – Rune Gebo – Partnerships.
Tatia (Orange) – Triangle (3) – Rune Anzus – Faith and Blessing.

Julie (Red) – Triangle (4) – Rune Hagalaz – Elemental Power.
Tess (Yellow) – Triangle (5) – Rune Berkana – Personal Growth.
Judy (Green) – Triangle (6) – Rune Algiz – Defence and Protection.
Dianne (White).
Liz (Indigo).

Marg (Violet) and Roger (Pink) were not part of the Atlantis Eight. *Lemurian Twelve Celestial Dolphin Family*, my Guide said. So Marg and Roger were among the Lemurian Twelve Celestial Dolphins.

There were two Celestial Dolphins yet to be revealed: one held the colour Purple — Healing Triangle (7) — Rune Perth — Quest and Initiation. I walked in the Heart in order to absorb this information and as I did so my mind filled with the words *Busselton, a heart speaks. The red rose whispers of passion. The white rose breathes of love*. I was trying to cope with the feelings stirred by having heard the princess, when my Guide sent me to a poem by John Boyle O'Reilly (1844–1890), which Barbara had posted to me years before:

The red rose whispers of passion,
And the white rose breathes of love;
O the red rose is a falcon,
And the white rose is a dove.

But I send you a cream-white rosebud
With a flush on its petal tips;
For the love that is purest and sweetest
Has a kiss of desire on the lips.

I was stunned, not able to grasp having heard the voice of the princess, then reading this poem sent across the world from Barbara highlighting intense past-life emotions held within Greta and Barbara. I was encouraged to hold the Amazonite gemstone, which I had been guided to refer to now as Truth Stone / Amazonite. *Revealing of more truths, sibling rivalry and family inheritance*, my Guide warned.

Although having to walk with crutches still, I was able to drive. In our post box I discovered a letter from Barbara for Mum. There had been no personal correspondence between them for years, as she had made it clear that she did not want to be told any personal news regarding Australia. Barbara wrote that Tim was to become a father, and I knew it would be a girl. I asked Mum to come with me to the lodge with Barbara's letter and, following my Guide's directions, we stood in front of the painting *Dolphin Dreaming*. I went to find my 1995 notes, and read aloud a specific entry when I returned: 'Twenty-Seven October — my last day at the Art Gallery. I was guided to buy an original watercolour *Dolphin Dreaming* by Tracey J Taylor. The painting featured three dolphins and the artist's name of Taylor was highlighted.'

This dramatic painting, with its two dolphins swimming with a smaller dolphin between them, and its blend of black and turquoise, was somehow connected with Barbara's news concerning Tim becoming a father and the name 'Taylor'.

Early on 22 May I was woken with the instruction that The Lovers pot from the Old Saddlery be placed on the jarrah table in the Dolphins Healing Room and the *Call of the Dolphin* tape played, and then changed to the *In Touch* tape. The cheap digital watch I had purchased with the ten-pound note Barbara sent me for my fortieth birthday stopped. I had only worn it when gardening. The dial remained illuminated, but it read '000'. My Guide was communicating with Greta and Barbara's soul energy.

The gardener who I employed to mow the pathways arrived, and for the first time he mowed the inner circle of the Solar Plexus Chakra. I felt a sense of achievement as I stood inside this now-cleared massive circle and admired the cray-slat formation. *There is no avoiding karma*, my Guide warned.

I slowly made my way back to the lodge. It was awkward walking with crutches and I was distracted by a rhyme that repeated over and over in my mind: *Think that the sun is illusion. Think that a diamond is dew. Think that hope is delusion, but know that my love is for you.* The word 'diamond' reminded me of Greta's Kimberley diamond necklace.

My Guide referred me once more to *Crystals for Transformation, Healing and Spiritual Growth* by Soluntra King:

Solar Plexus ... The colour is Yellow. The center of Personal Power ... The main area where emotions and desires are held. The intellectual centre, understanding the world around us. Where we disperse our energy or internalize our power ... (21)

Mum was working a long-stitch tapestry. 'Your chakra, the solar plexus, is complete,' I informed her. 'You must activate it now by reading this standing inside its inner circle,' and I handed her the book. We walked to the Healing Garden and down to the Solar Plexus Chakra itself. *There is no avoiding karma*, my Guide repeated. I relayed the warning to Mum.

'You have yet to find the lonely Egyptian child,' she said.

'And we have yet to fulfil Daddy's request for Barbara to be rescued.'

A visitor came to the garden, a joey kangaroo. It stayed near the lodge. *Symbolic of a leap in faith*, my Guide said.

She instructed me to place the Central Quartz / Atlantis Eight near the reddish brown leather Bible found in January of the previous year at the tip. The Bible was opened at the marked pages and the Central Quartz placed on the words within Psalm 110: 'The Lord has sworn / And will not relent, / You are a priest forever / According to the order of Melchizedek.' When I attempted to leave the room I was held for a moment. *Drawing forces together as a focus of energy*, my Guide said.

On 4 June I was drawn to a smoky quartz crystal and referred to Soluntra King's *Crystals for Transformation, Healing and Spiritual Growth*:

> Brings Spiritual sight and integration of past lives and future into the Now. (21)

My Guide requested that I lie down on the massage/healing table holding the smoky quartz and I soon drifted off into a deep sleep. I became aware of Julie and told her how it had been with Greta, and she understood. When I woke I accepted that I had needed to share and release all those deep personal hurts.

Five days later, when Mum and I were in Dongara, we wandered into a gift shop. There were many beautiful silk scarves on display, one with an exquisite embroidered red rose that caught Mum's attention. I nearly said, 'No, don't!' but stopped myself as she walked to the counter to buy it for Barbara's pending birthday. *You must trust the process. Rose energy*, my Guide insisted. On our return to the centre, I was taken to a friend's letter regarding Edgar Cayce's *Thoughts On Reincarnation – Physical Karma*:

> Karma is a Sanskrit word literally meaning action; in philosophic thought, however it has come to mean the law of cause and effect, or action and reaction, to which all human conduct is subject. There are various types of karma. One type might well be called Boomerang Karma because like the Australian boomerang, which when thrown returns to the thrower, a harmful action directed towards another person seems to rebound to the proprietor of the action. (33)

I walked in the area of the Boomerang/Karma and repeated Edgar Cayce's words aloud: 'A harmful act directed towards another person seems to rebound to the proprietor of the action.' This was linked to Barbara's reaction to Mum's rose gift. *Angry tide*, my Guide warned.

'The Atlantis Eight' having been highlighted, I pondered the number 8, and was referred to *A Dictionary of Symbols* by Tom Chetwynd:

> Eight – Completion ... the numeral '8' is sometimes said to represent the two spheres, heavenly and earthly, joined, touching. (8)

Several photographs of Greta's visit to Switzerland in 1977 were brought to my attention and I posted them to her. *Loss of a child, Pemberton, healing*, my Guide explained. I wondered if this message was linked with Cindy, or the lonely child of Egypt, and was taken aback when encouraged to write to my nephew Tim in England:

> 19 July 2002
> Dear Tim,
> Nanny tells me that you have begun the journey to becoming a parent and father. I remember the day you and Mark, your twin, were born. You were premature and I used the fact I was a uniformed police officer to get past the nursing staff to the delivery room to check that all was well with my sister and then to know how the delivery went and who had 'arrived' in the world. Your mum was recovering, but I established she was well and I was taken by the nursing staff to see the two incubators holding my twin nephews. You were so tiny and there was concern for your wellbeing. I stood by the glass panel and felt emotional. I prayed you both would be okay. That 'moment'

created a bond that never left me. When your child is born it will be a different bond but equally as strong or stronger. You are a young man filled with love and compassion. I know you will be a father and a partner who will love and support his family unit. I think about you both, knowing one day I will actually meet your partner and of course the next generation that will be part of Tim. Much love, Judy.

A week later I looked up into the clear sky and saw a flight of ibis in a V formation. One bird left the formation and turned towards me, flying straight over my head. The next day I was standing in the meditation room when another ibis flew past the window. It was so close that I saw every detail. The word 'ibis' stayed with me, as I had been given this word before. It was connected with a priest, or priests. I was taken to my notes of 11 February the previous year, when I was set a ten-day *Regime of purification*. On Day 9 I read a part from *The Temple of a Million Years* by Christian Jacq and recorded it:

> Two masked priests, one in the guise of a falcon and the other an ibis, stood either side of Ramses. They symbolized the god Horus, protector of royalty, and Thoth, master of hieroglyphs and sacred learning. Pouring the contents of two tall vases over the prince's naked body, they cleansed him of his humanity ... (29)

This was the message of the bird. My role as an Egyptian priest, in the guise of the ibis (symbolising Thoth), was my connection to the royal family and to the princess. *Integrity and misuse of power*, my Guide said. I had compromised my integrity as a priest and Greta had misused her power. *Golden thread is the child*, my Guide said. The emotional turmoil within our female child, born out of wedlock, was the thread that ran through our incarnations.

I touched the Isis Oracle Box containing the upturned Thoth Card and Greta's rejected turquoise gemstones. Before my hand left the box I was reminded again: 'Oracle – to speak, pray, among the ancients, the reply of a deity or god through an inspired priest, to some enquiry.' *You are an inspired priest*, my Guide said. I enquired if Cindy was the reincarnation of the child born out of wedlock to myself — the priest — and Greta — the princess. Confirmation was immediate: I was taken to the drawing Cindy had made of herself and sent to me on 10 August the previous year with the message that she missed me.

My mind re-lived our walks on the beach in Busselton when Cindy withdrew to sit on the sand. I would watch her, aware of her loneliness. *The lonely child of Egypt*, my Guide explained. I felt the distress of the child, the despair of the mother, the grief of the lover and the anger of the husband. Something traumatic had happened to Cindy — the lonely child of Ancient Egypt — and the knowing was held in the angry words *This is forbidden*. I re-read Greta's amended past-life heart issue notes:

> Heart Issue: Greta – dream – regal young woman with dark brown eyes – disposal – crocodile – karma / past life – male passions – lonely child – karmic truths – ten days, ten roses – page marker / Jerusalem – Egypt and priests – This is forbidden – Jude Priest – lovers – Temple.

Many clues had been revealed but there were soul elements yet to be disclosed. Fear and panic shot through my being when I re-read the outstanding clues:

> Heart Issue: Greta – disposal – crocodile – karma / past life – This is forbidden.

A new form of communication began using the blue/green dolphin given to me by Liz, the Indigo Dolphin, for my fiftieth birthday. This beautiful dolphin was on display in the meditation room near the blue dolphins globe. I turned it anticlockwise twice — symbolic of two years — then read my diary for this date two years earlier. Greta and I had travelled the South West together and I had received the words *Drawing forces together*.

My Guide directed me to go into the garden and wire together the tops of the cray-slat framework forming the two massive circles in the Solar Plexus Chakra. This task would take time, as I was not able to stand for long, but it was good to be working. Within days of my working within her chakra, Mum started talking about family and the unresolved controversy surrounding the sale of the Old Saddlery. She was annoyed and upset that, in order to hide their actions, Anne and Barbara had wrongly accused me of stealing money from the business, and expressed her need to go back to that time and resolve the issue. I did not connect this disturbance in Mum with her buying the rose silk scarf for Barbara's birthday in September, or our having activated her chakra. Mum wrote to her sister Val expressing her feelings, but Aunty Val's response was 'Leave it all.'

Mum believed Barbara might have the courage to admit she intended to misuse my power of attorney. I recalled how I had been hurt by the note of Barbara's put through the letterbox in Mum's apartment declaring her intention to take her children away from me. That was the most hurtful of the issues that had arisen since my fortieth birthday in 1986.

On 10 August I awoke wondering how Mum would be drawn into a confrontation with Barbara and was taken to Chamber Three of the Heart to move several slats within the flow of life force. A change of energy between Barbara and Mum was being encouraged.

The next day I was taken to stand in front of Mary Magdalene's image. A quiet, rushing sound came from the picture and words formed in my mind: *A request for help, golden thread*. Before I could absorb what had happened, I was instructed to make a sign for the Heart Chakra and to paint it pink, but I did not have the correct colour. Four days later Catherine Keogh, who had painted the Blue Rose Protective Shield, visited. She had the shade of pink paint required for the sign, which when finished was left at the base of Pulpit Board One. Roger drove in and walked to the sign. He looked at me and said, 'It is about time this went up.' He secured the sign to the Pulpit Board. I was encouraged to go into the lodge to read the Soul Energy (2) notes:

Soul Energy (2): Celtic 7 – pink rose energy – past lives / karma clearing – red rose energy – St Michael – Mary May Day '96 – 7 chakras – Buddha – Sacred 13 – runic energy – 7 Healing Triangles – pink – male energy – Celtic Entrance – maypole – Mary May Day '97 – Egyptian Goddess Nut – silver locket – Golden Rose Dolphin.

Over time, all the elements held within this soul energy had come into prominence. Roger, the Pink Dolphin, had played his part within the soul group.

I was instructed to travel south to Margaret River for a short break in bed-and-breakfast accommodation while Mum stayed in respite care. On the morning of 20 August I was outside in the garden when another guest, a Greek woman who I had met briefly the evening before, walked up to me and handed me some wild violets saying, 'Judy, you are free.' I remembered choosing a violet for a flower reading in Northampton in

October 1994. The issue raised following this reading had surrounded Barbara and my feelings towards her. I had returned to Dongara four days later with the wild violets.

When I collected Mum she again spoke of her concerns regarding the sale of the Old Saddlery. *Truth, sibling rivalry and family inheritance*, my Guide explained. I was sent to review the clues regarding the Crystal Pool and my past-life heart issue:

> Crystal Pool Energy: Supreme power – male passions – heart pain – conflict and loss – Egypt – heart's journey – Golden Rose Dolphin – karmic truths – page marker / Jerusalem – Egypt and priests – This is forbidden – Jude Priest – I had a dream and the dream was you – Egyptian wife – Temple – the protection of Isis – mother and daughter.
>
> Heart Issue: Judy – Jude Priest – I had a dream and the dream was you – Egyptian wife – lovers – birth of a child – deception – Truth of suffering – Star of David / Melchizedek – Temple – two roses – two people – Order of Melchizedek – Mary – princess – royalty – power – Egypt – Healing Heart Karma – celebration – campsite – power place – hunter – spear – badly wounded – protection of Isis – mother and daughter – successful birth.

Many clues had been revealed but there were soul elements yet to be disclosed:

> Crystal Pool Energy: This is forbidden – mother and daughter.
>
> Heart Issue: Judy – mother and daughter.

Six days later I turned the blue/green dolphin anticlockwise three times. On this date in 1999 I had been with Greta in Perth when she handed me the Healing Heart Karma necklace from Nannup. I was now instructed to take this gift out to the Healing Garden and place it under the Heart Chakra sign for a few minutes. *Healing Heart Karma, Heart Chakra*, my Guide said. She directed me to place the Healing Heart Karma necklace on the Jarrah Heart in the Dolphins Healing Room beside two lit white candles, indicating that there was encouragement for two past-life heart issues to be revealed and healed between a mother and daughter: Greta and her daughter Cindy, Mum and her daughter Barbara.

Tensions between Mum and her sister Val increased during their correspondence, resulting in a brief phone call from Barbara to Mum saying she really didn't have the time but had decided to ring Mum anyway. Mum's reply was to tell her that in that case she'd better get on with her busy day. On 10 September we posted the parcel with the rose scarf to Barbara. *Mary Magdalene's signature*, my Guide said.

Our parcel would arrive at Barbara's home on 18 September, three days before her birthday. On this day I was encouraged to light a new white candle in the Double Dolphin holder and place Merlin at its base. The joey returned and hopped around Mum's fence line all day. *A leap in faith*, my Guide said again, and I explained his presence to Mum.

Mum and I were guided to drive to Geraldton, order a new car and apply for a bank loan. Days later we drove a new blue Holden Barina back to Dongara. The feeling of affluence lifted our spirits, and we both understood we would soon be required to travel.

During Barbara's birthday I was encouraged to touch Merlin at the base of the Double Dolphin candle-holder, and I wondered what part he was to play in the scheme of things. Mum rang Barbara, singing the birthday song, but was met with an answering machine. The next day I lit the candle in the Double Dolphin holder and touched Merlin. *Angry tide*, my Guide warned.

On 25 September I turned the blue/green dolphin anticlockwise six times. On this day in 1996, during a meditation, I had seen Mary Magdalene's image but with both eyes open. I was being given warning of a coming situation where 'having one's eyes opened' would feature. The next day, an early morning disturbance of energy sent me to the Dolphins Healing Room at 4 am. I was to light the candle in the Double Dolphin holder, with Merlin at its base. At 8 am I stood in the meditation room in front of the print of St Michael and All Angels Church, Cornwood, and requested protection for the two pairs of mothers and daughters as their past-life heart issues surfaced.

Mum had been encouraged by my Guide to send a gift of a red-velvet heart filled with lavender to each of her sisters prior to Barbara's birthday on 21 September. The post brought thank-you notes from them but there was no response from Barbara regarding Mum's birthday gift.

I awoke on 5 October feeling anxious. *Something from Cornwall to arrive*, my Guide warned. I walked to the meditation room and found a book lying on the floor; it featured Cornwall and was titled *Angry Tide*. It had been pushed out from within the bookcase. Something from Cornwall was about to arrive and it held the vibrations of an *angry tide*. I was directed to take a diagram of the Egyptian Goddess Nut into the Dolphins Healing Room and place the Truth Stone / Amazonite at its centre. This crystal represented truth, clear understanding and a solid foundation. Two weeks had passed now since Mum had left her birthday message for Barbara.

The next day I dreamed of a duck. The dream chart in my bedroom explained that a duck symbolised an 'anonymous letter'. My attention was drawn to Merlin at the base of the Double Dolphin candle-holder, *Cornwall*, my Guide warned. It was at Tintagel in Cornwall with Mum in 1992 that I first heard the message *Arthur and Merlin*.

Two days later I awoke to the message *Two years are now finished*. It was two years to the day since I ended my friendship with Greta and I appreciated there must be a required time span in play. *Until the Atlantis influence returns*, my Guide confirmed.

The following day a postcard from Newquay in Cornwall arrived for Mum from her sister Val, describing a special day she and her husband had spent with Barbara. They had been driven to Cornwall by Barbara and her husband as a surprise on Sunday 29 September, the weekend after Barbara's birthday. Barbara had spent time with a family member who she knew was in contact with Mum. The postcard held the vibrations to create an *angry tide*. Barbara had used Mum's sister like an anonymous letter, to hurt her. I watched as she read its contents. Aunty Val was aware of the strained atmosphere between Mum and Barbara, Mum having shared with her the unresolved issues between them. Mum's hands shook with emotion and she struggled to speak. I said what was in both our hearts: 'Why would Aunty Val send this to you knowing Barbara is ignoring you?'

'I don't know,' Mum replied, with tears in her eyes.

'You went across the world in your eighties, to bring Aunty Val back from the brink. Why on earth would she have the need to send this to you, knowing it would hurt?'

Mum pushed the postcard away, and said again, 'I don't know.'

'Would Aunty Val allow her daughter to be wrongly accused of stealing, or in the case of you, Mum, allow her daughter to get away with obtaining her power of attorney by stealth? Not likely!' I said angrily.

'Acora,' Mum replied, 'he told you in the beginning everyone had been poisoned against you and he emphasised *everyone*. You are Barbara's smokescreen.'

'But why the need to hurt you?'

'Because I know the truth and no-one wants to hear the truth.' *Truth, sibling rivalry and family inheritance*, my Guide said. This was the past-life heart issue between this mother and daughter.

Before I could recover I was sent to my diary entry of 10 October and found that on this day the year before I had created a card that held the travel icon information 'The Guardian Angel — Our Lady of Tenderness', dried Barossa Dream roses and a dried pansy. Later I had found a hole in the Heart, and the words *Someone's heart felt the loss today* had come. Cindy had received my card 'Love is a Rose' that morning. I held the card and looked up at Mary Magdalene's image and waited for the soft, rushing energy *I will protect the child*. Although Greta, the lonely child's mother, had rejected Our Lady of Tenderness, Cindy was protected as she sought to resolve the past-life heart issues held in the angry sentiments *This is forbidden*. This was the past-life heart issue between this mother and daughter.

I placed the handmade card by the Central Quartz on the purple cloth beside Tatia's pouch containing the crystal energy of the Atlantis Eight. I was aware the Atlantis Eight held the vibrations of Our Lady of Tenderness / Mary Magdalene.

On 11 October I stood by the Heart Element, as this was the day the Four Years of Conflict were to end and the elements of repair to begin. The next day a photograph of Tim, then of Greta, were highlighted and placed on the purple cloth by the Central Quartz. *You will meet them again*, my Guide said.

The phone rang and I was asked to give a lecture to a group. Four days later thirty-eight people arrived. I had prepared the tractor shed by placing information sheets and enlarged photographs on the boards Terry had made for Foundation Day / Sunflower Fest '97. I was nervous, but soon lost the feeling when I began to explain the Healing Garden concept. One woman in the group asked me if I was a medium, and my mind went racing back to my father's brother Dick in England in 1988. Uncle Dick had pointed out my paternal grandmother's photograph and told me she was a medium, and one day I would speak out as she had done. I had been adamant I would do no such thing. I smiled at the lady, then looked across at Mum and she nodded her approval. 'Yes, I am,' I replied.

Hillarys Harbour Resort, my Guide said, following a request for me to drive to the Dongara Library and dowse their travel brochures. *Important messages*, my Guide said. Mum and I drove south to the resort, in a northern Perth suburb. The next day was stormy, but we walked to the shopping arcade and into the Crystal Shop. A tarot reader was offering readings; she sat us in chairs and spoke to both of us, although I selected the cards.

She told me I would write two books and I must learn to trust again. This would happen after I experienced the last ancient tears. I would have new energy then. She saw travel ahead. She went on to say there had been a lot of suffering for us, after making many sacrifices for our beliefs, but now we were stronger. A man in his thirties would come into our lives and we were to listen, but to take what he said with a pinch of salt. A lot of negativity would come towards us from overseas but we would reverse this with loving thoughts and actions. Love was the key to stopping the negativity. She told Mum that 'the Angel of seeing-things-as-they-really-are' was playing a part in her life right then.

While Mum rested I was instructed to buy a book, *Way of Karma* by Judy Hall, at the local newsagents. We drove back to Dongara early the following morning. On 19 October I was referred to this book and read:

> Three things strongly affect karma: desire, purpose and grace ... Desire (often called craving or wilfulness) is a powerful creator of karma ... The strength of desire can transcend death and pull a soul back into incarnation to deal with unfinished business or to recreate once again a situation where the desired object can, so it seems, be achieved ... Purpose is soul intention ... Purpose can overcome destructive desires ... and it can also compensate for difficult karma ... Grace strengthens purpose and helps it to manifest. Grace is an offer from the highest part of being to release karma ... (34)

Mum expressed a wish to share with Jan, Barbara's friend, how we both felt concerning everything that had happened since our leaving England in 1985, and she wrote her a letter. *Trust the process and all will be revealed*, my Guide said.

On 24 October I awoke from a dream trembling. A young woman was pregnant and I was one of two men fighting about this situation. It was a violent fight; we both wanted to win. I lost and began a dangerous walk away from the hurt. I was surrounded by swirling muddy water and shouted for help until people assisted me onto the steps of a tower. One of them asked me for money. I referred to my dream chart and discovered that muddy water represents sorrow and a tower represents success.

Five days later Victor Tanti, a reporter, rang wanting to interview me, and made an appointment for the next day. He conducted the interview in the tractor shed and at the Mary Seat. After he had gone I was guided to send Greta photographs of the children's wheelbarrows and write about my mentioning their names during future lectures. *There must be a willingness to fight for truth*, my Guide said.

On 6 November Victor Tanti's article, 'Medium didn't choose her path', featured in *The Geraldton Guardian*:

> Judy Roach didn't really choose to be a medium; it was more or less thrust upon her. Genetics might have something to do with it. There are other family members, her grandmother amongst them, who have also been in touch with ancient spirituality. In Ms Roach's case, her task is to act on what she describes as 'voluminous amounts' of information about building a healing garden … She started her garden … just north of Dongara, eight years ago and it's now only two years from completion … (35)

There was still no communication from Barbara. Six weeks had now passed since Mum's birthday gift had been delivered. *Another heart wound for Tess*, my Guide warned.

Mum received a newsy letter from her sister Val describing her trip to Cornwall with Barbara and how wonderful it had been. I watched with concern at the hurt on her face and wondered at Aunty Val's insensitivity. I was sent to my notes of 11 May 1993, Val's birthday. Mum and I were discussing family then, as now, and this date had been highlighted until we became aware that Aunty Val was supporting Barbara. Mum and I knew, having read the notes of our trip to England in 1992, that this was Barbara's seventh attempt to resolve a past-life issue regarding sibling rivalry and family inheritance. I read the 1993 message to Mum:

> There are great expectations of your success here. There have been six attempts in life experiences to bring Barbara's soul back to the Light. She will forever be in your debt as a soul participant in future growth, a lost soul due to envy.

Then I was taken to my notes regarding karma and Desire to read to Mum:

> Desire (often called cravings or wilfulness) is a powerful creator of karma … The strength of desire can transcend death and pull a soul back into incarnation to deal with unfinished business or to create once again a situation where the desired object can, so it seems, be achieved. Desire keeps the karmic wheel turning …

Mum and I understood that the wilfulness coming from within Barbara and Aunty Val was to create a situation between Mum and Barbara with a 'desired objective' in mind. This was the predicted 'seeing-things-as-they-really-are' situation. *Keep trusting the process and all will be revealed*, my Guide said. 'This is part of a bigger plan,' I told Mum.

In my post box I found a note from Greta. She was annoyed, saying that her children had not played any part in the development of the Healing Garden. On my return to the centre I was guided to lie down and rest. I went into a meditative state where I could see a rainbow. When I opened my eyes I saw the rainbow in my window; it was a multicoloured rainbow featuring a silver heart, a red heart and a dolphin sent to me by Cindy with her words 'Dear Judy, I hope you love me, Cindy.'

In my mind, I remembered Cindy watering the Area of Relationships, then she and I cutting the vetiver grass with tiny scissors, laughing. My heart filled with light as I saw her sitting in my wheelbarrow. I saw her run into the garden early one morning, ahead of her mother, and me picking her up. These images came and went like moving pictures. We had exchanged healing hugs when our lives became hard and it was Cindy I missed when I turned away from her mother. I was not to accept Greta's reactive past-life need to separate me from Cindy. But Greta was correct when she said her son had played no part, so I removed his wheelbarrow from the Healing Garden. *This is the golden thread, tension over the child*, my Guide said.

I replied to Greta describing the images and Cindy's involvement in the garden, and telling her I would not suppress the truth regarding my attachment to her daughter. The letter was due to arrive on 11 November. *There must be a willingness to fight for the truth*, my Guide said. Finally, I had acknowledged the lonely child after all these centuries.

Rose Cottage, Cindy, recovery, my Guide said. Cindy would be brought to Rose Cottage, a place I had yet to find. Recovery from what though?

I wondered with alarm. My Guide requested that the Rose Cottage plate be taken into the office and placed on seven Blue Rose Protective Shield photographs positioned in a fan-shaped formation with the Miraculous Medal / Mary Magdalene placed uppermost. I became apprehensive. Then the soft, rushing energy came and the words *I will protect the child*.

I lit a white candle in the Double Dolphin candle-holder and lit Seashore incense at its base. I watched in utter amazement, unable to believe what I was witnessing, when the incense smoke split into two separate halves! Half surrounded one dolphin, swirling in circles, the other half gradually enveloped the other dolphin, also swirling in circles. It was an awesome sight, and I understood that Greta and I were surrounded by the protective energy of Mary Magdalene, ensuring Cindy's safety.

The following day, 8 November, Mum received a response from Jan. She mentioned Barbara had spoken to her and asked her to pass on the message to Mum that she would be sending a thank-you note for her birthday gift, *some time*.

'Too little, too late,' Mum said, 'this situation must be dealt with now.' She sat at her table and wrote to Barbara.

Dear Daughter,
Today a letter came from Jan. She passed on a message from you that you intend to write to thank me for my birthday gift. Well, Barbara, it will be too little, too late. That was seven weeks ago. I bought the beautiful silk scarf with such love in my heart and was waiting with pleasure to talk with you. Judy had sent a family recipe book recommending a dish and I wanted to tell you about a minor change. I rang leaving a message on your answering machine but there has only been silence since.

I have no intention of spending the rest of my life allowing the undercurrent to go on between Judy, you and I, regarding the sale of the Old Saddlery. You flatly deny signing anything, maybe so. But Barbara, we all know, it takes a good six to eight weeks to build up to a sale. Anne had to have discussed her intentions with you to find a house and allow a buyer to complete a contract on the Old Saddlery.

So you had the intention to sign. Without you, Anne would never have contemplated these things. So it is a play with words. You let your sister down. You know that, she knows that, and I know that.

You were to act in Judy's best interest and you acted in Anne's, for whatever reason; neither Judy nor I are interested. The fact remains you let your sister down and yourself and the family were drawn into chaos. Anne rang, crying, to say she was letting Judy down after the sale was stopped by the solicitors. We have forgiven you and moved on. Now you must look at yourself and forgive yourself. When Judy returned to try and resolve the drama, you wrote her a note telling her that she was greedy and stupid and that you were taking your children away from her and she would be a lonely, old woman. A friend was with Judy at the time and read the note. You have to live with these words. Your sister loved you all so much and spent years fending for and supporting you and the children. Whatever was inside you when you wrote that must be a terrible thing to bear. Your children are not for you to hand out or take back.

Years later, you allowed the family to believe Judy was a liar and a thief, having taken money from the business. I was there when she rang and asked you to tell Anne and arrange for a transfer from Lloyds. I was there when Geoff Coyte, the bank manager, responded with the transfer from their joint account. It was to secure a position of employment here in Australia for Anne. You knew that and so did Anne. So to allow such a terrible rumour was unforgivable. I am taking you to task because of my love for you and my love for Judy. I love both my daughters the same and if it was Judy that had hurt you, I would be taking her to task. Continue with your silence if you wish, but at some time you will have to bring all these memories to the surface, face them and move on. I am not going to allow the situation to continue to block my life — or yours. Love Mum.

My Guide instructed that the letter was not to be posted until 11 November — the day Greta would receive my response to her child issue: her wrongful statement that Cindy had played no part in the development of the Healing Garden here in Dongara.

'There will be an eruption in England,' I said. *Trust the process and all will be revealed*, my Guide replied. She asked Mum to send copies of her letter to Barbara to her two sisters and to Jan, ensuring they would know the contents and intention of her letter. *Only truth, no untruths*, my Guide insisted.

On 9 November Roger brought huge carpets to repair the Star of Melchizedek and the Area of Relationships, confirming that the Element of Repair had begun.

Early the next day Mum came looking for me. She told me she had been woken twice in the night and on each occasion saw an incredible ray of blue coming towards her and soft, rushing energy that then moved through her. She heard the words *Mother to mother*. I took her into my office holding Tatia's leather pouch, which contained the eight crystals representing the Atlantis Eight. The clear quartz — not of the Earth plane — was now to be placed on an eighth Blue Rose Protective Shield photograph beside the fan of seven photographs, the Rose Cottage plate and the Miraculous Medal / Mary Magdalene. I understood that it was not only Cindy who needed protection but also my mother. *Truth and goddess energy*, my Guide said.

On 11 November I posted Mum's confrontational letter to Barbara. *Await the pending storm from overseas*, my Guide warned.

Prior to my fortieth birthday, in 1986, at the beginning of our journey, Mum and I had walked the beach at Middleton in South Australia waiting with dread to hear from England; now, sixteen years later, we walked the Healing Garden of Dongara in Western Australia waiting again with dread to hear from England.

Two days later Barbara's thank-you note to Mum for her birthday gift arrived, crossing in the post with Mum's confrontational letter. *Prepare to go south*, my Guide instructed.

On 15 November I awoke to the property vibrating with *another's* temper, and responded to Mum's call for help over the intercom. I found her standing at her kitchen table holding a chair and shaking with distress. I saw the apprehension in her eyes, led her to an armchair and held her hands until she was able to breathe normally again. 'Your letter has arrived at Barbara's home,' I explained gently.

My Guide instructed that I light a white candle and Mum re-read the letter aloud. I watched with admiration as her apprehension became determination and her voice strong. I went to hug her but my Guide insisted I wait — this was between a mother and her angry, resentful elder daughter.

'Barbara, God bless your soul,' Mum said, with a tremor in her voice.

She shuddered and I became anxious. 'What is it? What did you see?'

'I saw the turbulent resentment held within Barbara's soul.'

Mum was very affected by this. I recalled Acora warning her that Barbara's anger was harmful to her and watched with concern as this proved to be true.

I was sent into the office to wrap the Rose Cottage nameplate and was forced to struggle with disruptive energy linked with Cindy and the sentiments *This is forbidden*, and the pending *angry tide* from Barbara. These combined vibrations only calmed when the Rose Cottage nameplate was sealed. Mum was still breathless when I returned, so I took her into the Dolphins Healing Room and sat with her till she became calm.

'That was ghastly, Mum, just ghastly,' I said, aware of my rapid heartbeat. The instruction from my Guide, *Prepare to go south*, was now understood — we were to leave the centre for a few days. Early the next day, we headed south to Toodyay, driving until we found B&B accommodation overlooking the Avon Valley.

Three days later we were allowed to drive back to the centre, and I turned the blue/green dolphin anticlockwise three times. On this day in 1999 I had been with Greta in Busselton and Greta, Cindy and I had walked the beach holding hands with the child in the middle. We had lifted her into the air every few steps, all laughing at the pleasure of it.

On 21 November a reply from Barbara to Mum's confronting letter arrived. The envelope was dated 15 November, the day Mum and I woke to the vibrations of anger and were forced to leave the property. On the back of the envelope, for all to see, Barbara had written:

Your English Daughter Remember Her?

There it was out in the open — the sibling rivalry consuming Barbara's soul energy. Barbara had returned Mum's letter highlighting the issues with a pink marker in the form of a word or statement and enclosing a note filled with hurtful comments. Mum put the note down and pushed it away. I felt sick after reading it and sat holding her hands. I pushed the note as far away from me as possible.

'I now understand Mary Magdalene's message to you of mother to mother,' I said. 'Only you as her mother could love Barbara at this moment.' *Another damaging heart wound for Tess*, my Guide said.

We read through Mum's letter and Barbara's marked replies. At the very end of the letter, where Mum had written that she had no intention of allowing the undercurrents to go on, Barbara had replied, 'Your

Choice.' Where Mum had written 'So you had the intention to sign', regarding the contract for sale of the Old Saddlery, Barbara had replied 'Yes'. After all these years the truth had been revealed with that word.

I looked at Barbara's *confession*, having waited sixteen years, and it was a huge relief to read just that one word. Mum had achieved our aim: 'the revealing of the truth'.

I became emotional, saying, 'At last, the truth.'

Where Mum had written, 'Without you Anne would never have contemplated these things,' Barbara had replied, 'Rubbish'.

Where Mum had written, 'The fact remains you let your sister down and yourself and the family were drawn into chaos,' Barbara had replied, 'Rubbish'.

Where Mum had written, 'We have forgiven you and moved on. Now you must look at yourself and forgive yourself,' Barbara had replied, 'Rubbish'.

Regarding the note put through Mum's letterbox in which Barbara had stated her intention to take her children away, Barbara had written, 'This is a lie.' This was an extraordinary denial, as Paula had been with me when the note arrived and had read it. The person who delivered it knew of its existence, and I had returned the note to Barbara via Anne, who would have read it. Then I understood: I had returned the original to Barbara and this was why she was denying its existence, but I had taken a copy and sent this to our mother. 'You read her note, so to deny it now is futile,' I said.

Where Mum had written, 'You allowed the family to believe Judy was a liar and a thief … to allow such a rumour was unforgivable,' Barbara had written, 'Get Over It.' I stared in shock as I read this, unable to take in Barbara's response.

'She has no regard whatsoever for the harm she has caused me,' I said.

Within the sentence where Mum had written, 'I am taking you to task because of my love for you and of my love for Judy', Barbara had circled the words 'for you' and written 'Rubbish'. At the end of Mum commenting that Barbara could continue with her silence if she wished, but at some time she would have to bring all these memories to the surface and face them and move on, Barbara had written, 'I am not the one with the problem.' Where Mum said that she was not going to allow the situation to continue to block her life — or Barbara's, Barbara had written, 'Good'. And at the end of the letter, where Mum had written 'Love Mum', Barbara had crossed out 'Love'.

'Thank you for confronting Barbara,' I said. *You both trusted the process*, my Guide said. I repeated this to Mum and we understood Barbara's rage had finally exploded, causing her to admit that, yes, she had intended to misuse my power of attorney.

'Aunty Val played her part in the soul group by encouraging Barbara's resentment all these years,' I said. 'Then you flushed her out from hiding behind your two sisters.' Mum reached for her pen and calmly wrote:

Dear Barbara, Thank you for your post. At last, we have the truth concerning the sale of the Old Saddlery. Thank you, Mum.

I wondered at the Cornish connection until indignation surged through my heart, helping me understand. In a past life as a young boy I had been wrongly accused of theft and deported to Australia. I realised my sibling had found the means to remove me from their life, and I had no doubt now *who* that sibling was. Anne had said in the very beginning that Barbara had thought I would disappear. Mum's gift of the scarf embroidered with a rose (Mary Magdalene's signature), and Barbara ignoring the gift, had brought about the *angry tide* — and the revealing of truth. Mum had confronted Barbara's deep-rooted resentment, regaining her personal power, which had been taken away by stealth when she had been embarrassed into signing a power of attorney in 1985. I filed Mum's letter along with Barbara's angry responses.

At 6 am the next day the joey was waiting for me by the lodge gate. It looked to see if I was watching, then hopped into the Healing Garden and the Heart itself. I walked past it and down to the Egyptian Pulpit, where I waited. The joey then hopped down the pathway of the Heart Chakra / Pulse of Life / Goddess Nut after me. I stood still as I watched it approach. It stopped near me, putting out its face to be touched, and when I looked into its dark brown eyes tears of relief welled up from inside me. *Last of the ancient tears*, my Guide said.

The dispute between Barbara and me regarding the Old Saddlery was over. I would amend my notes regarding the final clue, 'mother and daughter', held in my Heart Issue notes and 'settled legal disputes' held in the goddess energy notes. I would not have come to this conclusion without my Guide's assistance and my remarkable mother. When I walked by the Heart Chamber, where the Joey had waited, I received the words *Judy, you are free*. I not only heard these words but now *felt* them. The part of my personality that had sought healing through the revealing

Egyptian Pulpit Heart Chakra / Pulse of Life – Goddess Nut / Goddess Isis

of truth was satisfied. But there were still clues held within Greta's Heart Issue notes and the Crystal Pool Energy notes yet to be resolved:

> Crystal Pool Energy: This is forbidden – mother and daughter.
> Heart Issue: Greta – disposal – crocodile – karma / past life – This is forbidden.

A week later Mum discovered an unpleasant message on the answering machine from Aunty Pat, attacking her for confronting Barbara. We were shocked. Mum replied with a short note to her saying we were happy to withdraw from the family at this time.

'How do you feel now, after yesterday and Aunty Pat's message?' I asked Mum.

'I lanced the festering boil, so emotions will run high.'

'Barbara has not admitted the whole truth,' I said. I reminded Mum — not that I needed to — that Barbara's signature was queried at the time of sale of the Old Saddlery, by the purchaser's solicitor, who asked who she was, and when he was told she held my Power of Attorney he asked to see it and discovered it did not cover the sale of a home and business, only a home, so he stopped the sale.

'Does this mean nothing is resolved between you?'

'Barbara admitted she'd intended to sign, and that released me,' I replied. 'You reclaimed your personal power by standing up to Barbara and your sisters. What happens now is up to the three of them, and their individual consciences.'

I was guided to draw an ankh and placed the Truth Stone / Amazonite at its centre on the jarrah table. The Miraculous Medal / Mary Magdalene was placed on this, encouraging the revealing of truth regarding the lonely child, Cindy. I went outside and discovered that a small area in the Heart Chamber was damaged where the Joey had waited. As I repaired it, I understood there was a small heart in need of repair — Cindy's heart.

It was 24 November 2002, and on this day in 1997, at 10 pm Egyptian time, the blue light had been transferred from Cairo by Greta. The next day at 4 am I sat in the Dolphins Healing Room staring at the Truth Stone / Amazonite and Miraculous Medal / Mary Magdalene remembering the arrival of the blue light five years before at 4 am Dongara time. The sensation of shock came, and I was forced to hold my breath as if I was drowning. I struggled to cope with intense panic. When this terrifying experience eased I was guided to go into Mum's extension to pick up my father's black waterproof torch, which was by her bed. *Dad and Daddy*, my Guide said.

I walked around the lodge in a state of severe agitation holding Daddy's torch and turning it on and off, on and off, not knowing what I was to do next, overwhelmed again by the feeling of panic. Then the emotion left, leaving me breathless, drained, exhausted and apprehensive. *Medical emergency*, my Guide warned.

The date '2 December' and 'Tim' were highlighted by my Guide.

Christina rang as I was setting up a newly purchased second-hand computer in my office and offered to come down and assist with the process — to ensure I could begin a draft of my proposed book *Entwining of Souls*. I was surrounded by my files of notes, diaries, photographs, diagrams, symbols and letters and boxes of slides. I left the office to find Mum.

'My Guide has asked me to write to Anne care of Barbara's address,' I said, ' to relay to her that Barbara has admitted her intention to misuse my power of attorney and confront her with the hurt and chaos they both caused in the family unit, and our lives.'

'How do you feel about this?' she asked.

'It feels good to be in a position to confront her with their duplicity.'

Roger and his wife, Mary, drove me to Geraldton Hospital on 18 December to have the plate removed from my right leg. Having the wound reopened was distressing. I was driven home the following day by the Carers' Service and again I was on crutches.

A Christmas card arrived from Cindy. 'Judy, I miss you,' she wrote.

I was woken at 3 am on Christmas Eve to look across at Mum's extension and, seeing her light was on, went over and encouraged her outside to stand under the moon in her nightgown and slippers. We were happy to stand in the light of the moon. I encouraged her to see its aura and after a while she was able to do so. 'It's a circle around the moon,' Mum announced with delight.

Then I encouraged her to visualise a shaft of light entering her body. We waited until she confirmed a forked shaft of light had moved through her. She said it was healing energy. We walked to the Standing Stone, where my Guide directed us to walk clockwise around it four times. We wondered where we would be on Christmas Eve 2006, and the response was *Rose Cottage*. 'Do you have any idea where Rose Cottage is?' Mum asked.

'No Mum, but remember that Rose Cottage was mentioned two years ago by my Guide when we were sent to Manjimup, and Ray from the caravan park drove us to the Diamond Tree.'

On Christmas morning Mum and I sat near our Christmas tree to open our gifts. There had been only silence from Barbara since Mum had written thanking her for the truth regarding the sale of the Old Saddlery. Mum's sisters did not ring either, with their usual Christmas greeting. This reminded us both of 1986 and our first Christmas after leaving England, when we were ignored. Barbara had not rung Mum at Christmas time in the seventeen years we had lived together in Australia. We brushed aside their silence and enjoyed our day. Among my gifts from Mum were a 2003 diary and a wrought-iron twin candle-holder. 'Twin' featured, and my Guide highlighted the date, '2 January'.

At 4.30 am on Boxing Day I was up playing the *Call of the Dolphin* tape, aware that I had not sent Christmas greetings to Greta. But, following her message to me to say she missed me, I had sent Cindy a birthday card for 2 January. I was guided to wheel Cindy's wheelbarrow onto the veranda by my bedroom, and I felt I was keeping her close by doing so.

We spent the last day of 2002 browsing through a brochure on Shark Bay.

On Cindy's eighth birthday I was taken to my notes of February 1994. Cathy and I were in the Blue Mountains and visited the Springwood Spiritualists Church and I received the message from a medium that a wheelbarrow was for me 'a link to a past life'. Wheeling Cindy's wheelbarrow brought on feelings of dread. It was as though she had been hurt and was in a wheelchair. The map of the Western Australian Kimberley coast was highlighted and I was then drawn to the words 'Kimberley Region'.

I was taken from this to lighting two turquoise candles in the twin candle-holder below the *Dolphin Dreaming* painting, then to sending a postcard to Tim with my email address, enquiring about the birth of his first child. Barbara's silence would surely mean Mum and I would not be given any further news. I checked my emails at the Dongara Library on 24 January and was thrilled to find a message from Tim describing the birth of his daughter Taylor on 2 December, the date highlighted in the previous year's diary. Taylor — this name had been brought to my attention before.

On 13 May the previous year, the concept regarding the Atlantis Eight and the Lemurian Twelve had been revealed. After learning this I had been sent to my post box in Dongara. I found a note from Barbara for Mum saying Tim was to become a father. (I knew it would be a girl.) Mum had followed me to the lodge with the note and we were encouraged to look at the painting *Dolphin Dreaming* by Tracey J Taylor. The name 'Taylor' was highlighted.

In the meditation room I studied the painting, with its three dolphins. There were two large dolphins and a smaller one swimming between them in the turquoise water. The understanding came that the two larger dolphins were Mum and me and the smaller dolphin was Tim. I was guided to hold on to Tim's news for Mum's birthday on 27 January.

Mum and I drove north to the Monkey Mia Resort in Shark Bay and spent the evening before her birthday sitting on the beach. We woke early next day and walked to the water's edge to wait for the arrival of the dolphins. Mum had now read Tim's email regarding the birth of her great-granddaughter Taylor. When the dolphins arrived I spoke out, saying 'I request that Mum and I gather in all the dolphins.' I had taken a photograph of Mum standing straight and strong alongside the white dolphin featured at the resort entrance, highlighting that she had regained her personal power. Barbara had responded to Mum's challenging letter with intimidating anger but we had faced it and pushed it to one side.

Barbara's animosity towards Mum had first been revealed in March 1986 when I returned to England to discover her photograph placed upside down. This image today replaced that unpleasant intention. Reacting to past-life energy is an explanation, not an excuse to harm or hurt.

Before we left Monkey Mia, we went shopping and bought two carved wooden dolphins, and on the morning of 30 January I placed them on the jarrah table. Then I was encouraged to send one of them to Tim, along with a silk scarf featuring a boomerang design — a symbol that required him to visit Australia. My Guide instructed me to place the Central Quartz near the brochure from Monkey Mia, where I had requested that Mum and I gather in all the dolphins, and I was requesting this again. The other dolphin I placed near Tim's photograph.

The previous year I had put photographs of Tim and Greta on a purple cloth with the Central Quartz and handmade card of Our Lady of Tenderness / Mary Magdalene. I was now to move Tim's photograph and the Monkey Mia Dolphin to stand alongside my drawing of the ankh, the Truth Stone / Amazonite and the Miraculous Medal / Mary Magdalene. The clear quartz — not from the Earth plane — I positioned under

Tim's image, indicating that more truths were to be revealed concerning Tim, Greta and Cindy. A photograph of Tim, Mum and me taken in Cockington, England, on 29 February 1992 I put by the dolphin family tapestry and the clear quartz — not from the Earth plane — indicating there was a connection between everything. I waited.

Lemurian Twelve, Celestial Dolphin Family, my Guide explained. Tim is the eleventh Celestial Dolphin and one of the Lemurian Twelve.

I placed the smoky quartz from Tatia's pouch by Tim's photograph and then returned it. This was Tim's vibrational crystal influence in the Lemurian Twelve: 'Brings Spiritual sight and integration of past-life into the Now.' I was sent to the Twin candle-holder under the *Dolphin Dreaming* painting to light its turquoise candles. *Turquoise*, my Guide insisted. I looked at the painting with its dolphins swimming in turquoise water and thought of Tim, then recognised that he was the Turquoise Celestial Dolphin.

My Guide referred me to my notes of January 2001, when Martin came and asked what the colour turquoise inside the Ankh Burial Chamber meant to me, and I was sent indoors to read about the Causal Chakra — Turquoise. I went to the Crystal Pool / Causal Chakra and sat by the Ankh Burial Chamber, understanding that Tim as the Turquoise Dolphin held the key to this chakra. My mother, his nan, had activated the Causal Chakra on 27 January the previous year, and I touched the turquoise triangle with a sense of relief. Tim had moved through the negativity in England to share the birth of his daughter Taylor, choosing to return to the positive and healing energy of the original Dolphin Family.

I read my notes regarding the past-life energy stored within this chakra to be reminded there were two elements yet to be resolved, 'This is forbidden' and 'mother and daughter' — the past-life heart issue between Greta and Cindy. *Miracle*, my Guide said.

I awoke two days later with the urgency to drive to the newsagency, where I was taken to a laminated poster of Egypt. I was to journey back to ancient Egypt using this poster as a directional guide. As I walked from the car, the poster flew out of my hands and across into the Crystal Pool / Causal Chakra, landing on the Ankh Burial Chamber. *Burial chamber*, my Guide said.

Mum – Yellow Celestial Dolphin

I pondered Roger's crystal influence as the Pink Dolphin in the Lemurian Twelve and in response I was taken to the Miraculous Medal / Mary Magdalene symbol, which Roger had painted the colour lapis lazuli. I was then guided to drive to Dongara to buy a small lapis lazuli cross and place it within the leather pouch. This was Roger's influence: 'Enhances psychic abilities and communication with the higher self and Guides.'

Then I pondered Marg's crystal influence as the Violet Dolphin in the Lemurian Twelve and in response was taken to a seventh small clear quartz. This joined the six quartz crystals inside the leather pouch. Marg's influence was the same as that of Liz, Dianne, Tatia, Christina, Julie and Mum: 'Because Rock Crystal bears the Divine Light in it, it attracts the Soul towards the Light.'

What was this place Lemuria? I wondered. My Guide sent me to Gerber's *Vibrational Medicine*:

> Lemuria existed at an early time in human history when the reincarnational cycle of dense physical form had only recently begun. In early Lemuria, people lived simple lives. Spirituality and the recognition of the God-force in all things was a part of daily life ... They were also extremely psychic, and could see auras and the spiritual light around all living things quite easily. Information flowed from their Higher Selves into waking consciousness with great ease ... Prior to the loss of Lemuria, many migrated to the land mass known as Atlantis, where one of the greatest civilizations of all time was evolving. (3)

I was puzzled when directed to send Rene, in Brittany, details of the property and enclose a diagram of the Seven Healing Triangles. I had been guided to spend time near the Celtic Entrance where the underground aquifer / ley-line ran through the property, and create a rectangular symbol filled with both soil and mulch. In each east-facing corner I placed a large flat limestone boulder, symbolising a birthstone. I then secured a piece of trellis to two star pickets across the centre of the rectangle, with six strands of fencing wire above it. The symbol of Algiz I created using timber, and I put it at its eastern end: Defence and Protection — my runic energy influence as the Green Dolphin. The first birthstone had been placed following Taylor's arrival in the world. The second birthstone had been placed after receiving the message *Cindy's birth*.

There was one more Celestial Dolphin to be identified — the final member of the Lemurian Twelve / Celestial Dolphin Family — who, apart from holding a colour key, held the runic influence in the Healing Triangle Perth (Purple) — Quest and Initiation. Greta's photograph remained on the purple cloth by Our Lady of Tenderness / Mary Magdalene.

On 14 February, the day for lovers, my Guide directed me to place the shells from the Monkey Mia beach on specific regions of the Nile River in the Egyptian Poster / Directional Guide in my office: the Temple of Kom Ombo in Upper Egypt, Sinai-Serabit Khadim in Middle Egypt and Sais in Lower Egypt. A surge of purple energy went through me and I was forced to speak aloud, 'I request the princess's help.' I was drawn to the Temple of Kom Ombo and the Angel Card Love.

The next day, the Temple of Kom Ombo was highlighted again. *Loving thoughts from the princess towards the priest*, my Guide said.

Two days later I was referred to my diary entry of 14 February the previous year and the message *The priest and the rose*. This was the past-life Egyptian romantic link I was accessing in order to reveal Cindy's past-life heart issue. The information alongside the wording 'Temple of Kom Ombo' was highlighted by my Guide:

> Kom Ombo – This double temple, built in Ptolemaic and Roman times ... is dedicated to ... the crocodile god Sobek and the falcon god ... Horus the Elder.

As I read the words 'crocodile god' my heart froze and panic shot across my chest, through my arms and down my legs, and it took a huge effort to shake free of the terrifying feeling. I was referred to notes recorded by my mother from a library book concerning the Egyptian god Sobek:

> He is depicted as a crocodile wearing a plumed head-dress or a part-human hybrid. His crocodile imagery suggests an ability to attack and kill with sudden speed. The Sobek cult was apparently extensive along the Nile valley.

Kimberley diamond, my Guide warned. I was encouraged to find the notes of November 1993 where she referred me to a part of the book *Kimberley Dreaming to Diamonds* by Hugh Edwards. I was to read the same words again ten years later:

It was dangerous to annoy a Wandjina, a being with lightning, storm and flood at his disposal. In cases of severe offence a cyclone was a grim possibility ... The Aborigines saw the Wandjina as supernatural beings. They had individual names like Bundjinmoro, at Manning Creek; Pindjuari, the crocodile Wandjina of the Oscar Ranges; and the Kaiara, the sea Wandjinas of Bigge Island and other sea caves. (4)

The message I was given then repeated: *There is a higher purpose to your life. A special contribution you can make.* The clues 'disposal' and 'crocodile' had been added to the first past-life heart issue notes, later revealed as Greta's heart issue. I remembered the feeling of dread as I wrote those two clues. Over the next ten years Greta's past-life heart issue had been updated and amended as the elements were revealed. It now read:

Heart Issue: Greta – disposal – crocodile – karma / past life – This is forbidden.

I feared for Cindy's safety, and in response was encouraged to move the pages of my desk calendar from the current month of February to October, and mark the date 3 October with a cross. On this page was a coloured image of a saltwater crocodile, and as I looked at it I felt the fear and panic again. Then it passed.

At 5 am on 19 February I was woken and told *You will be leaving.* This was followed by a request to open the tin containing my father's war medals. I looked under the medals and to my surprise found a Miraculous Medal. The word *Joy* followed and I understood Daddy was celebrating the rescue of Barbara. My having been sent to Daddy's torch in November the previous year, walking around the lodge turning its light on and off, indicated he was highlighting the word 'light' — confirming Barbara had been turned back to the Light when Mum had said, 'Barbara, God bless your soul.'

But the finding of Daddy's torch and turning it on had followed the emotion of panic, which accompanied the words *Dad and Daddy*. I was aware of its link to Daddy and Barbara, but the panic had come with the message *Dad*.

Two days later Mum and I met Marg and Christina at the Rose Café in Geraldton. I mentioned the first draft of my book *Entwining of Souls*. Marg studied me, then said, 'Judy, you are aiming for gold. You will be a teacher in the spirit world.'

On our return to the centre I sat in the Crystal Pool / Causal Chakra and looked at the Pyramid Formation with its Ankh Burial Chamber. There was still the past-life heart issue within Cindy waiting to surface. Martin had said the ankh given to me by Greta held the key: the burial chamber was in the shape of an ankh.

No burial, my Guide said. There had been no burial for the Egyptian female child born out of wedlock. So what had happened to the child? I wondered. *This is forbidden*, the unknown male responded angrily. *A heart in need of repair*, my Guide warned.

I became anxious. Then the soft, rushing energy came and with it the words *I will protect the child*. I was being reassured again that Cindy was protected as she sought to resolve the past-life personality issue within her with regard to the angry sentiment *This is forbidden*.

My Guide sent me to the purple cloth holding my father's Miraculous Medal, and I put it near Greta's photograph. A miraculous rescue regarding Cindy was assured. I then placed Cindy's drawing of herself on the purple cloth beside the Monkey Mia dolphin. *Purple Dolphin*, my Guide said.

Cindy is the twelfth and final Celestial Dolphin, one of the Lemurian Twelve, and holds the runic influence of the Healing Triangle (7) Perth — 'Rune of mystery, pointing to the secret and hidden beyond our conscious awareness …' I then pondered Cindy's crystal influence as the Purple Dolphin in the Lemurian Twelve and was taken to touch the moonstone: 'Truths, no untruths.'

I pondered Greta's crystal influence as the Rose Dolphin in the Lemurian Twelve. Rose quartz: 'Opens the heart … Compassion, Forgiveness and Acceptance.' I placed the moonstone inside the pouch and returned the clear quartz — not of the Earth plane — my crystal influence in the Lemurian Twelve, then pulled the cords together to seal the twelve energies within. At Monkey Mia in January I had asked that Mum and I gather in all the dolphins, and this had now been accomplished.

I looked up at Mary Magdalene's image and waited for reassurance regarding Cindy. The soft, rushing energy came and the words *I will protect the child*.

Miracle, my Guide confirmed.

I went outside and discovered there were many spider webs between the top two wires of the symbol containing the two birthstones and Algiz. I wondered what this symbol represented, and in response I found waiting for me in my post box a letter from Rene in Brittany. He had returned the diagram of the Chakra Garden and Seven Healing Triangles, having drawn a long line across the page, marking this area and writing 'Green Positive Magnetic (healing) Point' in the margin. In his accompanying note he said I had created a Green Positive Magnetic Energy Captor and he was thrilled for me. I was to stand within this area twice a day for fifteen minutes.

The next day, at sunrise, I stood on the second birthstone — Cindy, within the Green Positive Magnetic Energy Captor — for fifteen minutes, and was fascinated to find all six layers of wire were now a mass of spider webs; each with a spider at their centre basking in the first rays of the sun. This symbol held the energy of nature's magic and ancient wisdom, and I held my breath as I sought entry. I was referred by my Guide to the book *Medicine Cards*:

> Spider ... weaving webs of delight,
> Weave me a peaceful world.
> Carrying creation in your web,
> Waiting to be unfurled! (15)

*S*tart *writing again*, my Guide said.
I stood on Cindy's birthstone each day at sunrise and sunset, for the fifteen minutes, visualising her laughing and playing, then walked the property to absorb the energies of the eight chakras, before going to my office to continue the first complete draft of the manuscript *Entwining of Souls*.

The Healing Garden contained information for visitors on the Information Board and with Pulpit Boards and a gardener mowed the pathways. Vicki, a wwoofer in her mid-forties, was visiting on a regular basis and given the never-ending task of trimming the vetiver grass and weeding the Heart. Roger continued to bring materials to ensure the ongoing maintenance of all areas of the garden.

Everything was calm until I touched the box containing the Old Saddlery legal files, when I began to have bouts of nausea. I mentioned this to Mum, who suggested I take it to the Dolphins Healing Room and place it below the Blue Rose Protective Shield on the wall. There had been silence from Barbara and Mum's sisters since November, following Mum's confrontational exchange with Barbara regarding her part in the attempted underhand sale of the Old Saddlery. When I positioned the box under the shield, waves of nausea began, accompanied by violent shooting pains in my abdomen.

On 27 February, twelve months to the day from being in the Geraldton Hospital having the operation on my right leg (and, unknown to me at the time, the title being transferred to my sole name), I was in difficulty again. I did not say anything to Mum and went to my bedroom to lie down. By 5 pm the pain was so intense that I found it hard to cope and at 7 pm Mum came looking for me. She called an ambulance.

At the Dongara Medical Centre I was told I would be staying overnight and Mum was collected and brought to their respite room. My condition became worse and I heard the doctor say that I had a subacute small bowel obstruction. I was put in an ambulance and driven to Geraldton for emergency surgery. Carol Hope, the tarot card reader, was the rostered volunteer, and she sat with me. I understood it was serious and concentrated on slowing my rapid heartbeat. I was operated on at midnight and woke later with forty-nine staples in my body. The problem had come about, I was told, as a consequence of the gall bladder operation I'd undergone in England many years before. Loops of the small bowel that had stuck to the scar had been divided. They also told me the operation was a success.

I was driven back to the centre two days before my birthday in March. Mum was waiting for me, shaken by the experience. She would sit with me as I returned to my writing and I would share my thoughts with her. We understood emotions would be rekindled as we re-lived what had happened since purchasing the Old Saddlery in 1983.

On 10 June I was encouraged out into the Healing Garden before sunrise to say the Celtic prayer. I sensed energy around me, and then a blue circle formed at eye level some distance away. I held the image until a central blue dot formed and then waves of red patterns like a kaleidoscope moved towards the centre. I was thrilled and wondered what it was. *Blue Mary Ray Diamond Centre*, my Guide said.

By the end of June Mum's health had deteriorated, forcing her to spend time at the Dongara Medical Centre. Two valves in her heart were damaged and she was not coping with the medication to control her heartbeat. She would stagger and suffer energy loss, and was not able to return home for a few days. *The Rose Dolphin will return*, my Guide said.

The next day, 6 August, I was encouraged to find the stick-on window display of two dolphins I had bought in Denmark when travelling with Greta three years before, in July 2000. The dolphins were to be displayed in my bedroom window and two orange candles lit. I placed my left hand on the 'o' of the word 'Dolphins', and as I did so I lost all sense of time, aware only of the orange glow of the candles reflecting within the two dolphins. *Blue Mary Ray Diamond Centre*, my Guide said.

A month later she directed that the Central Quartz on the jarrah table be moved to the healing/massage table, and I was encouraged to play the tape *Violet 19*, sent to me by a visitor. *Wild places, quiet places, gathering of shamans*, my Guide said.

On 27 September my Guide highlighted the 'Rose Cottage' nameplate and sent me to the Healing Garden to make a request as the first orange and yellow rays of the sun appeared over the horizon. 'I pray that my companion from Atlantis join me,' I said.

One day towards the end of September I went into Mum's extension and found her on the floor. I rang for the ambulance and she was taken to Geraldton once again. I rang Aunty Pat to tell her and was met with a controlled, strained voice, but I ignored this and spoke only about Mum's deteriorating health. Flowers were delivered to the ward from Aunty Pat and Aunty Val, and later, after Mum had returned home, letters arrived from both sisters. Mum responded, and all three began to exchange childhood memories. Mum shared with Aunty Pat a dream in which she met my Grandmother Lilian, their mother, and the scent of Lily of the Valley was strong — Nanny's favourite perfume.

On 11 October I was given the direction to place the property on the market on 7 March the following year. Two weeks later the Central Quartz was to be moved from the healing/massage table to the Rose Cottage nameplate now on the Jarrah Heart. At the end of November, the nameplate was again brought to my attention and a postcard received from Vicki the wwoofer titled 'Birth of Lemuria'. *Important changes to your membership*, my Guide said.

During the first week of December Marg, the Violet Dolphin, visited. I thought about my having played the *Violet 19* tape a few months before. We drank wine from the goblets used by the Celtic Seven and walked the property by moonlight. The next day I found her sitting inside the Crystal Pool / Causal Chakra area. She told me she had received the message *Energy centre*.

On 17 December my Guide instructed me to put the 'Birth of Lemuria' postcard by the Double Dolphin candle-holder with a lit white candle and play the tape *Call of the Dolphin* followed by *Windjana Spirit of the Kimberley*, given to me by Greta in 1997. *Energy centre*, my Guide said.

Christmas week brought cards from the twins for Mum and me, and in Tim's card he enclosed a photograph of Taylor. This was the child predicted in the Ten Year Mary Magdalene Project '94. The prediction had mentioned a new child to enter my life, and highlighted 'Christmas'. Taylor was born on 2 December. A lot of contact was forecast: she had been chosen with a double meaning for being in my life.

On Christmas Eve I created a stunning 'ray' of silver and gold on the wall in Mum's extension. Standing near it, she read me her letter to Aunty Val, before I posted it, where she described this spectacular decoration, and wrote the following:

> Dear Val ... I have been given another lovely day. I accept that one day my heart will stop. I have no regrets and I want you to know that I am at peace within myself. Love Tess.

Days later we watched the sunrise to welcome in the New Year of 2004.

A birthday card for Mum arrived from Barbara. We assumed Mum's comments to Aunty Val had prompted this, breaking the silence. I handed it to Mum on 27 January as part of her birthday. Mum responded with a note, telling Barbara a female Buddhist monk had visited the garden on her birthday and handed her wildflowers, then had gone into the Heart to chant a Buddhist Heart Mantra. I discovered Tim had sent an email for Mum's birthday and spoke of his daughter Taylor as being a light of life. Mum's reply told him of how she'd awoken to find her extension filled with streamers, and no matter how old you become you are always a child within.

I was instructed to have our homes painted, starting with Mum's extension, and spent a lot of time ensuring all repairs were completed beforehand. The instruction had come the previous year to place the property on the market the day before my birthday in March.

Late in the evening of 20 February Mum became quite unwell again, and our doctor advised me to drive her to the Geraldton Hospital Emergency Unit, where I stayed until she was admitted. The next day a nurse told me to prepare myself. What does she mean? I wondered.

Mum and I were destined to move south near Manjimup and live in Rose Cottage by Christmas Eve 2006. Christina came, and we sat quietly talking as Mum moved in and out of consciousness; then I drove back to the centre to rest, but Mum was rushed to the Intensive Care Unit and I felt I must ring Aunty Pat. I returned to the centre but there was no sleep in me.

I sat on the Mary Seat in the darkness with Jessie curled at my feet. Mum had to get through this, so I asked my Guide for help and was quickly given the understanding that she was to be taken off all medications. I rang the hospital. The staff were not happy, but reluctantly agreed. I went to my bedroom and slept for a while before being shaken awake to find one of my Grandmother Lilian's handkerchiefs and Mum's Lily of the Valley perfume. I returned to the hospital and touched Mum's arm. She opened her eyes — there was so much trust and love in them. I took a deep breath and sprinkled drops of perfume onto the handkerchief, placing it by Mum's nose so that its scent would be drawn into her being. I whispered, 'Nanny says it is not your time.'

Ten days later I was allowed to drive Mum back to the centre, even though she was still weak. The local estate agent brought a prospective buyer to the property on 7 March, that is, on the day it was put on the market. This surprised us, but Mum had decorated her extension for my birthday breakfast, so there was an air of celebration around the place.

A curt note in a small white envelope arrived from Barbara, asking Mum if she wanted to start writing again. Mum replied saying the barrier was still there between the three of us because nothing had been resolved. She explained that this was not her way and, unlike Barbara, wanted everything out in the open. She added that she and I were more than willing to discuss how we felt and asked her if she was now willing to do the same. Unless the three of us sorted this out once and for all, she said, this attempt at reconciliation would not work. There was no response from Barbara, but later Aunty Pat left a message on our answering machine telling me, in not very polite terms, that I was the cause of everything negative that had happened within the family over the years.

'Their avoidance of the truth is just unbelievable,' I said.

'It is easier to blame you than face the truth.'

Months passed and, although Mum's general wellbeing had been affected, she was able to start her visualisation evenings again, and I watched her enjoy the company.

The property had been on the market since March, but no-one else had come to view it. Then, in the first week of October, a couple from Margaret River visited. The garden and our bed-and-breakfast licence were the attraction. They discussed with me the possibility of clearing the Heart Chakra / Pulse of Life / Goddess Nut and plant lavender, then made several offers. My Guide directed me to take the third, and completion was arranged for 15 November — six weeks before the completion of the Ten Year Mary Magdalene Project 1994.

Mum and I were sent south to buy a new brick-and-tile three-bedroom home in the small mining township of Greenbushes. This was not Rose Cottage, but we followed my Guide's instructions. I was surprised when guided to write to Barbara and tell her I had sold the centre and was preparing Mum for our move to the South West — and even more surprised when guided to write to her again a week later, making the observation that nineteen years before, at around this time, she had made two decisions that would change all of our lives. The first was to obtain Mum's power of attorney to assist her friend, Jack, the high-flier; the second was to obtain my power of attorney to assist Anne. There was no response to either letter.

On 15 November, as soon as the purchase money for the centre had been deposited, I repaid in full Roger's loan and then walked the property for the last time. A young Aboriginal man arrived from Geraldton to move us. We drove out of the centre with Jessie on the back seat and the manuscript in a blue box.

On our arrival at our new home I put the manuscript in my office, hung the Wild Geese / Soul Group print on the wall and placed The Lovers pot on display in the kitchen. The Butterfly Circle with its jarrah surround was stored in the garage, not placed under Mum's bed as usual, but I was aware that we were now living by a jarrah forest. I wondered if this symbol would remain in the garage until Mum's ninetieth birthday, January 2006, and the predicted completion of events between Mum and Barbara.

Important changes to your membership, my Guide said.

My Guide instructed that the *Dolphin Dreaming* painting be hung in my office, the massage/healing table set up in the sunroom, and Cindy's photograph put on the Jarrah Heart nearby. I was guided to send Greta a card with our new address.

An early Christmas card arrived from Aunty Pat for Mum, who responded by mentioning that nineteen years before she and I had arrived in South Australia with plans to stay for six months, but our lives were changed by dramatic events, and what was first viewed as a tragedy turned out to be what we now understood to be our destiny. *Completed cycle*, my Guide explained.

In the first week of December Mum came into the office, wanting me to read a letter she'd written to her sisters before she sent it across the world to them both.

> Dear Val and Pat,
> There will be terrible grief in my youngest daughter when I do not wake up one morning. The sadness for me will be that her motives have been misrepresented for the past nineteen years and I have been helpless to do anything about it. I know she has, in reverse, encouraged me to stay part of a family that has rejected her so cruelly. Tess.

On 14 December a card arrived from Greta, and I was instructed to send her a letter describing our move to Greenbushes and the prospect of Rose Cottage. *Completed cycle, Lemuria*, my Guide explained. Each day for a week the same message repeated: *Lemuria, energy centre*. Late on Christmas Eve my Guide directed that the White Dolphin symbol of Atlantis be hung outside by the front door and Mary Magdalene's image be hung in the sunroom / healing room. In our post box at the Greenbushes store / post office I discovered Christmas cards from Tim and Mark for both Mum and me. We were thrilled.

On Christmas morning Mum handed me one of her gifts, insisting I open it right away. It was a framed wrought-iron flower. I was confused, and looked over at her. She was smiling. 'It is the fleur-de-lis,' she said, 'flower of the lily.' *French connection*, my Guide explained.

'Its energy has created a surge of emotions,' I said.

My Guide requested that the fleur-de-lis be hung in the dining room, completing a triangle of energy in partnership with the White Dolphin and Mary Magdalene's image.

On Boxing Day I was woken early and told to drive south, and we found ourselves in the Bridgetown Jarrah Park inside a circle of jarrah trees. I was told to walk around an old tree stump nineteen times in reverse. *Release*, my Guide said. On our trip home I thought about the sunroom / healing room having jarrah doors and jarrah blinds, and understood that the Butterfly Circle was to be hung in this room on Mum's ninetieth birthday, in 2006.

On 27 December, the last day of the Ten Year Mary Magdalene Project '94, at 8 am, the time ten years before when I had channelled the project in Geraldton, I was encouraged to light a white candle in the sunroom / healing room and wait. *Something new and revolutionary*, my Guide said. *You must let go of the past, as I have great need of you.*

I spent the day creating a massive symbol in the back garden with the wwoofer, Vicki, who had maintained the Heart Chakra in Dongara and was visiting for a few days. Using railway sleepers, we created a triangle and a square, connected by eight round blocks of wood, symbolic of eight seats. *Atlantis Eight Formation*, my Guide said. I asked for the symbolic meaning of this. *Completion and new beginnings.*

My mind went back to 8 October three years before, a date imprinted in my mind when I awoke to the words *Two years are now finished*. I had ended my friendship with Greta on that day two years earlier and realised there was a required time span before we could meet again — *until the Atlantis influence returns*, I was told. I stood by the Atlantis Eight symbol and knew I had been moved beyond Ancient Egypt to the time of Atlantis.

On the first day of 2005 at 3.33 am Mum called out, and I went to her bedroom to discover her agitated following a visitation. She said she had been awake when a movement drew her attention. It was a slim woman wearing a fitted grey skirt with pleats. Her face was friendly, and Mum sensed that she was from the time of the cottage that had been demolished in order for our new home to be built. The woman spoke of Barbara, telling Mum her elder daughter was bitter, and she must try to persuade her to speak to her. I waited until Mum understood what she must do. She went to her notepaper and wrote:

Dear Barbara, how much longer do you need to keep us all separated? Mum.

The manuscript of my book was brought to my attention and I spent the weeks leading up to Mum's birthday reading our story. She asked that we spend her birthday alone. I wanted to take her on an adventure and was directed to travel the Pemberton Tram to the karri forest. We drove to the Diamond Tree later and remembered the message *Rose Cottage* of five years before.

Barbara did not respond to Mum, but sent a tape, *Celtic Sanctuary*, instead. Mum posted a note back to her in response.

> Dear Barbara,
> My birthday was filled with surprises; your gift *Celtic Sanctuary* was a surprise. Nineteen years ago I myself sought sanctuary in Australia. Love Mum x.

Mum explained it was a struggle to write, as she felt Barbara's angry energy trying to stop her, but she persisted. There was no response from Barbara. The time span of nineteen years had been highlighted many times, and I asked my Guide to explain. I was referred to my notes concerning Mary Magdalene, where I re-read that she herself had been exiled to Lyon in France in AD 44 and died in Provence in AD 63, a time span of nineteen years in exile. The words 'in exile' and Mum's words to Barbara, 'I myself sought sanctuary', were highlighted.

On 26 February I received a letter from Vicki to tell me she had taken a copy of the diagram of the Heart Chakra / Pulse of Life / Goddess Nut to Violet, an Aboriginal Elder in Perth, and she had told Vicki that it contained the black and red snake of tribal law.

During the next few months we were guided to travel the South West, leaving home in the early hours and returning late in the evening. Then, at the beginning of June, Mum's health became an issue: she became weaker and her weight loss dramatic. I stayed at home with her, walking Jessie in the local forest when she rested.

On 4 October I awoke to the message *Love and healing*.

I was in my office when I understood from references made on the TV that a child had been attacked by a crocodile in the Kimberley region. When I watched the report I was shocked to discover it was Cindy. I felt sick with apprehension until she appeared on the screen sitting in a wheelchair with her left arm bandaged. I did not recognise her: she had matured and there was a determined set to her mouth. Greta was standing behind and her brother beside her. My initial reaction was dismay, as I listened to how she and her brother had been on a boating trip with their father when they went swimming in a remote pool 240 kilometres north of Derby, about 24 kilometres from the mouth of the Sale River. The traumatic incident with the crocodile had happened at 2 pm on 3 October, the day marked on my previous year's calendar with the picture of a saltwater crocodile.

The story was reported in *The West Australian* the next day under the headline 'Brave Dad, brother foil croc attack.' Cindy had been grabbed by a crocodile and pulled under the water. Her father had dived to find and drag her to safety with the crocodile still holding on. Her brother then repeatedly hit the crocodile on its jaw until it let go. Cindy had been flown to Derby Hospital with deep wounds to her left arm and torso. I watched in both shock and relief as the story of her *miraculous rescue* was told by Cindy and her brother. Greta had flown to Derby, and I saw her put her hands to her face and shake her head, appearing unable to take in what had happened.

All night I paced our home, haunted by images of Cindy's body held in the mouth of a crocodile. I understood I had lived through this hell before. Greta and I had been betrayed by someone close and our secret affair discovered, and the true identity of the child was revealed. I realised the female child born out of wedlock in Ancient Egypt had been disposed of to the crocodiles of the Nile. There had been no burial. *This is forbidden*, had been shouted by the husband of the princess, as he angrily arranged for the disposal of the child that was not his. This explained the princess's eventual suicide. It was impossible to imagine the effect this unspeakable act would have had on the child, the grief-stricken princess and the guilt-ridden lover. I went over the horrific scene until I could control my anger and accept that a past life had been replayed, but with a very different outcome.

The clues 'disposal' and 'crocodile' had featured in Greta's past-life heart issue since November 1993, fourteen months before Cindy's birth on 2 January 1995. Greta's ex-husband had risked his life to save Cindy and return her safely to her mother. The past-life secret relationship triangle that connected Greta, her ex-husband and I had been revealed. I accepted that one of my roles in the Ten Year Mary Magdalene Project 1994 was to create the Healing Garden and its eight Chakras to encourage the revealing of this past-life karmic attachment held deep within those involved, to ensure the safety of the lonely child of Egypt and bring about healing.

The husband of the princess had returned in this lifetime as the biological father of the child and the traumatic past-life karmic triangle had been replayed, the requirement being that the child was to be saved by him from certain death by a crocodile. The personality within Cindy, seeking healing, had faced and braved the past. Cindy's determined stance came to mind; she had survived. I sent a 'Get Well' card to her in Derby Hospital. It would arrive on 7 October, four years to the day after I ended my friendship with Greta and Cindy and I were separated. The journey back to Cindy had begun.

I became quite concerned for Mum's wellbeing, and wrote to her sisters about the situation. Neither responded, but wrote to Mum instead. I no longer reacted to their rejections, as my only concern was for Mum and keeping them all in contact.

The Buddha statue that we'd brought from the Sacred 13 in Dongara was highlighted. *When the student is ready the Master will come*, my Guide said.

Julia called in. She and her partner were over from South Australia touring the South West. It had been many years since we had seen her, and I sensed that it was an important visit. Julia had met us in Adelaide when Mum and I arrived from London twenty years previously. A week later they visited again and asked to be allowed to come with us on the following day when I took Mum to the Bunbury Hospital for tests. It was good to have someone to share with, as my concern for Mum was increasing. Following their visit, Julia started to communicate with us on a regular basis and would ring to offer support.

Mum asked me to send Tim's daughter, Taylor, one of her tapestries — a sulphur-crested cockatoo — for her birthday on 2 December. During the first week of December I was guided to fill our home with Christmas decorations, and this helped lift Mum's spirits, especially when I brought a Christmas tree home and we decorated it together, creating a magical corner complete with flashing lights.

The New Year of 2006 began with the message *Rose Cottage*.

Mum was well enough to venture out, so I drove her to the Golden Valley Tree Park outside Balingup, where we sat under one of two huge English oaks. We talked about Rose Cottage, wondering when we would be moved there. She spoke of her hurt with regard to Barbara. I said I no longer felt I had a sibling, and this was a great relief and a good thing, as it protected me. Mu, in England all those years ago, had provided the means for me to cut the negative past-life, karmic umbilical cord that connected the two of us, and I understood this had ensured my freedom and enabled me to be strong all these years.

A week later I was woken with the message *Rose Cottage*. Three days after this I asked a local estate agent to put our home on the market. I was taken to a box, then to a parcel within it — it was the Rose Cottage nameplate. Christina rang sensing change, and I confirmed that Mum and I were on the move again. I spoke to her about Mum's pending ninetieth birthday and wondered what would happen between her and Barbara.

On 13 January we drove to Manjimup and went to the Roy Weston Real Estate office. When an agent sat us in front a computer to display all the properties they had for sale, a refurbished cottage with a green tin roof appeared on screen. *Yes, this one*, my Guide said. The agent said the cottage was beyond our budget, but I insisted we view it and the owner agreed. The modern three-bedroom cottage was close to the hospital, in a quiet street, with a sunroom at the rear and a garden in desperate need of development. I spoke to the Bridgetown agent regarding our property in Greenbushes, and he agreed to raise the asking price to a figure that would allow us to buy the cottage if someone would pay that much. *Red rose energy*, my Guide said.

As I read through the manuscript a day or two later I reached the part where I was at the permaculture conference with Julie in 1996. I had been encouraged to give her a red rosebud following my placing another one on the grave of a person named Gardner. 'Red rose energy' was being highlighted again, but in present time.

The next day Mum and I signed a contract to purchase Rose Cottage subject to the sale of our Greenbushes home. To our surprise I was directed to unwrap the Butterfly Circle and hang it in the sunroom. *Time for change*, my Guide explained. I was then guided to send a note to Greta to tell her Mum and I had found Rose Cottage in Manjimup. I was still trying to absorb this change of energy when its owner knocked on our door! He wanted to know why we didn't have a 'For Sale' sign outside. When I explained that all such matters were in the hands of our agent, he drove into Bridgetown, returned with the sign and erected it in the front garden. 'My Guide has everything under control,' I said to Mum.

Several days before Mum's ninetieth birthday, cards arrived — from Barbara, the grandchildren and great-grandchildren — and I added them to the correspondence from nieces, nephews and cousins and gifts from her sisters. Bouquet upon bouquet of flowers and roses were delivered and our home was filled with their scent. I hid all the gifts and set the table after Mum had retired. There was one gift missing — Barbara's. I knew Mum would be awake early so I went into her bedroom singing the birthday song. Then I walked her to the candle-lit kitchen table. She drew a deep breath when she saw the pile of communications.

I raced to the post office while she looked at them and, to my relief, there was a gift from Barbara.

The phone began to ring as her sisters and friends shared in this special day. I invited the wwoofer, Vicki, to lunch and Marg arrived as a surprise. The three of us toasted Mum with red wine. Marg asked Mum if she would like a flower reading; she selected a bloom and handed it to her.

Mum was told her spirit family were pleased with her. They were clapping and a large orchestra was playing as they celebrated her life. The front doorbell rang, and a magnificent arrangement of pink-and-gold flowers was delivered from the grandchildren and great-grandchildren. Something had changed: Barbara was the only person not to ring and neither Mum nor I was concerned.

The next day I was instructed to take down the Butterfly Circle. It had followed Mum since March 1986, when we first learnt about Barbara and Anne's deceptive actions in regard to the Old Saddlery. Mum watched as I removed the Butterfly Circle from the sunroom and packed it. We understood the very *action* of removing this heavy symbol was being emphasised. *Yes, the removal of the heavy emotional burden of Barbara's actions*, my Guide explained, *completing the predicted cycle of events between Barbara and her mother.*

Within days of her birthday Mum and I were in Bunbury seeing a heart specialist, who told Mum to stop all medication as she was showing signs of allergic reactions. The reactions persisted and again she was overwhelmed by health issues. The doctor found a medication to help, but her heart condition was taking its toll.

On 23 February I was walking Jessie in the forest when a raven followed us, calling out. *Magic afoot*, my Guide said. I came across a dead raven and was reminded of the raven that had died at the centre and was buried at the main entrance. *Welcome changes*, my Guide said.

I carried the raven home and buried it inside the Atlantis Eight Formation. The following day I was instructed to drive to Manjimup but *en route* visit the Mitre 10 store in Bridgetown. I was drawn to a rosebush whose label read 'Lovers Meeting' and directed to buy it — but after I had visited Rose Cottage. Later, at home, I was taken to Mary Magdalene's image, and then to placed petals from the rose around the Monkey Mia Dolphin. A week later we learnt that the centre in Dongara was for sale.

Mum and I enjoyed my sixtieth birthday at home. That evening I displayed the Hagalaz Cloth used in the transfer of the blue light from

Egypt in 1997 and placed the Central Quartz at its centre, then moved the Lovers Meeting rose petals from the Monkey Mia Dolphin to the crystal. *When the student is ready the Master will come*, my Guide said.

Vicki sent me details regarding a woman called Pauline, who lived near Margaret River and assisted with manuscripts in readying them for presentation to a publisher. My manuscript was in its basic stage. I placed the information about Pauline near Mary Magdalene's image and on 3 May I posted the manuscript to her. Who is this woman Pauline? I wondered. *Atlantis*, my Guide replied. *Trust the process.*

Five days later we sold our home and settlement day was set for 2 June. We organised a post box at the Manjimup post office and Mum wrote to her sisters to tell them our new address. I was encouraged to send it to Greta also. Pauline rang, and we spoke for the first time. I told her we were moving to Rose Cottage. She returned the manuscript later with the box filled with red rose petals. *Red rose energy*, my Guide said.

We followed the removal van to Manjimup. The Wild Geese / Soul Group print was hung in my office, The Lovers pot placed on the Welsh dresser in the dining area and the Butterfly Circle stored in the shed. Mum had given me a set of Bush Flower Essence Flower Reading Cards for my birthday, and I dowsed a card. When I turned it over I found it was 'Sturt Desert Pea — Grief and Sadness.' I put the card by the *Dolphin's Dreaming* picture before I hung it. *Someone you love very much will go out of your life*, my Guide warned. The painting held the three dolphins symbolic of Mum, Tim and me. A week later I was taken to the flower essence cards, and the one highlighted was 'Sydney Rose — Realising that we are all one — that there is no separation.'

I pruned the roses at the front of the cottage and placed the Lovers Meeting rose in its pot by the already established yellow and red rosebushes. On 18 June I planted it.

My Guide directed me to seek help from local services, as Mum's care was now a twenty-four-hours-a-day commitment. A respite service arranged to come once a week for three hours. At times Mum would rally, and when she did I took her out to areas selected by my Guide.

I had sent the manuscript to an assessor, and when it returned I was thrilled to read that she felt it was a remarkable story — one of a kind — although there was still a lot more work to be done. I placed the 1992 photograph of Mum and me at Cockington with Tim on the manuscript with the Truth Stone / Amazonite.

At the end of July a consultant visited from the nursery and began the process of transforming the back area into a native garden for Mum to sit in, wander around and enjoy.

'August 9' was highlighted as being important. When the day arrived, I awoke wondering what was to happen. The first instruction was to write to Pauline and ask about finding an editor for the manuscript. The second was to place the Lovers Meeting rose label on the Nannup Healing Heart Karma necklace, given to me by Greta. *A positive thought for the future, as anything is possible,* my Guide said.

Three days later Pauline rang and we discussed editors. On 24 August I drove to Margaret River to meet one, but knew at once that she was not the right person and was instead sent by my Guide to visit the Energy Beacon nearby, dedicated to the Egyptian Princess. Days later I drove Mum to Nannup for their Tulip Festival and thought about the Lovers Meeting rose and the Healing Heart Karma necklace.

I had written to Mum's two sisters and to Barbara sharing my concern for her health, but there had been no response. Then Aunty Val sent a note to say Barbara was dealing with a family issue and did not have time to write. 'Here we go again; their behaviour is unbelievable,' I said.

'If they are all so determined to shut you and me out then so be it,' Mum replied.

At the start of September I ordered two Pierre de Ronsard climbing roses — Rose for Romance — then bought two tall black garden obelisks to be placed in the flowerbed by the front veranda. The next day I erected them and planted the two romance roses. The label read: 'Pierre de Ronsard — a 16th-century French poet noted for his love poems.' *French connection,* my Guide said.

Four days later Mum became breathless and was taken by ambulance to the local hospital, but they found nothing seriously wrong with her. Although weak, she insisted on returning home. Later, I was sent to the White Dolphin symbol of Atlantis and guided to hang it in the enclosed veranda/sunroom where Mum would sit, and the *Call of the Dolphin* tape was played.

On Barbara's birthday, 21 September, I awoke drained, having cared for Mum in the night as she was distressed and unwell. I was woken by the word *threat* going through my mind, and I went into the kitchen to light a white candle and ask for protection. I understood I was to write the word 'threat' on a piece of paper, then burn it. 'Be gone from our lives,' came from within me, forcing me to speak aloud the sentiments of *another* — Barbara.

Pauline rang with the names of editors and when I dowsed I was given the name Betty. I sent an email to her and she responded by phone. She had retired but was keen to read the story, and there would be no charge. I posted the manuscript and she replied saying it would take time for her to work through its contents.

Selva the clairvoyant was available for readings at the local crystal shop and my Guide instructed me to go and see her. She greeted me warmly and I spent half an hour with her. She saw financial security around me and, although I was being severely tested emotionally, I was strong and determined. She looked at me and said, 'Your sister does not care about either you or your mother.' I did not comment and waited for her to continue. 'There is no energy around Tim. He needs your hand to guide him and he will come to Australia one day.' I told her we had moved to Manjimup to live there; she smiled and said, 'You have one more move and you will be surrounded by people. Two new friends to enter your life, young and strong, and your book will be published.'

Mum rallied and I drove her to Big Brook Dam to see the wildflowers and stand by the water's edge. I held her arm as we walked, aware of how fragile she had become. 'What will you do when I am gone?' she asked, concerned.

'You are not going anywhere,' I replied firmly.

On 10 October I returned from shopping to discover Mum on the floor. She was breathless so I called an ambulance. In the post I found a note from Barbara, telling Mum her husband was heading for surgery, but there was no enquiry as to Mum's health.

A week later she returned home. During the rest of the month she suffered bouts of angina and spent a lot of time in hospital. I would be by her side to keep her calm when she awoke and would stay all day. We returned to the cottage at the end of October and I replayed a message left on our answering machine. We were stunned to hear Aunty Pat ordering me not to contact Barbara with any news. She rang days later leaving yet another distasteful message questioning my truthfulness with regard to Mum's health. 'You will never be hurt and humiliated again,' Mum said.

She asked for paper and pen and wrote a note to her sisters. She told them I had spoken only the truth regarding her health; that the doctor had told her that her heart was worn out and time was not on her side. She continued by saying that no-one in the family would be given the opportunity to hurt or humiliate me ever again. *Part of the healing process for you both* my Guide said.

At the beginning of November Mum was taken into hospital and again I was left with the quandary of who to contact in the family regarding her declining health. *Contact Tim's twin*, my Guide said. I sent an email to Mark and wrote what was in my heart. He and Mum had been close, as they both shared a love of art and were artists themselves.

> 11 November 2006
> Dear Mark,
> Aunty Pat left a tense message on our answering machine again last night. At no time have I used the wording 'terminally ill' with regard to your Nan, that is used for patients with illnesses such as cancer. Your Nan is struggling physically and emotionally and I do not need to receive tense accusing phone calls. I am here looking after Nan and I know what is happening. I have no idea when Nan's last day will be but your Nan is very fragile and in my opinion her eldest daughter had the right to be told what is happening. After 21 years I am tired of the animosity aimed at me personally, and would have no trouble seeking a peaceful existence with just Nan and I and withdrawing from family altogether. I have no intention of making you piggy-in-the-middle and am relaying to you today that I am tired of the intrigues and drama of family. Judy.

There was no reply from Mark, but the hurtful messages from Aunty Pat stopped. 'We must ensure you are never humiliated again,' Mum said. *Part of the healing process for you both*, my Guide explained. The next day I found Mum sitting at the table writing.

> 16 November 2006
> Dear Val,
> Judy has arranged with our friend Julia, in South Australia, for you to be told when I do pass-over. We both hope it will be later rather than sooner. I am happy with the decision. We both feel it will be sudden rather than drawn out. Do you remember, Val, we decided we would rather keep our figures than our faces as we grew old? I remember our conversation so clearly. Love Tess.

Betty sent through pages of the manuscript with her comments and the exchange began that would last well into the pending New Year of 2007. Mum would lie on the single bed in the office next to the computer and sleep while I worked on our story. She sought to be near me and I sensed she was apprehensive regarding her declining health.

Healing hugs, my Guide said. I thought about Cindy and her healing hugs.

On 13 December a Christmas card arrived from Greta. As I was placing it by The Lovers pot, Pauline rang. I spoke to her about having been ordered not to communicate with Barbara by Mum's sister Pat regarding Mum's health, as Barbara had more important concerns. 'This would be with Barbara's encouragement,' she said. 'Is Tim part of this drama?' I replied that his name had not featured and I had not heard from him. 'He is a Celestial Dolphin, so he will be watching and listening,' she said.

Six days later, while Mum was sleeping, I walked to the Timber Park in Manjimup to the Aboriginal Circle, made of circular blocks of wood. I stood inside the circle and soon found myself stamping my feet in a rhythm *familiar* to me. I asked all the Noongar Ancestors to set Mum and me free of the negativity in England.

Marg rang on my arrival back at the cottage. 'Are you drawing on your vast spiritual knowledge?' she asked. I told her about the Aboriginal Circle.

Three days before Christmas Mum was rushed into hospital. I sat with her in the ambulance. It broke my heart to see her distressed, and I felt helpless. On Christmas Eve she insisted on returning home, as she did not want me to be alone on Christmas day. She had arranged with her carer to buy me a 'Comfort Candle', and we placed a red rose in a vase for our Christmas table setting. I drove her back to hospital the next day. It felt like an ongoing nightmare and I prayed that I would wake up and all would be okay again.

I was taken to my diary, and when I opened it a photograph of Tim fell out. *You will receive the comfort you need*, my Guide said.

On 2 January 2007 I received a late Christmas card from Tim:

Thinking of you always. Love – Peace – Respect. Tim.

Days later I woke to the words *Atlantis, another group of eight being summoned*. The Miraculous Medal / Mary Magdalene was highlighted and I placed it by The Lovers pot. Three days later I was sent to the Diamond Tree to touch it and to ask for help. Ten days after this I was guided to send Pauline the book *Discover Atlantis* by Diana Cooper and

Shaaron Hutton, which I had not been allowed to read. The following week I was encouraged to place dried Rose Cottage lavender inside The Lovers pot. Everything was connected, but how I did not know; then a note arrived from Cindy asking if I would like to meet with her.

Mum was home and responding to new heart medication. On her ninety-first birthday I drove her to the Diamond Tree and we sat drinking tea, watching the tourists climb this fire tower. I stood beside her and then drew her to me in a protective hug. She smiled and said, 'You could live in the forest couldn't you.'

Responding to Cindy's request to see me, I was guided to book accommodation in Busselton for 7 February, arranging for a carer to stay with Mum at the cottage. I wrote to Cindy and Greta rang in response. It felt strange to be talking to her after all this time but I was not disturbed. She suggested we meet before I met Cindy. I drove through Nannup on my way to Busselton, stopping to sit by the river for a while. When I walked towards the Equinox Café in Busselton, I saw Greta waiting. She smiled and I gave her a hug. I was aware we were studying one another as we talked, searching for something. Her mobile phone rang and she said, 'Yes, Judy is here.' She looked at me. 'Cindy is coming.' A rush of emotion surged through me and I left the table and walked off to stand alone by the sea.

Greta watched as Cindy raced to me and gave me a hug. I held her back from me and said, 'Thank God you are safe.'

She held my hand and then walked me to her mother. I was choked with emotion. Greta was aware of this and stood close, enabling me to draw on her energy. I made an excuse to leave, driving to another beach in order to allow the intense relief to surface. *In serving each other we become free*, my Guide said.

A few days later, as I was writing a card to Greta with our street address, Pauline phoned to say she was enjoying the book *Discover Atlantis* and suggested we meet at Nannup on 15 February. The phone rang again and it was Christina, to say she wanted to stay overnight on 14 February. It was clear that Christina and Pauline were meant to meet and we were all to meet in Nannup. I took Christina to the Diamond Tree as soon as she arrived; for some reason unknown to me this tree was linked symbolically to the diamond-shaped Central Quartz. The new Atlantis Eight were responding to the Central Quartz / Mary Magdalene energy.

When Christina and I arrived in Nannup, a tall young woman with wavy dark hair walked up to Christina and gave her a hug. It was

Pauline. She handed *Discover Atlantis* to Christina, then turned to me. 'Follow me,' she said. I looked back at Christina as I followed Pauline towards the river.

Christina shouted, 'I'll drive back to Perth then.' I waved and she drove off.

Pauline walked quickly to a bridge, then stood me in front of a 'Reconciliation Pathway' sign. I saw Aboriginal stepping-stones painted with their symbols. We walked the stones, then ate lunch in a café and talked about the manuscript. *Companion from Atlantis,* my Guide said. Awesome! I thought, but said nothing to Pauline. *Your friend through time*, my Guide confirmed. Mum was fascinated when I told her Pauline was my companion from Atlantis.

Greta rang to say she wanted to visit Mum some time.

Days later I became concerned when I was taken to a photograph of Mum taken outside St Mary's Church in Busselton and instructed to place it inside a gift box along with the string of pearls my father had given Mum. I was also to put in the box a copy of her will, in which she bequeathed the pearls to Barbara. My Guide told me to post the box to Barbara via Tim after Mum had passed over to spirit; then I was referred to *A Dictionary of Symbols* by Tom Chetwynd:

Pearl – The incorruptible product of the life's work ... *The soft flabby oyster makes the pearl which is revealed at the death of the oyster.* Man's flesh completes the cycle of life, and then disappears, leaving behind the enduring work, often formed from the grit of suffering. (8)

Formed from the grit of suffering, my Guide said. This was to be Mum's final gift and message left behind for Barbara.

Although post had arrived for Mum from her sisters and Barbara for her ninety-first birthday, the energy had changed since Mum had confronted Val and Pat the previous October regarding my being ordered not to bother Barbara with Mum's health concerns.

Mum was not strong enough to organise my birthday in March, but was firm with regard to the table setting, saying it must feature masses of flowers. *Love is the river of life*, my Guide said. I played the *Call of the*

Dolphin tape and lit the Dongara candle. The day before my birthday Mum insisted I drive her to Pemberton and walk her to a gift shop, where she made a purchase. When, later, I opened her gift, I found it was a banksia box in which she had placed my father's silver Mary capsule and eight dried red rose petals. *Mary Magdalene / Atlantis Eight,* my Guide said.

Betty rang to tell me she had finished reading through the manuscript and would be sending on the last few chapters with her recommendations.

Rose Dolphin and Rose Cottage, my Guide predicted.

Pauline rang and gave me the name of a celebrant. My Guide encouraged me to ring a funeral company in Busselton. I tried to remain calm when Mum was taken into hospital with chest pressure. When I visited her I told her I would be in Busselton the next day and not to worry. I did not tell her I was making arrangements for her funeral. As I drove to Busselton I was only vaguely aware of what was happening. My Guide was adamant that I make all the arrangements, and I followed her directions in a state of shock. Two days later I brought Mum home from hospital.

On 26 March Greta rang to inform me she was visiting Mum and would arrive at 10 am. I watched her drive into our driveway, get out of her car, then bend to touch the two Lovers Meeting roses in bloom. Greta, the Rose Dolphin, sat with Mum, the Yellow Dolphin, and held her hands. I understood she had come to say goodbye.

Easter was spent at home as I worked through the manuscript, and Mum helped me choose the photographs to be included, enjoying the memories. Two weeks later I placed Mary Magdalene's image alongside a photograph of Mum taken when she and I arrived in South Australia in 1985, at the very beginning of our journey. The soft, rushing energy came and with it the words *I will protect you both.*

The past-life energy of romance is in the air, my Guide said. I was encouraged to pick a Lovers Meeting rosebud and place it near The Lovers pot and the Healing Heart Karma necklace. The manuscript was drawn to my attention and I was taken to a page where, five years before, my Guide had said, *Until the Atlantis influence returns.* This was in answer to my question as to when Greta and I would meet again. I was also given the message that Cindy would be brought to Rose Cottage as part of her recovery. Pauline rang later to ask if she could read the manuscript yet again. I was surprised, but my Guide insisted this be allowed, so we arranged to meet in Busselton on 3 May. Pauline was waiting when I arrived and insisted that I leave the manuscript in my car and go with her. When I sat in her car she handed me a blue box, inside which I found a red rose with an incredible scent. It reminded me of Julie's red rose at the centre. Pauline told me she was going to take me somewhere and drove through several streets, then parked by the sea. I followed her and we walked the water's edge until she stopped.

'You know what you must do,' she said. My heart raced and I became emotional as I looked at the rose. Pauline smiled when I looked at her and, reluctantly, I placed the rose in the water. The retreating tide took it away. A shadow followed the rose, and I saw it was a stingray encouraging it to drift further out.

I was taken aback when Pauline asked where Greta was working and then drove us there. We walked into the café, where she was serving at the counter. I found myself introducing Pauline to Greta and watched them shake hands. Then I took in the enormity of what was happening. The Egyptian Princess was greeting my Companion from Atlantis, a move in energy and further back in time from the trauma of Ancient Egypt to the harmony of Atlantis.

We sat outside and Greta served us. 'I will bring Cindy to Rose Cottage soon,' she said. I looked across at Pauline and she smiled.

Days later Pauline rang and asked me if I had decided who would be speaking at Mum's cremation. I choked with alarm, unable to reply. She waited until I told her I could not even think about such things. 'You must organise everything,' she said. 'When your Mum leaves, you will be too distressed to cope.' I wrote to Julia, Marg and Christina and asked them to speak. Pauline rang again. She wanted to organise for us to meet on 14 May, when she would return the manuscript.

I became very distressed when Mum said, 'I want to die in your arms.' There was *another* near her, and I was aware of a calming energy. I wanted to say 'Don't leave me,' but the words would not form.

On 13 May, Mother's Day, my Guide sent me to the 'Comfort Candle' Mum had given me for Christmas. I saw written around it 'To someone special'. I lit candles and read my Mother's Day card to her. Early in the evening, when I went to sit by her, I felt intense pressure in my head; then a nosebleed started and blood poured over my clothes and onto the floor. Mum was frightened and I tried to calm her as I rushed to the phone to ring for help. My neighbour arrived, and she called another neighbour to sit with Mum before taking me to hospital. I was told I must stay in overnight, so my neighbour collected Mum and we were put next to one another. It had all happened so fast. In my mind came the assurance *I will protect you both*.

The next morning I rang Pauline from the hospital to tell her I would not be able to meet her. At lunchtime Mum suffered a massive heart attack and was rushed into the Intensive Care Room. I watched, helpless, as the nurses took over. Mum kept saying, 'Tell Judy I love her.' These were to be the last words she would say.

I rang Julia and she rang Aunty Val, as arranged. Pauline rang to say, 'I am there for you.' There was silence from England.

Mum remained motionless with eyes closed and her breathing shallow. I slept in her room on a mattress; during the night a nurse asked if I wanted to ring my family. 'I have no family, they were taken away by stealth,' I replied.

Later, I awoke restless and began to pace the corridor, until Pauline rang and told me she would be with me by lunchtime. Mum's breathing became erratic. Pauline walked in, went straight to Mum and held her hand, and my mother relaxed. It was such an obvious change that the nursing staff looked at me with questioning eyes. What is it about this woman? I wondered.

At 3.35 pm Mum's breathing became shallow and I alerted the nurse, who told me to prepare myself. When I took her hands she opened her eyes for the first time since the heart attack. I knew my Grandmother Lilian was near, and this time she would take Mum with her. Pauline put her hand on my arm and I drew on her energy and said, 'I love you Mum. I am safe, you can go now.' Mum's eyes questioned if I was indeed safe and when I nodded she closed her eyes and stopped breathing.

Anguish moved up through my chest and out of my throat. Pauline held me until it burst out of me. The doctor told me Mum had gone and I asked him to check her again. I had promised her I would do this. He examined her again and confirmed she had passed over. I did not stay: my mother had gone.

I rang Julia before leaving the hospital and she said she would ring Aunty Val again. Pauline drove me to the Diamond Tree and we walked in the forest and talked; then she drove me back to the cottage, where she encouraged me to talk more, and it was late when I went to bed. I did not want to be here without Mum so I concentrated on slowing down my heartbeat, determined to make it stop. I spoke my intent out loud, forgetting Pauline was in another bedroom. She came in and sat on the edge of my bed, as Mum would have done, encouraging me to talk and express my feelings. 'Your mother wants you to finish the book and reveal the truth,' she said.

Pauline left the next day, and I sat in the cottage wondering what to do. My world had stopped, but the world outside was still functioning, forcing me to make decisions. I found myself wandering in the main street of Manjimup not knowing how I got there and walking home quickly as Mum might be worried, only to find the cottage empty. My dog Jessie had died two days after my birthday and I missed her instinctive comforting ways.

I posted Mum's will and Daddy's pearls to Barbara, care of Tim.

Julia rang to say she was flying over from South Australia. Greta rang and she said she would bring Cindy to see me on 19 May.

I watched as Greta was again drawn to touch a Lovers Meeting rosebud, then she and Cindy walked through the obelisks under the romance roses. I had been guided to find the decorated soapstone box I'd bought at the Taj Mahal during my visit with Mum in 1985, and had written out the story for Cindy, concerning my handing Mum this gift, with the words, 'This box connects you to a child and this place.'

Cindy was this child and was to be given the box as a gift from my mother.

I watched Cindy's face as she opened the wrapped gift and was taken by surprise by her and Greta's reactions. They had spent their trip to Manjimup talking about the Taj Mahal and Greta's wish to visit. Cindy looked at me in wonder and Greta was not able to comprehend that I had handed her daughter a gift from the Taj Mahal itself. As they were leaving, Cindy said, 'I want to go to Tess's funeral.' She looked at Greta and she nodded.

Julia drove me to the Bunbury Funeral Parlour on 25 May in preparation for Mum's cremation — a private service. We were taken to the room where her oak coffin was waiting, surrounded by flowers. I was asked by a staff member if I wished to view and I declined, saying I wished to remember my mother as the vital, elegant woman she always was. Only my long-stemmed red rose was on the coffin.

I heard the *Call of the Dolphin* music playing as we turned into the Crematorium Gardens and I saw our friends and Celestial Dolphins waiting. We gathered inside and sat near a small table where Mum's photograph was displayed beside the Dongara candle-holder with a new long white candle. The music played until Mum's coffin rested at the front. Cindy then stepped forward, placing wildflowers on the steps, and then turned to look at me with love and respect in her eyes.

Atlantis Eight, my Guide said, highlighting that Mum, Marg, Christina, Greta, Cindy, Pauline and I were together, and Tatia would be lighting a candle in South Africa at the time I would be lighting the Dongara candle to begin the service.

My mother had recorded her wishes, requesting the Twenty-Third Psalm — 'The Lord is my shepherd' — and the anthem 'Jerusalem' by William Blake — 'And did those feet in ancient time / Walk upon England's mountains green? / And was the holy Lamb of God / On England's pleasant pastures seen?'

Mary Magdalene, the Messianic Queen, died the year Joseph of Arimathea built the Glastonbury chapel in her memory. A year later Mary's son dedicated it to his mother — but he had visited England before, and this inspired William Blake's poem and anthem.

In 1989 I had been sent to Glastonbury to absorb this energy, and was here now with my mother, aware *only* of her and my Red Rose / Mary Magdalene and the lit candle. Mum's coffin moved slowly through the curtain to the vibration of 'Jerusalem'.

I went to her photograph and whispered, 'I will hold you safely in my heart until we meet again.' Several minutes passed before I was able to blow out the candle.

Afterword

The narrative of this book ended, fittingly, with the passing of my remarkable mother following the completion of the Ten Year Mary Magdalene Project 1994. But, life being what it is, there are some loose threads in the story, and it might be wondered if any of them have since been woven firmly into the fabric of my life.

Some of the loose threads remain just that, examples being the promise that a soulmate would enter my life with whom I would find contentment and that I would also be making a significant connection with a man in his thirties. As yet that hasn't happened, but I am confident it will.

It has been different in the case of a similar promise: that two new friends would be coming into my life. In 2011 I was sent by my Guide to Nannup, where I connected with Pick-a-WooWoo Publishers and the two talented young women who run it. They have patiently guided me through the process that has led to the publication of *Entwining of Souls*.

Other threads: Selva the clairvoyant told me that Rose Cottage would not be my permanent home: there would be one more move, and in my new location in a valley I would be surrounded by people drawn there because of my energy. This does not appear to be in the offing at the moment, but my understanding is that it will happen when the time comes for me to begin channelling the concept for the Blue Mary Ray Diamond Centre.

There has been no change so far in my relationships with Barbara and Mum's sisters. It will be recalled that my Guide spoke of Barbara being 'turned back to the Light' following my mother's words in 2002 — 'Barbara, God bless your soul' — but like all humans she has free will, and from that moment on she would have been free to approach the ongoing conflict in such a way as to either dispel or incur karma. Any attempt on my part to heal the relationships will take place when the book is published and my version of what happened has been put into the picture. After that, any interactions with all family members will be based on the truth.

Since loaning Greta a rough draft of the book in 2008, which she returned, we met briefly in the street when my Guide sent me to

Busselton, and did little more than exchange greetings. I accepted then that I may never see her again. The pair of Lovers Pots symbolised our brief traumatic relationship in ancient times; their separation – I have one and she has the other – symbolise our release from each other and the negative karmic attachment we had been carrying. We are free to move on — 'on opposite sides of any river', to quote the Perth tarot card reader.

There has been no resolution with Cathy. When I confronted her after our legal issues had been resolved she said, 'No more, Judy.' There has been no further contact and I have no idea where she is.

I was directed by my Guide to revisit the former Celestial Dolphin Centre in Dongara with Christina and Marg following the passing of my mother, and we met the new owners, the property having been sold a second time. The woman stood by the Standing Stone with me as I explained the concept and informed her I was completing a book and felt readers would be drawn to visit the property after reading it.

All materials from within the Heart Chakra / Pulse of Life / Goddess Nut had been removed including the outline of the chambers, but the white-flowering planting along the outer walkways was left intact. All other elements such as the Rainbow Serpent were removed, but the symbols representing the constellation of Virgo remained intact apart from the Heart Element, which I replaced with a new pile of stones. Following my Guide's directions, Christina, Marg and I walked between the constellation symbols recharging its energy. I told them of the prediction that the Healing Garden of Dongara would be visited by clairvoyants and healers from around the world to recharge, but for me personally the point of its creation had been that it was instrumental in resolving traumatic past-life karmic issues.

My nephew Tim has not yet visited Australia, as promised, but I'm sure it will happen. However, I have had further contact with him. In February 2009 his daughter, Taylor, asked him to send her favourite toy to her Great-aunt Judy in Australia. He and I had started to communicate about life in general — absolutely no reference to the family conflict — but it was this initiative by Taylor that opened the door for me to go to England in September 2010 and stay with the family for a month. We were now face to face, but the conflict was still not discussed, nor did I meet my sister, who lived five minutes' walk away.

Within hours of my arrival he handed me a metal dolphin — I had never talked to him about dolphins — and then gave me a small metal tin he had made at school as a boy. Inside it were some sharks' teeth he had collected over the years, no doubt including one I had sent him from Kalbarri some time before. I knew he was handing me all his repressed emotions.

Tim took a week off work and we drove to Dartmoor, where we walked hand in hand to Scorhill Circle. Without any prompting or suggestion from me, he asked how many times he must walk the circle, and followed my direction that it must be seven times. He then walked to the nearby stream, where I had seen his image years before, washed his hands, took my hand again and walked me back to the car.

We drove into Mortonhampstead, where in 1992, on Tim's birthday, I had danced around their Dancing Tree alone, enjoying the sensation of celebration. Once again it was without any prompting from me that, as we passed the tree, he asked what it was, stopped the car and danced around it several times!

He asked where I would like to go next, and we drove towards Brent Tor. He again held my hand as we walked up the Tor to the church. I had sensed his energy with me years before when last I'd made the climb, and that same energy was intimately with me now. He stood by me to look at St Michael's leadlight window and I recalled in my mind having longed for the revealing of the truth and justice. Tim took a photograph; in the image there was a haze of pink that is no part of the actual window.

Another day, we drove into Cornwall to visit the place where he had scattered his father's ashes, and then onto to Sennen Cove. There we walked the beach hand in hand just as I had experienced it years before without him being present.

On 21 September, Barbara's birthday, I was sent to the 11th century Cockington Church, which Tim, Mum and I had walked past in 1992. Inside I was encouraged to light two candles in memory of my mother and father and ask for their blessing. My Guide insisted I take a photograph of the lit candles and keep it until after both Tim and Barbara had read my book. It is my understanding Tim will take his mother to this church and hand her this image, enabling her to reconnect with her parents and begin the process of emotional healing for her.

A few days before I left England Tim placed a red rose in my bedroom. It was hard to leave him.

In 2013 Tim's sister, Debby, wrote to me. I was instructed to reply and share the fact that at no time in the past 28 years had anyone asked for my perspective on the family drama, preferring to think badly of me;

but I had written a book that held the truth. Tim responded, asking me if I could tell him the truth over the telephone. It was a breakthrough for me that for the first time someone had considered I might have a point of view. I told him a phone call would not be appropriate: he must read the book.

Since then he has resigned from his job of 24 years – which had restricted his life. He is now free to travel with his family.

My Guide continues to guide me on a daily basis, and extraordinary happenings continue to occur. I will always follow her guidance as predicted.

September 2013

Notes

1. William Kowalski, *Eddie's Bastard*, HarperCollins, New York, 1999, pp. 275–6.
2. Denise Linn, 'Soulmates: The quest for your perfect mate', *Wellbeing Magazine*, No. 29, 1988.
3. Richard Gerber, *Vibrational Medicine: New Choices for Healing Ourselves*, Bear & Company, Santa Fe, 2001.
4. Hugh Edwards, *Kimberley Dreaming to Diamonds*, Tangee Publishing, Perth, 2005.
5. The Findhorn Community, *The Findhorn Garden Story*, 4th edn, Findhorn Foundation, 2008.
6. Sogyal Rinpoche, *The Tibetan Book of Living and Dying*, HarperCollins, New York / Rider, London, 1992, pp. 93, 146.
7. Ainslie Roberts (paintings) & Melva Jean Roberts (text), *Dreamtime Heritage: Australian Aboriginal Myths*, Rigby, Adelaide, p. 76.
8. Tom Chetwynd, *A Dictionary of Symbols*, Granada, London, 1982.
9. David V.Tansley, *Chakras: Rays and Radionics*, C.W. Daniel, Ashingdon, Essex, 1994.
10. 'Understanding our sacred symbols', *Eagles Wings*, vol. 4, no. 5.
11. Anna Flanders, 'Creating a wave of excitement', *The Geraldton Guardian*, 2 January 1997.
12. Judy Roach, 'All Roads Lead to Dongara', *Midwest Times*, 5 February 1997.
13. Merle Severy, 'The Celts', *National Geographic Magazine*, May 1977.
14. Jamie Sams, *Sacred Path Cards: The Discovery of Self Through Native Teachings*, HarperCollins, New York, 1990.
15. Jamie Sams and David Carson, *Medicine Cards: The Discovery of Power Through the Ways of Animals*, St Martin's Press, 1988.
16. *Nexus Magazine*, October/November 1996, p. 39.
17. Nancy Blair, *Goddesses For Every Season*, Element Books, Rockport, Massachusetts, 1995.

18. *Wanda Sellar, The Dictionary of Essential Oils*, C.W. Daniel, Ashingdon, Essex, 1992.
19. Dorothee L. Mella, *Stone Power*, Grand Central Publishing, New York, 1988.
20. Sheril Berkovitch, *The Crystal Workbook*, Labrys, Melbourne, 1992.
21. Soluntra King, *Crystals For Transformation, Healing And Spiritual Growth*, 2nd edn, Evenstar Creations, Kin Kin, Queensland, 1994.
22. Marice Sariola, *Icons*, <www.iconsbymarice.com.au>.
23. Patricia Jepsen Chuse, *Star of Melchizedek: Rhythm of the Perfect Man or Consciousness*, <www.melchizedeklearning.com>.
24. Laurence Gardner, 'The hidden history of Jesus and the Holy Grail', part 3, *Nexus Magazine*, vol. 5, no. 4, 1998.
25. Ainslie Roberts (paintings) & Charles P. Mountford (text), *The Dawn of Time: Australian Aboriginal Myths in Paintings*, Rigby, Adelaide, 1969.
26. *Laurence Gardner, Bloodline of the Holy Grail: The Hidden Lineage of Jesus Revealed, Element, Shaftesbury, Dorset, 1996.*
27. Christian Jacq, *Ramses: The Lady of Abu Simbel*, vol. 4, Grand Central Publishing, New York, 1996.
28. Christian Jacq, *The Black Pharaoh*, Simon & Schuster UK, London, 1999.
29. Christian Jacq, *The Temple of a Million Years*, Simon & Schuster UK, London, 2005.
30. Gary Zukav, *The Seat of the Soul, Rider Books, London, 1990 / Simon & Schuster, New York, 1989.*
31. David Taylor-Brown, *The Isis Oracle*, New Burlington Books, New York, 2001.
32. Alcyone, *At The Feet Of The Master*, Theosophical Publishing House, Adyar, Chennai, India, 1910.
33. *Edgar Cayce Readings*, Edgar Cayce Foundation, Virginia Beach, Virginia, 1971.
34. Judy Hall, *Way of Karma*, Thorsons, London, 2002.

35. Victor Tanti, 'Medium didn't choose her path', *The Geraldton Guardian*, 6 November 2002.
36. Elizabeth Kyle, 'EPONA' greeting card.
37. Helen Chryssides, 'Visions of Mary. Off the wall: The Anglican Church's first heavenly apparition has put Yankalilla on the miracle map', *The Bulletin With Newsweek*, 2 September 1997.
38. Nur Ankh Amen, *The Afrocentric Experience. Ankh: The Original Cross.* <http://thelovelykeish.tumblr.com/post/884388732/360degreeofurban-the-ankh-is-defined-as-the>.

Permissions

Permission to reprint material from the following sources is gratefully acknowledged:

Extract from pp. 275–6 (131 words) from EDDIE'S BASTARD by WILLIAM KOWALSKI. Copyright © 1999 by William Kowalski. Reprinted by permission of HarperCollins Publishers.

Extracts from 'Soulmates: The quest for your perfect mate' by Denise Linn, © *Wellbeing Magazine*. Reprinted by permission.

Extracts from *Vibrational Medicine* by Richard Gerber, M.D. Copyright © 1988 by Richard Gerber. Published by Inner Traditions – Bear & Company – <www.InnerTraditions.com>. Reprinted by permission.

Extracts from *Kimberley Dreaming to Diamonds* by Hugh Edwards. Copyright © 1991 by Hugh Edwards. Publisher Tangee Publishing. Reprinted by permission.

Extracts from *The Findhorn Garden Story* by The Findhorn Community © The Findhorn Foundation 1975, 2008 (fourth edition). <www.findhornpress.com>. Reprinted by permission.

Extracts *from The Tibetan Book of Living and Dying* by Sogyal Rinpoche, published by Rider Books. Reprinted by permission of The Random House Group Limited. Permission granted for use throughout the world excluding the US and Canada.

Extracts from *The Tibetan Book of Living and Dying* by Sogyal Rinpoche and edited by Patrick Gaffney & Andrew Harvey / Two brief quotes from pp. 93, 146. Copyright © 1993 by Rigpa Fellowship. Courtesy of HarperCollins Publishers. Permission granted for use throughout the US, Canada, Philippine Islands and open market.

Extract from *Dreamtime Heritage: Australian Aboriginal Myths*, paintings by Ainslie Roberts and text by Melva Jean Roberts (page 76). Copyright © 1975 by Ainslie Roberts and Melva Jean Roberts. Publisher Rigby Limited – ISBN 0-7270-0046-2.

Extracts from *A Dictionary of Symbols* by Tom Chetwynd. Copyright © 1982 by Tom Chetwynd. Publisher Paladin Books Granada Publishing Ltd – ISBN 0-586-08351-0.

Extracts from *Chakras: Rays and Radionics* by David V.Tansley, published by C.W. Daniel. Reprinted by permission of The Random House Group Limited.

Extract from *Eagles Wings* – Volume 4 Number 5 – 'Understanding our Sacred Symbols' – White Eagle Teachings USA – White Eagle Publishing Trust – <anna@whiteagle.org>. Reprinted by permission.

Article in *The Geraldton Guardian* 1997 'Creating a wave of excitement' by Anna Flanders and to the extent that WA Newspapers/*The West Australian* does or may hold copyright for the article, Permission is granted to reproduce the article as part of your forthcoming book.

Article in the *Midwest Times* 1997 'All Roads Lead to Dongara'. Copyright © Judy Roach.

Extracts from the May 1977 edition of *National Geographic Magazine* – <www.NationalGeographicStock.com> – Rights Release No RR3-147080-1.

Extracts from 'Hour of Power-Ritual of Joy' (p. 150), 'Moon Lodge-Retreat' (235), 'Fire Medicine-Passion' (307) from SACRED PATH CARDS by JAMIE SAMS. Copyright © 1990 by Jamie Sams & Linda Childers. Reprinted by permission of HarperCollins Publishers.

12 pages of text from MEDICINE CARDS – THE DISCOVERY OF POWER THROUGH THE WAYS OF ANIMALS © 1988 by Jamie Sams and David Carson. Reprinted by permission of St Martin's Press. All rights reserved.

From October/November Issue of *Nexus Magazine* 1996 (page 39) – diagram of The Egyptian Goddess, Nut. Permission granted – <editor@nexusmagazine.com>.

Extracts from *Goddesses for Every Season* by Nancy Blair, published Element Books, Rockport, Massachusetts, 1995.

Extract from The Dictionary of Essential Oils by Wanda Sellar, published by C.W. Daniel Company Limited. Reprinted by permission of The Random House Group Limited.

Extract from *Stone Power* by Dorothee L. Mella. Copyright © 1988 by Dorothee L. Mella – ISBN 9780446386968. Publisher Grand Central Publishing. Reprinted by permission.

Extracts from *The Crystal Workbook* by Sheril Berkovitch. Copyright © 1992 by Sheril Berkovitch. First published by Labrys, now published by Hihorse Pty Ltd. ISBN-0909223-97-1. Reprinted by permission.

Extracts from *Crystals For Transformation, Healing and Spiritual Growth* by Soluntra King. ISBN 9780646183879 – <Soluntra@evenstarcreations.com>. Reprinted by permission.

Icons painted by Marice Sariola, © Icons by Marice – <www.iconsbymarice.com.au>. Reproduced by permission.

Star of Melchizedek – Rhythm of the Perfect Man or Consciousness. Copyright © 1996 by Patricia Jepsen Chuse, University of Melchizedek – <www.melchizedeklearning.com>. Reprinted by permission.

Extracts from Volume 5, Number 4 (June–July 1998), *The Hidden History of Jesus and the Holy Grail* from a lecture by Sir Laurence Gardner, Kt St Gm, KCD – Part 3 (final) page 6, page 8, pages 7/8 and pages 4/5. <www.nexusmagazine.com>. Reprinted by permission.

Extract from *The Dawn of Time: Australian Aboriginal Myths* in paintings by Ainslie Roberts and text by Charles P. Mountford (page 50). Copyright © 1969 by Ainslie Roberts and Charles P. Mountford. Publisher Rigby Limited – ISBN 0-85179-304-5.

Extracts from *Bloodline of the Holy Grail. The Hidden Lineage of Jesus Revealed by Laurence Gardner.* Copyright © 1996 by Laurence Gardner. Reprinted by permission of HarperCollins Publishers Ltd.

Extracts from RAMSES: THE LADY OF ABU SIMBEL – VOLUME 1V by Christian Jacq. Copyright © 1996 by Editions Roberts Laffont. By permission of Grand Central Publishing. All rights reserved.

Extracts from *Ramses: The Lady of Abu Simbel* – Volume IV by Christian Jacq. We grant MBS Press permission to use the extracts mentioned, in the British Commonwealth – excluding Canada. Simon & Schuster UK Ltd. ISBN 0-684-82122-2.

Extracts from *The Black Pharaoh* by Christian Jacq. We grant MBS Press permission to use the extracts mentioned, in the British Commonwealth – excluding Canada. Simon & Schuster UK Ltd. ISBN 0-671-01805-1.

Extracts from *The Temple of a Million Years* by Christian Jacq. We grant MBS Press permission to use the extracts mentioned, in the British Commonwealth – excluding Canada. Simon & Schuster UK Ltd. ISBN 0-684-8237-0.

Extracts from The Seat of the Soul by Gary Zukav, published by Rider Books. Reprinted by permission of The Random House Group Limited. Permission granted only throughout the UK and Commonwealth, excluding Canada.

Extracts printed with the permission of Simon & Schuster, Inc. from THE SEAT OF THE SOUL by Gary Zukav. Copyright © 1989 Gary Zukav. This permission applies solely to publication of the above cited-work in the English language in the United States, its territories and dependencies, the Philippines and Canada.

Isis Oracle Gift Box and *The Isis Oracle* by David Taylor-Brown. Copyright © 2001 by David Taylor-Brown – Quarto Publishing. ISBN 86155-585-7.

Extracts from *At the Feet of the Master* by Alcyone. Copyright © 1910 by The Theosophical Publishing House, Adyar, Chennai, India. ISBN 0-8356-7113-5 (USA). Reprinted by permission.

Edgar Cayce Readings © 1971, 1993–2007 by Edgar Cayce Foundation. Reprinted by permission.

Extracts from *Way of Karma* by Judy Hall, published by Thorsons. Copyright © 2002 by Judy Hall – ISBN 0-00-711809-0.

The West Australian provides permission to use the article from Victor Tanti 'Medium didn't choose her path' within your book *Entwining of Souls*. © Courtesy of The Geraldton Guardian.

Quotation from the 'EPONA' greeting card. Copyright © Elizabeth Kyle. Reprinted by permission.

Extracts from 'Visions of Mary. Off the wall: The Anglican Church's first heavenly apparition has put Yankalilla on the miracle map' by Helen Chryssides. *The Bulletin With Newsweek*, 2 September 1997. Reprinted by permission.

Every effort has been made to locate copyright holders of material quoted, but this has not proved to be possible in every case.

Photograph and Illustration Credits

Pages 138 and 390. These photographs, capturing Mary's image at Medjugorje, Bosnia-Herzegovina, were supplied to the author by E. Trosser, to whom grateful acknowledgement is made. Copyright permission for the use of the images was sought by attempting to identify the tourist who captured them. MBS Press undertakes to make formal acknowledgement to the photographer upon being presented with proof of copyright ownership.

Pages 199, 201, 204, 205, 220, 221, 222, 225. Illustrations reproduced by permission of J. Firth, Yilgarn Traders.

Page 226. Diagram of the Egyptian Goddess Nut reproduced by permission of *Nexus Magazine* (October/November 1996 issue, page 39): <editor@nexusmagazine.com>.

All other photographs © Judy Roach.

About the Author

Judy Roach was born in 1946 in the manor Delamore House, in the Dartmoor village of Cornwood, Devon, England, and was educated at Stoke Damerel Grammar School for Girls in Plymouth. Between 1967 and 1972 she trained as a sexual assault specialist with the Devon and Cornwall Constabulary before being further trained in retail security with an international firm and heading Down Under in 1974. She quickly obtained employment as an assistant security manager and sought residency.

On returning to England in 1979, she was employed by Marks and Spencer as a mobile divisional head office detective before resigning in 1982 to restore a 14th-century building on the edge of Dartmoor and convert it into a very successful organic wholefood restaurant — the Old Saddlery. Spiritual disturbances within the energy of the building led her into the world of past lives, in particular to the traumatised trapped soul of a child.

Unforeseen events in England while she and her mother were visiting Australia in 1985 compelled them to remain there and led to the sale of the Old Saddlery in the following year.

Her psychic abilities increased dramatically when given access to her spirit Guide and becoming a Seeker after Truth. Between 1994 and 2004 she was encouraged by her Guide and Master Guide to develop the Celestial Dolphin Centre and Healing Garden of Dongara, Western Australia, under the umbrella of the Ten Year Mary Project '94. She lives in the Southern Forest region of Western Australia.

www.ingramcontent.com/pod-product-compliance
Lightning Source LLC
Chambersburg PA
CBHW051415290426
44109CB00016B/1308